KU-253-117

Grace, Talent, and Merit

Grace, Talent, and Merit

Poor students, clerical careers, and professional ideology in eighteenth-century Germany

ANTHONY J. LA VOPA

The right of the University of Cambridge to print and sell all manner of books was granted by Henry VIII in 1534. The University has printed and published continuously since 1584.

CAMBRIDGE UNIVERSITY PRESS

Cambridge

New York New Rochelle Melbourne Sydney

Published by the Press Syndicate of the University of Cambridge
The Pitt Building, Trumpington Street, Cambridge CB2 1RP
32 East 57th Street, New York NY 10022, USA
10 Stamford Road, Oakleigh, Melbourne 3166, Australia

© Cambridge University Press 1988

First published 1988

Printed in the United States of America

Library of Congress Cataloging-in-Publication Data

La Vopa, Anthony J.

Grace, talent, and merit : poor students, clerical careers, and professional ideology in eighteenth-century Germany / Anthony J. La Vopa.

p. cm.

Bibliography: p.

Includes index.

ISBN 0-521-35041-7

1. Educational sociology – Germany – History – 18th century. 2. Church and education – Germany – History – 18th century. 3. Occupational mobility – Germany – History – 18th century. 4. Social mobility – Germany – History – 18th century. 5. Professions – Germany – History – 18th century. I. Title.

LC191.8.G3L3 1988
370.19'0943 – dc19 88–1905
CIP

British Library Cataloguing in Publication Data

La Vopa, Anthony J.

Grace, talent, and merit : poor students, clerical careers, and professional ideology in eighteenth-century Germany.

1. Germany. Scholarship, 1740–1790
I. Title
001.2'0943

ISBN 0 521 35041 7

UNIVERSITY COLLEGE
LIBRARY
SWANSEA

Contents

Acknowledgments

The work on this book advanced despite numerous temptations to loiter along the way. At several critical junctures I received the kind of institutional and financial support that enables a scholar to devote himself wholeheartedly to his trade. I spent the spring semester of 1980 at the Shelby Cullom Davis Center for Historical Studies at Princeton University. Having arrived there with a vague aspiration to explore what seemed distinctive, if not unique, about German culture, I left with a thematic focus and a research agenda. My thanks to Lawrence Stone and his colleagues in the Department of History and to the other Visiting Fellows, who offered needed encouragement and were eager to share ideas. Three research trips to Germany were hosted by the Max-Planck-Institut für Geschichte in Göttingen. I join a long line of visiting scholars who have enjoyed the unusually generous hospitality of Professor Rudolf Vierhaus and his colleagues, notably Hans Erich Bödeker, Alf Lüdtke, Hans Medick, Jürgen Schlumbohm, and David Sabean. Supported in part by a fellowship from the American Council of Learned Societies, I spent the academic year 1983–84 at the National Humanities Center in the Research Triangle, North Carolina. It would be hard to imagine a more conducive environment for beginning a long writing project. The solicitude and efficiency of the center's staff were much appreciated, and special thanks are due several colleagues there – William Bouwsma, Timothy Breen, Jack Censer, Gladys Lang, and Kurt Lang – for bearing with my initial efforts to shape a coherent argument.

Doctor Walter Brod, the Institutsleiter of the Institut für Hochschulkunde, kindly arranged for a visit to Würzburg that proved both pleasant and fruitful. Frau Anneliese Bruns, the secretary of the Universitätsarchiv in Göttingen, oriented me to the archive and never once evinced skepticism about my seemingly endless requests for files. I was also fortunate to explore (all too briefly) the library and archive of the Franckesche Stiftungen in Halle. Other visitors will concur that Herr Jürgen Storz, the keeper of the these treasures, is a rare combination of *Gemütlichkeit* and expertise.

As important as the sojourns in Germany were, I conducted a good deal of the research at home. That I was able to do so is testimony to the competence and the tolerance of the interlibrary loan staff of the D. H. Hill Library at North Carolina State University, Raleigh.

Fritz K. Ringer helped sustain the project with his encouragement and his expertise. Four scholars – Charles McClelland, Gail O'Brien, Mack Walker, and K. Steven Vincent – read the manuscript in its entirety and improved it with gentle but constructive criticism. As each chapter materialized, Steve Vincent assumed the onerous responsibility of confronting me with its shortcomings. More critical, though, was his confidence in the viability of the larger project, particularly as I found myself leaving the terra firma of social history and entering a meandering course through the history of ideas. I thank him for his patience as well as his acumen.

Introduction

I

The eighteenth century lures some with its modern face, still fresh and innocent but reassuringly familiar. I backpedaled into the century, in pursuit of the less familiar. Stimulated but unsettled by an exchange of ideas with students of other national histories, I had become intent on following my own hunches – every German historian has at least one – about the peculiarities of the Germans. But the exchange had also made me aware of the insularity and stagnation of eighteenth-century German studies. If we are eventually to reach firmer historical ground for explaining what was and what was not peculiar about a national experience, it will be from new angles of vision on the German route from tradition to modernity, unobstructed by shopworn models and their present-minded criteria for modernization. Above all we need a more nuanced, densely contextualized understanding of the social meaning of German religious and secular cultures and the variations on their interplay over the course of the eighteenth century.

It was in pursuit of this agenda that I made "poor students" (*arme Studenten*) my point of departure and my recurrent object of reference. Poor students were a more or less substantial minority at Protestant universities, and one that attested to the tenacious traditions of a religious culture. Nonetheless they provoked censure and alarm in old-regime society. With their ambivalent presence as its focal point, the study developed in concentric circles, raying out from a specific social experience to the cultural norms and ideas that gave it meaning and in turn bore its imprint.

In the eighteenth century, the term "poor student" referred to a distinct species of young men. Students of theology, they went on to careers in the clergy, including its teaching branch. They owed their earlier education to charity in various forms, all products of the reform impulse that had sustained Lutheranism from its earliest days. Many had arrived at the universities on foot, like vagabonds, after days or weeks on the roads, trusting in God or the next benefactor for tomorrow's meal. They were distinguished from their more affluent *Kommilitonen* by the fact that they took their meals at "free tables" in refectories and local inns, by their need to earn extra cash as tutors in private homes, by their threadbare coats and soiled shirts. On closer inspection the species breaks down into outsiders and insiders. For the outsiders, academic education was a dramatic but risky leap into an alien world. Raised in the "lower" spheres of farming and the manual trades, they could expect to be relegated to the cellar of the learned estate – as pastors in villages and small towns and as teachers in the Latin schools. But among the exceptions were some of the stellar figures in eighteenth-century intellectual life; from the plebeian depths came Johann Joachim Winckelmann and Christian Gottlob Heyne, two of the giants in the renaissance of classical studies, and the three men – Christian Wolff, Immanuel Kant, and Johann Gottlieb Fichte – who largely account for Germany's eighteenth-century renown in academic philosophy.

As a practical definition, "poor student" also referred to sons of obscure clergymen following in their fathers' footsteps. These were often every bit as poor as outsiders, and no less dependent on charity. What made them insiders was the fact that they had been introduced to academic culture, at least in a minimal way, at home. Gellert, Lessing, Herder, and Jean Paul are perhaps the best examples of their contribution to German letters – a contribution that has long been recognized but still lacks the socially informed explanation it merits. Sons of clergymen who lacked propertied wealth, and who could not count on high-placed connections, also faced limited career prospects, though they were less disadvantaged than outsiders. But again the success stories were dramatic; one thinks of Johann Salomo Semler, the leading rationalist theologian of his generation, and Friedrich Gedike, the school director in Berlin who was appointed to the Prussian Superior School Board at age thirty-two.

Hence – to introduce a bit more sociological precision – only some poor students experienced *intergenerational* mobility, and whether and in what sense that mobility was "upward" (or "vertical") is a troublesome issue. I use the term "academic mobility" in an admittedly loose sense, to evoke the entire phenomenon. Academic mobility may strike some readers as providing an oddly constricted angle of vision onto the larger themes of the study; but in fact it is of strategic significance for conceiving the shape and structure of eighteenth-century German society and understanding the pertinent social referents and sources of tension for ideological divisions on issues of social order, individual freedom, and justice.

That significance has been obscured until recently by the very framing of questions and definition of terms. Eighteenth-century studies have been permeated with the same assumptions about a German "divergent path" (*Sonderweg*) that are now being contested in the more crowded ranks of nineteenth-century historiography.[1] What allowed England and France to

[1] Particularly important in provoking a reexamination of the *Sonderweg* model for the nine-

achieve the "maturity" of a liberal polity (the one by an evolutionary process, the other by revolution) – so the standard version goes – was a bourgeoisie with a capitalist center of gravity in a modern class society. Lacking such a center, and hence impotent in the face of a "feudal" aristocracy retaining its social hegemony and its monopoly of political power, German intellectuals orchestrated a bourgeois retreat into apolitical "inwardness" (*Innerlichkeit*).

French historians have been busy demolishing the conventional image of 1789 as a bourgeois "advent." In the search for a distinctly "bourgeois" mentality in eighteenth-century Germany, the choice between a liberal (or at least protoliberal) political consciousness and apolitical resignation (or escapism) has come to seem artificially constricting.[2] But the model of bourgeois modernization has proved remarkably durable, and not just in orthodox Marxist circles. In the 1920s and 1930s Karl Mannheim and his associates, despite their aversion to the economic reductionism of Marxism, gave the model a new lease on life in their historical "sociology of knowledge." The dichotomy between a feudal aristocracy and a progressive bourgeoisie has become inherent in secular visions of history as an inevitable (if sometimes retarded) march of progress and in the coupling of political progress to economic modernization. In our own era, as in the interwar years, the notion of an "apolitical" German *Sonderweg* has broad appeal among academics and intellectuals, preoccupied as they are with the crippling legacy of an authoritarian past.[3]

teenth century is David Blackbourn and Geoff Eley, *The Peculiarities of German History. Bourgeois Society and Politics in Nineteenth-Century Germany* (Oxford and New York, 1984).

[2] On the historiography of the French Revolution, see especially François Furet, *Interpreting the French Revolution*, trans. Elborg Forster (New York, 1981); Keith Michael Baker, "Enlightenment and Revolution in France. Old Problems, Renewed Approaches," *Journal of Modern History* 53:1 (Mar. 1981): 281–303; Colin Lucas, "Nobles, Bourgeois, and the Origins of the French Revolution," *Past and Present* 60 (1973), reprinted in Douglas Johnson, ed., *French Society and the Revolution* (Cambridge, 1976), pp. 88–131, which denies central importance to an aristocratic-bourgeois conflict in eighteenth-century France and argues that in this regard the Estates General elections in 1788 occasioned an abrupt turn to polarization. For examples of the changing image of the eighteenth-century German "bourgeoisie," see Rudolf Vierhaus, ed., *Bürger und Bürgerlichkeit im Zeitalter der Aufklärung*, Wolfenbütteler Studien zur Aufklärung, vol. 7 (Heidelberg, 1981). See also Franklin Kopitzsch, ed., *Aufklärung, Absolutismus und Bürgertum in Deutschland. Zwolf Aufsätze*, Nymphenburger Texte zur Wissenschaft, vol. 24 (Munich, 1976); idem, "Aufgaben einer Sozialgeschichte der deutschen Intelligenz zwischen Aufklärung und Kaiserreich," *Sozialwissenschaftliche Information für Unterricht und Studium* 5 (1976): 83–89.

[3] Norbert Elias, a student of Mannheim at Frankfurt, provides a classic application of the model in *The History of Manners*, The Civilizing Process, vol. 1, trans. Edmund Jephcott (1939: New York, 1978), pp. 8–29. A more eclectic but still characteristic product of the new "sociology of knowledge" is Hans Weill, *Die Entstehung des deutschen Bildungsprinzips* (Bonn, 1930). A more recent (and imaginative) analysis of the unpolitical *Bürger* is Wolf Lepenies, *Melancholie und Gesellschaft* (Frankfurt am Main, 1972), esp. pp. 76–114. In Hans J. Haferkorn's relatively complex Marxist framework, authors and their new "public" enter a problematic relationship as the literary market is drawn into the market economy of modern capitalism. But at the same time an emerging "free" literary intelligentsia, reflecting "the conflict

The two most important essays on the eighteenth-century intelligentsia – Hans Gerth's *Bürgerliche Intelligenz* and Wilhelm Roessler's *Die Entstehung des modernen Erziehungswesens* – represent positive variations on the same model. Gerth was a student of Mannheim, but one need only compare his dissertation with his mentor's more famous essay on conservative thought to appreciate its imaginative grasp of historical detail. Written as the collapse of the Weimar Republic was making the weaknesses of German liberalism painfully evident, *Bürgerliche Intelligenz* is remarkably detached from its era. Gerth found liberalism where others lamented its absence; he traced the origins of the imposing liberal movement of the mid-nineteenth century to a surrogate vanguard of university-educated officials born around 1770. Educational and professional experience, he argued, made this group precociously receptive to Western liberal ideas, and the "points of coincidence" between its bureaucratic "habitus" and the market orientation of capitalists eventually made for the fusion of these two bourgeois wings into a single liberal movement.[4] Roessler does not mention liberalism, but its conceptions of emancipation and enlightened progress hover over every page. What concerned him was the genesis of a modern ethos of personal autonomy and self-determination – a sense of "personal station," essential to the exercise of individual freedom and responsibility in the liberal sense. Again it was important to posit a convergence of *Bildung* and *Besitz*; by the early nineteenth century the new ethos had found a solid bourgeois (my word) foundation in the "new middle estate," which included university scholars, the broad ranks of officialdom, manufacturers, and members of the "newly emerging industrial and public professions."[5]

Much of the subtlety of both studies lies in explaining how changes in eighteenth-century aristocratic culture contributed to and were assimilated into a distinctly modern social consciousness. Likewise both scholars were too familiar with the variety of student life-styles at eighteenth-century universities to gloss over the distance between poor students and scions of upper bourgeois families. But for all the flexibility they introduced into the

between *Bürgertum* and *Aristokratie*," takes a "resigned path" into an "inwardness alienated from its literary-political possibilities." Hans J. Haferkorn, "Zur Entstehung der bürgerlich-literarischen Intelligenz und des Schriftstellers in Deutschland zwischen 1750 und 1800," *Literaturwissenschaft und Sozialwissenschaften*, vol. 3 (Deutsches Bürgertum und literarische Intelligenz 1750–1800) (Stuttgart, 1974), pp. 14, 128–29.

[4] Hans H. Gerth, *Bürgerliche Intelligenz um 1800. Zur Soziologie des deutschen Frühliberalismus*, ed. Ulrich Herrmann, Kritische Studien zur Geschichtswissenschaft, vol. 19 (Göttingen, 1976). This is a reprint of the thesis, with an informative introduction by Ulrich Herrmann on Gerth and the intellectual context. It can now be supplemented with Gerth's own retrospective view, in Joseph Bensman, Arthur J. Vidich, and Nobuko Gerth, eds., *Politics, Character, and Culture. Perspectives from Hans Gerth* (Westport, Conn., 1982), pp. 14–71.

[5] Wilhelm Roessler, *Die Entstehung des modernen Erziehungswesens in Deutschland* (Stuttgart, 1961). For another positive variation on the model, see Fritz Brüggemann, "Der Kampf um die bürgerliche Welt- und Lebensanschauung in der deutschen Literatur des 18. Jahrhunderts," *Deutsche Vierteljahrsschrift für Literaturwissenschaft und Geistesgeschichte* 3 (1925): 94–127.

overarching model, they upturned its verdict without questioning its basic categories and cleavages. The aristocracy is no longer a monolithic obstacle; but its "feudal" privileges, often linked awkwardly with "absolutism," remain the primary reference for understanding "bourgeois" resentment. Since both scholars are sensitive to distinctions within the university-educated *Bürgertum*, as well as between its milieu and that of commerce and industry, it is all the more striking that they devote so little attention to the social resentments occasioned by inequalities *among* commoners. The essential problem remains; within a *political* definition of a social category, various kinds of mobility into the intelligentsia and through its ranks tend to be collapsed into a single bourgeois "ascent," in turn marking a single species of emancipatory consciousness.

As useful as it may still be in some respects, the aristocratic-bourgeois fissure oversimplifies the structure of access to academic education and public employment. In the course of the eighteenth century, as the corporate identity of the "learned estate" (*Gelehrtenstand*) acceded to the professional jurisdictions of a modern "educated bourgeoisie" (*Bildungbürgertum*), that structure developed two fault lines, both registering strains. In the civil and judicial bureaucracies of some German states, a preference for pedigrees (or at least titles) in the higher echelons clearly provoked resentment among bourgeois law graduates. But this was a rivalry within a consolidation. As Gerth suggested, the law faculties of the late eighteenth century perpetuated both a service aristocracy, acquiring at least minimal academic qualifications to maintain its preeminence at the highest levels of government employment, and an entrenched *Bildungsbürgertum*, transmitting academic learning as a kind of family patrimony.

The German Enlightenment did pit the claims of individual talent and merit against the collective privileges of "birth"; but one need only sample its vast literature on educational reform to realize that much of the tension was being generated at the second, lower fault line – the one running *through* the *Bürgertum* and its clerical branch. It was this line that separated the outsiders among poor students – those inheriting neither *Bildung* nor *Besitz* – from the hybrid service elite. Straddling it – and registering its tensions – were the clergymen's sons who had inherited a measure of *Bildung* but nonetheless, in view of their fathers' paltry pastoral and teaching incomes, were genuinely poor.[6]

[6] On the bourgeois-aristocratic conflict, see esp. Johanna Schultze, *Die Auseinandersetzung zwischen Adel und Bürgertum in den deutschen Zeitschriften der letzten drei Jahrzehnte des 18. Jahrhunderts (1773–1806)* (1925: Vaduz, 1965). An important restatement of the case for such a conflict in the Prussian bureaucracy is Hans-Eberhard Mueller, *Bureaucracy, Education, and Monopoly. Civil Service Reforms in Prussia and England* (Berkeley, Calif., 1984); it should be compared with Hans Rosenberg, *Bureaucracy, Aristocracy and Autocracy. The Prussian Experience 1660–1815* (Cambridge, Mass., 1958). Particularly important for understanding the aristocratic wing of an emerging service elite is Charles E. McClelland, "The Aristocracy and

In the conventional models poor students are included in a sprawling *Bürgertum*; or in their plebeian profile, they become sons of a "proletariat"; or as products of a *Kleinbürgertum*, they represent a kind of bourgeoisie manqué. None of these approaches does justice to the fact that, in the corporate order of the old regime, certain disadvantages and rites of passage into the learned estate formed outsiders and insiders, for all the differences between them, into a distinct group. And yet the conventional alternatives also blur the duality that makes the category so intriguing. While all poor students lacked the advantages of propertied wealth, only some had to cross the widening chasm between the uneducated mass and the educated elite. One of the critical lines of demarcation in eighteenth-century society bounded the entire group; another cut straight through it.

Within this more variegated social topography, salient divisions on the familiar issue of "careers open to talent" come into relief; the eighteenth-century ideal of meritocracy can be seen patterning into neocorporate and egalitarian alternatives, both in need of detailed explanation.

II

Ralph H. Turner's contrast of the English and American school systems has been pivotal in widening the comparative approach to mobility from measurements of rates to a broader understanding of their social and cultural significance. In the "sponsored mobility" that prevails in England, Turner argues, a coherent elite and its agents control the induction of new recruits into its ranks by selecting them at an early age and requiring them to meet its standards.[7] With suitable adjustments for a very different time and place, this "ideal type" offers a useful handle on eighteenth-century academic mobility. The controlled induction of poor boys into the learned estate was not the centralized, standardized selection by examination that prevails

University Reform in Eighteenth-Century Germany," in Lawrence Stone, ed., *Schooling and Society. Studies in the History of Education* (Baltimore, 1976), pp. 146–73. The lower fault line has emerged clearly in recent contributions to the history of education; see Karl-Ernst Jeismann, *Das preussische Gymnasium in Staat und Gesellschaft. Die Entstehung des Gymnasiums als Schule des Staates und der Gebildeten, 1787–1817*, Industrielle Welt. Schriftenreihe des Arbeitskreises für moderne Sozialgeschichte, vol. 15 (Stuttgart, 1974); Detlef K. Müller, *Sozialstruktur und Schulsystem: Aspekte zum Strukturwandel des Schulwesens im 19. Jahrhundert*, Studien zum Wandel von Gesellschaft und Bildung im Neunzehnten Jahrhundert, vol. 7 (Göttingen, 1977); Fritz K. Ringer, *Education and Society in Modern Europe* (Bloomington, Ind., 1978), esp. pp. 81–91.

[7] Ralph H. Turner, "Sponsored and Contest Mobility and the School System," *American Sociological Review* 25 (1960): 855–67. An important attempt to elaborate and refine Turner's distinctions, particularly as they relate to specific educational systems, is Earl Hopper, "Educational Systems and Selected Consequences of Patterns of Mobility and Non-Mobility in Industrial Societies: A Theoretical Discussion," in Richard Brown, ed., *Knowledge, Education, and Cultural Change. Papers in the Sociology of Education* (London, 1973), pp. 17–69. See also idem, ed., *Readings in the Theory of Educational Systems* (London, 1971).

today; sponsorship was in the hands of the individuals – from the local teacher or pastor to the noble Maecenas – who distributed various forms of public and private charity and dispensed appointments. And yet as individualized as this patronage was and as esoteric as the initiation into old-style learning may seem from this distance, academic mobility had a discernible structure and cultural density. Much of Part I is devoted to reassembling the structure, to explaining the process of selection within it, and to defining the prescriptive terms of class inequality for patrons and clients.

This approach to the relationship between social structure and ideology is somewhat different from the one to which the new "social" history of education has been largely devoted. The field has been preoccupied with gauging the degree to which access to academic education has been "open," primarily by assigning pupils and students to the categories of a larger class structure, and with matching reform agendas to various social interests.[8] As handicapped as it has been by the fragmentary eighteenth-century data on students' social origins, quantitative research has confirmed that, within an overall pattern of elitism, there was limited but significant scope for academic mobility. What the field lacks – and this is ironic in view of its commitment to interdisciplinary research – is precisely the concern with social *process* and cultural *experience* that has entered the sociological literature on mobility in the past few decades. Turner was intrigued by the possibility that the actual structure of mobility in a particular national context reflected an "organizing folk norm" central to the culture. More recent studies have added complications to his essential distinction between "sponsored" and "contest" models; but they have also pursued his basic insight that perceptions of mobility are shaped not only by its measurable reality, but also by the cultural grids of norms and values within which it is idealized (or at least legitimated), or censured, or given an ambiguous value. Likewise sociologists have become increasingly aware that upward mobility via education is a kind of molting process. Whether the result is painful alienation or comfortable assimilation – whether there is a neat fit or an awkward disjuncture between the "inner" personality and its newly acquired social and cultural shell – the process cannot be simply extrapolated from "objective" data. Nor can it be deduced from our current ideological precon-

[8] On recent research in the field, see Konrad H. Jarausch, "The Old 'New History of Education': A German Reconsideration," *History of Education Quarterly* 26:2 (1986): 225–41. A useful synthesis is Peter Lundgreen, *Sozialgeschichte der deutschen Schule im Ueberblick*, Teil 1: *1770–1918* (Göttingen, 1980). On the universities, see esp. Charles E. McClelland, *State, Society, and University in Germany 1700–1914* (Cambridge, 1980), which synthesizes recent research and offers new perspectives. The most relevant analyses of structure and ideology in the above sense have been Müller, *Sozialstruktur und Schulsystem*; Ringer, *Education and Society*; Hans Georg Herrlitz, *Studium als Standesprivileg: Die Entstehung des Maturitätsproblems im 18. Jahrhundert* (Frankfurt am Main, 1973), which focuses on the issues raised by "poor students." See also Peter Lundgreen, "Bildung und Besitz – Einheit oder Inkongruenz in der europäischen Sozialgeschichte?" *Geschichte und Gesellschaft* 7 (1981): 262–75.

ceptions. It becomes critical to conceive of class as a series of relations rather than a static structure and to understand how cultural norms as well as structural conditions have constituted the historical experience of mobility.[9]

I have tried to excavate several layers of cultural ideology in this sense, with an eye to explaining both how they were shaped to a specific social milieu and how they came to bear its imprint. If the sociological literature on mobility convinced me of the need for such an excavation, it did not offer reliable signposts to the findings. The context of most mobility studies is the kind of modern "industrial" society that had hardly begun to emerge at the end of the eighteenth century. Until very recently one of the guiding assumptions was that the openness of modern classes -the fluidity of movement between them – signifies an egalitarian blurring of class distinctions.[10] At the rarefied altitudes of theory, unencumbered by historical empiricism, it has been easy enough to underline that assumption by contrasting the present with the rigidity of corporate hierarchies in a "preindustrial" past. In its broad outlines the contrast probably holds. Nineteenth-century industrialization, it still seems judicious to claim, brought an increase in mobility of all kinds, though the opportunities for dramatic social ascent over two generations may have remained quite restricted. Likewise a marked tendency toward closure – a tendency well illustrated by the large number of sons following in their fathers' footsteps in the eighteenth-century German clergy – can still fairly be considered an attribute of corporatism.

But sociologists are no longer so quick to assume that high mobility rates reduce either actual inequalities or perceived distances between classes. At the "preindustrial" end of the spectrum, Sylvia Thrupp observed more than a quarter-century ago that the legal demarcations in corporate hierarchies should not be mistaken for "effective barriers to mobility." Thrupp may have missed the mark in blaming the confusion on "a certain mechanical way of using the concept of class"; it was probably due more to a rigid conceptual polarity between corporate closure and class "openness." But

[9] The other seminal work was Seymour Martin Lipset and Reinhard Bendix, *Social Mobility in Industrial Society* (Berkeley, Calif., 1959). The most relevant recent contributions for my purposes were Pierre Bourdieu and Jean Claude Passeron, *Les héritiers: Les étudiants et la culture* (Paris, 1964); idem, *La réproduction: Eléments pour une théorie du système d'enseignement* (Paris, 1970); John H. Goldthorpe, *Social Mobility and Class Structure in Modern Britain* (New York, 1980); Keith Hope, *As Others See Us. Schooling and Social Mobility in Scotland and the United States* (Cambridge, 1984); Karl Ulrich Mayer, *Ungleichheit und Mobilität im sozialen Bewusstsein. Untersuchungen zur Definition der Mobilitätssituation* (Opladen, 1975); Cornelius J. Van Zeyl, *Ambition and Social Structure. Educational Structure and Mobility Orientation in the Netherlands and the United States* (Lexington, Mass., 1974).

[10] See esp. the syntheses of recent research in Hartmut Kaelble, *Historische Mobilitätsforschung. Westeuropa und die USA im 19. und 20. Jahrhundert* (Darmstadt, 1978), which takes a notably cautious posture toward prevailing assumptions about a traditional-industrial dichotomy; idem, *Soziale Mobilität und Chancengleichheit im 19. und 20. Jahrhundert* (Göttingen, 1983).

her basic point has been vindicated; while the preindustrial past remains a theoretical foil in mobility studies, historians have been busy demonstrating the extent of movement, vertical as well as horizontal, across permeable corporate boundaries.[11]

To read modern perceptions and norms back into a preindustrial context is to indulge in the present-mindedness we are all committed to avoiding. But if the historian assumes that the mobility in question, though tolerated de facto, had no legitimate place in the culture, he ignores deep-rooted cultural sanctions that developed *within* preindustrial societies and were inherent in their corporate values. This is not to deny a tenacious preference for "birth" in corporate ideology. That preference often found expression in moral censure of poor students and in alarmism about the threat their swelling number, their ambitions, and their apparent lack of "honor" posed to the integrity of the corporate order. And yet however limited and conditional the approval of poor students' presence was, it existed and requires a historical explanation in terms of cultural traditions. The traditional Latinity of the schools was vital to the permeability as well as the closure of the clerical order. Paternalism – the ideology that underpinned authority at all levels of the corporate hierarchy – gave patrons a moral right to deferential gratitude from the poor boys they sponsored; but it also set limits on the kinds of deference they had a right to expect and hence gave clients a moral basis for preserving a measure of personal integrity even as they acknowledged their dependence. It has become a truism that, in the orthodox Lutheran conception of "duty" and "office" (*Amt*), the entire emphasis was on accepting subordination in a "station"; much less attention has been devoted to the fact that the sponsorship of poor boys for clerical careers was a hallowed tradition in the Lutheran church, and we have only begun to appreciate how the Pietist revival of the late seventeenth and early eighteenth centuries revitalized that tradition.

To a degree the German sociological concept of an "intelligentsia" has bypassed the conventional dichotomy between industrial and preindustrial societies. Gerth and others have sought to give national and temporal specificity to Mannheim's broad-stroked historical sketches of "socially unattached" intelligentsias, particularly by examining the kinds of mobility to which recognizably modern forms of education and bureaucratic employment gave rise *before* modern industrialization got under way.[12] But again a

[11] Sylvia Thrupp, "Hierarchy, Illusion and Social Mobility," *Comparative Studies in Society and History* 2:1 (1959): 126–28. For examples of historical assessments of the extent and significance of intergenerational upward mobility, see also Stephan Thernstrom, "Notes on the Historical Study of Social Mobility," *Comparative Studies in Society and History* 10:2 (1968): 162–72; Lawrence Stone, "Social Mobility in England, 1500–1700," *Past and Present* 33 (1966): 16–55; Allan Sharlin, "From the Study of Social Mobility to the Study of Society," *American Journal of Sociology* 85:2 (1979): 338–60.

[12] For Mannheim's definition of the intelligentsia, see esp. *Ideology and Utopia. An Introduction to the Sociology of Knowledge* (New York, 1936), pp. 136–46.

certain present-minded oversimplification is striking from this distance. More or less aware of their ideological preferences, historical sociologists and historians have equated bourgeois "emancipation" from the collective constraints of old-regime corporatism with the rise of modern individualism.[13] The issue dividing liberals and Marxists is not whether individualism appeared, but whether it made the modern *Bürger* a truly progressive figure (the liberal version) or camouflaged his class consciousness behind an illusory commitment to universal rights and freedoms (the Marxist alternative).

Again the two major studies fall on the positive side of the spectrum – and again they see the academic and official intelligentsia as the vanguard in a larger process of bourgeois emancipation. To Gerth the original vision of a *Rechtstaat* – the one that paved the way for a distinctly political liberalism in the pre-March era – promised a rational legal framework for competitive achievement, posed against the constraints of "estates of birth." To Roessler the new individualism – the "personal station" – lay less in a commitment to individual achievement than in an ethos of personal autonomy and self-determination, defined in cultural terms but clearly inspired by a political ideal of individual freedom and responsibility. A flexible rationality with ever expanding horizons emancipated the new breed – appearing first in the intelligentsia and later in the commercial and industrial bourgeoisie – from both the patriarchal authority of the traditional household and the constricting solidarity of corporate membership.

Whether the emphasis is on the exercise of political freedom in a public realm, or on the private pursuit of self-interest in a competitive market, or on vaguer notions of self-fulfillment in an "achievement society," the concept of individualism radiates nineteenth- and twentieth-century values. Contemporary resonances, in fact, make the concept all the more treacherous. The classical liberalism of the nineteenth century is all too easily read back into the consciousness of previous generations, but at least can be said to have provided fairly clear-cut political and economic criteria for individualism. In our century this legacy has been absorbed into the elusive congeries of cultural values that is now being dubbed "expressive individualism." My point is not to deny that the eighteenth century gave rise to distinctly modern forms of consciousness; the study is in fact centrally con-

[13] On the many varieties of "individualism," see esp. Steven Lukes, *Individualism* (New York, 1973). Recent critiques are Thomas C. Heller, Morton Sosna, and David E. Wellbery, *Reconstructing Individualism. Autonomy, Individuality, and the Self in Western Thought* (Stanford, Calif., 1986), and Robert N. Bellah et al., *Habits of the Heart. Individualism and Commitment in American Life* (New York, 1986). Bellah and his associates provide a nuanced analysis of both "utilitarian" and "expressive" individualism in contemporary American culture and of their various conflations. It will become apparent that the "utilitarian" ethic they have in mind – i.e., one that sanctions and indeed requires the competitive pursuit of self-interest in a free market – is very different from what I shall call the utilitarian ethic of eighteenth-century German rationalism.

cerned with their emergence and their significance. But caution is required precisely because the century seems to offer so many breakthroughs to (or at least anticipations of) modern culture, because it introduced the vocabulary – the language of freedom, talent, and merit – that has become the lingua franca of private self-searching as well as public discourse, because the simultaneous persistence of old-regime traditions seems to throw the appearance of the modern into bold relief. All this makes it especially tempting to observe the eighteenth century through a lens of subsequent ideology, at once political and more vaguely cultural, that distorts and obscures.

Removing the lens is in part a matter of avoiding a simplistic *moral* dichotomy, equating modern forms of mobility with individual freedom at one end, traditional corporate membership with a complete lack of personal autonomy at the other. Set within this contrast, the traditional ascent of poor students into the learned estate is seen to require complete absorption into a corporate solidarity or, in a more cynical view, relentless opportunism (or "servility") in conforming to its standards. One needs to penetrate behind the edgy pieties of eighteenth-century stereotypes, to the moral dilemmas they caricatured. Then it becomes apparent that the concept of corporate "honor," as it found expression in traditional social norms and religious ideals, cut both ways. If it required assimilation within a corporate standard and deference to its guardians, it also demanded a core of personal autonomy and integrity.

III

The "new" history of education is committed to providing a dense social grounding for the study of pedagogical theory and educational reform thought, and this book is a case in point. But in the preoccupation with structure (narrowly defined), intellectual history tends to be allotted a token presence. That is another reason why the field is in danger of settling into a new insularity – and why I became resolved to widen the angle of vision. To approach mobility as a cultural phenomenon is also to recognize the formative role of ideas. An examination of a dense configuration of ideas – familiar eighteenth-century concepts of talent and merit, of calling in the religious sense, of vocation and profession – seemed essential to understanding how poor students were perceived and how they made sense of their lives. One form the ideas took *was* to explain the experience of academic mobility; that helps account for their vital meaning to individuals – a meaning that will be demonstrated again and again – and for their ascendancy in the larger culture. From that direction as well, a restricted vision opens out onto broader dimensions of the relationship between society and culture.

All citizens, the French National Assembly proclaimed in 1789, "are equally admissible to all public dignities, offices and employments, according to their capacity, and with no other distinction than that of their virtues and talents."[14] In a sense German poor students posed the questions about the nature of a truly just society, and above all about the proper way to reconcile social order and individual right, that the Declaration of the Rights of Man and the Citizen discreetly avoided. Did the opening of careers to talent mean "equality of opportunity" in the sense of procedural justice and hence was it, as the French Declaration seemed to imply, a simple matter of eliminating the legal privileges of "birth" that structured a corporate hierarchy? Or was the issue distributive justice, which might require an assault on the de facto privilege constituted by inherited wealth and education? Was talent, like property in one definition, an individual possession, to be allowed maximum freedom as a vehicle for individual self-interest and personal happiness? Or should it instead – by analogy with an alternative notion of property – be considered a trust, its legitimate use restricted by a collective definition of "public" need? Did talent and virtue form a natural pairing of equals, or was the legitimacy of talent contingent on the primacy of virtue?

We bring a certain skeptical detachment to the eighteenth-century enthusiasm for virtue, perhaps because it strikes us as quaint in the light of more recent developments. The celebration of "talent" is closer to home; having become integral to an amorphous but potent ethos of achievement in contemporary Western societies, it resists the imposition of critical historical distance. Students of eighteenth-century France have looked back from the Revolution to pinpoint the social appeal of opening careers to talent – to an ambitious "bourgeoisie" in the face of aristocratic privilege and, in more recent literature, to a Grub Street proletariat excluded from *le monde*. In the study of eighteenth-century Germany, appropriately enough, the question has been whether the ideology of a bureaucratic reform from above aimed at promoting or excluding talent from below. In a sense both approaches have been preoccupied with the familiar; while one isolates anticipations of revolutionary ideology, the other takes as its standard contemporary agendas for "equality of opportunity" (*Chancengleichheit*).[15]

In Germany, as elsewhere in Europe, "talent" was one of the lynchpins

[14] Georges Lefebvre, *The Coming of the French Revolution*, trans. R. R. Palmer (Princeton, N.J., 1967), includes the entire text of the Declaration of the Rights of Man and the Citizen. Quotation from Article VI, in ibid., p. 222.

[15] For France, the classic study, still very useful, is Elinor G. Barber, *The Bourgeoisie in 18th Century France* (1955: Princeton, N.J., 1973). On the Parisian subintelligentsia, see esp. Robert Darnton, *The Literary Underground of the Old Regime* (Cambridge, Mass., 1982). Particularly important for the issue of *Chancengleichheit* in Germany are Herrlitz, *Studium als Standesprivileg*; Müller, *Sozialstruktur und Schulsystem*.

in the Enlightenment triad of nature, human nature, and society; that makes our neglect of its contextual history all the more striking. We need to know how "talent" coupled or collided with other key concepts in eighteenth-century rationalism and to become better attuned to the social resonances in its various usages. Clearly the career opened to talent represented a secular aspiration, far removed from a Christian ethic of self-denial; but if we are to unearth the roots of a secular reverence for talent and merit, we have to be attentive to affinities as well as ruptures with the religious ideals of calling and service that were central to orthodox Lutheranism and its Pietist variant. Likewise, if we are to appreciate the "modern" implications of both religious and secular ideas, we need to understand how they contributed to a new ethos of "profession" – and to a new conception of professional careers – at the end of the century.

There is a certain irony to my exploration of these ideas. Sidestepping questions about whether Germany entered a *Sonderweg* in the conventional sense, I became intent on doing justice to the German twists in my story. The two agendas are in fact inseparable. As Gerth's essay demonstrates, the search for liberalism tends to go hand in hand with a tendency to assume that the modernizing function of the German intelligentsia, like that of its Polish and Russian counterparts, lay in importing Western ideas.[16] The very elasticity of the German language in the eighteenth century calls attention to a more subtle process – one in which an indigenous fund of meanings informed imported ideas (or at least European-wide ideas) with specifically German resonances and emphases at the same time that it was modified by them. In eighteenth-century Germany a secular ethic of vocation (*Beruf*) became the repository for a humanistic concept of "natural talent" and its corollary celebration of productive work, merit, and service, typical of Enlightenment rationalism. But *Beruf* had entered German culture as Luther's word for calling, and this received meaning, with all it evoked about the opposition between grace and "the flesh," had been intensified in the Pietist ideal of conversion.

One of the purposes of the book is to trace the cultural roots and social implications of a distinct way of thinking about and assigning value to mobility – a way that may strike some as blatantly contradictory rather than merely tension-ridden, but only because current thinking is so pervaded with justifications of mobility in terms of the calculated pursuit of self-interest in market competition, or the satisfaction of personal ambition in an achievement society, or the therapeutic strategies for "expressive" self-fulfillment. Hence we will be concerned with the underlying contin-

[16] See esp. Richard Pipes, "The Historical Evolution of the Russian Intelligentsia," in idem, ed., *The Russian Intelligentsia* (New York and London, 1961), pp, 47–62; Aleksander Gella, "An Introduction to the Sociology of the Intelligentsia," in idem, ed., *The Intelligentsia and the Intellectuals. Theory, Method, and Case Study* (London, 1976), pp. 9–34.

uities as well as the more obvious ruptures between the sacred and the secular versions of what Weber called "this-worldly asceticism." There are senses in which the ethic of calling provided an impetus for a positive estimation of individual achievement; but its "ascetic" impulse also helps explain why the achievement ethos had so little room for the values of modern individualism and above all for emphatic approval of personal ambition. The tensions within eighteenth-century ideologies of vocation, talent, and merit lay precisely in the fact that they sanctioned individual self-determination without relaxing an overriding insistence on collective imperatives. What is striking about even the more egalitarian visions of meritocracy in utilitarian rationalism – i.e., the rationales for opening careers to talent from below – is their tendency *not* to license the assertions of individual freedom, economic, social, political, and psychological, that have become central to individualism in the modern era.

Part III pursues mutations of this theme in the neohumanistic ideal of self-cultivation and uses them to shed new light on the transition from the traditional learned estate (*Gelehrtenstand*) to the nineteenth-century *Bildungsbürgertum*. Neohumanism offered a new cultural idiom for academic mobility, radically emancipatory (and indeed individualistic) in some respects, but nonetheless constrained and conditional in its own way. At the turn of the century, the rhetoric of *Bildung* also overlay and to a degree displaced utilitarian rationalism in the reform thought of teachers and clergymen, and particularly in their public arguments for a dramatic upgrading of the collective status of their occupations. I call these arguments "professional ideologies" and see them as another episode in the secularization of *Beruf* and the expansion of its social dimensions. The new concept of "profession" can be seen as a variation on a Western model, but my concern is with its distinctly German contours. The study comes full circle; we return for a closer look at the occupational worlds of the school and the pastorate. Here too the preoccupation with individualism has imposed blinders; we need to understand how professional ideologies, in the very process of posing their service ethics against old-style corporate selfishness, subtly recast corporate values. My analysis aims to lay bare the logic of this recasting and to account for its turn-of-the-century shift in idiom within the larger framework of the study. Again the presence of poor students – as a reminder of the plebeian legacy to be overcome or as a prefiguration of the egalitarian meritocracy that a modern profession ought to be – becomes a revealing angle.

My purpose was to penetrate modern ideological filters, not to extrude politics from the subject. Throughout the study I have tried to ground an understanding of political significances and ramifications in the social reality of poor students and in their specifically German cultural context. What came to seem misleading was the conventional choice between a political consciousness identified by liberal criteria and an apolitical retreat to "inwardness." To apply that choice to professional ideologies is to miss both the "political" and the "apolitical" in their logic; my question is why and how they laid claim to a privileged realm of public authority, at once political and above mere politics, for the kind of knowledge peculiar to professional disciplines.

The final chapter is a kind of coda, tracing variations on a range of issues through the thought of Johann Gottlieb Fichte. Fichte's trials as a young man were emblematic of the poor student's dilemmas, and his mature philosophy can be understood as a particularly radical attempt to resolve the social and political paradoxes in German conceptions of "careers open to talent."

IV

All experience is construed experience. I offer this much-cited observation by Clifford Geertz not to identify with a particular methodological orientation in social (or cultural) history, but simply to introduce a statement of purpose.[17] The study has been designed to explain how a particular social reality was construed within a dense fabric of ideas and how the process of construal contributed to the weave and texture of the fabric. Part of the appeal – and the challenge – of the research lay in coaxing a scattered and varied assortment of sources, published and unpublished, into a single interpretive framework. The assortment includes philosophical treatises, sermon collections, university lectures, school reform tracts, pedagogical literature, handbooks on tutoring, autobiographies and autobiographical fragments, private correspondence, diary fragments. My interpretive strategies in the face of this mélange may be open to the charge of opportunism; I like to think of them as judiciously eclectic.

Nonetheless comments on two specific strategies are in order. The reader should not expect a systematic essay in comparative history, but one way to let some fresh breezes into eighteenth-century German studies was to suggest comparisons with the intelligentsia across the border.[18] Eighteenth-

[17] Clifford Geertz, *The Interpretation of Cultures* (New York, 1973), p. 405. On the relevance of this approach to historical research, see esp. William H. Sewell, Jr., *Work and Revolution in France. The Language of Labor from the Old Regime to 1848* (Cambridge, 1980).

[18] C. B. A. Behrens, *Society, Government and the Enlightenment. The Experiences of Eighteenth-Century France and Prussia* (New York, 1985), is a systematic comparison, and its insights confirm the value of such research. Behrens is essentially correct, I think, in claiming that in Prussia the Enlightenment generated a preference for state-sponsored reform, whereas in France its disruptive and divisive impact prepared the way for the collapse of the monarchy in 1789. But her conception of "equality" in an emerging "bourgeois" society overlooks the German ideological fissure between defenses of de facto privilege and rationales for an egalitarian alternative, and she ignores the role of professional disciplines in forming a public consensus at the end of the century.

century France no longer offers itself as a convenient foil to Germany's "failed" bourgeois modernization; but recent research on the French Enlightenment also highlights by contrast the distinctive constraints of the German scene. Hence Rousseau will make several brief appearances; it is instructive to compare his pedagogical vision with what German pedagogy took it to be. Likewise there will be an occasional glance at the "gutter Rousseauism" of the Parisian "Grub Steet" intelligentsia in the 1780s and 1790s; their radicalism puts in perspective the egalitarian vision of their contemporaries among German school reformers.

In the course of cementing its partnership with other social sciences, historical research may have become all the more segregated from literary studies. My contribution to bridging this disciplinary chasm lies in interpreting a corpus of autobiographical literature in which, I must admit, I initially expected to find only illustrative ornamentation. What soon became obvious was that a literal-minded approach to autobiographical texts, estimating their historical value strictly by their "factual" reliability, would hardly do justice to their testimony about construed experience. It became necessary to approach the text as a more or less conventionalized kind of "fiction"; to seek social and cultural meaning in fusions and mutations of conventional forms; to bring the same concern with meaning and form to narrative structures, symbolic usages, and other literary properties.

The pivotal text was Karl Philipp Moritz's *Anton Reiser*. Now the object of a minor industry in literary studies, this combined autobiography and novel still lies off the beaten track for most historians. I first read it in Göttingen. It was one of those chilly summer evenings when archives, libraries, and cafés are closed and the homesick American scholar without a television finds himself resorting to more demanding ways of killing time. The setting may help explain why I became absorbed in Moritz's relentlessly gloomy narrative; but I also realized from the first page that his text was taking me deeper into the aspirations and miseries of eighteenth-century poor students than any other. *Anton Reiser* proved to be the richest vein in a sizable deposit of autobiographical literature – and I have mined it more than once in researching and writing this book.

PART I

Poor students

I

Realities and stereotypes

THE PROTESTANT LEGACY

The Lutheran university in Wittenberg was in danger of extinction, one of its professors acknowledged in 1801; but it could still take pride in the fact that Martin Luther's room in the ancient Augustinian cloister might have been the scene of the "first thoughts of Reformation." The room itself had been preserved – a reminder of the heroic era when Wittenberg had been the center of the German Reformation, in a university that had long since reverted to the status of an intellectual backwater in a sleepy provincial town. From the late 1570s onward the cloister building housed a royal refectory, originally designed to provide two square meals per day to 150 students. The recipients were to be "children of the poor" who "are capable in terms of natural gifts of intelligence and other gifts" and "can accomplish something worthwhile in studies," but "cannot attend a university because of their poverty or . . . cannot endure there long because of the great poverty and financial incapacity of their parents and kin."[1]

The cloister-turned-refectory is an appropriate landmark for the rise of a new clerical order in Protestant Germany and for the new and adapted forms of charity that created the order and replenished it from one generation to the next. Luther himself had pointed the way with his "school sermons" in 1524 and 1530, in response to a precipitate decline in attendance at town schools and universities. It was above all to ensure a large recruiting pool for the officialdom of church and state that he called for obligatory mass education. Most recruits for the new clerical order, he reasoned, would have to come from "the common people, who used to have their children educated for the sake of [clerical] livings and benefices," and especially from "the poor."[2] Philipp Melanchthon and a host of lesser-

[1] Johann Christian August Grohmann, *Annalen der Universität zu Wittenberg*, 3 vols. (Meissen, 1801–2), 1: 65–78. The number of stipends was lowered to 120 in 1584 and to 75 in 1588. See also Otto Kius, "Das Stipendiatenwesen in Wittenberg und Jena unter der Ernestinern im 16. Jahrhundert," *Ilgen's Zeitschrift für die historische Theologie* 35 (1865): 96–159.

[2] Martin Luther, "To the Councilmen of All Cities in Germany That They Establish and Maintain Christian Schools, 1524," *Luther's Works*, vol. 45 (The Christian in Society, II), pp.

known reformers acted on Luther's appeals by reorganizing the existing universities, establishing new ones, and creating a new *Gelehrtenschule* to groom the Protestant learned estate in evangelical piety and humanistic scholarship. The public and private charity they made available was intended primarily for aspirants to the clergy who were "poor" at least in the sense that their parents could contribute little or nothing to their education. Charity formed a series of more or less precarious footholds on the climb through schools and universities to clerical appointments. By the eighteenth century some of the footholds were noticeably shaky, and to educational reformers the entire facade was coming to seem hopelessly obsolete. But the structure was still intact; its very survival is testimony to the fact that charitable support for poor schoolboys and university students had been the product of a vital reform impulse and had become deeply rooted in Protestant culture. To map the footholds is to trace the paths of academic mobility that most poor students were still taking at the end of the eighteenth century.

Some of this charity was a product of direct intervention by the territorial states and their governing ecclesiastical bodies. In Saxony, for example, confiscated church properites were used to establish four *Fürstenschulen*, with free places for sons of *Bürger* as well as for scions of aristocratic families. The municipal secondary schools – known as *Lateinschulen* or *Gymnasien* – collected fees from most of their pupils, but the new territorial school ordinances of the middle to late sixteenth century provided for some free places in them.[3] Former church wealth was also channeled into municipal stipends (*Stipendien*), which used it to finance the studies of native sons. "Family" or "private" stipends were endowed in the wills of professors, prosperous merchants, *Bürgermeister* and other local notables, and widows from the same social circles. This combined demonstration of piety and familial loyalty persisted into the seventeenth and eighteenth centuries, though perhaps with decreasing frequency; it had become as characteristic of Protestantism as the endowment of masses for departed souls had been

347–78; idem, "A Sermon on Keeping Children in School, 1530," *Luther's Works*, vol. 46 (The Christian in Society, III), pp. 222–36. The perceived need for "a large recruiting pool" for the "proliferating bureaucracies" of church and state is emphasized in Richard Gawthrop and Gerald Strauss, "Protestantism and Literacy in Early Modern Germany," *Past and Present* 104 (Aug. 1984): 31–55. For background on early Lutheran educational reform, see Gerald Strauss, *Luther's House of Learning. Indoctrination of the Young in the German Reformation* (Baltimore, 1978).

[3] There are numerous examples in Georg Mertz, *Das Schulwesen der deutschen Reformation im 16. Jahrhundert* (Heidelberg, 1902). On the Saxon *Fürstenschulen* see Friedrich Paulsen, *Geschichte des Gelehrten Unterrichts auf den deutschen Schulen und Universitäten vom Ausgang des Mittelalters bis zur Gegenwart. Mit besonderer Rücksicht auf den klassischen Unterricht*, vol. 1 (3rd, enl. ed.: Berlin and Leipzig, 1919), pp. 298–303; Theodor Flathe, *Sanct Afra. Geschichte der königlich sächsischen Fürstenschule zu Meissen seit ihrer Gründung im Jahre 1543 bis zu ihrem Neubau in den Jahren 1877–79* (Leipzig, 1879); Karl Julius Roessler, *Geschichte der Königlich sächsischen Fürsten- und Landschule zu Grimma* (Leipzig, 1891).

to an earlier religious style. Typically the bequest stipulated that the recipient had to be "poor" or "needy" as well as deserving in other respects and that, in the absence of a relative who wanted to "study," the support should go to someone outside the kin network.[4]

The charitable impulse also found more informal outlets. In the eighteenth century it was still common for local families to provide free meals to a boy attending the Latin school, particularly if a relative or a friend of the family had been able to enlist his neighbors for this purpose. This modest gesture of charity, in fact, was within the means of local artisans and shopkeepers as well as clergymen and more prosperous residents.[5] More important, the poor pupil could in effect earn charity by training for and performing in the street choir – known as the *Currende* or *chorus symphonicus* – that was a standard feature of Protestant towns. Under the direction of the local cantor-schoolteacher (who shared in the proceeds), the choir elicited contributions by performing hymns in the streets, before the houses of local residents, particularly during the Christmas and Easter seasons, and in some communities by providing the music at weddings and baptisms as well. For some, choir membership was merely a musical apprenticeship for the lower office of organist or cantor; but to the more ambitious poor boys – those aspiring to university studies – it was a significant source of financial support. Thanks to the generosity of local audiences and, more important, to the frequency of the performances, the yearly earnings were often considerably more than small change. In the mid-eighteenth century, the first quarterly share Ernst Gottlieb Gossow received as a new choirboy at the Graue-Kloster Gymnasium in Berlin was eight thaler, which was precisely equal to his quarterly allowance from

4 The Protestant *Stipendien* were intended in part to eliminate pupils' and students' reliance on "begging"; see esp. Walter Heinemeyer, "Pro studiosis pauperibus. Die Anfänge des reformatorischen Stipendiatenwesens in Hessen," in idem, ed., *Studium und Stipendium. Untersuchungen zur Geschichte des hessischen Stipendiatenwesens*, Veröffentlichungen der Historischen Kommission für Hessen, vol. 37 (Marburg, 1977). The various kinds of *Stipendien*, particularly in Saxony, are discussed in "Stipendien," in Johann Heinrich Zedler, ed., *Grosses vollständiges Universal Lexicon Aller Wissenschaften und Künste*, vol. 40 (Leipzig, 1744), pp. 135–42, and are illustrated in detail in Moritz Metzer, ed., *Verzeichniss der für Studirende an der Universität Leipzig fundirten Stipendien und Beneficien* (Leipzig, 1876). For other examples of municipal and private *Stipendien*, see esp. Johann Daniel Schulze, *Stipendien-Lexikon von und für Deutschland*, pt. 1 (A-L) (Leipzig, 1805). Also useful is I. G. B., "Beytrag zur Geschichte der milden Gestiffte für Studirende," *Magazin der Sächsischen Geschichte* (1785): 300–8; (1786): 92–100, 266–78, 350–56, 472–80, 531–41, 661–64; (1787): 66–80, 286–95, 350–55, 450–56. Johann Christian Siebenkees, *Abhandlung von Stipendien und den Rechten derselben* (Nürnberg, 1786), is an informative but limited discussion of legal questions.

5 The most striking example is Karl Philipp Moritz, *Anton Reiser. Ein psychologischer Roman* (1785–90: Frankfurt am Main, 1979). See also Margarete von Olfers, "Berliner Gymnasiastenleben zur Zeit Friedrichs des Grossen. Aus den Erinnerungen Ernst Gottliebs v. Gossow," *Zeitschrift des Vereins für die Geschichte Berlins*, Neue Folge 51 (1934): 44–50. The decline in this kind of charity was occasionally noted.

home, and it soon increased to ten thaler.[6] Understandably boys feared being excluded from the choir when they reached puberty and their voices changed.

Local willingness to support choirs is one reason why the bulk of pupils at some schools – the Thomasschule in Leipzig is a striking example – managed to board away from home despite their parents' financial incapacity. Another way to earn cash was to instruct the younger children of local families. In towns like Lüneburg the *Hospitum* – the use of older "foreign" pupils for this purpose, in return for room and board – was a mutually beneficial arrangement for the school and prosperous local families. In addition to allowing the school to enroll outsiders, despite the lack of boarding facilities, it offered the families a convenient way to have their children instructed and kept under supervision at home.[7] By the eighteenth century this use of pupils as live-in tutors seems to have become less common, partly because students had replaced them in that role; but for "foreign" pupils and for local boys without means, private lessons at an hourly or weekly rate were still an important source of cash.

While choir membership and tutoring tended to distinguish poor schoolboys, more or less invidiously, from their more affluent mates, they also had the effect of integrating outsiders into the social fabric and cultural rhythms of local life. The young man who moved on to a university town advanced from the dependent status of a minor to the corporate freedom of an academic *Bürger* and entered a distinct student subculture known to coexist on uneasy terms with local society. But he was likely to enjoy outside support; there were probably more municipal and private stipends for students than for pupils, and the university itself was accommodating. The

[6] Olfers, "Berliner Gymnasiastenleben," p. 44. For the year 1681, the total proceeds for the choir from the Johanneum in Lüneburg, which had to share the local turf with the choir from another school, was about 193 thaler – a sum higher than the income of many schoolteachers. After the rector and cantor had taken their shares, there were 22 thaler for the eldest boy (the *Praefectus*) and 19 thaler for his assistant (*Adjunctus*). But there was a steep scale – from a little more than 1 thaler to 13 thaler – for the other eighteen regular members and two *Expektanten*, and the intake shrank considerably in the eighteenth century. Wilhelm Görges and August Nebe, *Geschichte des Johanneums zu Lüneburg* (Lüneburg, 1907), pp. 27–30. For a detailed firsthand description of a choirboy's life in Dresden, see Otto Richter, "Erlebnisse eines Annenschülers 1758–72. Aus der Selbstbiographie des Pastors Christian Heinrich Schreyer. Mitgeteilt von Otto Richter," *Dresdener Geschichtsblätter* 16 (1907): 154–84, which provides precise figures from Schreyer's account books on the considerable rise in income that came with seniority. On the sixteenth-century reform of the *Currende*, see Mertz, *Schulwesen*, pp. 433–36, 457–648. For the typical objections to the choir in the eighteenth century, see M. C. B. Suttinger, "Ueber die in der Lausitz bei den gelehrten Schulen gewöhnlichen Singechöre," *Neues Magazin für Schullehrer* 1 (1792): 244–49; Insp. Küster, "Antrag zur gänzlichen Aufhebung der Singechöre," *Annalen des preussischen Schul- und Kirchenwesens*, ed. Friedrich Gedike, 1:2 (1800): 260–76.

[7] Görges and Nebe, *Geschichte des Johanneums*, pp. 18, 44. On the Thomasschule see Otto Kaemmel, *Geschichte des Leipziger Schulwesens vom Anfange des 13. bis gegen die Mitte des 19. Jahrhunderts (1214–1846)* (Leipzig and Berlin, 1909), esp. pp. 84–88, 221–45.

matriculation fee was lower for *Bürger* than for noblemen, and in any case a poor student normally was exempted from all or part of the fee, particularly if he could produce a "testimony of financial incapacity" (*testimonium paupertatis*) from a local pastor or teacher. Likewise the stiff course fees for wealthier students in effect subsidized their poor *Kommilitonen*, who customarily paid little or nothing for the basic theology courses needed for the qualifying examination and, when they had won the special favor of a professor, were admitted gratis to his much more expensive "private" courses as well.[8]

By the end of the sixteenth century the refectory for poor students was a fixture of university life, from Tübingen in the southwest to Frankfurt/Oder and Königsberg in the northeast. As bothersome as it was from an administrative standpoint, feeding students seemed preferable to giving them cash in hand and allowing it to slip through their fingers. In the late eighteenth century the *Konviktorium* at Wittenberg was frequented by a very substantial portion of the student population; but like the institution it served, it was small and shrinking. But at larger universities the eighteenth-century refectory was, by the standards of the era, an imposing operation. By 1700 the eating hall in the Paulinerkollegium in Leipzig had eleven tables with a total of 132 free places, supported partly by the Saxon government and partly by family endowments. From midcentury onward, after seven more "free tables" had been added, the hall accommodated 216 students for two meals per day.[9]

Even if given a place at a free table, and even if exempted from matriculation and course fees, the student still needed cash to pay for a room, heating wood, lamp oil, laundry, the minimum in books and writing materials, and perhaps a few other necessities. As for cash stipends, many had never been generous enough to support a student, and many others, once barely sufficient for that purpose, had been eroded by inflation. On the

[8] It was indicative of the strength of this tradition that as late as 1792 students at Helmstedt had to be warned not to expect exemption from course fees as something owed them (a *Schuldigkeit*); "Akademische Gesetze für die Studirende auf der Julius Karls Universität zu Helmstädt," *Philologisches-pädagogische Magazin* 2 (1794): 207. See also Ludwig Heinrich von Jakob, *Ueber die Universitäten in Deutschland, besonders in den Königl. Preussischen Staaten* (Berlin, 1798), pp. 90–101.

[9] Carl Christian Carus Gretschel, *Die Universität Leipzig in der Vergangenheit und Gegenwart* (Dresden, 1830), pp. 184–88; Johann Daniel Schulze, *Abriss einer Geschichte der Leipzig Universität im Lauf des achtzehnten Jahrhunderts nebst Rückblicken auf die frühern Zeiten* (Leipzig, 1802), pp. 321–29. The establishment at Frankfort, launched in 1572 to provide two meals per day to 100 students, was reduced to 60 places in 1723 – and subsequently dropped the evening meal. Carl Renatus Hausen, *Geschichte der Universität und Stadt Frankfurt an der Oder, seit ihrer Stiftung und Erbauung, bis zum Schluss des achtzehnten Jahrhunderts* (Frankfurt/Oder, 1800), p. 156. On the "free tables" in Königsberg, see Daniel Heinrich Arnoldt, *Ausführlische und mit Urkunden versehene Historie der Königsbergischen Universität*, 2 vols. (Königsberg, 1746), 2: 262–319. The efforts to reform the refectory at Helmstedt are recounted in Marta Asche, "Das Konvikt an der Universität Helmstedt," *Braunschweigisches Jahrbuch* 47 (1966): 52–124.

other side of the ledger, though, students were adept at living on a shoestring and simply going without when pinched. Universities and their host towns accommodated a steep scale of student life-styles, evident in the estimated budgets that several professors published for the benefit of aspiring students and worried parents in the late eighteenth century. The five budget classes for Leipzig in the 1790s ranged from 120 to 800 thaler. The higher classes obviously were for the scions of aristocratic and upper bourgeois families, often accompanied on their university "tours" by servants and private tutors. In addition to paying substantial university fees and spending liberally on rent, food, and "entertainments," they took the expensive private lessons that less affluent theology students did not need and in any case could not afford. To judge by the estimates for Göttingen, it cost about as much per month to take riding or violin lessons as to rent a cheap furnished room. Limited to the cheapest ways of meeting expenses for necessities, the 120 thaler budget for Leipzig included 17 reichsthaler, 8 groschen for a small and barely furnished back room, 18 reichsthaler for a main meal that would leave a "strong" young man "not completely sated," and 6 reichsthaler for the basic courses and a book or two purchased at an auction.[10]

How far a cash stipend would stretch depended in part on the cost of living, which was known to vary from place to place. Göttingen's reputation as a particularly expensive university town, though perhaps exaggerated, was probably merited; to judge by the estimates for rent and food, even the cost of bare survival there was higher than at most other universities. The estimate of 100 thaler per year for Halle, published in 1795, was for the student who "must limit himself extraordinarily and deprive himself of many things." It kept rent at a very low 12 thaler, although 20 to 25 thaler was needed for a "mediocre" furnished room; allowed coffee "at most once a week"; required water rather than beer with meals; limited expenses for books and writing materials to 4 thaler; and left nothing for haircuts, shoeshines, and newspapers and journals.[11] Leipzig and Jena may have been a

[10] "Jährliche Kostenberechnung eines Studierenden zu Leipzig nach verschiedenen Massstäben mit erläuternden Anmerkungen," *Annalen der Teutschen* 2 (1791): 215–33 (originally published in Friedr. Glob. Leonhardi, ed., *Allgemeine theoretische-praktische Stadt- u. Landwirtschaftskunde* 1 [1789]: 49–63); Johann Christoph Röder, *Plan-tabelle bestehend in einer genauer Verzeichniss der Kosten aller nothwendigen und nützlichen Bedürfnisse eines hier (in Göttingen) Studierenden von 1768 bis 1769* (Göttingen, 1768). The reporter from Leipzig claimed that "more than 100 students" there managed with 40 to 100 reichsthaler.

[11] *Bemerkungen eines Akademikers über Halle und dessen Bewohner, in Briefen* (Germanien, 1795), pp. 262–79. This estimate had five categories, the highest at 500 thaler. In 1787 the Prussian government had published a minimal budget for Halle, intended to counteract the problem of student debts by impressing on parents the unavoidable costs of university life. It amounted to the modest sum of 149 reichsthaler – and that despite the fact that it included 32 thaler for course fees and 17 thaler for clothing (compared with 12 thaler and 8 thaler, respectively, in the 1795 budget). "Ueber dasjenig, was ein Student auf der Universität Halle, jährlich zur höchsten Nothdurft gebraucht," in *Novum corpus constitionum Prussico-Branden-*

bit more expensive than Halle, but the smaller backwaters like Frankfurt, Erfurt, and Wittenberg seem to have been comparable, if not cheaper. Karl Philipp Moritz, who spent two semesters at Wittenberg in the late 1770s, calculated that a student who had a free table and free lodging – both "very easy to come by" – could under extreme necessity manage with 30 thaler per year.[12]

Despite the variations among them, the budgets provide roughly congruent impressions of the cost of living for students at the cheaper universities. Even the student who had to pay for everything from his own (or his parents') pocket might be able to survive for less than 100 thaler, and certainly could scrape by with less than 125 thaler. These were not petty sums for families at the lower end of the income hierarchy; 600 thaler was a decent income for a village or small-town pastor, and most schoolmen earned considerably less. But with this scale of expenditure even an obviously inadequate stipend of 30 to 50 thaler per year meant a considerable alleviation. In cash terms, a place at a free table cut expenses substantially; food was by far the highest item in all the budgets – between one-third and one-half of the total, and usually two or three times more than rent (the next highest item).

In the absence of help from home, there were many ways to close the common gap between charity and unavoidable expenses, including proofreading for professors and publishers and hack translating. For students, as for pupils, the most common resort was tutoring. In 1784 the inspector of the *Konviktorium* in Wittenberg reported that some students turned to tutoring merely to gain access to good company and conversation in local families or to get extra cash for books; but it was one more unavoidable expedient for the "large portion of the needy" (including those with smaller stipends) who "are forced to resort to all means to get through the academic years in the most oppressive misery."[13] The availability of tutoring positions, like the prospects for securing a place at a free table, clearly was a

burgicarum, praecipae Marchicarum Berlin 8 (1791): 305–20. See also Joh. Chr. Förster, *Kurze Anweisung für ankommende Studirende auf die Universität Halle* (Halle, 1781), pp. 11–25. In 1820 a professor at Göttingen estimated that thirty years earlier a student might have been able to live "respectably" on 250 to 300 thaler; Friedrich Saalfeld, *Geschichte der Universität Göttingen in dem Zeitraume von 1788 bis 1820* (Hanover, 1820), p. 619.

[12] Hugo Eybisch, *Anton Reiser. Untersuchungen zur Lebensgeschichte von K. Ph. Moritz und zur Kritik seiner Autobiographie*, Probefahrten. Erstlingsarbeiten aus dem Deutschen Seminar in Leipzig, ed. Albert Köster, vol. 14 (Leipzig, 1909), pp. 72–73. See also "Ohngefähre Berechnung des jährlichen Aufwandes, den ein hier Studirender bürgerlichen Standes mit der möglichsten Ersparniss machen kann," *Wittenbergisches Wochenblatt*, Stück 51 (Dec. 23, 1768): 432; "Berechnung des jährlichen Aufwands eines Studenten mittleren Standes nach zwei Klassen," *Erfurtisches Intelligenzblatt*, 1769, Stück 8. On the inflation of costs, see *Zeichnung der Universität Jena. Für Jünglinge welche diese Akademie besuchen wollen* (Leipzig, 1798), pp. 56–59.

[13] "Von Informiren auf Universitäten," *Wittenbergisches Wochenblatt* 17 (1784): 285–89, 293–97.

consideration for the poor student choosing a university. In fact the abundance of such employment in Leipzig tended to compensate for its reputation as an expensive university town.

Use of credit was another way to make ends meet, at least temporarily. Numerous measures were proposed and enacted to alleviate the chronic problem of student debts – by protecting honest local tradesmen from irresponsible youths and by keeping innocent students out of the clutches of the unscrupulous. A tendency to incur debts liberally and to honor them very slowly, if at all, was characteristic of the ethos that many scions of noble houses brought to the universities. A similarly cavalier approach may have been common among bourgeois students from prosperous homes – because they were spendthrift about entertainments and had nothing left for necessities, or simply as a gesture of contempt for the local philistines. But credit was also an unavoidable resort for many of the poorer students, and in some cases a failure to pay debts was a measure of sheer penury. One reason for the financial straits of pastors and teachers fresh out of the university – aside from their paltry incomes – was that they were still paying off debts incurred as students.[14]

It was this world of student poverty and debt that Friedrich Richter (the later Jean Paul) entered in Leipzig in the early 1780s. Richter was the orphaned son of a poor village pastor, and his mother could contribute little to his support. A position at a free table was not to be had, he reported back to the rector in his hometown. Contrary to the rector's assurances, "tutoring positions are rare here – and the crowd of those who tutor is unbelievably large."[15] Though exempted from the usual fees and paying only 16 reichsthaler in rent (on condition that he vacate the room during the fairs!), Richter had to send an urgent plea to his mother for 20 reichsthaler at the end of his first semester. He had already "used credit very often," he explained, and would have to continue doing so for heating wood and "something warm" at breakfast and dinner. In August 1782, a little more than a year after he had arrived in Leipzig, he owed 24 reichsthaler at the inn where he took his meals, 10 to his landlord, and 6 to others – and requested another 8 thaler in Saxon currency from his mother to pay a laundress, a shoemaker to fix his boots, and a tailor to mend his torn beaver coat. In lieu of the usual expedients, Richter managed to survive

[14] On the problem of student debts, see Jakob, *Ueber die Universitäten*, pp. 62–65; Johann Georg Büsch, "Ueber die auf der Universität Halle neuerlich gemachte Verfügung zur Verhütung des Schuldenmachens der Studenten," *Hamburgische Adress-Comtoir-Nachrichten*, Stück 29–33 (1788): 225–27, 233–36, 241–45, 249–51, 257–58; Christoph Meiners, *Ueber die Verfassung und Verwaltung der deutschen Universitäten*, 2 vols. (Göttingen, 1801–2), 2: 238–61.

[15] Friedrich Richter to Rektor Werner, late May 1781, in *Die Briefe Jean Pauls*, ed. Eduard Berend, 2 vols. (Munich, 1922), 1: 6–7.

for more than three years at Leipzig on the earnings from his first satirical novels, but not without more debts and constant worries. "Since I have no money I am in pitiable circumstances," he reported gamely to his mother in June 1784, shortly before leaving the university, "but I have not a few debts and make an effort every day to add new ones to the old ones."[16]

"When I look out at my audience," a professor at Jena reportedly was in the habit of saying, "I get hungry because I see hunger pressed into almost every cheek."[17] He was not speaking in metaphorical terms. While charity in its various forms enabled many young men to study, it offered them at best subsistence. Coming to the end of a stipend, failing to find a tutoring position, or losing one, waiting in vain for a supplementary allowance from home or from a private benefactor – in these and many other circumstances the poor student faced the void. The Lutheran charitable legacy supported a makeshift world of student poverty, its hardships and anxieties perhaps exacerbated by an inflation of living costs in the eighteenth century. Its emblems of citizenship were the glass of water to wash down a skimpy meal, the boots desperately in need of repair, the tattered coat that made its owner too embarrassed to visit a respectable home. To be poor meant not only to be deprived of books and real luxuries like coffee and sugar, but also to be unable to replace worn-out clothing, or to buy enough heating wood to get through the winter, or to pay for medical expenses when illness struck.

Richter was a remarkably self-possessed and self-reliant young man, able to dismiss the stylishness of wealthier students at Leipzig as silly conformism and maintaining his wry humor in the worst financial crises. What Christian Gottlob Heyne recalled about his student years at Leipzig in the early 1750s, surviving on a meager, irregular allowance from a pastor back home, was the debilitating anxiety of hand-to-mouth survival. "Nature" had prevailed over physical illness, Heyne recalled; but his "gnawing distress" (*nagenden Kummer*) had induced a "deep" and lasting *Melancholie*, and indeed had made him "a prey of madness" (*ein Raub der Verzweiflung*).[18] Desperate to escape his poverty, he would have ended his studies prematurely after only two years if a tutoring position had not materialized. Heyne's reaction was no more typical than Richter's; but it is not surprising that poor theology students were known to limit their studies to the *Brotstudium* of basic courses so as to get through as quickly as possible – and that among them nostalgia for the years spent as *Kommilitonen* was rare.

[16] Ibid., pp. 34–35, 51–52, 131.

[17] Johann Friedrich Jakobi, "Gedanken über die gewöhnliche Erziehung junger Geistlichen," *Journal für Prediger* 5 (1774): 58.

[18] Arnold Hermann Ludwig Heeren, *Christian Gottlob Heyne, biographisch dargestellt* (Göttingen, 1813), pp. 23–28.

SOCIAL PROFILES

How far into the upper and lower reaches of the social hierarchy did the category "poor student" extend, and what are the salient distinctions within it? How is academic mobility to be understood within a larger structure of access to the universities?

At various points in the middle to late eighteenth century several universities began to use the occasion of students' matriculations to record fairly regularly the occupations or official titles of their fathers. The same information is available for some of the recipients of places at "free tables" at Göttingen. The limitations of this evidence, though perhaps all too obvious, should be underlined. The scattered sample of Göttingen *Stipendiaten* for the middle decades of the century, when enrollments in theology were at their peak, constitute only a portion of the poor students. As for the matriculation registers, fathers are identified only from 1768 onward at Frankfurt/Oder, from 1769 onward at Tübingen, from 1796 onward at Göttingen, and for the years 1768–71 and 1785–87 at Halle.

In the nineteenth century, declines in university enrollments usually were accompanied by disproportionate decreases in the percentages of students whose fathers lacked both university education and substantial property. Did the same relationship obtain for the drop in the decennial average in new enrollments at German universities from 4,270.5 in 1726–35 to 3,748.6 in 1756–65 and to 3,041.5 in 1796–1805?[19] Our information for

[19] The figures on the eighteenth-century decline in enrollments were originally assembled in Franz Eulenberg, *Die Frequenz der deutschen Universitäten von Ihrer Gründung bis zur Gegenwart* (Leipzig, 1904). I have used the adjusted figures, taking into account the approximate rate of interuniversity mobility, in W. Frijhoff, "Surplus ou deficit? Hypothèses sur le nombre des étudiants en Allemagne à l'époque moderne (1576–1815)," *Francia: Forschungen zur westeuropäischer Geschichte* 7 (1980): 173–218. On enrollment patterns and accompanying changes in the social origins of students in the nineteenth century see esp. Hartmut Titze, "Die zyklische Ueberproduktion von Akademikern im 19. und 20. Jahrhundert," *Geschichte und Gesellschaft* 10 (1984): 92–121. My research is not a corrective to earlier conclusions about the social origins of students in the late eighteenth century, but refines them by distinguishing between faculties; see esp. Konrad H. Jarausch, "Die neuhumanistische Universität und die bürgerliche Gesellschaft, 1800–1870. Eine quantitative Untersuchung zur Sozialstruktur der Studentenschaften deutscher Universitäten," in Christian Probst, ed., *Darstellungen und Quellen zur Geschichte der deutschen Einheitsbewegung im neunzehnten und zwangzigsten Jahrhundert*, vol. 11 (Heidelberg, 1981), pp. 11–58; Fritz K. Ringer, *Education and Society in Modern Europe* (Bloomington, Ind., 1978), pp. 81–91. A systematic comparison with recruitment patterns in eighteenth-century France would be premature, but three differences on the French side seem particularly significant. To the extent that the celibacy of the French Catholic clergy allowed for a kind of corporate self-recruitment, it was obviously more indirect (through nephews, for example, rather than through sons). At the same time the strong presence of sons of clergymen in the German law faculties had no counterpart in the French law faculties. And the urban concentration of German recruits for theology as well as law becomes more striking in view of the significant percentages of rural inhabitants (especially landowning "peasants") among the fathers of French parish priests. See, e.g., Richard L. Kagan, "Law Students and Legal Careers in Eighteenth-Century France," *Past and Present* 68 (Aug. 1975): 38–72; W. Frijhoff and D. Julia, *Ecole et société dans la France d'ancien régime. Quatre exemples Auch, Avallon, Condom*

Frankfurt and Halle includes years of limited recovery within the overall decline. There was little change at Halle; but at Frankfurt, where enrollments in theology decreased by 51.9 percent from 1781–85 to 1791–95, the percentage of students' fathers without university education fell from 52.8 to 33.3 (although the percentage of artisans rose slightly from 17.9 to 19.6). These findings suggest that the nineteenth-century pattern also held, though perhaps with less consistency, throughout the eighteenth century. To venture a conservative extrapolation: the percentages of theology students from families without *Bildung* and *Besitz* may very well have been higher in the earlier decades of higher enrollments, and in any case it is most unlikely that they were lower.

Aside from often being maddeningly vague, particularly when in Latin, designations of fathers' occupations isolate only one dimension of a family's social position; ideally we would also be able to rank each family in terms of its level of wealth, using the father's income and property ownership, and perhaps also the wealth the mother brought to the family. One can assume only a very rough correspondence between the hierarchies of official ranks in the ecclesiastical and civil bureaucracies and their hierarchies of wealth. Likewise the categories for artisans and shopkeepers, though not likely to include families with substantial propertied wealth, cover a wide range of incomes. But this handicap has a certain virtue; since the occupational distinctions can be correlated fairly accurately with differences in educational level, they isolate the most relevant social bifurcation for understanding what privileged access to the universities meant.

At all four universities, uneducated families were grossly underrepresented, given their obvious preponderance in the population at large. Most striking is the tiny number of students from the peasant and subpeasant masses of the countryside and the unskilled laboring classes in the towns. Aside from their enormous cultural distance from academic education, sheer poverty often prevented families at these levels from dispensing with the labor of school-age sons and supplementing charitable support with even a minimal cash outlay. The more prosperous peasant family, perhaps able to forgo a boy's labor contribution, was still handicapped by the urban concentration of academic schooling. In the towns the lower grades of many Latin schools introduced all pupils, including some local boys from uneducated families, to the rudiments of Latin. But the boy who attended the "German" or "lower" school of a village or small market town was instructed by a "schoolmaster" – usually the sexton or a local artisan – who lacked university education and might not have even attended a secondary school. Unlike the talented artisan's son, who could advance up the local school

et Gisors (Paris, 1975); Timothy Tackett, *Priest and Parish in Eighteenth-Century France. A Social and Political Study of the Curés in a Diocese of Dauphiné 1750–1791* (Princeton, N.J., 1977), esp. pp. 54–71.

grades, the talented peasant's or field hand's son had to be singled out and given special instruction by a discerning schoolmaster or, more likely, a local pastor. While most of the municipal stipends and many of the private stipends were restricted to sons of town *Bürger*, the rural family was more likely to have to pay boarding expenses, and to have to do so earlier.

At the other extreme is the clergy, distinguished by its disproportionately high representation. Its strong presence reflects two simple facts: that, de facto and sometimes de jure, sons of the university-educated officials of church and state had privileged access to the universities and that, within that elite, clergymen (including theology graduates in teaching positions) were by far the largest occupational group. Sons of clergymen, more than any other group, formed a bridge between the two major faculties; that in itself is eloquent testimony to the fact that the clergy had formed into a broad center of gravity in German academic and intellectual life. While the majority of clergymen's sons studied theology, others constituted more or less significant minorities of the law students in our samples (13.9 percent at Halle, 18.0 percent at Göttingen, 17.2 percent at Frankfurt, 22.4 percent at Tübingen). Where the theology faculty was larger than the law faculty, sons of clergymen were the single largest group in the student population; where the opposite obtained, they were second only to university-educated civil officials (Table 1.1).

Thanks to their inherited educational advantage, their parents' willingness and ability to shoulder the financial burden of a legal education, and perhaps their family connections in official circles, sons of clergymen were in a position to pursue prestigious careers in the administrative and judicial bureaucracies. What of the others – the great majority – who were following in their fathers' footsteps? The marked tendency toward corporate self-recruitment in the clergy must be understood within a skein of inter-generational career lines, tracing lateral as well as upward and downward movement in a steeply graded occupational hierarchy. At the higher echelons were the pastors of prestigious urban churches, the district superintendents and *Spezialen* (Württemberg), university professors, and councilors in the central consistories. Clerical "dynasties" often controlled appointments at these levels, and in any case the son of a prominent church official could expect to benefit from the looser but still vital family connections that propelled clerical careers.

Teaching positions, whose stingy local endowments and meager fees were notorious, formed the underlayer of the clergy. Barely adequate for the young theology candidates who used the schools as "waiting rooms" for pastorates, teaching incomes kept the older, married men who had been unable to escape on the edge of real poverty. The occupant of a poorly endowed village or small-town pastorate was more likely to receive contributions in kind and enjoy the use of parish lands, which cushioned his

Table 1.1. *Students' fathers: officials with university education*

	Total students	A. Clergymen[a]	B. Other university educated	A + B
Halle (1768–71, 1785–87)				
Theology	1,358	39.0(530)	8.4(114)	47.4(644)
Law	726	13.9(101)	41.3(300)	55.2(401)
Frankfurt/Oder				
Theology (1771–75, 1781–85, 1791–95)	251	47.0(118)	3.2 (8)	50.2(126)
Law (1771–72, 1781–82, 1791–92)	244	17.2 (42)	25.4 (62)	42.6(104)
Tübingen				
Theology[b]	566	53.7(304)	17.8(101)	71.5(405)
Law (1771–75, 1781–85, 1791–95)	174	22.4 (39)	53.5 (93)	75.9(132)
Göttingen (1797–98)				
Theology	46	50.0 (23)	10.9 (5)	60.9 (28)
Law	89	18.0 (16)	46.1 (41)	64.1 (57)

Note: Figures are percentages; subtotals in parentheses.
[a] Includes schoolteachers in Latin schools and *Gymnasien*.
[b] Includes both cloister school graduates and *oppidani* (see Table 1.2).

family against rising food prices; but in other respects he was hardly better off. Clearly members of the elite by virtue of their educational credentials, but comparable to, and perhaps even worse off than, artisans, shopkeepers, and peasants in their lack of propertied wealth, these obscure pastors and teachers occupied an ambivalent place in the social hierarchy of *Bildung* and *Besitz*. Their sons were the insiders among poor students. Some ended up at roughly the same level as their fathers, if only because they lacked family connections; but the opportunity for upward mobility was there, and those who pursued it successfully – who became superintendents, professors, and consistorial councilors – offer striking examples of meteoric careers in the eighteenth-century educated *Bürgertum*.

If in the clerical family at a modest income level charity eased the burden of educating an eldest son, it could become the sine qua non for the education of his brothers – especially if there were daughters in need of dowries. Particularly in the poorer clerical families, the early death of the father threatened catastrophe. After the widow had been provided for and debts had been paid, there might be little or nothing left in the legacy to finance the sons' education. But the same event that threatened to ruin career prospects also opened new doors to benefactors. To judge by the frequency with which they appear in our records (which are far from complete on this score), orphaned sons of clergymen were probably the most common recipients of stipends. Typically their benefactors were clergymen; the sense of responsibility for the offspring of deceased colleagues was a measure of corporate solidarity in the clerical order.[20]

If a comparison of students at our four universities yields roughly similar social parameters, it also points to differences in both the larger social context and the structure of academic mobility. These are best understood as eighteenth-century variations on what Ralph Turner, an American sociologist, has termed "sponsored mobility." In modern school systems, Turner has argued, the prevailing kind of mobility reflects one of two "ideal typical normative patterns."

> *Contest* mobility is a system in which elite status is the prize in an open contest and is taken by the aspirants' own efforts. . . . Under *sponsored* mobility elite recruits are chosen by the established elite or their agents, and elite status is *given* on the basis of some criterion of supposed merit and cannot be *taken* by any amount of effort or strategy. Upward mobility is like entry into a private club where each candidate must be "sponsored" by one or more of the members. . . . Contest mobility incorporates [a] disapproval of premature judgments and of anything that gives special advantage to those who are ahead at any point in the race. Under sponsored mobility, fairly early selection of only the number of persons necessary to fill anticipated vacancies in the elite is desirable.[21]

At first glance Protestant Württemberg might seem to offer a remarkably close – and precocious – approximation of the sponsorship type. Württemberg abounded in small towns, and scattered across its townscape were more than fifty Latin schools, most with only one or two clerical "preceptors" initiating boys into academic learning. On this broad foundation the clerical establishment, under the authority of the High Consistory in Stuttgart, had erected a very narrow stairway. The entryway was an annual territorial examination (*Landesexamen*), held in Stuttgart, with consistorial councilors

[20] For a striking example of the charity available to a deceased pastor's son, see Olfers, "Berliner Gymnasiastenleben," pp. 41–53, 74–77. The education of clergymen's sons will receive further attention in Chapter 2.

[21] Ralph H. Turner, "Sponsored and Contest Mobility and the School System," *American Sociological Review* 25 (1960): 855–58. Turner considered the "monopoly of credentials" in sponsored mobility to be typical of "societies with well entrenched aristocracies" or of "societies organized on large-scale bureaucratic lines permitting centralized control of upward social movement." Ibid., p. 858. But cf. the attempt to refine Turner's typology by relating variations in the structure of educational systems to "particularist" and "universalistic" ideologies of selection, in Earl Hopper, "Educational Systems and Selected Consequences of Patterns of Mobility and Non-mobility in Industrial Societies. A Theoretical Discussion," in Richard Brown, ed., *Knowledge, Education, and Cultural Change. Papers in the Sociology of Education* (London, 1973), pp. 17–69.

and university professors presiding. Only boys who passed this examination were admitted to the state-funded cloister schools, which in turn supplied the great majority of scholarship students with free room and board in the famous theological Stift at Tübingen.

By the early eighteenth century the *Landesexamen* had become a two- or three-day affair, with oral questionings in Latin and written translation exercises in Latin, Greek, and Hebrew (in descending order of difficulty). Even for the boy who had been prepared at home as well as in a Latin school, this was an imposing hurdle. In 1749 the state in effect turned the examination of younger boys into dry runs by providing for a maximum of five tries, beginning no earlier than age eleven and ending no later than age fourteen or fifteen.[22] If the pressure was eased by this graduated schedule, the stakes in the competition remained high. The stairway to which the *Landesexamen* gave entry – i.e., the cloister schools and the Tübingen Stift – was the only sure route to preferment in the Württemberg clergy.

This sacrosanct process of selection and training had originally been intended primarily to single out gifted boys without means, but had come to play a very different social role. From 1771 to 1800 56.7 percent of our sample – i.e., the 413 new students with fathers identified by office or occupation, from the two cloister schools (Bebenhausen and Maulbronn) that alternated in sending their graduating classes to the Stift – were sons of clergymen. Almost entirely absent were not only "peasant" families, but also the kinds of uneducated families in the artisan trades and shopkeeping that registered a significant presence at some other universities. Both the high degree of corporate closure and the almost total exclusion of the uneducated must be understood within a broader process of elite consolidation and entrenchment, reflecting the juridical and sociopolitical structure peculiar to Old Württemberg. The process becomes visible when one compares the cloister school sample with the sample of Württemberg subjects

[22] *General-Rescript* of May 3, 1749, in A. L. Reyscher, ed., *Sammlung der württembergischen Gesetze*, vol. 11, 2. Abteilung (Tübingen, 1847), pp. 206–10. On the Württemberg Latin schools, see esp. Reinhold Stahlecker, *Allgemeine Geschichte des Lateinschulwesens und Geschichte der Lateinschulen ob der Steig*, Geschichte des humanistischen Schulwesens in Württemberg, vol. 3 (Stuttgart, 1927). On the system for clerical education, see also J. Eitle, *Der Unterricht in den einstigen württembergischen Klosterschulen von 1556–1806*, Beihefte zu der Zeitschrift für Geschichte der Erziehung und des Unterrichts, vol. 3 (Berlin, 1913); Ellis Hesselmeyer, "Das Landesexamen," *Württembergische Vierteljahrshefte für Landesgeschichte*, Neue Folge 39 (1933): 293–328; Martin Leube, *Geschichte des Tübinger Stifts*, 3 vols. (Stuttgart, 1921–36); Gustav Lang, *Geschichte der württembergischen Klosterschulen von ihrer Stiftung bis zu ihrer endgültigen Verwandlung in Evangelisch-theologische Seminare* (Stuttgart, 1938). An excellent study of the corporate ethos of the clergy is Martin Hasselhorn, *Der altwürttembergische Pfarrstand im 18. Jahrhundert* (Stuttgart, 1958). Also useful are Chr. Kolb, "Zur Geschichte des Pfarrstandes in Württemberg," *Blätter für Württembergische Kirchengeschichte* 57 (1957): 74–190; Karl Müller, "Kirchliches Prüfungs- und Anstellungswesen in Württemberg im Zeitalter der Orthodoxie. Aus den Zeugnisbüchern des herzoglichen Konsistoriums," *Württembergische Vierteljahrshefte für Landesgeschichte* 25 (1916): 431–38.

studying law at Tübingen from 1771 to 1795. More than three-quarters (78.9 percent) of the 413 fathers of cloister school graduates belonged to the elite of *Honoratioren*, and slightly more of the 174 law students' fathers (80.5 percent) belonged to the same group. The *Honoratioren* were a legally recognized category, including some merchants in the major towns and "free" professionals in medicine, pharmacy, and law, but constituted essentially by the academic and official elite. Its core groups were the clergy (including pastoral assistants and Latin school teachers) and a range of civil officials that encompassed the higher personnel at court, in the administrative and judicial bureaucracies and in the estates' administration, as well as a unique group of "scribes" (*Schreiber*) in both state and municipal offices.[23] Sharing the same educational patrimony and often interrelated by marriage, families in the constituent groups of this elite crisscrossed in their use of higher education to insure their sons' futures. The most striking difference between the Stift and the law faculty lay in concentrations *within* the elite ranks; while 56.7 percent of cloister school graduates' fathers were clergymen and 18.1 percent were non-clerical officials with *Honoratioren*-status, the percentages of law students' fathers in these categories (22.4 and 53.5, respectively) were roughly the opposite (Table 1.2).

In the first half of the century, the fact that Stift graduates were waiting until age thirty and beyond for appointments had raised the specter of overcrowding in the clergy. The High Consistory's critical countermeasure had been a rescript in May 1749 reducing annual admissions to each of the two lower cloister schools from twenty-five to twenty until "[the] number of capable people" became "proportionate to the number of available offices." Boys who took the *Landesexamen* three times and still failed to qualify were to be rejected permanently – and in this decision, the rescript stipulated, "not the station and wishes of the parents, but the character and capability of the children" were to be considered. Yet the overriding point was not to bar the undeserving, regardless of their social origins, but to establish a social threshold for individual competition. In addition to limiting *any* family to one place per generation, the rescript specifically excluded sons of "common artisans" and "peasants" as well as those who could not manage the accessory costs of study, with the notable exception of

[23] The *Honoratiorenschicht* is described in Hasselhorn, *Pfarrstand*, esp. pp. 24–29. At the close of the century an informed observer broke down the clerical branch of the *Honoratioren*, in descending rank, into 3 consistorial councilors, 14 prelates, 37 professors, 39 superintendents, 16 town pastors, 560 pastors, 72 deacons, 72 preceptors, and 27 "assistants" (*Collaboratoren*). Balthasar Haug, *Das gelehrte Wirtemberg* (Stuttgart, 1790), p. 26. For further details on the structure of officialdom, see Friedrich Wintterlin, *Geschichte der Behördenorganisation in Württemberg*, 2 vols. (Stuttgart, 1902–6). Bernd Wunder, *Privilegierung und Disziplinierung. Die Entstehung des Berufsbeamtentums in Bayern und Württemberg (1780–1825)*, Studien zur modernen Geschichte, vol. 21 (Munich and Vienna, 1978), places the consolidation of the official elite within the context of a political struggle between the ducal government and the estates.

Table 1.2. *Fathers' occupations/offices of Württemberg subjects enrolled at Tübingen*

Occupation	Identified[a]	Unidentified	A. Clergy	B. Other *Honoratioren*		A + B	Local officials	Artisans	Other
				Officials	Other				
Law (1771–75, 1781–85, 1791–95)	174	14	22.4 (39)	53.5(93)	4.6 (8)	80.5(140)	2.3 (4)	—	17.2(30)
Theology Cloister school graduates (1771–1800)	413	7	56.7(234)	18.1(75)	4.1(17)	78.9(326)	9.0(37)	1.7 (7)	10.4(43)[b]
Oppidani (1771–75, 1781–85, 1791–95)	153	13	45.8 (70)	17.0(26)	3.3 (5)	66.0(101)	6.5(10)	7.2(11)	20.3(31)[c]

Note: Figures are percentages; subtotals in parentheses.

Source: Die Matrikeln der Universität Tübingen, ed. Albert Bürk and Wilhelm Wille, vol. 3 (1710–1817) (Tübingen, 1953).

[a] That is, in the 21 graduating classes with fathers regularly identified by occupation or office. Identifications were not available for 6 other classes from 1771 to 1800 (Bebenhausen in 1779, 1785; Maulbronn in 1772, 1778, 1784, 1788).

[b] Includes 8 merchants (*Kaufmann, Handelsmann, Mercator*), 2 innkeepers (*hospes*), 3 surgeons, 2 foresters (*Förster, Forstmeister*) 2 physicians, and 2 musicians. There were no peasants.

[c] Includes 8 merchants (*Kaufmann, Handelsmann, negotiator, traiteur*), 4 schoolmasters (*Schulmeister*), 2 surgeons, 1 physician, and 1 peasant (*Bauer*).

"children of poor pastors." The criteria for individual aptitude and "character" derived from the corporate ethos of an entrenched elite and obviously favored boys who already bore its imprint.[24]

The exclusion of sons of artisans had become hardened policy by the 1770s and remained so at least until the end of the century. If any other artisans' sons were admitted, the fathers would be in the category of local officeholders whose main occupations were not identified. A decree in 1788, in response to renewed concern about long waits for clerical appointments, specifically excluded all but the most exceptional sons of *Bürgermeister*, *Schulzen*, and other local notables from the *Landesexamen*.[25] As in the case of artisans, state policy may have hastened a trend already underway; with the reduction in the size of the cloister school classes, local officeholders among graduates' fathers dropped from 13.9 percent in 1771–80 to 10.6 percent in 1781–90 and to only 1 of 120 fathers in 1791–1800.

The other noticeable leak in the elite monopoly had already been plugged. In 1760, 35.6 percent (70) of the theology students at Tübingen were *oppidani*, or "town theologians," living outside the Stift and supported by their families or by private or municipal stipends.[26] To the High Consistory the fact that some of these students were sons of "*Professionisten*, artisans, schoolmasters and such people" made their competition with Stift graduates for scarce appointments all the more alarming. A decree in 1780, establishing a minimum age of eighteen for *oppidani* and requiring at least five years of university studies before they could take the consistorial examination, probably contributed to the sharp reduction in their number from 80 in 1771–75 to 57 in 1781–85 and 27 in 1791–95.[27] But in view of the social distribution of the 1771–75 sample, there had in fact been

[24] Reyscher, *Sammlung*, vol. 11, 2. Abteilung, pp. 206–10.

[25] Ibid., p. xxx; Hasselhorn, *Pfarrstand*, pp. 34–35. My findings should be compared with Hasselhorn's statistics (ibid., p. 30), which provide the father's occupations for the 3,208 candidates who took the qualifying examination for a pastorate before the Consistory in Stuttgart. Unfortunately his figures are for the entire century, with little indication of shifts over time. But with this broader measure of the social composition of the clergy, Hasselhorn finds the same tendency toward increasing closure. Only 106 sons of artisans took the examination in 1751–1800, whereas 199 had done so in 1700–1750 (ibid., p. 31). G. Bormann, "Studien zu Berufsbild und Berufswirklichkeit evangelischer Pfarrer in Württemberg. Die Herkunft der Pfarrer – Ein geschichtlich-statistischer Ueberblick von 1700 bis 1965," *Social Compass* 13: 2 (1966): 95–137, focuses on the nineteenth and twentieth centuries, but includes Hasselhorn's figures.

[26] Wunder, *Privilegierung*, p. 99.

[27] Reyscher, *Sammlung*, vol. 11, 3. Abteilung, pp. 499–504. Cf. Hasselhorn, *Pfarrstand*, p. 34. The family stipends are listed in Ferdinand Friedrich Faber, ed., *Die Würtembergischen Familien-Stiftungen nebst genealogischen Nachrichten über die zu denselben berechtigten Familien*, Heft 1–6 (Stuttgart, 1852–53); Albert Rienhardt, ed., *Die Tübinger Studienstipendien und ihre Verwaltungs- und Verleihungsvorschriften nebst Erläuterungen* (Tübingen, 1919). For a history of a family stipend, with interesting detail on how it was distributed, see Jürgen Schneider, *Die Studienstiftung des Biberacher Bürgermeisters Gottschalk Klock an die Universität Tübingen (1594–1962)*, Biberacher Studien, vol. 1 (Biberach, 1973).

little cause for alarm. Of the 70 fathers of *oppidani* with occupations identified, only 5 (7.1 percent) can be described as artisans (or *Professionisten*) and only 1 was a schoolmaster. On the other hand, 46 (65.7 percent) were *Honoratioren* and 29 (41.4 percent) were clergymen. It was obvious by the 1770s that boys who did not attend the cloister schools and the Stift, and whose families lacked connections in the clerical establishment, had little hope of preferment. The alternate route was in fact largely an auxiliary in the broader recruitment process, extending the possibility of a clerical career to sons of *Honoratioren* who could not get past the hurdle of the *Landesexamen* and to sons of clergymen whose brothers had already taken the main route.

Of the 234 clergymen-fathers in our cloister school sample, 167 (71.4 percent) were pastors, and there were as many pastoral assistants and teachers – 33 (14.1 percent) – as higher clergymen. These figures suggest that the *Landesexamen* opened the prospect of upward mobility to a significant number of sons of "poor pastors" and even poorer schoolmen. But "sponsored induction" into the Württemberg clergy turns out to be quite different from Turner's model, which assumed a "formally open class system that provides for mass education." As numerous as they were, the Latin schools on which the *Landesexamen* drew were not an eighteenth-century equivalent of the kind of mass education on which the "eleven plus" examinations in England – to cite Turner's example – have been built. Nor was eighteenth-century Württemberg an "open class society"; its state-imposed exclusion of the great mass of the population from higher education – an exclusion that would be unthinkable in contemporary Western societies – typified the legal demarcation of corporate boundaries within and between classes.

Hence the other similarity – the role of the state in centralizing selection with standardized examinations – is also only apparent. In contemporary societies, the state claims to play the role of impartial agent, even when it is in fact applying elite criteria of selection. In the administration of the *Landesexamen*, the cloister schools, and the Stift, the ducal government of Württemberg was far from claiming an independent and overriding authority over against corporate enclaves – and that despite the occasional emphasis on "merit" in its regulations. What the union of church and state meant instead was that state authority had become the instrument of a centralized corporatism. It was precisely because this corporate self-regulation was already in place, with the *Landesexamen* as its critical means, that "the state" was in a position to ban outsiders effectively in the course of the eighteenth century. In practice centralized induction allowed the clerical establishment, acting on behalf of a broader but still cohesive elite of *Honoratioren*, to institutionalize and formalize a markedly *endogamous* recruitment into its ranks.

In its territorial compactness, in the cohesiveness of its elite, and in the centralization of its selection and training of aspiring clergymen, Württemberg was unique. The data for the Prussian universities at Halle and Frankfurt represent the different kind of sponsored induction that prevailed throughout Protestant central and northern Germany. The essential difference was not in the initial access to academic education. Though perhaps less densely distributed than in Württemberg, small-town Latin schools also abounded in this landscape. In their socially mixed lower grades all pupils, including local boys from uneducated homes, were introduced to Latin; it was a standard complaint among reformers, in fact, that as a result these schools were swamping the universities with poor students who lacked the requisite intellectual capacity and adequate training.[28] What mattered was that the centralized screening effected by the Württemberg *Landesexamen* had no equivalent elsewhere. Whether a boy without means was deemed bright enough and otherwise suitable for academic studies hinged on teachers' judgments at the local level. Aside from the possibility of receiving a municipal or family stipend, both controlled by local notables, he could hope to be supported by a pastor or teacher, or a prosperous relative, or some other benefactor. And of course he could always turn to the street choir and tutoring.

The university was a more imposing financial hurdle, but the young man without support from his family or a stipend could enroll in a theology faculty in the reasonable expectation that some form of charity would come his way.[29] What distinguished Halle was the scale of its generosity. A newcomer founded in the mid-1690s, Halle had joined its neighbors – Wittenberg, Leipzig, Erfurt, and Jena – in a tight cluster of universities in the heartland of Protestant Germany. Partly at their expense, it had very quickly assumed a preponderant role in the training of the Prussian clergy. Under the leadership of August Hermann Francke, the Pietists who dominated the theology faculty in the early decades had introduced practical variations on the traditional provisioning of free tables. It was Francke who drafted the ordinance in 1704 that introduced a quarterly collection in every Prussian village and town for "royal" tables.[30] In 1695, the same year in which

[28] On the importance of the small-town Latin schools in Prussia, see Karl-Ernst Jeismann, *Das preussische Gymnasium in Staat und Gesellschaft. Die Entstehung des Gymnasiums als Schule des Staates und der Gebildeten, 1787–1817*, Industrielle Welt. Schriftenreihe des Arbeitskreises für moderne Sozialgeschichte, vol. 15 (Stuttgart, 1974), pp. 163–70. See also Hans Georg Herrlitz, *Studium als Standesprivileg: Die Entstehung des Maturitätsproblems im 18. Jahrhundert* (Frankfurt am Main, 1973), pp. 36–40, 57–59, 99–108.

[29] At Frankfurt in the second half of the century, university bodies and individual professors controlled or had a major say in the distribution of roughly thirty-one *Stipendien*, ranging from 34 thaler to 100 thaler per year, and most with tenures of two or three years. In addition the poor student might secure one of the sixty or so places at free tables; he merely had to submit a request in Latin to the rector and pass a minimal examination administered by the *Dekan* of the philosophy faculty. Hausen, *Geschichte*, pp. 136–47.

[30] By 1708 the number of tables funded by this collection had reached thirteen, each with twelve places.

he had founded his famous orphanage, Francke had received a 500-thaler grant intended primarily to support poor theology candidates. Soon after he began to dole out the cash, he realized that he could keep a closer watch on the recipients by having them teach and compensating them with meals in the orphanage refectory. With this tidy arrangement Francke was able to support a very substantial number of students *and* provide cheap but at least minimally competent labor for his schools. As the applicants increased, other kinds of work were found, especially recording lectures and sermons for future publication. Taking into account Francke's innovation, the royal tables, and three others supported by the provincial estates, the total number of Halle students using the free tables was nearly 500 by 1711 and had surpassed 600 by 1720. And even that fell short of the demand; by 1720 "extraordinary" free tables, without the obligation to work, were providing evening meals to 212 students and afternoon meals to more than a hundred others.[31] The press of supplicants may have eased in the middle decades of the century, when enrollments declined; but the orphanage refectory remained a magnet for a large number of poor students, and particularly for those to whom other sources of charity had not been opened.

Under the circumstances typified by Frankfurt and Halle, sponsored induction meant a dispersed, highly individualized exercise of patronage. It allowed clergymen (including teachers) a critical role, but was not under the direct and exclusive control of a clerical establishment. The result was, in comparison with Württemberg, a relatively *exogenous* recruitment. The percentage of clergymen's sons in our samples of theology students' fathers is a healthy 47.0 at Frankfurt and 39.2 at Halle – figures which testify not only to the educational advantage enjoyed by insiders, but also to the degree to which they were preferred in the distribution of charity. But this kind of patronage did extend charitable support to some outsiders, below the educational level of the academic and official elite. Hence the bridging position of the clergy at Halle and Frankfurt was quite different from its

[31] *Kurtze Nachricht von dem Gegenwärtigen Zustande der Frey-Tische Auf der Königl. Preuss. Friedrichs-Universität in Halle* (Halle, 1720), pp. 2–4; Johann Christoph von Dreyhaupt, *Diplomatisch-historische Beschreibung des Saalkreyses*, 2 vols. (Halle, 1749–50), 2: 31–35; Friedrich August Eckstein, *Chronik der Stadt Halle. Eine Fortführung der Dreyhauptschen Beschreibung des Saalkreises (Erste Lieferung)* (Halle, 1842), pp. 58–61. See also Francke's reports, in his *Der von Gott in dem Waysenhause zu Glaucha an Halle ietzo bey nahe für 600. Personen zubereitete Tisch* (Halle, 1722), pp. 5–24, and in Gustav Kramer, *August Hermann Francke. Ein Lebensbild*, 2 vols. (Halle, 1880–82), 1: 275–76, and 2: 486, 504–8. On the early history of the university, see Johann Christoph Hoffbauer, *Geschichte der Universität zu Halle bis zum Jahre 1805* (Halle, 1805); Wilhelm Schrader, *Geschichte der Friedrichs-Universität zu Halle*, 2 vols. (Berlin, 1894); Hans Hübner, ed., *Geschichte der Martin-Luther-Universität Halle-Wittenberg 1502–1977 (Abriss)*, Wissenschaftliche Beiträge der Martin-Luther-Universität Halle-Wittenberg 1977/3 (T 13) (2nd. rev. ed.: Halle, 1977). J. Dyck, "Zum Funktionswandel der Universität vom 17. zum 18. Jahrhundert. Am Beispiel Halle," in Albrecht Schöne, ed., *Stadt-Schule-Universität-Buchwesen und die deutsche Literatur im 17. Jahrhundert* (Munich, 1976), pp. 371–82, concentrates on the significance of the legal faculty.

position at Tübingen. The clergymen's sons in the law and theology faculties at Tübingen range across hierarchies of *Honoratioren* that are roughly parallel. At the Prussian universities, the hierarchies of the two faculties stand in an inverted relationship. In law, sons of clergymen occupy the lower and middle zones of a predominantly academic and official scale, extending up to higher officialdom in the administrative and judicial bureaucracies; in theology, they occupy the middle and upper zones of a more heterogeneous hierarchy, reaching down into the broad base of the social pyramid.

Even this kind of sponsored induction rarely compensated for the geographic and cultural isolation of poor boys in the countryside. It was more open and egalitarian than the Württemberg variety primarily in the sense that it admitted a significant minority of students from the uneducated and semieducated strata of the towns. Proximity to town Latin schools, access to various kinds of stipends, the literacy required in many artisan trades – these are probably the most important reasons that 18.4 percent of the identified fathers of theology students at Halle in the sample years and 20.3 percent of those at Frankfurt were artisans, although sons of peasants were a much smaller minority at Halle and were virtually absent from Frankfurt. More striking are the petty officials – 15.9 percent at Halle and 10.4 percent at Frankfurt. These were sextons and nonacademic schoolmasters (often combined occupations), employed by the parishes as pastoral assistants, and office clerks, copyists (not to be confused with the Württemberg *Schreiber*), tax collectors, and other employees in the subaltern ranks of state and municipal administration. Such employees formed only the tiny nucleus of what would become a large "new lower middle class" of petty officials in the next century. Unlike artisans, they were an overrepresented group, particularly in theology but also in law. Their advantage did not lay in wealth; petty civil and church offices were notoriously poorly paid, and indeed it is likely that students' fathers in this category were less well off on the average than the artisans. What mattered were three other factors: that many of the fathers had spent a few years in academic schools; that they tended to see their own offices as steppingstones for the family's ascent into the academic and official elite; and that their employment put them in close proximity to the state officials and clergymen who distributed charity, in many cases as their immediate subordinates (Table 1.3).

Sons of artisans and sons of petty officials represent different tendencies within a *relatively* exogenous sponsored induction. Only of the former can it be said without reservation that clerical careers were open to a significant minority of outsiders. The sons of petty officials, though marking a greater degree of openness than in Württemberg, also attest to the countervailing tendency toward closure; patronage was being extended to occupational groups that, although not university educated, formed an outer circle of scholastic credentialing and public employment. Yet it is a measure of the

Table 1.3. *Fathers' occupations/offices of German students enrolled at Halle and Frankfurt/Oder*

		A. Clergy			B. Other				E. Merchants,			
	Total[a]	Church	School[b]	Total	univ.-educated officials	A + B	C. Petty officials[c]	D. Artisans	industrialists, shopkeepers[d]	F. Army officers	G. Medical[e]	H. Other
Halle (1768–71, 1785–87)												
Theology	1,353	36.1(489)	3.0(41)	39.2(530)	6.5 (88)	45.7(618)	15.9(215)	18.4(249)	7.9(107)	0.3 (4)	2.3(31)	9.5(129)[f]
Law	726	11.6 (84)	2.3(17)	13.9(101)	41.3(300)	55.2(401)	10.6 (77)	6.1 (44)	9.6 (70)	3.7(27)	2.3(17)	12.4 (90)
Frankfurt/Oder												
Theology (1771–75, 1781–85, 1791–95)	251	38.6 (97)	8.4(21)	47.0(118)	3.2 (8)	50.2(126)	10.4 (26)	20.3 (51)	8.8 (22)	—	2.8 (7)	7.6 (19)[g]
Law (1771–72, 1781–82, 1791–92)	244	14.8 (36)	2.5 (6)	17.2 (42)	25.4 (62)	42.6(104)	12.7 (31)	5.7 (14)	11.9 (29)	5.3(13)	2.9 (7)	18.9 (46)

Note: Figures are percentages; subtotals in parentheses.

[a] To make the Frankfurt sample comparable with Conrad's, I have included all German students (and not simply Prussian subjects). The fathers of 29 theology students at Frankfurt and of 79 law students could not be identified by occupation. The equivalent figures for Halle were not available.

[b] The Frankfurt figures include 10 cantors (8 in theology), some of whom may not have had university education.

[c] Includes 110 *Lehrer ohne akademische Bildung* at Halle (99 of them in theology).

[d] Combines Conrad's *Kaufleute, Gastwirte,* and *Industrielle.*

[e] This category comprises the 23 *Apotheker* and 37 *Aertze* (some of whom may have been university-educated) for Halle; 2 *Apotheker*, 7 surgeons, 4 doctors (3 with the title "Dr."), and 1 professor of anatomy, at Frankfurt.

[f] Includes 12 *Rentier*, 72 *Bauern*, 9 "workers" (*Arbeiter*), 29 "domestic servants" (*Niedere Bedienstete*).

[g] Includes 3 "farmers" (*oeconomi*), 4 *Schulze*, 2 *Pächter*, and 2 estate inspectors.

Sources: Johannes E. Conrad, "Die Statistik der Universität Halle während der 200 Jahren ihres Bestehens," in *Festschrift der vier Fakultäten zum zweihundertjährigen Jubiläum der vereinigten Friedrichs-Universität Halle-Wittenberg* (Halle, 1894): 1–78; *Aeltere Universitäts-Matrikeln.* I. *Universität Frankfurt a.O*, vol. 2 (1649–1811), ed. Ernst Friedlaender (Leipzig, 1888). Conrad's total of 1,358 theology students is inaccurate.

marginality of this group, in contrast to the privileged access enjoyed by sons of university graduates, that in the sharp contraction of the Frankfurt theology faculty it decreased as other groups increased. The reduction in new enrollments – from 117 in 1781–85 to 57 in 1791–95 – was accompanied by an increase in the percentage of sons of university graduates (from 42.2 to 66.7), and of sons of clergymen in particular (from 42.5 to 62.8). Sons of petty officials dropped from 11.3 to 5.9 percent.

The social distribution of its students in 1797–98 made Göttingen in most respects more similar to Tübingen than to the Prussian universities (Table 1.4). Over the previous several decades, when enrollments in theology had declined sharply, the distribution of theology students by social origins may have shifted significantly. But aside from helping to explain the overall recruitment pattern, the distribution of the new public stipends for Hanoverian subjects is in itself an instructive hybrid of sponsored induction. The stipends were in the form of "free tables" in local establishments, and the number of places had grown from the original thirty-six, funded in the late 1730s, to fifty-eight by the mid-1760s. The recipients were selected by the five provincial estates (*Landschaften*), nine municipal governments, and two ecclesiastical endowments that funded their places. A substantial minority of places – roughly 31 percent – went to law students. Our sample for scattered years from the late 1730s to the end of the century includes all five of the *Landschaften* (controlling 64.0 percent of the stipends in our sample), both ecclesiastical endowments, and the towns of Hanover, Hedemünden, Northheim, and Ulzen.[32]

Though left to a variety of administrative bodies and lacking a centralized qualifying examination, the distribution of stipends was, in social terms,

[32] On the need to support poor theology students at Göttingen, see esp. Johann Lorenz von Mosheim's draft of statutes for the theology faculty (1735), in Emil F. Roessler, ed., *Die Gründung der Universität Göttingen: Entwürfe, Berichte, und Briefe der Zeitgenossen* (Göttingen, 1855), pp. 294–95. The establishment and distribution of the stipends is described in K. Knoke, "Geschichte der Freitische an der Georg-August-Universität zu Göttingen," *Zeitschrift des historischen Vereins für Niedersachsen* (1893): 1–164. The other towns were Göttingen, Lüneburg, Einbeck, Osterode, and Clausthal; the indications of fathers' occupations in their stipend records were too irregular to be of use. There is no extant document indicating whether the Hanoverian government had a policy about the kinds of families for which the "free tables" were intended. But the continued reliance on "free tables" in local taverns – rather than giving out cash or establishing a single refectory – was a via media; only the "truly needy" would be willing to acknowledge their need publicly in this way, but at the same time – unlike students reliant on refectories at other universities – they were not stigmatized as a separate caste of "paupers." See the records of deliberations about possible changes, in Göttingen Universitätsarchiv, KK III, a 1, Nr. 7; KK IV, II F 3a, Nr. 285; KK III, 9a 1, Nr. 23 and 24. In 1776 the Hanoverian Consistory, perceiving a shortage of suitable candidates for pastorates (and noting in particular that there were not enough pastors' sons entering the clergy), took the unusual step of instructing clergymen to encourage more young men without means to study theology. *Acta historica ecclesiastica nostri temporis, Oder gesammelte Nachrichten und Urkunden zu der Kirchengeschichte unserer Zeit*, 3 (1793): 295–300.

Table 1.4. *Fathers' occupations/offices of Hanoverian subjects*[a] *enrolled at Göttingen, 1797–98*

Occupation	Identified	Unidentified	A. Clergy	B. Other university-educated				A + B	C. Petty officials	D. Artisans	E. Merchants, industrialists, shopkeepers	F. Other
				State officials	Local officials	Other	Total					
Theology	46	3	50.5(23)[b]	10.9 (5)	—	—	10.9 (5)	60.9(28)	17.4(8)	8.7(4)	4.4(2)	8.7(4)[c]
Law	89	5	18.0(16)	35.6(32)	10.1(9)	3.4(3)	49.4(44)	67.4(50)	6.7(6)	6.7(6)	10.1(9)	9.0(8)[d]

Note: Figures are percentages; subtotals in parentheses.

[a] Includes students from the Bremen region (unless the independent city was clearly indicated), but excludes students from the Eichsfeld, Osnabrück, Hildesheim, Duderstadt, and Goslar.

[b] Includes 4 school rectors and 4 cantors.

[c] Includes 1 tenant farmer (*Pächter*), 1 musician, 1 artillery sergeant, and 1 miner (*Bergmann*).

[d] Includes 1 language instructor (*Sprachmeister*), 1 riding master (*Rittmeister*), 4 military officers, 1 estate owner (*Gute*), 1 farmer (*Landmann*).

Source: Die Matrikeln der Georg-August-Universität zu Göttingen, 1734–1837, ed. Götz von Selle, Veröffentlichungen der historischen Kommission für Hannover, Oldenbourg, Braunschweig, Schaumburg-Lippe und Bremen, vol. 9 (Hildesheim, 1937).

quite concentrated. It was largely in the hands of an academic and official elite, lacking the juridical defense barriers of the Württemberg *Honoratioren*, but nonetheless clearly demarcated and well entrenched. The elite bonded state bureaucracy, provincial (estate) administration, and municipal government to an unusual degree. Included were clergymen; higher officials, who bridged the spheres of the state bureaucracy and the *Landschaften*; and the law graduates who staffed the town magistracies.[33] Particular interests were especially well served by each kind of stipend. The magistracies that controlled town stipends, for example, tended to give top priority to caring for their member families, largely at the expense of the clergy; 16.7 percent of the town stipends in the sample went to local officials with academic education (as opposed to 9.5 percent overall), while 26.4 percent went to sons of clergymen (as opposed to 40.1 percent overall). More striking is that in general the distribution of stipends was by way of interlocking networks of patronage; officials, including those in the town magistracies, used their control over particular stipends to serve colleagues in other branches of the elite as well as fellow members of their own groups.

One result of this cooperation is that the rate of clerical self-recruitment among the *Stipendiaten* in theology – 50.3 percent of them were sons of clergymen – is close to the rate for the Württemberg cloister school graduates. Included among the sons of pastors, pastoral assistants, and schoolteachers were poor students who otherwise might not have been able to study. But again corporate closure must be understood within a larger process. As at Tübingen, law and theology are variations on the same process of elite reproduction; the difference between the faculties lies in the concentrations within the elite. While in theology the percentages of clergymen and civil officials with university education are 50.3 and 12.9, the equivalent percentages in law are 23.3 and 42.7 (Table 1.5).

Hence at Göttingen sponsored induction was less centralized than the Württemberg variety, but far less dispersed and particularized than the Prussian alternative. This was a hybrid in which most uneducated groups, including artisans, were hardly represented at all. The only significant exception is petty officials, who contributed 22.2 percent of the fathers in theology, 15.5 percent in law, and 19.7 percent in the combined total. While the social milieu of artisans was largely beyond the pale of an elite-controlled sponsorship, petty officials, aside from their other advantages, took orders

[33] This is the "state patriciate" whose ethos and life-style have been reconstructed in Joachim Lampe, *Aristokratie, Hofadel, und Staatspatriziat in Kurhannover* (Göttingen, 1963). Jonathan B. Knudsen, *Justus Möser and the German Enlightenment* (Cambridge, 1986), pp. 31–52, is a well-textured description of an equivalent elite of law graduates in Osnabrück. See also Ernst von Meier, *Hannoversche Verfassungs- und Verwaltungsgeschichte, 1680–1866*, 2 vols. (Hildesheim, 1973).

Table 1.5. *Fathers' occupations/offices of Hanoverian subjects receiving public stipends at Göttingen*

Occupation	Identified	Unidentified	Clergy	Other university-educated: State officials	Local officials	Other	Total	Petty officials	Artisans	Merchants, industrialists, shopkeepers	Other
Stiftungen											
Theology	17	2	56.2 (9)	18.7 (1)	18.7 (1)	—	11.8 (2)	12.5 (4)	—	—	11.8 (2)
Law	9	2	20.0 (2)	30.0 (3)	—	—	33.3 (3)	30.0 (2)	—	—	22.2 (2)
Total	26	4	42.3 (11)	23.1 (4)	3.8 (1)	—	19.2 (5)	19.2 (6)	—	—	15.4 (4)
Towns											
Theology	41	6	36.6 (15)	4.9 (2)	9.8 (4)	7.3(3)	22.0 (9)	14.6 (6)	17.1 (7)	4.9(2)	4.9 (2)
Law	31	2	3.2 (4)	16.1 (5)	25.8 (8)	6.5(2)	48.4(15)	6.5 (2)	3.2 (1)	12.9(4)	16.1 (5)
Total	72	8	26.4 (19)	9.7 (7)	16.7(12)	6.9(5)	33.3(24)	11.1 (8)	11.1 (8)	8.3(6)	9.7 (7)
Landschaften											
Theology	113	25	54.9 (62)	3.5 (4)	5.3 (6)	0.9(1)	9.7(11)	24.8(28)	2.7 (3)	—	8.0 (9)
Law	63	12	28.6 (18)	28.6(18)	11.1 (7)	1.6(1)	41.3(26)	19.1(12)	—	—	11.1 (7)
Total	176	37	45.4 (80)	12.5(22)	7.4(13)	1.1(2)	21.0(37)	22.7(40)	1.7 (3)	—	9.1(16)
Total											
Theology	171	33	50.3 (86)	4.1 (7)	6.4(11)	2.3(4)	12.9(22)	22.2(38)	5.9(10)	1.2(2)	7.6(13)
Law	103	16	23.3 (24)	25.2(26)	14.6(15)	2.9(3)	42.7(44)	15.5(16)	1.0 (1)	3.9(4)	13.6(14)
Total	274	49[a]	40.1(110)[b]	12.0(33)	9.5(26)	2.6(7)	24.1(66)	19.7(54)[c]	4.0(11)	2.2(6)	9.9(27)[d]

Note: Figures are percentages, subtotals in parentheses.

[a] On the scattered lists used for the sample, another 44 students were not identified by faculty, and 17 others enrolled in medicine.

[b] Includes 11 schoolteachers (3 of them cantors); 9 of their sons enrolled in theology.

[c] Includes 3 parish sextons (*Küster* and *Custodis*), 3 organists, and 2 schoolmasters; some of these may also have been artisans. Most of the others were clerks and tax collectors.

[d] Includes 6 surgeons, 4 physicians, and 5 army officers.

Source: Universitätsarchiv Göttingen, 9a, 2, Nos. 4 (Calenbergische Landschaft and Grubenhagische Landschaft), 5 (Lünebergische Landschaft), 6 (Hoyische Landschaft), 7 (Bremen- und Verdensche Landschaft), 16 (Stift Loccum), 17 (Stift St. Alexandri), 22 (Hanover), 23 (Hedemünden), 26 (Northeim), 28 (Ulzen).

from the sponsors and in many cases worked in the same offices. If the sons of petty officials were bona fide poor students, they were also far less threatening exceptions to the continuity of "birth" than outsiders. Their mobility was not a matter of crossing a great divide, but simply of advancing from the outer to the inner circle of public employment.

REFRACTIONS

Poor students were an actual presence in eighteenth-century society, and a significant one at some universities. But they also existed as a set of stereotypical images, encountered again and again in state regulations and in a wide variety of literature produced and consumed by the educated public. While the images reflect the social reality in some ways, they also refract it through explicit ideology and the still denser ideological medium of implicit cultural norms. The refractions should not be dismissed as mere distortion; they are prescriptive devices, revealing a good deal about the problematic identity assigned the poor student in the corporate hierarchy of old-regime society and the conditional terms for his acceptance in the learned estate.

Even those who called for a drastic reduction in the "crowd" of poor students were careful to note that the boy of low birth but "extraordinary" intellectual gifts – the true "genius," as he came to be called – must be allowed to rise to prominence, as he had always risen. In Protestant lore, Luther was the most illustrious of these exceptional cases; but in the course of the eighteenth century examples could be cited from a growing pantheon that included Christian Wolff, Christian Gottlob Heyne, Johann Joachim Winckelmann, and Immanuel Kant. At the other extreme, however, was the artisan's or peasant's son who brought a "mediocre" intelligence to academic studies and became at best "half-learned" (*halbgelehrte*). Was this type as exceptional as the triumphant genius, or was he typical of his kind?

The latter view prevailed in the mounting concern about an oversupply of poor students, apparently resulting from an "addiction to study" (*Studirsucht*) among the masses. The standard parable, evoked repeatedly as a warning to parents and teachers, made the poor student a tragic victim of misguided aspirations. Pushed into academic studies by ambitious parents or a well-intentioned benefactor, he relied on charity to eke his way through secondary school. He probably had to move on to the university prematurely, and in any case he had no choice but to get through university studies as quickly as possible by limiting himself to the bare minimum – the *Brotstudium* – of basic theology courses. Having enjoyed neither the contacts that gave access to polite society nor the means to appear respectably in it, he left the university still bearing the unmistakably boorish marks of his plebeian origins. He endured the years, perhaps decades, of waiting for preferment as a mistreated live-in tutor or "consoled himself with the advantages of his Latin life-style, as though it constituted a rise in station, while he ate the bread of charity with his uneducated relatives." If he did not become an entirely "useless" burden, he was relegated to one of the less desirable rural pastorates or a Latin school. The reward for years of sacrifice and delayed gratification was a paltry income, barely sufficient to support a family, and woefully short of his expectations. Clearly he would have made a better life for himself by staying on the farm or learning a decent trade.[34]

In its broad outlines this story can be taken as a reminder of three indisputable eighteenth-century facts of life: that employment opportunities for university graduates were scarce, that occupational choices were inflexible, and that in the underlayer of the learned estate – i.e., in the lower clergy, including its teaching branch – the educated man might not enjoy a standard of living "appropriate to his station." At the end of the century the self-employed author, living off the sale of his publications, was still a rare exception. In the absence of this alternative, it seemed a simple matter of common sense that the supply of university graduates had to be limited to the number of vacancies in the civil and ecclesiastical bureaucracies. To most observers the body of officialdom, as pitifully small as it was by contemporary standards, seemed already full-grown, if not overgrown. They did not anticipate the nineteenth-century growth of white collar employment in large-scale commercial establishments and public services. On the other hand, the student entering a theology faculty in his late teens or early twenties probably was already too old to find a respectable alternative to a clerical career; the trades and commercial employment usually required a long apprenticeship that began considerably earlier. If the student was of obscure origins and lacked family connections, clerical prestige and affluence were more a vague possibility than a guarantee; he was likely to find himself trapped for life in a remote pastorate or teaching position.

[34] See esp. "Von der Menge der Studirenden in Teutschland," *Hannöverisches Magazin* 1:100 (1763): 1585–1600; "Ueber die zu grosse Anzahl der Studierenden," *Berlinische Monatsschrift* 12 (Sept. 1788): 251–64; "Sollte man nicht der Studiersucht des gemeinen Mannes, besonders in der Theologie, Gränzen setzen?" *Neues Hannöverisches Magazin* 1801, Stück 24: 369–96, 401–12. For further references see Herrlitz, *Studium als Standesprivileg*, which remains indispensable for understanding the eighteenth-century spectrum of opinion on poor students and the social issues they raised. Also relevant is Grete Klingenstein, "Akademikerüberschuss als soziales Problem im aufgeklärten Absolutismus. Bemerkungen über eine Rede Joseph von Sonnenfels' aus dem Jahre 1771," in Grete Klingenstein, Heinrich Lutz, and Gerlad Stourzh, eds., *Bildung, Politik und Gesellschaft. Studien zur Geschichte des europäischen Bildungswesens vom 16. bis zum 20. Jahrhundert*, Wiener Beiträge zur Geschichte der Neuzeit, vol. 5 (Munich, 1978), pp. 165–204. The German perception of a spreading "addiction to study" had its analogue in France, and the latter was informed by similar social and political concerns; see Harvey Chisick, *The Limits of Reform in the Enlightenment. Attitudes toward the Education of the Lower Classes in Eighteenth-Century France* (Princeton, N.J., 1981).

If our perception of eighteenth-century poor students relied entirely on the impressions of contemporaries, however, it would be skewed in several ways. We would be led to think that through most of the second half of the century the number of poor students was at least holding steady, and perhaps rising dramatically. To judge by its recurrence in public discussion, the concern with the "addiction to study" seems to mount in the last third of the century, when the precipitate decline in enrollments at most universities certainly brought an absolute reduction in the number of poor students and probably decreased their percentage of the student population. This is not, to be sure, a simple matter of stereotype flying in the face of obvious fact. There were no enrollment statistics with which to follow the general trend. While most of the smaller universities were shrinking, it was equally obvious in the 1780s that larger institutions like Halle were growing again, and it was not clear that this trend had reversed itself until the mid-1790s. Perhaps more important, the impression of overcrowding in theology derived mainly from the fact that candidates faced long waits for appointments. In an employment market in which connections were indispensable, it was not hard to find victims of this problem, even when a decline in enrollments had lessened the competition. The long-suffering candidate might simply have had to wait for a vacancy in one of the few appointments within his patron's orbit.

Nonetheless the selectivity of perception – the alarmist preoccupation with some facets to the exclusion of others – is striking. On the basis of contemporary witness we would conclude that peasants' sons, though less common than artisans' sons, constituted a much more substantial portion of poor students than our data indicate. In the negative stereotypes of poor students, sons of clergymen simply do not appear. The censorious definition of "poverty" ignored the fact that sons of poor pastors and teachers figured large among the truly needy recipients of charity; its critical criterion was whether the family had been able to bequeath a certain minimum of academic education.

In its skewings of social fact, the image of the poor student was a vehicle for ideological preoccupations and prescriptive norms. Its significance lay in articulating the criteria for approving or, more often, condemning the ascent of men from uneducated and propertyless families into the learned estate. The prevailing assumptions are perhaps best understood by way of contrast with the argument that Johann Adam Bergk, a popular philosopher in Leipzig, advanced in 1800. Bergk was well aware that "the limitation of the freedom to study by the state" had been and would continue to be applied one-sidedly to "propertyless or even moderately propertied students." He diverted to their cause the two new currents flowing across the German intellectual landscape at the turn of the century: Kantian philosophy and Smithian economics. The responsibility of the state, Bergk argued, was simply to protect "the freedom of all according to the same laws." By excluding potential students because of their social origins, or for any other reason, the state would be unjustly acting on the wrongheaded notion that its purpose was "the promotion of the happiness of its *Bürger*." Aside from the principle of justice at stake, unlimited freedom to attend the universities was also "clever" state policy. Conceiving of the intellectual arena as a Smithian market, Bergk assured his readers that unlimited competition on the basis of free exchange would result in maximum progress in the search for "truth." Hence a state-imposed limitation on the number of university graduates represented the same artificial meddling with "nature" that was crippling national economies. The greater the number of toilers in the fields of scholarship, the more rapid their "progress."[35]

Bergk was careful to note that the state had the right and the duty to screen candidates for public offices, and he acknowledged that his market approach might occasionally produce an oversupply. But if the individual's happiness was his own responsibility, so was his failure to qualify for an office. In any case the market would soon readjust itself:

> If at some point the crowd of students becomes too large for all to be absorbed by the state, this lasts only a short time. New livelihoods and branches of work become available, which draw workers to them. Everything comes back into balance (*Gleichgewicht*), and the number of students decreases.[36]

The emphasis on maximum flexibility in career choices, and on open and free competition for social rewards, corresponds to Turner's "contest" model for mobility. But Bergk's contribution is rare, if not unique, in contradicting the attitudes toward poor students and their mobility that still prevailed in his generation. The received framework – the most obvious target of Bergk's argument – was the cameralist doctrine that had developed in the wake of the Thirty Years' War. The cameralists saw the need for a limited number of stipends for poor students, but also took as axiomatic that state intervention must prevent what Veit Ludwig von Seckendorff described as an "all too large crowd of those who want to study but make no real contribution in that area and at the same time avoid other respectable

[35] Johann Adam Bergk, "Ueber die Einschränkung der Freiheit zu studieren durch den Staat," *Monatsschrift für Deutsche; zur Bildung des Geschmacks, und zu froher Unterhaltung* 1 (1801): 3–16. The article is dated April 25, 1800. On Bergk see also Herrlitz, *Studium als Standesprivileg*, pp. 115–17. For a similar argument, but one appealing to a providential economy rather than a Smithian market, see J. Z. H. Hahn, "Bescheidene Prüfung der Cirkularverordnung Sr. Königl. Majestät von Preussen, Friedrich Wilhelm des Dritten, an allerhöchstdero sämtliche Regimenter und Bataillons, den Unterricht in den Garnisonschulen betreffend . . . ," *Monatsschrift für Deutsche* 1 (April 1800): 270–315, and 2 (May-July 1800): 44–80, 121–94.

[36] Bergk, "Ueber die Einschränkung der Freiheit," p. 15.

livelihoods, and thus end up useless and superfluous to the common weal."[37]

Unlike Bergk's Kantian state, the cameralist state was in the business of making its subjects happier, despite their selfish interests and misguided impulses. It promoted the common welfare by maximizing the contributions of myriad human energies and resources. In the cameralist utopia, every subject would willingly and industriously fulfill his "productive" capacity. The most intolerable vice was parasitical "idleness," whether embodied in the landed aristocrat who used his rents to support a life of leisure, or in the able-bodied beggar who could find gainful employment but preferred to avoid it, or in the "superfluous" university graduate who could not secure an official appointment but was not qualified for any other branch of productive employment. Central to the vision of state-promoted progress was a mechanistic notion of equilibrium, not unlike that of the Newtonian universe, but very different from the market self-adjustment of Smithian doctrine. The machine that was society could operate at maximum output only if the state kept its various parts in balance. The officialdom of church and state constituted one critical part, but in the aftermath of the devastation and depopulation of the Thirty Years' War the urgent need was to restore productivity in agriculture and the trades. Hence any real or potential expansion of the recruitment pool for officialdom, beyond what was absolutely necessary and "useful," was viewed with great alarm. Like the beggar, the poor boy who became a superfluous university graduate was doubly "useless"; in addition to requiring others to support him, he deprived society of a badly needed hand in the fields or the workshop.

Where the able-bodied beggar and the poor student differed was in their motivation. Since the beggar was too "lazy" to perform manual labor, he was willing to accept dependence on charity despite its degradations. The uselessness of the poor student was blamed on his parents' ambition to raise him above their own station; in his case laziness – the illusion that a clerical office promised a life of leisure – went hand in hand with social pretensions.[38] As in Bergk's alternative ideal, the role assigned the state was inseparable from the definition and evaluation of ambition. For Bergk the

[37] Veit Ludwig von Seckendorff, *Teutsches Fürsten Staat*, ed. Ludwig Fertig (1665 ed.: Glashütten im Taurus, 1976), p. 211. But see also Seckendorff's discussion of stipends for poor students, in ibid., pp. 350–52. For a striking example of the tenacity of cameralist assumptions about higher education, see Johann David Michaelis, *Raisonnement über die protestantischen Universitäten in Deutschland*, 4 vols. (Frankfurt am Main, 1768–76). The cameralist tradition is given due attention in Herrlitz, *Studium als Standesprivileg*.

[38] This association of social pretensions and laziness remained quite common; it is the leitmotif of Johann Moritz Schwager, *Leben und Schicksale des Martin Dickius*, 2 vols. (Bremen, 1775), an amusing satire about the son of a day laborer and a laundress who studies theology despite his stupidity, but does not quite manage to secure a pastorate. See also "Sollte man nicht der Studiersucht des gemeinen Mannes, besonders in der Theologie, Gränzen setzen?"

striving for advancement through academic studies, like the profit motive in Smithian economics, was a "selfish" motive force harnessed to a higher rationality; it functioned positively within a market dynamic that the state could leave to adjust itself. In the cameralist tradition, the only ambition meriting approval was the desire to become "more and more useful" to society in the exercise of one's capacities. "Lower" families using education to catapult their sons into higher stations, regardless of the resource needs of society, were in the grip of a blind "passion" that had to be curbed. Indeed the "mania for study" was blind in two senses; in addition to being oblivious to the danger of disequilibrium, it rested on an illusion about the prospects for "happiness" in the lower ranks of the learned estate.

This vision of the "well-ordered police state" inspired the German states' earliest efforts to reduce the "crowd" of poor students in the first half of the eighteenth century and remained central to the discussion of educational reform in the next half-century. What changed as cameralism merged with the broader currents of Enlightenment thought was the estimation of the productive capacity at the mass base of society. In Germany, as elsewhere, the preoccupation with repopulating agriculture and the trades persisted long after symptoms of overpopulation had begun to appear in both the countryside and the towns. But the mounting enthusiasm for "popular enlightenment" (*Volksaufklärung*) was fueled by the conviction that the practice of farming and *Handwerk*, though still requiring little more than rote physical labor, could become an informed application of "useful" scientific and technological knowledge, offering both intellectual satisfaction and greater pecuniary rewards to the "clever." Aside from their numbers en masse, the human resources of the agricultural and industrial populations were now seen to include the intellectual capacities of their individual members. The poor student with unexceptional but solid intellectual endowments – the kind of intelligence officialdom could dispense with, but farming and the trades needed to modernize themselves – represented a brain drain that had to be plugged.[39]

The cameralist approach to poor students became conventional wisdom in the mainstream of German Enlightenment thought because it suited an agenda of enlightened reform from above, aimed at modernizing society and the state without undermining their basic structure and lines of authority. Overcrowding was not a simple matter of numbers; it spelled the danger that sons of uneducated and propertyless families would displace families with education and property from the small and static sphere of public employment, in a society with virtually no other "appropriate" employment opportunities. As enthusiasm for reform spread in the educated

[39] This is a pervasive theme; see esp. "Von der Mengen der Studirenden"; "Ueber die zu grosse Anzahl der Studierenden."

public, this fear of pressure from below was at once reflected in and intensified by a heightened awareness that intellectual labor was the privilege of a tiny minority, its position easily shaken by rising expectations among the masses. It was above all this danger that the peasant boy-become-poor student – the young man who was driven by a misguided desire to escape the drudgery of farm labor and whose absence from agriculture weakened the base of the social pyramid – came to evoke. Uprooted from his inherited occupational milieu, he was a particularly sobering reminder that the enlightenment of the masses must be limited to safe dosages.

In this perspective the problem was not simply that uneducated but ambitious parents attributed far more prestige to clerical offices than their employment conditions warranted; the typical *Gelehrter* likewise failed to realize that agriculture and the trades were the most "useful" and "productive" branches of society, and hence did not accord the peasant and the artisan the "honor" they deserved. This was to award the artisan a new identity, quite different from the one he usually claimed for himself. Whereas the honor of a trade traditionally had rested on collective guardianship of a received skill, the emphasis now was on the individual's openness to innovation. The appeals for a more egalitarian social consciousness in this sense were meant to encourage a new interchange between manual and intellectual labor; but they also reconciled the enthusiasm for progress on several fronts with a marked nervousness about the possible social consequences of change. To project more "honor" for the common lot of occupations was to offer an ideological sweetener to the stern conclusion that the great majority of sons of the "lower orders" would have to remain in their stations of birth, whether they liked it or not.

But eighteenth-century stereotypes were not simply reactions against the threat posed by the sheer number of poor students. At issue was whether the poor student's specific attributes – his upbringing in an uneducated family, his experience of material hardship, his ambition to cross the gulf between the uneducated and the educated – made him peculiarly qualified or especially unsuited for membership in the learned estate. Did the poor student compensate for his disadvantages with unusual motivation and capacity for hard work? Was he in fact an embodiment of the work ethic that informed the celebration of "usefulness" in cameralism and permeated the Enlightenment ideal of "virtue" (*Tugend*)? Or did his family background and his experience of ascent preclude the self-assurance and sense of personal honor to be expected of an educated man? At this level the mainstream of public discussion accommodated positive as well as negative profiles, and it should not be surprising that clergymen and schoolteachers, including former poor students, contributed to both.[40] The clergy at once exemplified

[40] For the typical arguments on both sides, see Johann Samuel Fest, *Ueber die Vortheile und Gefahren der Armuth für Jünglinge auf der Academie* (Leipzig, 1784).

the general tendency to corporate closure in old-regime society and constituted a de facto career open to talent. From one standpoint, bright poor boys seemed especially suitable material for a kind of second-class citizenship in the educated *Bürgertum*. They had known hardship and deprivation since birth and had neither the time nor the cash for the amusements and "luxuries" that spoiled scions of prosperous families for the rigors of clerical life. This image combined a hard-nosed realism – in some cases, in fact, an almost cynical defense of poor students on the grounds that they obviated the need to improve clerical incomes – with a note of reverse snobbery. It conveyed a certain pride in the asceticism of the *Gelehrter*, withdrawn from the reigning materialism and hence devoted to his calling despite its lack of pecuniary rewards.[41]

In the negative to this positive image, the paramount concern was that the clergy was slipping down the social scale as wealth and conspicuous consumption became indispensable for admission to "polite" society. Poor students were in effect dragging down the order, when its urgent need was to upgrade itself with true refinement and "culture." Rarely was this objection couched in terms of biological inheritance of "base" traits. What the poor student lacked was the broad social and cultural "education" (*Erziehung*) that is perhaps better termed breeding. The same domestic simplicity that others found an inherent advantage meant, in this view, that there had been no opportunity to cultivate intellectual interests beyond the narrow scope of a *Brotstudium* or to acquire the conversational agility and bodily grace expected in polite society. Too inept socially and too poorly dressed to appear in respectable homes, the poor student could not compensate for these handicaps in school and at the university. He was too accustomed to being treated with "contempt" to command respect among well-educated people.[42]

In addition to projecting alternative social profiles of the clerical order, these stereotypes applied the social and ultimately moral criteria by which the actual ascent of poor boys into the clergy was sanctioned or deemed illegitimate by the larger society. As in the contrasting rationales of cameralism and Bergk's self-adjusting market, the essential opposition lay

[41] Ibid., pp. 19–27; Jeremias Nicolaus Eyring, *Gedanken zur Vertheidigung derer die ohne Reichthum studiren* (Göttingen, 1761), pp. 23–33; Thümen, "Ist es zur Verbesserung des öffentlichen Erziehungswesens durchaus nothwendig, dass keine guten Köpfe aus der niedern und ärmern Volksklasse studiren?" *Deutsche Monatsschrift* 3 (1798): 236; "Ein Wort für Studierenden aus niedern Ständen," *Neues Hannöverisches Magazin* 1801, Stück 56: 902–03.

[42] The concern about the declining status of the clergy is unusually explicit in Jakob Christoph Rudolf Eckermann, "Mittel und Vorschläge, die Menge derer zurückzuhalten, die sich jetzt aus den niederen Ständen, ohne natürlichen Beruf zum Studiren auf Universitäten, und in die Stände der Gelehrten eindrängen," in idem, *Kleine vermischte Schriften*, 2 vols. (Altona, 1799), 2: 399–432. See also Johann Christian Heinrich Krause, *Beantwortung der Frage: Wer hat Beruf, ein Gelehrter zu werden?* 2 vols. (Bremen, 1787–88), 2: 21–23.

between different perceptions of ambition as a motive force. In his positive guise, the poor student who ascended to a respectable office became a German academic version of the self-made man – not a victor in market competition, to be sure, but nonetheless a deserving achiever, and perhaps even an overachiever. It was to his advantage, and to the advantage of the order he would enter, that he had been detached from his original social moorings and could not rely on inherited property or family connections. He had to *earn* membership in the learned estate and hence had no choice but to groom himself for his destiny by winning the approval of teachers and benefactors, by disciplining his wants, and by applying himself assiduously to his studies.[43] The appeal of this image becomes understandable against the backdrop of "idleness" and "debauchery" that was considered typical of student life throughout the century. The well-motivated, hard-working poor student figured as a model for the eighteenth-century version of a "bourgeois" work ethic, rooted deep in the utilitarian values of cameralism.[44] As such he was also, ironically, a foil, underscoring the absence of that ethic among better-off students, including those from prosperous bourgeois homes.

To be driven by ambition in this sense was to be well motivated. But in the second half of the century negative images continued to predominate, and in their alternative estimations of what motivated the academic mobility of outsiders they asserted some of the deepest and most tenacious values of a corporate hierarchy. In his treatise on the universities Johann David Michaelis, a professor at Göttingen, acknowledged that the "ambition" of the exceptionally bright poor boy could make him a "very useful" scholar. But he also made poor students primarily responsible for student "disturbances":

> The rich [young man] is not by nature better than the poor one, and his temperament can be just as vicious, just as malicious, just as troublemaking [*schadenfroh*]; but he has too much to lose for him to be able to follow any impulse; and precisely his property, his honor [*Ehre*], his hopes are the surety to the public for the moderation of his behavior. The poor [young man] from lower origins, on the other hand, carries all his endowments quite theoretically [*recht philosophisch*] on his person, even his hopes, his fatherland are wherever he turns. If he has the desire to do the worst, such considerations do not hold him back. . . . Among a very large crowd

[43] See, e.g., Eyring, *Gedanken*, p. 24; Fest, *Vortheile und Gefahren*, pp. 13–18; Thümen, "Verbesserung," pp. 234–40. For an intensely personal variation on these themes, see Gottlob David Hartmann, *Sophron. Oder die Bestimmung des Jünglings für dieses Leben* (Mitau, 1773), which will receive detailed treatment in Chapter 6.

[44] On this ethic see esp. Wolfgang Martens, *Die Botschaft der Tugend. Die Aufklärung im Spiegel der deutschen Moralischen Wochenschriften* (Stuttgart, 1968).

of poor, only some will be really dangerous, but the others do from lack of breeding [*Erziehung*] what the man of better lineage will not easily do.[45]

In one image, the lack of ascriptive advantages made the poor student an exemplar of self-disciplined effort; in the other, it made him a reckless *Luftmensch*. Within the corporate ethos of old-regime society, moral self-discipline was seen to require a sense of personal "honor," which in turn was regarded as an essentially social and heritable attribute. While Michaelis blamed poor students for university disorders, it was more common to ascribe to them an analogous lack of moderation; they typified the *Luxus* that seemed to be spreading through society and corroding its hierarchical distinctions. In the traditional conception – a conception that often found its way into Enlightenment reform thought – social distinctions were finely calibrated stations, each marked by plainly visible emblems of consumption as well as by a corporate ethos. *Luxus* was not simply a matter of wasting time and money on useless luxuries. It was a state of mind – an unrestrained, virtually insatiable ambition to possess and enjoy the accoutrements of higher status – that did not respect the "appropriate" limits of station. By making its victims dissatisfied with the standard of living that their actual circumstances allowed and by spreading social envy at the same time that it produced personal discontent, *Luxus* threatened the legitimacy of the entire intricate corporate pyramid.[46]

The very aspiration to academic studies was a symptom of *Luxus*, an illegitimate ambition for the great mass of the population. But "overeducation" was also a catalyst; it was excessive in the sense that it tended to inflate expectations, to become the cause of new appetites for the refinements of life. For the poor student, as for the overeducated peasant lured to the city, uprooting exacerbated the problem. An interloper in his new station, he had not been raised to respect its self-restraints. This was one of the senses in which the *Studirsucht* was an "addiction." In 1710 Hieronymous Gundling, a law professor at Halle, had raised the specter of unrestrained expectations by comparing ambitious poor students with "the sick and thirsty, who demand to have their thirst satisfied with good, pure water but, precisely because they are so thirsty, sometimes drink muddy puddle water that increases rather than slakes their thirst, and thus makes

[45] Michaelis, *Raisonnement*, 3: 237–39. Meiners, *Verfassung und Verwaltung*, 1: 69–87, likewise argues for keeping the number of poor students at Göttingen within safe limits.

[46] See esp. "Sollte man nicht der Studiersucht des gemeinen Mannes, besonders in der Theologie, Gränzen setzen?" which typifies the eighteenth-century view of the poor student as symptomatic of spreading *Luxus* and ambition but also, from the vantage point of 1801, recalls nostalgically that thirty years earlier sons of the lower orders had been content to remain in their inherited stations. See also "Ist die Studirwuth, besonders in der Theologie, nicht einer der ersten Gründe von den jetzt herrschenden Unzufriedenheit?" *Neues Hannöverisches Magazin*, 1797: 865– 90.

them poor and miserable, without property and having to beg."[47] It made little difference that, as some observed, the poor student could not afford the luxuries that corrupted his better-off *Kommilitonen*; what mattered was that he craved what he could not have. Indeed his probable destiny made inflated expectations especially tragic; far from allowing a man to live above his station, the incomes of lower clerical offices were inadequate for the legitimate needs of an educated man.

The censure of ambition fused personal, social, and moral attributes. In the course of earning a right to office, the poor student as self-made man learned to subordinate himself to the superiors who sponsored him and to render them the proper deference. In the negative image, it was above all the prolonged "dependence" on patrons – on teachers and professors, on private benefactors, on the employers of private tutors – that made the poor student inveterately "base," despite his educational credentials. As a schoolboy and as a student still in need of charity, he owed his prospects to men who were in a position to act arbitrarily and exact a high price for their sponsorship. As a university graduate, seeking an appointment without family connections, he became "a slave of some people who make him some generous promises that they forget again a moment later."[48] Here "baseness" (*Niederträchtigkeit*) connoted servility, which was not to be confused with the deferential posture expected of social inferiors at all levels of a corporate hierarchy. Even the young man from a prosperous bourgeois home – the kind Michaelis preferred to form the core of the student population – depended on patrons for his career prospects. The perceived difference – and here stereotypes demonstrate how inseparable moral judgments were from consciousness of rank – was that he could be appropriately deferential, since his family legacy of "honor" constituted a foundation of moral autonomy. Ingrained norms enabled him to acknowledge his inferior position whenever necessary, but also prevented him from debasing himself in the pursuit of favors. The stereotypical poor student, driven by ambition, lacked this balance; he had no choice but to accept extreme dependence and pursue favors at any price. If "arrogance" was an affront to hierarchy, "servility" in a sense was more intolerable from a moral standpoint. Precisely because his need to ingratiate himself was not checked by an inherited sense of honor, the poor student could manipulate the patron-client relationship with flattery, feigned humility, and other forms of dissembling. Self-degradation – in accepting handouts and in tolerating the imperious

[47] Nicolaus Hieronymous Gundling, *Sammlung kleiner teutscher Schriften* (Halle, 1737), p. 117. Gundling made this comment in the announcement to his winter-semester lectures in 1710. See also Ferdinand August Weckherlin, "Der Junge muss studiren," in idem, *Wirtemberg. Pietismus. Schreiben. Schulen. Und Erziehung und Aufklärung überhaupt* (1787), pp. 75–91.

[48] "Von der Menge der Studirenden," p. 1593. See also Krause, *Beantwortung*, 2: 17–18; Fest, *Vortheile und Gefahren*, pp. 40–49.

treatment of benefactors – was also likely to involve a dishonest presentation of the self.[49] Whereas proper deference was sincere, servility undermined the social order because it was in this sense calculating. The irony was that its very lack of balance also made it clumsily transparent.

While this image reflected the realities of sponsored mobility to some degree, it also refracted moral categories through an elite social consciousness. Its censure exemplified a common tendency in the educated public – a public that drew very fine distinctions within its own ranks – to lump all uneducated families into a homogeneous and at least implicitly dishonorable mass. Yet in the eyes of the same public the self-employed artisan became a foil to the "dependent" poor student. The promising poor boy who took up a trade might not become wealthy, but at least he was his own man. His "independence," and indeed his freedom, gave him the honor the poor student lacked, albeit in a station well below the ranks of the learned estate.[50] This was to counteract one illusion – that academic studies and a clerical career brought prestige, affluence, and leisure – with another. The idyll of the independent *Handwerker* ignored the fact that most trades required a long period of subordination (and deference) in apprenticeship, that guild membership entailed a host of corporate restrictions, that overcrowding already exposed some trades to market forces and threatened others with the same kind of dependence. In this refraction, as in images of the poor student, stereotype drew selectively on the realm of social fact. What mattered was that the contented, self-respecting artisan was immune to ambition and its vices. He did not threaten a balance among the parts of the social body, and ultimately in the norms governing social relationships, that seemed essential but precarious.

[49] On the broader cultural significance of this theme and its historical connection with perceptions of mobility, see Lionel Trilling, *Sincerity and Authenticity* (Cambridge, Mass., 1972), pp. 12–25.

[50] See esp. Weckherlin, "Der Junge muss studiren"; "Von der Menge der Studirenden," pp. 1592–97. The recurrent emphasis on the advantages of the trades is also noted in Herrlitz, *Studium als Standesprivileg*, pp. 75–77.

2

Initiations

Poor students make frequent appearances in the historical record as objects of perception, but their lived experience is more elusive. In prescribing the conditions for their acceptance into educated society, prevailing stereotypes caricatured some of their motives and responses and ignored others. We are left wondering how the initiation actually formed boys and young men, and how they in turn made sense of and came to terms with its imperatives.

To an extent the initiated can speak for themselves about the expectations with which they entered academic studies, about the cultural legacy they brought from their homes to the school, about the dilemmas of poverty and dependence. There is no better entrée to the daily anxieties of the charity pupil than the reluctant request for money Johann Gottlieb Fichte sent his father, a village ribbon weaver, from the *Fürstenschule* at Pforta on April 1, 1775. Having proudly reported that he expected to receive one of the best grades in the annual examination, Fichte went on to explain in panic that his triumph would bring with it "the fatal custom" of having to treat eleven schoolmates to pastries.[1] But this is a virtually unique glimpse into school life from the pupil's standpoint, and even letters from the university years are rare.

Autobiographical witness is less immediate, more oblique. In one way or another, past experience has been filtered, patterned, and interpreted in the process of memory. Though often acutely conscious of their struggle upward from obscurity, the witnesses did not approach their life histories as case studies of the socialization and acculturation of the upwardly mobile. And yet certain preoccupations, inherent in the conventional *forms* of autobiographical texts, are revealing of how a structure of inequality and its cultural norms meshed in the experience of academic mobility. Most of our

[1] Johann Gottlieb Fichte, *Briefwechsel 1775–1793*, *Gesamtausgabe der Bayerischen Akademie der Wissenschaften*, III, vol. 1 (1968), pp. 6–7. The father had apparently offered to send garters (*Strumpfbändern*) for distribution, but Fichte gently declined. "Unfortunately such things are not sought after here as much as money," he noted, and he "would be mocked unbearably."

texts represent, to one degree or another, the cross-fertilization of two generic types in autobiographical literature from the mid-eighteenth century onward. One was the self-consciously literary narrative, its more or less fictive properties marking the influence of both the picaresque novel and the "novel of education" (*Bildungsroman*). Though the fusion of documentary "fact" and novelistic "fiction" rarely produced the shocking intimacy with which Rousseau mesmerized his readers, it did make the life history the vehicle for an introspective concern with the development of an individual personality. This literary form of individualism is in itself a significant expression of social consciousness; it conveys a new distance on and detachment from corporate traditions, and at the same time a certain critical awareness of class and its inequities.

But as late as the 1790s, when the life histories of prominent clergymen throughout Germany were being published in a clerical journal in Leipzig, the conventions of the older subgenre – the *Gelehrtenbiographie* – still shaped the selection and interpretation of detail.[2] In its pure form the *Gelehrtenbiographie*, perhaps intended only for members of the family and colleagues, was restricted to an account of a public career. Its social meaning lies precisely in its lack of critical distance – in the fact that it conveys the social texture of a corporate way of life from the inside. The very fact that the experience of poverty as a schoolboy and student was so common in the clerical order made for candor about the family's lack of means. If *la vie intime* is discreetly ignored, childhood and youth nonetheless receive considerable attention as preparatory stages for the assumption of a corporate identity. Parents are not seen as having molded a psyche in the modern sense; convention required that the author explain how parental example had contributed to his academic achievement and his commitment to a calling. We also learn how instruction and reading at home prepared for success in school; how the boy was introduced to Latin and the other subjects that formed the entryway to the learned estate; how certain teachers and professors shaped his intellectual development. Former patrons and

[2] From 1789 to 1795 a life history was published in each issue of the *Allgemeines Magazin für Prediger, nach den Bedürfnissen unserer Zeit*, ed. Joh. Rud. Gottl. Beyer (cited hereafter as AMP). Most were first-person accounts, and most of those written in the third person were also autobiographical. For background on the cross-fertilization of autobiographical subgenres and "novels" of various sorts in the eighteenth century, see esp. Klaus-Detlef Müller, *Autobiographie und Roman. Studien zur literarischen Autobiographie der Goethezeit* (Tübingen, 1976); Günter Niggl, *Geschichte der deutschen Autobiographie im 18. Jahrhundert* (Stuttgart, 1977). Also relevant is the secularization of the Pietist conversion testimonial, which will be considered in Chapter 5. The subtle analysis in David Vincent, *Bread, Knowledge, and Freedom. A Study of Nineteenth-Century Working Class Autobiography* (London, 1981), demonstrates the value of autobiographical literature for social history. See also Lucien Bély, 'L'Elève et le monde: Essai sur l'éducation des lumières d'après les mémoires autobiographiques du temps," *Revue d'histoire moderne et contemporaine* 28 (1981): 3–35, and, on the German literature, Petra Frerichs, *Bürgerliche Autobiographie und proletarische Selbstdarstellung* (Frankfurt am Main, 1980).

employers figure large; the public history of a career was an opportunity to acknowledge the generosity and guidance of some and to settle scores, more or less discreetly, with others.

As rare and scattered as it is, our autobiographical testimony at least has the virtue of offering a fairly wide spectrum of family origins, childhood milieus, and careers. Of the eleven most pertinent texts, two were written by sons of clergymen. Jakob Friedrich Reimmann (1668–1743) was one of seven children of a pastor in the Duchy of Magdeburg; the other – Johann Salomo Semler (1725–1791) – was the fourth son of the deacon (*Diakonus*) in the town of Saalfeld in Saxony. The fathers' occupations of the nine others were quite varied: a village schoolmaster in Thuringia, an innkeeper-farmer in Thuringia, a musician and petty official at the court of the Duchy of Weissenfels, a regimental musician and later village notary (*Lizentschreiber*) in Hanover, a tailor and farmer in Brandenburg, a miller-farmer in Süderdithmarsch, a village weaver in Saxony, a mason in Dresden, a small shopkeeper in Altona.[3]

All eleven authors had studied theology, but only four – Reimmann, Christian Heinrich Schreyer (1751–1823), Claus Harms (b. 1778), and Johann Samuel Fest (b. 1754) – had become pastors. The careers of two others – Semler and Johann Christian Edelmann (1698–1767) – chart the rapid advance of rationalist theology from a renegade doctrine, under fierce attack from the Orthodox establishment, to an entrenched and thoroughly domesticated academic school. For Reimmann, as for most poor students in later generations, teaching was an interim employment between university studies and a pastoral appointment. But Georg Friedrich Schumacher (b. 1771) and Wilhelm Harnisch (1787–1864) belonged to the new generation at the turn of the century to whom teaching offered the possibility of a lifetime career. Christian Gottlob Heyne (1729–1812) and Johann Gottfried Seume (1763–1810) also exemplified new career prospects – Heyne as the guiding spirit in the renaissance of classical studies at Göttingen, Seume as a well-known and fairly well remunerated man of letters. In the brief life of Karl Philipp Moritz (1757–1793) eight restless years as a gymnasium teacher in Berlin were sandwiched between unsuccessful efforts to join an acting troupe and a meandering career as a novelist and essayist.

The school days and university years of Schumacher, Harms, and Harnisch were noticeably different from those of Reimmann more than a century earlier. By then the reforms that would produce the nineteenth-century system of higher education were under way. But the basic structure of the patronage and charity that had been available to poor boys since the sixteenth century was still intact, and the academic culture into which they

[3] In four cases – Schreyer, Schumacher, Harms, and Seume – the early death of the father had plunged the family into financial straits.

were inducted had changed very little at most schools. Our first task is to identify these elements of continuity in the academic initiations of poor boys.

PATRIMONIES

How were poor boys initiated into learned culture in the eighteenth-century *Gelehrtenschule*? What were the differences in the formative experiences of insiders and outsiders?

Perhaps the most striking feature of the Latin schools and *Gymnasien* was their apparently bewildering juxtapositions of elements, some reminders of the schools' continuing integration into the society and culture of the old regime, others at least apparent anticipations of the structure and ethos of academic achievement in modern school systems. The typical hierarchy of grades, ascending from *Sexta* (or *Quinta*) to *Prima* (or to the still more rarified stratum of *Selectaner*), was in some respects a direct antecedent of the bureaucratic gradations in contemporary schools. But in most schools at the end of the century this hierarchy still reflected more the ranking within the teaching staff (with one or at most two teachers completely responsible for each grade) than a division by subject. The tidy correspondence between class gradations and age cohorts to which modern bureaucratic schooling has accustomed us was noticeably lacking. There was no standard age of exit; pupils were expected to spend a minimal period in the *Prima* before attending a university, but teachers constantly lamented their inability to prevent some boys from moving on too soon after entering that grade, or indeed from bypassing it entirely. Likewise there was no standard point of entry; both the age at which a boy entered school and the grade in which he began hinged on whether and to what degree he had been prepared at home by his father, an elder brother, or a tutor; and that in turn depended at least in part on his family's level of wealth and education.[4]

[4] There are a great number of local histories of Latin schools and *Gymnasien*. Especially useful are Julius Heidemann, *Geschichte des Grauen Klosters zu Berlin* (Berlin, 1874); Wilhelm Görges and August Nebe, *Geschichte des Johanneums zu Lüneburg* (Lüneburg, 1907); Georg Friedrich Grotefend, *Geschichte des Lyceums der Königlichen Residenz-Stadt Hannover während des Zeitraums von 1733 bis 1833* (Hanover, 1833); Otto Kaemmel, *Geschichte des Leipziger Schulwesens vom Anfange des 13. bis gegen die Mitte des 19. Jahrhunderts (1214–1846)* (Leipzig and Berlin, 1909). Wolfgang Neugebauer, *Absolutistischer Staat und Schulwirklichkeit in Brandenburg-Preussen*, Veröffentlichungen der Historischen Kommission zu Berlin, vol. 62 (Berlin and New York, 1985), includes a brief but informative discussion of town Latin schools and an extensive bibliography of secondary literature. Also helpful were the excerpts and summaries from inspection reports in the Prussian provinces, in Paul Schwartz, *Die Gelehrtenschulen Preussens unter dem Oberschulkollegium (1787–1806) und das Abiturientenexamen*, 3 vols., Monumenta Germaniae Paedagogica, vols. 46, 48, 50 (Berlin, 1910–12).

Like most other institutions of the old regime, the school attested to the vitality of corporate values and distinctions. It was not simply that certain forms of dress distinguished pupils preparing for university studies from other local boys. To advance up the grade levels – from *Tertia* to *Secunda*, and ultimately to *Prima* – was to ascend a hierarchy of jealously guarded privileges and to approximate more and more the corporate "freedom" of university students. Promotion brought the right to wear a cape, or to carry a stick in lieu of the student's sword, or to perform in public functions outside the school. But the eighteenth-century school is resistant to simplistic distinctions between tradition and modernity, since it fused these gradations of corporate identity and solidarity with an ethos of individual competition. The duality, it should be stressed, had been integral to the *Gelehrtenschule* since its inception. Eighteenth-century reformers, in their efforts to make the school an arena for individual achievement, envisioned an alternative to the corporate values of the larger society; but in fact they were providing new rationales for a longstanding reliance on competitive ranking to stimulate learning and reward individual performance.

Württemberg offers a characteristically eccentric variation on this duality. Each *Promotion* – i.e., each class admitted as a result of the annual *Landesexamen* – advanced as a group through the ranks of the cloister schools and the Tübingen Stift, with individual advancement only for the most exceptional cases. A few months after entering the first cloister school, pupils took an intensely competitive "translocation" examination, which ranked them within the *Promotion*. The first six had to maintain their ranking in the recurrent examinations for which the cloister schools and the Stift were famous, but could expect as their reward appointments to the most prestigious clerical offices. Thus competition not only was compatible with the formation of self-enclosed corporate subgroups; it also fixed a hierarchy within each class, reflecting and eventually helping perpetuate the corporate hierarchy of the Württemberg clergy as a whole.[5]

Elsewhere competition had a more autonomous function. Typically pupils were expected to spend a minimal period (usually two years) in each grade; but beyond that, in promotion from one grade to another both age distinctions and grade solidarities were secondary to individual achievement, which was evaluated in special "translocation" examinations as well as in daily classroom observations. At least until the *Prima*, when all the remaining pupils could be treated equally as prospective students, the order

[5]Gustav Lang, *Geschichte der württembergischen Klosterschulen von ihrer Stiftung bis zu ihrer endgültigen Verwandlung in Evangelisch-theologische Seminare* (Stuttgart, 1938); Martin Leube, *Geschichte des Tübinger Stifts*, 3 vols. (Stuttgart, 1921–36), 2: 69–75. On the importance of the first examination and on the intensely competitive spirit among cloister school pupils, see also David Christoph Seybold, *Hartmann, eine wirtembergische Klostergeschichte* (Leipzig, 1778), pp. 96–118. Seybold's mildly satirical novel is based on firsthand experience; it is a rich fund of detail on the corporate initiation into the Württemberg clergy.

of seating in the schoolroom reflected the teacher's ranking of performance, with weekly and sometimes even daily changes of place.[6]

The final complication was the medium for competition. Even in the lower grades (the *Sexta* and the *Quinta*), despite the presence of local boys who would not advance to academic studies, an hour or so per day was devoted to the memorization of Latin vocabulary, declensions, and conjugations. In the *Sekunda* and *Prima*, Latin occupied one-third to one-half of the instruction – roughly ten to fifteen hours per week. Aside from the time it commanded, Latin instruction dominated the curriculum in most schools because it formed the only competitive arena for promotions within and between grades. On this subject it becomes especially important to exploit autobiographical witness *despite* its prejudices and blinders. Most of the detailed descriptions are of schoolrooms in the last quarter of the century, and they reflect the standards of the educational reform movements already under way. To both utilitarian and neohumanistic reformers, the traditional Latinity was a *Schlendrian* characterized by rote, or "mechanical," memorization of vocabulary and grammatical rules, a "pedantic" preoccupation with form over content and meaning, and indifference to, if not outright hostility toward, the richness of life outside the schoolroom.[7]

Despite the growing enthusiasm for reform, most secondary schools at the end of the century – including the cloister schools in Württemberg, the Saxon *Fürstenschulen*, and the hundreds of small-town Latin schools – were still attached to this *Schlendrian*. They were more or less well-preserved monuments to the symbiosis of Lutheran piety and classical scholarship that had created the sixteenth-century *Gelehrtenschule*. Even the most rigidly traditional school, to be sure, seemed a pale realization of the institution that Melanchthon and his fellow humanists had envisioned. To sixteenth-century Protestant humanists, as to their Jesuit counterparts who had created the French collège, an unqualified commitment to Latinity had promised to segregate school life from worldly corruption by forming it into an all-encompassing, self-contained pedagogical universe. But even for boarders it had proved impractical to limit the language of daily intercourse, as well as instruction in class, to Latin. By the eighteenth century and perhaps earlier, in fact, some of the explanations required in Latin classes were given in German. Likewise the curriculum had not frozen into a sacrosanct corpus; long before the reform movements at the end of the century, there had

[6] In some schoolrooms, evaluation seems to have kept the pupils in perpetual motion.

[7] See, e.g., "Kurze Geschichte meiner Schuljahre vom Jahr 1760 bis 1766, auf einem damals berühmten Gymnasium," *Braunschweigisches Journal* 2 (1789): 319–49; Georg Friedrich Schumacher, *Genrebilder aus dem Leben eines siebenzigjährigen Schulmannes, ernsten und humoristischen Inhalts, oder Beiträge zu Geschichte der Sitten und des Geistes seiner Zeit* (Schleswig, 1841), pp. 78–89; the assessment of instruction in the Chemnitz lyceum is in Heyne's brief but revealing account of his childhood and youth, in Arnold Hermann Ludwig Heeren, *Christian Gottlob Heyne, biographisch dargestellt* (Göttingen, 1813), pp. 15–17.

been innovations, involving greater attention to the native language and its literature as well as to "practical" subjects like history and geography.[8]

While these adjustments had brought the *Gelehrtenschule* into closer alignment with intellectual trends and the needs of some of its patrons, they had not undermined its traditional raison d'être. In eighteenth-century society, the corporate status hierarchy overlapped to some degree with a class structure, reflecting the distribution of wealth and power; but it also enjoyed a degree of autonomy. Aside from its particular occupational function, the clergy was a branch of a fairly homogeneous learned estate. What marked off that estate publicly from the surrounding society was a distinctly formalistic and imitative mastery of language, a technical competence that, aside from any practical value it might have, was to be acquired and displayed as an honorific credential.[9] It is the continuing appeal of this kind of learning that most autobiographical accounts, taking their very different standards for social value from a modern definition of the learned professions, tend to ignore or dismiss. The authors may recall their excitement about being inducted into an esoteric ritual and may even acknowledge a certain pride in having excelled in it; but judging the ritual to have been useless, and perhaps even crippling, they did not dwell on the attractions of its routinism for boys of their background.

All this is not to deny that the Latinity of the schools was in a more or less advanced stage of ossification. Its coupling of status and learning had loosened as the German Protestant symbiosis of piety and "eloquence" lost its original vitality. Hence one of poor students' worsening dilemmas in the eighteenth century: the formal *Bildung* that had to compensate for lack of *Besitz* had been confined to a kind of learning that seemed increasingly obsolete and boorishly "pedantic." But the tradition came to seem absurd only very gradually, as the pace of change in the surrounding society quick-

[8] The best description of the traditional Latinity is still Friedrich Paulsen, *Geschichte des Gelehrten Unterrichts auf den deutschen Schulen und Universitäten vom Ausgang des Mittelalters bis zur Gegenwart. Mit Besonderer Rücksicht auf den klassischen Unterricht*, vol. 1 (3rd., enl. ed.: Berlin and Leipzig, 1919), pp. 345–87. Especially informative for eighteenth-century continuities and innovations in the traditional curriculum is Kaemmel, *Geschichte des Leipziger Schulwesens*. Latin instruction is also given some attention in Georg Jäger, *Sozialgeschichte des deutschen Unterrichts an höheren Schulen von der Spätaufklärung bis zum Vormärz*, Schule und literarische Kultur, vol. 1 (*Darstellung*) (Stuttgart, 1981); Joachim Gessinger, *Sprache und Bürgertum. Zur Sozialgeschichte sprachlicher Verkehrsformen im Deutschland des 18. Jahrhunderts* (Stuttgart, 1980), pp. 65–79. On the French tradition, see F. de Dainville, *La naissance de l'humanisme moderne* (Paris, 1940); Georges Snyder, *La pédagogie en France aux XVIIe et XVIIIe siècles* (Paris, 1965), pp. 31–83.

[9] See esp. R. Steven Turner, "The '*Bildungsbürgertum*' and the Learned Professions in Prussia, 1770–1830: The Origins of a Class," *Histoire sociale-Social History* 13:25 (May 1980): 105–35; Wilhelm Roessler, *Die Entstehung des modernen Erziehungswesens in Deutschland* (Stuttgart, 1961). Also relevant is the concept of "representative publicness" (*repräsentative Oeffentlichkeit*) in Jürgen Habermas, *Strukturwandel der Oeffentlichkeit. Untersuchungen zu einer Kategorie der bürgerlichen Gesellschaft* (4th ed.: Neuwied and Berlin, 1969), pp. 17–26.

ened and above all as educated men became enamored of utilitarian visions of progress. Though the number of dissenting voices among schoolmen increased with each new generation, it is safe to assume that until the last two decades of the century the silent majority remained staunchly traditionalist. That was not simply because many Latin schools, and above all those in small towns, were isolated from new trends in intellectual life. Relegated to offices offering so little in the way of wealth and public authority, the teachers, and particularly the older men who had been unable to escape to pastorates, had special reason to stand guard over the integrity of a formal credential.

Whether the typical product of a typical Latin school entered the university as a competent Latinist is another matter. To judge by the complaints of university professors throughout the century, the training in Latin as well as Hebrew and Greek in most secondary schools, and especially in the small-town Latin schools, was inadequate; the typical product could neither read extensively nor comprehend lectures in the language of scholarship. But if the schools fell woefully short of their assignment in that sense, their *Schlendrian* remained suited to the task of distinguishing future *Gelehrten* from the mass of uneducated laymen by endowing them with an honorific cultural property.

Particularly in schools within the Pietist orbit, there had been a tendency to replace the works of Vergil, Pindar, and other classical authors with soberly Christian texts, demonstrating the essentials of Latinity without exposing pupils to the prurience and noxious values of paganism. But in other schools the standard corpus of classical texts retained its place alongside the Lutheran catechism and Bible precisely because the ideal of "eloquence" it embodied required little attention to substantive meaning. Beyond the initial memorization of rudiments – of vocabulary, of declensions and conjugations, and of grammatical rules – one earned and displayed membership in the learned estate primarily by mastering form. The exercises in translation that occupied so much of the older pupils' time allowed for commentary on the author and his world; but their essential purpose was to develop "elegance" of style by imitating a master in the intricacies of Latin syntax, rhyme, and meter.

It was emblematic of this entire pedagogy that the pinnacle of achievement for the older schoolboys, often recalled in autobiographies, was the composition of Latin verse according to the classical rules of prosody. This kind of mastery was admirably suited to the recital of poems and the delivery of largely ornamental speeches at annual or semiannual public examinations, with parents and local dignitaries in attendance, as well as at festivities outside the school. By the end of the century German had often joined Latin in both versifying and speechmaking, and contemporary issues had been added to the traditional rhetorical repertoire from theology, ethics, and other strictly academic subjects. But the traditional learning could tolerate these intrusions without abandoning its essential social function, which did not require justification by appeal to the relevance of learning to everyday life, or even by appeal to its value for practical mastery of the native language. In a standard exercise, pupils were given an apparently odd assortment of words and phrases and had to fashion them into a piece of prose or poetry. In retrospect the exercise struck Schumacher as perfunctory and largely sterile, since it involved reassembling the easily recognizable pieces of a classical text. His teacher, the "old pedant" Henrici, would have found this objection puzzling; to him the point was not to induce the pupils to apply their language skills to contemporary life, much less to encourage originality of expression, but to require them to imitate an elegant style faithfully.[10]

Despite their shared condition of schoolboy "poverty" and their shared dependence on charity, insiders and outsiders had distinctive angles of vision on academic studies and the prospect of a clerical career. Even clergymen in poorly endowed rural pastorates and small-town teaching positions – though often worse off financially than artisans, small shopkeepers and landholding peasants – counted themselves solid members of the learned estate. As in the higher echelons, their corporate consciousness often rested on several generations of clerical lineage and was reinforced by marriage to clergymen's daughters. Inherent in their sense of superiority to the uneducated mass, including the more respectable artisanry and peasantry, was the expectation that the family's distance from these groups would be maintained, if not widened, in the next generation. This pride of "birth" is implicit in the brief accounts of ancestry with which Reimmann and several other clergymen's sons begin their life histories.[11] The son of a small-town lawyer, Anton Friedrich Büsching felt the need to trace his clerical heritage directly to his paternal grandfather Johann Leopold. His father, he recalled with unusual candor, had been too stubborn and volatile to develop a clientele and had squandered money on drink; but his own relentless devotion to hard work stood as proof that sons do not necessarily inherit their fathers' traits. In the long view, the father's failure was merely a temporary interruption of a family ascent:

> One might assume that [my grandfather] devoted himself to a teaching office in the church because this is usually the first step taken by a family of commoners when it decides to have its sons pursue university education. True, my grandfather thought just like other *Bürger* in this matter; but he was no artisan, and my family did not inherit through him the artisan mentality [*Handwerksgeist*], which often is

[10] Schumacher, *Genrebilder*, pp. 87–89, 123–24.

[11] Johann Jacob Reimmann, *Eigene Lebens-Beschreibung, Oder Historische Nachricht von Sich Selbst* (Brunswick, 1745), pp. 1–4. See also, e.g., Johann Salomo Semler, *Lebensbeschreibung* (Halle, 1781), p. 1.

apparent for a long time, and in many forms and ways, in the educated descendants of artisans. My grandfather's descendants did not lower themselves by marrying daughters of artisans for the money. My grandfather was in fact born for the office of clergyman.[12]

As Büsching suggests, the lack of substantial property in the lower clergy made educational credentials all the more vital to their corporate consciousness. As in higher ranks, it was more a foregone conclusion than a matter of individual choice that sons pursue clerical careers. The element of choice entered when it seemed possible to lift the family still higher by financing legal studies for at least one son, or when in the absence of family means and charitable support a boy had to be placed in a "lower" occupation.

Friedrich Gedike meant to point up his divergence from the corporate pattern when he recalled that his father, an obscure village pastor, had allowed him to "grow wild and without special instruction among the peasant boys of the village until age nine."[13] For most clergymen's sons, boarding life at school completed a process of social insulation. From early childhood they had been kept removed from street life, where boys' peer groups played such an important role in shaping the social consciousness of the "lower" *Bürgertum*. The complement to this insulation from plebeian influences was a methodical induction into learned culture, integral to the family's domestic life.[14] For boys destined to follow in their fathers' footsteps, the initiation sometimes took the form of an apprenticeship; the son might be introduced to the Hebrew or Greek he would need for biblical scholarship and might be required to record his father's sermons.

But the core – the vital link between family and school – was the introduction to Latinity. It was no accident that in Württemberg, where the unusually centralized selection for the cloister schools had allowed the cler-

[12] Anton Friedrich Büsching, *Eigene Lebensgeschichte* (Halle, 1789), pp. 4–5, 22–29. Heinrich Eberhard Gottlob Paulus was the son of a Pietist clergyman in Württemberg who had been suspended from office and "replaced this outer loss for his children richly through the care and effort with which all his time was now devoted to their education." The family had been lifted into the *Mittelstand*, Paulus recalled, by the grandfather, who was descended from "artisans in a very limited trade" but had by his own efforts become first an *Aktuarius* and then a *Stadtsyndikus*. AMP 7 (1793): 330–33.

[13] Friedrich Gedike, *Gesammlete Schulschriften*, 2 vols. (1789–95), 1: 241.

[14] On the peer groups of street life and the isolation of educated bourgeois children from them, see Jürgen Schlumbohm, "'Traditional' Collectivity and 'Modern' Individuality: Some Questions and Suggestions for the Historical Study of Socialization. The Examples of the German Lower and Upper Bourgeoisies around 1800," *Social History* 5:1 (Jan. 1980): 84–98. It may be correct to attribute a new interest in childhood and domestic education in the "bourgeois" family in the second half of the eighteenth century to a new "individualism," in turn reflecting intergenerational mobility and the achievement ethos that such mobility required; but social historians have tended to overlook the continuities with bourgeois domestic instruction as a vehicle of corporate inheritance. See, e.g., Heidi Rosenbaum, *Formen der Familie. Untersuchungen zum Zusammenhang von Familienverhältnissen, Sozialstruktur und sozialem Wandel in der deutschen Gesellschaft des 19. Jahrhunderts* (Frankfurt am Main, 1982), pp. 255–309.

ical establishment to tighten its grip on recruitment, the commitment to memorization and stylistic elegance was particularly rigid. From a distance of more than thirty years, Christian Friedrich Duttenhofer could forgive neither the monkish regimentation nor the "old-school *Schlendrian*" of the cloister school at Denkendorf. It struck him as absurd that he had begun to decipher the meaning of classical texts only by private effort and had "learned to botch together a host of Latin, Greek and German verses, and even occasionally a Hebrew version, before being given the slightest guidance, or a model, for his own essays in the German language."[15] But Duttenhofer was a particularly bitter witness; other former pupils credited the cloister schools' highly formalized initiation to Latinity, as antedeluvian as it had come to seem, with reinforcing the self-enclosed institutional regimen in preserving an unusually strong esprit de corps in successive generations of Württemberg clergymen. Aside from its disciplinary value, the traditional Latinity was vital because it put clergymen in a unique position to transmit an esoteric command of grammatical precision and stylistic elegance. Indeed clergymen in Württemberg not only groomed their boys assiduously in the requisite skills at home; they also accompanied them to the annual *Landesexamen* in Stuttgart, compared notes on the examiners' grading for the essays and translation exercises, and, to judge by the Consistory's prohibitions, occasionally could not refrain from prompting the candidates in the oral performances.[16]

Elsewhere in Protestant Germany, initial preparation for academic studies at home, often from an early age, was quite common in clerical families. Even families that were not particularly affluent could entrust instruction in Latin and other subjects to a private tutor, usually a theology candidate waiting for a clerical appointment. In some homes, particularly at the lower end of the clerical income pyramid, the lessons were primarily the father's responsibility. They might also become a family affair; mothers conducted memory recitations in Latin fundamentals as well as in catechism and scripture, and an older brother, already attending a local Latin school or returned home from the university, might also be enlisted. The future theologian Johann Salomo Semler was taught Latin vocabulary two or three times each week by an older brother until he was about six years old. In this case, and

[15] AMP 11 (1795): 90–91.

[16] There is a particularly vivid description of this corporate ritual in Seybold, *Hartmann*, pp. 66–72. Though sharply critical of clerical traditionalism in this novel, Seybold also acknowledged the advantages of a cloistered education; ibid., pp. 116–17. For other assessments of the cloister schools and the Stift, see Ferdinand August Weckherlin, *Wirtemberg. Pietismus. Schreiben. Schulen. Und Erziehung und Aufklärung überhaupt* (Stuttgart, 1787), pp. 294–304; Heinrich Eberhard Gott. Paulus, "Das Theologische Stift zu Tübingen in Beziehung auf die neuesten für dasselbe getroffene Verbesserungsanstalten," *Neues theologisches Journal* 5:1 (1795): 67–99. See also Martin Hasselhorn, *Der altwürttembergische Pfarrstand im 18. Jahrhundert* (Stuttgart, 1958), pp. 39–49.

probably in many others, the brother's drills were reinforced by the approval of the father, who rewarded the boy's efforts with a word of praise at the table, a small gift, or permission to go walking with him.[17]

For sons of the poorer pastors in villages and small towns, this distinctive cultural patrimony compensated for lack of propertied wealth. Preparing a boy at home spared the family school fees, and perhaps boarding expenses as well, in the early years, until he was ready to enter one of the higher school grades. His cultural advantage over outsiders lay in being introduced at home to the formalistic learning that set the standards for success in the schoolroom and in being in effect exempted from the need to prove himself at lower grade levels. Reimmann's father, who occupied a "small and insignificant" village pastorate in the Duchy of Magdeburg, instructed his son at home until he was ready to enter the *Prima*. Unable to manage boarding expenses, he then switched the boy from school to school in the hope that he would find a live-in tutoring position that would keep the costs to a minimum. Despite the obscurity of his career, the younger Reimmann proudly recalled, his father was a learned man who wrote "a lovely Latin style" and took pains to pass on the same skill to his son. "You are named Reimmann," the father had frequently reminded him, "and so for the sake of your name you must be diligent in learning to compose a good rhyme."[18] For the lower clergy, this devotion to the poetic trappings of humanism was a practical strategy as well as a source of aesthetic satisfaction.

This form of privileged access to higher education did not require wealth, but that is not to make it separable from the family's social position. The domestic grooming in Latinity must be seen operating within local networks; the father's colleagues among the local pastors and teachers, in addition to being potential sources of patronage and financial support, reinforced family-induced motivations for academic achievement. Semler took obvious pride in his native intelligence; but he also recalled how his talents had been nurtured within one of these networks as he progressed through the municipal school in Saalfeld. Thanks to the instruction he had received at home, he had to spend only a half-year in the *Quinta*. Cantor Frömer, his teacher in the *Tertia*, also gave him private lessons in "ornate syntaxes" (*Syntaxin Ornatan*) and helped his parents find him proper playmates among

[17] Semler, *Lebensbeschreibung*, pp. 10–23. For other examples of domestic instruction in clerical families, see Friedrich Gottlieb Welcker, *Das Leben Friedrich Gottlieb Welcker's. Nach seinen eignen Aufzeichnungen und Briefen*, ed. Reinhard Kekulé (Leipzig, 1880), pp. 15–24; AMP 1:4 (1789): 105–10 (Johann Christoph Döderlein); AMP 4:4 (1790): 443–47 (Johann Friedrich Jakobi); AMP 4:6 (1790): 651–55 (Franz Volkmar Reinhard); AMP 6 (1793): 619–31 (Christian Wilhelm Schneider); AMP 8:1 (1793): 194–205 (Johann Adolph Schinmeyer). Also helpful was Ute Beyer, "Das Erziehungsmilieu deutscher Pfarrfamilien des 19. Jahrhunderts," Magisterarbeit, Fachbereich Sozialwissenschaften, Universität Göttingen, ca. 1983.

[18] Reimmann, *Lebens-Beschreibung*, pp. 6–9.

the boarding pupils.[19] Semler explains why he advanced so rapidly to the status of *Primus* in Frömer's class, although he was only twelve or thirteen and there were eighteen-year-olds at that level:

> I at least learned Greek and Latin quite properly, with grammatical correctness. My merit was not so much that I excelled above all the others; I was much younger than most of his pupils, much more attractive in appearance, well supervised at home, always lively when he wanted me to be, in order to shame others. Add to that that he was a university acquaintance of my father, who had him visit almost every week, since they had more than enough to discuss about the theological affairs of their era, especially in the field of polemics.[20]

For schoolmen, learning, however minimal, was an especially precious patrimony. At the bottom of the clerical hierarchy of income and prestige, they nonetheless could emulate better-placed colleagues in beginning their sons' induction into the clerical estate. Sons of petty officials tended to share the same advantage; their fathers felt close enough to the academic and official elite to want the next generation to achieve full-fledged membership in it; and most of them, though not university-educated, had advanced far enough in Latin school to give their sons an initial push onto the same path.[21]

PATHS OF ENTRY

Even when charity was available, it is not immediately obvious why uneducated parents were willing to commit their sons to a career route requiring so much time and effort for such modest returns. Given the paltriness of many pastorates and most teaching appointments, academic mobility was no guarantee of upward mobility in economic terms, or indeed in social terms to the degree that status hinged on wealth. Religious zeal often overrode this sobering reality; in some cases, in fact, the sons had been dedicated to the church from birth. If they could not be expected to acquire substantial property, there was a less tangible but no less alluring advantage: academic education, in and of itself, was a highly valued status credential, distinguishing even the lowliest clergyman, as an "educated" man, from the man who made his living with his hands.

Here above all autobiographical witness allows us to penetrate censorious stereotypes that made the "addiction to study" symptomatic of rampant

19 Semler, *Lebensbeschreibung*, pp. 26–38.

20 Ibid., p. 27.

21 See, e.g., AMP 6 (1792): 241–47 (Samuel Friedrich Nathanael Morus); AMP 11 (1795): 83–84 (Johann Samuel Fest); AMP 12:2 (1795):90–96 (Carl August Gottlieb Keil); the "Entwurf einer Selbstbiographie," in *Friedrich August Wolf; Ein Leben in Briefen*, ed. Siegfried Reiter, 3 vols. (Stuttgart, 1935), 2: 337–38.

Luxus. The perception was not only that parents and their sons were blind to the advantages of respectable livings in the trades and farming; they were also deluded about the ease with which a poor boy could enter the clergy and about the affluence and leisure he could expect in office. But if delusions were at play, they were probably more about public authority and power than about affluence. In Heinrich Jung-Stilling's *Jugend* and Karl Philipp Moritz's *Anton Reiser*, two of the most novel-like autobiographies, the pulpit becomes the focal point for a boy's enthrallment with the prospect of becoming a clergyman. Both Heinrich, the village tailor's son, and Anton, the son of a regimental musician, enact their ambition by building makeshift pulpits at home and playing at being a preacher. During Anton's apprenticeship to a hatmaker, when he seems barred permanently from academic studies, Pastor Paulmann, a preacher at the local church, assumes God-like stature in his eyes. The rhetorical mix of reason and emotion in Paulmann's sermons seems to "carry away" his audience "irresistibly." What mesmerizes the boy is not the religious message itself, but the ability of a "public orator" with "ceremonial seriousness in his expression" to chastise the leading citizens for their "opulence" and their indifference to "injustice and oppression," and even to call to account individual families "by name."[22]

In Moritz's obviously stylized rendition of a childhood aspiration, the sermon becomes an opportunity to exercise power over privileged society, and indeed to take a certain verbal revenge on it; within its conventions as a public ritual, even a child of the powerless and underprivileged can hope to rebuke property (*Besitz*) with impunity, if he has acquired the requisite education (*Bildung*). This image surely exaggerates the critical consciousness of outsiders; but it also conveys their underlying fascination with the pulpit and preaching. Placed within the larger social and institutional hierarchy, pastorates were merely the lowest links on long chains of command. But the office looked quite different to a young boy who had no firsthand knowledge of the public "self-presentation" of the court and its aristocracy and lacked both the means to finance a legal education and the social contacts needed to parlay that investment into a prominent career in the judicial or administrative bureaucracy. His direct experience of collective public life was limited largely, if not entirely, to his local church. Within its walls, the preacher assumed nearly superhuman status because his office represented the only dramatic exercise of public authority to which he could legitimately aspire. The drama of the sermon, the central public ritual of the community, lay in its exhibition of an extraordinary command of educated language; hence it seemed all the more within reach of the outsider who excelled in language exercises in school.

[22] Johann Heinrich Jung-Stilling, *Heinrich Stillings Jugend, Jünglingsjahre, Wanderschaft und Häusliches Leben* (Stuttgart, 1968), pp. 94–95; Karl Philipp Moritz, *Anton Reiser. Ein psychologischer Roman* (1785–90: Frankfurt am Main, 1979), pp. 66–76.

The father in Wilhelm Harnisch's *Mein Lebensmorgen* might seem to conform to stereotype. An orphan raised by stepparents in poor circumstances, Harnisch senior had left his native agro-town in Brandenburg to learn the tailoring trade. He returned to marry an older widow from a prestigious, landowning *Bürger* family and to establish a prosperous trade as a "tailor of fashion," popular among the local nobility. Harnish remembers him as an ambitious, hard-driving man, sensitive about his wife's higher social rank and determined to pull himself up to it. By age eight Wilhelm was the only surviving child – of the eleven children by both marriages (!) – and hence it is not surprising that the father chose for him the clerical career to which he himself had aspired as a youth.[23]

The father's ambition for his son, Harnisch recalls, blended piety with mundane considerations. If he sought to win over the boy by contrasting the leisurely life-style of local clergymen with the long hours and six-day work weeks of artisans, he was also prompted by a less sanguine prospect:

> He had often heard of the precariousness [*Misslickkeit*] of the peasant estate; since damp years had caused setbacks to the family on the ancestral farm several times. He had experienced the misery of the lower estate of artisans as a child with his stepfather. He also realized that as he got older, and as younger masters who brought new fashions from Berlin appeared, his customers decreased. He went from four journeymen to three, to two, and to one; and in the end farming supported the household more than the trade. Add to that that I was the only son and that, in addition to the fact that the property was free of debts and in good shape, my father possessed some capital he had saved.[24]

As a prosperous tailor, Harnish may have harbored illusions about the greater affluence and leisure of the clergy. But as an increasingly hard-pressed artisan, pessimistic about the future of his trade, he sought to secure his son against the threat of social derogation. What mattered was the public *security* of the clerical office, the fact that its "service" income was neither a wage nor earnings from the sale of goods and hence, unlike the income from a trade or farming, was not directly vulnerable to the vicissitudes of market forces. It may be no accident that Harnisch senior watched his shop decline at the very end of the century, when the pace of the economic changes that threatened traditional small-scale artisanal production was quickening. But the same perception of decline is likely to have played a role in the choice of a clerical career by artisans' sons in earlier generations, since trades faced threats from overcrowding and mass production in domestic industry throughout the century. The father of Christian Gottlob Heyne was a linen weaver who migrated from Silesia to Saxony to escape religious persecution and was reduced to piecework at the mercy of mer-

[23] Wilhelm Harnisch, *Mein Lebensmorgen* (Berlin, 1865), pp. 16–19, 26–27.

[24] Ibid., pp. 32–33. The father also assumed, incorrectly, that a family stipend would be available.

chant capitalists. Though Heyne does not make the connection explicit, the family's descent to poverty and wage-earning dependence probably helps explain his resolve to study, despite his father's wish that he apprentice with him.[25]

In uneducated families, as in the lower ranks of the clergy, the early death of the father threatened to ruin a boy's prospects. Compared with occupations that had formerly seemed within reach but required an initial outlay of capital, the academic route to a clerical office might seem a fairly cheap alternative. For Claus Harms, a relatively well off orphan, the perils of market forces made the alternative all the more appealing. Having allowed his son to study Latin with a local pastor, the father had decided that he lacked the means to finance his education himself and did not want him dependent on affluent relatives, and that in any case the prospects for university graduates were too insecure. Claus had been quite content with this decision, since it seemed a "long way" from school to a clerical appointment and he preferred "commercial life" to "the often constricted life of a pastor." But after the father's sudden death in March 1796, the family sold the mill rather than face the competition from a new one being built nearby. Claus discovered that his legacy did not suffice to buy himself another mill. After experiencing hard physical labor as a hired hand on a farm he decided, at the relatively late age of nineteen, to invest his money in an academic education.[26]

The attraction of public security was not illusory. Nor was the push exerted by economic decline or by a sudden death; either turn of events could prevent a son from relying on his father's occupation as a path to social honor and could make the clerical office seem all the more attractive as an honorable, and accessible, alternative. If autobiographies are corrective in this sense, however, they leave no doubt that the social metamorphosis caricatured and ridiculed in stereotypes was thorough and often wrenching. Former outsiders were no less conscious of their superior status as educated men than were sons of clergymen; the difference was that their consciousness was rooted in an awareness of having departed radically from the norm, not in pride of caste. Even when parents made the choice, academic studies represented a rare and momentous fate, not a matter-of-fact entry onto an expected life course. More often the choice had required a dramatic turn of events, with a local pastor or teacher, or perhaps a relative, intervening to win over reluctant parents.

25 Heeren, *Heyne*, pp. 5–10. Schreyer recalled that during his childhood his father, a mason in Dresden, had sunk into poverty under the impact of the Seven Years' War; Otto Richter, "Erlebnisse eines Annenschülers 1758–72. Aus der Selbstbiographie des Pastors Christian Heinrich Schreyer," *Dresdener Geschichtsblätter* 16:3 (1907): 156, 172–73. See also Hans Georg Herrlitz, *Studium als Standesprivileg: Die Entstehung des Maturitätsproblems im 18. Jahrhundert* (Frankfurt am Main, 1973), p. 38.

26 Claus Harms, *Lebensbeschreibung* (Kiel, 1851), pp. 31–32, 40–43.

The boy's sense of his exceptional status had been reinforced by the social crossover it required. As he advanced into the higher school grades, he became detached from the peer groups of "street kids" to which boys of his background typically belonged. Heyne recalled that, when he first tasted success in the Chemnitz lyceum and began to apply himself, he was "distanced from contact with [his] comrades [*Kommilitonen*], among whom the most extreme ill-breeding and immorality of all sorts prevailed – as could only be expected of youth of lower origins and bad upbringing."[27] There is no more graphic measure of the process of detachment, and of the social gulf it interposed between the lower orders and the educated men who had left their ranks, than this image of former playmates. In other recollections the divergence is more gradual, even halting; but the perception of unbridgeable worlds is no less clear. As the son of a shopkeeper and a Reformed pastor's daughter in Altona, Schumacher might be regarded as a borderline case. Frau Schumacher, in severe financial straits after her husband's sudden death, found some compensation for her impoverishment in her father's local eminence. She was determined to keep her children off the streets, despite the lack of space in the cheaper lodging they had had to find. But this proved impossible in summer; her son was allowed to play rough games with "comrades of the crudest sort," although not without paying the price of hearing his mother's recriminations. At age twelve he entered the gymnasium, and although he was very slow to find new friends among his classmates his ties with street "comrades" were effectively cut. When it came time to be confirmed, he had to attend the catechism lessons given by the local pastor, and as a sixteen-year-old *Selectaner*, already practically considered a "young student," he found it humiliating to sit on the same bench with "boys" from the local *Bürgerschule*. Confirmation day "emancipated" him and "allowed [him] to throw [himself] entirely into the circumstances of the gymnasium pupils."[28]

As boys like Heyne and Schumacher grew older, the demands of school limited their ability to perform chores at home and in the shop. The very decision to pursue academic studies meant that in their early teens, when other boys of their background were entering their parents' work world in earnest, they were being detached from it. Claus Harms reached this crossroads at age fourteen, after being introduced to Latin by the local pastor. Since his father had decided against preparing him for a clerical career, he spent more and more time "at the mill and in the house, and in the fields in summer," and "books and reading no longer had a place, except for an occasional glance backward." His decision at age nineteen to attend a secondary school required a radical and difficult change of course.[29]

[27] Heeren, *Heyne*, pp. 16–17.

[28] Schumacher, *Genrebilder*, esp. pp. 9–15, 105–06.

[29] Harms, *Lebensbeschreibung*, pp. 31–43. Such changes of course can usefully be compared

Again the autobiographies convey a sense of sharp dichotomy even when the transition was halting. In *Anton Reiser* Anton's apprenticeship to a hatmaker, which intervenes between his initial stint in a Latin school and his years in a gymnasium, only serves to magnify the allure of a clerical career. At first he takes pleasure in entering a "definite station," with its distinctive corporate customs and its regularity of work rhythms. But the daily routine of the shop soon becomes a monotonous *Kreislauf*, and from within it the clergyman's *Laufbahn* seems all the more appealing. The very use of *Kreislauf* and *Laufbahn* – their contrasting images of a circular course and a straight-line advance – is meant to underscore the difference between the common lot of occupations and the only "career" with at least some hope of advancement open to poor boys.[30]

The outsider could help pay for his studies with tutoring, but his detachment from the everyday work world meant that he was in effect exempt from the contribution to the household economy expected of most boys of his age and background. This underlying family sacrifice reinforced his exceptional status and at least in some cases complicated his relationship with his parents. Schumacher's painful recollection of guilt feelings on this score was entangled with his lingering bitterness toward his widowed mother. Since the mother was unable to make ends meet with her small clothing shop, the two sisters – a younger sister, it should be noted, as well as an older one – had to earn wages as domestic seamstresses for a local stocking "factory." He was only eleven, but was "pained" by the incessant complaints that he "enjoy[ed] lodging and board in the domestic circle, but earned nothing." During his first years at the gymnasium, before he began to give private lessons, his mother took pleasure in his quick promotions; but that did not prevent her from "sighing" about each new payment of school fees.[31]

That the recollections of outsiders dwell on the competitive dimension of school life is not surprising; competition played a critical role in determining their fate. The clergyman's son in need of financial support might seem justified in pursuing academic studies by sheer force of family tradition,

with the one experienced by Johann Wilhelm Friedrich Hezel, a pastor's son, when – at the urging of his parents – his boyhood interest in "mechanical tasks" acceded to a concentration on studies; AMP 6 (1792): 418–19.

30 Moritz, *Anton Reiser*, pp. 52–65.

31 Schumacher, *Genrebilder*, pp. 36–38, 71–76. See also Schreyer's recollection of the conflict between his school work and his obligation to contribute to the family earnings by helping his stepmother with straw-plaiting (*Stroharbeiten*), in Richter, "Erlebnisse eines Annenschülers," p. 164. Winckelmann, the son of a "poor cobbler" in Brandenburg, also had had to resist his father's wish that he follow in his footsteps; Carl Justi, *Winckelmann in Deutschland. Mit Skizzen zur Kunst- und Gelehrtengeschichte des achtzehnten Jahrhunderts* (Leipzig, 1866), pp. 20–21. In Justi's account, it should be noted, Winckelmann's youth was in many respects typical of the poor student's path into the *Gelehrtenstand*.

even if his performance in the schoolroom was lackluster. The needy boy from an uneducated family had to stand out, to justify himself as a rare exception to the rule. And yet precisely because they had not entered the school from within a corporate culture, outsiders were especially conscious of and sensitive to its corporate ethos. If the exclusiveness of schoolboys confronted them with an imposing barrier, the very segregation of the group promised to compensate for their dubious origins. The school life that detached them from their peers in the mainstream represented another order of solidarity, superior to that of the streets.

Appropriately Moritz, the son of a regimental musician and probably our most extreme example of an outsider, evoked the appeal of this duality in especially rich detail. The young Anton lacks encouragement at home for his intellectual ambitions; but nonetheless, inspired by the apparently God-like stature of local clergymen, he identifies with schoolboys from "cultured families" rather than with the "street kids" from his own background. When he finally enters the gymnasium he craves acceptance by his classmates, but membership in one of the school's corporate subgroups is so desirable because it brings the right to compete and excel. This fusion of solidarity and competition is underscored when Anton's classmates reject him and drive him "entirely out of the ranks"; he feels excluded from "the long rows of benches in which pupils of wisdom sat, among whose numbers he thought of himself with delight, and with whom he once hoped to compete for the prize."[32]

But what accounts for the academic achievement of outsiders? Was their passage from popular to learned culture traumatic, or were there links that eased the transition? On these questions recent literature in the sociology of education and sociolinguistics can provide some guidance, so long as it is applied with close attention to the differences in structure, content, and context between modern higher education and the eighteenth-century German variety. Much of the literature is devoted to explaining why, despite the aura of objectivity in tracking pupils, there is a "differential elimination according to social class" in contemporary higher education. "Middle-class" and "working-class" pupils are grossly unequal competitors, since they bring different kinds and degrees of "cultural capital," and particularly of "linguistic capital," from home to school. The overwhelming class bias is not belied by the fact that the few working class children who do advance in higher education also tend to excel in it. These are the "over-selected" exceptions who prove the rule, and indeed at the cost of undergoing a painful, disorienting process of uprooting. Their later success was virtually

[32] Moritz, *Anton Reiser*, pp. 99–103, 114–15, 132–43, 173. See also, e.g., Schumacher, *Genrebilder*, pp. 48–71; Richter, "Erlebnisse eines Annenschülers," pp. 163–68.

ensured by the fact that they had to demonstrate the requisite academic aptitude to an exceptional degree at earlier stages.[33]

The notion of "over-selectedness" can be usefully applied to the outsiders among poor schoolboys. It points to the strategic role of cultural inheritance in sanctioning and perpetuating the social exclusiveness of academic education, but at the same time suggests that the cultural patrimony of some uneducated families was analogous to that of the educated *Bürgertum*. But there are critical differences in context. If contemporary social structures are resistant to a simple dichotomy between middle class and working class, the complex interplay of corporate status and class in eighteenth-century society makes such a dichotomy all the more inappropriate. The most damning grievance against contemporary schools is that their success in fostering an illusion of "objective" selection in a "fair" competition camouflages the brutal reality of class. As a result disadvantaged pupils, in effect barred from advancing, tend to blame themselves for personal failure. In the introductory grades of the eighteenth-century Latin school, one might argue, boys from uneducated families were spared this form of cultural hegemony, though they were conditioned in other ways to accept exclusion; the schools made no pretense of countering the role of ascription in their lives.

For the exceptions, the outsiders among poor pupils, academic mobility required the shedding of one social persona and the assumption of another. Autobiographies often bear witness to the persistent anxieties of this molting process; their perspective combines a posture of distanced superiority to popular life, and of alienation from its ignorance and drudgery, with nostalgia for the reassuring simplicity of a childhood world. But there were also continuities, facilitating the academic achievement of the over-selected and perhaps easing its traumas. For all the differences between the popular and the learned varieties of Protestantism, outsiders from pious homes can be said to have advanced within a cultural continuum from their early religious training at home to catechism and Bible lessons in the early school grades, and from there to mastery of fine points in theology and exegetical skills. Likewise the Protestant work ethic transcended social boundaries; outsiders prided themselves on the same devotion to hard work and the same self-discipline that had characterized their parents, albeit in a different

[33]See esp. Pierre Bourdieu and Jean Claude Passeron, *Les héritiers: Les étudiants et la culture* (Paris, 1964); idem, *La réproduction: Eléments pour une théorie du système d'enseignement* (Paris, 1970); Basil Bernstein, "A Socio-linguistic Approach to Social Learning," in idem, *Theoretical Studies towards a Sociology of Language* (Class, Codes, and Control, vol. 1) (London, 1977): 118–39; Michael Flude, "Sociological Accounts of Differential Educational Attainment," in Michael Flude and John Ahier, eds., *Educability, Schools and Ideology* (New York and Toronto, 1974), pp. 15–52; Henry A. Giroux, "Literacy, Ideology, and the Politics of Schooling," *Humanities in Society* 4:4 (Fall 1981): 335–61.

sphere. The family's history might reinforce this parental legacy of piety and "character" in various ways. In her piety and her ambition to recover a lost prestige, the clergyman's or official's daughter who had had to marry an uneducated man might long for the day when her son would "mount the pulpit."[34] The example of an uncle or grandfather, or even of a more distant relative, could inspire parents to commit their son to the clergy and at least could lend the son's aspirations a certain legitimacy. "It is obvious," Claus Harms recalled, that a great uncle on his mother's side who had reached the lofty rank of consistorial councilor "shown very bright in my family."[35]

These are hardly more than scattered hints – enough to suggest that certain aspects of childhood environment compensated for others in allowing the development of innate potential, but not enough to allow any precision about the relative importance of nurture and nature. But another inheritance had a quite specific importance in developing the linguistic competence, and particularly the initial memory skills, that the initiation to Latinity in school required. The fact that the material of Latinity – the vocabulary and grammatical rules of a "dead" language – was esoteric can easily obscure a continuity between this kind of learning and the restricted but intensive literacy to be found in some uneducated homes. The few odd books that parents acquired or inherited in such homes cannot be compared to the often extensive libraries collected by clergymen like Reimmann and Semler, often at considerable financial sacrifice. But the extent of domestic reading material is not the point; what mattered is that parents did take the trouble to teach the boy to read and that from an early age he became skilled at oral, verbatim recitation of the printed word from the few books available to him.

The domestic reading fare might include some secular material as well as current religious works. But this was essentially the kind of literacy uneducated but pious Protestant families applied to the Word and the devotions surrounding it, without necessarily accompanying reading with the regular use of writing or with instruction of the children in that skill. Its core materials were Scripture itself, the catechism, prayer books, hymn books, and sermons and devotional tracts passed down from generation to generation. Under the pervasive impact of Pietism this orientation to the printed word spread rapidly in the eighteenth century; but it remained compatible with the oral transmission of popular culture and may have reinforced it. Harnisch recalled how his father, who was "a fine storyteller

[34] Schumann, *Genrebilder*, is a particularly interesting example of the status consciousness of the clergyman's daughter.

[35] Harms, *Lebensbeschreibung*, p. 4. For another striking example of the importance of relatives, see AMP 11:6 (1795): 114–22 (Georg Friedrich Götz).

and often told long stories in the evenings," alternated the oral tradition with a domestic regimen of reading for his son's benefit:

In addition to church attendance the reading of Spangenberg's *Postille*, in which in question form the Sunday Gospels and Epistles are explained, belonged to the obligatory Sunday activities. Father knew them almost by heart; when I read he corrected me from his head. . . . On Sundays after dinner I would usually have to take his place in reading the explanation of the current Gospel and Epistle from Spangenberg's *Hauspostille*, which was a great burden to me. At times I carelessly passed over a phrase, to finish sooner. But I could not be secure about this daring move, since my father easily noticed it. There was also a small house library, beyond the Bible, *Hauspostille*, a morning and evening prayer book, and hymn book. My father enlarged it occasionally with a new book, bought from peddlars. . . . In the winter evenings I read from it, or my father told a story – in which case relatives from the neighborhood who did not work in the evenings came by.[36]

Harnisch did not look back fondly on his school days; though he excelled in mathematics, he was handicapped by a "weak memory" in the all-important Latin exercises. In comparing himself with rivals among the best pupils, he ignored the fact that his domestic reading duties had prepared him for the intensive, repetitive mastery and oral recitation of the printed word that the introduction to Latinity required. This connection between home and school is evident even when the father did not methodically groom his son for the clergy. For Heyne the two linguistic spheres were bound by a practical arrangement; an uncle paid for his private lessons in Latin on condition that he visit every Sunday to recite the Gospel he had "learned by heart."[37] Considered a "phoenix in learning" by the schoolmaster in his native village, Seume had not learned any Latin by the time he became a boarding pupil and discovered to his embarrassment that he was "quite raw in learning." But mastery of a collection of Latin proverbs (edited by his new teacher) formed a natural transition between the "ability

[36] Harnisch, *Lebensmorgen*, pp. 19–21, 41. In the Harms household, newspapers were not read, but a selection of the writings of Zollikofer, a contemporary rationalist preacher, had been added to the devotional literature. Harms, *Lebensbeschreibung*, pp. 34–35. Seume simply could not explain how his father, an innkeeper and farmer, had come to know "most of the passages of our most recent poets at that time," although "he read little and had little time for reading." Johann Gottfried Seume, *Mein Leben* (Stuttgart, 1961), p. 29. To the extent that the spread of literacy resulted from actual Bible reading in uneducated families, it may have been due more to the Pietist revival from the late seventeenth century onward than to the original Lutheran Reformation. Richard Gawthrop and Gerald Strauss, "Protestantism and Literacy in Early Modern Europe," *Past and Present* 104 (Aug. 1984): 31–55. The symbiosis of literacy and oral tradition is noted in ibid., p. 54. On popular reading habits, see also Rolf Engelsing, *Der Bürger als Leser. Lesergeschichte in Deutschland 1500–1800* (Stuttgart, 1974), esp. pp. 53–78; Rudolf Schenda, *Volk ohne Buch. Studien der populären Lesestoffe 1770–1910* (Frankfurt am Main, 1970). On the reading habits and intellectual horizons of artisans, see Helmut Möller, *Die kleinbürgerliche Familie im 18. Jahrhundert: Verhalten und Gruppenkultur*, Schriften zur Volksforschung, vol. 3 (Berlin, 1969), esp. pp. 248–78.

[37] Heeren, *Heyne*, p. 9.

to memorize biblical passages," which had earlier demonstrated his precocity, and his later outstanding performance in Latin exercises.[38]

Memorization only built the foundation for mastery of the "logical necessity" (Seume's phrase) of grammar, as it was applied in increasingly elaborate translation exercises (*Excerzitien*) from German to Latin and the intricate prosody of versification. Latin was the primary medium for what Basil Bernstein calls an "elaborated code" of academic learning, in contrast to the "restricted" codes of uneducated homes. In Bernstein's view of the critical relationship between family background and linguistic competence in school, each of these code types reflects and reinforces a class identity, which in turn is rooted in the structure of the child's social relationships within and through his family. The middle-class child is at an advantage because, thanks to a "person-oriented role system" at home, he is already oriented toward expressing himself verbally and winning approval for his individual intellectual performance. The "status-oriented role system" in working-class families and boys' peer groups inculcates a verbal mode that makes it very difficult to meet the school's requirements. It is above all in "linguistic code switching" that the academic achiever from a working-class family pays the price of a "change of social identity."[39]

The eighteenth-century educated *Bürger* was likely to have been far more authoritarian than Bernstein's middle-class parent; but for boys like Semler, relationships with parents and other adults in their social circles reinforced methodical domestic instruction and obviously were critical in motivating and equipping them to win the approval of teachers by demonstrating a distinctly academic linguistic competence. Likewise differences in the social and linguistic milieu of uneducated families clearly were reinforced by the child's early involvement in the peer groups of street life.[40] But for the exceptions – the few outsiders who succeeded in linguistic code switching – Latin made for a complication not envisioned in Bernstein's schema. Its central position as the medium for competition might have been expected to make their initiation into academic culture more difficult, and indeed more traumatic; but the autobiographical evidence suggests the opposite effect. In *Anton Reiser* Moritz recalls his difficulties in conversing with the clergymen who have taken notice of his intellectual prowess and are planning to sponsor his education:

> Since he had not learned the language of a polished manner and nonetheless did not wish to express himself in common terms, he used on such occasions book language, put together from *Telemachus*, the Bible and the catechism, which often gave his answers a distinctive mark of eccentricity [*Originalität*] in that, for example, on such occasions he took pains to say that he had been unable to overcome the

38 Seume, *Mein Leben*, pp. 16, 26–27.
39 Bernstein, "A Socio-linguistic Approach to Social Learning."
40 Schlumbohm, "'Traditional' Collectivity and 'Modern' Individuality," esp. pp. 83–98.

urge to pursue academic studies, which continually transported him, and now wished to make himself in every way worthy of the benefactions that were poured forth onto him, and to try to lead his life to its end in complete piety and honor.[41]

Moritz describes the linguistic self-alienation of the outsider. Eager to win approval by camouflaging his cultural deprivation, but unable to replace his "common" idiom with the idiom of polite society, he finds himself caught between codes. But the dilemma is in his native tongue; he had experienced his first academic triumph in the standard Latin memorization exercises, and here is his description of his later progress in the "old *Schlendrian*" as a *Sekundarer*:

Whoever had paid closest attention to the explanation [of grammatical rules] could do best in his so-called *Exerzitium* and thereby advance to a higher place.

As unusual as German expressions read together for the sake of Latin sounded, the exercise was basically useful and stimulated quite a competition. – Within a year Reiser came so far in it that he wrote Latin without a single grammatical error and thus expressed himself more correctly in that language than in German. Since in Latin he knew where to place the accusative and the dative. But in German he had never considered that "me" [*mich*] was the accusative and "to me" [*mir*] the dative, and that his mother tongue, just like Latin, had to be declined and conjugated. – Nonetheless he grasped, without noticing, some general concepts that he later could apply to his mother tongue.[42]

To Anton, the outsider, Latinity was central to the competitive as well as the corporate dimensions of school life. In Moritz's imaginative evocation, what is only hinted at in other recollections, usually inadvertently, becomes explicit. If High German had been the primary medium for school competition, the outsider, aside from having to shed his dialect, would have had to demonstrate mastery of the class-specific nuances of linguistic usage that already came naturally to boys from educated homes. Though Latinity was a corporate patrimony, there was also a sense in which its devotion to form over content ensured its detachment from everyday life at any social level. This very detachment made Latin instruction a relatively neutral pedagogical universe, minimizing social advantages. Eventually, of course, the outsider also had to master academic German. But as Moritz suggests, the initiation via Latin tended to have a spillover effect, even when, as was often the case, German instruction was neglected at school. If Latin reduced the outsider's competitive disadvantage, it may also have intervened to facilitate his transition from popular to academic culture in the native tongue.

Hence the corporate credential was double-edged. At the same time that Latinity marked the castelike segregation of the clerical order from the uneducated masses, it made the order permeable to the few outsiders who

[41] Moritz, *Anton Reiser*, pp. 115–16.

[42] Ibid., pp. 133–34.

could excel in its acquisition. In documenting the survival of this fusion of formalistic learning, corporate status, and mobility, most of the autobiographies also mark the process of breakdown and reconstitution that was well under way by the end of the century. That Heyne pilloried the pastor who had introduced him to Latin for fancying himself a "Latin versifier and therefore a learned clergyman," despite his almost total ignorance of the genuine classics, was to be expected.[43] Heyne's philological seminar at Göttingen was committed to replacing the old-style "pedant" with a new breed of schoolteachers. Moritz occupied neither world; having soured on his boyhood dream of becoming a clergyman, he could not make the commitment to a new professional identity that sustained many of his teaching colleagues. His distance on the clergy, unlike that of the reformers, allowed for an appreciation of the traditional Latinity in its natural habitat – as the exclusive property of a corporate group and the path of entry for the few outsiders initiated into its ranks.

[43] Heeren, *Heyne*, pp. 12–13.

3

The patronage chain: structure and ideology

The climb up the academic ranks to a clerical appointment was also an advance along a patronage chain, formed by the men who singled out bright boys without means, distributed the public and private charity that made possible their studies, and filled vacancies in clerical and teaching offices. These sponsors represented a many-tiered hierarchy of wealth, status, and institutional authority, both within the educated *Bürgertum* and in the social networks binding it to other groups. For poor boys, the corporate initiation into the clergy was also an experience of class inequality on more or less polarized terms. The social hinge in the initiation, patronage was also an instrument of class power.

The actual workings of patronage in eighteenth-century society have received little attention, despite its obvious importance in both securing the advantages of birth and creating channels for merit.[1] Instead class inequality has been conceived as a static hierarchy of wealth and power, and quantitative research has demonstrated how academic education reflected and perpetuated a social "structure" in this sense, above all by overrepresenting an academic and official elite and virtually excluding groups at the bottom. In the workings of patronage – in the skeins of personal ties and mutual loyalties between sponsors and poor boys – class can be comprehended as a process, a series of one-to-one relationships with a formative impact on consciousness. Clearly structural realities underlay those relationships and lent them coercive force; but it was cultural norms, at once sanctioning

[1] An important exception is Harold Perkin, *The Origins of Modern English Society 1780–1880* (Toronto and Buffalo, 1972), esp. pp. 38–56. Much of what Perkin has to say about the role of "vertical links" of patronage in structuring eighteenth-century English society and in keeping class solidarities and conflicts "latent" is also relevant to Germany. On the continuing importance of patronage in the upper ranks of Prussian officialdom, see Hans Rosenberg, *Bureaucracy, Aristocracy and Autocracy: The Prussian Experience 1660–1815* (Cambridge, Mass., 1958), esp. pp. 75–87.

inequality and setting limits to its terms, that made patronage seem a legitimate exercise of authority rather than an abuse of power.

In March 1782, nearly a year after he had begun his studies at Leipzig, Friedrich Richter recorded his particularly sharp reaction against the terms of clientage. Rather than join in the scramble for the usual kinds of financial support available to poor students, Richter explained to a friend, he had resolved to support himself and maintain his independence by writing satirical novels:

God deprived me of four feet with which to be obsequious enough to attract the benevolent gaze of a patron and some crumbs [*etliche Brosamen*] from his excess. I can be neither a false flatterer nor a fashionable fool, and cannot win friends with the movement of my lungs or my back. Add to that that most professors have neither time, nor opportunity, nor the will, nor the capacity to help; that the crowd of those who flatter and deceive makes access to them impossible for those who do not wish to do either; that it would betray pride if one wanted to snap at the opportunity to show them a good side – put all this together and you know my situation.[2]

There is something reassuringly modern about the uncompromising insistence on personal autonomy and self-reliance in Richter's individualism. If he was voicing a common aspiration in his generation, however, his defiant conclusion – that the conditions of clientage were incompatible with personal honor – was rare. Even the more critical clients – those who nursed bitter grievances about the particular abuses to which patronage had subjected them – did not question the need to accept dependence and render deference to a degree not easily reconciled with the criteria for personal autonomy in modern individualism. And yet at the other extreme, the eighteenth-century stereotype of the "servile" poor student is no less misleading; it does not do justice to former clients who, though far from denying the legitimacy of the basic terms that patronage imposed, at least implicitly indicted its more extreme requirements.

Most of our autobiographical texts record this ambivalent field of responses. They do not do so by providing an "objective" factual account or by conveying unmediated experience across the temporal distance between past and present. Autobiography has aptly been defined as "a cultural act of reading the self, rather than a private act of writing the self." Its social meaning lies in the subjectivity, and sometimes even in the "fictions," of the reading.[3] Ideology was indispensable to self-reflection in this sense; if

[2] Friedrich Richter to Pastor Vogel, Mar. 8, 1782, in *Die Briefe Jean Pauls*, ed. Eduard Berend, 2 vols. (Munich, 1922), 1: 39–40. Richter's other complaint seems more cryptic: "You must use money to make a patron understand that you need money; i.e., you must not be poor if you want to become rich. This I am lacking; and no distributor of outside charity regards me as needy enough to grant me outside funds, because I cannot send him my own money."

[3] The phrase is taken from Janet Varner Gunn, *Autobiography. Toward a Poetics of Experience* (Philadelphia, 1982), p. 31. See also the insightful remarks on the relationship between form

it made for distortions of the life history, it also mediated between past and present, individual consciousness and social reality. Only by filtering past experience through shared assumptions and norms did the reading of the self – and the projection of a present identity it entailed – acquire both personal and public meaning. In reading the experience of clientage, there was some room for individual protest, and even for a notion of injustice, within an ideological consensus; our autobiographies are not lacking in bitterness about patrons' abuses of power. But if ideology could not blot out such memories, it usually was absorbent enough to preclude a basic questioning of the role of patronage, and of the class realities it represented, in distributing educational and career opportunities.

FATHERLY PATRONS

In the sponsoring of poor students, as in so many other kinds of sponsorship in eighteenth-century society, noblemen often stood at the pinnacle of patronage hierarchies. Aside from controlling clerical appointments, particularly in the countryside, noble families offered many of the tutoring positions that supported theology candidates after their university studies. They also used their private wealth as well as their control over public charity to help ensure the flow of deserving young men into the church, even when it meant lifting them out of the very lowest social strata. It was a scholarship from "the prince" – i.e., from Carl von Mecklenburg, brother of the Hanoverian queen – that made it possible for Moritz to attend the Hanover gymnasium. In a classic example of noblesse oblige, Johann Gottlieb Fichte, the son of a village ribbon weaver in Saxony, was discovered at age nine by Baron Ernst Haubold von Miltitz, who on a local visit was impressed by the boy's ability to recite the pastor's sermons from memory. Within a few hours Miltitz had persuaded Fichte's parents to let him take charge of his education, and the Miltitz family was still contributing to his support when he began his university studies.[4]

But this kind of direct intervention from on high was rare, and even when it occurred the noble patron was likely to become a distant figure who entrusted responsibility for his client to others. Whether as intermediaries or, more often, as benefactors in their own right, clergymen – local teachers and pastors, superintendents, and other higher church officials – and local bourgeois notables formed the lower links of the patronage chains that led

and content in autobiography, in Jean Starobinski, "The Style of Autobiography," in Seymour Chatman, ed., *Literary Style: A Symposium* (New York, 1971), pp. 285–93. On issues of historical and literary interpretation of autobiography, see esp. James Olney, ed., *Autobiography. Essays Theoretical and Critical* (Princeton, N.J., 1980).

[4] Xavier Léon, *Fichte et son temps*, 3 vols. (Paris, 1924–27), 1: 33–34. See also Johann Gottfried Seume, *Mein Leben* (Stuttgart, 1961), pp. 23, 44–48.

into and through the schools. Bachelors and married clergymen without sons, unable to project their ambitions onto offspring, may have been particularly prone to helping promising local boys. Aside from such personal motives, this use of charity in the service of the church was sustained by its status as a longstanding tradition. In the same tradition university professors, in addition to using their connections to help launch the careers of poor students, secured them free tables and other kinds of support and let them take their courses gratis.

There is no richer source for the psychological and emotional texture of this world than Semler's *Lebensbeschreibung*, published in 1781. If there is any thematic coherence to Semler's lengthy, apparently rambling account of his childhood and youth, it lies in his explanation of how he fell prey to and subsequently escaped the Pietism that had gained dominance in his native town of Saalfeld. At both ends, the story turns on the perils and opportunities of patronage. A *Diakonus* in a small court town, well aware of the financial difficulties he would face in educating several sons for the clergy, Semler senior had planned ahead for the fourth son, Johann Salomo, by securing as his godfathers the local superintendent and the *Bürgermeister*. But both men had died by the time the boy was old enough to begin university studies. Meanwhile, under the leadership of the new superintendent and court chaplain, the "party of the children of God and the reborn" had gained favor at court. While others flocked into this party, Semler recalled with some pride, he recognized the new piety for what it was – a device to promote prospects at court, and a way for his schoolmates to "recommend themselves everywhere" without making the effort required in serious learning.[5]

Semler's father originally had been hostile to the movement, particularly since its antipathy to "human learning" ran directly counter to his own scholarly interests. But in the year before his son was to attend the university, Semler senior shifted course and began urging him to attend the "uplifting hours," preparatory to the requisite "conversion," at school. His father's change of mind, Semler surmises, may have been due to the realization that he "needed the support of stipends, or of the superintendent at court." Semler faced intense pressure, since the court placed great importance on the conversion of a local clergyman's son. At the same time he found himself in a painful conflict with his father. Having already imparted to his son a sense of corporate identity by grooming him at home to be a "learned clergyman," the father now disapproved of his preference for learning over piety. Semler senior was not appeased by his son's argument that the new piety was "a disturbance of [the pupil's] station" or by his charge – in an essay written, appropriately, in Latin – that the pupils

[5] Johann Salomo Semler, *Lebensbeschreibung von ihm selbst abgefasst* (Halle, 1781), pp. 6–7, 28–57.

singled out for praise were ignorant hypocrites. To win back his father's approval, Semler finally began to attend the uplifting hours. Put off at first, he gradually found that he "could really reject [his] judgment as a naturally sinful hostility to God" and "really accepted in all seriousness every step and stage of the new piety."[6]

When Semler later came under the spell of Sigmund Baumgarten, the great rationalist theologian at Halle, the shift of allegiance did not escape notice back home. His father had already had to sell some landholdings to support him and now feared that he was entering "a road on which support would be lacking." He explained this plight in a letter to Baumgarten, and in response the professor offered Semler his sponsorship. "I kissed his hand," Semler recalls, and "not without tears, which were the first offering and clear acknowledgment of my pure feeling." Later Baumgarten made him the tutor for his children, with free room and board in his household, and the young protégé "tried to make [himself] more and more deserving of the approval of such a fatherly man through every possible attention and readiness to serve."[7]

The cynical reader might ask how this young man, assiduous in winning the favor of the man who launched his academic career, differed from pupils back home who were trying to "recommend themselves everywhere" or indeed from the crowd of sycophants who provoked Richter's disdain. Of interest here, though, are the implicit distinctions in an elaborate self-justification. Semler attributed his conformity to his efforts to win back paternal approval and recalled it ending in subtle self-deception, not to be confused with the degrading opportunism that led others to feign piety. Likewise Semler explained his obeisance to Baumgarten, however self-serving it might seem, in terms of a genuine conversion (or, perhaps better, reconversion). The underlying point is that Baumgarten, unlike the Pietist superintendent, *deserved* outward displays of gratitude and deference and that in turn Semler, precisely because his motives were pure, merited his benefaction. While the other student-lodgers responded to Baumgarten's inquiries about the state of the household with an evasive "cleverness," Semler "won the special and great trust of this great man" by daring to speak "the pure truth."[8]

On one level Semler's account demonstrates the pressures for dependent clients to compromise themselves on matters of religious belief and observance. This use of patronage was a handy weapon in the Orthodox and Pietist defense against rationalist theology, which of course built patronage networks of its own as it established itself at the major universities.[9] But

[6] Ibid., pp. 51–62.

[7] Ibid., pp. 99–109.

[8] Ibid., pp. 108–9.

[9] Joachim Heinrich Campe, the future educational reformer, was one victim of the efforts

the worshipful portraits of men like Baumgarten, who assumed heroic stature on the academic battlefronts of the century, must be seen as heightened expressions of a common attitude toward patrons, rooted in prevailing social norms. Likewise a larger field of tension, less dramatic but more deeply woven into the social fabric, underlay the choice between purity of conscience and sycophantic "hypocrisy" – a field in which threats to personal integrity were inherent in the very terms of clientage.

This is not to deny more pragmatic reasons that the typical posture toward patrons in clerical autobiographies – the posture that Semler, for example, assumed toward Baumgarten – is one of reverential gratitude. Aside from the fact that most of the authors had already entered the clergy's elite ranks, and hence had much for which to be thankful, the public decorum expected of men in their positions kept a fairly tight lid on any lingering bitterness. But ideology also continued to endow patrons with a positive glow, even as Protestant justifications of their role in terms of providential intervention were constricted in appeal and diluted in substance by the ascendancy of rationalism. Vertical relationships linking generations, the patron-client bonds that propelled academic mobility were a highly appropriate locus for the ideology of paternalism that permeated eighteenth-century society. The language of paternalism appears again and again – in the occasional descriptions of patrons as "second fathers" and in the standard acknowledgments of their "fatherly" (*väterlich*) love, guidance, and support. If only because this underlying continuity tended to be made explicit in a formulaic language, it is dismissible as merely conventional ornamentation. But in its very conventionality, the language distills deep-rooted norms, critical to understanding why a degree of dependence and deference that might offend modern sensitivities was accepted as perfectly natural.[10]

It was the role of the father that provided the model for patrons, and the original filial posture of reverential gratitude that defined the proper posture of the client. With rare exceptions autobiographies recall fathers

to keep the troops in line; in the 1760s he paid for his open allegiance to the rationalists by losing his *Stipendium* at Helmstedt. Jakob Anton Leyser, *Johann Heinrich Campe. Ein Lebensbild aus dem Zeitalter der Aufklärung*, 2 vols. (2nd ed.: Brunswick, 1896), 1: 11–12. Wolff had claimed that the Pietist theologians at Halle had threatened to take away the *beneficia* of students who attended his lectures. *Christian Wolffs eigene Lebensbeschreibung*, ed. Heinrich Wuttke (Leipzig, 1841), p. 190.

[10]For a similar perspective on the possibilities for achieving a measure of personal autonomy within a patriarchal society, see Natalie Zemon Davis, "Boundaries and the Sense of Self in Sixteenth-Century France," in Thomas C. Heller, Morton Sosna, and David E. Wellbery, eds., *Reconstructing Individualism. Autonomy, Individuality, and the Self in Western Thought* (Stanford, Calif., 1986), pp. 53–63. Paternalist ideology, like the patronage it sanctioned, is in need of research. Indispensable is Otto Brunner, "Das 'Ganze Haus' und die alteuropäische 'Oekonomik'," in idem, ed., *Neue Wege der Verfassungs- und Sozialgeschichte* (2nd, enl. ed.: Göttingen, 1968): 103–27. For suggestive recent analyses, see Robert M. Berdahl, "Preussischer Adel. Paternalismus als Herrschaftssystem," in Hans-Jürgen Puhle and Hans-Ulrich Wehler, eds., *Preussen in Rückblick* (Göttingen, 1980): 123–45; Bengt Algot Sørensen, *Herrschaft und Zärtlichkeit. Der Patriarchalismus und das Drama im 18. Jahrhundert* (Munich, 1984).

who had commanded "respect," at home and in public, because they were "upright." This was a quality that allowed and indeed required strictness (often contrasted with the "tenderness" of the mother), but only so long as it was in the service of "justice" and did not preclude familial affection. Fathers were also almost always "pious," and usually "hard-working" as well. Such portraits are not so much attempts to etch individual personalities as variations on the ideal "head of household" (*Hausvater*) to which a considerable Protestant literature had been devoted. The very vagueness of the attributes made for a flexible ideology, transcending differences in domesticity between educated and uneducated families and even allowing sons to revere "upright" and "pious" fathers across the generational chasm between Pietism and "enlightened" religiosity.[11]

Despite the tendency to subsume concrete memories of family life under an abstract model, autobiographical detail often registers the tensions between ideal and reality. The stern exercise of authority within the family could be problematic; "upright" fathers were sometimes "irritable" or "hot-tempered," and in the anecdotes illustrating these traits strictness becomes "hardness," the exercise of justice shades into petty tyranny and violence.[12] Another source of tension lay in the fact that the domestic patriarch might very well be on the subordinate, dependent end of client-patron relationships outside the home. For all his filial respect, Semler cannot help censuring his father obliquely for succumbing to the epidemic of opportunism in Saalfeld. There is more sympathy than blame in Edelmann's recollection of his father's dogged passivity as a victim of the whims of court patronage; but it is not surprising that Edelmann senior's role as an authority figure is noticeably muted.[13]

If the memory of lapses and contradictions was often painful, however, the ideology survived despite them; it sufficed that the father had been a rough approximation of the model. A schoolmaster's son who had become a prominent theology professor at Leipzig recalled that his parents, realizing that they would not be able to bequeath any property, had always striven "to accustom him to order and subordination, so that he could please God

[11] There are many examples in the sample from the *Allgemeines Magazin für Prediger* (cited hereafter as AMP); see esp. AMP 11:4 (1795): 83–84 (Fest); AMP 10:5 (1794): 106 (Johann Christian Förster); AMP 12:3 (1795): 109–10 (Johann Friedrich Christoph Gräffe); AMP 6 (1792): 241 (Morus); AMP 7:2 (1793): 330–37 (Paulus); AMP 4:6 (1791): 651 (Reinhard); AMP 2 (1790): 85 (Johann Georg Rosenmüller). On the ideal *Hausvater* see Julius Hoffmann, *Die 'Hausvaterliteratur' und die 'Predigten über den christlichen Hausstand.' Lehre vom Hause und Bildung für das häusliche Leben im 16., 17. und 18. Jahrhundert* (Weinheim, 1959).

[12] Particularly striking is the tension-ridden portrait of the father in Seume, *Mein Leben*, esp. pp. 11–13, 18–20. See also Wilhelm Harnisch, *Mein Lebensmorgen* (Berlin, 1865), pp. 18–27.

[13] Johann Christian Edelmann, *Selbstbiographie*, ed. Bernd Neumann, Deutsche Autobiographien. Dokumente zum bürgerlichen oppositionellen Selbstbewusstsein von der Aufklärung bis zur Revolution 1848, vol. 1 (Stuttgart, 1976), esp. pp. 27–30.

and man and have the prospect of advancement even without wealth."[14] But there is no reason to assume that the boy's subjection to his father and the adult's posture toward patrons stood in a simple, one-way relationship of cause and effect. Autobiography records a more or less advanced stage in the process of self-construal, with memories of childhood and more recent experience continually interacting. The reverential view of patrons not only drew on an increasingly distant, idealized image of the father; it also nourished that image.

Paternalism had often been reinforced by continuing integration into the kind of domestic environment that was its proper setting. For many, ascending the patronage chain was not simply a matter of advancing from one sponsor to another; it was also a passage from household to household. The boy who had to leave home to attend a Latin school boarded with an uncle, with a local pastor, or, more often, with a teacher who adopted him as a protégé. Particularly among those who had pursued university careers, it had been quite common to find room and board at the university, sometimes gratis, with a professor. While some professors rented rooms to supplement their incomes, others offered room and board in exchange for services – tutoring, for example, or assistance on scholarly projects – or simply as a gesture of charity. Particularly in the latter cases, the professor was able to select a privileged few and extend his personal influence over them.[15]

For the boarding pupil or student, the patron, as head of household, was literally *in loco parentis*. If the requirements of subordination and deference were particularly stringent in this arrangement, they were attended by a measure of personal concern and familial warmth. These advantages are often recalled in autobiographies, and their absence is noted with regret when the boarder was not welcomed into the household circle.[16] It was above all in the exercise of authority as *Hausvater* that the patron, like the father, could fail to meet his client's expectation of paternal justice. When boarding with his cousin (a local pastor) as a schoolboy, Edelmann recalled in a telling anecdote, he had been bullied by a fellow boarder named Flegel. The cousin's initial response to his complaints – that the younger should accede to the older – seemed an "unwise decision" that only encouraged the bully to commit further abuses. The cousin then subjected both young men to a sermon, but its point was that Edelmann should take the initiative in making peace. Edelmann remembered himself as both a politic client,

[14] AMP 6 (1792): 241 (Samuel Friedrich Nathanael Morus).

[15] See, e.g., AMP 10:5 (1794): 106–11 (Förster); AMP 11:6 (1795): 114–15 (Georg Friedrich Götz); AMP 6 (1792): 619–20 (Schneider); AMP 12:6 (1796): 50a-50e (Johann Friedrich Zöllner); Heinrich Wilhelm Justus Wolff and Georg Karl Bollmann, *Heinrich Philipp Conrad Henke. Denkwürdigkeiten aus seinem Leben und dankbare Erinnerungen an seine Verdienste* (Helmstedt and Leipzig, 1816), pp. 8–40; Wilhelm Frhrn. von Blomberg, *Das Leben Johann Friedrich Reinert's, zuletzt Direktors des Archi-Gymnasiums zu Soest* (Lemgo, 1822), pp. 1–41.

[16] See esp. Seume, *Mein Leben*, pp. 28–36.

knowing how to "dampen [his] fire" when he might otherwise annoy his benefactors, and as a young man "easily aroused and hard to conciliate" when people refused to acknowledge that an injustice had been done him. The latter persona won out when the bullying became unbearable. He gave his persecutor a good thrashing – and years later still took pride in having resorted to violence. "A few hand slaps in the face had more effect on him," he recalled, "than the pastor with all his impotent sermonizing."[17]

In recounting this anecdote Edelmann was preoccupied by his polemic with the Orthodox establishment. "I would not have believed it," he added with a playful touch, "if someone had told me that in future times I would have so many Theological Flegels in front of my fist in a moral sense." But of interest here is a moral quid pro quo, assumed to be implicit in the exercise of paternal authority. The boy is seen to be justified in refusing to accept an assigned place in the generational hierarchy of the household, because its head had acted in blatant disregard for the justice of the case. Edelmann's grievance was not that the cousin's judgments were too harsh, but that they were arbitrary. He left the house rather than assume the supervision of the children, since he would not have been able to live with his cousin's "indulgent discipline" (*weiblichen Kinderzuchts*).[18]

If the sanctity of paternal authority precluded a critical questioning of the basic terms of patronage, it was not so potent as to expunge painful, even bitter memories imprinted along the way. Paternalist ideology, often reinforced by the ongoing experience of household membership, made the client's dependence seem a perfectly natural status; but it also set limits to the obligations of dependence. In a sense patron and client were using each other, though the client's need for a sponsor was obviously more urgent than the patron's need for a protégé to testify to his stature and benevolence. Paternalism infused this essentially instrumental relationship with sentiments of mutual loyalty and even intimacy, analogous to the ties of consanguinity. The "servile" client was guilty of violating this ideal by exploiting the instrumental relationship – by reducing it to manipulative, ultimately dishonorable calculation. But likewise the patron could abuse his power, whether by going too far in actively enforcing the client's dependence or simply by being indifferent to his dilemmas.

It was above all the latter that formed a gray area. Johann Samuel Fest, the son of an impoverished village schoolmaster, recalled how his experience as a charity pupil, surviving largely on "free tables" and the money earned as a choirboy, had nearly aborted his academic career:

When I was transferred to the second class I began after a while to frustrate again

[17] Edelmann, *Selbstbiographie*, pp. 16–18.
[18] Ibid., pp. 18, 20. On Edelmann's theological radicalism, see Walter Grossman, *Johann Christian Edelmann: From Orthodoxy to Enlightenment* (The Hague, 1976).

the expectations that had been placed in me. I was lacking several books needed to profit from the instruction of my worthy teachers Manniske and Hankel; thus at the same time I lost courage and began to lower my prospects merely to a position as a village schoolmaster, like most of the others; my voice, strained to the point of spitting up blood, changed into a vague screeching, and so my income to that point, perhaps not entirely fairly, was reduced by half and more; I wasted a good part of my time with copying, for which I had hired myself to a benefactor out of gratitude and for sheer lack of things to do outside school. I no longer distinguished myself and thus was overlooked. . . . The school, to which I did little honor, also began to lose its appeal for me, indeed because of the crudeness of many of my fellow pupils, especially in the second class. . . . I often slunk around sadly half the day by myself in isolated places, especially since I often did not know how I could clothe myself, and often was tempted to seek the wide world.[19]

Pupils like Fest had to live with a painful contradiction, inherent in the minimal charity with which they were made to suffice. While such charity made their studies possible, it did not enable them to meet some of the additional expenses that the status of pupil entailed. Inability to purchase books was not the only deprivation; as Fest suggests, the poor pupil, unable to dress respectably, faced humiliation in precisely the social circles from which he received support. When Edelmann voiced his resentment of the "avarice" of the "clerisy," exemplified by the tendency among his former patrons to offer advice in lieu of cash, it was the painful memory of this dilemma that surfaced. As a gymnasium pupil in Weissenfels, without any support from his family, Edelmann survived on "free tables" provided by, among others, the superintendent and the court *Diakonus*. Since he had to take his meals with "respectable people" every day, he used "all [his] patience and skill" to keep his "sorry wardrobe" in decent condition. But disaster struck; a classmate poured ink on the back of his only presentable coat, and his frantic effort to remove the stain with lemon juice only compounded the damage. This was no trivial accident; it "made me nearly melancholic," Edelmann recalled, "because I could neither attend classes nor take meals without wearing a shabby coat, and without being able to remove the dagger which I, as a gymnasium pupil, had to wear."[20]

When legitimate enforcement of the client's dependent, deferential status became subjection to stigmatizing "humiliations," the stereotype of the "servile" poor student became a self-fulfilling prophecy. Even Edelmann, though far more critical of former patrons than Fest, attributed his depri-

[19] AMP 11 (1795): 84–85. Roughly the same account, with a bit more detail, is in Johann Samuel Fest, *Biographische Nachrichten und Bemerkungen über sich selbst*, ed. M. Christian Victor Kindervater (Leipzig, 1797), pp. 22–33. Fest nonetheless had seen moral advantages in the poor student's hardships in his *Ueber die Vortheile und Gefahren der Armuth für Jünglinge auf der Academie* (Leipzig, 1784).

[20] Edelmann, *Selbstbiographie*, pp. 28–31. On the dilemma of shabby clothing, see also Otto Richter, "Erlebnisse eines Annenschülers 1758–72. Aus der Selbstbiographie des Pastors Christian Heinrich Schreyer," *Dresdener Geschichtsblätter* 16:3 (1907): 174.

vation to the "avarice" of patrons rather than to any conscious intent to humble him. In Schumacher's recollection of his boyhood, on the other hand, abiding respect for a fatherly patron has not canceled out resentment about intentional enforcements of humiliation. Schumacher thought of himself as a boy whom poverty had made "proud and defiant" rather than "servile." He saw these traits as an inheritance from his mother, the pastor's daughter determined to maintain appearances after her husband's death had plunged the family into poverty. Mother and son, he recalled, faced strikingly analogous threats to their pride from Herr Paap, a local "factory" owner who was appointed the mother's *Curator* and became the son's guardian after her death. Schumacher retained great admiration for this pious, well-read, intellectually imposing gentleman who had done so much to broaden his horizons; but he also felt victimized by Paap's extreme sensitivity, which tolerated "no offence, no impoliteness, and above all no failure to show respect for his person."[21]

The sense of victimization was in part vicarious. When her two daughters began working for Paap, Frau Schumacher had expected him to respect her "sense of honor" by allowing them to deliver the finished stockings privately. Instead he treated them as two more piecerate workers; they had to collect their wages at the appointed hour, with forty or fifty other women and girls. "He wished to break the pride of my mother," Schumacher recalled, "and did not know how deeply he thereby wounded her."[22] After the mother's death it was Paap who arranged a local subscription to finance the boy's academic studies. But when the first year's contributions were due, he also insisted that the boy collect them himself – and the haughty reception in some houses turned that obligation into a most humiliating experience. The same bitterness toward Paap that Schumacher attributed to his mother finds qualified expression in his attempt to come to terms with this trauma:

> And should I now beg?
>
> That is the way I felt, although I came to realize much later that this was not the right word. If one speaks of begging, that had already happened, and others had done it for me. One should speak here of a duty, perhaps voluntary and willingly assumed, that now had to be fulfilled. But I am not entirely persuaded that it was right to hand over this grim process to me. It would have been very easy to arrange the collection in another way; but my guardian seemed to believe that it would be arrogant not to do it myself. I had to go, as I was ordered. And, God knows, it was a painful road for me.[23]

[21] Georg Friedrich Schumacher, *Genrebilder aus dem Leben eines siebenzigjährigen Schulmannes, ernsten und humoristischen Inhalts, oder Beiträge zur Geschichte der Sitten und des Geistes seiner Zeit* (Schleswig, 1841), pp. 57, 103.

[22] Ibid., p. 37.

[23] Ibid., pp. 130–31.

It is implicit in this passage that the patron should not violate a fundamental sense of personal honor. Integrity in this sense was, or at least ought to be, compatible with dependent status as a client. Schumacher was still trying to decide whether by that standard the paternal authority exercised by Paap had been "right" or "just."

If the criterion of justice could be applied to the conditions of charity, it had special relevance to the personal judgments that determined the selection and promotion of charity pupils. In the absence of standardized evaluation procedures, reliance on patrons made a certain practical sense; in principle, if not always in fact, the individual sponsor was a credible judge, in a position to testify that his client was worthy of support. To a degree the intellectual and moral criteria applied in each sponsor's judgment were the expression of a collective social consciousness. Precisely because sponsored mobility was in this sense a "controlled" induction by the educated elite, sons of poor pastors had an advantage over outsiders in meeting the requirements for "character" as well as for academic aptitude. But only in the Württemberg *Landesexamen* did this collective judgment assume a centralized and standardized form. More typically sponsorship – whether for charitable support as a pupil or student or for a clerical appointment – was particularized; control from above was in the form of individuated judgments, with ample room for the play of personal preferences and quirks in advancing some and passing over or excluding others.

It was above all in the meshings of his relationships with individual patrons that the outsider, and to a degree the poor clergyman's son as well, experienced the contingency and vulnerability of his social inferiority. If most autobiographies stop short of questioning the justice of patronage as such, despite their occasional censure of individual patrons for injustice and abuse of power, that is because the particularism of paternalist ideology reinforced its claim to universal validity. At the same time that the paternal ideal elevated class norms to universal moral standards, it condensed the collective power of class into an apparently legitimate exercise of individual authority. But the particularism also made for a certain tension between the expectation of justice in the abstract and an awareness of social contingency in the concrete; in retrospect the workings of patronage became focal points for the role of the apparently arbitrary, or at least of the apparently accidental – whether for better or for worse and whether explained ultimately by reference to "providence" or to a more secular notion of "fate." Individual sponsorship worked both ways; while it made possible sudden discoveries of talent (or at least of a precocious ability to perform), resulting from chance encounters and quick (not to say overly hasty) impressions, it also meant that at any point on the long road to office the failure to win or maintain someone's approval could snap the patronage chain and leave an aspirant without prospects.

This was the problem Johann Gottlieb Fichte faced in 1790, when he left a tutoring position in Zürich in the hope of finding a pastorate in his native Saxony. Fichte traveled from Leipzig to Dresden to secure a very powerful patron in Christoph Gottlob von Burgsdorff, the president of the High Consistory, to whom he had once been recommended by his former patroness Frau von Miltitz. But in the interim, the president reminded him during his audience, Frau von Miltitz had "often raised complaints" about her former protégé. When Burgsdorff learned that her "pardon" still had not been secured, he could only offer the prospect of a teaching appointment in classical studies. Fichte promptly sent off an appropriately contrite plea for the needed pardon, but to no avail.[24] His subsequent letter to Burgsdorff from Leipzig was designed to circumvent this imposing hurdle without resorting to dishonest assurances of his religious orthodoxy, and without doing too much violence to his pride. The result is a tortuous balance of self-assertion and obsequiousness. He has searched for the truth, he assured Burgsdorff, in the conviction that, if he did enter a "false path," God would not abandon him there. As a former pupil of a Saxon *Fürstenschule*, he was eager to honor his debt to "the fatherland" by entering its clergy. Classical studies he rejected as "too small to fill [his] whole life." In the second draft of the letter he balanced this candid admission of ambition with a gesture of humility (and flattery) toward a "supervisor in matters of learning" for whom "nothing has weight but merits or the capacity to develop them."[25] He then came close to accusing Frau von Miltitz of a rash injustice, though in a wording that did not explicitly contradict Burgsdorff's good opinion of the lady:

> I believe that the displeasure of Frau v. Miltitz toward me is based largely on the fact that I have been described as a man who not only has learned nothing, but also is not capable of learning anything and becoming useful – a description that amazes me, since I have never stood in this repute with any of my teachers or, as far as I know, with anyone else. – I am of course aware of a host of rash decisions and impetuosities in my previous behavior – but no malevolence [*Bosherzigkeit*] or serious wrongdoing. But I cannot know what has been charged against me, since the reason for the displeasure toward me has never been communicated to me. I have previously written to Frau v. Miltitz, and have done so again recently, that I will dispense with a defense as well as an excuse, and request no more than a pardon. . . . In my case I can hardly hope for further support from Fr. v. Miltitz, but it would be the greatest good fortune for me just to have achieved a favorable opinion on her part.[26]

Apparently Burgsdorff was not convinced. "Every one of my projects has

[24] Johann Gottlieb Fichte, *Briefwechsel 1775–1793*, Gesamtausgabe der Bayerischen Akademie der Wissenschaften, III, vol. 1 (1968), pp. 140–47.

[25] Fichte to Burgsdorff, July 1790, in ibid., pp. 147–51.

[26] Ibid., p. 151.

evaporated," Fichte reported to his fiancée in Switzerland on August 12, 1790. His patriotism seems to have vanished with them; "Saxony," he added in the same letter, "no longer means anything to me, just as I am nothing to it."[27]

It was not uncommon for clients to have distant, indirect relationships with their sponsors, particularly when the sponsors were noblemen and high-placed bourgeois officials. In this kind of sponsorship, in fact, part of the problem was that judgment, if it was to be credible, had to rest on a claim to personal knowledge, even if acquired only through an intermediary or in brief encounters. Why Frau von Miltitz had turned against Fichte is not clear; this lofty patroness probably had not seen her husband's protégé since his boyhood (if at all). Fichte's letter to Burgsdorff was designed to establish the requisite personal relationship with a new sponsor, despite the weight he attached to Frau von Miltitz's appraisal. Hence its irony: having chided himself in Switzerland for revealing too little of himself to friends, Fichte now had to confide his discouragements, limitations, and ambitions to a virtual stranger.

On the lower levels of the patronage chain, and particularly in the schools, clients were likely to be under closer scrutiny. While this made for better-informed judgments, it also required that expectations be met constantly. Local pastors and teachers played a key role, since they observed potential recruits firsthand and could claim to be uniquely qualified to determine whether a boy had the intellectual endowments and moral qualities expected of a clergyman. Their withdrawal of approval, even when it did not bring a loss of financial support, could have a devastating effect simply because it deprived the boy of needed encouragement. It was through no fault of his own that Fest "no longer distinguished [himself] and thus was overlooked"; but the result was that he lowered his expectations and nearly sabotaged his prospects.

Edelmann's effort to set the record straight in the face of attacks from the Orthodox camp, and particularly in response to a hostile biography impugning his moral qualifications as a theologian, occasioned a striking example of this potential reversal. To assure readers of his earlier rectitude, he reproduced the letters of recommendation with which he had been provided as he advanced through school and into university studies. Most are formulaic assurances, explicitly meant to win him "patrons" and "benefactors" farther up the line. But there was one qualified exception, a letter from the rector and staff of the gymnasium in Altenburg, forwarded by his uncle after he had moved on to another school. It came at a particularly bad time; Edelmann was a superannuated pupil, already twenty-two years old, but his father was penniless and no other support for his university

[27] Fichte to Marie Johanne Rahn, Aug. 12, 1790, in ibid., p. 166.

studies had materialized. "I would not have been ashamed to submit myself as an apprentice to often unreasonable masters," he recalled, "if I believed that I could give up the school nonsense [*Schulfuchsereyen*] for good."[28]

In this state of mind Edelmann received the recommendation, which was a curious juxtaposition of perfunctory praise and candid disapproval. The rector and his colleagues eventually spoke of a "thoroughly deserving youth," whose "behavior" and "industry" had been "everywhere and continuously excellent." But at the outset their "reliability and good conscience" had required them to acknowledge that this paragon "had sullied himself with the dissipations of youth" and "was rightly considered one of the cankers and burdens of the school."

> I cannot decribe how agitated I became when the first three or four lines came into view; I did not know whether I was waking or dreaming, and it would not have taken much for me to tear the innocent paper into a thousand pieces out of anger and frustration. Since I was not aware of the things that appeared in the opening lines of this *Testimonium*. . . . In view of my little experience at the time, I also do not believe that I was to be blamed for doing bad, since people seemed to curse me when I felt I deserved praise. I will leave it to the reader to judge whether he would have reacted differently when, in expectation of a reliable witness to his good behavior, the opening lines came into sight.[29]

The remaining lines had calmed Edelmann down; but many years later, when he picked up the document once again, it reawakened the initial response to an injustice and its potentially catastrophic implication for a charity pupil.

ANTON REISER: THE WITNESS OF A VICTIM

Anton Reiser was conceived as a contribution to the magazine on "empirical psychology" that Karl Philipp Moritz launched in Berlin in 1783. Turning to autobiography in his late twenties, Moritz looked back on his childhood and youth not from the distance of a long career, but with a sense of their painful immediacy. Research has confirmed Moritz's claim to be writing a "biography" drawn "for the most part from real life"; the narrative records his life history with considerable accuracy, and its evocations of Anton's past psychological and emotional states derive in part from the author's own diaries.[30] But Moritz also introduced *Anton Reiser* as a "psychological novel."

[28] Edelmann, *Selbstbiographie*, pp. 23–25.

[29] Ibid., pp. 24–27. The recommendation was in Latin, but there is a German translation (ibid., pp. 463–65).

[30] Independent documentation on Moritz's life, including material directly related to the account in *Anton Reiser*, has been carefully presented in Hugo Eybisch, *Anton Reiser. Untersuchungen zur Lebensgeschichte von K. Ph. Moritz und zur Kritik seiner Autobiographie*, Probe-

He meant not only to evoke the world of "romance" and adventure the novel traditionally had taken as its subject, but also to alert the reader to an interpenetration of documentary fact and novelistic fiction. As morbidly introspective as it became, this fusion of fact and fiction resulted in a text of singular value as social testimony. Moritz's self-consciously literary experiment in autobiography produced a unique inversion of the *Gelehrtenbiographie*, distinguished from conventional contributions to the genre above all by its critical distance on class and the specific terms of inequality for outsiders.

Moritz had originally intended to supply raw data for the study of personality disorders, but he became increasingly involved in a kind of cautionary self-diagnosis – an effort both to account for his failure to develop a secure sense of self and to provide a sobering example of the escapist fantasies that had lured so many young men of his generation into poetry and the theater. At its most philosophical, the account is a remarkably precocious but abstract anatomy of existential *Angst*. But in view of his early aspirations and recent disillusionment, it is not surprising that Moritz also took pains to make his readers aware of the social sources and dimensions of his insecurity. Moritz had not entirely abandoned his childhood dream of becoming a renowned preacher when he ended his university studies at Wittenberg in 1778, after two semesters as a theology student. His efforts to secure a pastorate over the next few years were sporadic and fruitless. Meanwhile, like so many other young men in such circumstances, he had taken refuge in teaching, first at the royal orphanage in Potsdam, then as an instructor in the lower grades of the Gymnasium zum Grauen Kloster in Berlin. Moritz developed a genuine interest in the new pedagogy, and by the end of 1782 had advanced to the relatively well paid position of conrector at the Kölnische Gymnasium. But in 1784 he returned to the Graue Kloster as an "extraordinary professor," despite the drastic loss of income the move entailed, so as to have more time and freedom to write. Even this partial withdrawal did not prevent him from feeling trapped in the "miserable school dungeon," as he once put it, and increasingly his escapes took the form of distant travels, to the neglect of his teaching duties. In the summer of 1786 the gymnasium director, Anton Friedrich Büsching,

fahrten. Erstlingsarbeiten aus dem Deutschen Seminar in Leipzig, ed. Albert Köster, vol. 14 (Leipzig, 1909). See also Mark Boulby, *Karl Philipp Moritz. At the Fringe of Genius* (Toronto, 1979), esp. pp. 27–35, 51–77. Boulby's book is an excellent intellectual biography of Moritz, including an insightful analysis of the mix of fact and fiction in *Anton Reiser*. My interpretation isolates Moritz as autobiographer; it avoids the tangled issue of the relationship between *Anton Reiser* and his other writings, and particularly the two novels – *Andreas Hartknopf. Eine Allegorie* (1786) and *Andreas Hartknopfs Predigerjahre* (1790) – he wrote during the same period. On that subject see, in addition to Boulby's book, Robert Minder, *Glaube, Skepsis und Rationalismus. Dargestellt aufgrund der autobiographischen Schriften von Karl Philipp Moritz* (1936: Frankfurt am Main, 1974); Thomas B. Saine, *Die ästhetische Theodizee. Karl Philipp Moritz und die Philosophie des 18. Jahrhunderts* (Munich, 1971).

who had promoted Moritz's teaching career despite his eccentricities, lost patience and appealed to the magistracy to discipline him. This provoked Moritz to cut the cord; he left teaching – and Berlin – in a huff, to indulge his compulsion to travel in Italy.[31]

By then Parts 2 and 3 of *Anton Reiser* had appeared, and Moritz had become a self-supporting writer. That in itself was no small achievement, considering that the publishing market in the late eighteenth century still offered a meager basis for a free-floating literary intelligentsia. Having earlier abandoned his acting ambitions for want of dramatic talent, Moritz had now come to realize that he lacked the poetic imagination needed for truly creative literary effort. *Anton Reiser* can be read in part as the story of a young man who emulates Goethe's Werther in aspiring to artistic "genius" but, unlike his hero, has to face up to and live with his ordinariness. But this sober self-appraisal coexists with a relentless anxiety, generated within the field of tensions between conformity and deviation, normalcy and alienation, that are recorded in Moritz's diary excerpts from his early years in Berlin. Despite his distance on earlier pretensions to genius, Moritz found himself unable to be content with an appropriately modest but "useful" vocation. And yet – and here is the other tension line – his vaulting ambition to achieve literary fame is paralleled by a lingering ambivalence about entering the educated elite in any capacity.[32]

The most striking inversion of the standard *Gelehrtenbiographie* is the use of an erratic plot line to convey this ambivalence. Moritz, to be sure, was not the only former poor student to look back on his experience as an ordeal. But typically the author's candor about moments of discouragement, and even about plunges into despair, complemented his pride in having ascended nonetheless to a clerical or teaching office. If his new identity remained insecure, it was solid enough to form the ordeal in retrospect into a steady verticle advance through school grades and university studies into office. In *Anton Reiser* a plot line that is anything but straight reflects Moritz's very different perspective as an uprooted young intellectual. From the early days as a schoolboy in Hanover through the initial stint as a student at Erfurt, violent fluctuations in the protagonist's mood – between exultation and self-condemnation, vaulting expectations and despair – intersect with and usually are occasioned by jolting leaps and plunges in his actual circumstances and prospects. And the account ends with an emphatic, apparently catastrophic downturn. Gripped once again by the "theater mania" that has displaced his fascination with the pulpit, Anton leaves Erfurt to join an acting troupe – only to discover after weeks of wandering that the

[31] See esp. Boulby, *Moritz*, pp. 51–65, 137–43.

[32] "Aus dem Tagebuche eines Selbstbeobachters," *Gnothi sauton; oder, Magazin zur Erfahrungsseelenkunde als ein Lesebuch für Gelehrte und Ungelehrte* 7 (1789): 25–52. The entire *Magazin* has been reprinted by Antiqua-Verlag (Lindau, 1978).

troupe has disbanded. In fact this disappointment effectively stifled Moritz's theatrical ambitions. If he had been able to look back on it as a turning point, offering a positive sense of direction as well as negative lessons, the autobiography might have evolved into a genuine *Bildungsroman* of self-discovery and self-development in the fourth volume, completed after his return from Italy in 1790. But the volume closes with its hero facing the void, and Moritz did not return to the project; the inverted *Gelehrtenbiographie* is also, in one critic's equally apt description, an *Anti-Bildungsroman.*[33]

From an early age Anton identifies with schoolboys from "cultured homes" and finds humiliating the chores that other boys of his background – the "street urchins" – accept as a matter of course. This sense of estrangement from plebeian roots is reinforced by highly stylized, symbolic depictions of a bleak, foreboding urban physical environment, juxtaposed to the natural "freedom" of the countryside.[34] And yet at the same time Moritz stylizes a series of characters, all drawn directly from popular life, into heroic, almost saintly figures. In descriptions of the charity meals Anton receives as a Latin school pupil, a Cobbler Schantz is contrasted with the other local residents, who made "humiliation" the price of their generosity. Aside from making the boy feel genuinely welcome in his home, Schantz converses with him about "metaphysical" subjects in "the language of common life," without the obfuscations of "academic terminology" (*Schulterminologie*). If Schantz had become a teacher, "he would have been able to build the minds of those for whom he made shoes." The same mystique attaches to the "philosophical vinegar maker" whose evening circle Anton later enters. Despite his *Plattdeutsch* this obscure man speaks "correctly" and "nobly" about music and literature. Anton finds it inspiring that "a man of such knowledge and capabilities subjected himself with such patience and steadfastness of soul to his fate, which excluded him completely from the polite world and all [its] intellectual nourishment." Indeed the boy endows him with all the more value because his obscurity prevents his "luster" from being "lost amidst the crowd of other lights."[35]

Moritz was not sentimentalizing the common man, much less voicing

[33] Hans Joachim Schrimpf, "Karl Philipp Moritz," in Benno von Wiese, ed., *Deutsche Dichter des 18. Jahrhunderts. Ihr Leben und Werk* (Berlin, 1977), p. 892. See also idem, "Anton Reiser. Wege zum psychologischen Roman," in Benno von Wiese, ed., *Der Deutsche Roman*, vol. 1 (Düsseldorf, 1965), pp. 95–131. Though Moritz probably had not made a "conscious decision" to end the autobiography with the fourth part, Boulby notes, its "fall-away ending" was clearly "a calculated narrative effect." Boulby, *Moritz*, p. 35.

[34] Moritz, *Anton Reiser*, pp. 40–41, 88–89.

[35] Ibid., pp. 125–26, 269–71. See also the portraits of the former theology candidate Tischer and Doctor Sauer, in ibid., pp. 41–43, 397–401. On the significance of such figures, cf. Hans-Ulrich Schnuchel, "Die Behandlung bürgerlichen Problematik in den Romanen von Karl Philipp Moritz," in *Festschrift für Wolfgang Vulpius zu seinem 60. Geburtstag am 27. November 1957* (Weimar, 1957), pp. 93–98; Ruth Ghisler, *Gesellschaft und Gottesstaat. Studien zum 'Anton Reiser'* (Winterthur, 1955), pp. 121–26.

"democratic" aspirations from the social depths. These figures represent an alluring but ultimately illusory alternative; they have somehow escaped in spirit from the intellectually cramped, treadmill existence of the uneducated mass, without meeting the prevailing requirements for escape. While the account conveys the appeal of this prospect to an ambitious but insecure young boy, the narrator's distanced irony leaves no doubt that the boy was indulging in wishful thinking. Implicit in Anton's admiration is the ambitious poor boy's fear that he will suffer the obscurity of the excluded – that he will be rejected by the elite he aspires to join. The same fear informs the fantasy of becoming a "refined, polite, and well-bred peasant," which offers Anton solace at a particularly low moment when he is without "prospects" and on the edge of "madness." Likely to remain "lowered far beneath his station" if he persists in his studies, he prefers to imagine himself a peasant who has "far more education" than he needs and thus is "raised above his station."[36]

Moritz senior had eventually become a village notary, but until his son reached age fourteen he had been a regimental musician – an occupation that placed him closer to the urban underclass of wage earners than to the skilled artisanate. Hence Moritz had begun the ascent into educated society from an unusually low point, and that helps explain why he could not shed the feeling of being an interloper. In the early pages of *Anton Reiser* the humble social rank of the family is secondary to its internal constellation in explaining the roots of Anton's pathology. What deprives the boy of a secure sense of self is his parents' incessant domestic warfare, which leaves him neglected and unable to choose between fundamentally incompatible temperaments and religious sensibilities. Even his shabby clothing, the public emblem of his social humiliation, is attributed to this parental failure rather than to poverty; they had had the means to dress him more respectably, if they had not been so indifferent.[37]

But the reader is not asked to choose between psychological insight and social awareness; Moritz's diagnosis of a family syndrome, with its remarkable anticipations of modern pyschology, is inseparable from his unusually critical view of class relations. In tracing his pathology back to his domestic upbringing, Moritz departed radically from the conventional tendency to attribute self-discipline, piety, and other qualities of "character" to parental example. In retrospect, to be sure, he realizes that his father was more "just" than his loving but self-pitying mother. But there is more sympathy than respect in this portrait, and even the sympathy is qualified; the father

[36] Moritz, *Anton Reiser*, pp. 192–94. See also the description of Moritz's fantasies by a former pupil and friend, in Karl Friedrich Klischnigg, *Erinnerungen aus den zehn letzten Lebensjahren meines Freundes Anton Reiser. Als ein Beitrag zur Lebensgeschichte des Herrn Hofrath Moritz* (Berlin, 1794), esp. pp. 78–79.

[37] Moritz, *Anton Reiser*, pp. 15–23. On Moritz senior, see Eybisch, *Anton Reiser*, pp. 4–11.

UNIVERSITY COLLEGE LIBRARY SWANSEA

is not excused for depriving his son of the innocent joys of childhood by subjecting him to a mystical variety of Pietism or for failing to offer encouragement and financial help in the early years of his studies. It is the absence of a reverential (even if critical) posture toward paternal authority that makes for an unusual degree of social insight as well as psychological depth. The family syndrome that deprived Moritz of a secure sense of self also allowed him to look back on his experience of class inferiority without the usual ideological filter.

An exclusive concern with the effects of the family constellation would have put the emphasis on the peculiarity, if not the uniqueness, of Anton's pathology. But as the account progresses a very specific psychological diagnosis merges into a more general social analysis. The reader is reminded repeatedly that the meandering career of this ambitious poor boy, facing familiar obstacles on the climb into the learned estate, represents the class injustice of a society divided between the "cultured" elite and the uneducated mass, the privileged and the unprivileged. Moritz, to be sure, occasionally seems to sidestep this social issue by appealing to blind Fate to explain the momentous consequences that flowed from apparently trivial circumstances and events in Anton's life. The "romantic" compulsion to travel that Anton absorbed from his reading of picaresque novels, and that he pursues at several points in the narrative, clearly retained a certain hold on the mature author. By analogy Fate – the same Fate that orchestrates the traveler's adventures – offers an explanation for fortunate turns in career prospects; the friendly strangers on the road who rescue Anton from desperate straits have their parallel in Pastor Marquardt, who takes notice of him after a chance encounter on the street and secures his stipend, and in other sponsors whose behavior seems as fortuitous.[38]

If Fate is a secular *deus absconditus* in this sense, however, it also becomes the metaphor for an entirely different perspective. Anton takes a dark pleasure in solitary games in which he assumes the role of Fate and, closing his eyes, wreaks random destruction. On one such occasion the object of his destructive impulse – indulged this time by burning a toy city "built of small paper houses" – is the urban world Moritz's recurrent imagery of dark, narrow alleys and intimidating towers fashions into an oppressive environment. Here blind Fate becomes the vehicle for a muffled but audible cry of resentment against society – and the imaginary instrument of revenge. The vision of a town destroyed, the reader learns in an especially cryptic passage, "arose from a dark premonition of great changes, emigrations, and revolutions in which all things would receive an entirely different structure [*Gestalt*] and the existing monotony would cease."[39]

[38] Moritz, *Anton Reiser*, pp. 109–10. See also, e.g., the account of how Anton became a student at Erfurt, in ibid., pp. 394–400.

[39] Ibid., pp. 28–29.

In such passages *Anton Reiser*, like some concurrent contributions to picaresque literature in the late eighteenth century, endows a secularized Fate with "immanent social determinacy."[40] The focus of Moritz's social critique is easily distorted if his "novel" is taken as one more "bourgeois" protest against the survival of aristocratic privilege. That approach has often linked *Anton Reiser* with Goethe's *Die Leiden des jungen Werthers*, which took Moritz's generation by storm. Indeed one of the most famous scenes, taken in isolation, seems to encourage this pairing. The young nobleman Anton had been tutoring, probably assuming that his tutor was about to depart, abruptly took leave of him. Anton tried to account for the feeling of "life weariness" this apparent insult induced with abstract speculations about "the nothingness of human life," but the narrator knows better:

At bottom it was the feeling of humanity oppressed by social conditions [*bürgerliche Verhältnisse*] that overpowered him here and made life hateful to him – He had to instruct a young nobleman who paid him and could show him the door in a polite tone at the end of the hour if it pleased him – What crime had he committed before his birth that prevented him from becoming someone about whom a number of other people had to trouble and exert themselves? – Why was it he who played the role of worker, and another that of paymaster [*Bezahlenden*]? If his circumstances in the world had made him happy and content he would have seen purpose and order everywhere, but now everything seemed to him contradiction, disorder and confusion.[41]

The scene occurs soon after Anton has read *Werther* and is reminiscent of the more famous incident when Werther is asked to leave an exclusive gathering of the court aristocracy. But in fact there are characteristic differences, both in the social referents and in their literary signification. *Werther* can be read as one testimony among many that scions of upper bourgeois families resented the precedence still given to "birth," in the strict form of legal and de facto privileges attached to aristocratic lineage, over individual "merit." But as the son of a wealthy merchant, Werther is well aware that he gains "many advantages" from "class distinctions."[42] If Moritz is to be considered a "bourgeois" author at all, he represents the newcomers to the lowest ranks – the young men who entered the underlayer

[40] Günter Niggl, *Geschichte der deutschen Autobiographie im 18. Jahrhundert* (Stuttgart, 1977), p. 81. Moritz is not included in Niggl's discussion of the late developments in the "picaresque life history"; but parts of *Anton Reiser* clearly borrow from the genre and reflect the evolution that Niggl describes.

[41] Moritz, *Anton Reiser*, pp. 314–16.

[42] *Die Leiden des jungen Werthers*, in *Goethes Werke*, vol. 6 (Munich, 1973), pp. 63–69. On Goethe's social perspective, see esp. Dieter Borchmeyer, *Höfische Gesellschaft und Französische Revolution bei Goethe. Adliges und bürgerliches Wertsystem im Urteil der Weimarer Klassik* (Kronberg/Ts., 1977). The social meaning of Werther's behavior depends in part on the narrative perspective, which shifts within the novel and was adjusted in the revised edition; see Eric A. Blackall, *Goethe and the Novel* (Ithaca, N.Y., 1976), pp. 44–55. For a more extensive discussion of *Werther*, see Chapter 9.

of the academic and official elite from the plebeian depths. Anton overreacted to an unintended insult, the reader is reminded, because it triggered a series of associations with earlier humiliations, most of them perpetrated by clergymen-teachers who misjudged his intelligence. The nobleman is only secondarily an embodiment of the privileges attached to a family title and pedigree; his larger role is to personify "birth" in a looser sense – the world of privileged access to higher education that includes, for example, Pastor Marquardt's son and the son of an *Amtmann*, "well-dressed" and "of fine upbringing," to whom Anton had had to cede first place in confirmation class.[43]

Anton – and Moritz – experienced class inequality primarily as a recipient of the patronage and charity extended from this larger elite of "birth" to the lower depths. Moritz achieved a nuanced, multilevel exploration of the social psychology inherent in this experience by splitting the autobiographical self into a narrator and a third-person character (the Anton of the account). In the prospectus for his magazine on empirical psychology, he explained his rationale for adopting this obviously novelistic technique. If the novel traditionally opened a world of fantasy, the autobiographer must penetrate "his own actual world":

> But who gives the observer of man the coldness and serenity of soul to observe everything that happens as a play and the people who often injure him as the actors? Indeed, if only he himself were not comprehended in the game, and if only no envy of others' roles [*Rollenneid*] occurred? – But what should one do if he is oppressed by men or by his fate, and cannot go on? What better and nobler than to transport himself, just as if he had become another existence, entirely different from himself, who laughs at all things from a higher region. . . . Thus as soon as I see that no role will be given me, I place myself before the stage and am a calm, cold observer. As soon as my own situation becomes frustrating I cease to be self-interested and regard myself as the subject of my own observation, as if I were a stranger whose strokes of fortune and misfortune I hear being related with cold-blooded attention.[44]

This is an arresting passage, and not simply because it announces the "theater obsession" that would become a leitmotif of *Anton Reiser*. To be denied a part on the stage of life is to be "oppressed," whether by other men or by a "fate." But oppression brings a certain advantage; the self-analyst deprived of a social role can achieve a degree of detachment that

[43] Moritz, *Anton Reiser*, pp. 114–15. On Moritz as a "bourgeois" author, see esp. Josef Grolimund, *Das Menschenbild in den autobiographischen Schriften Karl Philipp Moritz. Eine Untersuchung zum Selbstverständnis des Menschen in der Goethezeit* (Zürich, 1967), pp. 15–16; Josef Fürnkäs, *Der Ursprung des psychologischen Romans. Karl Philipp Moritz' 'Anton Reiser'* (Stuttgart, 1977), esp. pp. 76–79.

[44] "Vorschlag zu einem Magazin einer Erfahrungs-Seelenkunde," *Magazin zur Erfahrungsseelenkunde* 1 (1782), no pag. For a different reading of this passage, see Saine, *Die ästhetische Theodizee*, pp. 100–1.

is somehow consoling. In this sense the narrative structure of *Anton Reiser* represents a therapeutic exercise as well as an experiment in diagnosis. The narrator's posture alternates between empathic reconstruction of Anton's world, as seen and experienced from within the confines of his consciousness, and a soberly realistic, uncompromising assessment of that consciousness. The latter posture in turn has its alternate modes, in considerable tension. The narration often points out instances of Anton's paranoid distortion and overreaction. But it also steps back (or out); the reader learns that, despite his self-destructive impulses, the protagonist was a helpless, unwitting victim of circumstances. With this splitting of the autobiographical self, Moritz was able to explore the tangle of causes and effects in the relationship between an individual psyche and the reality outside it, individual pathology and the responsibility of society. He does not unravel the tangle, but does find a loose end, a place to start. In the course of concluding that his "inner" pathology was the effect of his "exterior" circumstances, not their cause, he comes to see himself as a victim – as someone of whom "it can be said. . . in truth that he was oppressed from the cradle."[45]

Who – or what – was to be held responsible for his victimization? Moritz remained too plagued by self-doubt to provide a single consistent answer; instead he juggled the alternatives of blind Fate and social injustice, now allowing them to fly apart at random, now demonstrating adeptly how they might configurate into a single complex but logical explanation. But the overall thrust is clear enough; the complex structure of the narrative combines with its very monotony – its grim succession of similar episodes, related with "bare, reiterative monotonies" and "agglutinative tautologies" – to demonstrate the underlying vicious circle Moritz had succeeded in identifying. The origins of Anton's fundamental lack of "self-confidence" lie in a tangle of "oppressive" circumstances, with parental conflict and the stigma of poverty reinforcing each other. Only social recognition as an exceptional case – in school and ultimately with public acclaim as an intellectual – can compensate for this legacy. But upbringing and social disadvantages have denied Anton precisely the confidence in his own capabilities that his uphill struggle requires. Faced with the slightest setback, he becomes morbidly introverted and blames himself, despite an occasional

[45] Moritz, *Anton Reiser*, p. 15. See also Fürnkäs, *Ursprung*, which maps a complex relationship between the narrator and the "narrated figure," similar in some respects to my interpretation. Fürnkäs argues that, by demonstrating the protagonist's chronic lack of identity and by imposing continuity (in the absence of inner development) with a causal explanation of his pathology, this narrative structure reproduces the bourgeois domination-subordination relationships of the social order. This is an intriguing insight, but the study is symptomatic of the tendency to appeal to abstract socioeconomic categories – in this case capitalism – in lieu of detailed familiarity with the historical context. Fürnkäs includes an excellent analysis of "alienation" and "exploitation" in the apprenticeship to a hatmaker but, despite his characterization of Anton as an *Aufsteiger* from the *Kleinbürgertum*, ignores the more numerous examples of the patron-client relationship in academic mobility. Ibid., pp. 41–46, 72–85.

inkling that he is being victimized by "injustice." Self-destructive behavior, provoked by self-hatred, seems to confirm the social prejudices of others and thus brings still more rejection. The only escape is flight into "fantasy" – in "romantic" fiction, in poetry, and above all in the theater. While this escapism saves him from complete "madness," it is in the end another form of self-destructive withdrawal; it provides temporary escape, but does not break the circle of oppression.[46]

Moritz had cited Rousseau's *Confessions* as an example of the kind of autobiographical witness he had in mind, and his exploration of Anton's syndrome often seems to conjure up all too familiar variations on Rousseauian themes. Anton's initial encounters with injustice at home are suspiciously reminiscent of the famous recollections of the same experience in Rousseau's account. In Anton's alienated vision, as in Rousseau's, there is a sharp contrast between the oppression of urban life and the freedom to be found in isolated retreat into nature. But if Rousseau posed the innocence of passions, liberated in response to nature, against a coldly analytical Reason, Moritz gives this theme another twist. Under the scrutiny of the narrator's cold, clinical rationality the cult of nature becomes a pathological symptom, its delusions easily punctured.

Likewise there is a critical difference in the social angle. In both texts a "Young Man from the Provinces" is in desperate need of patrons but is repelled, at least in retrospect, by the inferiority and dependence of clientage.[47] But Rousseau was a largely self-educated man, and from an early age he had had to make his way in the great world without formal credentials. *Anton Reiser* achieves its greatest critical force when it examines the social psychology of class in the narrower, institutional world of the school – the world to which Moritz's experience, with the exception of a few brief interludes, had been confined. In Anton's series of humiliations as a schoolboy a familiar detail – the shabby clothing emblematic of poverty and dependence – is set within a particularly ironic context. Anton has to suffice with a "coarse old red soldier's coat" in winter because his benefactors, oblivious to the psychological impact of these stigmas, want to spare his scholarship money. The same insensitivity has led them to arrange the free meals with local families that become the daily scenes of his "shame" and feelings of "nothingness."[48]

To Anton the competitive environment of the Latin school at first seems to promise "more justice" than he can expect at home. His disillusionment advances in a downward spiral of apparently trivial but nonetheless fateful

[46] See the analysis of the "circulos vitiosus" in Grolimund, *Menschenbild*, esp. pp. 21–23. The description of Moritz's style is from Boulby, *Moritz*, p. 48.

[47] On this theme, see Lionel Trilling, "The Princess Casamassima" (1946), reprinted in idem, *The Liberal Imagination. Essays on Literature and Society* (New York and London, 1979), esp. pp. 59–62.

[48] Moritz, *Anton Reiser*, pp. 117–29.

incidents, their sequence worth tracing in some detail. As a scholarship boy, Anton receives free lodging in the home of the new rector, Sextroh, who at first has him assist in setting up a library and encourages his stumbling efforts to engage in learned conversation. But during his examination for promotion he is rebuked by Director Ballhorn for nervously turning a page of Cicero's *De officiis* too quickly and almost tearing it. The irony is that he is wrongly judged to lack respect for the very printed word that has been his refuge at home, and indeed for the very Latin learning he reveres. Anton's subsequent "timid" manner lowers him still further in the director's estimation. When his attempt to repress a "laughing expression" during morning prayers betrays "an extremely mistrustful, common and slavish fear," Ballhorn accuses him of "base" behavior. Already ashamed of being nicknamed "the rector's servant [*Famulus*]," Anton now becomes the object of his schoolmates' scorn. In a literal inversion of his ambition to cut a public figure on stage, he is denied a role in the school play. He loses all self-confidence and becomes "misanthropic" when Sextroh, judging that "at best he would only make a village schoolmaster," begins to use him as a domestic and attributes his failure to deliver a message to "sheer stupidity." Disappointed by the very behavior he has helped induce, the rector finally asks Anton to find lodging elsewhere. The victim blames himself, since he is still unable to explain his conduct as "a natural result of the extremely constrained circumstances in which he found himself." It is his need to escape debasement that makes the illusory world of the theater seem "more natural and agreeable."[49]

Moritz does not include these apparently trivial details as traces of an inscrutable Fate; they evoke the contingent terms of the patron-client bond, which in turn is a microcosm of the wider vicious circle of oppression and alienated withdrawal in the poor boy's relationship to society. Blind Fate becomes the metaphor for an arbitrary and hence unjust distribution of life chances. This perspective obviously does not make Moritz a spokesman for some kind of "proletarian" consciousness, or even for a "democratic" ideology; but it is equally misleading to interpret the "novel" as a symptomatic expression of "bourgeois" *Melancholie.* Such an interpretation collapses the distance between an uncomprehending protagonist, plunged into self-destructive depression, and an empathic but critical narrator, applying the rationalism that provided at least one compass for the mature author's self-awareness. In the narrator's hands, the solipsistic trials of a neurotic schoolboy occasion a highly self-conscious diagnosis of the social roots of *Melancholie.*[50]

49 Ibid., pp. 157–84.

50 Hans-Jürgen Schings, *Melancholie und Aufklärung. Melancholiker und ihre Kritiker in Erfahrungsseelenkunde und Literatur des 18. Jahrhunderts* (Stuttgart, 1977), esp. pp. 226–55. Schings rightly uses *Anton Reiser* as the centerpiece of an analysis of the Enlightenment's critique

Eager to identify and sponsor poor boys with the potential to join their ranks, men like Sextroh and Ballhorn also are quick to spot disqualifying signs of "baseness." Moritz's conception of "injustice" implicitly imputes a class bias to the criteria for character and "honor" that his teachers assumed to have universal moral validity. If Anton's family life has made him especially vulnerable to their judgments, he has also entered an especially treacherous environment. In his neurotic craving to rise above the crowd, he expects the approval and sponsorship of clerical patrons to be an objective reward, when in fact the school harbors a contradiction between the competitive ethos informing its examinations and promotion procedures and the arbitrariness, at once personal and social, inherent in the poor boy's reliance on sponsors. The result for Anton is not simply self-contempt; his vicious circle also brings a loss of confidence in his clergymen-teachers, which implicitly indicts the sponsored mobility over which they preside. Appropriately this theme – the establishment's loss of legitimacy in the eyes of the victim – is sounded again when Anton flirts with criminality at the lowest ebb of his fortunes. Forced to leave the rector's house and share a room with two other impoverished pupils who also regard themselves as outcasts, he joins them in plundering a cherry orchard. They regard the act not as "theft," but as "a raid into the enemy's territory."[51]

Typically the outsider justified himself within the terms of prevailing stereotypes, even as he exempted himself from their censure. He insisted on the modesty of his aspirations, and perhaps recalled with pride his "inner" refusal to abase himself. On one level Moritz's deviation from this pattern seems to lie simply in admitting what others deny; true to stereotype, Anton's behavior combines "presumption" and "servility." But in fact Moritz's inversion of the conventional form achieves a radical and searching negation of standard wisdom. Anton's "vanity" is not the inflated, illegitimate ambition of the overeducated poor student. Instead "oppression" has inflated a legitimate need for recognition into a self-destructive craving. The tragedy in fact is that, in his need to escape "oppression," Anton in effect opts out of conventional social climbing; lured by the theater, he catapults his ambitions entirely beyond the pale of respectable careers.

It is within this syndrome that Moritz gives a new specificity to the Rousseauian censure of "dissimulation" in social relations. Anton had joined the school choir – the traditional source of charity for poor pupils – "to acquire a new and honorable station," but soon discovered that most of its members

of *Melancholie* (considered inseparable from religious "enthusiasm" in the negative sense), but leaves its social context and implications vague. For a critique of the approach to eighteenth-century *Melancholie* as bourgeois psychological "compensation" for political impotence, see Wolfram Mauser, "Melancholieforschung des 18. Jahrhunderts zwischen Ikonographie und Ideologiekritik. Auseinandersetzungen mit den bisherigen Ergebnissen und Thesen zu einem Neuansatz," *Lessings Yearbook* 13 (1981): 253–77.

51 Moritz, *Anton Reiser*, pp. 197–99.

"develop a servile mentality . . . and never quite lose the trace of it." The same lack of self-confidence that fueled his delusions made it impossible for him to develop "what in young people is called an insinuating manner." Hence in his mouth, the reader learns, the "language of a polite manner" would have become "the most blatant servility" and obvious "flattery."[52] The moral danger here is not that false deference, betraying a lack of personal honor, threatens to undermine hierarchical values. Servile behavior has become the unjust price, the violation of the self, that society exacts from the ambitious but disadvantaged. One of the cruelest ironies is that, from the vantage point of the victim, the only alternative to *Niederträchtigkeit* - a word that always connotes servility as well as baseness – is morose withdrawal.

Anton's descent into *Melancholie* reaches its nadir in a scene with his father. The elder Reiser evinces a new interest in his son's success in school, but it receives a rude jolt when, on a visit to Hanover, he learns that Pastor Marquardt has given up on the boy:

> When his father left he [Anton] accompanied him out to the city gate and there it was that he [the father] repeated to him the "comforting" words of Pastor Marquardt and bitterly reproached him for not acknowledging the benefits bestowed on him, and pointed to the coat he wore as an undeserved present from his benefactors. This made Reiser angry; for the coat, which was of coarse gray cloth that gave him the appearance of a servant, had always been a hated object to him, and he therefore told his father that a coat of that sort, which he had to wear to his distress, could arouse no great feeling of gratitude in him.
>
> Thereupon his father, taught by Madame Guyon's writings to regard humiliation and mortification of self-conceit as sacred, fell into a kind of rage, turned away from him quickly and cursed him on the road. Reiser was now in a state of mind he had never been in before. . . . As he went back into the city he broke into blasphemy and was near despair, he longed to be swallowed up by the earth and his father's curse seemed to pursue him in earnest.[53]

Moritz's alienation from an entire structure of class relations finds expression in this passage. The elder Reiser is trying to play the stern father, but the narrator – and the mature author – have stripped away the moral legitimacy of paternal authority. The father's mystical-Pietist ideal of self-abnegation dictates a grateful, compliant posture toward patrons; but the crippling aridity of Pietist introspection has already been exposed as a root cause of the son's pathological insecurity. The personal integrity of men

[52] Ibid., pp. 121–22, 141, 153. On Moritz's view of dissimulation, see also "Vorschlag zu einem Magazin."

[53] Moritz, *Anton Reiser*, pp. 222–23. Cf. the analysis of the father-son relationship in Wolf Wucherpfennig, "Versuch über einen aufgeklärten Melancholiker: zum *Anton Reiser* von Karl Philipp Moritz," in Johannes Cremarius et al., eds., *Freiburger literaturpsychologische Gespräche* (Frankfurt am Main, 1981), pp. 177–79.

like Schantz and the vinegar brewer – men who have risen intellectually above their sphere without submitting to the humiliating dependencies of clientage – stands in painful contrast to the father's counsels. Anton's alienation is double-edged; if he loses confidence in the sponsors of ascent, he also cannot respect uneducated men like his father, who accept their terms.

More than any other source from the eighteenth century, *Anton Reiser* explores a social universe in which "birth," in its preeminently modern sense, means the privileged access to higher education afforded by heritable wealth and "culture." Moritz did not accompany his critique with a call for sweeping social change, or even with an appeal for the kinds of institutional reform that other educators of his generation were advocating. Instead the narrator merely assumes the role of enlightened pedagogue, warning his fellow educators not to damage their pupils' "feeling of inner value" by judging them too hastily.[54] What nonetheless makes this "psychological novel" unique, both as a literary achievement and as a social document, is its narrative tension between critical distance and imaginative empathy. While the one posture exposes a structure of inequality, inherent in the precarious workings of patron-client relationships, the other makes the reader appreciate why the self, even when it instinctively questions the legitimacy of a class structure, remains encapsulated within the terms of corporate sponsorship. On both counts Moritz's pedagogical antidote for injustice is likely to strike the modern reader as inadequate; it pales before his probe into the damaged psyche of a victim and his insight into the social process of victimization.

[54] Moritz, *Anton Reiser*, esp. pp. 176, 185. See also Moritz's remarks on his method of observing pupils, in *Magazin zur Erfahrungsseelenkunde* 1 (1783): 107–10; Fürnkäs, *Ursprung*, pp. 45–46.

4

The *Hofmeister*

At midcentury Johann Lorenz Mosheim, a leading theologian and advocate of ecclesiastical reform, devoted an entire chapter of his *Ethical Teachings of Holy Scripture* to the "dream" of creating a well-educated, dedicated clergy. The chief "obstacles" lay in the lack of natural gifts among recruits and the poverty many of them had to endure. Mosheim wanted theology students to remain at least four years at the university, until they were in their early to middle twenties, but considered thirty to be the minimum age at which they would be mature enough to assume pastoral duties. Rather than being "left to themselves" or "forced to find their bread in misery" in the interim, they should be housed, fed, and further trained in "certain well-ordered houses" supported by the state. Appointments would be distributed among the residents of these "nurseries of the church" according to their seniority and qualifications for particular offices.[1]

At the close of the eighteenth century, every theology candidate without independent means still faced the problem the "well-ordered houses" would have removed. In the hiatus between university studies and a clerical appointment – a hiatus that usually lasted at least a year or two, and often much longer – they had to find a means of survival. Some took teaching positions in the schools, which served as "waiting rooms" for the clergy proper throughout the century. The most common alternative was to join the crowd of live-in tutors in private homes, who usually received a token cash remuneration as well as free room and board.

The reliance on tutoring at the juncture between university studies and a clerical career has special importance for understanding the social experience of academic mobility. Tutoring was a well-established institution that had long served as a finishing school for young men with rough edges; but it nonetheless became the target for a reaction to the polite world, particularly in its aristocratic form, that mixed social anxiety with a defiant assertion of "bourgeois" cultural values. At the end of the century, the re-

[1] Johann Lorenz Mosheim, *Sitten-Lehre der Heiligen Schrift* (4th, rev. and enl. ed.: Helmstedt, 1753), pp. 517–27.

lationship between tutor and employer might still approximate a patriarchal ideal; but the same relationship also had become a neuralgic point – the link on the patronage chain that, more than any other, made paternalism seem hypocritical and indeed exploitative. While particular abuses of tutoring had long been satirized, in fact, the legitimacy of the institution itself was called into question and often denied in the last third of the century.[2]

In part changing perceptions of tutoring account for this development, and the new ideas about pedagogy and education that shaped those perceptions will receive attention in due course. Our concern here is with the fusions of learned and aristocratic culture that defined tutors' duties in particular households; with the class relationships that tutoring institutionalized; and with the employment markets leading to and from it. While these underlying stuctural realities made tutoring potentially advantageous for poor students, they also explain why it was often a traumatic interlude.

SCHOLARS AND COURTIERS

Perhaps the best-known treatment of tutoring in German literature is Jakob Michael Reinhold Lenz's *Der Hofmeister*. Written in the early 1770s, the play derived from the author's own experience as well as from the complaints of friends. In act 1, scene 4, we find Major von Berg fixing the salary for Läuffer, the new tutor, at 400 thaler over three years, although the lady of the house had promised him 450. When Läuffer objects, the major recalls that his predecessor settled for 250 thaler; "he was a scholar, and a courtier to boot, everyone gave him credit for that," the major notes, "and you've got a mighty long way to go, young man, before you match him." The predecessor's scholarly qualifications (and integrity) have already been thrown into doubt. Though he had assured the major that his son was "word-perfect in Latin," von Berg has just learned to his astonishment that the boy "can barely read" the language. This hardly matters to Frau von Berg; interested exclusively in Läuffer's courtly qualifications, she has already had him demonstrate "a low bow from the minuet" and a "pas," as well as his conversational command of French.[3]

[2] On the "crisis" in tutoring and its significance for the emerging consciousness of a bourgeois intelligentsia, see esp. Ludwig Fertig, *Die Hofmeister. Ein Beitrag zur Geschichte des Lehrerstandes and der bürgerlichen Intelligenz* (Stuttgart, 1979). Fertig's book is primarily a well-chosen sample of primary sources on tutoring. But his introductory essay, setting the subject within a framework of continuity and change, is in itself an excellent contribution to the cultural and social history of the eighteenth century. This chapter owes a great deal to its insights. The other major contributions, quite different in emphasis, are Hans H. Gerth, *Bürgerliche Intelligenz um 1800. Zur Soziologie des deutschen Frühliberalismus*, ed. Ulrich Herrmann, Kritische Studien zur Geschichtswissenschaft, vol. 19 (Göttingen, 1976), pp. 51–60; Wilhelm Roessler, *Die Entstehung des modernen Erziehungswesens in Deutschland* (Stuttgart, 1961), pp. 133–42.

[3] Jakob Michael Reinhold Lenz, "Der Hofmeister, Oder Vorteile der Privaterziehung," in

Such details ground the farcical elements of *Der Hofmeister* in an acerbic realism. In a popular handbook on tutoring, published in 1760, Anton Friedrich Büsching had cataloged a roughly similar range of the scholarly and courtly qualifications expected of tutors.[4] As early as 1740, more than thirty years before Lenz satirized this phenomenon, *Der Einsiedler* published a mock advertisement for a tutoring position on "an estate located to the north," offering a yearly salary of 20 reichsthaler with the prospect of a 2-thaler raise every three years. The tutor had to be a theology graduate who "above all is completely at home in mathematics, history, knowledge of the world [*Weltweisheit*], heraldry and all gallant branches of learning" – and who also "could serve as a complete master in riding, fencing and dancing."[5] In the mock correspondence Gottlieb Wilhelm Rabener published a few years later, a father describes the kind of "pretty, healthy" fellow he wants to a professor in Leipzig whose "reception room is always crowded with kowtowing creatures seeking tutoring positions":

> I require nothing more of him than that he have a good command of Latin, keep himself in clean laundry and clothing; that he can speak French and Italian, and writes a pretty hand, understands mathematics, composes verse, to the extent it's needed in the house, can dance and fence and, if possible, draw a little. He must also be well-grounded in history, and above all else in heraldry. If he also has traveled, all the better. But he must be willing to live on my estate and hire himself to me for at least six years. In return he will have free lodging in the same room with my children, will eat with the domestics, and will receive 50 gulden a year.[6]

Of the dozen candidates whom the professor lists, only one is actually qualified, and he has had the temerity to submit an itemized bill with separate fees for instruction in French, Italian, writing, mathematics, dancing, and fencing as well as for Latin. Fortunately the others – they include a young man who "reads Latin and Greek, but cannot speak any German" – are willing to settle for much less.[7]

One of the standard laments by the close of the century was that parents' inflated expectations were in absurd contrast to the paltry compensation and demeaning terms of employment tutors had to endure. The inflation of expected qualifications marks the multifarious functions tutoring assumed in the social and educational structure. While it is impossible to be

idem, *Werke und Schriften*, ed. Britta Titel and Hellmut Haug, 2 vols. (Stuttgart, 1966–67), 2: 13–19.

[4] Anton Friedrich Büsching, *Grundris eines Unterrichts wie besondere Lehrer und Hofmeister der Kinder und Jünglinge sich pflichtmässig, wohlanständig und klüglich verhalten müssen* (Altona and Lübeck, 1760), esp. pp. 36–43. There is an extensive selection from the 1802 edition of this book in Fertig, *Hofmeister*, pp. 217–34.

[5] Quoted in Fertig, *Hofmeister*, pp. 64–65.

[6] Ibid., p. 179.

[7] Ibid., pp. 180–85. See also Caspar Sincerus, "Schreiben von den Eigenschaften eines Hofmeisters," *Der Hofmeister* 1:39 (1751): 308–9.

precise about how widespread the employment of tutors had become or how it was distributed by class, the rough outlines of the phenomenon are clear enough from impressionistic evidence. The institution known as *Hofmeistertum* had originally been a distinctive feature of aristocratic households, but in the course of the eighteenth century the use of live-in tutors – whether called *Hofmeister* or distinguished from the prototype by the title *Informator* or simply *Hauslehrer* – extended deep into the *Bürgertum* as well. Private tutors are sought not only by noblemen, Büsching observed in 1760, but also by "officials, tenant farmers [*Pächter*], pastors in the countryside, and artisans in the towns."[8] It was probably a rare artisan who hired a live-in tutor, but there are numerous examples of Büsching's other categories of employers from the first half of the century. Over the next half-century this social dispersion of tutoring may have continued to advance, and in any case it became an entrenched feature of German life. It is particularly striking in the clergy; of the twenty-eight clergymen's sons who contributed autobiographical sketches to the *Allgemeines Magazin für Prediger*, twelve recorded that they had been instructed at home by tutors.[9]

Even aristocratic employers had a greater diversity of requirements than a standard catalog of tutoring skills and subjects could cover. One need only think of the social and cultural gulf separating ancient families at court from their much less affluent, often very distant cousins among the isolated *Landjunker*. Bourgeois employers were still more varied. Clergymen were likely to be more concerned than merchants about a tutor's expertise in scholarship. Even among merchants, the father grooming his son to follow in his footsteps has to be distinguished from the father dedicating his son to the church or preparing him for a judicial career. But the broad mid-section of employers was formed by the service elite, part aristocratic and part bourgeois, that dominated the higher levels of the civil and ecclesiastical bureaucracies by virtue of its more or less privileged access to academic education. In the course of the eighteenth century, it became increasingly apparent that the aristocracy could not rely solely on "birth" in the strict sense – i.e., on pedigree – to maintain its grip on the highest offices of state; it would also have to demonstrate, at least to a minimal degree, academic competence. Hence for aristocratic scions, as for sons of the emerging

[8] Büsching, *Grundris*, p. 6.

[9] Some of the clergymen's sons in the sample from the *Allgemeines Magazin für Prediger* (cited hereafter as AMP) may simply have neglected to mention their instruction by tutors. For other examples of the employment of live-in tutors by clergymen, see Karl Friedrich Bahrdt, *Geschichte seines Lebens, seiner Meinungen und Schicksale, von ihm selbst geschrieben* (Frankfurt am Main, 1790), pp. 36–76; Friedrich Gottlieb Welcker, *Das Leben Friedrich Gottlieb Welcker's. Nach seinen eignen Aufzeichnungen und Briefen*, ed. Reinhard Kekulé (Leipzig, 1880), pp. 16–21. There are numerous examples of the different kinds of families employing tutors in the AMP sample, and in Fertig, *Hofmeister*, pp. 3–90. See also Wolfgang Neugebauer, *Absolutistischer Staat und Schulwirklichkeit in Brandenburg-Preussen*, Veröffentlichungen der Historischen Kommission zu Berlin, vol. 62 (Berlin and New York, 1985), pp. 601–13.

Bildungsbürgertum, university studies became an increasingly common preparation for office. This explains why tutors employed by the nobility were expected to provide instruction in the academic fundamentals, and especially in Latin, despite the traditional aristocratic disdain for the "pedantry" associated with that kind of learning.

This was another step in an adaptation, not a rejection, of the aristocratic tradition. Since the late seventeenth century, the ideal of the "gentleman" had been modernized to include a familiarity with "cosmopolitan" and "gallant" subjects like philosophy, history, natural science, and geography. The properly educated "man of the world" was to be distinguished from the narrow scholar as well as from the well-born boor; this kind of cultivation did not dispense the nobleman from mastering the elaborate etiquette for which Versailles had set the standard. The etiquette had a formalism of its own, quite different from the emphasis on stylistic elegance in the traditional learned culture. The point of the "exercises" (*Exerzitien*) in dancing, riding and perhaps fencing was not simply to introduce the pupil to these specific accomplishments; they also groomed him in the bodily grace and self-control needed to accord people of various ranks the proper measure of exaggerated respect or self-assured superiority, reserve or familiarity. While the inclusion of Latin in domestic instruction reflected the increasing importance of academic credentials, French was still the lingua franca of aristocratic society at the turn of the century. Without it the young nobleman could neither participate in courtly society nor explore the realms of "worldly" knowledge, including the fashionable literature of the French Enlightenment.[10]

While the aristocratic scion might remain at home, under the tutelage of a *Hofmeister*, until he was old enough to attend a university, bourgeois families tended to use tutoring to prepare their sons for the schools. And of course bourgeois expectations leaned more to the scholarly end of the spectrum, particularly among the state officials and clergymen for whom academic education and official careers had become the twin pillars of status. But one should not be misled by expressions of moral distaste for the parasitical decadence of court life, despite the apparent appeal of this sentiment to bourgeois readers of the "moral weeklies." When contemporaries referred to "polite society," they meant a sphere far less exclusive than "the world" in the strict sense, but one marking the diffusion of at least some elements of courtly culture in the eighteenth-century *Bürgertum*. Manners might be less elaborate, but a certain bodily grace was indispensable – and the bourgeois scion could acquire it with dancing lessons, if not with lessons in riding and fencing. Italian was dispensable; but for the wealthy merchant, facility in French was a cosmopolitan cultural credential as well as a useful

[10] On continuity and change in the aristocratic use of *Hofmeister*, see esp. Fertig, *Hofmeister*, pp. 31–56, 141–62.

business skill. The same accomplishments distinguished the son of a prominent university professor or ecclesiastical official from the son of an obscure pastor.

Some of the tutors came from this same bourgeois world. Sons of prosperous merchants and prominent officials (including clergymen), they turned to tutoring after the university not because they needed a way to survive financially, but because they wanted a hiatus between their studies and career responsibilities in which to advance their learning and, as important, to broaden their education with travel. In such cases, particularly if the tutor accompanied his charge to universities, tutoring made possible a kind of "tour," a combined sampling of university life and introduction to polite society, at once analogous to and distinct from the cavalier's tour.[11] Observers tended to ignore this type, however, because it was the exception to the rule. More typically the tutor – whether he was the son of a clergyman or from an uneducated family – had been a poor student. His employment represented an important social trade-off in eighteenth-century society, as education came to play a central role in structuring and reproducing the social hierarchy. For an increasing number of families, both noble and bourgeois, the use of a live-in tutor was not an alternative to the schools and universities, but one manifestation of privileged access to higher education and official careers. Wealthier noble families might seek an all-purpose tutor, part scholar, part courtier, as a matter of convenience, although at least some of them instead hired different instructors for different subjects. For their less affluent cousins, convenience shaded into necessity; only by finding an all-purpose tutor, and thus avoiding the bills that Rabener's aspiring tutor had itemized, could they groom their sons for their station *and* equip them to meet the educational requirements for official careers. Precisely because the labor was so cheap, this particular advantage also extended deep into the *Bürgertum*. Even the rural clergyman who was not particularly well off could afford to pay a needy theology graduate 40 or 50 thaler per year in addition to room and board. In fact Büsching noted that it might be cheaper for a rural family to bring a tutor into the home than to support a son at a Latin school in town.[12]

At the same time tutoring positions, including those with markedly low compensation, at least offered a means of survival until a clerical or teaching appointment materialized. In that limited but important sense, tutoring was a necessary way station on the poor student's climb into the lower ranks of the educated *Bürgertum*. Hence the trade-off: poor students could find

[11] See, e.g., AMP 9:1 (1794): 89–90 (Carl Friedrich Stäudlin); AMP 7:5 (1793): 577–83 (Johann Joachim Bellermann); AMP 3:4 (1790): 434–39 (Georg Christian Ehrhard Westphal); AMP 12:3 (1795): 93–103 (Johann Friedrich le Bret).

[12] Büsching, *Grundris*, p. 17.

employment as tutors on a large scale only because their cheap labor was instrumental in the formation and maintenance of a bourgeois-aristocratic service elite, intermingling in a variety of ways elements from the educational ideals of two distinct corporate cultures. What becomes abundantly clear from the complaints on both sides is that, for employers and tutors alike, the trade-off exacted a high price. Employers had to put up with tutors who were in fact incompetent in the very subjects in which a theology graduate was supposed to be qualified. Even sympathetic observers acknowledged that the typical tutor, precisely because he had been poor, was less likely to satisfy his employer's expectations with respect to learning than a young scholar from a more affluent family. Aside from lacking training in the new pedagogy, he was likely to have used his limited time at the university to master the *Brotstudium*, to the virtual exclusion of everything else. Though he might have had to use Latin for at least part of his course readings, his actual training in it, and in the literature that exemplified its standards of elegance, had ceased with his departure from a Latin school.[13]

The more serious problem was that at this juncture the young man, incubated in learned culture since childhood, had to enter the culture of polite society, perhaps in its aristocratic form. In retrospect some tutors were grateful for the broadening experience, the opportunity to escape the narrow confines of the *Gelehrtenstand*, if only temporarily, and learn the ways of "the world."[14] But the mounting complaints about tutoring leave no doubt that for poor students, who were especially unprepared, this transition tended to exacerbate the immediate problem of adjusting to "civilian" life after several years as an academic *Bürger*. By its nature their education, including their university studies, could not compensate sufficiently for the fact that their families had had, at best, peripheral contact with polite society.

The boorishness resulting from this handicap should not be exaggerated. What polite society found particularly objectionable about student life was the same devotion to drinking, brawling, and other forms of disreputable behavior, calculated to provoke the "philistines," that made the universities dens of iniquity in the eyes of Pietists and havens of sloth in the more secular but no less moralistic judgment of Enlightenment reformers. But in fact many poor students probably had limited contact with this student subculture, since they were not likely to have the time and money its amusements required. Only a select few, though, seem to have enjoyed the kind

[13]See esp. the excerpt from Carl Müller, *Schädlichkeit der Hauserziehung für Erzieher, Zögling, und Staat* (Stendal, 1783), in Fertig, *Hofmeister*, pp. 204–7; August Wilhelm Friedrich Crome, "Ueber die Erziehung der Hauslehrer," *Allgemeine Revision des gesammten Schul- und Erziehungswesens*, vol. 10 (Hamburg, 1788): 18–23.

[14] See, e.g., AMP 10:5 (1794): 108 (Förster); AMP 6 (1792): 423 (Hezel); AMP 6 (1792): 243 (Morus); AMP 4:2 (1790): 216–24 (Christian Wilhelm Oemler); AMP 2:4 (1790): 88–89 (Rosenmüller).

of contact with professors, particularly in the latters' homes, that could polish the rough edges off young men whose social awkwardness stood in sharp contrast to their scholarly accomplishments. Aside from professors' reluctance to spare the time (and perhaps to endanger their daughters), there were practical obstacles on the students' side. Many eighteenth-century poor students probably confined themselves to the same austere, isolated work routine that Reimmann and his two roommates had followed at Jena in the late 1680s. Lacking proper clothing and required to "marshall every penny if [they] were to get through honestly and wanted to pay [their] bills for a room, food, heat, light, and such things," they had not had the "boldness" to make themselves known to professors. If poverty kept such students from the worst excesses that occupied their *Kommilitonen*, it also prevented them from appearing respectably in "cultured" homes.[15]

The literature on tutoring abounds in descriptions, some from firsthand experience, of the resulting "coarseness" and awkwardness of the poor student-become-tutor. Aside from inadequacies of dress, the young man was not likely to have had either the opportunity or the means to acquire the "manners," including the requisite bodily grace, that special instruction in dancing and other "exercises" inculcated. He had acquired, at best, the bare minimum in linguistic credentials. Claus Harms, who had kept his distance from professors and had had "absolutely no contact with families" as a student at Kiel, recalled his initial difficulties with everyday conversation in High German when he became the tutor to a rural pastor's children. At first he could only speak "book German" or resort to a student patois.[16] Harms adapted quite successfully, but for others, particularly in aristocratic households, the more imposing hurdle was French. Unlike the tutor's use of Latin, which was restricted to scholarly learning and usually to written communication, command of French meant the ability to use it as an everyday language of sociability. While elegance in Latin involved mastery of the stylistic intricacies of poetry and prose, fine distinctions and nuances in the spoken word – in pronunciation, forms of address, the use of *Complimenten* – distinguished an inbred facility in French from the telltale blunders of the interloper. In 1725 Johann Christian Edelmann was chosen to tutor the children of an Austrian family because he had managed to pick up a bit of French at Jena. He recalled his sense of impending doom as he traveled toward his assignment and became aware that the innkeepers and house servants were "incomparably more skilled and elegant" in the language than he was. Fortunately the parents were away when he arrived, and in two weeks he was able to learn enough French from his pupil so that he "did not have to be particularly ashamed to converse with them when they re-

[15] Jacob Friedrich Reimmann, *Eigene Lebens-Beschreibung; Oder, Historische Nachricht von Sich Selbst*, ed. Friedrich Heinrich Theunen (Brunswick, 1745), pp. 25–26.

[16] Claus Harms, *Lebensbeschreibung* (Kiel, 1851), pp. 57, 75–76.

turned."[17] Here is Carl Müller's assessment of the state of affairs more than fifty years later:

> Theology candidates have no command of French; they do not have the wealth that the complete mastery of this language requires, and I would have doubts about any young man whose prospects and wishes usually extend no farther than to a poor village pastorate if he were to purchase a French grammar for 12 groschen. Of what use is it to him in his small sphere? Usually they do not get far in learning the language; they make themselves laughable to those skilled in languages among their social superiors, and they lose a considerable portion of their time and means, which they could have more usefully applied to something else, more in accord with their future interests. But most take up the language a bit at the university, because they hear there that it is required in tutoring. You can imagine what kind of French instruction they give to the children of their *Herr Patronen*.[18]

The problem facing parents, then, was that cheap labor involved a built-in disadvantage, if not an outright contradiction. As observers on both sides pointed out repeatedly, it was absurd to expect the typical tutor, fresh from the university, to groom a boy in social accomplishments with which he himself had little, if any, familiarity. The absurdity was not limited to households with ancient pedigrees and great wealth. In his handbook on tutoring, August Hermann Niemeyer, a great nephew of August Hermann Francke and his successor as director of the Halle endowments, offered words of assurance to the young man who had been born in a "sphere where finer manners are [not] to be found" and who was "perhaps the only member of his family to distinguish himself with intellectual culture [*Geistescultur*]." It was not impossible to measure up to expectations in the "most restricted family circles" of "educated men of the learned estate." Perhaps thinking of his own clerical dynasty, Niemeyer employed a standard contrast between a certain moderation, associated with bourgeois domestic privacy, and the public display of aristocratic society. More "truly polished manners and genuine courtliness" were to be found in such bourgeois circles, he claimed, than in the "ostentatious society" (*Prunkgesellschaften*) of "the great world." Yet even in this modest environment the tutor needed, among other things, the habit of avoiding behavior that might be "displeasing" or simply "too noticeable"; a "natural respectability, a skilled bodily carriage, a certain noble self-awareness . . . from the awareness of having learned something and having nothing contemptible in one's character"; and enough "self-knowledge" to realize that one "still had much to learn."[19] Though meant

[17] Johann Christian Edelmann, *Selbstbiographie*, ed. Bernd Neumann, Deutsche Autobiographie. Dokumente zum bürgerlichen oppositionellen Selbstbewusstsein von der Aufklärung bis zur Revolution 1848, vol. 1 (Stuttgart, 1976), pp. 53–69.

[18] Fertig, *Hofmeister*, p. 206.

[19] August Hermann Niemeyer, *Grundsätze der Erziehung und des Unterrichts für Eltern, Hauslehrer, und Erzieher*, ed. Hans-Hermann Groothoff and Ulrich Herrmann (1796: Paderborn, 1970), pp. 50–53, 303.

to emphasize individual traits acquired through education, and not ascriptive advantages, the list underscores the difficulties of adaptation the poor student faced even in households of the educated *Bürgertum*.

But it was above all the chemistry in aristocratic households that made tutoring an important catalyst in the broader eighteenth-century process of defining and asserting a bourgeois consciousness. In the testimony of tutors in the second half of the century, that process can be observed gaining ideological momentum over several generations. In 1748, following his studies at Halle, Büsching had become the tutor to the eldest son of Friedrich Rochus Graf zu Lynau in the Vogtland. He had had little contact with other students at Halle, Büsching later recalled, but his "fortunate access to people of station of both sexes" had prepared him to profit from his new environment as "a school in which one could learn something new every day."[20] To judge by the handbook for tutors he published in 1760, Büsching's success was due at least in part to his willingness to render the proper kind and degree of deference to social superiors. His description of the ideal tutor leaned heavily toward the virtues of humility, patience, and "submissiveness" (*Unterwürfigkeit*).

But Büsching also advised the tutor to maintain a cautious via media. He must avoid "making a greater impression in dress" than was proper to a man of his station, but must always take pains to dress "cleanly" and "respectably." Though he should not presume an air of intimacy with his employers, he should also be careful not to degrade himself by becoming familiar with the servants. There was a pedagogical rationale behind this strategy of commanding respect while demonstrating acceptance of a subordinate household position and the social inferiority it bespoke. Büsching hoped that, by his example and the pedagogical authority his position of respect would ensure, the tutor might quietly counteract the unfortunate aspects of aristocratic culture with a dose of piety, devotion to work, moderation, and other solid bourgeois virtues.[21]

In 1774 Büsching found a tutoring position in the household of Herr von Holzendorf for his nephew and later son-in-law August Friedrich Wilhelm Crome. The son of a pastor, Crome was forced to this step by lack of means, after only two years at Halle. In his autobiography he recalled that he entered "the meandering track of the tutor's life" woefully unprepared to "adapt [himself] to the way of life and mentality of a strange family from the higher orders," but nonetheless soon won his employer's "respect" and "trust."[22] In a long article, published in an educational reform journal

20 Anton Friedrich Büsching, *Eigene Lebensgeschichte* (Halle, 1789), pp. 102, 107–26.
21 Büsching, *Grundris*, esp. pp. 29–36, 45–46, 59–65, 93–94.
22 August Friedrich Wilhelm Crome, *Selbstbiographie* (Stuttgart, 1833), pp. 39–40.

in 1788, Crome drew on his acquaintance with the less fortunate circumstances of others (and probably on the darker hours in his own eight years of experience as well) to sketch a grim picture of the tutor's lot. Like Büsching, he entertained hopes of inculcating bourgeois virtue, if the pupils had not already been "corrupted" by exposure to the "sensual pleasure and follies of the great world." But where Büsching implicitly acknowledged a conflict, Crome saw an obvious clash between aristocratic and bourgeois culture. And while Büsching hoped for quiet victories, his nephew's warning was that the tutor could not afford to engage in battle; his dependent position made him virtually powerless to change "the givens" in the "character of the parents" and the "tone of the household." The tutor, to be sure, could to a degree compensate for his lack of "exterior" power by demonstrating "true inner qualities of understanding and the heart" – but only if he exercised strict self-control in not revealing his "disapproval" of, and "aversion," to the "givens." In view of the helplessness of most tutors and the fact that social pressure often prevented parents with the best intentions from treating them with the proper respect, state intervention offered the only hope for significant improvement.[23]

It was Crome's counsel of "compliance" and "self-control" that provoked another tutor into print in 1789. "It is almost as though Herr Cr. accepted for the tutor the relationship of the serf to the lord," this anonymous contributor protested, and that only encourages "the great crowd of nobles . . . who are known to already regard any commoner [*Bürgerlichen*] as a born subject." While the author acknowledged that "fine manners" and "an educated taste" were incompatible with "the uninhibited student tone," his essay dripped with reverse snobbery toward aristocratic culture. He saw it as the duty of the pedagogue to "rescue" his pupils from its "corrupting" embrace. Upon assuming his duties he had found two "extremely weak boys who lived and moved in etiquette, welcomed me with courtly compliments, and affected a composed manner, as though they were nearly thirty years old." He was particularly contemptuous of the courtly equation of "exterior respectability" with "the activity and movement of the body, as the dancing master has put them through their turns in the minuet" and with "a measured stiffness that requires affected bendings of bodily parts for giving and taking, saying yes and no." In a little more than three years, if he can be believed, his unbending determination had prevailed over the parents' "deeply rooted prejudice," although he feared that it had already been too late for the older boy. His alternative, it should be noted, had not been to intensify the boys' "literary training," which he also dismissed as premature and hence "unnatural"; instead he subjected them to an en-

[23] Crome, "Erziehung der Hauslehrer," esp. pp. 23–33, 48–59, 75–78, 98–103, 123–30.

tirely new regimen, involving rigorous physical exercise and disciplined curiosity about the natural world around them.[24]

Büsching was an early leader in school reform, and in fact his handbook begins with an effort to persuade wealthy families of the advantages of public schools over private tutors. But by the end of the century the handbook, despite its muted disapproval of aristocratic excesses, was being dismissed by the younger generation as too accommodationist. In the response to Crome's essay, the aristocratic etiquette that had long set the standards for polite society has become decadent, artificial. Its bodily poise and self-control – the courtly manner against which the awkwardness of the poor student had traditionally been gauged – is now seen as empty formalism, stifling natural expression. The pedagogical alternative is evoked in a distinctly ideological idyll, with an enlightened pedagogue, by virtue of his moral superiority, reversing the traditional power relationship between aristocratic employer and bourgeois tutor. Whether the author was as victorious as he claimed is beside the point; he offers a striking example of the bourgeois domestication of Rousseau's "natural" pedagogy in the German Enlightenment and demonstrates its tendency to counter the longstanding hegemony of aristocratic culture by claiming universal validity for its own norms.

But among poor students in the closing decades of the century this ideological posture coexisted with, and indeed may have become a measure of, continuing social anxiety in the face of aristocratic standards, particularly in the immediate household context in which the tutor confronted them. There is no more revealing testimony of the mix of defiance and anxiety than Johann Gottlieb Fichte's correspondence from the early 1790s. After completing his studies at Leipzig, Fichte survived for nearly a decade as a tutor in various households in Saxony, Switzerland, Warsaw, and West Prussia. The diary he kept as a tutor for Herr Ott, the owner of an inn (*Gasthof*) in Zürich, reveals a young man who, like Crome's respondent, pits modern pedagogy against the prejudices of his employer; but Fichte also sees it as part of his mission to improve the tone of a bourgeois household with some of the aristocratic refinement he has acquired. The latter approach can at least be inferred from one of the grievances that the son, probably echoing his mother, lodges; "my rules at table are so affected," Fichte records the

[24] "Einige Bemerkungen zu der Cromischen Abhandlung: Ueber die Erziehung durch Hauslehrer, im 10ten Theil des Revisionwerks, von einem Hauslehrer," *Braunschweigisches Journal* 1:4 (Apr. 1789): 432–57. See also Fertig, *Hofmeister*, pp. 68–74. The response to Crome's essay can also be usefully compared with Johann Kaspar Velthusen, "Antwort eines Hofmeisters auf einige Briefe seines Freundes, die Beschäftigungen der Kinder in und ausser der Lehrstunden betreffend," *Hannöverisches Magazin* 4:8 (1766): 114–27 and 4:9 (1766): 130–35. Velthusen leaves the impression that in his efforts to apply the new pedagogy he enjoyed the full cooperation of his employer, an *Amtmann* near Bremen. But Velthusen was the son of a prominent merchant, and he subsequently married the *Amtmann*'s daughter.

boy as complaining, that one would think "a count or baron," and not "free Swiss," was being educated.[25]

Fichte's battles with Frau Ott make all the more striking his reaction to the challenge of his next position – the one in Warsaw. In the first audience, his new employer, Countess von Plater, was obviously disappointed to learn that he was not fluent in French, the language of the household. He would never have resolved to make the trip from Leipzig, Fichte protested in a letter of explanation, "if anything beyond Latin, history, geography, mathematics, and the mediocre knowledge of the French language that men of letters in my country possess had been demanded of me." Rather than apologize for his French, he stood on his "merits" as a scholar "who had seen enough of the great world to know its dangers but not enough to have acquired its mores" and "who has preferred for a long time to know some disciplines in depth than to know many superficially." Despite the countess's readiness to work out an accommodation, either in her own household or with another employer in the area, he preferred "to depart for [his] fatherland or another land where thoroughness [*Gründlichkeit*] and German are still valued."[26]

By 1794 Fichte had secured a university appointment at Jena and was finally beginning to settle into an academic career. His brother Gotthelf, who was still living at home, wanted to follow in his footsteps. Fichte agreed to sponsor him, but insisted that before joining him in Jena Gotthelf "develop [his] body and his manners" so that he "could appear in society without offense."[27] In a letter meant to impress on Gotthelf the difficulties this "trial" would entail, Fichte moved from the specific problem of mastering "the learned languages" at a relatively late age to a fascinating glance back at his own ascent:

> . . . you have still another disadvantage [in learning French] that others do not have, since your native dialect is the corrupt Saxon and, what is worse, the extremely corrupt Saxon of the Ober-Lausitz. I myself, though I left the region in early childhood, have had trouble purifying even my German speech so that my native land is no longer detected; you will never do that. And I have never been able to speak French well. . . . Another critical point is that the polite behavior of the great world is already necessary, and will become increasingly necessary, for the learned man who wants to belong to the higher class rather than remaining among the common learned *Handwerker*. Since the learned estate is beginning to raise itself to an ever higher rank, and before you enter it this phenomenon will advance much farther. Whoever is lacking on this score will be made laughable, precisely because the

25 Hans Schulz, *Johann Gottlieb Fichte als Hauslehrer*, Pädagogisches Magazin, Heft 709 (Langensalza, 1919), esp. p. 33.

26 Fichte to Katharina von Plater, June 10, 1791, in Johann Gottlieb Fichte, *Briefwechsel 1775–93*, Gesamtausgabe der Bayerischen Akademie der Wissenschaften, III, 1: 227–28; Fichte to Dewitz, June 12, 1791, in ibid., p. 232.

27 Gesamtausgabe, III, 2: 150–53.

excessive power of the learned is regarded adversely. . . . Such polished behavior is not learned in the later years, since the effects of early education are ineradicable. (Perhaps mine are no longer noticeable; but that is due to my very early life in the Miltitz house, my life in Schulpforta, among mostly better-raised children, my early learning of dancing, etc. And yet even after my departure from the university, I still had some "peasant" manners, which have only been eradicated by many travels, by much tutoring in various lands and houses, and especially by my great attention to myself. And yet, do I know whether they have been completely eradicated? –)[28]

There is no contradiction between the self-doubt that surfaces in this passage and Fichte's earlier defiant rejection of aristocratic standards. His underlying self-assurance lay in the certitude that, despite his background, he represented a new breed of "thorough" German scholars. Having begun with the problem of mastering "the learned languages," he made no mention of Latin. The former pupil at Schulpforta was now confident of his superiority to "common learned *Handwerker*"; he had come to regard the Latinity in which he had been groomed as the vestigial stigma of caste inferiority. If politesse was a necessary accompaniment of the new learning, courtly manners were not; Fichte was pointing to the formation of a new social elite – one into which a new learned estate, emancipated from its corporate ghetto, would be assimilated without being required to display the superficiality embodied in a French-speaking Polish countess. Tutoring had not simply helped qualify Fichte for such an elite; it had also reinforced the insecurity that made this alternative vision of "the great world" so appealing. He knew firsthand that, for the poor student, leaving academic culture to meet the standards of "the world" as a tutor was still a traumatic experience.

PATRONS AND MARKETS

Why did tutoring come to represent in concentrated form the insecurities and humiliations of academic mobility? Only part of the answer lies in the sensitive position the institution occupied in the cultural field of tensions formed by learned and aristocratic traditions. For the rest, it becomes necessary to locate tutoring on the patronage chain that led from obscure origins to clerical careers and to examine the convergence of three factors – class distance, household membership, and the employment market – that made it an especially problematic link.

In 1725 Edelmann, already thirty years old, was "driven" from a tutoring position in Austria in which he had spent three very pleasant years by the "unthinking desire to become a pastor" and the realization that his present employer could not be of any help.[29] The practical reality he faced explains

[28] Ibid., p. 151.
[29] Edelmann, *Selbstbiographie*, pp. 86–87.

why tutoring was largely the preserve of theology students and why it meant another stage of "dependence" for most of its recruits. While such employment would have required a detour from the standard career track for students of law and medicine, the director of the pedagogical institute in Halle explained to Minister von Zedlitz in 1781, it was attractive to the theology student precisely because "so many positions are the most direct route to a pastorate."[30] Aside from providing a means of survival after university studies, the employer could offer a young man in pursuit of a clerical appointment the family connections he lacked by birth.

The likelihood of this kind of patronage clearly was one of the criteria by which students distinguished among more or less attractive positions. Indeed Niemeyer admitted "secure prospects for an earlier or later promotion" as a "conditionally valid" reason for taking a position, so long as the prospects did not "have to be purchased with demeaning conditions, for example a pitiful salary, or even more scandalous promises."[31] Niemeyer was thinking primarily of aristocratic houses, whose role in filling clerical vacancies, particularly in the countryside, ranged from the right of appointment to indirect influence by way of relatives and friends. But the clergymen who hired tutors could also be distinguished in this regard. Carl Friedrich Bahrdt recalled that in the early years the tutoring position in his home attracted only sorry specimens; but the caliber of tutors improved as his father, a pastor in Leipzig, "accumulated enough credit, by virtue of the well-known regard in which he was held by the magistracy and at court, so that he was in a position to help in the promotion of a young man."[32]

It was this dependence on the employer's patronage that Lenz satirized in the opening scene of act 2 of *Der Hofmeister*. Privy Councillor von Berg (the major's brother) has just rebuked Pastor Läuffer for allowing his son to encourage the nobility to "regard their tutors as domestic servants." When Läuffer objects that a university graduate, while waiting for "the divine call," must have "a vantage point from which to spy out some public office" and that "a patron is very often the means to his preferment," the councilor retorts:

> There never was a nobleman took on a tutor without showing him the fair prospect of preferment beyond an avenue of eight or nine years' servitude, and when you've gone your eight years he did like Laban and pushed the prospect back as far again. Fiddlesticks! Learn your trade and be honest men. The state will not leave you standing long in the marketplace.[33]

30 Christian Gottfried Schütz, *Geschichte des Erziehungsinstituts bei dem theol. Seminariums zu Halle* (Jena, 1781).

31 Niemeyer, *Grundsätze*, p. 300.

32 Bahrdt, *Geschichte seines Lebens*, pp. 55–56.

33 Lenz, *Werke und Schriften*, 2: 27–31. At the close of the scene Läuffer hands von Berg a letter from his son, explaining that "the prospects of a blissful future to compensate for all the tribulations of [his] present condition" prevent him from quitting. On the promise of

There is also a positive side to the story, ignored in satire but gratefully acknowledged in many clerical autobiographies. Particularly for the young man of obscure origins, the patronage of the prominent "house" in which he was employed, or of its relations or friends, could indeed open a door to the clergy that might otherwise have remained shut – and could continue well beyond the initial appointment. As the tutor for a young nobleman, Johann Joachim Spalding, the son of a village pastor in Pomerania, became acquainted with a Herr von Bohlen, who made him a welcome guest on his estate and became "one of the principal causes of [his] temporal happiness and [his] advancement."[34] Johann Georg Rosenmüller, the son of a towel maker and village schoolmaster, was helped to his first pastorate by Privy Councilor von Lindeboom, the employer in his third tutoring position. From his vantage point as a professor and superintendent in Leipzig, Rosenmüller noted that he "had many proofs of [the Lindeboom house's] favorable disposition toward him not only then, but in the present."[35]

The glow of success was not the only reason that this kind of patronage took on a positive coloration, at least in retrospect. It was inherent in tutoring that the client was also a dependent member of the household, and hence the institution was an especially appropriate locus for the ideology of paternalism sanctioning patron-client relationships at all levels. When Büsching visited a friend who was tutoring two young noblemen, the father, favorably impressed and eager to secure his future services as a tutor, told him that "although [Büsching's] parents were still alive, he wished to be [his] guardian."[36] Here paternalism took the form of noblesse oblige; but in bourgeois households the live-in tutor could also be the object of paternal benevolence. In fact Niemeyer felt that parents were more likely to be "fatherly" toward the tutor "in the middle estate, in more quiet family circles, in the countryside, or in smaller towns" than in "very large houses."[37]

In both noble and bourgeois households, the employer's power as patron could be legitimated by his exercise of authority as *Hausvater*. But there were also reasons that the family's relationship to its tutor could make a mockery of the paternal ideal. Patronage meant personal sponsorship on the basis of personal knowledge, but even at earlier stages of academic mobility it was sometimes paradoxically impersonal. At the level of tutoring, the patronage networks that carried poor boys through the schools and universities interlaced with networks distributing graduates in employment

preferment, see also Martin Duns Scotus, "Fürschlag, einen Informator recht zu gebrauchen," *Der Hofmeister* 3:23 (1753): 181.

[34] Johann Joachim Spalding, *Lebensbeschreibung*, ed. Georg Ludewig Spalding (Halle, 1804), pp. 18–19.

[35] AMP 2:4 (1790): 85–90. For other examples see footnote 14.

[36] Büsching, *Lebensgeschichte*, pp. 88–89.

[37] Niemeyer, *Grundsätze*, p. 303.

markets. The tutor came into contact with relatives and friends of his employer – people already predisposed to him by the family connection, to be sure, but otherwise virtual strangers – who could suddenly launch his career. This is Carl Friedrich Bahrdt's explanation for his father's meteoric career, despite his lack of the qualities needed to be "a great scholar" and to "display himself in brilliant offices." Following his poverty-stricken student years at Wittenberg and Leipzig, the father became a tutor in the household of Count Fleming. Quite unintentionally, thanks to an impromptu speech at a family wedding, he won the favor of Count von Hohendorf, the president of the High Consistory in Dresden. He was "nearly chased from one position to another" by this new and very powerful patron, until he became a pastor, professor, and superintendent in Leipzig.[38]

The problem lay in the matching of tutors and families, where a much greater element of impersonality made for fiascos as well as happy combinations. While the market for clerical employment tended to be regional, there was an international market for aspiring tutors from central Germany, extending to Switzerland in the west and Austria, Poland, and even Russia in the east. It was not uncommon for the tutoring position, even if it was not in one of these far-off lands, to be at a considerable distance from the student's university. Some professors – including Francke at Halle, Gellert at Leipzig, and Niemeyer – were particularly well known and widely used mediators between parents and aspiring tutors, and many others performed the same service on a smaller scale.[39] These "brokers" often acted on behalf of relatives and friends, and when possible they recommended favorites with whom they were closely acquainted. But many aspiring tutors, particularly among the poorer students, had minimal contact with professors. In any case the sheer scale of the tutoring market meant that mediators often lacked firsthand knowledge of at least one of the parties.

In 1725 a Professor Beck at Jena was asked to find someone for a position on an estate in distant Austria. He gave the nod to Edelmann, whom he did not know, on the strength of a recommendation from the language instructor with whom Edelmann had lodged and a brief *Testimonium* about his academic diligence and "honest life" from another professor.[40] This proved a mutually satisfactory match; but more than sixty years later Karl Traugott Thieme explained why "it will always remain a true accident if a family and tutor come together and through the union of both parties their economic and moral needs are satisfied":

> How many tutoring positions in Germany and in other lands bordering on Germany are not filled merely with a recommendation? People turn to a professor at a university, who is named to someone. The chosen one is sent travel money and made

[38] Bahrdt, *Geschichte seines Lebens*, pp. 11–20.
[39] On "tutoring brokers" (*Hofmeistermakler*), see esp. Fertig, *Hofmeister*, pp. 60–62.
[40] Edelmann, *Selbstbiographie*, p. 53.

to come. And now, after the contract is concluded and its fulfillment has begun, the wares are inspected for the first time. The insight and probity of the author of the recommendation does not ensure a happy result in such a process, since it is not possible for a professor, and for any other scholar who in addition is not himself an educator, to get to know all the wrinkles [*Falten*] of all the people who want to be supported by him in one or two ceremonial visits – wrinkles that develop only in daily and familiar contact. I myself was once sent to a noble house by such a Maecenas, who had seen me only once in his entire life, when I relayed a letter to him. I am in the best position to know how it worked out.[41]

Often enough, particularly when the position was a distant one, parents literally met for the first time the young man who was to reside with them and instruct their children when he arrived to assume his duties. What determined the resulting chemistry was not simply the newcomer's relationship with the father. As a household resident, entrusted with the children's education, the tutor necessarily was in a delicate, potentially volatile relationship with the entire family. It was above all the sensitivity of this position that led Büsching and Niemeyer to conceive of the household as a mine field in which the newly arrived tutor would have to find his bearings and plot his course with great caution. Ideally the tutor assumed his proper place in the hierarchy over which a patriarch presided; in fact he might find himself caught in the crossfire between a strict but distant father and an indulgent mother, constantly working behind the scenes to soften the paternal regimen. Or as in Lenz's *Der Hofmeister*, he might have to cope with a mother's blindness to her son's faults and a father's preference for his daughter. It is not surprising that, in discussions of the dangers lurking within households, mothers figure prominently; they tended to be sticklers on the points of etiquette in which tutors were found wanting, but at the same time they were less educated than their husbands and hence less likely to appreciate the tutor's learning and pedagogical expertise. And as Fichte's diary graphically records, for the mother determined to make life impossible for a tutor, the children were a very handy weapon.[42]

Given the sheer variety of domestic circumstances, tutoring positions resist a simple classification by the class origins of the employees and the wealth or status of the employers. It was not uncommon for a former tutor who had occupied two or more positions to recall markedly different experiences, attributable more to specific characteristics of each family's domestic life (or lack of it) than to differences in their social ranks. But this

[41] M. Karl Traugott Thieme, "Ueber das Verhältnis zwischen Eltern und Privatlehrern," *Braunschweigisches Journal* 3:9 (Sept. 1789): 18–21. If things worked out badly, Thieme noted, the young man could move on and had only lost a little time. He ignored the possibility that an aspiring clergyman had lost an opportunity for sponsorship.

[42] Büsching, *Grundris*, esp. pp. 55–58; Niemeyer, *Grundsätze*, esp. pp. 307–10; Schulz, *Fichte als Hauslehrer*. See also the warnings about mothers in Crome, "Erziehung der Hauslehrer," pp. 142–43, and by Müller in Fertig, *Hofmeister*, p. 209.

variety in itself helps explain why tutoring was a particularly hazardous venture for the poor student. The very fact that a particular family constellation, aside from its importance in making a position "pleasant" or intolerable, could become critical for his later career prospects was a measure of his extreme dependence on social superiors.

If observers were struck by the myriad possibilities, they also emphasized that poor students were the most likely victims of a tendency to carry the terms of dependence and deference beyond their proper limits. "The *Hausvater*," Thieme explained, "believes that it is part of the duty of a subordinate [*Subaltern*] to adapt himself to the whims of those on whom he depends, to make no demands contradicting the circumstances in which he finds himself, but instead to accept in modesty or humility the degree of respect that it is considered proper to bestow on him."[43] In its extreme application, this belief reduced the tutor literally to one more domestic servant. Even this kind of treatment could seem logical enough from the parents' standpoint. Since the tutor was a live-in employee, compensated with money as well as with room and board, his position was quite comparable with that of servants. A certain respect for the tutor's learning might nonetheless prevent parents from reducing him to that level; but counterbalancing such respect might be contempt for his family origins, particularly if his learning was not accompanied by social graces, and the considerable license allowed employers in dealing with a young man dependent on their patronage to secure his future.

These were the circumstances in which tutors exhibited the kinds of behavior that seemed to confirm stereotypes of the poor student. If Crome and other critics are to be believed, the most common reaction was a "fawning subservience," a willingness to please, even to the point of accepting the degradation of "domestic" status, far beyond the deference an educated man owed the parents of his pupils. In such behavior the tutor's past and future – his heightened awareness of plebeian origins when confronted with the standards of polite society, and his urgent need to win the approval of potential sponsors – reinforced each other. On the other hand, it is not surprising that some tutors invited the charge of presumption, if not arrogance, because they were too eager to bridge the class difference with an air of familiarity or were too quick to react against any imagined slight. "The tutor," Thieme explained, "believes that he can rightly demand to be treated with special discretion as a learned man and as a person of importance for the welfare of the family."[44] Even if he did not arrive with a lofty notion of his pedagogical mission, he could stand on his dignity as a "learned man," particularly if his employer was a pretentious but ignorant *Landjunker*

[43] Thieme, "Ueber das Verhältnis," p. 28.

[44] Ibid. See also Crome, "Erziehung der Hauslehrer," esp. pp. 42–43; Müller's remarks on "domestic relations between tutors and their patrons," in Fertig, *Hofmeister*, pp. 207–11.

or, as in Fichte's Swiss experience, a commercial *Bürger*. Whether the reaction was servility or touchy pride, the difficulties of adjustment were heightened by the fact that an academic *Bürger*, who often had had little or no contact with family life, suddenly had to exchange his "freedom" for subordination within a household.

How could the tutor distinguish the real from the imaginary slights that his subordination entailed? Years later Wilhelm Harnisch acknowledged that his employer, a Frau von Waldow, must have had reason at first to be impatient with his "student coarseness" and "lack of higher, finer social education." But Harnisch also recalled the stings of her snobbery. His "otherwise good room" had "very poor furnishings," and on their frequent outings she required him to sit beside the coachman. He felt constrained to "give notice" when a friend on an overnight visit was assigned to a servant's bed.[45] The tutor's assigned status was clear enough when he had to eat with the servants or was never included in social events, or when he was actually expected to deliver messages and perform other menial tasks. But there were other details, not quite in the same category, that might or might not require an indignant response. Surely tutors instructing scions of great houses should not be expected to address them with ceremonial titles, as was sometimes required. But how could the instructor acknowledge his pupils' vastly superior social status without damaging the respect and authority he needed to teach them? Should the tutor have to sleep in the same room with his charges, or should he insist on separate quarters? If he did dine with the parents and their guests, how should he regard the request that he do the carving?[46]

As the interchangeable use of *Hausvater* and *Prinzipal* indicated, the tutor was both subordinate to a head of household and in a relationship of market exchange with an employer. The imbalance of the latter relationship was the most common explanation given for his extreme dependence and vulnerability, and with good reason. The immediate market situation sometimes allowed a prospective employee to bargain for better terms; but in general employers were in a position to require a great deal and offer petty compensation and to exploit the situation in other ways. They were at the right end of a supply-demand ratio *and* could offer their support at the next stage, in the employment market for aspiring clergymen.

Yet this does not suffice to explain the great variety in tutors' cash compensations or in the living and working conditions they faced.[47] The point is that household and market combined in different ways. While some em-

45 Wilhelm Harnisch, *Mein Lebensmorgen* (Berlin, 1865), pp. 144–53.

46 See esp. Crome, "Erziehung der Hauslehrer," p. 66.

47 For the variety of cash compensations and other arrangements, see, e.g., Harnisch, *Lebensmorgen*, p. 144; Büsching, *Lebensgeschichte*, pp. 107–8; Harms, *Lebensbeschreibung*, pp. 74–77; Paul Luchtenberg, *Johannes Löh und die Aufklärung im Bergischen* (Cologne and Opladen, 1965), p. 35.

ployers clearly exploited the buyers' market to pay the bare minimum, others demonstrated paternal benevolence by paying more than the market required. Ideally the tutor need not hesitate to accept a position on the basis of an informal agreement or a contract leaving much to be filled in later; he could rely on the *Hausvater*'s sense of justice and responsibility toward an educated young man making a vital contribution to his household. In reality, the informality of household authority was a boon or a trap. Once he came to be regarded as "an older son of the house," Claus Harms recalled, he was more than willing to forget his contracted salary and "live out of the pocket" of his pastor-employer, "generously or sparingly as circumstances allowed."[48] But to judge by the warnings in handbooks, Lenz dramatized a literal problem as well as a symbolic dilemma when he had Läuffer's employers relentlessly whittle down the salary he had been promised verbally. When specific duties had not been spelled out (and they often were not), the responsible pater familias would avoid overburdening a young man who was receiving modest compensation and needed time to continue his studies and prepare for his qualifying examination. But aside from the extreme case of being assigned domestics' tasks, it was a frequent complaint that the use of tutors as "children watchers" at home and on outings, beyond the hours devoted to instruction, left them little time for themselves.[49]

If the employer could exercise his paternal authority in ways that held his market power in check, he could also use that authority to exploit the tutor's market vulnerability. The complexity of this situation explains why suggestions for improving the tutor's lot tended to oscillate between two alternatives, without fully embracing either one. On the one hand, employers were urged to accept the tutor as a young but knowledgeable "friend" of the family, and prospective tutors were advised on how to develop the qualities of character needed to achieve that status. The term "friend" evoked a degree of equality and trust vis-à-vis the parents, and particularly the father, that not only lifted the tutor out of market dependence, but also detached him unquestionably from the domestic help. But tutors also were advised to secure formal, preferably written contracts, stipulating the cash salary and other forms of compensation, the subjects of instruction, and other rights and obligations, *before* taking a position.[50] That

[48] Harms, *Lebensbeschreibung*, p. 76. The conflict between the tutors' market exploitation and the paternalism of the household context is emphasized in Fertig, *Hofmeister*, pp. 94–95. "In view of the market situation," Fertig observes, "the claim that they [the tutors] were contained within the 'entire household' ['*ganzen Hause*'] became mere ideology."

[49] Martin Duns Scotus, "Fürschlag"; Büsching, *Grundris*, pp. 50–52, 103–6; Niemeyer, *Grundsätze*, pp. 57–72; Crome, "Erziehung der Hauslehrer," pp. 92–93, 134–35; Müller's complaints, in Fertig, *Hofmeister*, p. 214.

[50] See, e.g., Niemeyer, *Grundsätze*, esp. pp. 300–4; Crome, "Erziehung der Hauslehrer," passim; Thieme, "Ueber das Verhältnis," passim.

solution held the danger of enclosing the tutor entirely within a market exchange, with no place for paternal benevolence; its advantage lay in inhibiting paternal authority from making the tutor's market vulnerability all the worse.

As Lenz's satirical blade slashes through the reigning platitudes in *Der Hofmeister*, the market vulnerability of tutors becomes only one dimension of their exploitation, and paternalist ideology seems hardly worth dismissing. But the play also registers the ambivalence of the exploited. Läuffer is alternately the creature of a privileged establishment and the victim of his own pretensions and lack of integrity. Lenz does not ask the audience to choose between social injustice and individual culpability; he is content to expose the tutoring syndrome in all its absurdity. At the outset Councilor von Berg, the voice of good sense, is confident that "the state" can find appropriate employment for truly useful young men and that public schools will be an effective antidote to the aristocratic arrogance that tutoring perpetuates.[51] But the ensuing plot is anything but a realization of this enlightened reform agenda. When Läuffer finds a salvation of sorts as an apprentice to Wenzeslaus, the local village schoolmaster, it is by emulating an ascetic ideal that is at once heroic and ridiculous.

Läuffer had taken refuge with the schoolmaster after getting his employer's beloved daughter pregnant. With this twist in the story Lenz introduces an inspired caricature, affectionate yet biting. Relegated to the bottom edge of the *Gelehrtenstand*, Wenzeslaus embodies its anachronistic corporate dignity and underscores its marginality. Where Läuffer's learning is largely counterfeit, Wenzeslaus is a pedant of the old school, sprinkling his conversation with Latin and Greek phrases as well as biblical references. Unlike the young miscreant, who fancies himself a man of the world, his new mentor has never questioned the clerical identity of his caste. Läuffer has aped the decadence of "the world" by becoming a libertine (of sorts) as well as a fop; Wenzeslaus has had to remain celibate, and has silenced the stirrings of the flesh with a regimen of sausage and water, pipe smoking, and brisk walks in the fields. The older man finds his "reward" – his solid contentment – in his "good conscience"; his example provokes Läuffer to see himself for what he is, "a slave in a braided coat."[52] Where Läuffer cringes before his social superiors, Wenzeslaus confronts them as a moral equal and insists that they respect the sanctity of his home.

The caricature is complete when Läuffer, overcome with remorse and inspired by his mentor's celibacy, castrates himself. Wenzeslaus is overjoyed; he hails his apprentice as a "second Origen," a "most chosen instru-

[51] Lenz, *Werke und Schriften*, 2: 24–31.
[52] Ibid., p. 57.

ment," and confesses that he would not hesitate to do the same "were [he] not already beyond the years when the Devil lays his subtle snares for our first and best powers."[53]

Lenz's genius defies reduction to ponderous sociological statements; as a social observer he achieves his most incisive ironies when the comedy becomes most farcical. Läuffer aspires to be a "reborn" Wenzeslaus, but his physical mutilation is more a culmination than a rebirth. Castration is a grotesque reminder of the mutilation of the self – the servile dissimulation – to which ambitions and pretensions have reduced him. In a double-edged irony, what Läuffer envies as Wenzeslaus's "golden freedom" is in fact the freedom of renunciation. As grotesque as the castration is the fact that this obscure schoolmaster has eschewed self-mutilation (in both the physical and the figurative sense) only by embracing a life of relentless self-denial. Wenzeslaus preaches an ethic of self-denial that was coming to seem absurd and intolerable to the young malcontents of Lenz's generation. But as the schoolmaster reminds us, it was an ethic with deep religious roots; and in the course of the eighteenth century its imperatives had acquired new sacred as well as secular idioms.

[53] Ibid., pp. 80–82. René Girard, *Lenz, 1751–1792. Genèse d'une dramaturgie du tragi-comique* (Paris, 1968), emphasizes the avoidance of didacticism in Lenz's dramatic art. But cf. his analysis of the social meaning of *Der Hofmeister*, and particularly of the significance of the castration and Wenzeslaus; ibid., pp. 223–91.

PART II

Calling, vocation, and service

5

The calling: August Hermann Francke and Halle Pietism

In the formation of a modern German social vocabulary, as in so many other passages to modernity, the eighteenth century was the crucible. Words that had evoked the legal structure and the ethos of a corporate hierarchy for centuries came to host the more familiar meanings that still attach to them, though without losing resonances from their old-regime origins. "Station" (*Stand*) – a word that figured large in eighteenth-century efforts to assign poor students a social identity and location – is a case in point. Well into the nineteenth century *Stand* remained in common use as a social and political category, at once absorbing and modifying the new language of class; that in itself is a measure of the persistence of corporate values. But often enough this was corporatism in a new key; by the late eighteenth century *Stand* was being used to recast the "estates of birth" in a utilitarian profile, with professional corporations ranked by function rather than by historic rights. Likewise *Bürger* could no longer be defined simply by reference to a specifically German urban order; it also conveyed notions of "public" rights and obligations, most of them French and English in origin, that had universal application.[1]

[1] See, e.g., Oswald v. Nell Breuning, "Ständischer Gesellschaftsaufbau," in *Handwörterbuch der Sozialwissenschaften*, vol. 10 (Stuttgart, 1959), pp. 6–11; Manfred Riedel, "Bürger, Staatsbürger, Bürgertum," in Otto Brunner, Werner Conze, and Reinhart Koselleck, eds., *Geschichtliche Grundbegriffe: Historisches Lexikon zur politisch-sozialen Sprache in Deutschland*, vol. 1 (Stuttgart, 1972), pp. 672–75; Mack Walker, "Rights and Functions: The Social Categories of Eighteenth-Century German Jurists and Cameralists," *Journal of Modern History* 50:2 (June, 1978): 234–51; the introduction to Zwi Batscha and Jorn Garber, eds., *Von der ständischen zur bürgerlichen Gesellschaft. Politisch-soziale Theorien im Deutschland der zweiten Hälfte des 18. Jahrhunderts* (Frankfurt am Main, 1981), pp. 9–38; Ursula Becher, *Politische Gesellschaft. Studien zur Genese bürgerlichen Öffentlichkeit in Deutschland*, Veröffentlichungen des Max-Planck-Instituts für Geschichte, vol. 59 (Göttingen, 1978). For insightful comments on changes in the ideological usage of *Stand*, see also Robert M. Berdahl, "Anthropologie und Geschichte: Einige theoretische Perspektiven und ein Beispiel aus der preussisch-deutschen Geschichte," in Robert M. Berdahl et al., eds., *Klassen und Kultur. Sozialanthropologische Perspektiven in der Geschichtsschreibung* (Frankfurt am Main, 1982), pp. 263–87. On the evolution of the entire political vocabulary see Jürgen Schlumbohm, *Freiheit. Die Anfänge der bürgerlichen Emanzipationsbewegung in Deutschland im Spiegel ihres Leitwortes (ca. 1760–1800)*, Geschichte und Gesellschaft, vol. 12 (Düsseldorf, 1975). Also relevant for comparative purposes is William

In our efforts to sort out continuity and change and to understand the interplay of indigenous and imported cultural meanings, the operative word is *Beruf*. More than eighty years ago Max Weber demonstrated the need to explore the Protestant ethic and its more or less inadvertent contributions to modern forms of rational self-discipline by way of the ideal of calling.[2] Our concern is with a different, though surely related, lineage; academic mobility found ethical sanctions not in the spirit of capitalism, but in the spirit of academic achievement. Throughout the eighteenth century *Beruf* lay at the center of the religious and secular ethical codes with which poor students made sense of academic mobility and came to terms with its dilemmas. Likewise it was the focal point of the larger ideological field within which Protestant and Enlightenment culture perceived and took stock of their presence.

Accommodating the new without divesting itself of the old, this single word remained at the center of things across a century of change. By the end of the century *Beruf* was at once a sacred and an emphatically secular term, straddling an enormous range of meanings. As "calling" *Beruf* still conveyed the dual emphasis Luther had given the Protestant ethic. It gave spiritual value to work in this world, but only when the work was an assignment (or "office") that the Lord had imposed and his abject subject had accepted. As "vocation" *Beruf* posited more or less secular criteria for identifying people by their work – i.e., by their function in a social division of labor – and did so in a variety of more or less connotative ways. To say that someone practiced a *Beruf* might simply mean that, according to certain objective indices, he should be numbered in a specific occupational group; nothing need be implied about his subjective relationship to other members of the group, to the larger society, or to his work. But *Beruf* as vocation might also evoke the ethical commitment to work that enjoyed quasi-sacred status in the Protestant Enlightenment, and by the end of the century it was also beginning to convey the corporate ethos of a distinctly modern professionalism. A *Berufsstand* might still be coterminous with an "estate of birth" (*Geburtsstand*), or it might be the vehicle for individual talent and achievement. The former usage pointed to the old-regime hierarchy of corporate privilege; the latter conjured up eighteenth-century visions of meritocracy. Even in such visions, social ascription might be considered a relevant "external" dimension of *Beruf*, helping determine the individual's assumption of an occupational and social identity; but it was generally assumed that the

H. Sewell, "Etat, Corps, and Ordre: Some Notes on the Social Vocabulary of the French Old Regime," in Hans Ulrich Wehler, ed., *Sozialgeschichte Heute* (Göttingen, 1974), pp. 49–68.

[2] Max Weber, *The Protestant Ethic and the Spirit of Capitalism*, trans. Talcott Parsons (1904–5: New York, 1976). On *Beruf* see esp. Karl Holl, *Die Geschichte des Wortes Beruf*, Sitzungsberichte der Preussischen Akademie der Wissenschaften, vol. 29 (Berlin, 1924); Werner Conze, "Beruf," in Brunner et al., eds., *Grundbegriffe*, 1: 490–507; the insightful comments in Herwig Blankertz, *Bildung im Zeitalter der grossen Industrie* (Hanover, 1969), pp. 28–32.

individual owed his "inner" *Beruf* – i.e., his vocation in the subjective sense – to nature, not to social inheritance.

It was this increasingly dense ideological field that shaped perceptions of poor students and gave meaning to their own experience, and that their presence and experience in turn helped shape. Our task will be to trace the linear movements, twists, and turns in this interaction across the eighteenth century. This is in part a matter of tracking a process of secularization, but that term can obscure as much as it explains. It should be kept in mind that the humanistic ideal of a "natural" vocation – an ideal recovered in the Renaissance and resting on the revered authority of classical antiquity – was to be found at both the sacred and the secular ends of the spectrum.[3] Vocation in this sense had been grafted onto (and subordinated within) Lutheran Orthodoxy long before it became a leitmotif of Enlightenment thought. From this angle *Beruf* was not so much secularized as given new, or at least more specific, social contours.

The career of "calling" in the eighteenth century is not one of steady eclipse. At Halle and other centers of the Pietist movement, the century opened with a remarkable religious revival. What is striking about the early generations of Pietist mentors is their emphatic reassertion of the profoundly antisecular implications in the Lutheran ideal of calling and their particular concern with applying those implications to the circumstances of poor students.[4] Among university-educated men, Lutheran Pietism was eventually eclipsed by secular rationalism, but not before thousands of Lutheran clergymen and teachers over several generations – men who had studied at Halle for at least a year or two – had absorbed its spirit. The ascendancy of the rationalist alternative is not a simple story of discontinuity; it will also be necessary to identify underlying continuities between the sacred and the secular – continuities that help explain why in Protestant Germany the secular ethic of vocation assumed the forms it did.

There is no lack of analysis of the theological pedigree of the Pietist ideal

[3] For an excellent contrast of the humanistic concept of vocation with the Protestant ideal of calling, see Richard M. Douglas, "Talent and Vocation in Humanist and Protestant Thought," in Theodore K. Rabb and Jerrold E. Seigel, eds., *Action and Conviction in Early Modern Europe. Essays in Memory of E. H. Harbison* (Princeton, N.J., 1969), pp. 261–98.

[4] The movement is conventionally dated from the publication of Philipp Jakob Spener's *Pia desideria* in 1675, and Spener's appointment as pastor of the Nikolaikirche in Berlin heralded its brief but consequential ascendancy in Prussia. For introductions to Pietism see Martin Schmidt, *Pietismus* (Stuttgart, 1972); idem, *Wiedergeburt und neuer Mensch*, Arbeiten zur Geschichte des Pietismus, vol. 2 (Bielefeld, 1969); F. Ernest Stoeffler, *German Pietism during the Eighteenth Century* (Leiden, 1973). On Francke and Pietism in Prussia, see esp. Carl Hinrichs, *Preussentum und Pietismus. Der Pietismus in Brandenburg-Preussen als religiös-soziale Reformbewegung* (Göttingen, 1971); Klaus Deppermann, *Der hallesche Pietismus und der Preussische Staat unter Friedrich I (III)* (Göttingen, 1961); Wolf Oschlies, *Die Arbeits- und Berufspädagogik A. H. Franckes (1663–1727)*, Arbeiten zur Geschichte des Pietismus, vol. 6 (Witten, 1969); Franz Hofmann et al., *August Hermann Francke. Das humanistische Erbe des grossen Erziehers* (Halle, 1965).

of calling or of its psychological dynamic.[5] If the significance of the ideal for poor students and academic mobility is to be understood, it must be seen taking shape at the very center of the Pietist movement from the late seventeenth century onward. That center was the Prussian town of Halle, and its presiding figure was August Hermann Francke. Francke arrived in Halle in 1691 as a young clergyman, appointed to the pastorate of the neighboring community of Glaucha; by the time he died there in 1726 the theology faculty at the new university bore the stamp of his formidable personality, and the cluster of schools and other institutions attached to his celebrated orphanage bore witness to the dynamism of his reform ideology. It was above all Francke who made the Pietist ideal of calling the locus for a vision that seems paradoxical, if not contradictory, in the light of our modern secular order of values. In the very process of making mobility from below an indispensable means of reform, Francke's ideology reinforced the censure of personal and social ambition in the larger culture.

THE *SELECTUM INGENIORUM*

Within a decade of his arrival, Francke was envisioning Halle as the "city upon a hill" from which the second Reformation would emanate. His far-reaching expectations found expression in a proposal for a "universal seminar" in 1701 and in the more extensive reform blueprint known as *Der Grosse Aufsatz*, drafted in 1704 and revised several times thereafter. In both documents the essential step toward a "universal improvement" of Christendom was a regeneration of the clergy, and that in turn required a "*selectum ingeniorum*" from the Halle orphanage and affiliated schools. The existing institutions, Francke complained in 1701, are only "a small sketch of a great work." Because of the chronic lack of funds, "the finest temperaments and alert minds [*excitate ingenia*] cannot be selected from year to year," and in the school complex "the natural gifts that God has implanted in them cannot be sufficiently investigated." For the same reason the theology faculty had to turn away "many students . . . in whom a good talent is observed." The

[5] To scholars who have focused on the psychological dynamic of conversion, Francke's Pietism, like other varieties, prepared the way for a fascination with the self and individual psychology at the end of the century. See, e.g., Fritz Stemme, "Die Säkularisation des Pietismus zur Erfahrungsseelenkunde," *Zeitschrift für deutsche Philologie* 72 (1953): 144–58; Hans R. G. Günther, "Psychologie des deutschen Pietismus," *Deutsche Vierteljahrsschrift für Literaturwissenschaft und Geistesgeschichte* 4 (1926): 144–76; Tadeusz Namowicz, "Pietismus in der deutschen Kultur des 18. Jahrhunderts. Bemerkungen zum Pietismusforschung," *Weimarer Beiträge* 13 (1967): 169–80. The two indispensable studies on the wider influence of Pietism are Robert Minder, *Glaube, Skepsis und Rationalismus. Dargestellt aufgrund der autobiographischen Schriften von Karl Philipp Moritz* (1936: Frankfurt am Main, 1974); Gerhard Kaiser, *Pietismus und Patriotismus im literarischen Deutschland. Ein Beitrag zum Problem der Säkularisation* (Wiesbaden, 1961).

universal seminar would in effect replace the existing faculty, and with a proper selection process and sufficient financial support the school complex would funnel into it "poor children to whom God has lent a particular inclination and aptitude for a useful discipline."[6]

In 1701 Francke hoped to support as many as a thousand students in the universal seminar, but the enormous increase in charitable contributions that it required did not materialize. The essays nonetheless were momentous; they laid out the ends and means of a vital reform impulse, essential to the legacy of Halle Pietism to eighteenth-century intellectual life. Though the phrase *selectum ingeniorum* echoed the humanist pedagogical tradition, the more direct and relevant antecedent for Francke's plan was eminently Lutheran. In the 1520s Luther had been faced with a crisis, created in part by his own fulminations against Romanist "monkery" and "priestcraft." Since many parents now felt that the clergy no longer offered their sons viable careers, attendance at the academic schools and the universities was declining drastically. When Luther called for a compulsory educational system, with church resources and private charity used to support "promising" pupils, he assumed that most recruits for a new clerical order, as for its Romanist predecessor, would come from the "the common people" and especially "the poor." "Lords and other important people," he reasoned in his "Sermon on Keeping Children in School" in 1530, needed heirs to maintain "the temporal authority," and in any case were too corrupted by luxury and power to understand the spiritual office.[7]

Neither Luther nor Francke, it should be stressed, saw the recruitment of poor boys for the clergy as a step toward the realization of a general principle of equality of opportunity. Formulating such a principle would have required a fundamental questioning of the inherited privileges of "birth," in the loose sense of family wealth as well as in the strict sense of pedigree, that underpinned a society of orders. While Luther's rhetoric

[6] A. H. Francke, "Project zu einem Seminario universali," in Gustav Kramer, *August Hermann Francke. Ein Lebensbild*, 2 vols. (1880–82), 2: 489–96 (*Anhang*); Otto Podczek, ed., *Der Grosse Aufsatz: August Hermann Franckes Schrift über eine Reform des Erziehungs- und Bildungswesens als Ausgangspunkt einer geistlichen und sozialen Neuordnung der Evangelischen Kirche des 18.Jahrhunderts*, Abhandlungen der Sächsischen Akademie der Wissenschaften zu Leipzig, Philologisch-historische Klasse, vol. 53, no. 3 (Berlin, 1962).

[7] Martin Luther, "A Sermon on Keeping Children in School, 1530," *Luther's Works*, vol. 46 (The Christian in Society, III), pp. 222–23, 229–36. See also idem, "To the Councilmen of All Cities in Germany That They Establish and Maintain Christian Schools, 1524," *Luther's Works*, vol. 45 (The Christian in Society, II), pp. 347–78. Luther impressed on parents that it was their Christian duty to dedicate sons to the church; but he was not above the more mundane pitch that, in view of the plethora of vacancies, their sons "can easily get as good a living from the preaching office as from a trade." Gerald Strauss, *Luther's House of Learning. Indoctrination of the Young in the German Reformation* (Baltimore, 1978), concentrates on popular education, but notes views similar to Luther's among other reformers. Ibid., pp. 24–25, 44, 177–79. Strauss also demonstrates that the humanist tradition had some influence on Protestant pedagogy, although reformers incorporated it at the cost of tension with their evangelical morality. Ibid., pp. 48–70.

occasionally struck an egalitarian note, he saw upward mobility via academic education as the exceptional case needed to refurbish a tiny elite; for the most part he interpreted 1 Corinthians 7:20 to mean that intergenerational continuity of stations should remain the rule in the society at large.[8] The very organization of Francke's school complex reflected the same assumption. In the late 1690s he had established the Paedagogium, specifically intended to prepare sons of the nobility and other "prestigious families" for the positions of authority they would inherit. It was an expensive boarding school, accommodating eighty-two pupils by 1727, and Francke had been careful to assure prospective customers that it was entirely separate from the schools in his *Stiftungen*.[9] The complex included an enormous German school at the elementary level; by 1720 it had 621 pupils, most of them local children who would enter the trades. There was also a Latin school that was preparing its pupils, including a substantial number of boarders, for the university. Special Latin school classes, which included sixty of the ninety-six orphan boys in 1706, exemplified the kind of selection process Francke had in mind. But the selected orphans were and remained a minority in the Latin school, which had 350 male pupils by 1720. Thus a special channel for poor but gifted orphans ran through a structure whose divisions reflected basic inequalities of wealth among the various school populations. Francke's more ambitious plan assumed the survival of that structure; its significance lay in widening the channel to include poor sons of artisans and other families in the social mainstream.[10]

Within the larger framework of Prussian (and German) society, the increase in the number of exceptions to the rule that Francke's *selectum ingeniorum* promised was insignificant. But exceptions require justifications, and here Francke's vision marks a subtle but important shift in emphasis from the Lutheran tradition. While Luther had seen the "general calling" as a reception of divine grace, lifting the true Christian into a spiritual realm above natural corruption, he had assigned the "particular calling" in an office or occupation to the radically distinct and inferior temporal sphere where no amount or kind of human effort could merit salvation. Nonetheless the particular calling was essential to a Christian life at every stage. Calling in this sense was the primary locus of the "cross" – i.e., the sufferings and

[8] In 1530 Luther did call for the training of poor boys for offices in the "temporal government" as well as in the church, so that rulers and nobles would be reminded that they owed their positions to "God alone" rather than to "nobility of birth." *Luther's Works*, 46: 250–51. See also the remarks on Luther's view of the social order and social mobility in Lewis W. Spitz, "Luther's Social Concern for Students," in Lawrence P. Buck and Jonathan W. Zophy, eds., *The Social History of the Reformation* (Columbus, Ohio, 1972), pp. 258–62.

[9] Kramer, *Francke*, 2: 486; August Hermann Niemeyer, *Geschichte des Königlichen Pädagogiums seit seiner Stiftung bis zum Schluss des ersten Jahrhunderts* (Halle, 1796).

[10] Deppermann, *Der hallesche Pietismus*, pp. 89–90; Kramer, *Francke*, 2: 507 (*Anhang*). For descriptions of the entire complex, see Oschlies, *Arbeits- und Berufspädagogik*, pp. 16–21, 41; Hinrichs, *Preussentum und Pietismus*.

trials – that prepared for the state of grace. With the reception of grace it became the medium through which the Christian expressed the "love of neighbor" to which faith impelled him and, in so doing, helped realize God's design.[11]

Particularly in the early years Luther used this doctrine to justify an impressive agenda of social and political reforms. But his reform impulse was inhibited by his theological dualism; if the world demonstrated God's continuous work in creation, it was also the arena in which man's bestial nature inevitably found expression. At the same time, in the face of social unrest and political disorder, Luther and his fellow reformers became increasingly concerned with the reestablishment of authority – and it was that concern that came to dominate the Orthodox doctrine of calling. *Beruf* became virtually synonymous with "office" (*Amt*); both terms came to emphasize conscientious fulfillment of assigned duties in the established order, and particularly obedience to the divinely ordained authorities of church and state.[12]

To Francke nearly two centuries later, the Lutheran Reformation seemed to have bogged down soon after its inception. The mission of Halle Pietism in the face of "universal corruption" was to spearhead the "universal improvement of all estates."[13] In the service of that mission, the doctrine of calling, though remaining solidly Lutheran, incorporated a work ethic that bore close resemblance to the Puritan ideal of "continuous labor in the calling" as "the self-affirming activity of the Godly" and promised a similar "utopia of men without leisure."[14] The calling no longer was limited to duty in the traditional sense; it required an intensely self-disciplined, never-waste-a-minute, almost feverish activity in a lifelong occupation or office, maximizing use of time and effort in the service of "the common welfare." Francke's own tight, strenuous daily schedule testified to his virtual mania about the efficient use of time. "When I begrudge someone an hour of my life," he warned students who might want a private consultation with him, "I consider that I am extending him a great gift."[15] His approach to the

[11] The best theological explication of Luther's doctrine of vocation is still Gustaf Wingren, *Luther on Vocation*, trans. Carl C. Rasmussen (Philadelphia, 1957). See also Ivar Asheim, *Glaube und Erziehung bei Luther. Ein Beitrag zur Geschichte des Verhältnisses von Theologie und Pädagogik* (Heidelberg, 1961); Hellmut Lieberg, *Amt und Ordination bei Luther und Melanchthon*, Forschungen zur Kirchen und Dogmengeschichte, vol. 11 (Göttingen, 1962).

[12] This increasing concern to restore authority is emphasized in Strauss, *Luther's House of Learning*.

[13] Kramer, *Francke*, 2: 489–90 (*Anhang*); Podczek, *Der Grosse Aufsatz*, pp. 43, 70–76.

[14] Michael Walzer, *The Revolution of the Saints. A Study in the Origins of Radical Politics* (New York, 1970), pp. 210–11. See also Walzer's comments on the Puritan attitude toward social mobility, in ibid., p. 215.

[15] August Hermann Francke, *Lectiones Paraeneticae, Oder Oeffentlichen Ansprachen An die Studiosos Theologiae auf der Universität zu Halle*, 7 vols. (Halle, 1726–36), 4: 4–7 (cited hereafter as LP).

schooling and discipline of children was in the same spirit, although softened by a certain forbearance toward their natural weaknesses.[16]

Neither the activism of the individual nor its result had value in itself; each should be the expression of the true Christian's love of neighbor, inspired and nourished by faith, and a sign that he had entered the state of grace. But "improvement" meant concrete, practical changes that promoted and were part of the very process of spiritual regeneration. Francke's "universal" vision projected not only a religious revival extending far beyond Germany, but also a host of social and institutional reforms whose emphasis on education, on the application of advanced science, and on rational efficiency marked the influence of seventeenth-century Utopian literature. In the light of that vision, the Halle complex – with its schools, its new ways of organizing and funding poor relief, and its medical and astronomical facilities – was the radiating symbol of universal improvement as well as its operational center.[17] It was this reform activism, deeply rooted in the Lutheran tradition but also pointing well beyond it, that justified and indeed necessitated Francke's *selectum ingeniorum*. Since only the clergy could be the "leaven" of the revival, there was an urgent need to enlist available talent, particularly by selecting and supporting talented poor boys.

To Francke academic mobility promised to become a means to the sanctification of the world; in the service of that vision his pedagogy, despite its obvious rejection of the secular preference in the humanistic tradition, sought to realize the humanistic ideal of "natural" growth by organizing a program of methodical instruction within a carefully devised institutional structure. In the Pietist order of priorities development of innate, "natural" capacities was legitimate only as a process subordinate to "true cultivation of character," which required the radical effacement of self that Francke called "the breaking of the will."[18] But the same paradox had a positive logic; a disciplined, austere education, precisely because it was designed to break the will, allowed and could go hand in hand with the development of innate potential. The most striking feature of Francke's pedagogy, in fact, is its insistence on adapting to the peculiar "nature" of each child as well as to the natural stages of childhood. Teachers had to distinguish among the "temperaments" (*Gemüter*) of the children not only "to know more about how each can be controlled and whether each should be treated more strictly or more softly," but also "to discover the capacity of the intelligences and what in particular each child is skilled for, so that the gifts that God has implanted in each can be awakened and applied to the common welfare

[16] *A. H. Francke. Pädagogische Schriften*, ed. Hermann Lorenzen (Paderborn, 1957), esp. p. 32. On Francke's view of work and *Beruf*, see also Hinrichs, *Preussentum und Pietismus*, pp. 13–15, 342–45; Oschlies, *Arbeits- und Berufspädagogik*, esp. pp. 198–206.

[17] The rationalistic influence of seventeenth-century academies and utopian literature is given due emphasis in Hinrichs, *Preussentum und Pietismus*, esp. p. 45.

[18] *Francke. Pädagogische Schriften*, pp. 15, 30–33, 45–47.

[*gemeinen Nützen*]."[19] And intelligence was not an undifferentiated quantum; it subdivided into particular aptitudes, or "gifts," varying in strength and developmental schedule from pupil to pupil. Francke's most important departure from prevailing school arrangements was meant to capitalize on these variations among the pupils. Rather than each age group receiving instruction in all subjects from the same teacher, each subject had its hierarchy of classes through which the pupil progressed. As a result of teachers' observations and periodic examinations, the pupil might find himself at different class levels in different subjects, corresponding to his varying abilities and achievements.[20] Thus, in the broader selection process to which the *selectum ingeniorum* for the clergy pointed, several finely graded channels would have matched individual combinations of gifts to appropriate callings.

POVERTY, PATRONS, AND GRACE

While Francke was laying his plans for universal improvement, he was also seizing the more immediate opportunity to build a model theology faculty at Halle. Hardly more than a token presence in the early years, theology students contributed 41.8 percent of the university's average annual matriculations in 1721–30; they had become more numerous at Halle than at any other German university. What had allowed this unprecedented concentration was Francke's "free tables" for student-tutors and a variety of other charitable arrangements. The students who appeared "ten or more at a time" at conference hours, Francke observed in 1704, "have no idea how they are going to subsist and endure in view of their extreme poverty" – and many had to leave immediately or rush through their studies for want of support.[21] The influx was proof of the new university's success in competition with its regional rivals. Nonetheless Francke's superiors in Berlin had misgivings about it; a royal *Patent* in 1708 regretted that too many sons of peasants and artisans were attending the universities and instructed local school officials to weed out aspirants betraying "stupidity, laziness, and lack of enthusiasm or motivation."[22] But thanks largely to Francke's organizational talents, the *Patent* did not prevent the Halle faculty from continuing to grow at a rapid rate.

[19] Ibid., pp. 17, 40–41, 51, 83.

[20] Oschlies, *Arbeits- und Berufspädagogik*, pp. 124–27; Hinrichs, *Preussentum und Pietismus*, p. 65.

[21] Podczek, *Der Grosse Aufsatz*, pp. 44–45. On the enrollment figures see Chapter 1.

[22] Hans Georg Herrlitz, *Studium als Standesprivileg: Die Entstehung des Maturitätsproblems im 18. Jahrhundert* (Frankfurt am Main, 1973), pp. 36–37. To Nicolaus Hieronymous Gundling, a law professor at Halle, the *Patent* seemed urgently needed to prevent the academic proletariat that the university's misguided largesse threatened to create. See his *Sammlung kleiner teutscher Schriften* (Halle, 1737), pp. 112–21; Waldemar Kawerau, *Aus Halles Literaturleben*, Culturbilder aus dem Zeitalter der Aufklärung, vol. 2 (Halle, 1888), pp. 98–100.

And yet if Francke continued to see the hand of God in his success, he also came to regret some of the moral costs. By the turn of the century this theme was being sounded with increasing urgency in the weekly series of *Admonitory Lectures* (*Lectiones Paraeneticae*) he offered the theology students at the new university. Begun in 1693, most of the lectures focused on the Pauline Epistles, and they are permeated with the central doctrines of grace, faith, and calling that Luther derived from those texts. Francke continued to use this format to discuss technical problems of exegesis; but it also became the occasion for concrete, often acerbic applications of the Pietist ethic to the circumstances of the audience. Fortunately student-stenographers earned their meals by recording these exercises in scholarship and homiletics.[23]

That the central message of the *Lectures* was the necessity of undergoing conversion (*Bekehrung*) is not surprising. To the Pietists, as to the Puritans, the conversion experience was the crucible in which a merely "exterior" Christianity – the kind of religion orthodox Lutherans observed – melted away and an entirely new, "inner" religiosity of self-renunciation and faith was fired. Among the second generation of Pietist mentors, it was above all Francke, indulging the same passion for schematic order that he brought to institution building, who anatomized the experience into distinct stages and psychological states: the state of self-deception and false security; the preparatory "atonement struggle" (*Busskampf*), advancing from the crisis of faith to anxiety-ridden contrition and thence to a full awareness of "natural corruption" and a genuine hatred of sin; the "breakthrough" (*Durchbruch*) to renunciation of self and receptivity to God's grace; the gift of faith; the resulting "calmness" (*Gelassenheit*) as a servant of the Lord.[24] Nor is it sur-

[23] Francke and his son published an abundant sample (LP), ranging from 1701 to 1725, which is available on microfilm in German Baroque Literature, no. 1440, reel nos. 458 and 459 (Research Publications, Inc., Woodbridge, Conn.). For a painstaking reconstruction of the chronology and themes of the *Lectures*, see Friedrich de Boor, "Die paränetischen und methodologischen Vorlesungen August Hermann Franckes (1693–1727)," 2 vols., Dissertation, Martin-Luther-Universität Halle-Wittenberg, 1968. The original manuscripts are no longer available, but de Boor concludes that revisions in the published sample seem to have been limited to stylistic improvements. Francke returned to the subject of the "condition of the university" in 1709, 1710, 1713, and 1716, and the heading for 1716 specifically mentions that "the university is threatening to plunge into chaos because of the large number of students." Ibid., 2: 76, 85, 103, 119. A. H. Francke, *Timotheus zum Fürbilde Allen Theologiae Studiosis dargestellet* (Halle, 1695), is a summary of the earliest lectures. A later distillation is *Idea studiosi Theologiae* (1712), reprinted in *August Hermann Francke. Werke in Auswahl*, ed. Erhard Peschke (Witten-Ruhr, 1969), pp. 172ff. For a useful survey of Francke's views on theological studies and university reform, with copious references to the *Lectures*, see Erhard Peschke, "A. H. Franckes Reform des theologischen Studiums," in *August Hermann Francke. Festreden und Kolloquium über den Bildungs- und Erziehungsgedanken bei August Hermann Francke aus Anlass der 300. Wiederkehr seines Geburtstages 22. März 1963* (Halle-Wittenberg, 1964), pp. 88–115.

[24] There are particularly vivid depictions of the conversion experience in LP, 1: 237–47, 261–308. See also the descriptions in Oschlies, *Arbeits- und Berufspädagogik*, pp. 184–92; Erhard Peschke, *Bekehrung und Reform: Ansatz und Wurzeln der Theologie August Hermann Franckes*, Arbeiten zur Geschichte des Pietismus, vol. 15 (Bielefeld, 1977), pp. 111–14.

prising that, in the particular forum of the lectures, Francke depicted the experience as a compressed, dramatic series of events and conveyed such a powerful sense of urgency, if not desperation, about it. While in the orphanage and affiliated schools conversion could be a gradual process beginning in childhood, the students who formed his lecture audience had already become adolescents and young adults in a thoroughly corrupt world. If they were to be transformed into "servants of the Lord," they had to run the gamut, from crisis to "breakthrough" and beyond, during their brief stay at the university.

But the lectures reveal a good deal more about the man and the ideology. Francke was not simply an evangelist, warning against the false security of merely exterior observance; he was also a disciplinarian, organizing new ways to monitor student life. As a scholar himself, he wanted the new generation of pastors and teachers to be "textual theologians," well trained in their discipline and its auxiliaries; but he was also determined to extirpate the kind of "brain theology" and attendant scholarly ambitions to which he had once fallen prey. As an academic reformer, Francke was bent on instituting a well-ordered and complete program of theological studies. But the growing presence of theology students was not accompanied by any fundamental changes in the structure of access to university education or in the routes to clerical appointments. Francke could not alter the basic conditions and terms of sponsored mobility and hence could not exempt students from either the pressures of poverty or the caprices of patronage. He himself, in fact, was a well-known "broker" between aspiring tutors and parents. In the *Lectures*, the various elements of the conversion experience – the requisite preparation, the nature of the transformation, its consequences – mediated the tensions inherent in Francke's reform ideology and allowed him to reconcile a limited application of reform with the constraints of social and institutional reality.

To Francke the other German universities were "the holes from which the corruption most often bubbles," the "puddle of all scandal and abomination." Their students abused the privilege of academic freedom to enjoy a kind and degree of license unique in German society. Halle promised to set a new example because, under Pietist tutelage, it would combine depth of religiosity with disciplinary thoroughness. By 1703 – the first year of the only complete lecture series in the published sample – Francke's disappointment was finding expression in two negative images of the Halle theology student, often conflated in his jeremiads but representing very different causes for alarm. The one more familiar to contemporaries – the image of the untamed adolescent, part clown, part savage, that Francke and others refracted through their moralism – portrayed a collective life-style among students that seemed impervious to university and state prohibitions. Student codes of honor defended in duels and brawls, against both *Kom-*

militonen and the townsfolk; eccentricities of dress and manner calculated to scandalize the local philistines; drinking and pipe-smoking bouts in the local haunts; festivities, preferably in the early morning hours, complete with mock processions, ribald songs, and blaring trumpets – all this was included in what Francke called "debauchery" (*asoterie*).[25]

When Francke identified the principal carriers of this plague as newcomers from the schools and neighboring universities, he was shunting the blame for Halle's troubles onto other institutions, but with good reason.[26] The very circumstances of the university's growth dictated that it could not be a self-enclosed, controlled experiment. The bulk of the students could neither be produced in-house nor screened at the door; they poured in from the typical Latin schools and *Gymnasien*, where older pupils already had adopted student ways before arriving at Halle, and, more important, from Jena, Leipzig, and other nearby universities where "debauchery" held sway. If the new university could not quarantine itself from the student subculture, it could purify itself by enforcing an unprecedented degree of paternalism. Unlike theology students at other universities, Francke liked to boast, those at Halle had to report for counseling periodically to the faculty, whose professors were expected to keep track of their morals as well as their academic progress.[27] Again Francke exacted the maximum advantage from his charity; the member of a "free table" was under the supervision of an inspector and his seniors and was required to submit a twice-yearly conduct report, including his "entire manner of living" as well as his studies and describing how he "disposed of the entire week from hour to hour."[28] If all else failed, Francke warned repeatedly, he would be hauled before the faculty. The very frequency of the warnings, combined with Francke's generally bleak assessment of the situation, suggests that the measures taken had limited effect.

This new disciplinary regime might be considered an attempt to produce formal compliance in lieu of genuine piety, but Francke saw it as an instrument in a necessary stage toward the reception of grace. Conversion was a dramatic process, with intensely emotional peaks and troughs, but it was not a sudden, once-for-all wrenching from sinfulness to godliness. The keynote of Francke's exhortations was "struggle" (*Kampf*, *ringen*), by which he meant a daily, methodical exercise of self-discipline in which the indi-

[25] In his own litany, debauchery broke down into "scuffling, dueling, fighting, brawling, gluttony, boozing, whore-songs, *Runda* singing, immoderate tobacco smoking, nocturnal reveling, and the like." LP, 1: 96. See also LP, 1: 36–40, 58, 162–64, 193–214; LP, 2: 132–33, 334; LP, 4: 151–52, 243; LP, 5: 105–6. For background on the student subculture, see August Tholuck, *Das akademische Leben des 17. Jahrhunderts mit besonderer Beziehung auf die protestantisch-theologischen Fakultäten Deutschlands* (Halle, 1853–54), pp. 266–73.

[26] LP, 5: 258–59, 287–89.

[27] LP, 6: 21–23.

[28] August Hermann Francke, *Der von Gott in dem Waysenhause zu Glaucha an Halle ietzo bey nahe für 600. Personen zubereitete Tisch* (Halle, 1722), p. 51.

vidual overcame his "corrupt" natural tendencies and progressed toward the breakthrough. The student wallowing in *asoterie* had yet to engage the enemy. In a paradox typical of Pietism, the more advanced stage – avoidance of "the exterior gross sins and disgraces" – remained mere sham until it resulted from a genuine conversion; but it nonetheless was an indispensable step toward that experience. The victory of grace over human nature culminated a sustained warfare, with a ceaseless interaction between "exterior" and "interior," objective condition and subjectivity. Receptivity to grace – and hence the capacity for the inner transformation that must underlie behavior and sanctify a particular, or "exterior," calling in the clergy – lay through an "atonement" struggle against both the Old Adam within and the seductions that mired him in the world. In the rigors of that sustained preparation, Francke had both an urgent need and a powerful justification for a uniform, detailed enforcement of moral standards – one that, had it been successful, would have purified student life.

Within a decade of the university's founding, however, the image of a more insidious threat had begun to take shape in the *Lectures*. By 1703 Francke was already harking back to the early days, when the theology faculty had had "scarcely a handful of students." The early student had typically been eager to confide in his professors, he liked to recall, and had achieved the "breakthrough" to "thorough renunciation" before their very eyes. In the contrasting "chaos" of the present, the student-libertine took second place to the hard-working student-scholar who was "neither warm nor cold" in his Christianity, who felt "good stirrings" (*gute Bewegungen*) but got "stuck" in a "halfway condition," who neither undertook "a great metamorphosis" nor allowed "a great relapse."[29] Here the conviction Francke had derived from the pivotal experience of his own life fueled his disappointment about developments at Halle. By 1687 – the year of his conversion – Francke was a *Magister* in theology and a versatile linguist and was teaching at Leipzig. As the properly reared son of a judicial official, he probably had acquired little direct experience of the horrors of the student subculture; in his classic descriptions of his conversion struggle, he acknowledges the hard-core temptations of the flesh more as token villains than as formidable adversaries. For Francke love of "the world" had meant primarily "concern for the future, ambition, a desire to know everything, a search for human favor and friendship." "My intention," he recalled, "was to become a prominent and learned man"; he had made learning his "idol," not realizing that "all scholarship learned at the feet of Gamaliel is to be regarded as dreck in relation to the overflowing knowledge [*Erkenntnis*] of Jesus Christ in our hearts."[30]

[29] LP, 2: 145–49; LP, 3: 172–75; LP, 4: 77–87, 113; LP, 7: 150.

[30] The complete text of Francke's conversion account, with useful editorial information, is in *Francke. Werke in Auswahl*, pp. 5–29. See esp. pp. 23–24, 28–29. An abridged version is

It was the same academic pride and ambition that Francke saw becoming the order of the day at Halle. The very size of his audience was one of its most vexing symptoms. Moved from his private quarters to a public auditorium to accommodate the growing number, the lectures soon were attended by less than half of the theology students; apparently the others felt that his message was not "scholarly" enough to be worth their time.[31] Francke's reaction was to appeal constantly to the essential spirit and overriding objective of reform, though without sacrificing one of its principal means. While conversion had taught Francke to put things in their proper place, it had not turned him away from scholarship. Like other Pietists, he dismissed much of Lutheran Orthodoxy as mere pedantry and sophistry and felt that clerical training should concentrate on the practical requirements of pastoral care among the uneducated masses. But since pastoral practice required men who had a clear grasp of the basics and were well equipped to interpret scripture, it was critical to his reform plans that Halle achieve the "solidity" and "good order" in theological studies that other universities lacked.

Elsewhere students were simply left to their own devices or consulted a professor who herded them into his own courses. At Halle it was essential that the student acquire a thorough competence in Greek and Hebrew, master the fundamentals in public *Collegia* on theology, church history, and philosophy before sampling more abstruse fare, and complete a full course of study before entering a clerical office. Keeping a diary would encourage the student to gauge his academic "progress" as well as his advance in piety and to achieve *constantia* in both.[32] If Francke's via media was an alternative to mere scholarship, it was also meant to avoid anti-intellectualism. While the spirit of scripture could not be absorbed through "natural effort" and "mere study and knowledge," he warned in 1703, pretensions to mysticism were as misguided as pedantry. There was no substitute for basic familiarity with literal content, and in that sense every clergyman must be a "good textual theologian." To Francke, as to Luther, spiritual progress – progress in the "living knowledge" of Christ that he distinguished from mere rational understanding – lay through the abject appeals and intense wrestling with self that occurred in "prayer" (*Gebet*), not through scholarship. But the necessary hour or two of prayer each day need not interfere with an orderly and moderate commitment to study.[33]

Yet there was no middle ground. Academic learning was either an aid to spiritual progress or one of its most dangerous obstructions. Every the-

in Marianne Beyer-Fröhlich, ed., *Pietismus und Rationalismus*, Deutsche Literatur, Reihe: Deutsche Selbstzeugnisse, vol. 7 (Leipzig, 1933), pp. 17–29.

[31] LP, 1: *Vorrede* (no pag.); LP, 4: 48; LP, 5: 77, 248–49.

[32] LP, 3: 18–19; LP, 4: 32–33, 111–12, 164.

[33] LP, 1: 42, 130–34; LP, 2: 33, 201–04; LP, 3: 126–27; LP, 4: 118–44. On Luther's view of prayer, see esp. Asheim, *Glaube und Erziehung*, pp. 168–74.

ology student, Francke urged in 1708, must have "a fire" lit in his heart, and that fire must drive him relentlessly to achieve "a proper state."[34] In a sense the student-libertine, who could entertain little doubt about the depraved state of his soul, had an advantage over the hard-working, scholarly type. "When the Lord converts an academic," Francke quipped, "he works a true miracle." The great danger – a danger that Francke knew from personal experience – was that the scholar could so easily mistake rational understanding and erudition for faith and get stuck "halfway." Trapped in a state of "hidden and subtle self-deception," he concentrated on his "exterior calling" as a student and might never achieve the "breakthrough" to "fundamental renunciation." To rescue students from this pitfall, Francke, using every resource of language and metaphor at his command, elaborated the opposition between nature and grace, human will and divine mercy, at the core of Lutheran theology. Faith was not an intellectual achievement, earned through "mere knowledge," but a matter of "tasting" the "divine power." It was something instilled in "the heart" – i.e., in the affective seat of the personality – not developed in the "brain." To rely on "our own power, capacity, reason, wit, understanding, or whatever else it is called" was to fail to realize that the intellect, so long as it remained part of the natural self, was depraved.[35] The freedom of the converted Christian lay not in intellectual choice, but in the transcendent conviction – the freedom from doubt – that impelled action.

Francke's injunctions not only point to his own experience; they also register his sensitivity to the larger set of cultural norms that so often made poor students an object of alarm and censure in old-regime society. He had to confront the specter of academic ambition and its attendant vices in the very process of grooming learned clergymen. At times, to be sure, he seems to have been recalling the seductive pleasures of intellectual achievement for its own sake. But more often Francke equated intellectual zeal with personal ambition, the overly zealous scholar with the careerist. One indication that present-day students are avoiding "renunciation," he complained as early as 1703, is that their only concern is to secure "good and well-endowed pastorates."[36] While the original flock had been eager to renounce the world, this crowd worried about pleasing "patrons" and not missing opportunities for "advancement." In 1709, at the end of a typical litany of the upcoming generation's faults, he admitted that students had not actually "degenerated from the early, good type." In the early days "the good" was more apparent among a smaller number, whereas now, with many

[34] LP, 4: 21.

[35] LP, 1: 127; LP, 2: 179–83, 221–22, 272–73, 336; LP, 5: 17; LP, 6: 24–26, 257; LP, 7: 136–37, 275, 305–6, 370–73.

[36] LP, 1: 128–29. See also LP, 2: 366–71; LP, 4: 77–87; LP, 5: 318–19; LP, 6: 20.

more students, "the evil is clear and the disorders are more striking."[37] But as this rare concession suggests, Francke's nostalgic perspective reflected to a degree the actual evolution of the university. As the theology faculty had expanded and student-faculty relations had become more impersonal, the original dynamic, crusading spirit had given way to a more routinized enterprise. The gathered community of saints seemed to have become one more place where young men, eager to secure clerical livings as soon as possible and hoping to enter the better ones, acquired the necessary certification.

For all his disillusionment, Francke was not issuing another cry of alarm about "the addiction for study." Quite the contrary; the reformer, eager for an army of missionaries, welcomed the large and growing number of theology students despite his awareness that, as he reckoned in 1703, scarcely one in a hundred felt certain about having a "calling" to be "teachers of churches."[38] In an unusual interpretation, he used Paul's dictum in 1 Corinthians 7:20 to persuade students who came to doubt that they had an "inner vocation" for the clergy that they must nonetheless persevere. Likewise he warned them not to become so involved in soul-searching that they put their studies in abeyance and sacrificed precious time at the university. Unless God pointed the student in a new direction by instilling a "divine certainty" that flowed from faith, he could be sure that a change of careers would be one more indulgence of "self-love" and "fleshly," or "natural," desires. His only hope was that, with the proper combination of prayer and study, he would at last achieve the breakthrough that would make the "exterior" *Beruf* an expression of the inner fire.[39]

But if the student who seemed to have wandered into the study of theology "by chance" had to persist in it, he also had to accept the possibility of a lifelong assignment on one of the bottom rungs of the clerical ladder. Echoing Luther's theology of the cross, Francke repeatedly reminded his audience that the clergyman in a state of self-renunciation would welcome persecution and even martyrdom. He was preparing them not only for the real prospect of harassment at the hands of an Orthodox establishment, but also for the material deprivations and personal frustrations to be expected in the less desirable clerical livings. Like Luther, Francke evoked the ancient Christian ideal of a divinely ordained social organism, its every member performing an essential function, and saw a providential economy of gifts

[37] LP, 4: 414–15.

[38] In many cases, he noted, the father had made the decision, and with the sole thought that "other employments in the world are very uncertain but there has to be a pastor in almost every village." For others the "fleshly motive" was simply to avoid learning a manual trade regarded as "contemptible." LP, 5: 62–63.

[39] LP, 3: 247–55; LP, 4: 29–32; LP, 5: 64–68. It is striking that Francke diverged here from Christian Kortholt, one of his former teachers, who had felt that such unsuitable candidates should be encouraged to leave the clergy. Peschke, *Bekehrung und Reform*, pp. 47–48.

behind individual differences in intelligence and other endowments. His preferred use of the phrase "natural gifts" (or just "gifts") in this context, rather than the humanistic "natural talents," is revealing. "Gift" implied something that ought to elicit gratitude rather than pride or personal satisfaction. In the Lutheran economy of salvation, it was something the donor "lent" for His own purposes rather than for the recipient's advantage.

To be sure, methodical self-examination would in effect enable the student to fathom God's design by identifying his particular gifts, and one purpose of self-discipline was to fulfill his calling by developing those gifts to the fullest. But in the *Lectures* these positive notes were muted; Francke was more emphatic about warning zealous students not to "step beyond their limits," not to "force something for which they are not skilled by nature."[40] There was room for a great diversity of personalities in the clergy; "since there are all kinds of opportunities to apply one's received *Talent* for the communal use of the church, we need all kinds of people, all kinds of *ingenia*, not only outstanding ones but also mediocre ones and common ones."[41] Each student was urged to accept the assignment that God matched to his capacities, and indeed Francke warned that the student whose "pride in studies" had made him reluctant to "serve in a minor office" had to continue to "stifle the source [*Grund*] of his self-love" even after conversion.[42]

The push of ambition was inseparable from the pull of patrons; here too Francke's admonitions were shaped to the specific experience and norms of academic mobility. Precisely because the denial of the self in conversion insured against academic careerism, it also promised, paradoxically, to anchor social identity in the unassailable personal integrity – the "honor" in both a moral and a social sense – that the "servile" poor student was reputed to lack. The immediate problem was that the careerist, aside from trying to transgress his limits, was vulnerable to the temptation to end his studies prematurely. Students were eager to escape their material hardships as soon as possible, and patronage, far from allowing an orderly placement of candidates as they reached "maturity," often forced them to choose between leaving the university grossly unprepared and missing a precious opportunity that might never come again. Indeed students who arrive at the university without means expect the faculty to come to their aid immediately, Francke complained with the petulance of a besieged benefactor, and some even request more than they need out of fear that their provisioning will not hold out. Why can they not trust in the Lord?[43] In the same vein

[40] LP, 6: 240–47; LP, 7: 312–13, 331–42. See also *Francke. Werke in Auswahl*, pp. 188–89. On Luther's view of *Gaben* see Lieberg, *Amt und Ordination*, pp. 79–80.

[41] LP, 4: 50.

[42] LP, 7: 312.

[43] LP, 3: 372–75; LP, 5: 157–58; LP, 7: 138–39. On the *vocatio mediata*, see esp. Lieberg, *Amt und Ordination*, pp. 143–45.

he castigated needy students who were persuaded to leave the university unprepared by the offer of a clerical appointment or a position as a private tutor. "If they would change themselves and improve," he predicted, God would direct their teachers to grant them "some kind of needed *beneficia*" and "would provide means and ways for them to first put their affairs in better order, even if they had to survive on a pittance."[44]

In the Lutheran doctrine implicit in these passages, the "mediate" calling (*vocatio mediata*) to a particular office in the clergy came through men. Francke was entirely orthodox in applying this doctrine of mediation to endow the role of patronage in clerical appointments with a higher meaning; but in his hands it counteracted students' inclination to succumb to patrons' more inconvenient demands. Students must wait to "be sent"; those who "run after" vacancies before they are ready, Francke warned in 1703, are "running ahead" of the Lord.[45] The major problem was the fear of ruining prospects back home. When students are threatened with losing an appointment and forfeiting "the favor of this or that mortal *Patron*," he complained in 1709, "they drop, so to speak, like flies." Indeed "patrons back home need only write a stern letter and threaten to withdraw their hand," he added in the next lecture, and their clients "prefer to let pass the most beautiful opportunity [to continue their studies], rather than the mere contract that a human being can offer."[46] Whether the patron's letter was a premature temptation or the real calling depended on whether the student had the inner conviction and "calmness" (*Gelassenheit*) resulting from conversion and thus could act as a servant of the Lord. Again the ideal was the passive instrument, not the active seeker. The providential design that guided young men to the theology faculty at Halle, despite their base motives, would also guide them to the right places at the right times.[47]

Francke's ethic promised a truly Christian freedom in two senses. It provided relief not only from intellectual doubts, but also from the social and moral dilemmas inherent in the poor student's dependence on patrons. At the same time that the ideal of passivity offered immunity from the more dishonorable exigencies of place seeking, it reconciled Pietist reform ideology with the realities of hierarchy. Above all in this sense – and in keeping with the Lutheran doctrine of calling – the Pietist ethic of self-denial sanctioned sponsored mobility in its received form; in the very process of advancing reform, it would insure against the servile, calculating self-interest as well as the arrogance that such sponsorship was known to unleash. This was not to divest the patron-client bond of its paternalist sanction, but to insist that, in the event of conflict, a higher order of paternalism must take

[44] LP, 4: 44–46.
[45] LP, 5: 69–73.
[46] LP, 4: 87, 103. See also LP, 1: 171; LP, 7: 300–4.
[47] LP, 3: 291.

precedence. The instrumentalism of the social relationship was subsumed under its sanctification as a providential instrument; for that very reason, the client's abjection before patrons was precluded by the Christian servant's abjection before God the Father.

The strictures about patronage are especially striking examples of the harmony between exegesis and practical reform exigencies pervading the *Lectures*. Francke was intent on keeping virtually all of the recruits God sent his way. The self-denying, passive trust in providence he sought to instill would both prevent them from leaving the university too early – i.e., before undergoing conversion and completing the full course of study – and ensure their willingness to accept "minor positions" once they did leave. But he was not engaged in an opportunistic manipulation of Lutheran doctrine. Guiding and lending consistency to every specific admonition was the central ideal of the converted Christian, embracing a life of reformist activism precisely because he had renounced the Old Adam and become a completely selfless servant of the Divine Will. As striking as the eclecticism of Francke's highly structured program for conversion is his dexterity in channeling heterodox borrowings into the mainstream triad of justification by faith, rebirth, and calling.[48] If he confronted students with an uncompromising ethic, he at least offered them a way of making sense of sponsored mobility, and of responding to its real pressures and choices, within a received fund of meanings.

LEGACIES

In *The Protestant Ethic and the Spirit of Capitalism*, Max Weber sought to unravel a skein of lineages between the Protestant ideal of calling, particularly as it developed in Calvinism, and modern capitalist forms of rational self-discipline. One unfortunate result of the controversy the essay aroused (a result that cannot be laid at Weber's doorstep) is that the filiations and ruptures between the ethic of calling and other modern forms of work discipline have received remarkably little attention.[49] Are there analogous affinities between the calling and the ethos of self-disciplined achievement in modern academic education and professional life, or is their relationship a simpler one of irreconcilable opposition? Historians have hardly begun

[48] Peschke, *Bekehrung und Reform*, pp. 39–40, 142–44. My reading of Francke's theology, it should be stressed, is limited to the *Lectures*, which may exaggerate his faithfulness to Luther. In the most thorough and careful treatment of the subject, Peschke characterizes Francke's thought as "*einem eigenwilligen Lutherverständnis*," corresponding considerably to Luther's intentions in the "*formale Ansatz der Gedankenführung*," but often diverging from them in the "*inhaltliche Durchführung*." Ibid., pp. 148–49.

[49] There is a substantial literature on Weber's thesis; a useful sample is S. N. Eisenstadt, ed., *The Protestant Ethic and Modernization. A Comparative View* (New York, 1968).

to explore this subject, although it is arguably at least as important as the relationship between the Protestant ethic and the spirit of capitalism.

Even for such an inquiry Weber's essay remains instructive as an exercise in cultural excavation, whatever one might think of his findings. He demonstrated the need to distinguish between manifest content and latent impulse, and the subtlety of his argument lay in explaining how these had sometimes collided and sometimes joined forces in the passage from the sacred to the secular. It will become apparent that the secular ethic of vocation in eighteenth-century Germany owed a great deal to latent impulses in the ideal of calling. But the social meaning of calling also lay in its explicit injunctions and their application to specific kinds of work discipline, and there Weber's preoccupations may have set a bad example. Weber argued that the ideal of "ascetic" service to the community required a rational self-discipline, relieving anxiety about election and eventually, in its secular metamorphosis, sanctioning entrepreneurial success; he largely ignored the fact that in the same ideal of service there was no legitimate place for the pursuit of individual self-interest that is sanctioned in modern commercial life. Even as an end in itself (much less as a means to a selfish end), Weber acknowledged, capitalist acquisitiveness was not tolerated in the Protestant ethic; but critics have argued that he should have given far more weight to that explicit restraint.[50]

Understanding the significance of the Lutheran-Pietist ideal of calling for academic and professional achievement likewise requires attention to manifest content. The danger is that, in the search for wellsprings of recognizably modern attitudes, the ethical core of the ideal will be slighted. It is instructive to compare early Pietism – i.e., the Pietism of Francke's generation – with the relatively late stage of Puritanism with which it coincided. The reformist zeal of Francke and others does not exhibit the tendency to combine the formulas of Orthodoxy with a new tolerance for the "natural man" and his "worldly aspirations" that scholars have attributed to contemporary Puritan divines.[51] What the *Admonitory Lectures* express most emphatically, and with a great deal of social specificity, is the opposite impulse. Francke took pains to reject any accommodation with the world and spelled out the implications of that rejection for the only "particular" calling that offered

[50] See esp. Walzer, *Revolution*, pp. 303–6, and Anthony Giddens's introductory comments in Weber, *The Protestant Ethic*, pp. 8–12.

[51] Douglas, "Talent and Vocation," pp. 295–98; Robert S. Michaelson, "Changes in the Puritan Concept of Calling or Vocation," *New England Quarterly* 26 (June 1953): 315–36. To judge by an excellent study of the Mathers, the evolution of Puritanism in New England was more complex. Cotton Mather, who was Francke's contemporary and conducted a correspondence with him, advocated an "American Pietism" that was open to "secular" trends in some respects but placed increasing emphasis on man's natural depravity and total helplessness in the conversion process. Robert Middlekauf, *The Mathers. Three Generations of Puritan Intellectuals 1596–1728* (New York, 1971), esp. pp. 191–319.

poor young men significant access to higher education and public employment. In a sense, Francke was reacting against the very success and ambition of his academic enterprise. The decline of religious fervor at Halle assumed a particularly scandalous form in student debauchery; but its more alarming symptoms were the preoccupation with career prospects at the expense of sanctification that seemed to accompany rapid growth of the faculty into a less cohesive, more impersonal institution and the intellectual pride that students contracted in the very process of acquiring academic competence. Francke was intent on advancing reform without admitting the personal aspirations that academic mobility might produce. Using every opportunity offered by Pauline texts, he drew the appropriate implications from the opposition between grace and nature that Luther had made fundamental to Protestant theology.

In Francke's ideology, as in early Puritanism, a repudiation of "the world" was combined with an activist ethic of work *in* the world. Both orientations are intended in Weber's celebrated phrase "this-worldly asceticism." What Francke's *Lectures* make especially manifest is the kind of uncompromising antisecular "asceticism" to which Weber, in his preoccupation with the motive forces behind entrepreneurial activity, had to give little weight. On the level of explicit ideology, this asceticism was posed with special urgency against the more indirect, subtle affirmations of worldly achievement and success. In its substance, Francke's paradoxical ideal – what might be called the state of active passivity – was hostile to such affirmations in academic education and professional careers as well as in capitalist acquisitiveness. The *Lectures* not only left no room in the converted "heart" for deriving "inner" satisfaction from intellectual achievement; they also shut the door tight against the conscious pursuit of "external" social and professional rewards. The higher meaning Francke ascribed to the opportunities and pressures of patronage lay not in opening career prospects, but in testing the aspiring clergyman's complete passivity in the face of a providential design.[52]

What seems paradoxical about this ethic from the modern perspective is precisely what made it so appealing to both poor students and their sponsors in the social and cultural context of the old regime. By breathing new vitality into Lutheran tradition, the Pietist ethic of calling once again made academic mobility a critical instrument of reform *within* the established hierarchy. To students facing extreme dependence on the titled, the educated, and the propertied, the ideal of self-denial promised the core of personal integrity that was indispensable to social "honor"; but it did so without sanctioning an outlet for personal and social aspirations that might threaten hierarchy and controlled sponsorship. To attribute this significance to the

[52] On the difference between Halle Pietism and Puritanism, at least as Weber interpreted the latter, see also Hinrichs, *Preussentum und Pietismus*, esp. pp. 12, 342–51.

ethic, however, is not to imply that as a motive force it operated in a state of pristine purity. To receptive students in the heyday of Pietism, one suspects, the injunction to self-denial was more a standard by which to measure the persistent impurity of motives (and the extent of guilt) than an attainable goal.[53] To judge by autobiographical literature from the second half of the century, the ethic continued to figure in poor students' efforts to justify themselves; but the same literature suggests that it could survive only at the price of becoming more or less alloyed. In the chemistry of its bonding with other values, the ideal of passive receptivity came to function more as a kind of solvent, removing any taint of selfish motivation from social ascent, than as an expression of the categorical ethic Francke had preached.

This bonding is obvious enough in the first three volumes of Heinrich Jung-Stilling's autobiography, despite (and in part because of) his obsessive protestations to the contrary.[54] As the grandson of a peasant-charcoaler and the son of a village schoolmaster-tailor, Jung-Stilling recalled, he had once regarded a clerical office as "too far beyond his sphere"; but in his late twenties, after several frustrating years spent alternating between village schoolmastery and tailoring (and finding satisfaction in neither occupation) and a disastrous stint as a private tutor, he had taken the highly unusual step of studying medicine. The first volume – the *Jugend* – was written in 1772, immediately after he had completed his studies at Strasbourg and had begun a medical practice in Elberfeld. He was already deep in debt, and over the next few years – i.e., the period when he wrote the *Jünglingsjahre* and the *Wanderschaft* – it became apparent that his chosen profession offered him neither social recognition nor financial security.[55]

[53] For other examples of the Pietist approach to students, echoing Francke's injunctions, see Johann Jacob Rambach, *Wohlunterrichteter Studiosus Theologiae, oder gründliche Anweisung, Auf was Art das Studium Theologicum zur Ehre Gottes und Nutzen der Kirche Jesu Christi, wie auch selbsteigner Seligkeit auf der Universität anzufangen, zu mitteln und zu enden sey* (Frankfurt am Main, 1737); "Student, Studenten, Studirende," in Johann Heinrich Zedler, ed., *Grosses vollständiges Universal Lexicon Aller Wissenschaften und Künste*, vol. 40 (Halle and Leipzig, 1744), pp. 1185–97.

[54] Johann Heinrich Jung-Stilling, *Heinrich Stillings Jugend, Jünglingsjahre, Wanderschaft und Häusliches Leben* (Stuttgart, 1968) (cited hereafter as Jung-Stilling). This Reclam edition includes an informative *Nachwort* by Dieter Cunz. The fourth and final volume (the *Häusliches Leben*) was published more than a decade later, in 1789; it marks a quite different stage of his life, and there is general agreement that it is distinct from the first three volumes.

[55] Even if his ambition had been to study theology, Jung-Stilling later noted, his father's "entire wealth would not have sufficed to support [him] for a mere two years at the university." *Rückblicke auf Stillings bisherige Lebensgeschichte*, reprinted in Johann Heinrich Jung-Stilling, *Lebensgeschichte*, ed. Gustav Adolph Benrath (Darmstadt, 1976). p. 605. On his decision to study medicine, see also his letter to Lavater (Apr. 29, 1780), reprinted in ibid., pp. 660–61, and still another account (1788), reprinted in ibid., pp. 673–74. The *Jugend* had originally been conceived as a contribution to a literary society in which Jung-Stilling had participated as a student in Strasbourg, and it was pitched to the tastes of those friends whose "foundations of religious faith were very shaky." If the religious message was suitably decked out in "romantic, flowery costume," he reasoned, even the skeptical might be persuaded that there was

Jung-Stilling reacted to this disappointment by becoming all the more intent on proving that, following a meandering series of misfortunes and self-deceptions, he had at last entered his assigned calling. The novelistic technique of presenting himself as a third-person character, which had originally conveyed his nostalgia for an idyllic childhood, now served to demonstrate his passivity as an instrument of the Lord. The early failures and mistakes of a zigzag life course, and eventually the tribulations medicine had to offer, became necessary trials along a providential path.

Jung-Stilling's Pietism has strong traces of the Quietist variety to which his father had exposed him, but his autobiography attests above all to the continuing influence of the Halle spirit in his generation. It can be read as a self-consciously literary variation on conventional conversion testimonials, which had provided much of his childhood reading. The dramatic turning point comes on the Sunday afternoon when Heinrich, at age twenty-one, feels his soul penetrated by an "unknown power" and makes "a solid and irrevocable resolution with God to abandon himself entirely to His direction and cherish no more egotistical desires." His previous "trials" as a schoolmaster and tailor, he has already learned, have been meant to purge the craving for "honor" and "fame" that has "corrupted" his intellectual inclinations. From this point on, the plot becomes a series of miraculous interventions, and despite the obvious difference in circumstances the explanations of Heinrich's motives and decisions read like a textbook case of Francke's do's and don'ts for theology candidates.[56]

When he accepted a tutoring position in the household of a wealthy merchant, Heinrich followed once again "the old corrupt motive" that seduced him like "a kind of serpent . . . that strove to bring reason [*Vernunft*] to its aid." This final trial seemed to offer an opportunity to learn polite manners, but instead subjected him to poverty and social contempt.[57] Like a sleepwalker, "without knowing why and without having a direction," he finally left the household and set out on the road. In retrospect the author realizes that he had at last entered the miraculous path to a medical career. It will be marked by a succession of providential signs, culminating in the financial contributions from friends and patrons, usually arriving when he is on the brink of destitution, that vindicate his trust in the Lord and allow him to survive at Strasbourg.[58]

something truly miraculous about his ascent from a peasant family to a medical degree. It was Goethe, another former member of the society, who edited the manuscript and, to its author's surprise, arranged for its publication in 1776. Goethe removed or changed "religious pieces" as well as much that was "flat and superficial," Jung-Stilling later reported, but the surviving "ornaments" (*Verzierungen*) were his own. Ibid., pp. 654–55, 660–63, 686–87.

[56] Jung-Stilling, pp. 162–64, 209–10. For background on Jung-Stilling's Pietism see esp. Hans R. G. Günther, *Jung-Stilling. Ein Beitrag zur Psychologie des Pietismus* (2nd rev. ed.: Munich, 1948), esp. pp. 32–63.

[57] Jung-Stilling, pp. 211–20.

[58] Ibid., esp. pp. 220, 230–33, 247–50, 269–83.

And yet the dilution of Francke's categorical ethic is evident in the very form of this testimonial. In the conventional testimonial – the kind Francke himself had written – the point is to bear witness to the "general" calling to be a Christian that comes with the infusion of grace. Narrative detail is used primarily to mark the progress of the *Busskampf* – the struggle against the natural self – that precedes the "breakthrough"; it is a foregone conclusion, usually meriting little or no attention, that henceforth the Christian's immediate calling will reflect his transformation.[59] The received form was inadequate to Jung-Stilling's urgent need to justify an erratic ascent from peasant origins into the world of academic careers. His entire emphasis is on the protagonist's quest for the immediate calling for which all his experiences seem to prepare. Notably lacking in the "atonement struggle" is the introspective detail of an intense wrestling with the natural self. The breakthrough is not a culmination, but a pivot, enabling him not only to confront and eventually prevail over the corrupt motives behind false steps, but also to find personal satisfaction in the appropriate career.

Within this adapted form, the repudiation of rational calculation is undercut by a convenient, if tortuous, calculus of "inner" motivation and "exterior" direction. In Jung-Stilling's scheme of things, to be sure, the happy ending of the third volume (the beginning of his medical practice) actually punctuates the central paradox; objective social ascent has become permissible only because it is not motored by ambition – because the protagonist has ceased to desire it. But as Heinrich undergoes each trial and escapes each false step, the paradoxical implication is that the truly passive servant of the Lord will be spared such misfortunes. And the increasingly miraculous aura of the account tends to obscure the mundane reality that, thanks to Heinrich's reputation as an eye surgeon and his religious affiliations, his medical studies are completely financed by a network of Pietist merchant families in and around Elberfeld.[60] In the effort to prove his transcendence of ambition and to dispel any suspicion of self-interested calculation in his relations with benefactors, Jung-Stilling reduces the mediating role of patronage in a providential design to the purse strings of a cast of *patroni ex machina*.

This tension between dogmatic assertion and underlying motive has its parallel in Jung-Stilling's use of "urge" or "drive" to describe his inner

[59] On the evolution of the conversion testimonial as a genre, see esp. Gunter Niggl, *Geschichte der deutschen Autobiographie im 18. Jahrhundert* (Stuttgart, 1977), pp. 6–13, 62–74. As Niggl observes, even the earliest testimonials, though usually focused on the period before the "breakthrough," tended to give room to secular life alongside the formulaic religious account.

[60] The major contributor was his father-in-law, despite Heinrich's protestation to him during the courtship (and the author's retrospective assurance to the reader) that he was not angling for a way to finance his studies. Jung-Stilling, pp. 259–66, 269–83, 299. See also the justification of his "courtship" and first marriage in Jung-Stilling, *Lebensgeschichte*, pp. 660–61.

dynamic. When the young Heinrich laments that he does not have an intellectual *Beruf*, he is made to admit that his *Trieb* for learning is tied to a craving for social prestige. But when faced with the prospect of a "constant hell" as a peasant-tailor, he had protested to his father that "it would be horrible [*entsetzlich*] if God had implanted *Triebe* and inclinations in my soul and denied me the guidance to satisfy them as long as I live."[61] It becomes apparent that Jung-Stilling regarded a certain level of intellectual satisfaction as a legitimate need. The result is a tension-ridden justification for social ascent; operating in muted counterpoint to Heinrich's subjection to "duty" – to the Pietist self-effacement to which he progresses from trial to trial on a more explicit thematic level – is a natural inner entelechy, implying a right to develop innate potential. If *Beruf* was the assignment imposed from above, it was also the medium for self-realization through intellectual work.[62]

Jung-Stilling was an extreme case, and a somewhat eccentric one. More secular than this neo-Pietistic witness and more representative of the experience of poor students is Anton Friedrich Büsching's *Lebensgeschichte*. Here the underlying tone is one of muted self-satisfaction at the close of an eminent career, and in its glow the author's ascent from below has acquired a certain linear simplicity. A founder of the new discipline of political geography, Büsching had left a professorial appointment at Göttingen to spend twenty-six years as a consistorial councilor and well-paid director of a prestigious gymnasium in Berlin. In 1784, in a remarkably blunt article on the question "Who should attend the university?" he called for the opening of *all* academic careers (not just the clergy) to talent. Low family origins

[61]Jung-Stilling, pp. 94, 123, 129, 147, 162–64. The ambiguous language became more precise in Jung-Stilling's later *Rückblicke* (1804). Trying to summarize his autobiography from "the true angle of vision," Jung-Stilling distinguished himself from the exceptional man who determines the course of his own life by single-mindedly pursuing a "basic drive" that is purely "natural." His own *Grundbetrieb*, he insisted, had been the purely religious kind – the urge to serve "Jesus Christ, His religion, and His Kingdom" – that the Lord implanted from without, and its fulfillment had required the complete eradication of his "natural" appetite for "highly frivolous enjoyment of physical and intellectual-sensual pleasures." But by then Jung-Stilling was intent on defending his own increasingly dogmatic brand of neo-Pietism; his "true angle" imposes a rigid interpretive grid on the autobiography, distorting more than it clarifies in the first three volumes. And it is striking that, even in the *Rückblicke*, Jung-Stilling found no inconsistency in assuming that neither tailoring nor schoolmastery had been his true calling because he had found them "boring" and had practiced them "without desire [*Lust*], but merely out of a sense of duty." Jung-Stilling, *Lebensgeschichte*, pp. 599–602, 606–7. See also Günther, *Jung-Stilling*, pp. 70–74, and the insightful remarks on the "rationalization" implicit in Jung-Stilling's attempt to unite the traditional Pietist "structure of providential design" with "the modern idea of entelechy," in Niggl, *Geschichte der deutschen Autobiographie*, pp. 74–75.

[62] Not surprisingly Jung-Stilling's autobiography has often invited comparison with Moritz's *Anton Reiser*. See, e.g., Niggl, *Geschichte der deutschen Autobiographie*, pp. 65–75; Gotthilf Stecher, *Jung-Stilling als Schriftsteller* (Berlin, 1913), pp. 122–28; Klaus-Detlef Müller, *Autobiographie und Roman. Studien zur literarischen Autobiographie der Goethezeit* (Tübingen, 1976), pp. 127–68, 202–6; Bernd Neumann, *Identität und Rollenzwang. Zur Theorie der Autobiographie* (Frankfurt am Main, 1970), pp. 120–30.

and lack of means, he argued, should be irrelevant; all that mattered were a "good head," a "dominating drive" to learn, and "a good temperament."[63] In the "life history," published five years later, he offered his own career as a case in point. Büsching's father had studied law at Jena and Halle, but despite family connections he had become an obscure lawyer in his hometown. Temperamentally unsuited for a law practice, and finding relief from his recurrent fits of depression in drink, he squandered most of the family stipend that was supposed to finance his son's education. Büsching went to Halle in 1743 as one of the scholarship boys in the Latin school and went on to become a student-instructor compensated at one of the free tables.[64]

Büsching also looked back on a dramatic turning point, and his recollection of it was interwoven with an unusually candid account of his troubled relationship with his father. Though he explains his self-discipline in part as a reaction against the elder Büsching's heavy drinking, he also suggests that his own "liveliness" and "wildness" as a boy might very well have resulted in a similar lack of moderation. What saved him was his participation in the "hours of edification" (*Erbauungsstunde*) of a Pietist conventicle under the guidance of two local pastors. He could recall the exact day (January 30, 1741) on which he and a friend, meditating while waiting for one of the pastors, concluded a pact in recognition of their conversion. Its immediate effect was to allow him to defy his father in good conscience when the latter, furious at discovering his son's involvement in sectarian "enthusiasm," threw him out of the house. Thanks largely to the charity and intercession of fatherly Pietist mentors, he was able to begin his studies at Halle.[65]

Büsching's conversion had not simply given him an emotional center of gravity in the face of severe tensions at home; it had also led him to approach an uncertain future with the trust in the Lord that Francke had preached to his students. Nearly a half-century later, he remained convinced that his life and career represented a vindication of that trust. "Divine providence" had brought him the patrons and financial support that had made possible his education and had miraculously produced the required fees for his *Magister* degree. Likewise it had provided for the "access to people of station of both sexes" that had contributed so much to his social grooming and had proffered the tutoring position that had furthered his entrée to aristocratic society and had opened new career doors.[66]

"My example," Büsching observed, "can encourage young people who

[63] Anton Friedrich Büsching, "Beantwortung der Frage: Wer soll studiren?" *Magazin für die Erziehung und Schulen, besonders in den preussischen Staaten* 1 (Halle, 1781): 91–107 (also in *Archiv für die ausübende Erziehungskunst* 11 [1784]: 189–202).

[64] Anton Friedrich Büsching, *Eigene Lebensgeschichte* (Halle, 1789), esp. pp. 20–27, 78.

[65] Ibid., pp. 51–62.

[66] Ibid., esp. pp. 89–94, 102, 107.

want to devote themselves with head and heart to learning but have little or no means of support to attend schools and universities away from home with joyous trust in God, and to hope with certainty that they will be able to pursue their goal and wish."[67] In this life perspective, as in Francke's *Lectures*, the normal workings of patronage were critical junctures for providential intervention. And yet for all the importance he attributed to conversion as a pivotal experience and for all his insistence on his own "joyous trust," Büsching emerges from his autobiography more as a hard-driving, adept social climber than as a passive instrument of providence. Precisely because he is secure in his belief in providential intervention, he can celebrate his ascent without acknowledging the propelling force of his own ambition – and without admitting anything "servile" about his obvious readiness to cultivate the "people of station" who had the power to smooth his way.[68]

The other requisite quality of temperament was a willingness to "consider a life of hard work and effort the happiest life." Büsching assumed an impressive workload and maintained a strenuous daily schedule; it was apparently with good reason that younger colleagues in the 1770s and 1780s regarded him as a kind of workaholic. "Work is one of my life needs," the concluding précis of his "character" ended, and "the drive for it is greater than for any sensual pleasure."[69] It was above all in this sense that Pietist religiosity had prevented him from following in his father's footsteps. But if Francke's uncompromising struggle with the natural self had originally played a role in Büsching's this-worldly asceticism, it no longer seemed relevant by the time he recalled his conversion from the distance of a successful career. Behind his almost formulaic humility as a servant of the Lord lies his unmistakable pride in his own disciplined achievement.

Büsching's acknowledgment that he still drew personal meaning from a boyhood conversion may have startled some of his readers, though it was accompanied by assurances that this formative experience had not seduced him into a sectarian variety of Pietism. By the time he wrote the autobiography he was a solid citizen of the academic and clerical establishment

[67] Ibid., p. 102.

[68] Ibid. One advantage of private tutoring, Büsching had observed in his handbook on the subject, was "an acquaintance with various people . . . of whom divine providence will make use for further advancement of [the tutor's] exterior welfare." It was "more advantageous and praiseworthy to wait for a call [*Beruf*] in joyous trust in God, constant industry and respectable behavior" than to "offer oneself" for a tutoring position; but it would not hurt to move to a city in which many tutors were sought and "make oneself known through modestly demonstrated competence when the occasion arises." In keeping with this delicate balance, Büsching's list of the "natural powers of the soul" required of a tutor included "modesty" and "deference" as well as "cleverness" and "industry." Anton Friedrich Büsching, *Grundris eines Unterrichts wie besondere Lehrer und Hofmeister der Kinder und Jünglinge sich pflichtmässig, wohlanständing und klüglich verhalten müssen* (Altona, 1760), pp. 25, 29–36, 48.

[69] Büsching, *Lebensgeschichte*, p. 102.

of the German Enlightenment, where it was much more common to explain the trauma of conversion as misguided religious enthusiasm, if not as self-serving hypocrisy. While his personal testimony was meant to qualify the prevailing stereotype of Pietism, his underlying ethical orientation points to a very different species of eighteenth-century Protestant culture.

6

Vocation: the natural self and the ethic of reason

"How easy it was for me to return home," Israel Hartmann wrote to his nineteen-year-old son Gottlob David in October 1771, "as soon as I had the slightest sign [*Spur*] that you would let God work in your heart."[1] Hartmann had accompanied his son to Tübingen, where he was to begin his studies in the theological Stift after four years as a cloister school pupil. Long overdue, the sign proved illusory. The extensive correspondence between father and son records a classic discord, already audible several years before 1771 and reaching the point of shrill exasperation on both sides during Gottlob David's two-year tenure at the Stift.

"I dedicated you as the firstborn to the service of the church," Israel Hartmann reminded his son in December 1771, and as a child "you wanted to hear of nothing else." But by the end of his first semester Gottlob David was pleading with his father to allow him to leave the Stift after the initial two-year course in philosophy, so that he could pursue an academic career in that subject outside Württemberg. Aside from balking at the prospect of at least three more years as a penurious student, he was unwilling to endure the intellectual "slavery" and "oppression" imposed by the Orthodox clerical establishment of his fatherland. If required to remain in Tübingen to complete his theological studies, he warned his father, he would have to confine himself to his room for the duration.[2] In the fall of 1773, after completing a *Magister* degree in philosophy, he accepted a teaching appointment at the gymnasium that Duke Peter of the Curland had recently established in Mitau. The site of the Duke's modest court, Mitau was a

[1] Israel Hartmann to Gottlob David Hartmann, Oct. 1771, in Israel Hartmann Nachlass (cited hereafter as HN), p. 353. The Nachlass is available in Hauptstaatsarchiv Ludwigsburg. My references are to the archival pagination, which follows the chronological order of the letters. For a brief portrait of the son, see C. J. Wagenseil, "Nachricht von Hartmanns Leben und Charakter," in Gottlob David Hartmann, *Hinterlassene Schriften*, ed. C. J. Wagenseil (Gotha, 1779): v-xlvi. A useful biography is Wilhelm Lang, *Gottl. Dav. Hartmann. Ein Lebensbild aus der Sturm und Drangzeit* (Stuttgart, 1890).

[2] See esp. HN, pp. 369, 391–402, 431–34. Gottlob David added pointedly that, even if he completed his theological studies, his prospects in the Württemberg clergy would not have improved, since he would still refuse to toe the Orthodox line.

frontier outpost among princely residences. The father had bitterly opposed this change of course and had come very close to breaking off relations with him entirely. He was never to see his son again; already ill with consumption, Gottlob David died in Mitau on November 5, 1775, at age twenty-three.

Israel Hartmann may have had a change of heart after his son expatriated, but until then he was an unreconstructed Pietist.[3] Having experienced conversion at an early age, he grew increasingly impatient and alarmed as it became apparent that his eldest son was not following suit. Before their conflict surfaced, his invocations to atonement and self-denial took the form of carefully penned poems (*Carmen*), and he expected Gottlob David to demonstrate his piety as well as his skill in rhyme and meter by responding in kind. Francke does not figure among the authors he urged on the boy, although they did include Spener as well as Bengel, the great luminary of Württemberg Pietism. But it is testimony to the far-reaching influence of the Halle ethic that the father's letters echoed Francke's specific admonitions to the poor students in the Halle theology faculty. The son should welcome the cross of "dear poverty"; it would protect him from the seductions of the flesh and the world, as it had protected his father. Like Francke, Hartmann expected the aspiring clergyman to be self-disciplined and "industrious" in his studies without succumbing to the vanity and ambition with which learned men were so easily infected.[4] When Gottlob David tried to secure an appointment outside Tübingen through friends, his efforts seemed one more indication that he had contracted these vices. "Persevere in Tübingen," the father wrote, until "He who gave you the gifts calls you away" with "a more certain, unsolicited call."[5]

Lack of money was a constant irritant in this generational conflict. The fifth and youngest son of an oxen dealer, Isreal Hartmann had become a schoolmaster, without a university degree, in the royal orphanage in Ludwigsburg in 1755. His wife was the daughter of one of the preceptors in the lowest ranks of the Württemberg clergy. The family had reached the outer fringe of the network of families that virtually monopolized places in the cloister schools and the Stift, but it proved very burdensome to secure full membership among these *Honoratioren* for the eldest son while raising a brood of younger children on a meager teaching income. In August 1770, Hartmann calculated that he had devoted 25 gulden in less than six months to the boy's support at the cloister school. He figured on contributing 50 gulden per year – one-third of his cash salary – to his upkeep at the Stift,

[3] On the change of heart, see esp. Israel Hartmann's letter of Aug. 22, 1774, in HN, pp. 472–74. Thanks to the intercession of Lavater, who visited him in Ludwigsburg, Hartmann was persuaded that his son was following a providential path and came to regret his earlier harsh judgments. On Lavater's relationship with the son, see Chapter 9.

[4] HN, esp. pp. 43–57, 270–71, 319–20.

[5] Ibid., esp. pp. 428–38.

and even with that aid the son had to resort to credit. Not surprisingly the elder Hartmann's letters are filled with laments about inflation and mounting debts and pleas for economy.[6]

Even at the height of their quarrel, Israel Hartmann had to concede that his son "behave[d] [himself] better than others infected with the plague of *belles lettres* [*der Seuche der schönen Wissenschaften*]."[7] The allowance from home may seem exorbitant in view of the fact that room and board were free, but the young man was not indulging in the drinking, gambling, and other forms of "debauchery" that landed so many other students in debt and outraged the fathers who had to pay bills. The austere discipline of the cloister schools and the Stift left little scope for such amusements, and in any case Gottlob David was not the type. This father's problem was that his son was an ardent and unrepentant book buyer. In September 1770, when he was still a schoolboy, Gottlob David estimated that his annual book costs amounted to 20 gulden. It was little comfort to Hartmann senior that 7 gulden came from a small stipend and the other 13 was allowance money Gottlob David had saved by not drinking wine at meals. "Your brothers and sisters also want to have food and clothing from your father," the mother protested in a rare appearance, and "books we cannot eat."[8]

Financial difficulties aside, Israel Hartmann was unwilling to finance his son's "book addiction" because he disapproved of his reading habits. To the father reading, like the writing of *Carmen*, was a devotional ritual, an exercise in piety. Reacting to a book of verse the son had sent him, Hartmann contrasted good poetry, which flowed from the "spirit" and "life" of grace, with the arrogance and empty intellectualism of the "latest, most learned" poets. Instead of throwing away money on the most recent biblical commentaries, his son should "read in prayer the writings of Luther, Arndt, Spener, Bengel, and effect what God wants to make of you through their witness and the witness of your conscience." Gottlob David protested in defense that Arndt and Bengel sufficed "for a pious man," but not for the "scholar" he aspired to become, and that his purchases were limited to "old books" required in his studies. But the items he finally admitted to buying included, in addition to editions of classical authors and philological works, Voltaire's *Henriade*, Iselin's *Geschichte der Menschheit*, and Moses Mendelssohn's *Philosophische Werke*. The father also complained about "novels" and "very harmful and corrupting writings" by Wieland.[9]

What lured Gottlob David away from his theological apprenticeship and implanted his new aspiration to serve humanity in "philosophy" was the

[6] Ibid., pp. 278, 307, 358–65. On the parents' social background see Lang, *Hartmann*, p. 10.

[7] Israel Hartmann's letter of June 1, 1773, in HN, pp. 428–29.

[8] Agnes Rosina Hartmann's letter of July 13, 1771, in ibid., pp. 343–45. For Gottlob David's estimate of expenses see ibid., p. 280.

[9] Ibid., pp. 121–23, 145–47, 248–50, 274–75, 339–48.

literature of the Enlightenment. In 1773, while still at the Stift, he drew on this reading to produce a long and intensely personal treatise entitled *Sophron. Oder die Bestimmung des Jünglings für dieses Leben.* It was dedicated to Johann Joachim Spalding, whose *Ueber die Bestimmung des Menschen* inspired the title. Spalding's brief meditation was highly popular in rationalist theological circles; applying recent English and French thought, it guided the reader through an exercise in introspection that led from the "perfecting" of his natural capacities and fulfillment of his innate altruistic impulse to belief in God and an eternal reward.[10] Torn between his father's expectations and his own aspirations, Hartmann had become preoccupied with the first part of the exercise. He addressed *Sophron* to "the youth of [his] fatherland" and took it upon himself to explain how a young man ought to select the appropriate "way of life" by identifying the natural inclinations and talents that constituted his inner vocation.[11]

It was this debut in popular philosophy that confirmed Israel Hartmann's worst fears about the state of his son's soul. In several letters Gottlob David tried to demonstrate that his view, though stated "philosophically" and "psychologically" rather than "theologically," was compatible with his father's beliefs. But understandably the father took it personally when he read that the "assignment from above" was "what is true or false according to healthy human reason," not "what men dream about in the obscurity of their hearts." Hartmann senior acknowledged that the book might be beautifully written (it was not), but found it woefully lacking in the realization that "human nature and being [*Wesen*] is completely corrupted by Adam's fall." "Concentrate on being a genius," he concluded scornfully, and "never again think of theology."[12]

With the publication of *Sophron*, Gottlob David may very well have eliminated any chance for a clerical or academic career in Württemberg. The court chaplain rebuked him for insulting the educational institutions of his fatherland and embarrassing his parents, and at one point the Consistory in Stuttgart threatened to institute legal proceedings against the publisher.[13] But this reaction was a measure of the smug local patriotism and rigid

[10] Johann Joachim Spalding, *Bestimmung des Menschen (1748) und Wert der Andacht*, ed. Horst Stephan (Giessen, 1908). The tenth edition of *Bestimmung* had appeared in 1768. For a convenient summary of Spalding's argument, see Alexander Altmann, *Moses Mendelssohn. A Biographical Study* (London, 1973), pp. 130–34.

[11] Gottlob David Hartmann, *Sophron. Oder die Bestimmung des Jünglings für dieses Leben* (Mitau, 1773). The book was dedicated to Spalding.

[12] HN, pp. 409–19, 440–41. On the margin of his letter of Feb. 23, 1773 – the one in which Israel Hartmann had accused his son of defying both divine and paternal authority and had written, "Now I will not write to you anything more about God and his Word, and wish to know nothing more of this matter, and this your father writes to you in all seriousness" – he had later noted: "Oh, how entirely differently I ought to have always written, if I had only seen better; oh, prejudice and the judgment of others, how you plague the heart of a father." Ibid., pp. 418–19; Lang, *Hartmann*, p. 52.

[13] HN, pp. 442, 457–58; Lang, *Hartmann*, p. 62.

Orthodoxy for which the Württemberg clerical establishment was renowned. In a more accurate, though unkind, appraisal, one reviewer noted that Hartmann's "boring" and "drowsy" style "not seldom slides off the thoughts it wants to embrace" and that he had "sown only very thinly with his own thoughts."[14] If the book's "philosophy" was too derivative to establish Hartmann as an original thinker, it was too commonplace to provoke an official reaction, pro or con, or even to attract a wide readership outside Württemberg. In Protestant central and northern Germany, the ethic of vocation to which Hartmann had imparted so much youthful ardor was already a mainstay of public discourse and clerical consciousness. Our concern is with the ideological framework and implications of *Beruf* in this secular sense; with its radical departures from the ethic of Pietism; and with less obvious filiations, easily obscured by the terms of generational conflict.

NATURE, SOCIETY, AND ART

To Gottlob David Hartmann vocation was a voice within, but it spoke to "the reason" through nature rather than to "the heart" through grace. Heeding its message was a matter of identifying and developing the innate endowments evoked by the word "talent." The semantic triangle formed by vocation, nature, and talent is one of the "unit ideas" the Enlightenment throughout Europe filtered into modern consciousness. Of its immediate sources, the best known was John Locke's *Some Thoughts Concerning Education*, which was published in 1693 and may have been available in German as early as 1708.[15] In this widely read essay, Locke urged that "nature," discernible in childhood and even in infancy, be the overriding authority in pedagogy and likewise that it be the determining factor in choosing a boy's future "way of life." But the originality of Locke's contribution to pedagogy lay in deriving remarkably concrete and common-sensical precepts from an ancient tradition. The root idea of *vocatio* and its basic implications for pedagogy and occupational choices were to be found in the writings of Quintillian, Cicero, and other Roman authors, and had received considerable attention in Renaissance humanism. Even educated Germans

[14] Quoted in Lang, *Hartmann*, p. 111.

[15] For a list of the German printings of *Some Thoughts Concerning Education*, see *The Educational Writings of John Locke*, ed. James L. Axtell (Cambridge, 1968), pp. 102–3. The first German edition Axtell found was in 1729, but he notes the possibility of editions in 1708, 1709, and 1710. Axtell's critical edition includes an excellent introduction to the work and its intellectual context. On the importance of Locke for eighteenth-century German pedagogy, see esp. Rosemarie Wothge, "Eine Studie zur bürgerlichen Pädagogik des 17. und 18. Jahrhunderts. Dargestellt am Kommentar zu Lockes Schrift über die Erziehung in Campes Revisionswerk," *Wissenschaftliche Zeitschrift der Martin-Luther-Universität Halle-Wittenberg*, Gesellschafts- und Sprachwissenschaftliche Reihe, vol. 4, no. 3 (Halle, 1954–55), pp. 485–91.

who had not read Locke had been exposed to this tradition as schoolboys. One of its classic statements was Cicero's *De officiis*, perhaps the most widely used text in the Latin schools.[16]

The concept of "talent" owed its survival in part to academic Latinity, but its appeal extended far beyond this philological context. What is striking, in fact, is that in the course of the century the concept assumed increasing significance in German public discourse despite the condemnation of the Latin schools' deadening pedantry by former pupils, and particularly by the reform-minded pedagogues among them. Like the concept of nature of which it was a part, "talent" was an ideological construct. The point may be all too obvious, but there has been remarkably little elaboration of it in eighteenth-century studies. Even for France, where in 1789 the Declaration of the Rights of Man and the Citizen proclaimed careers open to talent, the prerevolutionary meanings and usages of the term have not received focused attention.[17] This neglect is not explained simply by the preoccupation until recently with social and economic conditions; it also reflects our inability to achieve critical distance on a particularly vital legacy of eighteenth-century thought. In the light of subsequent critiques of "liberal" thought, the normative assumptions informing eighteenth-century concepts of "liberty" and "equality" seem clear enough. "Talent" forms a more immediate link with eighteenth-century discourse; aside from its place in the various political ideologies to which the century gave rise, it remains fundamental to a pervasive cultural ideology of achievement in western societies. Whether and how talent ought to be rewarded is the obvious ideological issue; the object of the controversy retains special status as a fact of

[16] On the humanistic conception of *vocatio* and its classical sources, see esp. Richard M. Douglas, "Talent and Vocation in Humanist and Protestant Thought," in Theodore K. Rabb and Jerrold E. Seigel, eds., *Action and Conviction in Early Modern Europe. Essays in Memory of E. H. Harbison* (Princeton, N.J., 1969), pp. 261–98. For early efforts to draw social implications from the concept of "inner" *Beruf* (in the sense of natural vocation), see the article on "*Beruff*" in Johann Heinrich Zedler, ed., *Grosses vollständiges Universal Lexicon Aller Wissenschaften und Künste* 3 (1733), pp. 1449–51; the article on "Lebens-Art," in ibid., 16 (1737): 1272–77; "Betrachtungen über den Beruf," in Johann J. Schwabe, ed., *Belustigungen des Verstandes und des Witzes* (2nd ed.: Leipzig, 1742), pp. 27–39.

[17] The discussion of natural "aptitude" in Noëlle Bisseret, *Education, Class Language and Ideology* (London, 1979), is relevant to an understanding of the historical role of "talent" as an ideological construct. But Bisseret's historical analysis focuses on the nineteenth century, and the social framework for her brief discussion of the eighteenth century is simplistic. More attention has been devoted to explaining in social terms the ideological appeal of "careers open to talent" as an objective of reform (or revolution). Still indispensable is Elinor G. Barber, *The Bourgeoisie in 18th Century France* (1955: Princeton, N.J., 1973). See also Robert Darnton, "The High Enlightenment and the Low-Life of Literature," in idem, *The Literary Underground of the Old Regime* (Cambridge, Mass., 1982), pp. 1–40; idem, *Mesmerism and the End of the Enlightenment in France* (New York, 1976), pp. 83–125. For insightful comments on the significance of this issue for the German intelligentsia, see Hans Erich Bödeker, "Thomas Abbt: Patriot, Bürger und bürgerliches Bewusstsein," in Rudolf Vierhaus, ed., *Bürger und Bürgerlichkeit im Zeitalter der Aufklärung*, Wolfenbütteler Studien zur Aufklärung, vol. 7 (Heidelberg, 1981), pp. 221–53.

nature, an elemental reality that, like the force of gravity, must be accepted at face value. To approach the concept itself as ideology is not to deny the reality of its object of reference, but simply to recognize that the very identification of the reality was, and remains, a process shaped by and oriented to a specific social context. Welcomed as a criterion for distributing rewards by appeal to the natural order of things, "talent" appropriated nature for particular social purposes.

It will become apparent that in this regard talent proved remarkably flexible, but the first task is to account for the general appeal of the concept within a larger ideological field. In the eighteenth century "talent" was the corollary to "service" and "merit," both denoted by *Verdienst*. The pairing of *Talent* and *Verdienst* became standard as the assumptions and logic of cameralism fed into Enlightenment reform thought and shaped its ends and means. From the mid-seventeenth century onward, cameralist theorists, faced with the dismal aftereffects of the Thirty Years' War and eager to promote recovery, schematized society into the interlocking parts of an intricate machine. The hand guiding the machine was the state, and it would operate at maximum efficiency only when it effectively harnessed the potential contributions of its members. There was, to be sure, a tension inherent in this view. Expansion of the whole required equilibrium among the parts; as the overarching authority, responsible for maintaining equilibrium, the state in effect committed itself to perpetuating the existing hierarchy of orders, with status derived from the inherited privileges attached to membership in a family or corporation (or both). Yet the cameralists also tended to rank occupational groups according to the relative importance of their contributions to the public welfare. From this standpoint, the status of the group should hinge on its function in a division of labor, and the status of the individual should be in recognition of his performance in a functional role.[18]

In "an enlightened age and a sophisticated nation," a contributor to *Der Teutsche Merkur* wrote in 1774, the station of the *Bürger* should be "personal" rather than "hereditary," and "merited" (*verdienstlich*) rather than

[18] A key transitional figure was Johann Heinrich Gottlob von Justi, who was particularly fond of mechanistic metaphors; see especially his "Rede von dem unzertrennlichen Zusammenhange eines blühenden Zustandes der Wissenschaften mit denjenigen Mitteln, welche einen Staat mächtig und glücklich machen," in idem, *Gesammelte Politische und Finanzschriften über wichtige Gegenstände der Staatskunst, der Kriegswissenschaften und des Cameral- und Finanzwesens*, 3 vols. (Kopenhagen, 1761–64), 2: 169. On cameralism see esp. Marc Raeff, *The Well-Ordered Police State. Social and Institutional Change through Law in the Germanies and Russia, 1600–1800* (New Haven, Conn., and London, 1983), which has superseded the older literature and was particularly helpful for this study. Also relevant are Andreas Flitner, *Die politische Erziehung in Deutschland. Geschichte und Probleme, 1750–1880* (Tübingen, 1957); Manfred Heinemann, *Schule im Vorfeld der Verwaltung. Die Entwicklung der preussischen Unterrichtsverwaltung von 1771–1800* (Göttingen, 1974), pp. 18–42; Geraint Parry, "Enlightened Government and Its Critics in Eighteenth-Century Germany," *Historical Journal* 6:2 (1963): 178–92.

"accidental"; "the entire hierarchy of ranks and of the various stations should be constituted according to the classification of services [*Verdienste*], and the relative amount of each capacity and work, and of the value of the thing thereby accomplished, should be the true and actual standard for all civic honor."[19] A sophisticated society was a rational one, tapping the full potential of its human resources and in turn granting every individual the reward he "merited" by virtue of the "service" he rendered. Between these two meanings of *Verdienst*, "talent" offered the vital link. It was a kind of base currency of social exchange, referring human activity in all its variety to a single natural source of energy and creativity, but at the same time, in its differentiation into myriad kinds and degrees, enabling occupational groups and their members to earn their particular shares of "merit" for the equivalents in "service."

In the traditional Christian conception of hierarchy, incorporated into Lutheranism, function also figured as an organizing principle; if the rank assigned each part of the social body reflected the Divine Will, it also was in recognition of the value of a specific contribution to the entire organism. But the emphasis was on maintaining in this world the conditions of law and order in which the true Christian could prepare for the next, within a framework strictly bounded intellectually and in a state of economic stasis. Christian Wolff typified the very different orientation of cameralism when he defined the "common welfare" as a process of "unhindered advance to greater perfections."[20] Perfecting society meant not only increasing its population and expanding its wealth by encouraging commercial activity and introducing new technology, but also channeling more of its intellectual and moral energies into creative, productive activities. Underlying this shift in emphasis was a marked difference in the perception of the relationship between nature and society. In the traditional Christian conception, the society of orders was "natural" only by analogy; it reflected, on the microcosmic scale of human society, the same principles of hierarchy that located man on the chain of being ordering the entire cosmos. One of the attractions of the new, more dynamic vision was that it replaced analogy with a direct cause-and-effect relationship; in its pairing of merit and talent, the social hierarchy would rest on and derive legitimacy from the actual distribution of natural endowments among its members.

The principle of natural equality was essential to this vision; but in eighteenth-century discourse, it rarely had as one of its inferences a drastic leveling of social distinctions. As obvious as the commonality of the basic

[19] J. H. Majer, "Beitraege zur Geschichte der Menschheit, aus den Annalen der Teutschen," *Der Teutsche Merkur* 6:3 (June 1774): 244–45.

[20] Christian Wolff, *Vernünfftige Gedancken Von dem Gesellschaftlichen Leben der Menschen und Dem gemeinen Wesen* (4th ed., 1736), in idem, *Gesammelte Werke*, ed. J. Ecole et al., Abteilung 1 (Deutsche Schriften), vol. 1 (Hildesheim, 1975), p. 3.

endowments constituting human nature was an infinitely varied and grossly unequal distribution of natural aptitudes, at once necessitating and making justifiable a hierarchical distribution of labor. But the more immediately relevant implication was that in such a functional hierarchy "birth," at least in the strict sense of the privileges attached to lineage, would accede to "merit." In the "moral weeklies" of the mid-eighteenth century, this implication already informed the ideal of the "virtuous" and "patriotic" *Bürger*, his devotion to productive work in sharp contrast to the parasitical idleness of a court aristocracy.[21] In this confrontation of bourgeois and aristocratic norms, in fact, talent had the advantage of denying one ideological invocation of nature by resort to another. Its strength as a criterion for social ranking lay in its status as an elemental force, anterior to social conditioning; as such talent negated, from within nature itself, the mystique of pedigree – of biological inheritance and the superior qualities it supposedly transmitted – in aristocratic ideology.

To enthusiasts of the meritocratic alternative, talent was a raw material of virtually incalculable potential – an energy resource as yet largely untapped, but available to fuel a dynamic society. Precisely because its dispersion did not coincide with the distribution of inherited statuses and rights, talent could be harnessed outside and even in opposition to traditional social reproduction. If talent offered a natural principle for social organization in this sense, it also formed a bridge from the natural self to a social correlative. In its transformation from potential into socially productive capacity, talent became a kind of *Eigentum*, or "property," with which the individual projected his "inner" self onto an objective social role and earned a corresponding reward. This productive use of an innate endowment was sharply distinguished from the idleness of the wealthy heir, simply living off the rents from his landed property. It was more analogous to the enterprising landowner's improvement of his holdings, both to enhance his own income and to contribute more to society. The social "honor" generated by property in this sense was not a function of birth, but a reward earned in and through the practice of a vocation.

What appropriated the raw material of talent for society – and what made it the object of a vast pedagogical literature – was the "art" *(Kunst)* of

[21] For a particularly interesting example of the preference for personal *Verdienst* over heredity, see J. G. H. von Justi, "Abhandlung von dem Wesen des Adels und dessen Verhältniss gegen den Staat, und insbesonderheit gegen die Commerzien," in idem, *Politische und Finanzschriften*, 1: 147–92. The ideology of the "moral weeklies" has been reconstructed in Wolfgang Martens, *Die Botschaft der Tugend. Die Aufklärung im Spiegel der deutschen moralischen Wochenschriften* (Stuttgart, 1968). On the functional definition of merit, see also Mack Walker, "Rights and Functions: The Social Categories of Eighteenth Century German Jurists and Cameralists," *Journal of Modern History* 50:2 (June 1978): 234–51; Bödeker, "Thomas Abbt"; Ulrich Herrmann, "Die Kodifizierung bürgerlichen Bewusstseins in der deutschen Spätaufklärung – Carl Friedrich Bahrdts *Handbuch der Moral für den Bürgerstand* aus dem Jahre 1789," in Vierhaus, ed., *Bürger und Bürgerlichkeit*, pp. 321–33.

pedagogy. To characterize a form of expertise as a *Kunst* in the eighteenth century was not to assign it to one side of the dichotomy between "art" and "science" that has since become common. The new pedagogy also claimed the solidity and respectability of a *Wissenschaft*, or scholarly discipline, grounding the practice of its expertise on an academic foundation of theory. It would be a "scientific" discipline in the elementary sense that its principles, like those governing the study of the physical world, would derive from an objective, inductive analysis of nature. If pedagogy could not achieve that status in the immediate future, that was because the methodical, empirical observations of childhood that would yield its "system" of "rules" had not yet been undertaken.[22] Equipped with an understanding of the system, the pedagogue would approach childhood as a sequence of growth phases with its own laws; but the application of that understanding to an individual subject was an "art" requiring a deft practitioner and leaving ample room for creative insight and inspiration. The initial challenge of the art lay in reading nature, in interpreting the particular text through which nature inscribed itself on the "soul" of a particular child. Its axiomatic assumption – the one that made science and art virtually inseparable – was that irreducible natural elements like talent, though easily hidden beneath the world of social appearances, were open to scrutiny by the "enlightened" pedagogue, whether he be an informed parent or a trained teacher.[23]

Inspired by this agenda for a scientific art, and often encouraged by their reading of Locke, the early contributors to the pedagogical literature of the eighteenth century observed infancy and early childhood with a confidence that seems extraordinarily naive in our post-Freudian age. Gottlob David Hartmann was simply providing another example of this confidence, and of the lack of hard data behind it, when he mapped the "capacity of sensation" exhibited in early childhood into five neat categories.[24] The earlier the reading of nature began, it was assumed, the less the view of innate endowments would be cluttered and obstructed by socially acquired "hab-

[22] On both "art" and *Wissenschaft* see, e.g., Ernst Christian Trapp, *Versuch einer Pädagogik; mit Trapps hallischer Antrittsvorlesung Von der Nothwendigkeit, Erziehung und Unterrichten als eine eigne Kunst zu studiren*, ed. Ulrich Herrmann (1780: Paderborn, 1977). On the emergence of a secular conception of a pedagogical art, see Günther Dohmen, *Bildung und Schule. Die Entstehung des deutschen Bildungsbegriffs und die Entwicklung seines Verhältnisses zur Schule*, vol. 2 (*Die Entstehung des pädagogischen Bildungsbegriffs und seines Bezugs zum Schulunterricht*) (Weinheim, 1965).

[23] On the responsibility assigned to parents in this regard see, e.g., "Beruff"; "Betrachtungen über den Beruf."

[24] Hartmann, *Sophron*, pp. 49–75. As Hartmann's references remind us (ibid., pp. 45–46, 75–99), the efforts to anatomize innate capacities were inspired in part by the example of Juan Huarte's celebrated *Examen de ingenios para las ciencias* (1575), which Lessing had translated into German in 1752. On the revival of interest in this work in eighteenth-century Germany, see Martin Franzbach, *Lessings Huarte-Uebersetzung (1752). Die Rezeption und Wirkungsgeschichte des 'Examen de ingenios para las ciencias' (1575) in Deutschland*, Hamburger and Co. romanistische Studien, B, vol. 29 (Hamburg, 1965). On Huarte's significance in the humanistic tradition of *vocatio* see Douglas, "Talent and Vocation," pp. 283–85.

its" and "prejudices" – and the easier it would be to prevent dangerous ones from taking root. Indeed Christian Wolff went so far as to claim that the bodily movements of the suckling infant, by revealing "natural impulses," gave a window onto the entire "temperament."[25]

In addition to reading nature, the pedagogical art respected its schedule. This was one of the keynotes of reform, aimed directly against the "mindless routine" (*Schlendrian*) that still prevailed in most schoolrooms. The schoolteacher who relied on rote memorization, reinforced with heavy doses of physical punishment, was guilty of mistaking the child for a deficient adult. Instead of engaging in a misguided effort to compensate for deficiencies, the enlightened pedagogue accepted childhood as a natural stage of life with its own laws of development. It seemed especially absurd that young pupils had to memorize Latin vocabulary and recite complex rules of Latin grammar before they could have any notion of their application. Children who excelled under this regimen were in danger of becoming "pseudo-scholars," their heads crammed with undigested information, and many others lost interest precisely because this artificial, forced instruction deadened their natural curiosity. Adapting its knowledge of natural stages of growth to the particular developmental schedule of each pupil, the pedagogical art advanced the child from one level of difficulty to another only when he was "ripe" or "mature" enough. It would make the learning process relatively easy – not in the sense that it would dispense with disciplined effort from teacher and pupil, but in the sense that neither would have to struggle fruitlessly to outstrip a natural pace.[26]

If the pedagogical art had been defined exclusively as devotion to nature, however, it would not have commanded so much attention and become the basis for a plethora of schemes for reforming private and public education. In an essay on "natural endowments" in 1785, Moses Mendelssohn made explicit an operating distinction usually left unspoken; a human skill (*Fertigkeit*) is "natural" if it is "acquired without deliberate exercise and learning," but should be called *künstlich* "insofar as purposeful institutions, exercise and learning must be planned with the intention of bringing [it] to this or that degree of realization."[27] If the art of pedagogy adapted to nature, it also contributed the deliberate cultivation without which a natural entelechy might not be realized. The alternative to the artificial and therefore sterile, if not counterproductive, methods of the old dispensation was

[25] Wolff, *Vernünfftige Gedancken*, p. 73.

[26] The attack on traditional Latinity and the new approach to language learning will receive more attention in Chapter 7.

[27] Moses Mendelssohn, "Giebt es natürliche Anlagen zum Laster," in idem, *Schriften zur Philosophie, Aesthetik und Apologetik*, ed. Moritz Brasch, 2 vols. (Hildesheim, 1968): 2: 254. On Mendelssohn's concept of pedagogy see Dohmen, *Die Entstehung des pädagogischen Bildungsbegriffs*, pp. 117–27. Neither the ambivalence about raw "nature" in the child nor the impulse to control it were uniquely German; see D. G. Charlton, *New Images of the Natural in France. A Study in European Cultural History 1750–1800* (Cambridge, 1984), pp. 145–53.

not pure spontaneity, but the cultivator's skilled, self-conscious, methodical manipulation of raw material – channeling natural impulses and drives in the right directions, coaxing into life some that might otherwise atrophy, perhaps suppressing or even eradicating others. Ultimately it was the resulting duality that made the relationship between pedagogue and pupil so appealing. The pedagogical relationship offered itself both as a kind of natural incubation, relatively detached from potentially obstructive social influences, and as a vehicle for socialization. The mediating role of art was to accomplish both tasks at once; in the very process of insulating natural energies, it appropriated them for social purposes.

It was as a handy instrument for this mediation that children's play received so much attention in pedagogical discussion, from Christian Wolff's advice to parents in his treatise on "social life" to the observations of Basedow and other "philanthropinists" a half-century later. Like the infant's bodily movements, the child's choice of games and his behavior in them could be read as nature's inscription. While the spontaneity of play made for a particularly opaque text, it also lent the authority of nature to attacks on the rigid, forced instruction to which pupils were commonly subjected. Locke had pointed to the alternative; rather than complying reluctantly with coercive methods, the child could be induced to participate if instruction was given a degree of spontaneity and its objects were taken from the child's own world. One way to follow nature in the development of raw talent into ability, as in the fashioning of innate temperament into moral character, was to make the work of learning "like play" in this sense.

Even here, though, the pedagogue was a manipulator, intruding on the child's natural preserve with the priorities of society. The paradox of his art lay in its calculated spontaneity, its simulation of the natural "freedom" peculiar to childhood in a strategy adults conceived and directed from on high, for the advancement of social purposes. Likewise play itself – the actual exercise of natural freedom – could not be left undisturbed; German pedagogues also took seriously Locke's corollary dictum that play be made "like work." Parents who read Wolff on this subject learned that it did not suffice to avoid games that might "corrupt"; games could inculcate "desire for work" and "aversion to idleness" by keeping children busy, and could be used "to accustom [them] to activities like those that will be necessary later in serious affairs."[28] With the same aim in mind, Basedow urged parents to make their children's games "more useful," although without "limiting the freedom of playing harmlessly according to their pleasures."[29] If

[28] Wolff, *Vernünfftige Gedancken*, pp. 78–80.

[29] Johann Bernhard Basedow, *Elementarwerk*, ed. Theodor Fritzsch, 3 vols. (1909: Hildesheim and New York, 1972), 1: 23–24. There is a similar discussion of the pedagogical potential of "play" in Trapp, *Versuch*, pp. 200–14. See also Rosemarie Wothge, "Der Kommentar zu Rousseaus 'Emile' in Campes Revisionswerk," *Wissenschaftliche Zeitschrift der Martin-Luther-Universität Halle-Wittenberg*, Gesellschafts- und sprachwissenschaftliche Reihe, vol. 4, no. 2 (Halle, 1954–55): 252–53.

limited to suitable games, and if organized properly by an unobtrusive pedagogue, play could inculcate purposeful work habits and prepare for their later application in a productive occupation. Appropriated by and for the pedagogical art, a natural freedom would simulate a social imperative.

The role assigned parents in the new pedagogy reflected the same duality. From one angle the family was the fundamental human cell, closer to nature than any other social unit. The repeated appeals to parents to become self-conscious and methodical about domestic instruction were based in part on the assumption that the family, because it could be a relatively natural context for the practice of the pedagogical art, offered the best hope for preventing the child's social environment from atrophying or, worse, "corrupting" his innate potential. Particularly in the child's early years, parents had to be constantly on their guard against the intrusion of "prejudice," "superstition," and bad example, whether those dangers were embodied in wet nurses and other domestic servants or in misguided relatives.[30] The very intimacy of the familial context put parents in a unique position to read and cultivate nature as well as to protect it. Typical in this regard is the pedagogical idyll Johann Georg Hamann wrote as a young man, before his conversion experience reordered his priorities. Cast as a father's pedagogical "accounting" to his son, it devoted roughly equal attention to the mother because of her greater proximity to the child's natural state in his early years. The father is proud to acknowledge that her observations of "the smallest details" guided his efforts "to found [the son's] insights on the simplest concepts of nature and on the sensations of [his] soul."[31] While cultivation was a rational art, the family offered uniquely fertile soil precisely because its relationships were governed by the spontaneous, almost instinctual affinities inherent in consanguinity. The ideal pedagogical relationship was bonded by "love" and intimate "trust"; the more cultivation could find nourishment in these quintessentially familial ties, the more accessible nature became – and the more easily it could be molded with at least apparent respect for the child's natural freedom, rather than in coercive opposition to it. "We became . . . indispensable to each other," Hamann's ideal father cum pedagogue recalls of his relationship with his son, and "this mutual confidence became very useful to me in educating you constantly without it being obvious."[32]

The appeal of the new pedagogy lay in its potential to fuse nature and society into a productive harmony; that is why its enthusiasts continued to model the ideal teacher on the stern but loving father, bringing to bear social authority but relying more on "trust" than on coercion, long after they began to emphasize the advantages of public schools over domestic

30 See esp. Wolff, *Vernünfftige Gedancken*, pp. 74–77.

31 Johann Georg Hamann, "Briefe eines Vaters," in idem, *Sämtliche Werken*, ed. Josef Nadler, 6 vols. (Vienna, 1949–57), 4: 214.

32 Ibid., p. 215.

education. There is no better example of this pedagogical mediation than the pivotal role assigned parents, and particularly the father, in the transformation of raw talent into social *Verdienst*. The rationality of the parent-as-pedagogue lay in part in his ability to extrude irrational social conventions, including his own "prejudices," from the choice of a "way of life" for his son. In insisting that his son follow in his footsteps, despite the boy's reluctance or lack of the requisite capacities, the typical father was acting out of blind devotion to family tradition or simply to indulge his own ego. From this angle, in fact, families constituted an irrational and grossly inefficient realm of accident; family inheritance left the assignment of social places to the random distribution of biology and hence prevented society from reflecting nature's distribution of human resources and maximizing their productive use in a division of labor. The responsibility of the father-as-pedagogue was to identify innate capacities and "drives" in his child – "inner" endowments that could be deduced neither from the family's genetic inheritance nor from its social status. In channeling these endowments into preparation for an appropriate occupation, however, he acted as a trustee of the more rational society in the making. To launch his son into a career higher up the social ladder, simply because he had the means to do so and was attracted by the prestige it would bring, was as irresponsible as to force him to remain in the station of his birth. Instead he should determine where the boy's innate potential could be realized in the most "useful" contribution. The decisive consideration was not the conventional reward to be reaped, but the service to be rendered.[33]

THE SACRED AND THE SECULAR

It is only on "peripheral matters," Gottlob David Hartmann assured his father in May 1773, that "we are still not entirely in agreement."[34] But over the next several weeks Israel Hartmann actually took the trouble to read *Sophron*, and it confirmed his suspicion that he and his son were in irreconcilable conflict. Though overstated in the son's pleas for reconciliation, the underlying affinities in their beliefs merit attention; but on the

[33] See, e.g., Wolff, *Vernünfftige Gedancken*, pp. 57–83. The perception of a potential conflict between personal "happiness" and social "usefulness," which shaped much of the discussion of natural vocations in the second half of the century, was often absent from earlier contributions; the article on "Beruff" in Zedler's *Lexicon*, for example, saw the Divine Will, the pursuit of personal happiness, and "the need of society" as perfectly compatible considerations in the "duty" to choose a vocation. But nine years later, in "Betrachtungen über den Beruf," "inclination" (*Neigung*) and "duty" (*Pflicht*) are in a more uneasy relationship. For a symptomatic example of the later awareness of complexities, see Johann Georg Krünitz, "Lebens-Art," *Oekonomisch-technologische Encyklopädie. Oder Allgemeines System der Staats-Stadt-Haus- und Landwirtschaft*, pt. 67 (1795).

[34] HN, p. 423.

level of literal meaning, the father's conclusion was inescapable. Their conflict is an unusually graphic reminder that Pietism and rationalism brought radically different premises to the ideal of *Beruf* and collided on all the vital questions it raised.

To Israel Hartmann, as to Francke, human nature was literally depraved; to be "reborn" meant, in the literal sense of the verb *bekehren*, to turn away from nature and toward the supernatural, to transcend the natural state by becoming the receptacle of a supernatural power. If the "gift" of talent was to make its proper contribution in God's design, it had to be liberated from the individual self in the act of renunciation. The ultimate goal was a "living knowledge" of God that Pietism posed against rational analysis; until sanctified in the reception of grace the exercise of reason, like the use of talent, was as much a part of natural corruption as any other "fleshly" self-indulgence. While the scriptural source for this vision was the Pauline Epistles, Enlightenment thought affirmed the assumptions and values of a distinctly secular humanism and found an alternative to scriptural authority in the pedagogical treatises of pagan antiquity. Its inner voice of "vocation" sprang from nature, pure and simple. Natural talents and drives were good in themselves, or at least were neutral forces to be harnessed to ethical ends, and their development realized an entelechy entirely within the natural sphere. In the actualization of talent in a this-worldly work ethic – in the individual's projection of his innate self onto a social environment – reason was or at least should be the governing natural power.

At least from one angle, these antinomies gave diametrically opposed meanings to "art" in relation to "nature." "What matters," Francke reminded his audience in 1701, is "grace, not art," and "divine wisdom, not human will."[35] Within the economy of conversion, art in this sense, precisely because it relied on the cultivation of nature rather than on an infusion of grace, meant sterile artificiality, a futile attempt to realize in human nature powers it did not possess. In Enlightenment thought, the pedagogical art eschewed contrivances that were artificial in the sense of being unnatural; its purpose was not to transcend nature, but to cultivate it.

The continued reliance on *Beruf* to designate both calling and vocation in eighteenth-century discourse should not obscure these radical discontinuities in meaning. The antinomies are in themselves unexceptional measures of the distance separating Pietist religiosity from the rationalist sensibility of the Enlightenment; but they mark a sea change in academic culture, and they underscore the significance of academic mobility, as a common but nonetheless problematic experience, for understanding that change. Yet the Pietist legacy also helps explain why change took certain directions; in more or less subtle but decisive ways, its mode of religiosity

[35] LP. For background on this contrast see Dohmen, *Bildung und Schule*; vol. 1 devotes considerable attention to the Lutheran and Pietist conceptions of a "pedagogical art."

laid the groundwork for a secular concept of "inner" vocation and shaped its ethic. It was critical that Halle Pietism neither confirmed the conservative bent of Lutheran Orthodoxy nor turned in upon itself, like the Quietist variety. Instead, in pursuit of its reform vision, it sanctioned and indeed sanctified an activist work ethic in the world. Enlightenment thought, to be sure, rejected Francke's vision of a converted Christian community in favor of secular objectives; but the secular justifications for opening careers to talent in terms of "useful" work and "merit" in public service nonetheless were analogous to, and derived considerable impetus from, the spirit of "universal improvement" and Francke's rationale for a *selectum ingeniorum*.

This direct line of descent in reform thought does not exhaust the kinship; there were also more indirect, less obvious filiations and affinities between the sacred and the secular, as in the relationship Max Weber identified between the Puritan ideal of calling and its secularized role as a motivating force in economic life. In the preface to the fourth volume, written in 1790, Karl Philipp Moritz announced that *Anton Reiser* "actually deals with the important question: to what extent is a young man in a position to choose his *Beruf* himself."[36] In keeping with the utilitarian rationalism he had absorbed in Enlightenment circles in Berlin, Moritz held the obsessive inwardness of Pietism, along with the protoromantic cult of the artist, responsible for his insecurity and morbidity. In their place he was now turning his fascination with his own psyche to positive, or "useful," purposes; his sobering case study would join a growing body of pedagogical literature – what might be considered an early species of modern vocational guidance – on the need for the child, with the assistance of watchful parents and professional teachers, to discover his natural talents and inclinations and prepare himself accordingly for the appropriate occupation.[37]

On one level, this orientation signified a rejection of Pietist religiosity; but it also points to vital links between the sacred and the secular ideal of

[36] Karl Philipp Moritz, *Anton Reiser. Ein psychologischer Roman* (1785–90: Frankfurt am Main, 1979), p. 331. On the formative influence of Pietism on Moritz, see Robert Minder, *Glaube, Skepsis und Rationalismus. Dargestellt aufgrund der autobiographischen Schriften von Karl Philipp Moritz* (1936: Frankfurt am Main, 1974), esp. pp. 118–81.

[37] See, in addition to Hartmann's *Sophron*, Krünitz, "Lebens-Art"; Hermann Daniel Hermes, *Versuch über die richtige Bestimmung der für die Jugend zu wählenden künftigen Lebensart* (Breslau, 1774); Johann Christian Heinrich Krause, *Beantwortung der Frage: Wer hat Beruf, ein Gelehrter zu werden?* 2 vols. (Bremen, 1787–88); Jakob Christoph Rudolf Eckermann, "Die gewöhnlichsten Fehler, welche bey der Wahl des künftigen Standes begangen werden," in idem, *Kleine vermischte Schriften*, 2 vols. (Altona, 1799), 2: 93–142; idem, "Ueber die Erziehung der Kinder, in Rücksicht auf die Wahl ihres künftigen Standes," in ibid., pp. 143–206. Much of this literature was focused on academic studies, but its rationales for occupational choices obviously had broader social implications. On the issue of vocational choice and preparation as it applied to *Handwerk* see Karl Wilhelm Stratmann, *Die Krise der Berufserziehung im 18. Jahrhundert als Ursprungsfeld pädagogischen Denkens* (Ratingen, 1967). Also relevant is Walter Hornstein, *Vom 'Jungen Herrn' zum 'Hoffnungsvollen Jüngling.' Wandlungen des Jugendlebens im 18. Jahrhundert*, Anthropologie und Erziehung, vol. 14 (Heidelberg, 1965).

"inner" calling, implicit in the frequent coupling of "piety" and "study" in Francke's notions of "progress" and "maturity." While the Pietist's examination of conscience, with its battle against the natural self, should not be confused with a preoccupation with cultivating natural potential, the two share an introspective impulse, an attentiveness to the inner voice. The highly self-disciplined form that this introspection assumed in the "atonement struggle" left its mark on its rationalist counterpart; the continuity is apparent, however inadvertently, in Moritz's diary excerpts as well as in underlying associations in *Anton Reiser*, and in the methodical, painstaking self-examination Gottlob David Hartmann, another self-conscious apostate, demonstrated to his young readers in profuse detail in *Sophron*.[38]

Despite the difference between the Pietist's view of "gifts" as natural inscriptions of God's design and the humanist's homage to "talents" within a purely natural design, Pietism and humanism meet in the concern with identifying the individual's innate endowments as a prerequisite to determining his life course and proper role in society. To Francke this concern was, of course, secondary; the clerical calling had room for "mediocre" and even "common" intelligence, since the sine qua non – the grace that came in conversion – could make any Christian an effective instrument of the Lord. Likewise "gifts" included qualities of "temperament" (*Gemut*) that could compensate for lack of superior mental qualities in the less scholarly branches of the clergy. Nonetheless, under Francke's leadership, a categorical rejection of secular priorities had not prevented Halle Pietism from appropriating and lending its imprimatur to two fundamental assumptions of the pedagogical art: that the artistry lay in applying general precepts to the particularity of each child's cluster of aptitudes and that, at least in the pedagogical province, recognition of "merit" should reflect the natural distribution of inborn capacities, not a social distribution of ascriptive advantages. Hence it is no accident that the reorganization of school grades by subject – the new system with which Francke tried to achieve a *selectum ingeniorum* – was also a standard item on the agenda of school reform at the end of the century. For all its hostility to merely secular learning, Francke's "system" had set an important institutional precedent, familiar to many from their own experience at Halle, for the translation of humanist pedagogy into practical institutional changes.[39]

To Francke, a Christian pedagogy had to achieve two kinds of maturation:

[38] Karl Philipp Moritz, "Aus dem Tagebuche eines Selbsbeobachters," *Gnothi sauton; oder Magazin zur Erfahrungsseelenkunde als ein Lesebuch für Gelehrte und Ungelehrte* 7:3 (1789): 24–52; Hartmann, *Sophron*, esp. pp. 7–17, 199–204, 315–26.

[39] The secular rationales for the new "class system" will be examined in Chapter 8. Particularly interesting as a bridge figure is Anton Friedrich Büsching. Deeply influenced by Pietism as a boy and educated at Halle, Büsching became a pioneering school reformer of the rationalist persuasion as a gymnasium director in Berlin. For his advocacy of the "class system," see esp. his *Ausführliche Nachricht von der jetzigen Verfassung des berlinischen Gymnasii* (Berlin, 1768).

the spiritual breakthrough for which the atonement struggle prepared, and the development of innate capacities of mind. Operating in complete independence from any natural schedule for intellectual growth was the providential intervention that effected conversion; but natural maturation was also a reflection of the Divine Will and, if in the providential timetable it remained a premature state unless and until sanctified by grace, it also ensured efficacy in the Lord's service. There is no better example of both the tension and the harmony in this relationship than the testimonial Johann Georg Hamann recorded in London in 1758, in the immediate aftermath of a particularly condensed and wrenching conversion experience. Hamann had spent several years as a private tutor, broadening his education with reading in contemporary philosophy and literature and applying the precepts of the new pedagogy without great success. Now, in the light of grace, he lamented "the misuse of [his] natural powers" in an aimless wandering through *belles lettres* and "the vestibules of scholarship." Relying on his intellect and assumimg that he should be searching for his own happiness, he had been seduced away from a clerical calling and had failed to find an appropriate alternative. "I have been a premature fruit in all my activity, deeds, undertakings and calculations," he wrote, "because they were dared and begun without God and have reached a hole [*Loch*] rather than finding an end."[40] But a newly achieved passivity in the face of the Divine Will did not prevent Hamann from regretting bitterly the earlier abuse of his natural powers at the hands of school "pedants." In one of the schools he had attended as a boy in Königsberg, he recalled, the teachers had damaged his "natural liveliness and capacity" by dragging him prematurely into the "labyrinth" of Greek and Latin philology.[41] The digression occasioned by this memory is as much a reflection of Hamann's earlier pedagogical enthusiasm as it is a witness to his recent disillusionment:

A proper schoolmaster must go to school with God and himself if he wants to exercise the wisdom of his office; he must imitate God as he reveals himself in nature and Holy Scripture, and, by virtue of both, in the same way in our soul. The all-powerful God, to whom nothing costs anything, to whom nothing is too expensive for human beings, is the thriftiest and slowest God. The law of his economy of time, in which he awaits in patience the fruits, should be our standard. Is this law a matter of what or how much children and we humans in general know? It is all a question of how. He says to young men: in the hour in which it will be necessary for you to speak, it will be given to you first and foremost how and, after that, what

[40] J. G. Hamann, "Gedanken über meinen Lebenslauf," in idem, *Werken*, 2: 20–21, 27. On Hamann's conversion, see Fritz Thoms, *Hamanns Bekehrung*, Beiträge zur Förderung christlicher Theologie, vol. 37 (Gütersloh, 1933), which rightly emphasizes continuities with his earlier sensibility, but may exaggerate the Lutheran (as opposed to Pietist) character of his religiosity.

[41] Hamann, "Gedanken," pp. 13–14.

you should say. To us humans, this order seems to be inverted, but it is certainly God's own and sanctified by his own path.

To the pure everything is pure; natural taste can distinguish the quality of foods, natural moderation can determine their proportion, but the kindness and the Will of God, through which and with which we ourselves experience enjoyment, is the work of faith alone and the condition of the divine blessing. We sow not entire plants, not even their entire fruits, but rather nothing more than the smallest part of the seeds; and this itself is too superfluous, so that it must rot – the body of it – before it can send shoots up. But it does not shoot up if the ground is not prepared and the season is not taken into account. The thriving of the seed depends more necessarily on these conditions than on their nature. Therefore the methods of instructing children cannot be simple enough; as simple as they are, there is always much superfluous, lost and antiquated.[42]

Hamann goes on to describe a proper order of studies, from early reading to the learning of foreign languages as "an aid to the mother tongue" and a graduated exercise in reasoning. The cryptic Magus of the later writings is foreshadowed in these lines; but the juxtaposition of economic and organic metaphors conveys essentially the same dualistic conception of maturity that guided Francke's pedagogy. Hamann censured the old *Schlendrian* not only for its hubris in trying to bring to fruition human powers that on their own must "rot," but also for failing to recognize that such powers will not grow at all without cultivation in conformity with their natural schedule. In this he was typical; Pietism gave renewed emphasis to an underlying compatibility between the Lutheran economy of salvation and the much older humanistic concern with sequential progress in the natural man. Above all in this sense, the Pietist ethos was instrumental in the transmission of root ideas of natural vocation to an enlightened pedagogy. In its more conventional forms, the new pedagogy was equally accommodating; emphatically secular in dispensing with grace as the vital force for inner growth, it continued to derive the authority of nature and her schedule, at least implicitly, from a providential design.

In Halle Pietism natural intellectual growth in the humanistic sense was thoroughly subordinate to, and could not intrude on, the quite separate maturation of a *conscientia* at the core of the human personality. The irony is that this view of spiritual progress reinforced, indirectly, the humanistic appreciation of individual intellectual achievement that it rejected in principle. Francke's *Admonitory Lectures* are fraught with the tension between an eminently Lutheran insistence on a doctrine of justification, denying any role to human merit, and an evocation of the struggle toward conversion as a battle to be won or lost, a process whose outcome hinged on the individual's ability to confront his inner life squarely, to discipline himself,

[42] Ibid., pp. 14–15.

and to persevere. Here paradox – to add one more to the list – borders on contradiction; the individual had to *achieve* a state of completely helpless, passive receptivity to grace. The reverberations of this exaltation of achievement through struggle are especially audible in the frequent argument that the poor young man was more likely than the scion of a wealthy family to become a well-motivated, disciplined, hard-working student; like the sinner in the face of "the world" and "the flesh," he had to practice self-denial and develop a certain dogged tenacity in the face of disadvantages and hardships.[43]

This argument is focused on social virtues, but it also points to a deeper connection between the sacred and the academic. In its ideal of "piety" through conversion, Halle Pietism in effect structured and sanctioned a religious psychology of achievement. This psychology not only had its corollary in the insistence on disciplined study within the Pietist ethic itself; it also helped produce an autonomous secular counterpart in meritocratic approaches to academic performance. Not surprisingly, this inadvertent contribution largely escaped notice as Pietism and rationalism entered ideological confrontation in the course of the century. Pietists were increasingly preoccupied with distinguishing their ethic of self-renunciation from what they saw as the especially pernicious "fleshly" motivation to achieve in academic life, and rationalists with pitting their standards for serious academic endeavor against what they saw as the self-deceptions and hypocrisies of religious "enthusiasm."[44]

One of the few exceptions was the author of *Anton Reiser*. Moritz remained an ambivalent rationalist, on one level diagnosing Pietist enthusiasm as a species of psychological pathology, but on another not so estranged from his Pietist upbringing as to forget the earlier grip of its aspirations. In the early pages of *Anton Reiser*, Moritz's literary imagination drew on childhood experience to suggest how such aspirations and academic motivation could intertwine. There is a recurrent analogy between progress in "the work of conversion" and intellectual achievement in school, which held out to Anton the prospect of "a great career" and "a path to fame." Anton makes the decision to "convert himself" after reading a book on the stages of growth in piety from age six to fourteen. "Advancement in piety," Moritz recalled, "was made to seem like a matter of ambition [*einer Sache*

[43] See, e.g., Anton Friedrich Büsching, "Beantwortung der Frage: Wer soll studieren?" *Archiv für die ausübende Erziehungskunst* 1 (1784): 191–92; Johann Samuel Fest, *Ueber die Vortheile und Gefahren der Armuth für Jünglinge auf der Academie* (Leipzig, 1784), pp. 10–18.

[44] In Jung-Stilling's autobiography, academic achievement is a profane temptation that must be withstood, although on another level it is implicitly sanctioned (see Chapter 5). For the rationalist scholar's attitude toward Pietist "enthusiasm," see, e.g., Johann Salomo Semler, *Lebensbeschreibung* (Halle, 1781), pp. 47–62, and Nösselt's autobiographical recollection of a Pietist "awakening" at Halle, in August Hermann Niemeyer, ed., *Leben, Charakter und Verdienste Johann August Nösselts, nebst einer Sammlung einiger zum Theil ungedruckter Aufsätze, Briefe und Fragmente*, 2 vols. (Halle, 1809), 2: 31–35.

des Ehrgeizes], as when one is happy to ascend ever higher from one [school] grade into the others." When Anton learned that he would soon be withdrawn from the Latin school to begin an apprenticeship, the same analogy operated in reverse; his academic self-effacement – his deliberate efforts to "go down a place every day" in the class ranking – produced a sham display of religiosity, and in the end his piety became "nothing but a timorous constrained thing and could make no real progress." Moritz noted the ironic discrepancy between this implicit psychology and its theological grounding; when Anton "read somewhere how unnecessary and harmful self-improvement was, and that one simply had to be passive and let the divine grace take effect," his anxiety was not relieved.[45]

DUTY IN A NEW KEY

Pietism had in effect admitted an ethic of disciplined achievement through the back door; for that the Enlightenment ideal of vocation was indebted to it. But the affinity was double-edged. The devotion to "duty" (*Pflicht*), also central to the Enlightenment ideal, required another kind of self-discipline, well short of the radical self-effacement Francke's ideology enjoined but nonetheless analogous in its social implications. In this connection a truly pivotal figure was Christian Fürchtegott Gellert, who held a professorial position at Leipzig from the mid-1740s until his death in 1769. To a later generation of literary men, Gellert epitomized the superficiality of an earlier breed of courtly *Gelehrten*; but in his own era he probably reached a larger segment of the educated reading public than any other university-based author. His popularity was due in part to his dexterity in weaving the new strands of Enlightenment thought into the broad cloth of Lutheran Orthodoxy and in part to his skill in popularizing a comfortable, if not entirely persuasive, synthesis in fables, letters and lectures free of the more erudite preoccupations of academic theology and moral philosophy. Likewise he occupied an unusual social position. Known for elegance in manners as well as in literary style, he was a favored guest of and counselor to the prominent aristocratic and upper bourgeois families whose sons gave the student body at Leipzig its "gallant" tone. But Gellert was also in a position to appreciate the circumstances of the large contingent of poor theology students at Leipzig, who supplied many of his listeners at lectures and many of the aspirants to the tutoring appointments with which he was entrusted. The son of an obscure pastor, he had attended the Saxon *Fürstenschule* at Meissen as a scholarship pupil and had become well acquainted with poverty in his student years.

The series of "moral lectures" (*Moralische Vorlesungen*) Gellert gave each

[45] Moritz, *Anton Reiser*, pp. 20–21, 43–47.

year, like Francke's *Admonitory Lectures*, addressed the particular circumstances and choices of a student audience.[46] But academic and literary circles in Leipzig at midcentury – self-consciously classical in style, eclectic in substance – were far removed from the evangelical militancy of Francke's Halle. Within the overarching framework of an "ethics of religion," Gellert's lectures elaborate an "ethic of reason" – one that is advanced by grace to an exercise of pure virtue that the natural self cannot reach, but in the direction in which natural inclinations and faculties have already impelled it. Taken in isolation, many passsages read as homilies on a secular and distinctly bourgeois work ethic, with "merit" and "virtue" made a function of social "usefulness" in a vocation. Much of the guidance offered on domestic education, clearly influenced by Basedow and several other contemporary pedagogues, typifies the concern with inculcating purposeful work habits in and through natural cultivation.

Appropriately Gellert had also found inspiration in Spalding's *Ueber die Bestimmung des Menschen*, which he characterized as "an ethics of reason often scooped out of an ethics of religion." What is striking about his overall appraisal of human nature, however, is its contrast to the optimism of the rationalist theologian. Inspired by Shaftesbury, Spalding saw no need for the self-renunciation that only grace could effect. The individual could "perfect" his intellectual faculties without selfishly pursuing his "advantage," since on the scales of sovereign reason "natural self-love" was more than counterbalanced by an altruistic impulse, no less natural and "of such power that it makes itself the master of [his] entire soul . . . [and] devours all other feelings."[47] In Gellert's scheme of things, the same impulse – he called it *Menschenliebe* – is innate but "very attenuated"; it pales before the host of more powerful impulses that all too easily cross the boundary between legitimate self-love and blind selfishness and establish a tyranny over the human soul.

In his approach to the social psychology of ambition, Gellert was pulled between, on the one hand, an eminently Christian view of the Old Adam and, on the other, his partial agreement with rationalists like Spalding that Christian virtue was compatible with a rational pursuit of "happiness." The result is some rather tortuous moral counseling for the future clergymen and government officials who formed his audience. In his parting lecture each semester on "the faults of students," he reluctantly admits that the natural "appetite for honor" (*Ehrbegierde*) is a neutral impulse, potentially

[46] The *Moralische Vorlesungen* were published in 1770 as vols. 6 and 7 of *C. F. Gellert's Sämmtliche Schriften*, 10 vols. (Leipzig, 1769–74). The standard source for the details of Gellert's biography is Johann Andreas Cremer, *Christian Fürchtegott Gellerts Leben*, which is vol. 10 of the *Schriften*. On Gellert's conception of *Beruf*, see also Hornstein, *Vom 'Jungen Herrn' zum 'Hoffnungsvollen Jüngling,'* pp. 82–101. Hornstein underestimates the importance of the Lutheran tradition in Gellert's ethics.

[47] Spalding, *Bestimmung*, pp. 19–22.

conducive to virtue as well as vice; but he gives the actual "striving for honor" little room for legitimate play as a motive force in society. While "ambition" (*Ehrgeiz*) is conceded to be a powerful spur to academic achievement, it also is one of the "low motives" that bring so many unqualified people into the learned estate. Like Francke, Gellert blamed the pull of ambition for the many "half-learned" university graduates who had ended their studies before "the maturation of [their] powers." Their frustrated and disappointed expectations produce social alienation, in the form of the "learned misanthrope."[48]

The same emphasis pervades the *Moralische Vorlesungen*. There is, to be sure, an "obligatory appetite for honor"; the individual must seek the approval and respect he needs to "accomplish more good." But it is a measure of the strains within Gellert's ethical synthesis that the striving for social approval in pursuit of personal happiness is more problematic. If ambition in this sense is a "permissible" means to a "legitimate" end, it is also a dangerous indulgence in "selfishness."[49] In the final analysis the striving for social recognition, like the pursuit of material gain, is assigned to the realm of natural appetites-become-passions (*Leidenschaften*), which tyrannize the will and make it deaf to the call of reason:

> The surest path of honor is the way of constant duty, the careful training and application of [one's] gifts for [one's] happiness and others' best. . . . the permissible natural striving for honor can easily be corrupted into the evil pursuit of ambition [*Ehrgeiz*] and arrogance. We are ambitious when we seek fame and prestige for our own sake as a purpose, and not as a means to higher good aims, and thus make ourselves our God. . . . If the appetite for honor is to remain good, it must be moderated and ennobled by the virtue of humility before God and man.[50]

It was with this danger in mind that Gellert warned the future parents in his audience not to implant ambition in their children by encouraging them to outdo others in learning. In the discussion of pedagogy, in fact, the "motive power of *Ehrbegierde*" seems to join those "impermissible inclinations" which "the child . . . does not receive through the senses but brings into the world in his heart." It becomes an integral part of natural corruption, and the pedagogical art must suppress it in the very process of inculcating "industrious" habits.[51]

There is nothing about a conversion struggle in Gellert's ethic, and indeed in some respects education seems to obviate the need for such a

[48] "Von den Fehlern der Studirenden bey der Erlernung der Wissenschaften, insonderheit auf Akademien," in Gellert, *Schriften*, 5: 116–24. See also the opposition of "duty" and "selfishness" (or "vanity") in "Lehren eines Vaters für seinen Sohn, den er auf die Akademie schickt," in Christian Fürchtegott Gellert, *Werke*, ed. Gottfried Honnefelder, 2 vols. (Frankfurt am Main, 1979), 2: 310–26.

[49] Gellert, *Schriften*, 6: 326–50, and 7: 408–50.

[50] Ibid., 6: 348–49.

[51] Ibid., 7: 490–542.

struggle. And yet his assessment of human nature rested ultimately on the Lutheran doctrine of human depravity. In the face of natural corruption, only the atonement and reception of grace that "changes and renews the entire heart" could guarantee true virtue. In keeping with this orthodoxy, the virtue of "humility" (*Demuth*) – the antipode of ambition, and the only antidote to its dangers – lay in recognizing that natural "gifts" were a "divine loan," to be honored by accepting whatever role providence assigned.[52] And yet for all its sincerity, Gellert's Lutheran Orthodoxy often merely brackets an "ethics of reason" that is allowed considerable autonomy. Atonement and grace aside, "virtue" and above all dedication to "duty" emerge from a struggle *within* the natural man. Whereas Francke had warned that the seductive powers of reason were an instrument of depraved nature, Gellert exhorted his listeners to develop reason into a sovereign authority, preventing natural appetites from becoming selfish passions by suppressing or at least moderating them. To exercise the reason was to become increasingly able to subordinate self-interest to the overriding "good" of the collectivity and hence to choose "duty" over "the striving for honor." And in this "the heart" offered itself as a powerful ally; if it harbored "impermissible appetites," it also had an innate capacity to feel the difference between right and wrong.[53] The "ethics of religion" completed and sealed a victory of "duty" over selfishness that intellectual and emotional capacities, in mutually beneficial interaction, had far advanced. In this sense, the role of reason and conscience, on their lower but autonomous level, paralleled that of grace. They made possible a kind of self-denial entirely within the natural self.

Gellert began to ready his *Moralische Vorlesungen* for publication in 1769, just six months before his death. He was well aware of the impact of Rousseau's *Emile*, published seven years earlier, but the book does not figure among his recommended readings.[54] Where the two moralists meet is in their censure of ambition and their rejection of the usual rationales in its defense. Neither entertains the possibility, so appealing to many other eighteenth-century moral philosophers, that the individual's calculated pursuit of self-interest, though admittedly a poor substitute for disinterested virtue, could be beneficial to the general welfare if allowed to operate under the guiding hand of a natural harmony. Rather than finding in "the striving for honor" an instrumental rationality of potential benefit to society, they condemn it for enslaving reason to selfish and ultimately insatiable passion. But these apparently similar judgments reflect entirely different views of the relationship between the natural self and society. To Rousseau society itself is responsibile for perverting the passions; ambition arises when in-

[52] Ibid., 7: 451–89.
[53] Ibid., 6: 34–53.
[54] See his comment on Thomas Abbt's view of Rousseau, in ibid., 6: 253.

equality, through the medium of the imagination, induces artificial needs that can be satisfied only by entering false social roles of callous domination and degrading dependence. Hence the radical strategy when Emile enters adolescence and is finally ready to begin his moral education: if he is to remain a morally autonomous, compassionate human being despite social pressure, the development of his natural self must be prolonged as long as possible in isolation from society. Emile will learn the trade of carpentry not to fill an assigned role, but in order to earn a decent living without succumbing to the degradations and the false presentations of self that the effort to scale the ladder of social inequality requires.[55]

Gellert did not conceive of education as a prolongation of natural innocence; its task was to tame the natural self as early as possible, in the very process of cultivating it. The value of introspection lay not in preserving innocence against the threat of social corruption, but in repressing and emasculating some properties of the natural self while cultivating others. In subordinating the self to the Divine Will, reason and the conscience dictated that the dutiful Christian *Bürger* accept, in all humility, a station in the social hierarchy. This is not to say that Gellert was uncritical of social inequality; inherent in his Christian vision was a moral condemnation of status consciousness as an expression of "pride" and of its dissimulating efforts to conceal faults and demonstrate "merit" where none existed. But in these respects society simply reflected the innate depravity of the natural man; this is very different from Rousseau's verdict that the emergence of inequality had spelled the end of natural innocence. To the extent that Gellert imagined a more just society in a secular sense, it was one in which inequality would more accurately reflect the distribution of merit. But he was far more concerned with urging resignation on those who did not receive the social recognition they deserved. Like Emile, the dutiful Christian *Bürger* could remain aware of his "inner worth" despite society's prejudices; but for that very reason he could be satisfied with a social identity and attendant rewards far below his actual merit. Here above all "duty" meant a rational exercise in self-denial – and the only guarantee of "happiness" lay in the good conscience that devotion to duty brought.

Emile found a more receptive, though still skeptical, audience in the next generation. But it was the set of relationships in Gellert's ethic of reason – his couplings of merit and duty, duty and rational self-denial, ambition

[55] Jean-Jacques Rousseau, *Emile*, trans. Barbara Foxley (Everyman ed.: London and Toronto, 1977). My interpretation of Rousseau is particularly indebted to Judith Shklar, *Men and Citizens* (Cambridge, Mass., 1969); idem, "Jean-Jacques Rousseau and Equality," *Daedalus* 107:3 (1978): 13–25, which emphasizes Rousseau's view of social mobility as "psychologically destructive"; Nannerl O. Keohane, *Philosophy and the State in France. The Renaissance to the Enlightenment* (Princeton, N.J., 1980), pp. 420–49. On the idea of a harmony of self-interests see, in addition to Keohane's extended analysis, Arthur Lovejoy, *Reflections on Human Nature* (Baltimore, 1961).

and selfish passion – that shaped the ethic of vocation in the German Enlightenment in the last third of the century. While the new idiom of vocation was easily detached from Gellert's Orthodox framework, its priorities and emphases attested to the underlying resilience of the Lutheran tradition. The ethic also drew on the cameralist legacy, and it was the combination that gave it such vitality. In their naively optimistic moments, the cameralists had tended to assume that in a rationally ordered society individuals' "perfecting" of their natural endowments and the "perfecting" of society would stand in a harmonious relationship of mutual benefit. But when the irrational pursuit of ambition threatened to drain resources from the base of the social pyramid and overcrowd its upper strata, and hence to upset the equilibrium needed for a socially productive use of talent, the welfare of the collectivity took precedence over individual self-interest.

The philanthropinists associated with Basedow also had no doubts on this score. In his *Versuch einer Pädagogik* (1780) Ernst Christian Trapp, the first professor of pedagogy at Halle, argued that education should satisfy both the individual's natural drive for "happiness" and his society's requirements for usefulness. But the latter would be the decisive consideration in a society matching "capacities" and "inclinations" to its "needs"; the individual "usually can become everything he must become," but not "more than he must become."[56] In a lengthy essay published in 1785, Peter Villaume, a gymnasium teacher in Berlin, applied a more explicit and consequential logic to the same issue. The individual has an inalienable right to "perfect" his "natural powers," Villaume argued, but only to the point where his duties in a particular social role enter. Beyond that point society, which has nursed and protected his development, can require that it be sacrificed to "usefulness" (*Brauchbarkeit*). One implication was that a few boys of lower origins – the exceptionally talented ones – should be allowed to rise into the learned estate; the other was that the "ennoblement" of the rest could not exceed the requirements of usefulness in their inherited stations.[57]

One way to ensure society's rights over its members was to give the state coercive authority in its name. Villaume went very far in this direction; in his scheme – one he admitted was an indulgence in *Projektenmacherei* – the state would simply arrogate to itself the traditional role of the family in assigning young men to occupations.[58] But in addition to justifying this coercion from without, Villaume imagined an inner compulsion, a secular

[56] Trapp, *Versuch einer Pädagogik*, esp. pp. 14–23, 45.

[57] Peter Villaume, "Ob und inwiefern bei der Erziehung die Vollkommenheit des einzelnen Menschen seiner Brauchbarkeit aufzuopfern sei," in Herwig Blankertz, ed., *Bildung und Brauchbarkeit. Texte von Joachim Heinrich Campe und Peter Villaume zur Theorie utilitärer Erziehung* (Brunswick, 1965), pp. 69–142.

[58] Ibid., pp. 133–36.

echo of Gellert's ethics of reason, completely liberated from any reliance on the Lutheran economy of salvation:

In order to bring the human being to the point of willingly doing his duty, he must be taught to realize the reasons for and uses of his obligations. The "you should" is all very well and correct, and spoken in the name of God it has some effect. But it is a little hard, and then one counts on the Divine patience and mercy, so that it is not intrepreted too strictly. It would be much better to demonstrate quite clearly the necessity of duties in and for themselves and their superiority, to present God not as a legislator, but rather as a good teacher and counselor, as a father who warns his children about harms. Then one receives more desire to fulfill the imposed duty. And if it is further taught that behavior in itself is punished, without God's agency, and that therefore it is not at all a matter of reconciling God and receiving forgiveness from him, but rather of avoiding or compensating for harms: then one is more self-conscious, one thinks more about the improvement of behavior.[59]

This conception of duty, equating disinterested service with a "higher" rationality, was not limited to a particular educational movement; it pervaded pedagogical discussion and became the standard fare offered by popular moralists. Typical was the essay Jakob Christoph Rudolf Eckermann, another schoolman, devoted to distinguishing rational from irrational "dissatisfaction." It was perfectly legitimate and indeed commendable to use "all rational means" to "advance a step higher on the ladder of perfection," so long as the object was "to become more and more useful and active for oneself and others." But in its irrational form, the aspiration to become more useful was often motored by "the sense pleasures of a greater life of luxury." The latter included, to note one example among many, the obscure rural pastor's amhilion to secure a "higher" appointment to a town pastorate.[60] In his encyclopedia article on "way of life" (*Lebens-Art*) Johann Georg Krünitz preached that "each member of a society" had "a holy duty to unite with the concern for his own welfare the striving for the welfare of society." It was essential, Krünitz advised parents, that on the question of his future occupation the child feel that he was making a "free decision," even when they were actually making it for him. What should be decisive was the "inner worth" of a *Beruf* and "a feeling of duty [and] deeply felt reverence toward the design of providence" – not considerations of income and status. It was precisely at this juncture, in fact, that the domestic practice of the pedagogical art, in mediating between nature and society, leaned most noticeably toward the latter. Parents who selected for their child an

[59] Ibid., p. 129.

[60] Jakob Christoph Rudolf Eckermann, "Ueber die Unzufriedenheit, ihre Quellen und die Mittel wider dieselbe," in idem, *Kleine vermischte Schriften*, 2 vols. (Altona, 1799), 1: 313–406. The essay was originally published in 1777. Eckermann had been a school rector in Eutin, and in 1782 became a professor of theology at Kiel.

appropriately "useful" occupation had not exhausted their social responsibility; they also had to equip him morally to distinguish, as they could, between irrational self-interest and the rational imperatives of the collectivity.[61]

Again the contrast with Rousseau is instructive. Rousseau threw the corruption of contemporary society into bold relief by evoking two alternative models. In the egalitarian idyll of domestic self-sufficiency, usually in a rural setting, the family is able to fulfill the pedagogical assignment given to a tutor in *Emile*; it produces morally autonomous, socially independent adults because it is as isolated as possible from civilization and its false needs. In the Spartan Republic, socialization "denatures" the individual in the course of merging his will into a collective conscience. The domestic-rural model requires a context of material and cultural stagnation; that is the only way social gradations will remain minimal and the natural man can be kept relatively immune to artificial needs. The Spartan model, on the other hand, promises to realize the rationalist ethic of duty with a vengeance; its collective solidarity leaves no space for the individual expressions of creative talent that were commonly considered indispensable to progress in eighteenth-century reform thought.

In contrast, the German ethic of vocation was designed to organize a social dynamic for progress – economic, intellectual, and ultimately moral – within a steeply graded hierarchy. Its model society occupied that in-between state, more civilized than natural, that Rousseau abhorred, and its limited reconciliation of nature and society was designed to promote natural potential within an elaborate order of social inequality. What the ethic did *not* do was justify a *right* to achieve personal happiness through work and its rewards; that would have required society to allow the individual to realize his natural self in whatever social identity he chose. Unwilling to grant an entitlement to self-fulfillment in this sense, the German Protestant variant of utilitarian rationalism sought to prevent a felt need for it from arising. The emphasis was on subordinating the natural self to a socially defined common welfare, in the very process of tapping productive potential. No longer reliant on the power of grace to effect self-denial, *Beruf* enlists reason, in the form of an ethic of disinterested duty, to counter the threat of ambition. This ethic was as characteristic of reformers who were committed to opening all the learned professions to talent as it was to defenders of "birth"; however egalitarian the vision of meritocracy, the priority of "talent" over ascriptive advantages operated within an overriding emphasis on "service" over "reward." No longer enjoined to apply his "gifts" as a passive instrument of the Lord, the individual was expected to

[61] Krünitz, "Lebens-Art," pp. 47–57, 82–87. See also Joachim Heinrich Campe, *Theophron, oder der erfahrne Rathgeber für die unerfahrne Jugend* (2nd ed.: Wolfenbüttel, 1786), pp. 1–88.

contribute his "talents" as a willing and if necessary self-effacing instrument of society.[62]

The academic mobility of poor boys from uneducated families was not the only example of an irrational "striving for honor" or "ambition." Also censured were the selfish "striving for gain" in commerce and prominent families' reliance on nepotism to maintain their hold on prestigious and lucrative offices. But the ethic had special relevance to the problematic mobility of poor students into the clergy and its teaching branch. In their case ambition seemed especially misguided and alarming, since the expectations of social honor and material comfort (*Luxus*) that fueled it collided so rudely with employment realities. Given the contrast between the obvious public importance and the shabbiness of many pastorates and most teaching offices, it seemed especially appropriate to define the "merit" of their occupants more in terms of an "inner" conviction of worth than in terms of merely "exterior" enjoyment of rewards. Here, in fact, self-discipline in academic achievement and self-denial in the performance of duty converged in a positive stereotype. The poor student was likely to remain dedicated to service in a lower office, despite its deprivations, precisely because he already had had to discipline himself to endure poverty and to achieve academically despite it.[63]

In the second half of the century, as Orthodoxy gave way to rationalism in the clerical establishment, this ethic achieved something like the status of an official ideology. How broadly and deeply it took root in the lower ranks of the clergy cannot be gauged; but to judge by autobiographical witness, the ethic often joined with the surviving belief in providential intervention to shape clergymen's conceptions of their careers and keep ambition beyond the pale of legitimate motive forces. It is a measure of the authority of its conception of duty that young men who rejected the standard clerical career paths nonetheless felt the need to justify themselves in its terms. In the few cryptic but revealing diary fragments Moritz published in 1789, one glimpses the underlying continuity with Pietism. The fragments begin in 1778, when he was teaching at the royal orphanage in Potsdam, and continue through his first four years as a gymnasium teacher in Berlin. By 1789 Moritz had written most of *Anton Reiser*; he could dismiss earlier attempts at self-honesty in the diary as a "higher degree of self-deception," and indeed found in it only "forced religiosity and morality." In *Anton Reiser* he diagnosed his Pietist upbringing as a source of his path-

[62] Typical are the comments on "honour" and "ambition" in Georg Joachim Zollikofer, *Sermons on the Dignity of Man, and the Value of the Principal Objects of Human Happiness*, 2 vols. (2nd ed.: London, 1807), I: 122–42. The egalitarian version of meritocracy will be discussed in Chapters 7 and 8.

[63] See, e.g., Fest, *Ueber die Vortheile und Gefahren*, pp. 13–27; Jeremias Nicolaus Eyring, *Gedanken zur Vertheidigung derer die ohne Reichthum studiren* (Göttingen, 1761).

ological insecurity and escapism; but in the diary fragments he was still a confused young man, instinctively carrying the ethical orientation of Pietism over into the rationalism he was adopting. Whereas the later autobiographer becomes increasingly convinced of a poor boy's victimization at the hands of social "circumstances," the diarist is still finding fault with himself at every turn. Not yet able to censure society for requiring a false presentation of the self as the condition of its charity, he castigates himself for being withdrawn and "morose."[64]

Where the diary fragments and *Anton Reiser* complement each other is on the theme of vocation. Moritz's religious path to this theme is evident in the opening fragments, where the resolution to "account" to God for time spent echoes, and probably had its origins in, the traditional Pietist examination of conscience that Francke had urged on his audience. But in Berlin Moritz was drawn into the Enlightenment orbit of Mendelssohn, Spalding, and other luminaries, and the diary soon records his efforts to take stock of himself in rationalist terms. The efficient use of time is no longer a responsibility to God, but a means to "satisfaction with self." Steady application in a *Beruf* looms so large in the search for this satisfaction because it promises to solve two problems at once. On the one hand, it would draw him out of his recurrent self-isolation; professional dedication and normal sociability are a linked pair, the mutually reinforcing elements of a secure identity. But Moritz also oscillated between acceptance of lifelong obscurity as a schoolman and vaulting ambition, which produced scattered writing projects left unfinished. Consistent dedication to his *Beruf* offers a healthy middle way – an exit from isolation, but at the same time an antidote to "the appetite for honor" (*Ehrbegierde*) and its "tormenting thirst for fame."[65]

On August 4, 1779, Moritz recorded his impatience "to expand [himself], to cut [himself] loose from the yoke that drags [him] under." More than three years later, on September 11, 1782, he welcomed the return after a long absence of the "sweet, sweet feeling of exercising my duty"; "Who would have believed even four weeks ago," he asked himself, "that I could sweeten the hours of my *Beruf* so much as to make them the most blessed hours of my life?" – and he wondered whether he "could transform even this desert into a paradise."[66] Despite the occasional satisfaction he derived from professional dedication, Moritz did leave teaching – and Berlin – in 1786. But in the writing of *Anton Reiser* the rationalist ethic of vocation remained a guiding presence. While its pedagogical affirmation of the natural self provided a standard by which to diagnose "injustice" and "oppression" in the experience of a poor boy, its ethic of duty prevented an in-

[64] Moritz, "Aus dem Tagebuche eines Selbstbeobachters," pp. 27–29, 45–47.

[65] Ibid., pp. 26–35. On the influence of the Berlin Enlightenment on Moritz, see esp. Mark Boulby, *Karl Philipp Moritz: At the Fringe of Genius* (Toronto, 1979), pp. 60–81, 116–50.

[66] Moritz, "Aus dem Tagebuche eines Selbstbeobachters," pp. 40, 49.

dictment of social victimization from becoming a brief for a right to individual self-determination.

A decade earlier Gottlob David Hartmann, appealing to the same ethic, had echoed the Lutheran-Pietist ideal of calling in the very act of repudiating its doctrinal basis. Despite its lack of political focus, *Sophron* was an act of rebellion; Hartmann drew on his own experience and that of other promising young men to call into question the pedagogical as well as the theological authority of his elders. The clerical teaching establishment, he protested with specific reference to the cloister schools in Württemberg, neglected and indeed stifled creative talent. Too often pedantic teachers limited their approval and encouragement to boys who merely conformed to their myopic requirements for passive obedience and rote memorization of Latin vocabulary and grammatical rules.[67]

The other authority Hartmann was defying was, of course, his father. His precocious intellectual self-assurance can be gauged from the fact that, in the face of Hartmann senior's incessant recriminations, he never once conceded guilt. But in their correspondence, the son's stubborn self-assertion went hand in hand with a deep-seated need to justify himself to his father, if only by protesting that he had not strayed as far from the Pietist path of righteousness as might at first appear. In *Sophron* both reactions find expression in the discussion of parents' proper role in selecting a "way of life" for their sons, and the result is some of the most tortuous passages of a book not remarkable for the concision of its argument. While the calling comes "indirectly" through nature rather than "directly" through God, his young readers were counseled, the most important medium through which God distributed his assignments was the will of parents. But if parents proved unable to identify rationally a son's natural "capacities and inclinations" and channel them in the proper directions, the son could and indeed must make a rational choice himself, even against their will, once he reached his eighteenth birthday. This was to make parental authority conditional on competent exercise of the pedagogical art, and in effect to make the obedient but rational son arbiter of his own fate. "For myself," Hartmann concluded lamely at one point, "I am decided to satisfy my parents whenever possible, when we are not too much in contradiction with one another."[68]

But the ideal of disinterested service survived – and, one suspects, helped make possible – Hartmann's repudiation of his inherited faith. Having received more than enough paternal rebukes for his fleshly pride and ambition, Hartmann took pains to defend himself against this charge in his book. Taking stock of the natural self was in its way an examination of conscience; the youth could and must distinguish his "main impulse," which he could be sure operated in tandem with talent in impelling him to a

[67] Hartmann, *Sophron*, pp. 30–47.
[68] Ibid., pp. 248–61.

particular occupation, from the mere "gushings" of illicit "passions and appetites." What parents must impress on their sons was not "the glitter of a station," but the duty to "serve as much as possible [their] fatherland and its members." "Personal happiness" lay not in the pursuit of "honor" and other rewards, but in the consolation of "doing [one's] duty in the most unpleasant conditions."[69]

The implication for his own life, Hartmann had insisted in letters, was that he might very well have to accept ascetic obscurity as a teacher of philosophy, so long as he was in a position to espouse "the truth." Just as his father had been grateful to "dear poverty" for protecting him from the seductions of youth, so now the son thanks the same "benefactress of [his] youth" for inuring him to austerity and keeping him isolated from "high society" (*grosse Gesellschaften*).[70] Hartmann was not a prodigal son, despite his refusal to honor his father's will by accepting the yoke of a clerical calling. His self-examination bore witness that the active exercise of reason, no less than the passive reception of grace, expunged corrupt motives of self-interest.

[69] Ibid., pp. 7–16, 199–204, 315–26.
[70] HN, pp. 407–20; Hartmann, *Sophron*, pp. 265, 308–9.

7

Meritocracy: language and ideology

THE LOGIC OF NEOCORPORATISM

At the beginning of *Emile*, Rousseau explains why "the chief thing" in his pedagogical strategy is "to prevent anything from being done":

> In the social order where each has his own place a man must be educated for it. If such a one leave his own station he is fit for nothing else. His education is only useful when fate agrees with his parents' choice. . . . where social grades remain fixed, but the men who form them are constantly changing, no one knows whether he is not harming his son by educating him for his own class.
>
> In the natural order men are all equal and their common calling is that of manhood, so that a well-educated man cannot fail to do well in that calling and those related to it. It matters little to me whether my pupil is intended for the army, the church, or the law. Before his parents chose a calling for him nature called him to be a man. Life is the trade I would teach him. . . . In vain will fate change his station, he will always be in his right place.[1]

It was only as an import, domesticated for native consumption, that *Emile* found a broad audience among German educational reformers. Its German domestication in the last third of the century confirmed the pertinence of Rousseau's distinction between the human being (*Mensch*) and the "citizen" (*Bürger*), but reversed his priorities. This was in part because the rationalist preoccupation with "duty" in the German Enlightenment implied a radically different relationship between the natural self and society. But the difference was not simply one of theory; while Rousseau purposely excluded from his pedagogical idyll the concrete issues posed by schooling, German reformers were engaged in efforts to create out of the existing institutional chaos a several-tiered educational system, maximizing "usefulness" at all levels of society and training a small elite of "state servants" to staff the civil and ecclesiastical bureaucracies. Hence the social specificity implicit in the term *Bürger* – the specificity Rousseau ignored on principle – became

[1] Jean-Jacques Rousseau, *Emile*, trans. Barbara Foxley (Everyman ed.: London and Toronto, 1977), p. 9.

unavoidable. It had to be confronted not only in defining the particular occupational roles into which various school types would channel their pupils, but also in determining how far down the social hierarchy recruitment for the academic schools should reach.[2]

If the ideological lines of division on the latter issue often seem blurred, that is because they formed within a broad framework of consensus and ran through a shared vocabulary. Eighteenth-century faith in progress – in the power of enlightened education to achieve a great leap forward in economic productivity as well as in social mores – did not include the expectation that opportunities for "white collar" office work would proliferate in the private sector. Public employment, it was assumed, neither could nor should be expanded significantly; if it was not already a bloated sphere, draining human resources needed elsewhere, it was in imminent danger of becoming so. The issue was not whether to open the floodgates – to allow a much larger number of aspirants to participate in an open-ended contest – but whether and how to reorganize a channel for sponsored mobility that was already highly restricted and might have to be narrowed still further.

Reformers also were acutely aware that public employment was accommodating a variety of social interests and these might prove irreconcilable in the long run. Depending on where one looked, official careers were an increasingly important source of income and prestige for the aristocracy, the preserve of an educated and affluent *Bürgertum* with few career alternatives, and the only significant path of "higher" opportunity for talented (or at least ambitious) sons of the uneducated and propertyless. It was the perception of pressure and strain within this social constellation that made the real or potential problem of overcrowding seem urgent. Involved in disagreements about the social parameters of recruitment for higher education were very high stakes in a zero-sum game. At the more crowded end of the ideological spectrum were arguments for social exclusiveness; the academic schools would admit only the "extraordinarily intelligent" boy – the true "genius" – from the lower orders, and most poor boys from uneducated families – talented as well as unqualified boys who could rely on charity to climb up the ranks under the present dispensation – would be excluded. But by the 1790s there was also a minority argument, scattered but vocal, for a relatively egalitarian selection process. Propertied families would be required to make room for talent from below in a competitive

[2] On these issues see esp. Hans Georg Herrlitz, *Studium als Standesprivileg: Die Entstehung des Maturitätsproblems im 18. Jahrhundert* (Frankfurt am Main, 1973); Karl-Ernst Jeismann, *Das preussische Gymnasium in Staat und Gesellschaft. Die Entstehung des Gymnasiums als Schule des Staates und der Gebildeten, 1787–1817*, Industrielle Arbeit. Schriftenreihe des Arbeitskreises für moderne Sozialgeschichte, vol. 15 (Stuttgart, 1974); Detlef K. Müller, *Sozialstruktur und Schulsystem: Aspekte zum Strukturwandel des Schulwesens im 19. Jahrhundert*, Studien zum Wandel von Gesellschaft und Bildung im Neunzehnten Jahrhundert, vol. 7 (Göttingen, 1977).

academic arena, narrowing periodically on the ascent to the universities and extending to legal as well as theological studies.

The choice was between two distinct versions of meritocracy, formed *within* a widely shared preference in principle for individual "merit" over "birth."[3] At issue was not whether "birth" in its strict senses, as it sometimes figured in defenses of corporate privilege, should enjoy legitimate advantages. Instead the semantic field formed by "merit," "talent," and related terms proved as serviceable for the claims of "birth" in a looser sense as for attacks on inherited privilege. To appreciate the salient ideological fissure, it becomes necessary to observe how in the logics of two quite distinct normative orientations, as in alternative grammars for a single language, a shared vocabulary resonated with different meanings and produced incompatible conclusions.

Even those who assumed that at the broad base of the social pyramid talent was a rare commodity usually stopped short of explaining social inequality by appeal to genetic differences. The more common assumption was that nature, in its distribution of raw intelligence, was oblivious to social distinctions. At the same time, the very nature of the situation precluded a traditional corporate defense of the inherited legal rights distinguishing "estates of birth" (*Geburtsstände*) in the strict sense. The claim to a legal right to inherit office might make sense in France, where the state had resorted to *venalité* on a massive scale; but it made little sense in the German states, where most public offices had not become family patrimonies. Family connections obviously mattered, but the virtual requirement of university training, reinforced in the course of the century by the introduction of qualifying examinations for legal as well as clerical careers, left no doubt that "merit" played a role in appointments.[4]

If legal privilege was not at stake, "property" in various forms lay at the heart of the matter. The underlying question was whether the lower boundary for access to higher education should confirm, at least implicitly, that legitimate advantages adhered to inheritance of a certain level of wealth and educated culture. Immanuel Kant's famous essay on "the relationship

[3] This distinction has usually been ignored in studies of bourgeois-aristocratic conflict; see, e.g., Johanna Schultze, *Die Auseinandersetzung zwischen Adel und Bürgertum in der deutschen Zeitschriften der letzten drei Jahrzehnte des 18. Jahrhunderts* (1925: Vaduz, 1965).

[4] See, e.g., Hans Rosenberg, *Bureaucracy, Aristocracy and Autocracy. The Prussian Experience, 1660–1815* (Cambridge, Mass., 1958); Wolfram Fischer and Peter Lundgreen, "The Recruitment and Training of Administrative and Technical Personnel," in Charles Tilly, ed., *The Formation of National States in Western Europe* (Princeton, N.J., 1975), pp. 456–561; Peter Lundgreen, "Gegensatz und Verschmelzung von 'alter' und 'neuer' Burokratie im Ancien Regime. Ein Vergleich von Frankreich und Preussen," in Hans-Ulrich Wehler, ed., *Sozialgeschichte Heute* (Göttingen, 1974), pp. 104–18. Despite *vénalité*, it should be noted, the French universities were also becoming "mandatory stepping-stones" for legal careers in the eighteenth century; Richard L. Kagan, "Law Students and Legal Careers in Eighteenth-Century France," *Past and Present* 68 (Aug. 1975): 45.

of theory to practice in political right," published in 1793, lays out the essential duality of what would become the nineteenth-century liberal position; it confirms an overriding right of property in the very process of fashioning a case for opening careers to talent and hence straddles our relevant line of demarcation. Rather than emphasizing the individual's obligation to subordinate his self-interest to collective imperatives, Kant's rational order subjects everyone equally to "external" coercive laws that guarantee each the right to pursue his happiness as he perceives it. He concludes from this "uniform equality of human beings as subjects of a state" that "every member . . . must be entitled to reach any degree of rank which a subject can earn through his talent, his industry and his good fortune," and that "his fellow subjects may not stand in his way by *hereditary* prerogatives or privileges of rank and thereby hold him and his descendants back indefinitely." The radical thrust of this formula lies in Kant's willingness to bring center stage an implication of the new pedagogy more often left in the wings. Talent figures here as a nonheritable form of property, and its owner is granted an inalienable right to develop it. In the dedication of this innate endowment to a socially recognized and rewarded role, as in the use of physical property, there can be no *legal* perpetuation of social distinctions. Indeed Kant goes on to argue that, like heritable wealth, the socially productive exercise of talent in "any skill, trade, fine art or science" allowing economic independence is a form of property distinguishing "citizens" with political rights from mere "subjects."[5]

But characteristically Kant makes injustice a matter of individual intentions – or, more precisely, of the interaction between moral wills – rather than attributing it to a social structure. "Good fortune," like "talent" and "industry," *entitles* the individual to a particular social rank, and it includes "fortuitous external property." Whereas the hereditary enjoyment of legal privilege implicates the individual in an illegitimate form of collective coercion, the inheritance of wealth does not involve moral coercion, either by a collectivity or by the individual to whom the wealth happens to devolve. In fact wealth, by virtue of its externality, is a more "fortuitous" advantage than talent, which is inherent in the person. Precisely because Kant makes inherited property a social accident in this sense, rather than a result of moral intention, he regards it as a legitimate means in the individual's exercise of "freedom" – *not* an illegitimate legal bar to others' pursuit of happiness.[6] Hence the countervailing implication for academic education and the careers to which it led; while society – or the state in its name –

[5] Immanuel Kant, "On the Relationship of Theory to Practice in Political Thought (Against Hobbes)," in *Kant's Political Writings*, ed. Hans Reiss and trans. H. B. Nisbet (Cambridge, 1970), pp. 74–78. The essay was originally published in the *Berlinische Monatsschrift* 22 (1793): 201–84.

[6] Kant, "On the Relationship," pp. 75–76.

cannot tolerate legal obstructions to the rise of talent from below, it must tolerate the de facto advantage afforded by family wealth. Legal equality of opportunity must operate within social inequality of access.

What distinguishes Kant's essay from the conventional wisdom in discussions of educational reform over the previous several decades is its emphasis on freedom – and right – rather than duty. The essay was quite typical in its acceptance of de facto advantage. For all its censorious association of wealth with *Luxus* and selfishness, the reform literature, even at its most radical, did not conclude that the introduction of legal equality of opportunity was incompatible with the survival of private property as a principle of social organization, or indeed with the existing distribution of wealth. Some reformers, to be sure, accepted the gulf between a propertied elite and a propertyless mass reluctantly, as a regrettable but irremovable social fact; they did not share Kant's confidence that the "fortuitous" advantages of wealth left others free to pursue their happiness. In 1788, in a brief essay on the role of the state in education, Peter Villaume lamented a situation in which "wealth and poverty, privileges and oppression stand in tense contrast to each other" and "the excess of a few requires the oppression of many." The state, he argued, should not reinforce this injustice with legal barriers to social ascent, but should alleviate it with a legal equality leaving "all roads open to everyone." The alleviation would hardly be overwhelming; the brutal fact was not only that the lack of "capacities from nature" would of itself keep some in "the lowest classes," but also that the sheer "lack of means to raise themselves up" would "keep many more in lowliness."[7]

But Villaume's tone of grim cynicism about the "force of circumstances" is very much out of tune with the respect for property in the broad mainstream of reform thought. In the prevailing version of meritocracy – the one I shall call neocorporate – normative assumptions endowed property with a superiority that Kant was careful not to grant it. A certain level of wealth not only constituted a legitimate advantage, in Kant's morally neutral sense; it also gave a positive *moral* sanction to de facto privilege in access to academic education. In a youthful essay Johann Georg Hamann made neocorporate logic unusually explicit in assigning a critical role to a certain kind of inheritance. Hamann's theme was the contrast between the "family egotism" (*Familiensucht*) of an ancient aristocracy, now relying on lucrative offices in the state to compensate for the obsolescence of its military ethos, and the "family spirit" that entitled established commercial families to recognition as a true nobility of merit. Aristocratic greed found expression in the nepotism and other kinds of corruption that secured honors for children

[7] Peter Villaume, "Beschluss der im achten Stück abgebrochenen Anmerkungungen über die Frage: Ob der Staat in Erziehung mischen soll?" *Braunschweigisches Journal* 3 (1788): 7–24.

despite their "stupidity and lack of worth." The commercial "family spirit," on the other hand, implanted "the seeds of civic virtue [*bürgerlicher Tugend*]," which gave priority to "the honor of the estate to which we dedicate ourselves and its advantages for society" over "our self-maintenance and selfishness." Such a spirit was neither a genetic byproduct nor a product of schooling; it consisted of "an outstanding strength of certain natural gifts or impulses, which are made hereditary and are continually replanted through the impressions of domestic example and the education arising from it."[8]

By midcentury it was quite common to associate bourgeois "merit" with a commercial ethos, "birth" with the corruption of an official aristocracy. With suitable adjustments, though, Hamann's line of reasoning also could justify the entrenched position of an academic and official elite that included a branch of the aristocracy. This neocorporate logic had its deepest roots and widest resonances in Hanover, where the law faculty at the new university in Göttingen played an increasingly important role in perpetuating both a service aristocracy at the highest altitudes of the civil and judicial bureaucracies and a "state patriciate" in the middle zones. In the third volume of his treatise on the universities, published in 1773, Johann David Michaelis, a professor at Göttingen, devoted a long discussion to the causes and effects of an oversupply of university graduates. Michaelis, in effect demonstrating how social pressures were shaping perceptions of this problem, built an elaborate case for what he considered the proper mix of students from the aristocracy, the "middle estate," and the poor. Precisely because "nature distributes intelligence without partisanship for or against the accidents of wealth [*Glücksgüter*]," he argued, the state normally could meet the limited need for educated professionals without reaching down into the "really poor."[9] The crux of the matter was to limit the extremes of motivation brought to university studies and later careers. Michaelis was quite content that students from wealthy aristocratic families, destined for the highest government offices, were and would remain a minority. Aside from the fact that the instruction they had received from tutors was usually deficient, the same wealth and pedigree that allowed them the leisure for study also gave them little incentive to become industrious scholars. The problem with poor students, on the other hand, was not simply that they could not afford books and had to pass through the university too quickly. In their case incentive was in excess; if ambition drove them to work hard to prove themselves, it also made them approach learning merely as a means

[8] Johann Georg Hamann, "Beylage zur Dangeuil," in idem, *Sämtliche Werke*, ed. Josef Nadler, 6 vols. (Vienna, 1949–57), 4: 230–38. See also Philip Merlan, "J. G. Hamann as Spokesman of the Middle Class," *Journal of the History of Ideas* 9:3 (1948): 380–84.

[9] Johann David Michaelis, *Raisonnement über die protestantischen Universitäten in Deutschland*, 4 vols. (Frankfurt am Main, 1768–76), 3: 170.

to their social ascent. More important, ambition combined with lack of "upbringing" to deprive them of the sense of personal "honor" that made other students amenable to discipline.[10] The core of the student body, Michaelis concluded, should be constituted by sons of educated, "moderately prosperous" families in the "middle estate" – young men whose self-discipline mixed in the proper proportion the incentive to achieve and the inbred check on behavior guaranteed by "[their] property, honor, and hopes":

> The advantage of the middle estate is: it brings education [*Erziehung*], perhaps also more school preparation to the university; it can remain there the proper time, and can provide itself with the most necessary aids in books and instruction; it is still not too proud, and does not simply rely on the capital from which it lives, or on birth, with which it can enjoy preferment without merits, and thus feels the same necessity as the poor to really learn something, and to acquire merit; it takes the middle road.[11]

In an article published nearly two decades later, Friedrich Wilhelm von Ramdohr, an aristocratic councilor on the Hanoverian court of appeals, used a similar rationale to defend the existing division of labor within a bourgeois-aristocratic monopoly. Von Ramdohr conceded that "birth" was "the most accidental of all advantages" and likewise that the compensating importance attributed to "personal merit" was too intimately bound up with prevailing views of the "inner worth, value, beauty . . . of man" to brook contradiction.[12] Nonetheless he presented his educated bourgeois readers with the reasons that noblemen, though not to enjoy an exclusive right to the "highest offices" of state, should continue to be preferred for them. An aristocratic monopoly would encourage throughout society a caste spirit, its blind devotion to "hereditary forms, prejudices and rights" precluding the innovations on which enlightened progress depended. But open competition with well-educated commoners would give too much impetus to ambition, which was necessary to keep the state "machine" in "proper motion" but, in excess, might "bring it to a complete stop." Here, in fact, von Ramdohr warned envious bourgeois officials that their sons could be swamped from below; "only the forgoing of the highest offices by well-bred non-nobles maintains in the lower orders the modesty by virtue of which they do not press too strongly into the middle-level positions."[13]

The efficient functioning of the machinery required a "corporate spirit,"

[10] Ibid., pp. 174–92, 237–39.
[11] Ibid., pp. 187.
[12] Friedrich Wilhelm von Ramdohr, "Ueber das Verhältniss des anerkannten Geburtsadels deutscher monarchischen Staaten zu den übrigen Klassen ihrer Bürger in Rücksicht auf die ersten Staatsbedienungen," *Berlinische Monatsschrift* 17 (1791): 158. For an interpretation of this article within the standard framework of aristocratic-bourgeois rivalry, cf. Klaus Epstein, *The Genesis of German Conservatism* (Princeton, N.J., 1966), pp. 193–97.
[13] Von Ramdohr, "Ueber das Verhältniss," pp. 145–52.

by which von Ramdohr meant a collective commitment to a particular functional role. Corporate spirit did not guarantee the individual practice of "virtue," and indeed rarely allowed the individual to grasp the connection between his own work and "the general good." But if it lacked higher rationality of that kind, it more than compensated with "habitual, competent observance of purposefulness for the fulfillment of a specific assignment." What the nobleman brought to high office was the breadth of vision and versatile sociability that only an upbringing in the public arena of "the world" – of the network of aristocratic households through which he had passed – could inculcate. To the daily routine of office work the educated bourgeois brought the scholarly precision, devotion to detail, and orderly work habits that he had first imbibed from his parents in the intimate privacy of their home. The best way to promote both kinds of merit was to allow families to remain in the same stations (*Stände*) for generations; "thereby [people] receive a certain experience, grasp, skill, even a doctrine of ethics and behavior peculiar to their situation, which they bequeath to their offspring for further development."[14]

Obviously the neocorporate version of meritocracy had important variations, reflecting bourgeois-aristocratic rivalries *within* the elite. In von Ramdohr's reasoning, the same blend of "birth" and "merit" that secured the educated bourgeoisie a preserve at one level of public employment also justified aristocratic preferment at the very top, and thus in effect put a lid on bourgeois official careers. In the bourgeois version, the liberality of the gentleman acceded to the intellectual and moral qualities guaranteeing disciplined achievement in school and professional competence in office. This claim to superiority – or at least to equality – rested on a particular kind of domesticity, superior to the family life of the lower orders by virtue of its "culture" but also differing from the "publicness" of the aristocratic household in its relative privacy and modesty. To a degree von Ramdohr affirmed this domestic source of merit; but in his notion of a bourgeois corporate spirit, it became a convenient foil for an aristocratic capacity for statesmanship transcending mere professional competence – and deriving from a kind of "liberal" education that neither bourgeois domesticity nor training in school could provide.

But the various twists given to neocorporate logic should not obscure its value to both the service aristocracy and educated bourgeois officialdom. Individual merit took precedence over the privileges attached to a legal status only because it bore the social impress of a less formal but no less concrete kind of corporate membership. In this looser sense "birth," in both its educated bourgeois and its aristocratic form, became the vital source for the ethic of public service that would sustain and justify a functional

[14] Ibid., pp. 147–48.

hierarchy of merit. Particularly in its bourgeois guise, in fact, the value of this familial transmission of a collective tradition lay in injecting ambition into the social body in a controlled and therefore tolerable dosage – as the individual expression of a corporate sense of "honor," and therefore as a motive force fundamentally different from the unrestrained appetite for advancement and its rewards with which uprooted poor students menaced the social order.

In this way privileged access to academic education and public offices – a form of privilege both groups enjoyed de facto – was sanctioned without appeal to genetic superiority or a historical legal right. For the son of a modestly affluent bourgeois official, as for the scion of a far more wealthy aristocratic family, the "accident" of heritable wealth combined with the collective cultural legacy embodied in the family to produce a decisive – and perfectly legitimate – advantage. Differences aside, upbringing in a particular kind of family milieu became in both cases the critical variable between the natural self and the meritorious *Bürger* in a particular station, between innate endowments and the social and ultimately moral characteristics needed in school and office. In this conception of "merit," the pedagogical emphasis was on socialization rather than natural entelechy, a corporate ethos rather than individual performance. Like the aristocratic household, the more confined and modest bourgeois family was the pivotal socializing agent, inculcating collective habits and norms – and not the domestic incubator for natural growth. Hence there was no need to exclude poor students as a group on the shaky grounds that they lacked talent; "merit" was a matter of transforming raw talent into dedicated service, and poor students were less likely to do so than their better-off counterparts because they lacked the requisite social experience.

Meritocracy in this form may have been especially well suited to the social configuration in Hanoverian public employment, but it figures more or less explicitly in much of the educational reform literature throughout Germany. One of the marked tensions in reform thought lay precisely in its simultaneous commitment to an abstract principle of "merit," implicitly detaching the individual from his particular social affiliations so as to take the measure of his true value, and association of meritorious qualities and qualifications with specific groups.[15] Though often betraying the crank's penchant for absurdly intricate detail, Johann Bernhard Basedow's oscillations between abstract principle and concrete social applications are typical of this larger tension. What gave his reform thought a certain internal consistency in its eighteenth-century context was the normative grammar of neocorporatism. To Basedow, a revolution in the organization and the cur-

[15] There are numerous examples of this tension in Helmut König, *Zur Geschichte der bürgerlichen Nationalerziehung in Deutschland im letzten Drittel des 18. Jahrhunderts*, Monumenta Paedagogica, vol. 1 (Berlin, 1960).

ricula of the schools and universities was the only effective antidote to the "corruption" of contemporary society. His kinship with Rousseau lay above all in the ascetic cult of natural simplicity that informed his ideal of the "patriotic" *Bürger*. If his moral censure applied to the society as a whole, it was often aimed specifically at the *Luxus* – the self-indulgence and conspicuous consumption – that turned children of wealthy families into selfish, enervated adults. It was this kind of family upbringing that the reformed gymnasium would counteract in preparing future students; Basedow insisted that its pupils be boarders, removed from parental authority and "reared and trained" by the state, and that they avoid "the seductive display of the rich" by wearing military-like uniforms.[16]

But this moral censure of wealth operated within the typical perception of its "advantages." Basedow simply equated the "more cultured" families with "the propertied" and in so doing made a certain level of wealth the prerequisite for the moral qualities as well as the cultural advantages the word "*gesitteten*" connoted. Sounding the usual alarm about an oversupply of university graduates, he followed neocorporate logic to the conclusion that all but the most exceptional poor boys must be excluded from academic studies. In his organizational blueprint for a public educational system, as in those of most of his contemporaries, school types reflected and would perpetuate class divisions. In addition to the state-subsidized "lay schools," providing rudimentary instruction to the great mass of peasants' and artisans' children, there would be completely separate, more expensive "common schools" for children of "more prominent" *Bürger* – and only the latter would channel pupils into the gymnasium.[17]

Both the individual and the collective species of merit guided Basedow's intricate – one might say tortuous – planning for the Philanthropinum, the experimental school he established in Dessau in 1774. As a result an institution that in some respects suggested in microcosm a radical negation of the status quo – a meritocracy based strictly on individual merit – also gave substance to the neocorporate alternative. The pupils were divided into two groups: the majority of *Pensionisten*, from wealthier families paying their tuition and their room and board, and a minority of charity pupils known as *Famulanten*. A system of "merit points" was to grade academic performance and conduct with objective precision, and to underscore its objectivity all pupils had to wear a uniform. But only the outstanding *Famulanten* could hope to avoid becoming domestic servants, and only by receiving special training to enter teaching. Assigned to one or more *Pen-*

[16] Johann Bernhard Basedow, *Ausgewählte pädagogische Schriften*, ed. A. Reble (Paderborn, 1965), esp. pp. 61–62. Reble's edition includes an excellent introduction to Basedow's life and work (pp. 253–64).

[17] Ibid., pp. 20–21, 33–42. See also Albert Pinloche, *La réforme de l'éducation en Allemagne au 18ème siècle. Basedow et le philanthropinisme* (Paris, 1889); Rosemarie Ahrbeck-Wothge, *Studien über den Philanthropismus und die Dessauer Aufklärung* (Halle, 1970).

sionisten, the younger *Famulant* would spend nine of his seventeen working hours each day preparing for and cleaning up after meals, waiting on tables, and performing other menial tasks. In this way, Basedow explained, "the youth learn gradually in the early years to command rationally and obey well, and yet each is satisfied with his station." Not surprisingly the ranking of pupils by merit – or, more precisely, by merit points gained or lost – was to be observed only two days per week. On the other days they were to be ranked by "wealth," measured by the extent to which families contributed to the institution beyond room and board, and by "station" (*Stande*). The latter criterion was a particularly curious hybrid; outstanding older *Famulanten* selected to become teachers would occupy the first places, to be followed, in descending order, by "counts, imperial lords, nobility, *Bürgerschaft*."[18]

LANGUAGE, TALENT, AND MATURITY

In one form, mastery of language was the crux of the traditional corporate initiation into the *Gelehrtenstand*; in another, it lay at the heart of a new pedagogical fascination with the external expressions of an inner entelechy. There was no better example of the child's natural development of rational powers than his acquisition of his native language. In the course of the century, this obvious alternative to the "mechanical" routinism (*Schlendrian*) of old-style Latinity became all the more appealing precisely because it promised to reconcile nature and society, to cultivate the quintessentially human in the *Mensch* while equipping the *Bürger* for social life. But at the same time that the phenomenon of language itself, as a peculiarly human skill, remained a focal point, the pedagogical approach to language was particularly sensitive to the fracturing of a shared vocabulary of talent, merit, and vocation into alternate ideologies. To a degree new departures in language instruction could be accommodated within an essentially ascriptive definition of merit as a collective inheritance; but they also were critical in generating an egalitarian ideal of individual achievement and in pointing to a dramatic reversal of the neocorporate relationship between family and school.

Here again Gottlob David Hartmann's *Sophron* is a convenient landmark. Hartmann's confidence that the conscientious youth could take stock of his own capacities was fueled by a large measure of contempt for the judgments of teachers. Included in *Sophron* was a letter from a friend, recalling from bitter personal experience how "neglected geniuses" were subject to nar-

[18] Basedow, *Schriften*, pp. 215–23. On the "merit" system see also Hermann Lorenz, "Die Meritenbücher und Meritentafeln des Philanthropinums zu Dessau," *Mitteilungen der Gesellschaft für die Erziehungs- und Schulgeschichte* 12 (1902): 93–120.

row-minded, pedantic evaluations in school. Able to recall all the complications and accessory facts of an event, the friend nonetheless had been judged to have a poor memory; retention of words was considered "the true touchstone of capacities" in the rote Latin exercises that had monopolized his early instruction. Since "the learning of languages" will always be "more the work of memory than of rational understanding," he concluded, it was not a reliable measure of intelligence.[19]

Hartmann obviously identified with this victim of injustice, but in 1773 it was still impolitic for a young graduate of Württemberg's cloister schools to denigrate their hoary traditions in print. Elsewhere in Germany, though, Hartmann's grievance had been a commonplace among former Latin school pupils for several decades. Discontent with the prevailing "mindless routine" (*Schlendrian*) had become one of the driving forces behind the reform movement. By the 1790s this sentiment was fragmenting into two camps, one bent on dislodging study of the ancient languages from its sacrosanct position in the Latin schools, the other committed to its preservation, in suitably regenerated form, as the core of academic education. But the split into "philanthropinistic" and "neohumanistic" agendas should not obscure an underlying pedagogical consensus on how to teach language, whether native or foreign, modern or ancient. It was above all in the formation of this consensus that pedagogical theory and schoolroom practice met and entered creative dialogue.

While many schoolmen were especially attached to old-style Latinity as their only emblem of corporate honor, many others contributed to the development of new approaches to language instruction. Despite the emphasis on formalism in their training, the content of classical texts may have induced a certain receptivity to reform; in its approach to language, as in its other preoccupations, the new pedagogical literature was simply elaborating the ancient humanistic ideal of a "natural" pedagogy with which Latinists were already familiar. Not surprisingly, sons of clergymen were prominent among reform-minded schoolmen, including those at the more egalitarian end of the spectrum. From the vantage point of their later efforts to master more modern forms of learning, they often looked back on their domestic grooming in the mental habits of Latinity more as a handicap than as an advantage over outsiders. If as boys they had been groomed within a clerical world, as teachers, particularly in the lower grades, they were exposed to the social pluralism of town schools. Having shared with outsiders a precarious dependence on charity and patrons, they had reason to appreciate the meaning of social disadvantage.

[19] Gottlob David Hartmann, *Sophron. Oder die Bestimmung des Jünglings für dieses Leben* (Mitau, 1773), pp. 39–43.

The seminal figure among these pastors' sons was Johann Matthias Gesner. In most respects a *Gelehrter* of the old school, his career typifying the received traditions of academic mobility, Gesner nonetheless was remarkably precocious in developing and applying the pedagogical redefinition of language that would impel egalitarian reform. His father died in 1703, when he was only twelve, and like most other gymnasium pupils in such circumstances he had to make the rounds as a choirboy to earn his keep. As a theology student at Jena he attached himself to Johann Franz Buddeus, who took him into his household as his children's tutor. His mentor's theology was sufficiently tinged with Pietism to incur the wrath of Wolffian rationalists as well as the suspicion of Orthodox theologians. But Buddeus's vital legacy to Gesner was the scholar's interest in the humanistic tradition of vocation, not the converted Pietist's faith in the calling. It was that tradition, with its emphasis on reading nature's inscription in each child and respecting natural stages of development, that had informed Buddeus's dissertation on the "cultivation of intelligence" in 1699.[20]

In 1713 Gesner began his academic career by assembling a compendium of precepts from classical and more recent sources (including Locke) for use in the pedagogical seminar Buddeus planned to establish. This initial foray into the new pedagogy was followed by two decades of experience as an innovative schoolman. In 1730 Gesner left the rectorate in Ansbach to succeed Ernesti as rector of the Thomasschule in Leipzig, which, unlike its neighbor, the Nikolaischule, accommodated a large number of charity pupils.[21] His professorial appointment in Göttingen in 1734 was made in recognition of his editions of classical texts, and by the time he died in 1761 he was the presiding figure in a renaissance of classical scholarship. But his pedagogical interest and commitment to school reform remained. From his famous philological seminar came many of the first generation of reform-minded schoolmen in the middle decades of the century. The seminar was concerned as much with equipping future teachers with pedagogical

[20] There is a synopsis of Buddeus's dissertation in Martin Franzbach, *Lessings Huarte-Uebersetzung (1752). Die Rezeption und Wirkungsgeschichte des 'Examen de ingenios para las ciencias' (1575) in Deutschland*, Hamburger and Co. romanistische Studien, B, vol. 29 (Hamburg, 1965), pp. 49–50.

[21] Karl Hermann Bernhard Pöhnert, *Joh. Matth. Gesner und sein Verhältnis zum Philanthropismus und Neuhumanismus* (Leipzig, 1898), is a useful study of Gesner's reform thought in its intellectual context, though it may exaggerate the influence of Christian Thomasius on Gesner. Pöhnert rightly emphasizes the continuities between Gesner and the philanthropinists; the basic approach to method in language instruction is a case in point. For brief profiles of Gesner as a reformer see Friedrich Paulsen, *Der gelehrte Unterricht im Zeichen des Neuhumanismus, 1740–1892*, Geschichte des Gelehrten Unterrichts auf den deutschen Schulen und Universitäten vom Ausgang des Mittelalters bis zur Gegenwart, vol. 2 (3rd, enl. ed.: Berlin, 1921), pp. 16–30; Otto Kaemmel, *Geschichte des Leipziger Schulwesens vom Anfange des 13. bis gegen die Mitte des 19. Jahrhunderts (1214–1846)* (Leipzig and Berlin, 1909), pp. 309–31.

skills as with grooming future philologists in new methods of textual criticism.[22]

Gesner's eclectic enthusiasm for reform lacked the militant professionalism and the aggressively egalitarian ideal of competitive achievement to be found among some younger schoolmen in the last third of the century. In Leipzig he had been accepted into the same mixed circles of scholars, literary men, and prominent officials that Gellert would enter in the 1740s. Like Gellert, he came to typify the courtly *Gelehrter*, integrated comfortably into polite society despite his obscure origins as a pastor's son and the hardships of his early years. While pupils "of low station and little wealth" must be made aware that "their own virtue" could compensate for lack of "external advantages," he noted in his plan for a reformed gymnasium, they must also be reminded that "they have reason to use all proper means to win the favor and friendship of such persons whose birth and station open an easy way to prestigious positions of honor."[23] Likewise, as a powerful patron in his own right, Gesner expected clients to acknowledge his kindness with the usual deference.

But the patron's conventional view of rank and sponsorship went hand in hand with the reformer's far-reaching ambitions. Gesner saw no contradiction in imbuing his pupils with the cameralists' eminently utilitarian ideal of service in this world at the same time that he inculcated "piety." As a former poor student engaged in sponsoring the upcoming generation, he was actively committed to promoting talent from below. A far more accomplished classicist than his mentor Buddeus, he was well acquainted with the theoretical preference for natural entelechy over social ascription and the corollary willingness to allow boys and young men some freedom in choosing their "destinies" in the humanistic conception of vocation.[24] These commitments and intellectual orientations likewise found expression in his reform blueprint for the gymnasium. Its lower grades were in fact an early version of a common school; pupils "of all varieties of extraction, age, quality [*Beschaffenheit*] and destiny" would be exposed to the same core curriculum, with little room for private instruction, from their entry at age six or eight to their departure for academic studies or occupational life in the trades and commerce at age twelve or fourteen.[25]

Gesner also agreed with many of his contemporaries that the traditional

[22] Paulsen, *Der gelehrte Unterricht*, pp. 25, 42–43. Jeremias Nicolaus Eyring (1739–103), a member of the philological seminar and later director of the gymnasium in Göttingen, was particularly important in transmitting the more egalitarian implications of Gesner's reform thought. Appropriately his *Gedanken zur Vertheidigung derer die ohne Reichthum studiren* (Göttingen, 1761) was dedicated to Gesner. See also Herrlitz, *Studium als Standesprivileg*, pp. 64–66.

[23] J. M. Gesner, "Bedenken wie ein Gymnasium in einer Fürstlichen Residenzstadt einzurichten," in idem, *Kleine Deutsche Schriften* (Göttingen and Leipzig, 1756), pp. 368–69.

[24] Pöhnert, *Gesner*, pp. 39–41.

[25] Gesner, "Bedenken," pp. 356–64.

introduction to Latinity in the early school grades was doubly harmful, in that it lured the unqualified into the learned estate while leaving others with a lasting "contempt" for the language and its literature. Where he was truly innovative was in pursuing the practical implications of his alternative conception of language and its significance for human nature. Gesner would have agreed with Hartmann that the traditional Latinity narrowly equated intelligence with memory but would have found wrongheaded his conclusion that language learning could not be "the work . . . of rational understanding." In this regard the courtly scholar was more in tune with intellectual trends than the rebel of the next generation; Gesner's reform thought typified the eighteenth-century fascination with verbal communication as the essence of uniquely human mental capacity. The uniqueness of man lay in his reason, Gesner wrote in 1751 in commemoration of the founding of a Society for the German Language; "Language is the direct tool of reason . . . and indeed in a certain sense the soul itself, insofar as it can emerge from its concealment and enter into communion with other souls."[26] In the light of this standard, the technical competence required in old-style Latinity represented a "mechanical" and irrational defiance of what made man truly – and naturally – human. The actual content of texts – the human meaning they were meant to convey – had become the occasion to display technical mastery of formal rules. In Gesner's alternative approach, the language would function once again as the verbal means to a rational end, the tool for constructing meaning. Words were referents to substance, and grammar a structure for understanding; this was what he meant when he insisted that "mastery of words" and "knowledge of contents" were inseparable.

In applying this dictum, Gesner helped prepare the way for neohumanism as well as for the utilitarian brand of reform it opposed. While German would finally be given due attention as the appropriate medium for "useful" knowledge in a common school, a suitably reformed Latin instruction, using original texts, would give advanced pupils an understanding of the philosophical and ethical contributions as well as the aesthetic achievements of classical antiquity. And there was another reason for Gesner's disapproval of the reliance on memorization; if Latin instruction was to realize the classical ideal by adapting to the schedule of a natural entelechy, it must emulate the sequential development through which the pupil had already advanced in his native tongue. The natural strategy was to begin by having pupils comprehend meaning from "cursory" reading of texts and lectures in Latin, in place of the usual "static" dissection for philological and stylistic detail, and to make explicit only later the abstract grammatical rules they had already intuited. Pupils were not ready for this kind of initiation until

[26] J. M. Gesner, "Auf dem Stiftungstag der deutschen Gesellschaft," in idem, *Schriften*, p. 158.

the higher grades, following a general education in German, although they might earlier begin to acquire the rudiments.[27]

In the last third of the century, partly by way of his own students, Gesner's basic principles came to permeate reform thought. Their popularity did not prevent the emergence of competing agendas for changing the content and sequential order of the traditional Latin school curriculum. Basedow claimed that from an early age pupils could learn quite naturally to read and speak Latin in a variety of "useful" school subjects, without attention to grammatical or literary niceties, and to prove his point liked to exhibit his daughter Emilie, who had begun the language as a four-and-a-half-year-old.[28] His method was designed to rescue Latin from its honorific obsolescence, so that it could finally become the international language of everyday intercourse among the learned that it was supposed to be. Other philanthropinists argued that Latin could no longer play that role in the complex world of modern academic disciplines and professions; it was simply another form of expertise, still essential to a few scholarly disciplines but irrelevant to most. Among Latin school reformers, the more common view was that the study of classical languages and their literature should remain the shared experience of all educated men, but that it should not begin until a general education in the mother tongue – the same education given to pupils destined for nonacademic walks of life – had been completed.[29]

Underlying the gamut of curriculum plans, however, was a consensus on two deceptively simple notions: that memorization must accede to understanding in the learning and use of languages and that the "natural" developmental schedule of childhood and early youth – the schedule that the new language learning followed – was the proper standard for measuring intellectual maturation. These were not simply matters of scholarly taste and pedagogical preference; they had potentially radical implications for the social composition of the academic elite as well as for its role in the larger society. In the traditional Latin school, verbatim memorization of words, phrases, and rules was essential to the imitation of elegant models. To eliminate it was to change beyond recognition the transmission of Latinity as an honorific emblem of corporate membership.

[27] See esp. J. M. Gesner, "Vorschläge von Verbesserung des Schulwesens," in idem, *Schriften*, pp. 309–15; Pöhnert, *Gesner*, pp. 77–92. On the larger political and social issues involved in creating a German literary language and reforming language instruction, see Joachim Gessinger, *Sprache und Bürgertum. Zur Sozialgeschichte sprachlicher Verkehrsformen im Deutschland des 18. Jahrhunderts* (Stuttgart, 1980).

[28] Basedow, *Schriften*, esp. pp. 48–52; Pinloche, *La réforme de l'éducation*, pp. 105–9. The daughter was named, of course, in honor of Rousseau. Basedow had wanted to name her "Praenumerantia Elementaria Philanthropia," since her birth coincided with subscriptions for his *Elementarwerk*; but his wife had objected.

[29] For the controversy about Latin see, e.g., Ernst Christian Trapp's objections in *Allgemeine Revision des gesammten Schul- und Erziehungswesens* 16 (1792): 44–144. The issues are well summarized in Gessinger, *Sprache und Bürgertum*, pp. 75–85.

The ideological coloration of this change depended on the social angle. To make the living language the model for academic talent and achievement was necessarily to introduce a new dependence on the daily linguistic practices of social life and on the class distinctions they at once announced and helped perpetuate. If the criteria for evaluating inborn facility and potential in the native tongue were in principle "natural," they too – no less than the moral criteria for merit – often simply elevated the neocorporate bias for "cultured" homes to the status of a universal standard. Some found a reform of Latin instruction appealing precisely because it promised to reduce the opportunity for the occasional outsider without means, his verbatim memory perhaps already exercised in religious reading, to distinguish himself in a competitive arena that was detached from daily social life. A critical step in curing the entire learned estate of its monkish "pedantry" would be to remove the stereotypical artisan's (or peasant's) son who, in his eagerness to compensate for his family's lack of culture with academic feats of memorization, made himself a caricature of the pseudo-learned Latinist.

But verbatim memorization was also the vital link between domestic instruction in educated families and school learning; from that angle, in fact, it represented the critical advantage that sons of clergymen – including those whose fathers, in addition to lacking property, had a very tenuous interpretive grasp of classical texts by any standard – enjoyed over outsiders. It was precisely here that some reformers drew egalitarian implications from the new approach to language learning. In part this was a matter of rejecting the narrow equation of academic talent with verbal memory – the equation Hartmann found so unfair – in favor of a more differentiated standard. The value of Latin now lay primarily in the window it opened onto literature, philosophy, and several other branches of the classical corpus. In the lower grades, German would serve as the medium of access to a much broader range of subjects that included arithmetic, geography, and perhaps history. The use of language in different contexts now reflected the various modes of intelligence needed to grasp various contents; and in the selection of talent for a variety of professions and disciplines, it was possible to apply a different standard of maturity for each context.[30]

Perhaps more momentous was another implication. The kind of verbatim erudition young boys from educated homes could bring to school now attested not to their greater suitability for academic studies, but to their parents' misguided efforts to defy nature and make them prematurely

[30] The more variegated and flexible approach to academic intelligence and "maturity" is especially striking in the deliberations on the Prussian *Abitur*; see esp. Paul Schwartz, *Die Gelehrtenschulen Preussens unter dem Oberschulkollegium (1787–1806) und das Abiturientenexamen*, 3 vols., Monumenta Germaniae Paedagogica, vols. 46, 48, 50 (Berlin, 1910–12), 1: 72–115. For background on changing conceptions of academic "maturity," see Herrlitz, *Studium als Standesprivileg*.

learned. It was typical of this shift that in 1784 Philipp Julius Lieberkühn, the young rector of the Latin school in Neuruppin, warned that such efforts often did more harm than good – and that parents should not judge their sons' progress by the false standard of the amount of material memorized.[31] Carl August Böttiger, another young schoolman, attached a quite specific social pedigree to the same error and explained why it was incompatible with the mission of a public school:

Of course much in the mindless routine of teaching and educating children, especially in the more refined orders, would have to be altered and eradicated. The eight year old boy would not yet be reciting Latin flourishes like a parrot, and perhaps in his tenth year would not be able to relate anything about the Roman dictator and Jupiter's love affairs with the beautiful Europa; but he would know already from his own experience a hundred other things that are indispensable to him as a human being and a *Bürger* for his entire life. . . . But isn't the profile of the future *Gelehrter* discernible even in the earliest instruction of the child in its usual form? If in general all our pedagogical efforts, urgings, and writings for more than two decades have not been completely empty twaddle and an idle speculation in blueprints [*nichtige Lustbaumeisterey*], then it is to be hoped that the truth spoken and ruminated on countless times will finally be made more and more practical, i.e., that the boy must first be developed as a human being and a *Bürger* without regard for his future destiny, which he should not yet have at this age, until a certain year when language study and academic preparation must begin. . . . That would obviously remove the objection of many parents that the boy who will probably have a desire for studies cannot be familiarized early enough with all sorts of elegant purses, and that the head in which learning will soon find entry must be turned and cleaned from sunrise on with the brooms of vocabulary books and grammars.[32]

Taking language acquisition in the native tongue as its model, the new pedagogy defined its "art" in terms of a gradual, unforced progress, with the variety of inborn capacities that constituted academic talent revealing themselves in their proper time and maturing at their proper pace. In one sense the new approach to language induced a pronounced shift away from earlier pedagogical enthusiasm. Gone was the confidence that nature's inscription could be read in the earliest years of life; now the emphasis was on how deceptive the apparent signs of natural talent and inclination could be, particularly in young children, and on the need to postpone vocational

[31] Philipp Julius Lieberkühn, "Ueber die nothwendige Verbindung der öffentlichen und häuslichen Erziehung," in idem, *Kleine Schriften, nebst dessen Lebensbeschreibung und einigen charakteristischen Briefen an Hn. Professor Stuve*, ed. Ludwig Friedrich Gottlob Ernst Gedike (Züllichau and Freystadt, 1791), pp. 198–200.

[32] Carl August Böttiger, *Ueber die besten Mittel, die Studiersuch derer, die zum Studieren keinen Beruf haben, zu hemmen* (Leipzig, 1789), pp. 35–36. For other classic statements of the "natural" approach to language instruction, see Johannes Stuve, "Ueber die Erziehung," in idem, *Kleine Schriften gemeinnützigen Inhalts*, 2 vols. (Brunswick, 1794): 1–115; Thieme, "Von methodischer Erlernung der Sprachen," *Archiv für die ausübende Erziehungskunst* 7 (1780): 133–58, 225–306.

choices at least until the early teen years. In the case of a young man aspiring to academic studies "caution cannot be exaggerated" and "the understanding . . . cannot be overly prepared or overripe," Böttiger counseled, since it takes close examination over a long period to distinguish "quickly passing flirtations and impulses to imitate" from "true inner inclinations."[33] The irony is that this new modesty provided a powerful reason for enhancing the public authority of the school over its pupils' futures, at the expense of the family, and hence for loosening it from its traditional social moorings. The later the juncture at which the academic initiation began, the less importance would adhere to the cultural impetus educated homes could provide their sons. Instead pedagogical judgments, based on the observation of nature unfolding gradually in the neutral arena of the school, would be decisive. At least in this sense, the school would operate independent of its pupils' family backgrounds not only in determining the pace of advancement, but also in selecting the truly qualified.

[33] Böttiger, *Ueber die besten Mittel*, pp. 30–35. For the new note of caution, see also, e.g., Johann Georg Krünitz, "Lebens-Art," *Oekonomisch-technologische Encyklopädie. Oder Allgemeines System der Staats- Stadt- Haus- und Landwirtschaft*, pt. 67 (1795), pp. 58–70; Trapp's comments in *Allgemeine Revision* 16 (1792): 57. Especially important in this regard was Christian Garve's essay on "the examination of capabilities" (1779), which sensibly emphasized how deceptive the signs of nature in children's behavior could be; "Versuch über die Prüfung der Fähigkeiten," in Christian Garve, *Sämmtliche Werke*, 13 vols. (Breslau, 1801), 7: 9–88.

8

The egalitarian alternative: theory and practice

THE NEW BREED

"We would in a short time see entirely different men around us," Immanuel Kant observed in an advertisement for Basedow's Philanthropinum in 1777, "if once that educational method were in full swing that is derived wisely from nature itself, and not slavishly copied after the old custom of rude and inexperienced ages." What was needed, Kant argued, was not "gradual improvement" in the conventional schools, but the "quick *revolution*" that only an experimental school like Basedow's could accomplish.[1] But from a social standpoint, the agenda for a pedagogical "revolution" bypassed the experimental schools of the late eighteenth century; in the emergence of an egalitarian rationale for meritocracy, they were largely irrelevant. They might be designed to counteract the arrogance of lineage and great wealth, but they were too dependent on the financial support of affluent and educated parents to question in more fundamental terms the neocorporate equation of inherited advantages with "merit."

That questioning arose at the two extremes – the domestic setting of private tutoring and the public setting of town schools – that experimental institutions were designed to avoid. In the last decades of the century, many wealthier families still preferred tutoring to the Latin schools, and particularly to their lower grades. The widespread reliance on this institution gave poor students firsthand experience not only of the "public" style of the aristocratic household, but also of bourgeois domesticity in its more affluent forms. In the second half of the century it was still common for experience as a tutor to complete a young man's relatively unproblematic induction into polite society. But tutors who had grievances against employers, or who knew of the tribulations of others in their circles of friends and acquaintances, were led to question the very link between family up-

[1] *The Educational Theory of Immanuel Kant*, ed. and trans. Edward Franklin Buchner (Philadelphia and London, 1904), p. 242. The communication originally appeared in a Königsberg newspaper on Mar. 27, 1777. Kant was apparently enthusiastic enough about the Philanthropinum to be willing to collect subscriptions for it locally.

bringing and merit on which neocorporate logic turned. The underlying social reality – the painful collision between the university graduate's self-image as an educated man and his more or less openly enforced dependence and inferiority as a household employee – was not new. But now resentment could be articulated, at least privately, in a new idiom; the tutor was likely to be a fledgling practitioner of the pedagogical art, already familiar with the writings of Rousseau, Basedow, and others, or at least eager to compensate for his deficient preparation for his new "calling" by reading the literature recommended in tutoring handbooks. For a convert to the new pedagogy, it was difficult to conform to stereotype by retreating into a traditional corporate identity; he now had a critical standard by which to judge his own outmoded corporate initiation to learning at the hands of "pedants." But he had also acquired a compensatory weapon, a new vantage point from which to take the measure of the world he was entering. To young men unsure of and threatened by the requirements of polite society, the "natural" jurisdiction occupied by pedagogy offered a certain invulnerability, a claim to individual honor on the basis of education and expertise rather than wealth and breeding.[2]

This reaction is almost caricatured in the anonymous response to Crome's essay on tutoring in 1789. In the hostile setting of an aristocratic household still bent on grooming its two young scions in stiff courtly manners and "premature" literary learning, the young pedagogue poses as a custodian of nature. He does not hesitate to credit himself with "rescuing" the boys from physical enervation and moral corruption.[3] The tone is unusually militant, not to say arrogant; but this young Rousseauian probably differed from many other tutors of his generation more in his willingness to lay out his battle plan than in his basic posture. Even among tutors calling for some kind of modus vivendi with employers, there is the same tendency to describe – or, perhaps better, to fantasize – the pedagogical relationship of "love" and "trust" between tutor and pupil as an intimate, almost conspiratorial alliance against misguided parents, too blinded by prejudice or enslaved by the conventions of their station to appreciate the rationality of the pedagogical art and the gratitude owed its practitioner. The target of tutors' moral censure was not always the aristocratic household, although its "display" and its social conventions did come to embody artificiality in

[2] See esp. Ludwig Fertig, *Die Hofmeister. Ein Beitrag zur Geschichte des Lehrerstandes und der bürgerlichen Intelligenz* (Stuttgart, 1979), pp. 57–98; Hans H. Gerth, *Bürgerliche Intelligenz um 1800. Zur Soziologie des deutschen Frühliberalismus*, Kritische Studien zur Geschichtswissenschaft, vol. 19 (Göttingen, 1976), pp. 51–60. But cf. Wilhelm Roessler, *Die Entstehung des modernen Erziehungswesens in Deutschland* (Stuttgart, 1961), pp. 134–42.

[3] "Einige Bemerkungen zu der Cromischen Abhandlung: Ueber die Erziehung durch Hauslehrer, im 10ten Theil des Revisionswerks, von einem Hauslehrer," *Braunschweigisches Journal* 4:4 (Apr. 1789): 432–57. See also Carl Müller, *Schädlichkeit der Hauserziehung für Erzieher, Zögling und Staat* (Stendal, 1783).

the extreme. Posed against the material austerity and moral rigor of a truly natural environment – the kind in which good work habits and devotion to duty were cultivated – was the *Luxus* to be found in the affluent *Bürgertum* as well as the nobility. The very claim to penetrate behind the social shell to an inner reality made tutors with this orientation appreciate and perhaps even exaggerate their pupils' innate potential. From their standpoint, the great tragedy of wealthy scions was not that pedigrees and family connections sometimes compensated for their innate mediocrity, but that often their great potential for service in the eminent offices for which they were destined was not being tapped. But this perception was in itself a direct challenge to the assumptions of neocorporatism; family wealth, far from facilitating the transformation of raw talent into merit, was seen to work against it.

By generating this disenchantment with domestic education, the tutoring experience helped make the schools an appealing alternative and reinforced the growing enthusiasm for creating a truly public educational system. But it was in the efforts to reform the towns' academic schools – the Latin schools and the *Gymnasien* – that organizational blueprints for "careers open to talent" took shape in the last third of the century. Of the many administrative initiatives these efforts produced, the most dramatic was the introduction of a screening examination for university studies in Prussia in December 1788. Though this *Abitur*, or "maturity" examination, stopped short of actually excluding aspiring students on the basis of its results, and hence was of little practical significance, it was a benchmark. Its introduction confirmed that in Prussia, as in several other North German states, the reform of higher education had become a central objective of enlightened state policy. But the lengthy deliberations preceding the *Abitur* made it clear that at virtually every turn reform confronted the issue of social access to academic studies. On that issue the shared language of talent and merit overlay a deep ideological fissure.

What occasioned the deliberations was a memorandum to the new Superior School Board (*Oberschulkollegium*) in Berlin from Chancellor von Hoffmann at Halle on the pressing need to dam up the flood of young men entering the universities without adequate preparation. This was a common concern in university faculties; it went hand in hand with alarm about overcrowding, and particularly about swelling numbers of poor students. That this particular appeal issued from Halle was appropriate. Since the era of Francke an abundance of "free tables" and other forms of charity had given the university a well-deserved reputation as a poor students' haven. "We know from long experience," the university faculty reported in its contribution to the *Abitur* deliberations, "that every year a crowd of poor, badly instructed young men, capable at best of paying the costs of the trip, come to us in the hope of making it through here with charitable endowments and the support of kind people."[4] A recent recovery in enrollments, especially in theology, had peaked in the mid-1780s, and the precipitous decline that would characterize the 1790s was not yet apparent.

In Prussia and elsewhere there was a broad consensus among reformers that, if a rigorous selection process was to be achieved, preuniversity schooling had to be centralized. The chief culprits were the many small-town Latin schools; their teachers were inclined to delude themselves about the academic potential of favorities, and in any case parents bent on a university education for their son were free to ignore teachers' advice. Most of these institutions would have to be shut down or converted into *Bürgerschulen*, offering advanced commercial training to the kinds of pupils who were being misled into academic studies. But was the point to eliminate all the unqualified, including wealthier boarding pupils who attended the higher grades after preparation at home? Or was the exclusive target poor boys, able to advance academically precisely because the local presence of a Latin school allowed their parents to avoid boarding expenses? Likewise the young men who advanced to the *Prima* and left for the university "prematurely" included sons of wealthier parents – people whom teachers dependent on school fees could not afford to contradict – as well as charity pupils eager to get through the hardship years as quickly as possible. Should requirements for "maturity" be applied equally to all, or only to the latter?

The introductory grades of Latin schools and *Gymnasien* had come to play a dual role in urban life: to begin the academic preparation of those few boys destined for the universities and to provide elementary instruction of a relatively high quality to other sons of local *Bürger*. Unable to divide their younger pupils into academic and nonacademic classes, the schools simply gave rudimentary instruction in Latin to all. The result – reformers never tired of pointing out – was a disastrous promiscuity, at once social and cultural; the false glitter of Latin as a status credential, combined with the example of better-off classmates, seduced into academe sons of artisans and shopkeepers who would be far more "useful" elsewhere.[5] But if there was to be a segregation into Latin and elementary grades from the start, on what basis? If Latin instruction was postponed until a higher grade, could not the introductory grades become a socially mixed common school from which a talented few were selected for advancement to academic studies?

Rarely did the introductory grades include children of the large urban

[4] Paul Schwartz, *Die Gelehrtenschulen Preussens unter dem Oberschulkollegium (1787–1806) und das Abiturientenexamen*, 3 vols., Monumenta Germaniae Paedagogica, vols. 46, 48, 50 (Berlin, 1910–12), 1: 72–73. Schwartz used archival records to summarize the deliberations in detail; ibid., pp. 72–115.

[5] For the typical objections to the small-town Latin schools, see Carl Ludwig Friedrich Lachmann, *Ueber die Umschaffung vieler unzweckmässigen so genannten lateinischen Schulen in zweckmässig eingerichtete Bürgerschulen, und über die Vereinigung der Militärschulen mit den Bürgerschulen* (Berlin, 1800).

underclass in unskilled wage labor and casual employment; if these received any schooling at all, it was usually from licensed "schoolmasters" in "German" schools or special pauper schools or from the many unlicensed practitioners. But young sons of artisans, shopkeepers, and other uneducated but more "respectable" *Bürger* did sit in the same schoolrooms and receive the same instruction as pupils from wealthier, better-educated families. In a limited but important sense this pluralism – with pupils' families ranged on both sides of the bifurcation between the propertied and the propertyless, the educated and the uneducated, academic and popular culture – constituted a social laboratory for translating pedagogical theory into practice. More or less consciously, teachers weighed the relative importance of "natural" aptitudes and social – i.e., ascriptive – attributes in evaluating academic performance and potential.

Ideological differences among teachers reflected the assumptions and norms they brought to this day-to-day evaluation. In discussions of the traits required for academic studies, the "will" and the "intellect" often assumed the status of fundamental categories in a scientific anthropology. But this distinction between volition and mental capacity, like the distinctions among mental faculties, was quite conventional; if it retained strong resonances of the Lutheran-Pietist ethic, it also left ample room for the play of social biases. In fact there was no clearly drawn and fixed boundary between scholastic estimations of intelligence and moral appraisals of character. Equally elusive was the line between the innate and the acquired – between natural "motivation" (*Neigung*) and "impulse" (*Trieb*) and cultivated habit – within the territory of the will. Neocorporate logic assigned the family and the school complementary roles within a shared ethos; but it did so by elevating certain marks of "refined" speech, bodily carriage, dress and comportment – attributes specific to certain kinds of domestic upbringing – to the status of universal standards for academic potential and "maturity." The schoolmen who routinely applied these standards included former outsiders; it was a measure of the thoroughness of their induction into "cultured" society that they regarded themselves as the rare exceptions to the rule, the few who had been able to shed plebeian traits from an early age.[6]

To a degree the same ideological norms and class-defined criteria came into play in the more egalitarian approach. One thinks of Heinrich Philipp Sextroh, an orphaned pastor's son and the rector of the gymnasium in Hanover when Moritz was a pupil there. If Moritz is to be believed, Sextroh's commitment to sponsoring the "truly capable," regardless of station,

[6] See, e.g., Jakob Christoph Rudolph Eckermann, *Kleine vermischte Schriften*, 2 vols. (Altona, 1799); Johann Christian Heinrich Krause, *Beantwortung der Frage, Wer hat Beruf, ein Gelehrter zu werden?* 2 vols. (Bremen, 1787–88). The arguments for exclusiveness are emphasized in Hans Georg Herrlitz, *Studium als Standesprivileg: Die Entstehung des Maturitätsproblems im 18. Jahrhundert* (Frankfurt am Main, 1973).

did not prevent him from mistaking the insecurity of the outsider for "baseness."[7] More striking, though, are the positive themes. The tendency to find an untapped reserve of superior intelligence among poor boys had its corollary in the claim that they brought to academic studies the requisite motivation, self-discipline, and sheer endurance that better-off boys often lacked. This was to turn the tables – to make social disadvantages a unique source of virtue. At this end of the spectrum, the former outsiders among schoolmen were also commenting on themselves; the virtues attributed to new prospects reflected the self-image of men proud to have struggled through despite handicaps and hardships. If they felt they had *achieved* by dint of character as well as talent, they also were acknowledging that their strength of character was rooted in their plebeian background. In his positive stereotype of disadvantaged pupils, as in his autobiographical self-image, the former poor student tended to identify with his milieu of origin in the very process of claiming an earned right to have risen above it.[8]

In the last third of the century, the criteria used to qualify or disqualify outsiders became bound inextricably with competing definitions of the academic and official elite and its proper role in the larger society. The emphasis on imitative stylistic elegance in a dead language, the public rituals of academic life, the maze of titles – these and other traditions with which the learned estate defined its public identity in terms of honorific display rather than practical expertise were now becoming symbols of obsolescence. Basedow's reform tracts caused such a stir in the 1770s, despite the eccentricity of some of his specific proposals, because they focused this sentiment. It was the failure to demonstrate "usefulness," Basedow and his fellow philanthropinists argued, that was responsible for the obvious loss of prestige that learning and the learned had suffered in their century. The educated minority would restore itself to a position of leadership in society when it adjusted its learning to contemporary needs and committed itself to realizing its potentially enormous contribution to the public welfare. Scholars must leave their corporate ghetto and become one part, albeit the controlling part, of a well-functioning machine. Aside from inculcating the public "virtue" (*Tugend*) and the "patriotism" that would fuel this machine, the new schools would realize the cameralist vision of technological, economic, and ultimately cultural progress by forging a new union between modernized academic disciplines and actual labor in offices, shops and

[7] Karl Philipp Moritz, *Anton Reiser. Ein psychologischer Roman* (1785–90: Frankfurt am Main, 1979), pp. 157–201. On Sextroh see also Hugo Eybisch, *Anton Reiser. Untersuchungen zur Lebensgeschichte von K. Ph. Moritz und zur Kritik seiner Autobiographie*, Probefahrten. Erstlingsarbeiten aus dem Deutschen Seminar in Leipzig, ed. Albert Köster, vol. 14 (Leipzig, 1909), pp. 30–31. Sextroh had written a tract on the need to sponsor talented poor boys.

[8] See, e.g., Jeremias Nicolaus Eyring, *Gedanken zur Vertheidigung derer die ohne Reichtum studiren* (Göttingen, 1761); Johann Samuel Fest, *Ueber die Vortheile und Gefahren der Armuth für Jünglinge auf der Academie* (Leipzig, 1784).

fields. Above all in this sense, school reformers aspired to reconnect learning with "life."[9]

This reform enthusiasm projected a vast attitudinal shift, appealing precisely because it promised an entirely new relationship between learned and popular culture without implying any basic changes in the structure of class relations. It became standard rhetoric to berate academics for their traditional disdain of mundane affairs and urge them to cultivate a new respect for the truly "productive" orders. Typically Basedow and others hoped to inculcate this respect in boys from "cultured" homes without exposing them to potentially damaging contact with boys from "lower" families; the main fare in exclusively academic institutions could be spiced – and the world of agriculture and the manual trades could in effect be simulated – by introducing work (or play) in school shops and gardens.

But by the 1780s the attack on the traditional Latin school as a kind of hothouse, artificially insulating its charges from the demands and challenges of real life, was being incorporated into a larger theoretical shift with far-reaching implications. While continuing to pose a choice between an open-ended, multifaceted education of the "human being" (*Mensch*) and the carefully bounded and targeted fashioning of a *Bürger*, Peter Villaume and other philanthropinists also sought to minimize the tension between these agendas. In part they were acknowledging the Rousseauian alternative to a strictly utilitarian approach: there was, after all, a shared *Menschheit* – a core human nature anterior to all distinctions in social identity and more fundamental than differences in innate talent – and the pedagogical effort to realize it must be common to all forms of elementary education. In a more comfortable modification of utilitarian priorities, the tendency to break down the category *Bürger* into particular occupational groups, each with its distinctive educational needs, was balanced by a new "patriotic" emphasis on shared participation in the productive division of labor that constituted the "state" or, in more modern parlance, the "nation." As the basis for that commonality reformers now posited a single fund of "useful" knowledge, habits, and ethical qualities essential to the future *Gelehrter* and official as well as to the future merchant, tradesman, or artisan. From both angles a sharp dichotomy between rudimentary instruction for the great mass and a segregated academic training for the educated elite no longer seemed tenable. Instead the education of the *Mensch* and the *Bürger*, in his larger profile, seemed to imply a cultural continuum – a single pyramid, with higher levels differing from the base in degree rather than in kind. In the translation of this vision into blueprints for public educational systems, a deliberate social pluralism would replace the existing makeshift variety. If the Latin schools' introductory grades already accommodated pupils from

[9] See esp. Johann Bernhard Basedow, *Ausgewählte pädagogische Schriften*, ed. A. Reble (Paderborn, 1965), pp. 13–31, 100–5.

a wide variety of family backgrounds, they would now constitute a trunk institution – what will be called a common school – branching up into various nonacademic and academic occupational alternatives.[10]

It was a measure of the strength of neocorporate logic that, in the eyes of many of its enthusiasts, the new common school would not culminate in an egalitarian selection process; though initially sitting in the same classrooms and learning the same subjects, pupils from various backgrounds would simply advance to socially segregated tracks. But in the 1780s a more radical version emerged – one in which the advantage of a common school, accommodating all future *Bürger*, lay precisely in allowing a markedly egalitarian approach to "talent" and "merit." Its advocates were a distinct group of younger men; born in the 1750s, they entered careers as schoolmen in the late 1770s and the 1780s. They were roughly the contemporaries of the "Grub Street" radicals of Paris – the young intellectuals who found themselves beyond the pale of the patronage that distributed pensions and academy appointments and who on the eve of the Revolution were pouring their bitterness into *libelles* exposing the corruption of *le monde*.[11] But the radicalism of young German schoolmen was far removed from "gutter Rousseauism"; they espoused a more respectable kind of egalitarianism, reflecting a world of schools and official appointments very different from the Parisian literary underworld.

These were sons of obscure pastors, schoolteachers, and tradesmen, representing the lower ranks of the clergy's recruitment pool in wealth, and sometimes in educational level as well. For them, as for denizens of Grub Street, the rise from obscurity hinged on patronage. But they were the protégés of the rationalist theologians who had come to dominate the uni-

[10] See, e.g., the essays by Villaume and Joachim Heinrich Campe in the *Allgemeine Revision des gesamten Schul- und Erziehungswesens*, reprinted in Herwig Blankertz, ed., *Bildung und Brauchbarkeit. Texte von Joachim Heinrich Campe und Peter Villaume zur Theorie utilitärer Erziehung* (Brunswick, 1965). For background, see esp. Helmut König, *Zur Geschichte der Nationalerziehung in Deutschland im letzten Drittel des 18. Jahrhunderts*, Monumenta Paedagogica, vol. 1 (Berlin, 1960), pp. 108–18, 160–81.

[11] Robert Darnton, "The High Enlightenment and the Low-Life of Literature," in idem, *The Literary Underground of the Old Regime* (Cambridge, Mass., 1982): 1–40; idem, *Mesmerism and the End of the Enlightenment in France* (New York, 1976), esp. pp. 83–125. This generation of schoolmen might also be usefully compared with their French contemporaries among the Oratorians and the *Pères de la doctrine chrétienne*, who staffed a substantial portion of the *collèges*. The latter had long enjoyed a distinct identity as teaching orders, and in the course of the eighteenth century the reform sentiment in their ranks seems to have developed within a relatively smooth transition from clerical corporatism to secular professional organizations. In contrast German schoolmen were relegated to a marginal status – and, in theory at least, a merely transitional one – within the clerical order as a whole; their assertion of professional identity required a self-conscious repudiation of clerical traditions (see Chapter 10). R. R. Palmer, *The Improvement of Humanity. Education and the French Revolution* (Princeton, N.J., 1985), esp. pp. 49–51; Jean de Viguerie, *Une oeuvre d'éducation sous l'ancien régime: Les pères de la doctrine chrétienne en France et en Italie 1592–1792* (Paris, 1976).

versity faculties; thanks to these sponsors, and perhaps to contacts acquired in tutoring positions, they became solid if lowly citizens in the official ranks. Their favorable attitude toward poor boys reflected a certain pride in their own educational and career achievements, which proved that innate talent and hard work could compensate for lack of social advantages. By the time they had entered the universities, the theological battles with Lutheran Orthodoxy that had preoccupied their elders seemed to have been largely won.[12] The new frontier – the one in which "enlightenment" would be carried out of its university enclaves and into the mainstream of life and in which the new man, long projected in rationalist theology, might actually materialize – was pedagogy.

Coming of age in the 1770s, the younger generation of schoolmen had been enlisted for reform by Basedow's appeals and the reports of his celebrated Philanthropinum in Dessau. But when they left the universities, it was not to found more experimental schools; they faced the very different challenge of teaching in municipal Latin schools and *Gymnasien*. In their immediate local world, privilege was represented not by a German equivalent of *le monde*, but by the wealthier and better-educated parents on whom they depended for school fees. Their enthusiasm for the new pedagogy was nourished by Rousseau's *Emile*, as well as by classical treatises and Locke's *Some Thoughts Concerning Education*. As that enthusiasm evolved into a militant professionalism, it generated a paradox that would have struck Rousseau as very curious – and that may seem equally puzzling in the light of our tendency (which owes much to Rousseau) to pit the "natural" against the institutional and the bureaucratic. The essence of the pedagogical art lay in identifying a natural distribution of human resources, otherwise hidden and untapped beneath the social surface, and in developing individual potential in conformity with nature's schedule. In its capacity as a kind of incubator, the school's "public" identity and its "natural" jurisdiction fused; both were pitted against a social status quo represented by the narrow, selfish interests of particular groups and families. Hence the paradox: only if the school achieved truly public status as an arm of the state could it constitute the alternative – i.e., natural – jurisdiction needed to turn raw talent and other innate capacities into "useful" merit, despite countervailing pressures in the surrounding society. Pupils would become the objects of a new bureaucratic rationality, at once intensified and softened by their teachers' fatherly personal concern, as the pedagogical art structured this public space into a controlled, monitored arena for competitive achievement.

Philipp Julius Lieberkühn, one of the gymnasium directors asked to submit an opinion on the prospective *Abitur* in Prussia, belonged to this new

[12] On the theological preoccupations of the older generation, see esp. Karl Aner, *Die Theologie der Lessingzeit* (Halle, 1929).

breed. The son of a small-town rent collector in Brandenburg, Lieberkühn had been a charity pupil and had gone on to become a protégé of the rationalist theologians at Halle. In 1778, at age twenty-four, he left a tutoring position to accept an appointment in the Latin school in Neuruppin, a small town in Brandenburg, and six years later, in recognition of his reformist energies, he advanced to the directorship of a large gymnasium in Breslau.[13] By the end of his tenure in Neuruppin he was calling on the state to create a truly meritocratic selection process for academic studies. For poor boys whose talents required "a more refined education," he argued, public support must replace the traditional forms of charity:

> The poor but capable boy cannot be simply referred to the generosity of private people; often he lacks the necessary channels and arts; indeed it is often to be wished that he not have to allow himself to be oppressed and corrupted by the humiliations that such acts of charity not seldom entail. Hence the state will take him in its arms, and must support him from the public wealth of society.[14]

We are left wondering whether Lieberkühn had experienced such "humiliations" himself as a charity pupil. In any case his alternative system of public support implicitly transferred to the state, as a kind of surrogate father, the paternal authority that had traditionally sanctioned the role of individual – or, in his terms, "private" – patrons. This preference for public over private sponsorship had its parallel in Lieberkühn's explicit denial of the traditional authority of the family vis-à-vis the school. If his views marked the social consciousness of a former poor student, they also reflected the disillusionment and frustration of an enlightened pedagogue. In Neuruppin, a faction in the magistracy bent on a reform of the local school after years of neglect had appointed Lieberkühn and Johann Stuve, a friend of the same age, despite their youth and inexperience with "public" schools. Promised a free hand to push through innovations, the two young zealots soon came up against the opposition of local families. In Lieberkühn's second public report on the school, published in the same year they arrived, the optimistic appeals for parental cooperation already stand in odd juxtaposition to laments about the intractable "prejudices" they faced and the "cabales" and personal "slanders" they had to endure.[15]

It was standard procedure in "enlightened" educational literature to be-

[13] Stuve provided an informative biography of his friend in Philipp Julius Lieberkühn, *Kleine Schriften, nebst dessen Lebensbeschreibung und einiger charakteristischen Briefen an Hn. Professor Stuve*, ed. Ludwig Friedrich Gottlob Ernst Gedike (Züllichau and Freystadt, 1791), pp. 514–36. Lieberkühn's father was described as a *Ziesemeister*, which I have taken to be a misprint for *Zinsemeister*.

[14] "Ueber die nothwendige Verbindung der öffentlichen und häuslichen Erziehung," in ibid., pp. 178–82.

[15] Ibid., esp. pp. 53–54. On the Neuruppin reform effort and local opposition, see also "Nachricht von der Neu-Neuruppinischen Schule," in Johann Stuve, *Kleine Schriften gemeinnützigen Inhalts*, ed. Joachim Heinrich Campe (Brunswick, 1794), pp. 3–28.

rate the "public" for its its blind attachment to tradition. When Lieberkühn sounded this theme over the next several years, however, he departed markedly from the typical assumption that wealthier and better-educated families, however obscurantist, were more accessible to "reason" than the uneducated lower orders. His reports and essays make it abundantly clear that the local opposition to reform had emanated primarily from prominent and better-off families, accustomed to regarding the Latin school as their special preserve, and that his ideal of a public institution took shape and hardened accordingly. Even in "houses of good tone and enlightenment in other respects," he noted in 1784, "a host of prejudices and false principles" prevailed in the education of children. Since in making decisions about their children's futures parents, far from being guided by "the signs of nature," followed the dictates "now of selfishness, now of fear of embarrassment, now of vanity, now of prejudice," the state must "in general lead and arrange as much as possible" in matching individual capacities to the needs of society. Included in this indictment was the artisan who let his son be lured into the learned estate by its exterior glitter; but it was indicative of the focus of Lieberkühn's local battles that his particular grievance was against the same wealthier parents who coddled their children at home and expected teachers to give them preferential treatment in school.[16]

From this social and professional vantage point Lieberkühn sought to transform the makeshift necessity of social pluralism in the traditional Latin school into the virtue of a socially integrated common school. The danger that such mixing would corrupt well-bred boys was exaggerated, he argued, since parents gave too much importance to "exterior manners and respectability."[17] And in any case a public setting had an overriding advantage over private education:

> The feeling of differences in station and birth, which is so often a source of pride and hardheartedness, disappears or is moderated in public schools. Here all are treated according to the same laws, whether they are prominent or obscure; the only thing that matters is whether they are more capable, more orderly, more industrious, more decent, more noble-spirited, in order to be more loved and valued by their teachers and fellow pupils. Here the boy of prominent birth learns to know and appreciate children of all stations. He is persuaded from firsthand observation that these often have greater capabilities, more pleasing manners, and more noble attitudes than him and his like. . . . Even the variety of minds and characters has something uncommonly beneficial for the education of youth. Noble competition

[16] "Ueber die nothwendige Verbindung," pp. 178–79; "Ueber den Werth und die Rechte der öffentlichen Erziehung," in Lieberkühn, *Schriften*, pp. 282–99. But cf. the account of the Neuruppin reform in Wolfgang Neugebauer, *Absolutistischer Staat und Schulwirklichkeit in Brandenburg-Preussen*, Veröffentlichungen der Historischen Kommission zu Berlin, vol. 62 (Berlin and New York, 1985), pp. 545–47, which notes – incorrectly, I think – that "the opposition had its social anchorage in the urban underclass [*Unterschicht*]."

[17] "Ueber den Werth," pp. 264–73.

[*Wetteifer*] finds there a far greater and far more harmless sustenance than in private education, because it has there a larger field and a more proportioned stimulation. Finally, the publicness of treatment and life has a much stronger effect on young temperaments! It has indeed the happy result of producing in them early something of that noble community spirit [*Gemeingeist*] that is a precious trait of the human being.[18]

If parents tried to bring their social weight to bear on the school, Lieberkühn responded by walling off its public space from such "private" interference. In principle, if not in fact, an egalitarian competition, subjecting pupils from a great variety of backgrounds to the same "impartial" standards of evaluation, would neutralize social differences in the selection of the meritorious few for advanced studies. In assigning the school a key role in the creation of a national community, Lieberkühn remained solidly within the utilitarian reform tradition. The promotion of talent still derived its legitimacy from the needs of the social order, and the well-educated, virtuous *Bürger* was still the embodiment of the Enlightenment's ethic of disinterested service. But in the very process of explaining how a common school would inculcate a "spirit of community" and an ethic of service, Lieberkühn endorsed with unqualified enthusiasm the motivating force of competitive achievement – the open use of "love of honor" (*Ehrliebe*) to spur the individual to outdo his fellows – that was more often associated with illegitimate "ambition." Again the difference between private and public was decisive; the same motivation that produced a selfish caste mentality in a private setting, his logic implied, had precisely the opposite effect in the school, where it could be stimulated and channeled under public control.

In Lieberkühn's school impartial standards of evaluation encompassed moral behavior as well as intellectual performance. Since education was to produce virtuous *Bürger* devoted to the public welfare and since the new learned estate would constitute a moral as well as an intellectual elite, it was central to the school's mission to develop and assess "character." In an effort to evaluate character with the same objective precision applied to academic grading, teachers were to use every opportunity to "probe deeper into [the] soul" of each pupil. In Neuruppin each teacher had to observe the behavior of specific pupils at home, at least by making inquiries with parents, and keep a record of their transgressions in special "conduct books." These records were discussed at weekly teachers' conferences and were figured into the rector's monthly "public judgment" of each pupil at a "ceremonial assembly."[19] The procedure may very well have been one of the causes of friction between Lieberkühn and local parents in Neuruppin. He continued it at Breslau, despite parental opposition. Aside from ignoring differences in rank, birth, and wealth in making these "public judg-

[18] "Ueber die nothwendige Verbindung," pp. 188–89.
[19] Ibid., pp. 190–91.

ments," he explained in a report in 1787, he and his staff also tried to avoid a more subtle kind of prejudice "nourished by a host of socialized ideas [*vergesellschafteten Ideen*]." It was because they were so confident of being "impartial" that they proceeded with that "lack of inhibition" that many found "almost too much."[20]

For centuries the use of competitive ranking to motivate schoolboys, particularly in Latin instruction, had coexisted uncomfortably with the Christian ideals of humility and self-effacement that Lutheranism had sought to inculcate and Pietism had emphatically reconfirmed. When it came to intergrade promotions, competitive standards, if they had been applied rigorously at all, had been limited to poor boys in need of charity, while wealthier parents were left free to enter their sons when they chose, push them through rapidly, and send them on, prepared or not, to the universities. To Lieberkühn the application of a single standard was a crucial means of creating, in the school and ultimately in the larger society, a community transcending class divisions. The novelty of his approach lay, first, in making the motivating force of competitive achievement central to the school's moral education and, second, in making "objective" standards for promotion through the ranks, and ultimately for admission into or exclusion from the academic and official elite, binding on all.

This strategy not only offended wealthier and better-educated parents; it also diverged from other reformers' neocorporate assumption that a private familial right – parents' right to use their property to their children's advantage – took precedence over the public authority of the school. While Lieberkühn often spoke of the need for "cooperation" between school and family, he clearly assigned the family a subordinate role in preparing children to meet the school's public – and universal – standards.[21] What in neocorporate logic was a collective ethos, ensuring merit in school, was now seen as obstructive self-interest and prejudice. The family could prepare children for the school only to the extent that it transcended its particular identity and suppressed its selfish motives. Domesticity must become the natural alternative to corrupting socialization – hence assuming the role that pedagogy, in one of its theoretical orientations, had always assigned it. As a public institution, the school was now seen to command a socially neutral jurisdiction for the exercise of rational expertise. It had become the public arbiter between the individual and the collectivity – between the socially detached pupils who were the objects of its pedagogical art and the social needs they would be selected and trained to fulfill.

While this standpoint clearly was in the minority, even among reform-minded teachers at the end of the century, it was not limited to Prussia. In

[20] "Nachricht von der im Elisabethanischen Gymnasium zu Breslau üblichen Censur der Schuljugend," in Lieberkühn, *Schriften*, pp. 413–33.

[21] See, e.g., "Ueber den Werth"; "Ueber die nothwendige Verbindung."

an essay on school reform published in 1789, Georg David Koeler, the young rector of the gymnasium in Detmold, likewise called for a selection process strictly on the basis of individual talent and merit, with public support for qualified but needy pupils. This arrangement would have "something natural" about it, Koeler observed, whereas now public and private education operated independently and often at cross-purposes.[22] Here again an enthusiast of the pedagogical art, committed to following the "signs of nature," had developed his militant conception of a public school in reaction to the private prejudices and "whims" of local parents with means.

In the emergence of an egalitarian alternative, the shift in focus from experimental schools to the social realities of conventional local institutions was critical. There is no better example than developments in Dessau, which had hosted Basedow's celebrated experiment since 1774. By 1784 the Philanthropinum was still struggling to secure a sufficient number of paying customers, and Basedow, too quirky to establish a modus vivendi with his colleagues, had washed his hands of it. The ducal government entrusted C. G. Neuendorf, a young member of the staff, with the task of creating a public school system for Dessau itself and its host duchy. In Neuendorf's approach, as in Lieberkühn's, the school's utilitarian and national missions – its identification and promotion of talent for the public welfare and its dissemination of the fund of knowledge and virtue common to all *Bürger* in a national community – were complementary. He began by turning the introductory grades of the Lutheran municipal school into a common school (*Hauptschule*), its curriculum leading to a reformed gymnasium as well as to other alternatives and its pupils taking the same basic subjects until age sixteen. This integration of school levels into a cultural continuum was matched by a centralized schema for the duchy as a whole; in addition to drawing on Dessau itself, the common school would be supplied with talented pupils from other town and village schools, which were given a similar if less ambitious curriculum. To this end Neuendorf planned to provide a substantial amount of public support for needy pupils. Government generosity proved limited, but it is a measure of his egalitarian intent that by the early 1790s forty-six pupils in the *Hauptschule* – one-quarter of the total – enjoyed free places.[23]

Carl August Böttiger was one of the youngest of the egalitarian reformers who came of age in the 1780s. Best known as a classical scholar and ar-

[22] Georg David Koeler, *Ueber die Policey und äussere Einrichtung der Gymnasien* (Lemgo, 1789), pp. 21–25, 63. On Koeler's reform activity, see also Volker Wehrmann, *Die Aufklärung in Lippe. Ihre Bedeutung für die Politik, Schule, und Geistesleben* (Detmold, 1972), pp. 103–5.

[23] Walter Schöler, *Der fortschrittliche Einfluss des Philanthropismus auf das niedere Schulwesen im Fürstentum Anhalt-Dessau 1785–1800*, Diskussionsbeiträge zu Fragen der Pädagogik, Heft 7 (Berlin, 1957), is an informative account of Neuendorf's reform effort and its departures from Basedow's original objectives, based in part on archival records. See esp. pp. 58–85.

chaeologist, he was appointed director of the gymnasium in Weimar in 1791 and became one of the minor luminaries in Goethe's firmament. But it was as the twenty-nine-year-old rector of a lyceum in the small town of Guben and as a well-read enthusiast of the new pedagogy that Böttiger published an essay on the vocation for academic studies in 1789. The essay is not altogether consistent; if in some ways it confirms the egalitarian thrust of a secular rationalism, it also points up – quite unintentionally – the inhibiting strictures of the new orthodoxy. Böttiger employs a common distinction between "inner" and "exterior" *Beruf*; but now the language of *Beruf*, incorporated entirely into a humanistic idiom and given a new social specificity, is emptied of its distinctly German root ideas in the Lutheran-Pietist tradition. Rather than explain how the grace of conversion sanctifies the performance of duty in a Christian office, Böttiger asks how "natural capacity" and "inclination" and the availability of financial means (as well as good health) are to be weighed in admitting boys to academic studies. No longer resonating with sacred meanings, the dichotomy between subjectivity and objective condition in *Beruf* now poses an unabashedly secular choice between natural entelechy and social ascription, innate merit and "birth." This was one of the many areas in which "a certain compensation" should operate, Böttiger argued: "the lack on one side can be sufficiently replaced by superfluity on the other." Just as the boy with "outstanding wealth" but a "weak or only very mediocre mind" should not be excluded, so too the poor boy with "outstanding capacity and motivation" should be considered to have been given a "free pass" by "nature."[24]

In practical terms, Böttiger's compromise was a variation on the usual double standard, not an egalitarian resolution of the issue. Indeed the opening pages of his essay read as a classic eighteenth-century cry of alarm about an oversupply of university graduates. Framing the problem against the standard cameralist model of social equilibrium, he laments the fact that *Luxus*, now penetrating into "the huts of the lowliest of the people," is spreading the craving to "shake off the dust of low birth" and "climb higher" by way of the "ladder of studies."[25] But Böttiger's double standard was a practical concession, not an application of neocorporate norms. What finds expression as the argument advances is the social consciousness of the village pastor's son-become-militant professional – the young man who, for all his disapproval of rampant social climbing, conveys his intensely moralistic pride in his own achievement and his resentment of social privilege in an aggressively positive stereotype of poor students. When Böttiger asks

[24] Carl August Böttiger, *Ueber die besten Mittel, die Studiersuch derer, die zum Studieren keinen Beruf haben, zu hemmen* (Leipzig, 1789), pp. 24–25. See also Karl Wilhelm Böttiger, *Karl August Böttiger; eine biographische Skizze* (Leipzig, 1837). Böttiger was the son of a conrector and later *Diakonus*. For a different evaluation of his reform tract, but one likewise emphasizing its internal inconsistencies, see Herrlitz, *Studium als Standesprivileg*, pp. 11–15.

[25] Böttiger, *Ueber die besten Mittel*, pp. 5–15.

where the state finds truly qualified servants, his bitterness surfaces and his rhetoric takes flight:

Go to the universities, to the capitals and all those places where a colorful throng of civil and clerical candidates, like an army of bees around a blooming apple tree, swarm around the district courts, the chancelleries, and the consistories. Ask the most industrious, the most deserving, the most modest among them about their ancestry, their parentage. Without doubt sons of prominent families constitute the smallest portion of these, although of course for that reason the most precious. Most of them certainly come out of the common and lower orders. In their case it usually was not decided in the early years what they should study and whether they should study at all. The father perhaps said: first we have to see whether my son is suitable, and whether something can be made of him. So the son regarded the opportunity to study as a blessing [*Wohltat*], gathered all his powers, and learned what he could. But the prominent scion brings with him into the world the calling [*Beruf*] to the station of his parents, experiences the certainty of it with his first pair of pants, as a boy, when only a little effort suffices, envelops himself in school nonsense and pedantry, and during every hour in school calculates slyly whether he can use this or not. Out of this comes inevitably that race of bumble bees who only buzz and cannot prepare any honey, that sad breed of monkeys [*Aftergeschlecht*], of superficial half-learned, sugary creatures [*Süsslinge*] and papa's boys, who camouflage their emptiness with the often very ambiguous services of their fathers and, when they have obtained an office with cunning, begging, or sneakiness, are a pain and an agony to themselves and other men. And it is incumbent on the state to fill its offices with healthy and hard-working men. It cannot desire that the reward for the industrious be dissipated by yawning loafers and lustful *Sybariten* and enjoyed by brittle-nerved weaklings.[26]

Böttiger in effect inverted the prevailing order of stereotypes. Blind selfishness remained the essential vice in *Luxus*; but it was now an attribute of wealth, not a plague spreading through the lower orders. Pseudo-learning, more commonly ascribed to poor students, was now typified by the prominent scion. The onslaught of metaphor reminds us that there is a linear descent from Hartmann, the young philosopher who published *Sophron* in 1774, to the young schoolmen of the next decade. In its denial of the prevailing neocorporate logic, the egalitarian rationale for meritocracy represented a genuinely radical alternative. Equally striking, though, is that the alternative emerged almost entirely *within* a larger orthodoxy. The young protégés were applying the same rationalist ethic of vocation to which their elders were committed, and in essence they evoked the same utilitarian

[26] Ibid., pp. 55–57. Böttiger continued: "Thus it is a benefit for human society if that emaciated race of men, more and more decadent with each generation if it is kept pure [*aecht*] – a type that, knowledgeable people assure us, is so frequent in the refined and prominent orders – is enlarged with fresh members of unweakened intellectual and physical power from the common orders, which are corrupted little or not at all, and thus the paralyzed machine is redriven with new energy and activity."

idiom to justify its radical social implications. If their egalitarian commitment to the natural man contradicted the Lutheran-Pietist ethic of self-denial, their emphasis on the "public" dictates of service nonetheless echoed that ethic. The kind of ambition they openly encouraged – the kind that would motivate academic achievement – was safe precisely because it operated within the structured and therefore controlled competition of the school. Incubated in that environment, the appetite for "honor" would not be a selfish passion; it would be subordinated to, and indeed enlisted in, the development of moral character, which still took the dedicated and disinterested *Bürger* as its ideal.

But here lay the implicit tension in Böttiger's eclectic defense of poor boys; if one of his lines of argument remained within utilitarian logic, others replaced the conventional insistence on collective imperatives with an appeal to individual right. In its search for qualified officials, Böttiger argued at one point, the state need concern itself only with intellectual capacity; it cannot "guess beforehand what objective motivates each aspirant to academic studies." It should not be held against some that they "regard academic studies merely as a necessary means to a future livelihood and a convenient key opening for them the otherwise inaccessible doors to a well-endowed and comfortable state or church living."[27] Böttiger was not simply denying the neocorporate premise that certain kinds of familial inheritance ensured a superior purity of motive; he in effect accepted self-interest as a legitimate motive and extended to poor boys an equal right to pursue it. And when he likewise denied that the state could limit the opportunity to prove merit to "a single class of men," it was not simply because of the potential damage to the public welfare. Böttiger considered the "entitlements" (*Ansprüche*) to intellectual "perfection of the self" to be "inalienable" in the "civil condition." Such perfection was achieved above all in the learned estate, and "in this regard the son of the lowest of the people, as a human being, has the same legitimate claims [*Ansprüche*] as the son of the most prominent."[28] Here for once civic duty and human right – the service required of the *Bürger* and the realization of the natural self to which the *Mensch* was entitled – became coextensive in the rationale for opening careers to talent.

FRIEDRICH GEDIKE: PROFILE OF A SCHOOLMAN

Several schoolmen who contributed to the Prussian *Abitur* deliberations in 1788 approached reform in a more or less egalitarian spirit. Lieberkühn was one of them, but on this occasion he chose to keep the social impli-

[27] Ibid., pp. 54–55.
[28] Ibid., pp. 52–54.

cations of his argument muted. Friedrich Gedike was more explicit about the need to promote talent from below; and as the councilor entrusted with drafting the regulation, he was in a key position to translate this preference into institutional reforms.

Born in 1755, Gedike too belonged to the generation of reform-minded schoolmen who came of age in the 1780s. He had come to Berlin in 1775, as a twenty-one-year-old fresh out of the university, and four years later had been appointed director of the Friedrichswerdesche Gymnasium. In 1787, at age thirty-three, he had reached the apogee of a meteoric career; already a member of the Lutheran High Consistory, he had become the junior councilor on the new Superior School Board. The young schoolman found himself at the pinnacle of the clerical pyramid, far above the offices to which most of his colleagues in the schools could aspire. His route to Berlin, his integration into its intellectual and official establishment, and his reform efforts as a schoolman are worth reconstructing in some detail. Gedike's career marks with special clarity the convergence of social consciousness, professional commitment, and pedagogical theory that produced an egalitarian version of meritocracy; but it also explains why this kind of egalitarianism, as progressive and even radical as it was in context, remained so restricted and self-restrained.[29]

Gedike's father, a village pastor in the Prignitz (Brandenburg), died when he was nine. He spent the next seven years in an orphanage in Züllichau under the directorship of Gotthilf Samuel Steinbart, whom he came to revere as his "second father." Founded by Steinbart's grandfather in 1709, the orphanage had originally been a Pietist enterprise, inspired by Francke's success in Halle. Under the grandson it was devoted to providing bright but "helpless" orphaned sons of "pastors and other men in public offices" with the education they otherwise could not afford. Gedike's career seemed to Steinbart a dramatic proof that, as he noted in a report on the institution in 1786, such boys "show more industry and effort than children of parents with means precisely because they realize very early that they can rely on no one and must depend on their own competence."[30]

[29] Gedike sketched his career in his *Gesammlete Schulschriften*, 2 vols. (Berlin, 1789–95), 1: 240–46. See also "Jubelrede von den Freuden des Schulmannes; bei der hundertjährigen Jubelfeier des Friedrichswerdeschen Gymnasiums (Dec. 1788)," in ibid., pp. 469–92. A well-balanced portrait is Harald Scholtz, "Friedrich Gedike (1754–1803). Ein Wegbereiter der preussischen Reform des Bildungswesens," *Jahrbuch für die Geschichte Mittel- und Ostdeutschlands* 13/14 (1965): 128–81. For insightful analyses of Gedike's reform thought, see Herrlitz, *Studium als Standesprivileg*, pp. 99–108; Detlef K. Müller, *Sozialstruktur und Schulsystem: Aspekte zum Strukturwandel des Schulwesens im 19. Jahrhundert*, Studien zum Wandel von Gesellschaft und Bildung im Neunzehnten Jahrhundert, vol. 7 (Göttingen, 1977), pp. 98–109.

[30] Gotthilf Samuel Steinbart, *Pädagogisches Sendschreiben über die Verbesserung der gelehrten Schulen. An Herrn Friedrich Gedike* (Berlin, 1781), pp. 3–4; idem, *Nachricht von der jetzigen Verfassung der Erziehungsanstalten in Züllichau nebst einer Anzeige seiner Grundsätze über den Unterricht und die Erziehung auf Schulen* (Züllichau, 1786), p. 4.

With Steinbart's charity, a traditional expression of corporate solidarity – the kind that had saved so many sons of deceased clergymen from social derogation – became the instrument of a new partisanship. Steinbart was a well-known member of the rationalist clerical establishment, with connections in Berlin as well as Frankfurt. With his encouragement, Gedike distinguished himself as a pupil in the Paedagogium attached to the orphanage and in 1771 entered the theology faculty at Frankfurt. There Toellner, a well-known rationalist theologian, became his "fatherly" mentor and "generous patron." Toellner was succeeded in 1774 by Steinbart, who took his former pupil into his household as a tutor. The next vital link on this patronage chain was formed when, on Steinbart's recommendation, he received a tutoring appointment in the home of Probst Spalding and, through this new and well-placed sponsor, entered the social circuit of the Berlin Enlightenment. Having groomed the young man with "daily instructive conversation" for a year or so, Spalding secured him a teaching appointment in 1776 at the Friedrichswerdesche Gymnasium, a school under his supervision, where he would become rector and director three years later.[31]

Spalding and Gedike were linked as patron and client, mentor and disciple, but their entries into big-city life had been strikingly different. The son of a village pastor in Swedish Pomerania, Spalding had come to Berlin in 1764, at age fifty, as the newly appointed *Probst* of the Nikolaikirche and a councilor in the High Consistory. The first few years had been an ordeal, its anxieties still quite vivid when he wrote an autobiographical fragment nearly a quarter century later. To a man acutely aware of his lowly birth and provincialism and plagued by a sense of intellectual inadequacy in his new appointments, the obligatory dinners at "prominent" homes had been excruciating. In 1787, as a seventy-three-year-old, Spalding was still regretting that "almost into old age" he had been "shy and embarrassed in the presence of people of higher estate [he] did not know from continual contact."[32] In 1783, roughly eight years after his arrival, Gedike began a series of twenty-eight "letters" on Berlin, published anonymously in the *Berlinische Monatsschrift*. He emerges from them as a self-confident man about town, entirely at home in the social networks of a predominantly bourgeois intellectual establishment. In Berlin, he noted with obvious self-satisfaction, the educated bourgeois loses "that slavish astonishment in the face of the great World, with which so many *Gelehrte* are familiar only third-

[31] See esp. Gedike's tributes to these patrons in *Schulschriften*, 1: 240–42.

[32] Johann Joachim Spalding, *Lebensbeschreibung von ihm selbst aufgesetzt*, ed. Georg Ludewig Spalding (Halle, 1804), pp. 70–81. See also H. Plard, "Un 'père conscrit' du luthéranisme éclairé: Johann Joachim Spalding (1714–1804)," *Etudes sur le XVIIIe siècle* (Université Libre de Bruxelles. Groupe d'étude du XVIIIe siècle, 1983): 43–60. The most important monographic study is Joseph Schollmeier, *Johann Joachim Spalding. Ein Beitrag zur Theologie der Aufklärung* (Gütersloh, 1967).

hand, through hearsay" and that "feeling of helplessness about looking [its] blinding suns straight in the eye."[33]

How explain why a young, inexperienced provincial had integrated with notable ease into an urban society his elder colleague had found so threatening? This is not simply the difference between habit-ridden middle age and flexible youth; part of the answer also lies in the fact that the initiations were separated by eleven eventful years. Spalding was well known to the educated reading public by 1764; but nonetheless, in a city still dominated by Pietism and Lutheran Orthodoxy, his appointments had required something of a coup on the part of the handful of clergymen who had established a foothold for rationalist theology. As late as 1780 the rationalist faction had provoked a fierce protest movement among the laity as well as the clerical majority by trying to replace the traditional hymn book with one to their own liking. In the early years, Spalding might have been oversensitive about being regarded as a provincial curiosity; but now he became a principal target of public attacks that did not stop short of personal vilification. From Gedike's account of this "hymn book war" in the "letters," we learn that the Orthodox campaign had won the day in most parishes and could easily be provoked into another eruption.[34]

Clearly religious enlightenment had not become a groundswell from below by the mid-1780s. Instead it had secured powerful sponsorship from above in the person of Minister Karl Abraham von Zedlitz, who had brought church and school affairs under his aegis in 1770. "It does honor to the government," Gedike could confidently report, that enlightened clergymen like Spalding occupied "the most prestigious positions" and that "selections surely will be made according to the same principles in the future."[35] The

[33] "Sechzehnter Brief," *Berlinische Monatsschrift* 3 (Jan.-June 1784): 471 (cited hereafter as BM). The first "letter" was published in vol. 2 (July-Dec. 1783), and the twenty-eighth in vol. 5 (July-Dec. 1784): 180–85. Gedike never identified himself publicly as the author, but internal evidence, particularly in the discussions of the Berlin schools, makes his authorship virtually certain. The letters have been attributed to him in Scholtz, "Gedike," p. 129, and Müller, *Sozialstruktur und Schulsystem*, p. 99. Gedike has been identified as the probable author in Ursula Schulz, *Die Berlinische Monatsschrift (1783–1796). Eine Bibliographie* (Hildesheim, 1969), pp. 110, 162.

[34] See esp. "Vierzehnter Brief," BM 3 (Jan.-June 1784): 351–72. "The hymn book war was driven to raging fury," Gedike wrote, and "the lampoon [*Pasquill*] against Spalding and Teller, which was posted on the gallows, revealed such bitterness and deep-rooted spite that it was apparent the author would have been capable of an assassination for what he conceived to be the honor of God." "Vierter Brief," BM 2 (July-Dec. 1783): 545. On this episode, see also Walter Wendland, "Die praktische Wirksamkeit Berliner Geistlichen im Zeitalter der Aufklärung (1740–1806)," *Jahrbuch für Berlin-Brandenburgische Kirchengeschichte* 9/10 (1913): 320–76, and 11/12 (1914): 233–303; and the analysis of the new hymn book in Paul Sturm. *Das evangelische Gesangbuch der Aufklärung. Beitrag zur deutschen Geistesgeschichte des 17. und 18. Jahrhunderts* (Bremen, 1923).

[35] "Vierzehnter Brief," pp. 364–65. On Zedlitz and the ecclesiastical and educational reform he promoted, see Conrad Rethwisch, *Der Staatsminister Freiherr v. Zedlitz und Preussens höheres Schulwesen im Zeitalter Friedrich des Grossen* (2nd ed.: Strasbourg, 1886).

relevance of this change was not simply that it made Berlin a more congenial place intellectually for a young rationalist like Gedike; it also made for a much smoother social initiation into the big city than Spalding recalled. As a young tutor in Pomerania, Spalding seems to have been spared the degrading treatment at the hands of aristocratic employers that embittered others. Instead he had fond memories of this stage of his life; aside from securing well-placed patrons, he had won the respect and even the friendship of the well-born to the extent of becoming a guest for months at a time in the von Wolfradt and von Bohlen households. This initiation and his imposing credentials as an author make it all the more striking that Spalding felt inadequate as a dinner guest of the "prominent" in Berlin. A fifty-year-old veteran, he was still plagued by the anxiety that educated commoners, and particularly provincials of obscure family origins, experienced in the face of *die Welt* and its standards of politesse.[36]

By the mid-1770s there were new routes of ascent into less threatening elite circles. The personal sponsorship of patrons was still the sine qua non, but by the time Gedike's generation came of age Spalding and other rationalist clergymen had formed a "party," entrenched in key positions. This elite was in turn connected with likeminded colleagues in the provinces, and particularly in the theology faculties at Halle and Frankfurt/Oder, who passed on to it young protégés. If this patronage network enlisted young men for the cause, it also made their transition from the provinces to the big city relatively unproblematic. The clerical elders sponsored their induction into the larger social circuits of the Berlin Enlightenment – circuits in which aristocrats participated in a predominantly bourgeois style of sociability, self-consciously free of the traditional aristocratic preoccupation with rank and formality. From there it was but a step to the more riské salons and clubs of the 1780s – the ones the elders might prefer to avoid.[37]

The young man who profiled himself in the Berlin "letters" was to a degree free of his elders' intellectual inhibitions as well as their social anxieties. But the "letters" also remind us that Gedike remained deeply involved in the family squabbles of the clerical order that had groomed him. He conceived of the city in terms of its parishes as well as its clubs. Where he differed from Spalding and other mentors on the religious issue, as on the issue of opening careers to talent, was in his more thoroughgoing rationalism. Chiding them obliquely for their intolerance of Deists like Carl Friedrich Bahrdt, he went so far as to express the hope that Berlin would

[36] Spalding, *Lebensbeschreibung*, pp. 5–35.

[37] For a similar career pattern, see the biography of Gedike's contemporary and friend Johann Friedrich Zöllner (b. 1753) in *Allgemeines Magazin für Prediger* 12:6 (1796): 50a-50e. On the predominantly bourgeois social networks that created regional centers for the German Enlightenment, see Hans Erich Bödeker, "Strukturen der Aufklärungsgesellschaft in der Residenzstadt Kassel," in *Mentalitäten und Lebensverhältnisse: Beispiele aus der Sozialgeschichte der Neuzeit. Rudolf Vierhaus zum 60. Geburtstag* (Göttingen, 1982), pp. 55–76.

one day have the honor of hosting the first "church of natural religion" in Germany. Such a church, he noted, would also prevent the "theoretical atheism emanating from France" from winning converts – though fortunately the Berlin atheists, thanks to their "German thoroughness," were "not burdened with the enthusiasm [*Schwärmerei*] and intolerance" of the Parisian breed.[38]

If Gedike's Deism rested securely on the superiority of German sobriety over "French fashion whims," it also heightened his awareness that the Berlin Enlightenment lacked a popular base. On this score he had the same perspective on the larger society as his less urbane and theologically more cautious elders. Mixed in with his appreciative comments on the quick-wittedness of uneducated Berliners are two negative images of the urban mass, neither giving cause for optimism. Massive in-migration from the provinces, he reported, was swelling the ranks of an uprooted proletariat (my word), "without fatherland, beliefs, morals, and principles," with the result that "the most unnatural contrast between virtue and vices, culture and barbarism, [is] to be found here in the highest measure." And then there was the "mob" (*Pöbel*) that followed Orthodox demagogues – the one that had so fiercely opposed the introduction of an eminently sensible hymn book. It was epitomized by the attendant (*Aufwärterinn*) in his building, who was always moved to tears by a "shrieking and very incoherent" Orthodox preacher – though she once admitted that she had heard very little of the sermon and had understood less.[39]

Like his mentors, though perhaps with less blatant contempt, Gedike took an instinctively elitist, defensive posture toward the uneducated mass. What distinguished his social vision was not the partisan rationalism of the Deist, but the professional militancy of the enlightened pedagogue. At first, he acknowledged, he had been reluctant to enter an occupation as maligned and as poorly rewarded as teaching and had been determined to escape at the first opportunity. But satisfaction in office and promotion "with rare speed" (his own phrase) changed his mind. Imbued with the "philanthropinistic" spirit, but critical of the more gimmicky features of Basedow's experiment in Dessau, he had become one of the leading spokesmen for the generation of schoolmen who were beginning to overhaul the Latin schools.[40] At the Friedrichswerdesche Gymnasium Gedike, taking up the work his predecessor had begun, revived an institution that had been in decline for decades by reorganizing its finances, improving its teachers' incomes, and enhancing its reputation among "the public." In 1780 there were 43 new enrollments and 94 pupils in all grades; five years later the figures were 67 and 176, respectively. When Gedike had begun at the

[38] "Zwölfter Brief," BM 3 (Jan.-June 1784): 268–78.
[39] "Zweiter Brief," BM 2 (July-Dec. 1783): 453–55; "Vierzehnter Brief," p. 364.
[40] Gedike, *Schulschriften*, 1: 470–81.

school, there had been only one pupil in the *Prima* and three in the *Sekunda*, since it was customary to advance directly to the university from a lower level. In addition to enlarging the school's clientele, Gedike obviously had been successful in persuading parents to send their sons into the higher grades, and indeed to keep them there a few years.[41]

Gedike's attitude toward talented poor boys derived in part from his own experience. He had benefited from the corporate tradition of charitable support for colleagues' orphans within the clergy; indeed his opportunities might very well have been more constricted if his father had lived. Openly grateful for the sponsorship that had launched an orphan without means into a brilliant career, he expected upcoming generations of poor students to justify their exceptional status with dedication and achievement in useful work – as he was doing. If the ethic of service was to sanction this kind of mobility, it had to be enforced with particular stringency. What also struck Gedike when he looked back on his childhood, however, was that he could very easily have been passed over. "Until my ninth year," he recalled, "I grew up wild and without special instruction, among the peasant boys of the village." In Steinbart's orphanage "a considerable time elapsed before a shaft of light penetrated [his] soul, which had a thick cover and at the start gave [his] teachers little hope of any enlightenment." Only when he began to receive instruction from Steinbart himself in the Paedagogium did he "advance as quickly as earlier [he] had been slow and remained behind."[42]

Whereas Steinbart celebrated his protégé in neocorporate terms, as a shining example of the "outstanding minds" to be found among his fellow clergymen's orphaned children, Gedike was more impressed by the fact that, despite his parentage, his initial helplessness in the face of the requirements of school learning had made him akin to boys from uneducated homes. His case seemed an instructive reminder of the danger of "premature" judgments, overlooking the native talent that cultural disadvantages easily obscured. This perspective on his own life reinforced the pedagogical strategy he derived from scholarly and professional interests. As a young man Gedike had entertained the hope of becoming a classical scholar, and his earliest publications were translations of classical texts. As a schoolman he sustained this interest, but increasingly channeled it into pedagogical contributions. Philological concerns, the pedagogical theory to be gleaned from Greek and Roman authors, practical experience in the schoolroom – all pointed to the need for a theoretically sound and prac-

41 Friedrich Gedike, "Geschichte des Friedrichswerdeschen Gymnasiums," in idem, *Schulschriften*, 1: 157–252; "Nachtrag zu der Geschichte sowol des Friedrichswerdeschen als des Berlinisch-Kölnischen Gymnasiums," in ibid., 2: 289; "Praktischer Beitrag zur Methodik des öffentlichen Schulunterrichts," in ibid., 1: 92–94.

42 Ibid., 1: 241.

ticable approach to language instruction. The result was several essays confirming the basic principles Gesner had already distilled from classical texts, albeit with refreshingly concrete observations from his own teaching. Gedike joined the growing chorus of attacks on the traditional "chaos" of "words and phrases, rules and exceptions, elegances and barbarisms, uses and variants [over which] memory brooded with happy self-complacency while the other intellectual powers slumbered comfortably."[43] In addition to exercising these other powers, language learning must be the medium for absorbing content and grasping meaning. And of course it had to respect nature's timetable; the learning of Latin, like mastery of the mother tongue, broke down into "speech, understanding of books, writing [and] critical knowledge," and "the most natural method . . . is to ascend the four stages in their natural order, one after the other."[44] The actual initiation into academic learning could be postponed until age fourteen or sixteen; by then pupils were ready to ascend this "stairway of method" quite rapidly – and late developers like himself would not have been excluded at an earlier juncture.

To Gedike, as to Lieberkühn and several other contemporaries, the "public" status of a common school lay in constituting a socially neutral arena for competitive achievement, from which the truly talented and meritorious would advance to academic studies. Hence it seemed a real advantage that the gymnasium he took over in 1779 was a typically urban hybrid of elementary and academic grades. The school encompassed a broad range not only in its pupils' ages (from eight to twenty-one), but also in their parents' stations, "lower as well as higher." The fact that he himself had benefited enormously from his tutoring experience in the Spalding household did not prevent Gedike from protesting wealthier families' reliance on tutors. Aside from making the schools' financial situation more precarious, they were depriving their sons of the respect for "personal merit" and the motivation to achieve that only competition in the socially heterogeneous environment of a public institution could inculcate. His school discipline did make one concession to differences in family background; more severe punishments were sometimes needed to achieve the desired effect on boys accustomed to "harsher treatment" at home. But in all other respects there was to be "complete uniformity" in the "moral treatment" as well as in the academic evaluation of pupils.[45]

[43] Friedrich Gedike, "Ueber die Verbindung des wissenschaftlichen und philologischen Schulunterrichts," in ibid., 1: 20–21. See also "Von der lateinischen Sprache," in idem, *Aristoteles und Basedow; oder, Fragmente über Erziehung und Schulwesen bei der Alten und Neuen* (Berlin and Leipzig, 1779), pp. 157–206, and several other essays in the same volume.

[44] Gedike, "Von der lateinischen Sprache," p. 169.

[45] Gedike, "Praktischer Beitrag," pp. 92–94. Though unable to end poor boys' dependence on charitable proceeds from the school choir, Gedike took special care to see that this dictum applied to them.

It was in this sense that Gedike, for all his affinity with his elders' perspective on the larger society, represented an egalitarian alternative. At the same time his agenda for meritocratic reform distinguished him from more discontented (or at least disoriented) contemporaries, less willing to embrace utilitarian rationalism and the commitments it required. One of his newly found friends was Karl Philipp Moritz, another young provincial employed in Berlin as a teacher and an intellectual who frequented the same social circles. They seem to have made an oddly complementary pair – Moritz occasionally (or, perhaps better, fitfully) striving to emulate Gedike's devotion to professional responsibilities, Gedike sharing to a degree his friend's openness to the Sturm und Drang sensibility their elders detested. But the differences are more striking. Moritz aspired to literary fame and in life-style, though not in ideological posture, seems to have periodically become a kind of one-man Grub Street. Out of sheer frustration he flagrantly neglected his teaching duties, and in 1786 he finally escaped to Italy. By then Gedike was convinced that he had found his true vocation in teaching and had earned a reputation as a hard-driving schoolman and administrator.[46]

Unlike Moritz, who had reason to see himself more as a psychological victim of patronage than as one of its beneficiaries, Gedike knew very well that his career was a stunning example of what personal, informal sponsorhip could accomplish. The morbidly introspective Moritz – despite his grim view of the class injustice inherent in conventional patron-client relationships – did not share contemporary reformers' interest in an internal reorganization of the school, or their vision of the public school's larger institutional role in opening careers to talent. As a teacher his antidote to "injustice" was to establish terms of personal intimacy and even friendship with his pupils. To this end he kept a diary that probed beneath the often deceptive surface behavior of each pupil and gave access to his inner self by recording his physical, intellectual and moral traits. Gedike likewise expected his teachers to keep diaries, but his overriding concern was with monitoring and classifying. The markedly bureaucratic impulse in his approach to reform, as in Lieberkühn's, was a measure of determination to institutionalize a meritocratic ideal. The usual workings of personal sponsorship in the school acceded to an intricate evaluation system, in theory subjecting pupils to the judgment of collective expertise rather than to personal preference. While a degree of personal intimacy between teacher and pupils would limit the impersonality of this system, it would also en-

[46] Moritz's life-style in Berlin is described in Karl Friedrich Klischnig, *Erinnerungen aus den Zehn letzten Lebensjahren meines Freundes Anton Reiser. Als ein Beitrag zur Lebensgeschichte des Herrn Hofrath Moritz* (Berlin, 1794). See also Mark Boulby, *Karl Philipp Moritz. At the Fringe of Genius* (Toronto, 1979).

hance the experts' ability to gather the necessary data for evaluation of "character."

The diaries kept by teachers in the lower grades, with daily notations about the pupils' behavior, were the basis for the monthly and quarterly grades on "behavior, attention and industry" that determined intragrade ranking and were solemnly announced by the director at an assembly each month. For intergrade promotions the director also conducted examinations to gauge academic progress. Here above all, in the hierarchical articulation of academic competition, the implications of the "natural" approach to language learning that shaped Gedike's entire pedagogy were realized. From 1780 onward the traditional horizontal division among teachers, each responsible for the entire curriculum in his grade, acceded to vertical demarcations by subject, each with its hierarchy of grades. Within limits the twice-yearly "translocation examination" allowed a pupil to advance more rapidly in some subjects – the ones in which he demonstrated exceptional facility and effort – than in others.[47] Hence in gradually realizing the potential in each *Mensch* and identifying the particular station he should enter as a *Bürger*, the school could monitor a variety of intellectual aptitudes as well as moral qualities. And if the transition to the gymnasium and its classical curriculum did not occur until the teen years, the late developer would have the opportunity to compensate for a slow start.

For all its intellectual vibrancy, Berlin was not Paris, although it was much closer to the French capital in that regard than a court city like Dessau or provincial outposts like Neuruppin and Guben. Gedike might have included Paris when he observed that "the young *Gelehrte* who have to support themselves solely with literary piecework [*Handarbeiten*], and who are present in large crowds in Vienna, Leipzig, and elsewhere, are hardly to be found here at all." To him the absence of a Grub Street helped account for the happy compromise in Berlin's intellectual life, at once progressive and soberly moderate, in contrast to the fashionable, superficial extremism of the French capital.[48] Within a few years the contrast would prove more dramatic than he could have foreseen; the Prussian capital simply had not produced an equivalent of the radically subversive political culture unleashed in revolutionary Paris.

In its "Jacobinical" version, the "gutter Rousseauism" of Grub Street merged an ideological reverence for natural talent into an apotheosis of the People. The replacement of literary "aristocrats" with men of true talent

47 See esp. Gedike, "Praktischer Beitrag," pp. 97–108. See also Scholtz, "Gedike," pp. 144–53.

48 "Funfzehnter Brief," BM 3 (Jan.-June 1784): 463–69. See also "Neunter Brief," in ibid., pp. 52–53; "Zehnter Brief," in ibid., pp. 145–46.

and merit from the lower depths became inseparable from – and derived its impelling force from – the leveling ideology of a mass groundswell.[49] Obviously Gedike, the enlightened Berliner looking down on a population that seemed alternately barbaric and in the thrall of an obscurantist Orthodoxy, had a different angle of vision. His social consciousness typified the more limited egalitarianism of German schoolmen in his generation. In addition to preferring competitive achievement to ascription, they associated the disadvantaged with the requisite virtues – the driving motivation and self-discipline needed in academic studies – that coddled sons of wealthier families lacked. But this was to endow *individual* talent at the bottom with a kind of inverted social (and moral) advantage; it did not make the People in the mass the repository of Virtue.

Likewise Gedike, far from sharing Grub Street's visceral hatred for the presiding figures of an Enlightenment establishment, was quite sincere in acknowledging publicly the "fatherly" guidance and benefaction of Steinbart, Toellner, and Spalding. For him and others, reverential gratitude toward the elders above them was the complement to a sense of threat from below. The combination helps explain why the Grub Street vision of opening careers to talent in a full-scale assault on an entire establishment played no role in their reform thought. Like Lieberkühn and others, Gedike looked to a reform from above – the imposition of a public educational system by an enlightened state bureaucracy – to regenerate the official intelligentsia from within. The selection of talent would be a more centralized process; but it would still be a sponsorship from above, with an elite setting and enforcing standards for admission. The essential difference was that the new criteria for selection, by virtue of their rationality, would be legitimate and that new, more bureaucratic procedures would ensure their objective application.

This is not to deny that there was something radical about the egalitarian alternative. It went beyond the usual attack on legal privilege to reject the privileged access to academic studies and public office conferred de facto by inherited wealth and education. But the very fact that this egalitarian preference for natural talent over social ascription could be argued, however cautiously, at the very highest level of bureaucratic policy making, and indeed by a young protégé of the Enlightenment clerical establishment, is a measure of its respectability. The egalitarian version of meritocracy was

[49] Darnton quotes Grégoire: "True genius is almost always *sans-culotte.*" Darnton, "The High Enlightenment," p. 39. On the apotheosis of the People, see also François Furet, *Interpreting the French Revolution*, trans. Elborg Forster (1978: Cambridge, 1981), esp. pp. 25–61; Lynn Hunt, *Politics, Culture, and Class in the French Revolution* (Berkeley, Calif., 1984), esp. pp. 19–51. Even in revolutionary France, it should be noted, this leveling ideology represented a radical extreme; on the entire spectrum of educational reform ideologies and blueprints in the early 1790s see Palmer, *Improvement of Humanity*, pp. 79–176, and F. Stübig, *Erziehung zur Gleichheit: Konzepte der "éducation commune" in der französischen Revolution* (Ravensburg, 1974).

a respectable position, though still a minority one, precisely because it remained within the utilitarian discourse that enjoyed the status of an official ideology in wide circles of the civil and ecclesiastical bureaucracies. Gedike did note that fears about an oversupply of students might be exaggerated, since there would be an increasing need for clerical employees in government offices. But even that observation exemplified the overriding consensus. Reformers might disagree on how wide the educational channel into academic and official employment should be and on how much mobility from below could be accommodated within it; but the underlying assumption that society could not tolerate a spillover – an excess population of educated men, "useless" and perhaps dangerous – was beyond challenge. While the development of natural talent might be considered as inalienable a right as the use of property, the scope for its legitimate exercise was circumscribed by the opportunities to demonstrate merit – or, perhaps better, to render service – in public employment.

To characterize Gedike as a solid citizen of an official establishment is not to imply that he was an uncritical adherent of old-regime absolutism. As it was celebrated in his "letters," the Prussian monarchy set a progressive example for the rest of Germany by showing itself responsive to an "enlightened," often critical public opinion; that was why the reforms from above emanating from government ministries in Berlin seemed legitimate.[50] But if reform required the support of a broader educated "public," it also had to receive the imprimatur of the state through the regular bureaucratic channels. The *Abitur* deliberations were an opportunity to take a large step in that direction. But they also required caution; the junior colleague had to plot a course his seniors would accept, or at least would not find alarming.

The opinion that seems to have had the most impact on the senior members of the board had been submitted by Immanuel Kant, in his capacity as *Dekan* of the philosophy faculty at Königsberg. Kant had limited himself to the practical proposal that for intergrade promotions collegial decisions replace the often arbitrary judgments of school rectors and had urged that the "very poor" pupils who lacked "natural gifts and a noticeable drive to learn" be persuaded to leave academic studies in the *Tertia* or the *Sekunda*. This solution was perfectly consistent with his argument a few years later that propertied wealth, like native talent, was a legitimate advantage. If Kant had singled out poor boys while implicitly exempting their better-off schoolmates from the same scrutiny, he also had taken care not to make poverty a sufficient reason for excluding talent.[51]

But that was not the senior board members' reading of Kant's opinion.

[50] See esp. "Vierter Brief," pp. 542–48; "Fünfter Brief," BM 2 (July-Dec. 1783): 548–52; "Fünfzehnter Brief," pp. 463–69.

[51] Schwartz, *Gelehrtenschulen*, 1: 74.

Within the shared language of merit and talent, their ideological nuances were distinctly neocorporate. Von Irwing, the president of the Superior School Board, tilted Kant's proposal in the course of noting its merit; in a new promotion system the exclusion of boys in "slight financial circumstances" would apply not only to "unqualified heads without industry," but also to the "more capable heads" in whom "industry" could not be "awakened in a specific time." Gedike's mentor Steinbart, who came to Berlin from Frankfurt for the occasion, favored a common school, its "useful" elementary education preceding Latin instruction; but the way to the higher, academic level would be barred to children of "common people" who had not demonstrated exceptional gifts or outstanding industry.[52]

To appreciate Gedike's caution in the face of this sentiment, one need only contrast his proposals with the opinion submitted by G. N. Fischer, the young rector of the cathedral school in Halberstadt. Fischer began by attributing the academic "immaturity" of university students to abuse of social privilege as well as to the pressures of poverty and charity; while poor boys lacked the means to remain longer in school or could not postpone the use of stipends or free tables, boys from prominent families advanced to the university too soon because their studies were a mere formality. He proposed that the state intervene with examinations at two critical junctures. The first would come when pupils were in their early teens, immediately after confirmation; only those who passed it would be admitted to academic studies, and only those judged "not too immature" could try again. The transition to university studies a few years later would be commanded by two examinations, one given by the school and the other by the university, and again those judged too "immature" to prepare for another try would be irrevocably excluded. To date, Fischer noted, state regulations had been designed to keep the lower orders at a safe distance from university studies and not to exclude the unqualified. He left no doubt that his screening examinations would redress the balance.[53]

Gedike's proposals took up Fischer's scheme, but qualified it for official consumption. The initial screening examination would come at age fourteen; that was not too late for pupils without real potential for academic studies to shift to trades and commercial employment but was late enough to allow talent time to mature gradually, despite social and cultural disadvantages. In keeping with the prevailing double standard, Gedike limited this examination of innate talent – or, more precisely, of intellectual capacity – to boys of "lower" origins who would later be dependent on public support. At this stage, in other words, the right of wealthier families to advance their sons up the academic ladder, despite teachers' evaluations, would not be questioned. Gedike was willing to make this concession because the next

[52] Ibid., pp. 95–100.
[53] Ibid., pp. 90–91.

hurdle – the actual qualifying examination for the university, which would gauge maturity in the sense of academic accomplishment to date – would apply to all aspiring students without exception. Here, Gedike emphasized, higher officials, applying professional standards in the name of the state, must have the power to bar the "immature" without regard for their social origins; otherwise the examination would be regarded as a "mere formality" and the number of "ignorant young men" entering the universities prematurely would only increase.[54]

But it was precisely on this point that President von Irwing demurred, on the grounds that such a measure would be regarded as a "despotic" limitation of the "natural freedom of parents and even of pupils." Underlying his opinion was the usual neocorporate respect for property; but in the face of his younger colleague's reform zeal, the veteran chose to couch his objection in terms of sober political realism, seasoned with more than a little cynicism. The leaving examination could serve only as a guideline for parents and professors, not as a coercive measure:

> If one wished to extend the purpose of the school certificate, so that the young man who failed to acquire it would not merely be advised against attending the university but actually barred *vi legis*, this objective in many cases could not be realized, or if it should be pushed through with force, the matter would at bottom have something too despotic about it. . . . what hatred such a strict measure would provoke in the public. We are not dealing here merely with common people and reasonable parents, but often with prominent and wealthy parents who would decry such a law as an illegal attack on their rights over their children. The public wants to retain the right to have their dear children become good-for-nothings.[55]

In the end the board opted not to consider an initial screening examination. As for the qualifying examination – i.e., the actual *Abitur* – introduced in 1788, its social implications were noticeably lopsided. Certification of "maturity" was not required for admission to university studies, but was made a prerequisite for use of public stipends and "free tables."[56] The junior colleague had deferred to his elders.

[54] Ibid., pp. 103–5.
[55] Ibid., pp. 99–100, 106–7.
[56] Ibid., pp. 113–27.

PART III

New departures

9

Orthodoxies and new idioms

Friedrich Gedike's career was eclipsed as rapidly as it had soared. In 1788, just a few years after the celebration of Prussian "freedom" in the Berlin "letters," Johann Christoph Woellner, the royal favorite who replaced Baron von Zedlitz, launched a crackdown on the "enlightened" party. Though one of the most exposed targets, Gedike kept his offices until his early death in 1803. But survival had required that he steer clear of his elders' protests against Woellner's notorious edicts and that he give up the coeditorship of the *Berlinische Monatsschrift* in 1790.

This jolting change of course in Prussia was only one of the reactions against Enlightenment rationalism at the end of the century. To a proto-conservative like Woellner, Gedike's generation of reformers seemed bent on destroying sacrosanct traditions; but the same men, despite their youth, seemed wedded to a dessicated orthodoxy in the light of the fusion of Kantianism, Idealist philosophy, and classicism that has come to be called neohumanism. It was "self-cultivation" (*Bildung*) in the neohumanistic sense that would inspire the creation of the nineteenth-century gymnasium and university and would become the badge of membership in a modern *Bildungsbürgertum*.

The new ideal of *Bildung* was a secular recasting of calling, self-consciously pagan in its introspection, as well as a quasi-religious reaffirmation of work discipline in vocation. Within this many-sided ideological prism, emancipatory and restrictive impulses, egalitarian and elitist preferences coexisted; and the refractions formed a particularly complex pattern as they projected onto the social structure and experience of academic mobility. It was above all in the implications for poor students, and particularly for outsiders, that *Bildung*, from one angle, offered a radical alternative. Its uncompromising cultural individualism not only rejected the prescriptions of traditional corporate sponsorship; it also pronounced illegitimate the new conditions for ascent into a modernized academic and official *Bürgertum* in utilitarian rationalism. And yet from other angles onto the prism, *Bildung* represents variations on familiar themes. Fused into a single ideal were a new reverence for personal autonomy, its aestheticism diametrically opposed to rationalist imperatives for "usefulness," and an ethos of work discipline that has often been overlooked. The former confronted the outsider with subtle transfigurations of neocorporate biases into universal standards; the latter condemned his "ambition" in the light of an ideal of disinterested commitment to *Beruf* and its transcendent purpose.

There is still another social dimension to the prism of *Bildung*, likewise reflecting the problematic presence of poor students and equally revealing of continuities and changes in perceptions of their mobility. If self-cultivation became an idiom for individual achievement, it also served as an ideological lever for the *collective* mobility of the two occupational groups in which poor students were concentrated. Here above all it is simplistic to conceive of the ascendancy of *Bildung* as a retreat into privatism (or *Innerlichkeit*); if the new idiom often took that apolitical direction, it also superseded utilitarian rationalism at the core of new public ideologies, and indeed as the rhetorical strategy of a "professional politics" (*Standespolitik*). *Bildung* not only offered rank-and-file schoolmen and pastors an impeccable credential for membership in a new elite of educated professionals and an unshakable scholarly standard for mobility within structured professional careers; it also promised to reconcile the private interest of the group with the public interest and to magnify the specific occupational locus and bureaucratic location of the professional man into the public authority and vision of the educated *Bürger*.

But this is to anticipate twists in the new departure of the 1790s. Our first task is to account for the ideological dynamism of the departure – by explaining how it had been anticipated in the Sturm und Drang movement two decades earlier and how neohumanism at once echoed and superseded that initial generational protest.

MERIT VERSUS GENIUS

There is no point trying to admonish a *Genie*, Israel Hartmann lamented in a letter to his son on June 26, 1773.[1] Hartmann was using a fashionable term derisively, but with the encouragement of several mentors Gottlob David was beginning to take very seriously its application to his person and circumstances. There was a new fascination with "genius," and the young Hartmann – already beginning to make his mark as a poet and philosopher, and in correspondence with Johann Jacob Bodmer and several other prominent figures – was a likely candidate.

One of Hartmann's mentors was the Swiss pastor Johann Caspar Lavater,

[1] Israel Hartmann Nachlass (Hauptstaatsarchiv Ludwigsburg), pp. 440–41 (cited hereafter as HN).

who interceded with his father and gave him refuge in Zürich for several months before his departure for Mitau. Lavater used the portrait done during this visit, along with another sketch and two silhouettes, for "a profile portrait of a young genius" in the first volume of his *Physiognomical Fragments*. To Friedrich Nicolai, who had great hopes for physiognomy but was skeptical of Lavater's version of it, one of the sketches was so unlike the face of the young man who had visited him in Berlin as to make "correct judgment" impossible.[2] But Lavater was not daunted by such literalmindedness; the Zürich visit had convinced him that Hartmann had the potential to become "the greatest poet," and perhaps "a great philosopher" as well. Though hardly reminiscent of the fierce, soaring eagle with which genius was commonly compared, Hartmann's physiognomy displayed to Lavater "great, strong, immovable power" and the "incisive force of lightning, not of the slow, laborious researcher."[3]

After Hartmann's visit, Lavater had made the acquaintance of Johann Wolfgang Goethe, another young candidate for genius. Despite his initial resentment of this formidable rival, Hartmann began to come under Goethe's spell on his visit to Frankfurt on the way to Mitau. He was one of the many young men of the 1770s who was overwhelmed by *Die Leiden des jungen Werthers*. In the wilds of the Curland he found his own Charlotte, the divorced daughter of a local count, with whom he took to reading the novel again and again. "The book will remain my friend," he wrote Lavater in February 1775, several months before his death:

> I often long to be on the other side of the grave. . . . I have taken Werther's walks, wander around the fields nights in a sleigh I drive myself. Now I would allow myself to die for Goethe. . . . Lavater, have you found no similarity between me and Goethe? . . . Werther's *Leiden* are now daily nourishment for my spirit. I still want to complete a few matters, and then I would welcome an end to the farce. I feel now more and more pressingly, strongly, that nothing in this world can make me happy. And if all my wishes were fulfilled, my heart is itself the source of all the misery I carry around. In brief, things will never go well for me in this world. I bear now not only my own malady – I bear the fate of many others on and in my heart. I have not found any noble person who was happy.[4]

It is not surprising that Hartmann succumbed with such éclat to the "Werther-fever" sweeping through educated German youth. The counter-

[2] Johann Caspar Lavater, *Physiognomische Fragmente, zur Beförderung der Menschenkenntniss und Menschenliebe, Erster Versuch* (Leipzig and Winterthur, 1775), pp. 258–59. A facsimile of this edition has been published by Orell Füssli Verlag, Zürich, 1968. Nicolai's comments are in Martin Sommerfeld, *Friedrich Nicolai und der Sturm und Drang. Ein Beitrag zur Geschichte der deutschen Aufklärung* (Halle, 1921), p. 371.

[3] Lavater, *Physiognomische Fragmente*, pp. 258–59.

[4] The letter continued: "I hear that Goethe is now with you, and I am glad for you and him. Ask Goethe to write to me – a long letter, and as often as possible." It is quoted at length in Wilhelm Lang, *Gottl. Dav. Hartmann. Ein Lebensbild aus der Sturm und Drangzeit* (Stuttgart, 1890), pp. 107–10.

point to his stubborn resistance to his father was a youthful eagerness to please intellectual arbiters like Lavater, and one suspects that on his tour of cities en route to Mitau the intellectual posture that had seemed so defiant within the provincial confines of Württemberg came to seem quite tame and commonplace. But *Werther* had induced an abrupt change in the idiom of martyred youth; Hartmann's correspondence records with unusual clarity the shift in values and sensibility from idealistic rationalism to Sturm und Drang and its cult of genius. He was doing exactly what Goethe himself found so annoying and critics found so alarming – equating the author with his character and taking the character as a model to be emulated. To the young rationalist "the world" had been an arena in which to struggle against forces of obscurantism; the Werther-enthusiast was irreconcilably alienated from its "farce." Having offered his own self-examination as a guide to "the youth of [his] fatherland," Hartmann now saw himself exemplifying the young man's inconsolable misery of the heart. Rational introspection had become self-absorption in feeling, and preferably in suffering. There is a special irony to Hartmann's longing for the grave; a few years earlier the young philosopher had posed his ethic of duty in this world against his father's pious longing for "[the] home to which I am called and invited."[5]

Sturm und Drang was more a flash point on the literary landscape than a sustained movement. Its intellectual debt to Hamann and other mentors was considerable, but its actual nucleus of Young Turks was the circle that formed around Goethe and Herder in Strasbourg in 1770. By 1774, when *Werther* appeared, the group was already dissolving, and in the next year it lost its center of gravity when Goethe entered an entirely new phase at the Weimar court. But in the late 1770s and the 1780s the Sturm und Drang cult of genius became the idiom of protest for a youth culture, often emulating Werther more in style than in substance, but nonetheless alarming to parents and educators. Now the rationalist camp faced a new threat on two fronts. Unbridled indulgence in feeling and emotion at the expense of reason was no longer limited to Pietist "enthusiasm"; it was also embodied in the Wertherian cult of sensibility. Typically Joachim Heinrich Campe lumped the "so-called *Kraftgenie*" together with "enthusiasts" and "*Schwärmer*" in 1785 and issued one more warning about "this fashionable sickness that has gripped half of cultured Germany in the last twelve years."[6]

[5] Gottlob David to Israel Hartmann, June 10, 1771, HN, pp. 319–20.

[6] Joachim Heinrich Campe, "Von der nötigen Sorge für die Erhaltung des Gleichgewichtes unter den menschlichen Kräften," reprinted in Hermann Blankertz, ed., *Bildung und Brauchbarkeit. Texte von Joachim Heinrich Campe und Peter Villaume zur Theorie utilitärer Erziehung* (Brunswick, 1965): 49–55. The best introduction to Sturm und Drang is still Roy Pascal, *The German Sturm und Drang* (Manchester, 1953). I am emphasizing the ruptures between Enlightenment rationalism and Sturm und Drang on specific issues; cf. the argument for underlying continuities in Janine Buenzod, "De l'*Aufklärung* au *Sturm und Drang*: continuité ou rupture?" *Studies on Voltaire and the Eighteenth Century*, ed. Theodore Bestermann, 24 (1963): 289–313. Also useful for the elements of generational conflict and youth protest in the move-

And now the rationalist ethic of useful work – the ethic contradicted implicitly by idle aristocrats – was openly derided by young commoners aspiring to "genius" in the Sturm und Drang sense. Neohumanism would profit from this clash of values; it was in a defensive reaction against the Werther-fever that the rationalist ethic of vocation hardened into the kind of rigid, cut-and-dry orthodoxy that young men are wont to find oppressive.

Lavater may have been too eager to identify specimens of genius, but he had absorbed the mood of Sturm und Drang and could distill it with appropriately hyperbolic rhetoric. *Genie* was a "spirit" (*Genus*) of inspiration, not a "mere talent," he observed in his essay on the subject in the same volume of "fragments" containing Hartmann's portraits.[7] Lavater did not mean to deny that genius, like talent, was inborn, or that its development realized an inner entelechy. What the new cult of genius rejected was the analytical approach to talent and other natural "powers" in the rationalist conception of vocation. The "intelligence" designated by *Genie* in the rationalist sense derived from the humanistic concept of *ingenium*. As the phrase *selectum ingeniorum* implied, *ingenium* was a universal but highly varied human property that could be sorted into types and gauged along a hierarchical continuum. The genius was distinguished from the average run of human beings in the sense that, by virtue of being endowed with one or several kinds of intelligence to an extraordinary degree, he stood at the summit of the continuum. Long after Sturm und Drang this usage survived in the argument that only the "extraordinary genius" from the lower orders should be admitted to academic studies.

Posed squarely against this usage was the new equation of *Genie* with *Genus*, or "spirit," in the sense of inspiration. Whether inspiration was an actual infusion of a supernatural power, like the grace of conversion, or simply a natural reflection of divinity, it made the rare genius qualitatively distinct from and superior to the common lot of humanity. If creativity made geniuses as a group an incomparable breed, originality made the individual genius sui generis. This insistence on uniqueness went hand in hand with a cult of mystery; whereas natural talent was open to scrutiny by the trained observer, the wellsprings of genius lay hidden in the deepest

ment is Richard Quabius, *Generationsverhältnisse im Sturm und Drang*, Literatur und Leben, Neue Folge, vol. 17 (Cologne and Vienna, 1976). On the new concept of "genius," Hellmuth Sudheimer, *Der Geniebegriff des jungen Goethe*, Germanische Studien, Heft 167 (1935: Kraus Reprint, 1967), is dated but still indispensable. For background see esp. Pierre Grappin, *La theórie du génie dans le préclassicisme allemande* (Paris, 1952); Bronislawa Rosenthal, *Der Geniebegriff des Aufklärungszeitalters (Lessing und die Popularphilosophen)*, Germanische Studien, Heft 138 (1933: Kraus Reprint, 1967). Arno Koselleck, "Persönlichkeitsidee und Staatsanschauung in der deutschen Geniezeit," *Historische Vierteljahrsschrift*, Neue Folge 24 (1927): 33–58, is more interesting as a period piece than as an analysis of the political dimensions of the genius cult.

[7] The fragment on genius has been reprinted in *Johann Caspar Lavaters ausgewählte Werke*, 2 vols., ed. Ernst Staehelin (Zürich, 1943), 2: 198–203.

recesses of the personality. While its products left no doubt of its presence, the thing itself could not be analyzed or even described in rational terms. Unlike *ingenium*, genius could not be broken down into constituent powers or faculties; whether conceived as the irreducible core of a creative personality or as its integrating force, it was a unitary phenomenon. Talent was amenable to pedagogical cultivation, but genius was not. It could not be learned, and indeed its creative potential was realized only if it enjoyed an inviolable right to autonomous and spontaneous growth.[8]

In the Sturm und Drang celebration of creative spontaneity, condemnation of the aristocratic society of the German courts figured large. The courts' etiquette and snobbery epitomized the artificiality of social conventions, and their preference for neoclassical aesthetic rules, in slavish imitation of French culture, were seen to stifle artistic genius. But the cult of genius was not simply a rebellion against tradition; it was as opposed to the priorities and values of a "bourgeois" world in the making as it was to the outworn social and aesthetic forms of the old regime. To emphasize one of these orientations to the exclusion of the other is to oversimplify Werther's posture toward society. His path to suicide becomes inexorable when he is snubbed by the court aristocracy at Count C.'s soiree, and he reacts with eminently bourgeois disdain for the social pretensions of mere pedigree. But his bête noire – the man who stands between him and his beloved and whose presence reminds him constantly of everything he despises – is a conscientious, hard-working bourgeois official. Albert is a "useful member of society"; one of "those cool and composed gentlemen," he embodies the rationalist ideal of "merit" in and through "productive" or "useful" work. Ultimately it is in reaction to the ethical imperative of this ideal – and not to the strictures of court etiquette – that Werther becomes convinced of an irreconcilable conflict between the subjectivity of the artist and the rules of society.[9]

In the revised version of *Werther*, Goethe took pains to invoke pity for a victim driven to an act of madness, not admiration for a hero led by a special clarity of vision to the ultimate act of defiance. But the conflict between potential creativity and an unresponsive society remains, and in that sense genius still seems fated to alienated isolation. More common was

[8] On the etymological roots of "genius," see esp. Grappin, *La théorie du génie*, pp. 110–21; Rosenthal, *Der Geniebegriff des Aufklärungszeitalters*, pp. 15–56. The new cult of artistic creativity is succinctly described in Isaiah Berlin, "The Counter-Enlightenment," in idem, *Against the Current. Essays in the History of Ideas*, ed. Henry Hardy (New York, 1980), pp. 17–19.

[9] Klaus R. Scherpe, *Werther und Wertherwirkung. Zum Syndrom bürgerlicher Gesellschaftsordnung im 18. Jahrhundert* (Bad Homburg, Berlin, and Zürich, 1970), is a reading of *Werther* as "anti-bourgeois" in this sense, though Scherpe also rightly stresses that a sentimentalized version of the Werther-cult was easily assimilated into the "bourgeois" order. But cf. Peter Müller, *Zeitkritik und Utopie in Goethes "Werther"* (Berlin, 1969).

the image of the "eagle," the Promethean figure whose flight above and beyond his contemporaries brought benefits to mankind, or at least expressed the spirit of his nation. But even in this truly heroic guise, the genius was a loner and an outsider; if his individualism did not thrive on brooding alienation from his contemporaries, it at least required the freedom to operate outside – and above – conventional social roles.[10]

Rationalist critics of *Werther* were especially alarmed by its ending, and not simply because it seemed to bring the emotional trauma of unrequited – or at least largely unacknowledged – love to an absurd conclusion. They also recognized the choice of suicide for what it was – the ultimate repudiation of the ideology of merit through service (*Verdienst*), with its emphasis on duty over individual right, at the core of their vision of a rational, productive, and dynamic society. In 1775, in his first antidote to the incipient "fever," Friedrich Nicolai had an older admirer of Albert ask a young Werther-enthusiast to imagine the protagonist "as a man in society" who would be wrong to "regard himself as isolated and the men around him as aliens." Since Werther "enjoyed the benefits of society from the time he lay at his mother's breast," the young man is reminded, "he owed it duties in return"; "to withdraw from them was ingratitude and vice" and "to exercise them would have been virtue and consolation."[11]

Werther made it abundantly clear that the cult of genius, at the same time that it rejected the authority of tradition in aesthetics, repudiated meritocratic visions of progress. Whether "merit" in the rationalist sense was conceived as a heritable property, as neocorporate ideology would have it, or as a principle requiring the opening of careers to talent from below, made little difference. In the contrast between "genius" and the egalitarian approach to merit, in fact, the opposition of radically different kinds of individualism becomes especially evident. The rationalist conception of merit was individualistic in the sense that, in principle if not in practice, it evaluated the person in detachment from his social moorings. In its pedagogical application, however, it also broke individuals down into constituent talents and other endowments, sorted them into classifications, and targeted them for particular stations – hence the opposite celebration of the absolutely unique, unitary, and autonomous in the genius cult. What made classification and targeting indispensable in a rational meritocracy was the need to integrate merit thoroughly into a particular social collectivity.

[10] See esp. Sudheimer, *Der Geniebegriff des jungen Goethe*, pp. 446–59; Pascal, *The German Sturm und Drang*, pp. 136–55.

[11] Nicolai's *Freuden des jungen Werthers. Leiden und Freuden Werthers des Mannes* (1775), is reprinted in the appendix of Scherpe, *Werther und Wertherwirkung*. Quotation on pp. 18–19. On Nicolai's reaction to *Werther* see also Horst Möller, *Aufklärung in Preussen. Der Verleger, Publizist und Geschichtsschreiber Friedrich Nicolai*, Einzelveröffentlichungen der Historischen Kommission zu Berlin, vol. 15 (Berlin, 1974), pp. 120–33, which includes an excellent discussion of the "bourgeois" value system and conception of social progress that Nicolai defended.

In such a society, function had precedence over inherited right, and hence the legal barriers between corporate enclaves in old-regime society would be removed. But even when social groups were described as "classes" rather than as legally constituted "estates," observers were not thinking of broad class divisions; degrees of merit had to be differentiated within an intricate hierarchy of functional groups, each performing a specific service.

Where the neocorporate and egalitarian versions of meritocracy differed was on the degree to which education would make the higher levels permeable to new blood from below. What they shared – what reflected in both visions of modernity the tenacity of old-regime social norms – was the tendency to conceive of functional groups as corporate-like collectivities. The distinct identities of the occupational groups ranged along the social hierarchy were not simply a matter of specialized activities and forms of expertise, although these certainly were central to their definition. A "class" – or a "station" in the new sense – also embodied a distinct *Lebensart*, or "way of life"; like traditional corporations, though without their legal definition, it observed and transmitted a distinct sociability, demonstrated its rank with precisely calibrated habits of consumption, and applied prevailing moral standards in a singularly concrete way. It was the need to target individuals for occupational roles requiring particular intellectual, social, and moral qualities – and not just the force of internal logic – that sustained and directed the analytical thrust of the new pedagogy. In theory, the individual's cluster of innate endowments formed a uniquely integrated self, and pedagogical cultivation respected its entelechy as an organic whole. But depending on the specific social objective, the strategy of cultivation was to exercise an innate endowment or leave it dormant, give it free reign or keep it tightly bound, as though it were a detachable part.

In the contempt for the "mechanical" in Sturm und Drang, this mutual dependence between a pedagogical approach to the individual personality and the rationalist vision of an efficient social order was one of the more exposed targets. Used fondly by cameralist enthusiasts of the "well-ordered police state" since the seventeenth century, the metaphor of the social machine now evoked the brutal subordination of individual self-realization to the requirements of a dynamic but artificial and ultimately lifeless order. In the early 1770s, when Sturm und Drang burst on the scene, the basic tendencies caricatured in images of mechanistic sterility were only beginning to find expression in agendas for educational reform. Basedow's Philanthropinum did not open until 1774, and Ernst Christian Trapp's *Versuch einer Pädagogik*, which would have made a splendid target, did not appear until 1780. But the irony is that in the 1780s the Sturm und Drang attack came to seem prophetic. This was in part because the transition from pedagogical theory to practice had advanced very rapidly; now schoolmen like Lieberkühn and Gedike, committed to engineering an egalitarian selection of talent in and through the schools, were beginning to use their new organization of school grades and their elaborate examination systems to classify with a vengeance.

At the same time the theory itself was hardening into an orthodoxy, even as it sought to accommodate to some degree a Rousseauian respect for the natural man. The commitment to corporate-like functionalism was complicated and modified by a growing recognition that the essential qualities of the "human being" (*Mensch*) must not be sacrificed to the specific social assignment of the *Bürger*. To the measure that the philanthropinists and other reformers began to envision an introductory "general education" for children of all backgrounds in a common school, however, it seemed all the more urgent to reaffirm that in a concrete society the "perfecting" of the *Mensch* had to be more or less "relative" or "modified," depending on the specific occupational role he would assume as *Bürger*.[12] The need for this delicate balance was the essential message of Moses Mendelssohn's brief but intricate essay on "enlightenment" in the *Berlinische Monatsschrift* in 1784, though it was cast in philosophical rather than pedagogical terms. One side of Mendelssohn's argument was that "the essential destiny of the human being" could not be realized in any *Bürger* unless the basic cognitive and speculative faculties he called "enlightenment" were developed to a degree. A state was in an "unhappy" situation, he went so far as to observe, when the enlightenment "indispensable to humanity" could not be "diffused through all stations."[13] But Mendelssohn had a certain minimum in mind; beyond it, he stressed, the orderly development of a nation's *Cultur* – of its fund of practical capacities exercised in social interdependence – required a graduated distribution of enlightenment:

> Station and occupation in civil society determine the duties and rights of each member, and according to the measure that these require a different skill and competence, different inclinations, drives, sense of sociability and customs, another *Cultur* and refinement [*Politur*]. The more throughout all stations these are in agreement with their vocations [*Berufe*] – i.e., with their respective assignments as members of society – the more *Cultur* the nation has.
>
> They require, however, from each *Individuum*, in proportion to his station and occupation, different theoretical insights and a different competence to acquire them, a different degree of enlightenment. The enlightenment that concerns the

[12] Typical was the schema proposed by Baron von Zedlitz, the Prussian minister; see his "Vorschläge zur Verbesserung des Schulwesens in den Königlichen Länden," *Berlinische Monatsschrift* 10 (1787): 97–116 (cited hereafter as BM). There are many other examples of this approach in Helmut König, *Zur Geschichte der Nationalerziehung in Deutschland im letzten Drittel des 18. Jahrhunderts*, Monumenta Paedagogica, vol. 1 (Berlin, 1960).

[13] Moses Mendelssohn, "Ueber die Frage: Was heisst aufklären?" in idem, *Schriften zur Philosophie, Aesthetik und Apologetik*, 2 vols. (1880: Hildesheim, 1968), 2: 248–49. Cf. the discussion of "corporate Enlightenment" in Jonathan B. Knudsen, *Justus Möser and the German Enlightenment* (Cambridge, 1986), esp. pp. 3–19.

human being as human being is general, without distinction among stations; the enlightenment of the human being considered as *Bürger* modifies itself according to station and occupation.[14]

Mendelssohn's essay was a characteristic product of the Berlin Enlightenment, and it also voiced the prevailing sentiment among educators in the rationalist camp. His essential distinction and compromise were elaborated with meticulous logic in Peter Villaume's essay on the proper relationship between "perfecting" and "usefulness" in 1785.[15] But the epitome of hardened orthodoxy was Joachim Heinrich Campe. As a theology student at Helmstedt, Campe had been persecuted for his rationalist views, but the Werther-fever soon came to seem at least as exasperating as Lutheran obscurantism. *Die Freuden des jungen Werthers* struck him as an effective antidote; he was reputed to have recommended to young men of his acquaintance that they tear out the original pages of their *Werther* volume and replace them with Nicolai's parody.[16] Depending on the angle of vision, this philanthropinist either spoke plain and sober truths to the youth of his day or confirmed to them that the rationalist ethic led to an absurdly rigid and artificial schematism.

Campe's collaboration with Basedow in Dessau in the mid-1770s had been short-lived, and the school reform over which he presided in Brunswick from 1788 onward was soon paralyzed by local clerical opposition. He had considerably more success as an author and publisher. With the collaboration of Villaume, Trapp, and Stuve, he launched the famous *Allgemeine Revision* in 1785 to provide an encyclopedic survey of the current state of pedagogy and school reform. In one of his several contributions Campe, like Mendelssohn, tried to reconcile the general education of the *Mensch* with the specific socialization of the *Bürger*. The former required that the "original" or "natural" intellectual and emotional powers of the individual (*Individuum*) be developed as far as pedagogy allowed. Here Campe's emphasis, in fact, might be taken to acknowledge, albeit on a quotidian level, the unitary conception of personality in the genius cult; original powers had to mature in a state of "equilibrium" (*Gleichgewicht*), and in that regard the pupil's social circumstances and destiny should be

[14] Mendelssohn, "Ueber die Frage," p. 248. Mendelssohn went on to acknowledge that "the enlightenment of the *Mensch* and the enlightenment of the *Bürger* could come into conflict," since "certain truths that are useful to the human being as human being can sometimes be harmful to him as *Bürger*."

[15] Peter Villaume, "Ob und inwiefern bei der Erziehung die Vollkommenheit des einzelnes Menschen seiner Brauchbarkeit aufzuopfern sei?" reprinted in Blankertz, ed., *Bildung und Brauchbarkeit*, pp. 69–142.

[16] Ibid., p. 16. Campe had been a student of Teller at Helmstedt in the mid-1760s, and this rationalist association had cost him his stipend. Jakob Anton Leyser, *Joachim Heinrich Campe. Ein Lebensbild aus dem Zeitalter der Aufklärung*, 2 vols. (2nd ed.: Brunswick, 1896), 1: 11–12.

irrelevant.[17] But "derivative" or "inessential" powers were another matter; the development of these, like the diffusion of Mendelssohn's "enlightenment," must be "tapered to each pupil in accord with his future *Berufe*, and to such subjects as lie within the boundaries of his future *Berufen*." The future peasant or artisan could undergo the same "intensive" cultivation of his original powers as the future statesman, Campe explained, so long as the "extensive" development of his derivative powers differed by degree. While intensity referred to the concentration of "exercises," extension pertained to the "subjects" to which a power was applied. The educator, taking into "exact account" each pupil's "individual destiny," must "conduct the exercises in no other subjects than those that lie within [his] future sphere of activity."[18]

Campe acknowledged that premature and excessive development of "powers of comprehension," at the expense of the "power of sensation," could produce caricatures of the dutiful *Bürger* – the kind of men who, dead to "feeling" and "natural instinct," "perform their occupational tasks out of duty, eat, drink and sleep out of duty, love their friends out of duty, embrace their wives out of duty, and likewise concern themselves with their children out of duty." But on the more complicated battleground that men of good sense now faced, the other threat lay in the preponderance of "the power of feeling" over "the powers of comprehension," which was typified by the *Kraftgenie* as well as the religious "enthusiast."[19] Campe's essay typifies the uneasy mix of metaphors that had come to characterize rationalist pedagogy. Innate potential was still a "seed" or "kernel," and its realization still followed an entelechy of natural maturation. But now humanistic language attributed an organic vitalism to mechanical relations of forces, and at the same time a mechanical schematism was imposed on organic process. It was a reflection of the overriding social imperative to classify and target that, for purposes of pedagogical strategy, the individual soul was conceived as a particular cluster of commonly shared and readily comparable "powers," not an organic whole animated by a unique and inimitable vital force. Even Campe was not so enamored of mechanistic psychology as to claim that the evaluation of intellectual faculties and other powers was given to quantitative precision; but pedagogical analysis approached them more in terms of measurable degree than in terms of qualitative difference. Like a configuration of mechanical forces, intellectual and emotional powers could be weighted for the purpose of maintaining "equilibrium" (*Gleichgewicht*) – or, indeed, in an internal adjustment of the machinery, one power could be harnessed at maximum strength while others were allowed much less

17 Campe, "Von der nötigen Sorge," pp. 19–67.
18 Ibid., esp. pp. 41–45, 57–67.
19 Ibid., pp. 49–55.

exercise. One could speak of "imagination" and "feeling," like "reason" and "memory," as forces to be harnessed "intensively" or "extensively," given more or less density or diffusion.

The relative strengths of the powers themselves could be gauged only approximately, but a rational pedagogy could be considerably more precise about the kinds and degrees of knowledge used to exercise them. The reform literature abounded in increasingly detailed proposals for the curricula proper to various school types, leading to various occupational spheres; most of the proposals turned on the assumption that doses of intellectual and moral enlightenment could be matched to degrees of "relative perfecting," whether the target was the inherited station in which a pupil would remain or the higher one to which he would ascend. In 1788, with this aim in mind, Campe proposed an essay contest on the question "What kind of physical, literate and moral training, and what branches of knowledge and skills in the present state of the world, should be peculiar to each class of men in Germany if the public welfare as well as individual welfare is to be promoted?" In response to skeptics, he insisted that the usual larger social categories – the "main classes" of peasants, *Bürger*, and learned men – did not suffice; each occupational station had its own *Moral* and should be more or less circumscribed intellectually. His proposed ten categories distinguished "lower stations of townsmen" from the "middle *Bürgerstand*" (in turn separated into urban and rural) and broke down the learned estate into officials and state personnel, jurists, doctors and surgeons, and educators and schoolmen. "Nature," Campe acknowledged, produces only "individuals," each "a class by itself"; but nonetheless it was both possible and necessary to "classify."[20]

Rationalists like Campe were provoked into unintentional self-caricature; but their reaction, as alarmist as it was, at least recognized that in the more extreme expressions of the genius cult the rejection of "civil society" was categorical. In Sturm und Drang, contempt for the "mechanical" extended well beyond the rationalist ethic of service in the abstract; ultimately what made the individualism of the genius asocial, if not antisocial, was the incompatibility between his creative spontaneity and the occupational differentiation of a modern division of labor. Hence the strain of nostalgia for vanished patriarchal societies in Sturm und Drang – the kinds of deference such societies had in fact required of most men paled before the freedom they seemed to have allowed the heroic few. This kind of freedom, in its setting of lost simplicity, was posed against the rationalist vision of a more complex social hierarchy, at once functional and corporate-like, that seemed

[20] Joachim Heinrich Campe, "Beantwortung einiger Einwürfe, welche in den Schlesischen Provinzialblättern gegen eine von mir aufgestellte Preisfrage, über die einer jeden besondern Menschenklasse zu wünschende Art der Ausbildung und der Aufklärung, gemacht worden sind," *Braunschweigisches Journal* 1:3 (Mar. 1788): 338–73, esp. pp. 347–49, 361–73.

to promise regimentation rather than liberation. What made the assumption of occupational roles in the rationalist world so repugnant was its combination of imperatives – its reduction of personal "merit" to the acquisition of a particular form of manual or intellectual expertise and its simultaneous insistence on the assumption of a multidimensional identity, moral as well as intellectual, within a clearly circumscribed "sphere." While the requirement of expertise seemed to consign the natural man to an abysmally narrow, truncated form of self-realization, the all-encompassing requirements of corporate integration were no less antithetical to "individuality" and creative originality. The one arbitrarily bounded his horizons; the other threatened to engulf him.

The genius – whether he realized himself in art or in deeds – defied this fate. In fact the creative artist and the heroic man of action were not as different as might at first appear. Great art emanating from inspiration rather than mere craftsmanship was the highest form of action, in that it jolted mankind forward. Heroic action could have a similarly creative impact, precisely because it was not confined to conventional occupational life. The celebration of "action" (*handeln*) in Lenz's review of Goethe's *Goetz von Berlichingen* is anything but a call to practical life; Lenz juxtaposes a utopian vision of restless, passionate vitalism, God-like in its creativity, to the grim alternative of present reality:

> We are born – our parents give us bread and clothing – our teachers imprint on our brains words, language, scholarly disciplines. . . . a place becomes vacant in the republic, where we fit in – our friends, relatives, patrons go to work and happily push us into it – we revolve for a while in this place, like the other wheels, and push and drive – until in the ordinary course of things we are deadened and finally must make room for a new wheel – Gentlemen, that is without fanfare [*ohne Ruhm zu melden*], our biography – and the human being remains nothing but an excellently fabricated [*vorzüglichkünstliche*] machine that for better or worse fits the large machine we call the World, the realities of life, the ways of the world.[21]

Lenz uses "the World" not to designate the public arena of the courtier, but to evoke the routinized existence of men who have to work for a living. In this Rousseauian lament the smooth operation of the social machine is ensured by the lifeless artificiality of the socialized man. In Sturm und Drang, as in rationalism, nature is an ideological construct for finding fault with the social order; but the angle of vision has shifted radically. To Werther and his admirers, nature is not the rationalists' source of raw talent and other "powers," amenable to cultivation in the interest of conventional "productivity." As the mysterious, awe-inspiring source of the creative art-

[21] "Ueber Götz von Berlichingen," reprinted in *Jakob Michael Reinhold Lenz. Werken und Schriften*, vol. 1, ed. Britta Titel and Hellmut Haug (Stuttgart, 1966), pp. 378–82. The quotation opens the essay. See also Lenz's "Briefen über die Moralität der Leiden des jungen Werthers," reprinted in ibid., pp. 383–402.

ist's emotional and imaginative sustenance, it is the refuge from a bourgeois ethic of "useful" productivity. Where rationalist advocates of meritocracy found a principle for imparting a new hierarchical order to social complexity, the enthusiasts of genius found a standard against which to condemn complexity itself. As the focus of the critique shifted, so did the positive estimation of the lower orders. In the rationalist order, the "productive" laboring classes earned a new dignity by enhancing their usefulness with new forms of expertise. "Enlightened" in that popular sense, they joined the educated elite in a hierarchical continuum of knowledge and occupational functions. The *Stürmer und Dränger* were no less oblivious to the grim realities of manual labor, but not because they were entranced by the prospect of economic and technological progress. In their idylls peasants and artisans have occupations only in a formal sense; their main function is to people natural settings, posed against society.[22] Goethe knew from personal experience that the celebration of genius was inseparable from this cult of "the simple folk"; Werther has more affinity with peasants than with his educated peers because, like children, peasants represent the innocence and spontaneity of the natural man.

The larger quarrel was about the shape of things to come; it pitted a reverence for creative spontaneity, often utopian in its projections of a brave new world, against the more sober ideal of conventional work in a rationalist meritocracy. For the *Stürmer und Dränger*, as for later victims of the Werther-fever, the immediate obstacles to artistic creativity were the offices that educated young men were expected to assume. Goethe, the son of a merchant patrician in Frankfurt, had been destined for a legal career. The families of several others – Herder, Lenz, Klinger – were far less affluent, and hence they had had no choice but to study theology. For Lenz and Klinger military life, aside from promising opportunities for heroic action, was appealing as a way to make a living without entering a standard clerical or teaching career. In 1788 Campe captured this aspect of the youth rebellion when he warned against "genius-addicts who prefer their own enjoyment and spiritual efficacy to occupational tasks."[23] His term linked the new specter to a longstanding stereotype of poor students; like ambitious young men "addicted to study," geniuses threatened the social order with their insatiability. But whereas the former brought to their offices unrealistic expectations about status, affluence, and leisure, the latter were horrified by the very thought of official employment and wanted to avoid it entirely. To become a clergyman or, perhaps worse, a civil official was to

[22] See esp. Pascal, *The German Sturm und Drang*, pp. 49–50.

[23] Joachim Heinrich Campe, "Beschluss der Prüfung der Rheberg. Abhandlung im Febr. und März der Berlinschen Monatsschrift 88.," *Braunschweigisches Journal* 3:10 (Oct. 1788): 233.

enter the machine in its most bureaucratic – i.e., in its most mechanistic – form, where subordination to superiors brought "slavery" in the extreme and the conventional routine of occupational life meant tunnel-visioned, lifeless clerical work.

In the 1780s defensive rationalists, alarmed that Werther-fever was spreading this sentiment among the young, laid all the more stress on service and duty in their ethic of vocation. Personal happiness lay in service to others, which was to define it essentially as a good conscience, attainable only in the performance of duty in a particular sphere. In this sense Campe, denying that subordination in a *Beruf* was "slavery," likened it to "the slavery of love."[24] But the assurances that service in the abstract contributed to the public good were complemented by sober, if not grim, depictions of its concrete occupational settings. There was no denying that the daily routine of officialdom was monotonous, that the expert's preoccupation with trivial detail often did preclude a broader vision, that bureaucratic subordination often did require blind obedience. Precisely because the true "genius" could not adapt to such humdrum work, in fact, he was considered less "useful" to his contemporaries than the young men of "average" or "unexceptional" intelligence who typically attended universities and went on to official careers. The task of public education was to prepare the average for reality. It was essential to their "happiness" as well as their "usefulness" that their intellectual development and, perhaps more important, the cultivation of their emotional life respect the boundaries circumscribed by their later assignments. Their occupational "spheres," though broader than those of uneducated men, were no less carefully mapped and bounded on the functional hierarchy.[25]

This common-sensical approach was calculated to puncture the pretensions of genius without inflating the expectations of careerists. But now this-worldly asceticism – a spirit that had long informed the rationalist ethic of vocation – acquired new scope. Asceticism was no longer simply a matter of forgoing social recognition and financial reward; in the more soberly realistic depictions of the official's daily routine, it became questionable whether the work in itself could be the vehicle for self-expression that earlier enthusiasts of "talent" had expected it to become. Rationalists who preached this kind of self-denial were not likely to inspire youth.

[24] Ibid., p. 240.

[25] Ibid., pp. 240–41; Campe, "Von der nötigen Sorge," pp. 45–47, 53–57. This somber, almost resigned attitude toward the constraints and sheer monotony of academic and bureaucratic work is given special emphasis in Villaume, "Ob und inwiefern bei der Erziehung," pp. 85–106. It has not received sufficient attention in analyses of the "bourgeois" reaction against *Werther*; see, e.g., Scherpe, *Werther und Wertherwirkung*; Möller, *Aufklärung in Preussen*, pp. 120–33.

THE APPEAL OF SELF-CULTIVATION

In 1808 Friedrich Immanuel Niethammer published an elaborate explanation of neohumanism, itemizing the reasons why its ideal of "self-cultivation," or *Bildung*, was superseding the philanthropinistic alternative so popular only two decades earlier. Acting as the recently appointed Protestant school councilor in Munich, Niethammer wanted to establish a clear rationale and agenda for the educational reform the Bavarian government had undertaken under Napoleon's aegis.[26] His book marks the point at which an emergent ideology was patterning into formulaic statements – the kind that could be incorporated into state laws and applied in organizational blueprints for schools. As careful as he was to acknowledge the virtues of the opposing camp, Niethammer ignored the degree to which concepts of "general education," developed in the later stages of philanthropinism, had paved the way for neohumanism. But he was correct on the essentials: an alternative ideology had crystallized at the turn of the century, and the future belonged to its reform agenda.

The shift was in language as well as in ideas. In the 1790s the new semantic universe of neohumanism was already forming in the writings of Wilhelm von Humboldt, Friedrich Schiller, and several lesser figures. Genuine cultivation – i.e., *Bildung* in the new sense – was posed against mere instruction or training, and indeed against mere education (*Erziehung*) in the rationalist sense. The key words of Enlightenment orthodoxy – merit, service, duty, usefulness – were ignored, or dismissed contemptuously, or given entirely new connotations. To prepare children to assume social and civic identities as *Bürger* was to intrude on and perhaps abort their "ennoblement" as human beings. Only *Humanität* – and not merely *Menschheit* – could express the new reverence for the "human" with sufficient abstraction from the merely "civil" or "material." The relative concept of the "individual" gave way to the ideal of absolute "individuality" (*Individualität*) – to the "unique particularity" (*Eigenthümlichkeit*) of each "personality" (*Persönlichkeit*).

In Schiller's *Letters on the Aesthetic Education of Man* the characteristic neohumanistic mix of philosophical abstractions and organic images achieved dazzling and ultimately mystifying complexity.[27] Schiller wrote the *Letters* in the mid-1790s, when he was in his midthirties. He had been too young to contribute to the initial surge of Sturm und Drang, but as an

[26] *Friedrich Immanuel Niethammer: Philanthropinismus-Humanismus*, ed. Werner Hillebrecht, Kleine Pädagogische Texte, vol. 29 (Weinheim, 1968). Ernst Hojer, *Die Bildungslehre F. I. Niethammers; ein Beitrag zur Geschichte des Neuhumanismus*, Forschungen zur Pädagogik und Geistesgeschichte, vol. 2 (Frankfurt am Main, 1965), is a reliable intellectual biography of Niethammer. Still useful for biographical detail is Michael Schwarzmaier, *Friedrich Immanuel Niethammer, ein bayerischer Schulreformator*, 1. Teil: *Niethammers Leben und Wirken bis zum Jahre 1807*, Schriftenreihe zur bayerischen Landesgeschichte, vol. 25 (Munich, 1937).

[27] Friedrich Schiller, *Ueber die ästhetische Erziehung des Menschen*, ed. Wolfhart Henckmann (Munich, 1967).

enthusiast of *Bildung* he was relatively old. Most of the early neohumanists – the men who channeled several new departures in German academic life into a distinctly new educational ideology – constitute another well-defined generational subgroup. Born in the mid-1760s, they underwent formative experiences as university students in the 1780s. Only a decade or so separated them from egalitarian reformers like Gedike and Lieberkühn; but academic preoccupations and tastes were changing with increasing rapidity, and hence a mere decade could make a crucial difference. By the time Niethammer and his contemporaries reached the universities, the revival of classical studies under Christian Gottlob Heyne, Gesner's successor at Göttingen, was well under way, and Friedrich August Wolf at Halle was beginning to produce a coherent interdisciplinary program for a "science of antiquity" (*Altertumswissenschaft*). Humboldt (b. 1767) had come to Göttingen in the spring of 1788 ostensibly to study law and cameralism; but it was his participation in Heyne's famous philological seminar that shaped his future career as a scholar and educational reformer.[28] Friedrich Jacobs (b. 1764) had been a member of the seminar a few years earlier. He went on to become a gymnasium teacher in Gotha and in 1807, on Niethammer's recommendation, a professor in the lyceum in Munich. His inaugural address for the latter office typifies the militant rhetoric of the neohumanistic schoolman.[29]

In the 1770s, when Gedike and his contemporaries attended the universities, Immanuel Kant was an obscure professor in distant Königsberg. In the 1780s, with the publication of the major treatises, Kantian philosophy exploded onto the academic scene – and the early neohumanists were among its first converts. In 1800 Reinhold Bernhard Jachmann, who had studied under the master himself at Königsberg, became the first director of the Conradium, an experimental school on an estate outside Danzig. A few years later Jachmann and his younger colleague Ernst Passow, a former pupil of Jacobs, set about transforming the curriculum of the Conradium to demonstrate how self-cultivation through classical studies could contribute to national regeneration.[30]

[28] See esp. Clemens Menze, *Wilhelm von Humboldt und Christian Gottlob Heyne* (Ratingen, 1966). Humboldt was not a regular member of the seminar. Menze also emphasizes the differences between the holistic conception of *Altertumswissenschaft* that Humboldt and others developed and Heyne's less theoretical approach to classical studies.

[29] Friedrich Jacobs, "Zweck einer gelehrten Schule," in Rudolf Joerden, ed., *Dokumente des Neuhumanismus I*, Kleine Pädagogische Texte, vol. 17 (2nd ed.: Weinheim, 1962), pp. 32–45. This is an excerpt from Jacobs's *Antrittsrede* in the Munich lyceum in 1807, published in Friedrich Jacobs, *Vermischte Schriften*, 9 vols. (Gotha, 1823–62), 1 (1823): 108ff. For biographical detail see Jacobs's "Nachrichten aus meinem Leben," in ibid., 7 (1840): 3–298. See also Jacobs's defense of Heyne against Friedrich August Wolf and his disciples in ibid., 6 (1837): 583–90.

[30] The reform of the Conradium under Jachmann and Passow has been analyzed in Klaus Sochatzy, *Das Neuhumanistische Gymnasium und die rein-menschliche Bildung. Zwei Schulre-*

Humboldt was at Göttingen when he began to study the *Critique of Pure Reason* systematically. But it was the much smaller university at Jena, under the influence of Goethe's Weimar circle, that became the mecca for Kantians in central Germany and generated "idealist" offshoots in the 1790s. Niethammer (b. 1766) had come to Jena from Tübingen in 1790 to study with Kant's disciple and interpreter Karl Leonhard Reinhold, and two years later he began teaching in the philosophy faculty.[31] He was joined there in 1795 by another Kantian, Johann Heinrich Gottlieb Heusinger (b. 1766). In the same year Heusinger's article on "the education of the human being and the *Bürger*" in the *Philosophisches Journal*, edited by Niethammer and Johann Gottlieb Fichte, offered a succinct statement of the neohumanists' position.[32]

The neohumanistic ideal of *Bildung* drew on many other sources, but it was inspired above all by the new classical scholarship and the ethical imperatives of Kantian and Idealist philosophy. While its intellectual pedigree is easily traced, the social contours of its appeal are more elusive. *Bildung* owed its widespread ascendancy at the turn of the century in part to a chameleon-like capacity to refract the social norms of several groups at once. The ideal can arguably be explained as a neoaristocratic surrogate for pedigree and courtly breeding; as a distinctly bourgeois assertion of educational achievement and personal merit in the face of aristocratic pretensions; as a hybrid, at once aristocratic and bourgeois, legitimating a mixed elite.[33] If the new idiom for well-rounded cultivation was particularly appealing to a

formversuche in ihrer weiterreichenden Bedeutung (Göttingen, 1973). On Jachmann see also Karl-Ernst Jeismann, "'Nationalerziehung.' Bemerkungen zum Verhältniss von Politik und Pädagogik in der Zeit der preussischen Reform, 1806–1815," *Geschichte in Wissenschaft und Unterricht* 19 (1968): 201–18.

[31] See esp. Hojer, *Die Bildungslehre F. I. Niethammers*, pp. 21–33.

[32] Johann Heinrich Gottlieb Heusinger, "Etwas über den Ausdruck: Erziehung zum Menschen und Bürger," *Philosophisches Journal einer Gesellschaft teutscher Gelehrten* 1:3 (1795): 211–32. For Heusinger's biography see *Allgemeine Deutsche Biographie* 12 (1880): 335–36.

[33] For the variety of social explanations of *Bildung* see Hans Weil, *Die Entstehung des deutschen Bildungsprinzips* (1930: Bonn, 1967); Hans Rosenberg, *Bureaucracy, Aristocracy and Autocracy. The Prussian Experience 1660–1815* (Cambridge, Mass., 1958), esp. pp. 182–92; Wilhelm Roessler, *Die Entstehung des modernen Erziehungswesens in Deutschland* (Stuttgart, 1961); Fritz K. Ringer, *The Decline of the German Mandarins: The German Academic Community, 1890–1933* (Cambridge, Mass., 1969), esp. pp. 86–127, and Ringer's review of W. H. Bruford, *The German Tradition of Self-Cultivation: 'Bildung' from Humboldt to Thomas Mann* (New York and London, 1975), in *Central European History* 11 (1978): 107–13; Ralph Fiedler, *Die klassische deutsche Bildungsidee. Ihre soziologischen Wurzeln und pädagogischen Folgen*, Studien zur Soziologie des Bildungswesens, vol. 7 (Weinheim, ca. 1972); Rudolf Vierhaus, "Bildung," in Otto Brunner, Werner Conze, and Reinhart Koselleck, eds., *Geschichtliche Grundbegriffe: Historisches Lexikon zur politisch-sozialen Sprache in Deutschland*, vol. 1 (Stuttgart, 1972), pp. 508–51; Charles E. McClelland, "The Aristocracy and University Reform in Eighteenth-Century Germany," in Lawrence Stone, ed., *Schooling and Society. Studies in the History of Education* (Baltimore, 1976), pp. 146–73; Charles E. McClelland, *State, Society, and University in Germany 1700–1914* (Cambridge, 1980), pp. 111–22. Sochatzy, *Das Neuhumanistische Gymnasium*, is another important contribution to this subject.

restless intellectual like Humboldt, who shunned a bureaucratic career, it also had much to offer the nobleman in office facing the same occupational demands as commoners. Like the "worldly" grooming of the gentleman, *Bildung* represented a form of superiority over the mere expert; but at the same time, in an era when the accomplished courtier was derided for his superficiality and dilettantism, it offered the seriousness of a lofty ethical purpose and the respectability of scholarly depth. The dilemma of the educated commoner in the face of aristocratic pretensions was that he could not become what the nobleman simply was; in the words of Goethe's Wilhelm Meister, "he is obliged to make himself useful in one direction and must therefore neglect everything else."[34] Now he could acquire a modern surrogate for the breeding aristocrats had enjoyed by privilege of birth – a kind of cultivation achieved through personal effort, before assuming a professional identity.

Poor students are deprived of a distinct profile in these interpretations. In the requirements for *Bildung*, it is assumed, there was a new and powerful reason to stigmatize them as outsiders, their origins disqualifying them from crossing the line between the cultivated elite and the uneducated mass. Or they are lumped together with sons of the educated, affluent *Bürgertum* in a sprawling "bourgeois" category of social aspirations. There has been little effort to explain exactly how self-cultivation addressed their presence or to reconstruct the meaning it imparted to their experience. This particular angle could enhance our understanding of the entire phenomenon; it exhibits with special clarity the mix of egalitarianism and elitism, emancipatory and constraining impulses, in the ideal of self-cultivation.

Hans Gerth's discussion of neohumanism does include a distinction between upper bourgeois students and those with more restricted opportunities:

> The breadless and socially homeless writers [*Literaten*], the schoolmasters and tutors, secretaries, theologians from birth like Winckelmann and Heyne, directed themselves in their misery to the normative utopia of a hellenic humanity; since the question of slavery was not raised – this omission can be noted now that we have Nietzsche's alternative picture – one conceived of an exalted existence above historical precariousness, "noble simplicity and quiet greatness" became the signature of harmoniously and ethically perfected "nature." . . . Education in literary scholarship and aristocratic worldliness – admired in the nobility by the rising bourgeois – fused, fired by the enthusiasm of "disrupted" theologians who salvaged lost religious substance in the utopian elements of moral cultivation. They turned to this study when they began to doubt the religious beliefs with which they had been

[34] *Goethes Werke*, vol. 7, ed. E. Trunz (Munich, 1973), p. 291. For interpretations of this theme, see Gonthier-Louis Fink, "Die Bildung des Bürgers zum 'Bürger.' Individuum und Gesellschaft in 'Wilhelm Meisters Lehrjahren'," *Recherches Germaniques* 2 (1972): 3–37; Stefan Blessin, "Die radikal-liberale Konzeption von 'Wilhelm Meisters Lehrjahren,'" *Deutsche Vierteljahrsschrift für Literaturwissenschaft und Geistesgeschichte* 49 (1975), Sonderheft: 190–225.

inculcated at home. Philology and literary scholarship, in union with philosophical and historical studies, led through service in the schools and to a university career, and the constellation change in mobility opportunities favored this upheaval [*Umbruch*], which signified more for the individual than a change of field does today.[35]

Our impressions are no less scattered than Gerth's, but we can at least sharpen his images by asking how the new idiom challenged or confirmed received attitudes toward poor students, and how it addressed their circumstances. Likewise we can ask how it compared with alternatives, and particularly with the utilitarian ethic of vocation that had gained wide ascendancy in clerical circles and at the universities by the time neohumanism began to emerge. Gerth's diagnosis of *Bildung* as a utopian substitute for "lost religious substance" is as vague as it is suggestive. Rationalism surely was corroding religious belief, but did not its own reform ideology – the pedagogical mission of Gedike's generation – already provide a potent substitute for lost religious substance? How explain in this context the attraction of "the normative utopia of a hellenic humanity" to the kind of theology student who owed his education and career prospects to charity and patronage?

In neohumanism, as in rationalist reform thought, the egalitarian impulse aimed at creating opportunities for individual mobility, not at leveling a class structure. On that score, both ideologies anticipated the modern "liberal" ideal of equality of opportunity. In lieu of a commitment to basic structural changes, they both burdened the school with an awesome role as a socially neutral jurisdiction, in effect canceling out within its walls the advantages and disadvantages that "birth" would continue to transmit outside them. But within this common framework, *Bildung* was the self-conscious alternative to a hardened rationalist orthodoxy. Coming of age in the 1780s and 1790s and confronted with the defensive, cut-and-dry utilitarianism the Werther-fever had provoked, the neohumanists echoed Sturm und Drang but gave their own dissent a sharper focus. In the face of increasingly elaborate plans for classifying and targeting future *Bürger*, they refused to allow occupational training of any kind – even the preparation of future scholars was not excepted – to intrude on the cultivation of the "human being." At bottom this was a philosophical preference; inspired by a Kantian respect for the unconditional freedom of the self-realizing subject, the neohumanists condemned the rationalist conception of pedagogical cultivation for reducing the subject to the mere passive object of its manipulation. Their ideal was as opposed in principle to classification designed to create an egalitarian meritocracy as it was to corporate inheritance of stations. In the education of the *Mensch*, neither social origins nor

[35] Hans H. Gerth, *Bürgerliche Intelligenz um 1800. Zur Soziologie des deutschen Frühliberalismus*, Kritische Studien zur Geschichtswissenschaft, vol. 19 (Göttingen, 1976), pp. 43–44.

future social role were relevant; since the individual was an absolutely unique "personality," defying classification, his self-realization could not be kept "incomplete" or made "one-sided" by a "mechanical" pedagogical intervention. *Bildung* was a completely open-ended *process* of organic growth, and its goal was a well-rounded, "harmonious" configuration of *all* innate endowments.

As in rationalist pedagogy, raw nature was cultivated; but now society was denied the right to subordinate a natural entelechy to a social objective. In theory – practice was another matter – the neohumanists considered the innate "destiny" of the individual inviolable. To the extent that inner growth could be directed, it was only by self-discipline from within. The *Kunst* lay with the subject, who formed himself into a work of art by molding sensual, emotional, and intellectual attributes, perhaps exercising centrifugal force in their raw state, into an integrated, harmonious whole. It was in pursuit of this essentially aesthetic ideal of holistic self-realization that the neohumanists endowed classical studies with unique educational value. The new *Altertumswissenschaft* was to be entirely different from the traditional classicism of the schools. In the old dispensation, Greek, when it had been taught at all, had been a poor relation of Latin, limited to the New Testament; now the language and literature of the ancient Greeks constituted the core material for a "general human education." The object was not imitative mastery of stylistic elegance, but interpretive grasp of original texts in their historical and cultural context.

Though agreeing with Campe and others on the need to ban rote language learning from German schoolrooms, the neohumanists had nothing but contempt for utilitarian plans to remove classical studies from the secondary education of future scholars and officials. But they also found inadequate the usual defenses of the ancient languages among rationalist reformers. They did not regard language learning simply as a matter of exercising the intellectual faculties needed to become truly "human" or to master an educated profession. Nor did they think the ancient languages remained indispensable simply because they gave access to the fund of knowledge with which all learned men had to be familiar. The educational value of a language lay in its interpenetration of sensual substance and logical form. In its artifacts the concreteness of vocabulary and the abstraction of grammar had fused into a model for "harmonious" *Bildung*. Ancient Greek deserved special reverence because it had achieved this fusion to a unique degree and hence was the most appropriate medium for achieving an equivalent unity in the individual personality.[36]

The uniqueness of the language reflected the harmonious fusions of the

[36] See, e.g., Jacobs, "Zweck einer gelehrten Schule," pp. 36–39; Wilhelm von Humboldt, "Ueber das Studium des Alterthums, und des griechischen insbesondere," in idem, *Werke*, 5 vols. (Stuttgart, 1961–69), 2: 9–10.

culture. What fascinated the young Humboldt and others about classical Greece, and particularly about Athens, was that its culture seemed a perfect marriage of the sensual and the intellectual; that it was natural, and indeed childlike, without being crudely primitive, sophisticated without being artificially refined. As in the pedagogical "art," the ideal reconciled organic entelechy and deliberate cultivation; but now a historical culture became a rebuke to both the crudely materialistic and the artificially cerebral in modern civilization. Committed to restoring harmony to the individual and ultimately to society, the neohumanists considered an exclusive concern with the intellectual content of the classical corpus to be as "one-sided" as the traditional Latinist's preoccupation with stylistic elegance and memory learning. Grasping the "character" of "a many-sided nation in all its variety," the young Humboldt observed about the study of Greek culture, required that "one . . . put oneself in motion with his united energies" – that the student "cultivate the human being" by "strain[ing] all powers equally."[37] In 1807 Friedrich Jacobs attributed precisely the same value to Greek studies in his inaugural lecture at the Munich lyceum. The culture as a whole offered a model for the new ideal of "personality," and integrated self-cultivation lay in penetration of its unitary "spirit." In more practical terms, neither the language itself nor its artifacts could be appreciated in isolation; the well-balanced exercise of all innate capacities lay in a union of philological mastery, facility in literary interpretation, and historical understanding.[38]

The neohumanists tended to avoid the word *Verdienst*, because it reduced the "value" of the individual to his "merit" in the sense of social usefulness. But *Bildung* was not a substitute for virtue; their axiomatic assumption – the assumption around which Schiller wove his argument in the *Letters* – was that the development of character in an ethical sense lay *through* the well-rounded cultivation of aesthetic sensibility. As in rationalist psychology, a capacity or potentiality was a *Kraft*; but the connotations of that word hinged on the larger metaphor with which the structure of the inner self was conceived. It was the approach to human *Kräfte* as "powers" or "forces," to be allotted relative strengths, that the neohumanists found "mechanistic" about the rationalist strategy for inculcating character. Even when rationalists conceded the need for "equilibrium" to a point, the ultimate goal was an internal hierarchy of domination and subordination, with sovereign "reason" keeping a tight rein on socially dangerous "instincts" and "passions." To the extent that neohumanists thought in terms of forces and counterforces at all, their ideal was a multivalent balance. But their preference was for emphatically organistic metaphors in which *Kräfte* became vital energies,

[37] Humboldt, "Ueber das Studium des Alterthums," p. 7. On Humboldt's ideal of *Bildung* see Bruford, *The German Tradition of Self-Cultivation*, pp. 1–28.

[38] Jacobs, "Zweck einer gelehrten Schule."

in relationships of interpenetration and symbiosis. The way to cultivate character was not to subordinate some *Kräfte* to others, but to allow sensual and affective energies to be given nobility of form in the very process of nourishing reason with the full richness of their substance. In the aesthetic counterpart of organic metaphors, self-cultivation was a process of blending qualities; the richer the blending of sensual and intellectual experience, substance and form, the greater the "perfection" of the individual in a moral as well as an aesthetic sense. Or one spoke of a symmetrical structure, as when Humboldt compared the internal harmony of "the moral person" to the "symmetry" of "a beautiful painting or a beautiful statue."[39]

What this ideal promised poor students was emancipation from the cultural norms and ethical imperatives applied so stringently to their circumstances. If mastery of the traditional Latinity won them admission into the clergy, it also stigmatized them with a corporate identity that seemed increasingly obsolete. Self-cultivation through the new classical studies meant liberation from this stigma; the cultivated man would have the combination of depth and breadth – of scholarly grasp of language and its texts and intuitive appreciation of their "spirit" – that the learned "pedant" so obviously lacked. But *Bildung* was not aimed simply against the requirements and constraints of traditional corporatism; like the *Stürmer und Dränger*, the neohumanists also rejected the fusion of corporate and functionalist norms in rationalist visions of the complex division of labor in a progressive society. To reject rationalist standards for "usefulness" was to deny society an overriding right to exact a price for permitting mobility. Whether a poor boy could cultivate himself – and whether he could thereby rise above his parents' station – was no longer contingent on his willingness to accept an assigned place. Heusinger, the son of an obscure deacon (*Diaconus*), could not have made this implication clearer in his refutation of Villaume's argument for "usefulness":

So long as a child is still a child, i.e., so long as imperfections in the powers themselves hinder him from using them as they could and should be used, he is incapable of concluding a legally valid contract [with society] before the court of reason, and thus has no station in human society. . . . The station of the father cannot be inherited by his children, and indeed for that reason H. V. [Villaume] does not want to determine a child to be a doctor simply because his father was one. Children are born free, and remain so through their entire childhood and youth; their free will,

[39] Humboldt, "Ueber das Studium des Alterthums," p. 14. For Humboldt's classic statement of this aesthetic ideal see *The Limits of State Action*, ed. J. W. Burrow (Cambridge, 1969). The ideal is well explained in Bruford, *The German Tradition of Self-Cultivation*, pp. 1–28; Clemens Menze, *Die Bildungsreform Wilhelm von Humboldts*, Das Bildungsproblem in der Geschichte des europäischen Erziehungsdenkens, vol. 13 (Hanover, 1975), esp. pp. 18–58; Paul R. Sweet, *Wilhelm von Humboldt. A Biography*, 2 vols. (Columbus, Ohio, 1978–80), 1 (1767–1808): 103–42. See also J. W. Burrow's insightful introduction to Humboldt's thought in *The Limits of State Action*, pp. vii-xliii.

which in this case is guided presumably by their talents, selects an occupation they wish to learn. When they have learned it they enter society, make known their skill and their resolve to serve society with it, thereby assume duties they previously had not had, and in my opinion only from this point on can they be reckoned to have a station, if one wants to speak about stations. . . . Hence the station does not determine the measure for the powers of the child, but rather the powers determine the call [*Ruf*] to one of a variety of stations. [40]

For all the debt to Pietist introspection in the neohumanists' exalting of spirituality over materialism, the natural self was now an absolute value to be unfolded, not the seat of corruption. But *Bildung* also signified rejection of the alternative rationalist ethic; the road to moral integrity lay not through rational self-denial in one form or another, but through unfettered exercise of the freedom inherent in subjectivity and harmonious development of all innate instincts and faculties. A young man aware of his inner "merit" in the rationalist sense might win respect despite low origins and dependence on charity, but at the cost of accepting a truncated identity. Now *Bildung* offered an aesthetic refuge from the humiliations of poverty and dependence, and an ethical guarantor against the "servility" they often induced, that sanctioned the fullest possible cultivation of the inner self.

The equation of functional specialization with fragmentation of the personality, and of Enlightenment rationalism with a "mechanical" spirit; the reverence for the organic and the unique; the insistence on subjective autonomy – all these themes are reminiscent of Sturm und Drang. But if *Bildung* represented a further crystallization of the Werther-fever in these senses, it also allowed accommodations with the established social order that the cult of genius had foreclosed. Its social orientation did not take the form of an interest in concrete conditions, much less in specific issues of inequality and exploitation; one need only peruse the literature to realize how little the early neohumanists' disdain for the daily treadmill of material production drew on direct observation of its realities. But on a philosophical level they were intent on avoiding the self-absorbed and ultimately self-destructive subjectivity to which the cult of genius, in its more extreme forms, seemed to lead. If genius needed brooding isolation, self-cultivation throve on constant and ever varied interaction between the subject and objective reality. Subjectivity acquired substance for its inner articulation in its very self-projection into external forms.

The distance between this ideal of creative and ever varied self-expression and the demands of occupational life often seemed unbridgeable. The cultural achievement of classical Greece, Humboldt observed, had been made possible by the relatively primitive level of its material culture and its reliance on slaves in so many occupations; the combination had allowed it to

[40] Heusinger, "Etwas über den Ausdruck," pp. 221–22.

avoid the complex division of labor on which modern societies depended, and hence had spared its citizens the modern disease of "one-sided" and "mechanical" development.[41] Schiller found a tragic irony in the advancement of the human species since the Greeks; it had been achieved only by fragmenting "humanity" into specialized intellectual and manual activities that alienated the individual from himself and required "whole classes of people to unfold only a part of their endowments, while the others, as in stunted plants, are indicated only by slight traces."[42]

If in this perspective physical labor was the worst kind of drudgery, the bureaucratic work for which most educated men were destined seemed hardly less stultifying. In *On the Limits of State Action*, written shortly after he had left an apprenticeship for the legal bureaucracy in disgust, Humboldt castigated the ever expanding army of functionaries whose "partly empty, partly narrow employment" dealt only with "symbols and formulas of things." Preferring "things" to people, he lamented, bureaucrats "relapse into machines" and mistake the "trivial" for the "momentous," the "contemptible" for the "dignified."[43] As a leisured aristocrat, Humboldt may have had an inbred distaste for the routine and detail of office work; but the tendency to condemn a paternalistic state for dehumanizing its officials as well as its subjects – for reducing its servants to one more class of victims – pervaded early neohumanism. Again there is a clear echo of Sturm und Drang; the very repetition and elaboration of this image of mechanical lifelessness suggests that, at least in some circles of educated youth, alienation from the standard career tracks had become endemic. To Schiller the "state" not only embodied mechanical fragmentation; it bore primary responsibility for the accelerating advance of a functional division of labor. "If the public order makes the office [*Amt*] the measure of the man," he asked, "is it any wonder that other endowments of the temperament are neglected in order to devote all care to the ones that bring honor and reward?" Schiller's use of *Amt* was meant to connote the specific conditions

41 Humboldt, "Ueber das Studium des Alterthums," pp. 12–15.

42 Schiller, *Ueber die ästhetische Erziehung des Menschen*, pp. 90–91. Roy Pascal, "'Bildung' and the Division of Labor," in *German Studies Presented to Walter Horace Bruford* (London and Toronto, 1962): 14–28, emphasizes that Schiller, Humboldt, and others accepted the necessity of the modern division of labor "with a deep-seated feeling of unease that at times rises to passionate protest," and that their preoccupation was with the crippling effects on the individual rather than with "social effects." Pascal's analysis is remarkably prescient in suggesting similarities and differences between this reaction in "the Germany of the Goethe period" and the thought of the Scottish Enlightenment. This comparison can now be fruitfully pursued in the light of recent efforts to understand the Scottish Enlightenment by reference to the eighteenth-century reactions against "specialization" in the tradition of civic humanism. See esp. Istvan Hont and Michael Ignatieff, eds., *Wealth and Virtue: The Shaping of Political Economy in the Scottish Enlightenment* (Cambridge, 1983); J. G. A. Pocock, *Virtue, Commerce, and History. Essays on Political Thought and History, Chiefly in the Eighteenth Century* (Cambridge, 1985).

43 Humboldt, *The Limits of State Action*, pp. 34–35. On Humboldt's brief stint as a bureaucrat, see esp. Sweet, *Wilhelm von Humboldt*, 1: 83–89.

of bureaucratic employment as well as the broader Lutheran conception of duty in a station; he went on to condemn the "spirit of official business, enclosed in a uniform circle of objects and narrowed there still more by formalities," and the official whose "powers of imagination, confined to the uniform circle of his occupation, cannot expand itself to any other way of conceiving of things."[44]

But the early neohumanists combined a palpable sense of alienation from occupational life, and indeed a precocious insight into self-alienation, with a new optimism about the potential for regeneration. Their efforts to institutionalize the ideal of *Bildung* represent in extreme form the paradox of the German domestication of Rousseau. They were so insistent on extruding all social demands from secondary education, even in the higher grades, because they wanted the school to allow the prolonged natural incubation Emile had experienced in isolation from society. But if in this sense they were more purist, and more literalminded, about Rousseau's pedagogical message than rationalist pedagogues, they also exhibited a most un-Rousseauian acceptance of the fact that at the end of his incubation the young man must enter an artificially fragmented world of conventional occupational roles. Understandably Heusinger objected to Villaume's claim that Rousseau had not intended to prepare Emile for "civil society." But his own reading of the "just" and enlightened future Rousseau had in mind was hardly less willful. The young man would commit himself to an occupation only when he reached adulthood and was ready to enter a "legally valid contract" with society:

> He is a completely useful member of a legal and truly developed human society, and only awaits the moment of need to serve it as statesman, as soldier, as clergyman; that is, in order to devote himself exclusively to a station, he looks around himself to see where in society there is an empty place. True, this Emile possesses no complete knowledge in any discipline, no completed skill in any art, when he enters human society as a man; nonetheless he can (first) perform services for society and (second), if that does not apply, his educator has seen to it that he has good will, self-control, independence, and developed talents, so that he can make himself qualified for whatever office he seeks or the society hands over to him.[45]

Rousseau might have wondered how this young German philosopher reconciled his commitment to social justice with his acceptance of conventional social roles, and certainly would have been bemused by the prospect of Emile entering a military or clerical career. Rousseau's utopianism was a strategy of uncompromising moral condemnation; in the face of the degeneracy of the modern world, he used Emile's education to evoke an alternative society that might never exist. The utopian element in neohu-

[44] Schiller, *Ueber die ästhetische Erziehung des Menschen*, pp. 91–94.
[45] Heusinger, "Etwas über den Ausdruck," pp. 228–29.

manism lay in its confidence that future Emiles would neither be permanently alienated by an artificial and morally corrupt social order nor hopelessly overwhelmed by its demands. They would regenerate it from within. Here lay the great potential of a truly "human" education as an antidote to modern civilization. By realizing an inner revolution in myriad individuals, *Bildung* would transform their social existence without a concerted effort to change the external structure of things.

In the 1790s Humboldt looked to friendships and other forms of personal union for an anticipation of this vision. Such relationships would combine the intimacy needed for mutual nourishment with "personal independence"; they promised social interaction among equals, with each "participat[ing] in the rich collective resources of all the others" but "striv[ing] to develop himself from his own inmost nature, and for his own sake."[46] This kind of intersubjectivity would not only dissolve the caste boundaries of the traditional corporate order; the vague expectation was that it could also humanize a modern functional hierarchy, and indeed at work as well as in private life. But the more pronounced tendency among the early neohumanists was to expect work itself in all its forms to be transformed from an alienating activity into a vehicle of creative self-expression. In 1788 August Wilhelm Rehberg, another Göttingen product, anticipated this theme in an essay on the unique value of classical studies for all educated men. The antidote to young men's "dissatisfaction with [their] occupation and station" lay not in pedagogical efforts to "pull human beings down to the level of their occupations," but in a "higher cultivation" surpassing occupational requirements. *Bildung* enriched work as well as leisure; able to "elevate himself through scholarly insight above what the state expressly demands of him," the cultivated man would impart his personal creativity to the daily routine of office work.[47]

Rehberg sharply distinguished educated from popular modes of cultivation, but a few years later Humboldt gave the same ideal of revitalized labor universal application. When he argued that work of any kind should be performed for its "intrinsic worth," he meant not that it was valuable in and of itself, but that its only truly human value lay in nourishing the inner self and allowing its realization in external forms. So long as work was regarded "merely as a means" to "ulterior advantage" – whether it be the

46 Humboldt, *The Limits of State Action*, esp. pp. 16–19, 32–33. On the importance of "social bonds" in Humboldt's thought, see esp. David Sorkin, "Wilhelm von Humboldt: The Theory and Practice of Self-Formation (*Bildung*), 1791–1810," *Journal of the History of Ideas* 44:1 (Jan.-Mar. 1983): 55–73, and Burrow's comments in Humboldt, *The Limits of State Action*, pp. xxxvii-xli.

47 August Wilhelm Rehberg, "Sollen die alten Sprachen dem allgemeinen Unterricht der Jugend in den höheren Ständen zum Grunde gelegt, oder den eigentlichen Gelehrten allein überlassen werden?," BM 11:2 (Feb. 1788): 122–24. For background on Rehberg see Klaus Epstein, *The Genesis of German Conservatism* (Princeton, N.J., 1966), pp. 547–94.

individual's "happiness" or the betterment of society – it would remain an "alien" imposition. But in the harmoniously integrated personality, work would "spring from a man's free choice" and thereby be spiritualized:

The more unity a man possesses, the more freely does his choice of these external matters spring from his inner being, and the more frequent and intimate is the cooperation of these two sources of motive, even when he has not freely selected these external objects. . . . In view of this consideration, it seems as if all peasants and craftsmen might be elevated into artists; that is, men who love their labour for its own sake, improve it by their own plastic genius and inventive skill, and thereby cultivate their intellect, ennoble their character, and exalt and refine their pleasures. And so humanity would be ennobled by the very things which now, though beautiful in themselves, so often serve to degrade it.[48]

If the neohumanists had faith that work would be transformed by the new man, they also were confident that the new man would devote himself to work. Self-cultivation meant neither selfishness nor self-indulgence; rather than opting for individual freedom over responsibility to a collectivity, neohumanism claimed to reconcile the natural freedom of the *Mensch* with the social responsibility of the *Bürger* in an ideal of self-discipline without self-denial, duty without coercion. Every person embodied a unique ideal of "humanity," and in the very process of approaching realization of that ideal in and through self-cultivation, he offered something invaluable to the collectivity. In that sense his contribution to a specific society lay in the fulfillment of his duty to himself and to his species. That he would accept this duty – that he would freely choose to honor his responsibilities in a specific vocation – was not a matter of wishful thinking; aesthetic harmony guaranteed character, and hence the cultivated man did not need specific social imperatives. He would devote himself to purposeful work not because some of his "powers" had been subordinated to others, but because his very sense of himself as an integrated personality – the identity resulting from a balancing and blending of powers – would preclude narrow self-interest and lead him to find a social outlet for his creativity.[49]

If voluntary commitment to duty in this sense was a natural product of *Bildung*, the inculcation of self-discipline was inherent in its pursuit. The philanthropinists had deluded themselves, Niethammer argued, in their efforts to incorporate "play" into instruction so as to make it "easy." There is more than a hint of the traditional Lutheran conviction of human depravity

[48] Humboldt, *The Limits of State Action*, p. 27. Menze, *Die Bildungsreform Wilhelm von Humboldts*, pp. 28–58, also discusses Humboldt's ideal of work. On *Bildung* as an antidote to the modern division of labor, see also Johann Heinrich Gottlieb Heusinger, *Versuch eines Lehrbuchs der Erziehungskunst. Ein Leitfaden zu akademischen Vorlesungen* (Leipzig, 1795), pp. 105–08.

[49] See esp. Humboldt, "Theorie der Bildung des Menschen," in idem, *Werke*, 1: 235–40; idem, *The Limits of State Action*, pp. 16–21; Heusinger, "Etwas über den Ausdruck," pp. 219, 224–25; idem, *Versuch eines Lehrbuchs*, pp. 112–13.

in his insistence that the pedagogue, in addition to guiding his pupil in self-cultivation, must inculcate work discipline methodically as a "second nature," counteracting natural tendencies toward laziness.[50] For once Niethammer underestimated the manipulative impulse in rationalist pedagogy; struck by its naiveté about human nature, he missed its calculated effort to inculcate work habits in and through carefully selected and controlled play. At the same time, though, he ignored the neohumanistic expectation that the link between the *Mensch* and the *Bürger* – the middle term between Rousseauian incubation and the later assumption of an occupational role – would be a commitment to discipline in work, flowing from *Bildung* itself. For all his fondness for "idleness," the young Humboldt was determined to avoid an aimless life of leisure, and for all the breadth of his intellectual interests he did not wish to be a mere dilettante. When he extolled the new "science of antiquity" in the mid-1790s, it was in response to its call for the kind of "hard study" for which he felt a deep personal need. Only through the self-disciplined mastery of an exacting field of scholarship, requiring both depth and versatility, could the individual hope to reach the ultimate goal of absorbing the essence of the Greek achievement and thereby fashioning himself into a work of art.[51]

Humboldt was a leisured nobleman in search of a life purpose; but in his generation this scholarly reincarnation of the work ethic also exercised a strong appeal on commoners in need of a justification for their intellectual and social aspirations. In Jacobs's inaugural address of 1808, the celebration of the rigors of classical studies is well on the way to becoming the ethos of the reformed gymnasium. "The lofty goal is not reached by the rose-strewn path of convenience," the new lyceum professor warned his audience; "the more active the material, the more difficult and persevering the struggle demanded by the work of art of free human cultivation."[52] Expertise in philology and textual editing was as essential to this struggle as an aesthetic awareness of form. To Jacobs, of course, the ultimate quest for "the spirit of antiquity" made this kind of academic rigor fundamentally different from the formalism and rote memorization of the old dispensation; he did not anticipate the new routinism that would soon characterize the nineteenth-century gymnasium. But his apotheosis of classical *Bildung* helps

[50] *Niethammer: Philanthropinismus-Humanismus*, pp. 244–49. On the significance of work in Niethammer's pedagogy, see also Hojer, *Die Bildungslehre F. I. Niethammers*, pp. 120–23.

[51] Humboldt, "Ueber das Studium des Alterthums," pp. 6–7, 22–24. See also idem, "Theorie der Bildung des Menschen," pp. 237–38.

[52] Jacobs, "Zweck einer gelehrten Schule," pp. 35, 40–45. This neohumanistic variation on the work ethic is largely ignored in Fiedler, *Die klassische deutsche Bildungsidee*, which emphasizes the elitist social consciousness exhibited in the ideal of *Bildung* and rightly finds one of its expressions in a hostility to modern specialized labor, especially in its industrial forms. Fiedler's contribution remains insightful despite its onesidedness on this and other issues. See also Theodor Litt, *Das Bildungsideal der deutschen Klassik und die moderne Arbeitswelt* (Bonn, 1955).

explain why the neohumanistic celebration of individual freedom so easily became an official rationale for bureaucratic regimentation.

THE CONSTRAINTS OF SPONSORSHIP

In its abstract formulations, the ideal of *Bildung* gave emphatic preference to the innate "destiny" of the individual over social ascription. Its departure from the received alternatives lay in extending to the natural self an unconditional right to autonomous self-realization. In this sense self-cultivation was conceived as an emancipatory process, and one with radically egalitarian implications. But neohumanism, by the very nature of its individualism, eschewed the institutional innovations with which eighteenth-century reformers from Francke to Gedike had tried to evaluate and promote talent. This in turn made it all the more important that, in its application to academic education, the ideal of *Bildung* proved a receptive vehicle for class-defined norms. The results were evident well before the product of neohumanistic reform ideology – the nineteenth-century gymnasium – assumed hardened form. The sponsorship of talent from below was subject to a new set of conditions and restraints.

When the upheavals of the early nineteenth century created the opportunity to organize new educational systems in the German states, even Humboldt modified his earlier opposition to state meddling in education. Reform from above seemed essential, if only as a transitional means of establishing the public status of the schools.[53] But within this overarching commitment to state sponsorship, the bureaucratic impulse – the commitment to structuring a process of competitive achievement and selection within the school – weakened noticeably.[54] The new "systems" of evaluation and promotion had been designed to counter the "accidents" of birth by making the school the truly public jurisdiction for a rational – and objective – expertise. Now the expertise itself was considered "mechanical" and misconceived; the real threat to individual self-realization was seen to lie in a manipulative pedagogy, in the service of arbitrary social imperatives. From this angle, in fact, the domestic education made possible by a certain level of wealth tended to be regarded not as an obstacle to the inculcation of a competitive ethos, but as a buffer against pedagogical tyranny.

[53] Humboldt's view of the proper relationship between society and the state in education may have retained an underlying consistency by way of his "nascent nationalism"; see Sorkin, "Wilhelm von Humboldt."

[54] A striking example is Karl Salomon Zachariä, *Ueber die Erziehung des Menschengeschlechts durch den Staat* (Leipzig, 1802). Zachariä argues for individual self-determination and opening careers to talent, but only in principle. The role of the state as promoter and guarantor of "freedom" in the neohumanistic sense seems to preclude state intervention to organize an egalitarian selection process in public education.

With this shift in perspective, the enthusiasm for a common school lost a powerful rationale. In the early nineteenth century the neohumanistic version of the common school, with its emphasis on equipping all children with a "general human education," became all the more appealing in the face of the urgent need to forge national solidarity; but its enthusiasts did not see a need to organize a single competitive arena for pupils of all backgrounds. To Niethammer and others, in fact, the very notion of distinguishing pupils by their greater or lesser progress through a single introductory curriculum seemed to sacrifice concrete individuality to an artificial standard. And it is not surprising that neohumanistic reformers also ignored eighteenth-century schemes for organizing multiple hierarchies of grades, allowing the pupil a different pace of advancement in each subject; they rejected the dissection into modes of intelligence, and the matching of these to specific occupational requirements, implicit in this kind of classification. Instead the study of classical languages and literature was restored to its preeminent place, albeit in the new form of *Altertumswissenschaft*, because in theory it was uniquely suited to the concentrated and integrated exercise of all faculties. In pupils' progress in this core subject the neohumanists found an ideal measure of the kind of maturation needed for academic studies – one that testified to self-discipline at the same time that it reflected the integral unity of the personality.[55]

This principled opposition to bureaucratic classification within the schools was quite compatible with a commitment to centralizing the channel to university studies. By the turn of the century the need to concentrate pre-university education in a few large urban centers was recognized by reformers of all persuasions. If the philanthropinists blamed the many small-town Latin schools for perpetuating an obsolete Latinity, Heyne and others complained that the same institutions were the major obstacle to a revival of classical studies. Typically a social bias guided the sentiment for eliminating these schools, and it was nowhere more prominent than in a petition submitted to the Hanoverian government by seven professors at Göttingen, Heyne included, in February 1788.[56] Inspired by the recently issued *Abitur*

[55] For a striking example of this shift, see Sochatzy, *Das Neuhumanistische Gymnasium*, pp. 71–80, 147–48. For background on neohumanistic school reform in the early nineteenth century, see esp. Helmut König, *Zur Geschichte der bürgerlichen Nationalerziehung in Deutschland zwischen 1807 und 1815*, 2 vols., Monumenta Pädagogica, vols. 12–13 (Berlin, 1972–73); Karl-Ernst Jeismann, *Das preussische Gymnasium in Staat und Gesellschaft. Die Entstehung des Gymnasiums als Schule des Staates und der Gebildeten, 1787–1817*, Industrielle Welt. Schriftenreihe des Arbeitskreises für moderne Sozialgeschichte, vol. 15 (Stuttgart, 1974).

[56] The petition is in the Universitätsarchiv, Göttingen, 4 II a, file 31. The other signators were Ludwig Timotheus Spittler, J. G. H. Feder, Christian Meiners, Johann Peter Miller, Gottfried Less, and G. Planck (the last three were theologians). See also the analysis of the petition in John Stroup, *The Struggle for Identity in the Clerical Estate: Northwest German Protestant Opposition to Absolutist Policy in the Eighteenth Century*, Studies in the History of Christian Thought, vol. 33 (Leiden, 1984), pp. 155–58. Heyne had already voiced his approval of re-

in Prussia, Heyne and his colleagues hoped to counteract what they saw as a precipitate "decline" in the quality of theology students in recent years. Since students were hopelessly incompetent in Greek and Hebrew, they complained, they avoided the more advanced (and expensive) courses and limited themselves to a minimal "bread and butter" study (*Brotstudium*). One way to limit access to academic education to the truly qualified was to introduce the early, binding screening examination that the Prussian Superior School Board had just considered but rejected. But the problem was not simply oversupply; the theology faculty faced the particular dilemma that it was populated largely by poor students whose preparation was especially inadequate, and many of these issued from the numerous "corrupted" Latin schools in small towns. Hence it was also essential that academic education be centralized in two or three Latin schools in larger towns and that most of the others be converted into *Bürgerschulen* for future commercial employees and artisans. The object was not to exclude poor students altogether, the petition noted, but to admit only those with "quite exceptional natural gifts."[57]

The philanthropinists pronounced the study of dead languages irrelevant to the future professional responsibilities of most educated men, including theology candidates destined for obscure pastorates. In the very different perspective of the Göttingen professors, mastery of Greek and Hebrew (as well as Latin) was indispensable for the scholarly training in theology required of all clergymen. What was new was not the professorial lament about decline, but the expectations informing it. The Göttingen professors were intent on realizing a reform that had eluded Francke and others; the traditional *Brotstudium* – the kind with which poor students had had to suffice for centuries – would accede to an ambitious scholarly training. Minimal mastery of stylistic elegance in Latin, perhaps supplemented with a smattering of New Testament Greek – the kind of competence that even a poor boy could pick up in a small-town Latin school – would no longer substitute for ability to read and critically evaluate original texts.

The ideal of *Bildung* was only beginning to take shape in 1788, but the Göttingen petition already points to the relationship between class identity and learning that neohumanistic school reform would establish. To Heyne and his colleagues, the inadequacies of students were not due simply to a specific lack of academic training; they represented a larger cultural impoverishment, in turn rooted in material deprivation. A psychology of pov-

formers' plans to eliminate small-town Latin schools; see Christian Gottlob Heyne, "Nachricht von der gegenwärtigen Einrichtung des Königl. Pädagogii zu Ilfeld," *Archiv für die ausübende Erziehungskunst*, Theil 9 (1783): 52–53.

[57] The widespread use of tutors exacerbated the problem, the petition noted, and indeed perpetuated a kind of vicious circle. In addition to ensuring the inadequate education of their own children, families employing poor students who had learned "little or nothing" at the university were making it more difficult for the schools to attract capable men.

erty – the same trauma of deprivation that Heyne himself had experienced but overcome – seemed to make most of its victims unsuitable material for the universities. It was above all their presence that threatened to undermine the clergy's identity as a truly learned profession.

There was nothing new about viewing a certain minimum of wealth as a prerequisite for academic studies. The significance of the Göttingen petition lay in applying the usual social distinction between "means" and "poverty" to a new departure in humanistic learning and in regarding the presence of poor students as all the more problematic in the light of its heightened standards. Over the next two decades this perspective assumed central importance in the emerging ideology of *Bildung*. As both the corporatism of the learned estate and the courtly etiquette of the aristocracy lost their cultural authority, educated *Bürger* and noblemen in the government bureaucracies, for all their in-house rivalries, began to merge into a single service elite with comparable educational credentials. It was above all in this realignment that *Bildung* found its social locus. But its role in redefining the relationship between elite and mass was complex. Rationalist pedagogues like Campe and Villaume had conceived of a hierarchy of more or less educated occupations, ranged along a continuum of "useful" knowledge. The neohumanists' objection was that, in the social organization of such knowledge, the continuum would pattern into rigid fragmentation; the preoccupation with confining education to occupational training threatened to replace old-style corporatism with a new form of caste mentality. In their counterideal of *Bildung*, "general human education" would integrate the new elite into a national community. And yet an educational ideal that was posed against occupational fragmentation also cut a deep fissure across the entire society. Most obvious was that, with the renewed prestige attributed to esoteric languages, learning once more had an exclusive credential. But more decisive was the unique educational value attributed to classical studies, which implied a qualitative difference between the general education of the mass and academic *Bildung*. The implication was that one of the clearest lines of demarcation in an emerging class structure would divide the small elite of truly cultivated from the great mass of uninitiated.

The tendency to sanction a new class bifurcation in these terms is especially clear in Niethammer's book. Niethammer faulted the philanthropinists for two closely related errors: they abstracted an artificial ideal of humanity from the traits of myriad unique personalities, and they arbitrarily used occupational requirements to determine the relative degree to which the individual could realize that ideal. But in the very course of arguing against the rationalists' bureaucratic mode of classification, Niethammer came up with his own. The new school was, after all, an institutional setting; it simply could not take a unique approach to each pupil, despite the fact that the differences among individuals were of kind rather than degree.

Niethammer's compromise was to sort all pupils into two "main classes," depending on whether they were innately suited for "intellectual" or "manual" work. Committed to the universality of *Bildung* as an educational goal, he took pains to insist that for both groups the essence of education lay in stimulating intellectual activity. But the two classes nonetheless required fundamentally different orientations and materials; whereas the one learned to understand and change "the exterior world of matter" through "practical" subjects, the other cultivated and objectified an inner world of "spirit" with a literary and philosophical education focused on classical studies. Hence the new ideal of individuality required a basic choice about the proper kind of cultivation – and not, as the rationalists would have it, about the proper degree of enlightenment. The main thing was to maintain the distinction; whether it took the form of separate institutions was irrelevant.[58] Niethammer's efforts at clarification notwithstanding, the reader is left wondering whether his confidence about sorting pupils into two categories could be reconciled with his respect for individuality and the mysteries of natural entelechy – and why his two-class schema is not to be distinguished from rationalist classification merely by its brutal simplicity.

To say that the new class line was clear is not to imply that it would necessarily be unbridgeable. Rehberg wanted the educated elite to be distinguished unequivocally; that was why all educated men, and not just future specialists in the field, would share the same induction into classical studies. But the new credential was not to be the exclusive property of upper bourgeois and aristocratic families; since classical *Bildung*, unlike the traditional Latinity, commanded the respect of educated aristocrats as well as commoners, it would facilitate the climb from obscure origins to higher stations.[59] Rehberg's point was well taken, but it ignored the capacity of *Bildung* to assume a neocorporate coloration. It was a short step from evocations of a qualitatively superior inner realm – the realm to which classical studies gave access – to the assumption that *Bildung* should normally begin with an upbringing in relative affluence, free from the harsher necessities of material life, or at least that it required an early induction in a "cultured" home. Niethammer took that step at the end of his book, despite his earlier argument against allowing "thousands of accidents," including differences in parents' status and wealth, to decide pupils' fates:

> The first class includes – in addition to those pupils whose inner calling for an intellectual profession is unmistakable in view of outstanding intellectual capacity – those who are not favored with eminent intellectual gifts by nature but are endowed by fate with material goods and, free from the necesssity and pressure of

[58] *Niethammer: Philanthropinismus-Humanismus*, esp. pp. 284–302, 398–406. On Niethammer's concept of an educated elite see also Hojer, *Die Bildungslehre F. I. Niethammers*, pp. 87–91.

[59] Rehberg, "Sollen die alten Sprachen," esp. pp. 272–75.

external conditions, have the time and the means to apply to an extensive intellectual cultivation. If the latter do not have a clear place in the schema, there can nonetheless be no justified objection to this expansion of the division, since such external circumstances of the individual, like his inner characteristics, are to be regarded not as mere accident; rather both are to be regarded as assignments of a higher order that must be reckoned to the unalterable destiny of the individual.[60]

In Niethammer's reasoning the "accident" of heritable wealth, originally considered an intolerable obstruction, first becomes a legitimate advantage in Kant's morally neutral sense and ultimately figures as an intrinsic moral entitlement. The result – the new variation on the neocorporate preference for "birth" as the familial capacity to transmit a superior culture – marked one of the normative continuities underlying the shift from merit in the rationalist sense to self-cultivation. The "exterior" vocation still imposed harsh necessity on some, while allowing freedom to others. Niethammer's hybrid logic – his abstract preference for innate "talent" over "birth" and his simultaneous justification of ascriptive privilege – would remain typical of neohumanism.

Here again neohumanism often seemed to point to a radical alternative. To project a new kind of social interaction, respecting the inviolable autonomy of the individual personality, was not only to reject rationalist pedagogical manipulation; in principle the underlying instrumental character of the patron-client bond – its reduction of the other to a mere "means" – was no less objectionable, and the affective terms of its paternalist ideology were far removed from the new ideal of intimacy. And yet the rationalist objections to personal sponsorship, as ambivalent as they had been, had little echo in neohumanistic reform. More than antipathy to the rationalists' bureaucratic alternative was at work; patronage was an appropriate medium for the implicit cultural paternalism with which neohumanism applied its standards for cultivated "personality" from above.

What is striking is the authoritative subtlety with which class bias informed those standards. Well-educated commoners and aristocrats could agree that the insistence on merely "external" observance of form in courtly culture obscured the true merit of individuals. But in their Rousseauian reverence for a more "natural" sociability, the neohumanists did not mean to deny the need for standards of polite behavior. At the same time that the subject internalized the "stuff" of external reality, he realized himself in external forms. In the latter process his deeply rooted aesthetic sensibility found pleasing expression in his entire comportment. Hence Schiller found a moral justification for social "appearance" so long as it was "aesthetic." Rousseauian critics of the age went too far, he protested, when they extended their condemnation of "falseness of manners" to "politeness" (*Höf-*

[60] *Niethammer: Philanthropinismus-Humanismus*, pp. 406, 423–24.

lichkeit); reacting against the false expectation that "merits" would always be reflected in "appearance," they refused to allow the inner structure of the personality to assume "pleasing" form.[61]

As an alternative to stiff courtliness, the grace in bearing and speech that expressed the "inner" nobility of the cultivated man was "natural"; but it was also defined more or less explicitly by contrast with the crudity of plebeian society. Hence for the outsider, not familiarized with standards of polite discourse and comportment at home, form could be a pitfall rather than a means of self-expression. The poor boy's consistency in demonstrating self-discipline could easily be overshadowed by the survival of telltale physical awkwardness. In the old classicism, facility in the native tongue was assumed to be a byproduct of training in Latin; but the reverence for Greek in neohumanism went hand in hand with a systematic effort to establish High German as an educated and literary language. Indeed neohumanism heightened a new concern with form in the spoken as well as the written word – not as imitative mastery of models, but as the social "art" of communicating an intensely "individualized" intellectual and emotional substance. For the boy from an uneducated home, this was not simply a matter of shedding a dialect or mastering the logic of grammar and syntax. Form was a vehicle for grasping the substance and meaning of texts, and now it was assumed that a well-defined corpus of German "classics," distinguished from merely popular and commercial fiction, would complement the treasures of antiquity. If the outsider was no longer required to assume the stigma of an obsolete corporate identity, he also could not rely on feats of memory to compensate for inability to grasp the nuances and intricacies of a literary culture. His academic "maturity" and potential were now gauged partly by his ability to express himself comfortably in the literary idiom of his native tongue.[62]

The authority of these more or less implicit standards lay precisely in the fact that they were considered aesthetic rather than social – that the apparent universality and neutrality of an aesthetic ideal obscured its role in imposing class norms. In this sense the new ideal of *Bildung* offered a variation on the longstanding neocorporate argument that only "extraordinary" or "exceptional" boys from uneducated homes should be admitted to academic studies. What had changed were the criteria for distinguishing the rare

[61] Schiller, *Ueber die ästhetische Erziehung des Menschen*, pp. 178–79.

[62] On the need for a German classical corpus, see *Niethammer: Philanthropinismus-Humanismus*, pp. 304–25; Hojer, *Die Bildungslehre F. I. Niethammers*, pp. 138–39; Sochatzy, *Das Neuhumanistische Gymnasium*. On the new standards for "art" in spoken language, see Joachim Gessinger, *Sprache und Bürgertum. Zur Sozialgeschichte sprachlicher Verkehrsformen im Deutschland des 18. Jahrhunderts* (Stuttgart, 1980), pp. 75–89. Herder – though not a neohumanist – typified their tendency to equate the "natural" with the "artful," and both in turn with polite (though not courtly) sociability; see especially "Von der Ausbildung der Rede und Sprache in Kindern und Jünglinge" (1796), in *Herders ausgewählte Werke*, 6 vols. (Stuttgart), 3: 272–79.

exceptions from the rest – from the peasant's or artisan's son who might be as bright as pupils with means, but nonetheless was disqualified from advancing. Where there had been a distinction between the few exceptionally bright and the many more merely bright poor boys, there was now a distinction between the innately "noble" and the innately common. In the former view, the social value of intelligence was seen to hinge as a rule on the moral character formed in a particular kind of family. In the latter, intelligence and character merged into a broader cultural ideal of personality – and the social bias was all the more implicit.

Again the aesthetic had its ethical counterpart. To the extent that neohumanism freed poor students from traditional censure, it was not by allowing an "honorable" role to the motive force of ambition. Quite the contrary; neohumanistic individualism – and here is one of its many curious paradoxes from the standpoint of other kinds of individualism – rejected the rationalist ethic of self-denial in favor of a still higher order of disinterestedness. In 1807, in his departing address at Gotha, Jacobs extolled the teacher's satisfactions in imparting the "greatness and heights of antiquity" to the "sensitive souls of an uncorrrupted youth," free of all "world cleverness" and "hypocritical falseness" and "distant from all confusion of the conditions that ranks, estate and property bring into life."[63] But familiar social norms at once informed and found confirmation in this vision of the school as a haven of natural innocence. They were given oblique but clear expression in Jacobs's address on "the education of the Hellenes for morality," delivered in Munich in 1808. The superiority of ancient Greece over modern societies, he began, lay in valuing the "unselfish striving for knowledge" for its own sake, as a form of "free, self-sufficient play," over the pursuit of both material gain and "reputation."[64] One of its foundations was training in gymnastics:

> The *Gymnasien*, as schools of competition, served to purify ambition [*Ehrgeiz*]. To stimulate competition and at the same time keep it within bounds is one of the most difficult tasks of the new art of education. . . . Without this consideration any ambition that strives for the rewards of virtue without virtue, and that seeks the recognition due to worthiness through vain deception and all kinds of hypocritical falseness, is corrupting. This pitfall threatens the kind of ambition that is oriented only to knowledge, when it can by no means always be recognized whether the attitude it seeks to attain is a worthy goal, since it happens all too easily that a lower goal, enveloped in the fog of deception, appears lofty. In contrast the *Gymnasien* of the ancients were a center of the most open and upright striving; and as this striving was noble in itself and directed to a happy subject, without regard for further use

[63] Friedrich Jacobs, "Abschiedsrede im Gymnasium zu Gotha vor der Abreise nach München gehalten den 24ten October, 1807," in idem, *Vermischte Schriften*, 1: 93–94.

[64] Friedrich Jacobs, "Ueber die Erziehung der Hellenen zur Sittlichkeit," in ibid., 3 (1829): 3–5.

or future reward, no deception was thinkable, but rather the struggle was in every way honorable, and the reward merited by strict fulfillment of prescribed conditions.[65]

This idyll attests to the importance of academic competition and achievement in neohumanistic ideology, but also resonates with longstanding misgivings. Ambition, still paired with the grubby pursuit of commercial gain, is at the opposite pole from a disinterested intellectual quest. Its lack of integrity – its dishonest social presentation of the self – has become a violation of an ideal of aesthetic harmony as well as a moral offense. While the basis for moral censure shifted, the fundamental dilemma confronting the outsider remained; he was still open to the charge of calculated dissimulation, though the very need to impress potential sponsors made it difficult to avoid such behavior. And the irony is that the "useful" *Bürger* of the rationalist ethic was no longer a virtuous alternative to the "selfish," dissembling climber. Judged by the new standard of "honorable" disinterestedness, this kind of devotion to duty was not essentially different from an approach to learning merely as a means to personal advantage; both were crudely instrumental and materialistic, and both contradicted the new reverence for "inner" nobility as an end in itself. Academic achievement bespoke inner nobility only when it sprang from a higher purity of motive. This was a test of character that was difficult to apply and that few could be expected to pass.

[65] Ibid., pp. 23–24. The claim that humanistic scholarship, particularly in the form of classical studies, inculcated a uniquely disinterested self-discipline would become commonplace in nineteenth-century apologias for "liberal education." See Ben Knights, *The Idea of the Clerisy in the Nineteenth Century* (Cambridge, 1978), pp. 178–213. Knights also emphasizes the social bifurcation between the initiated and the mass that this ideal implied, and notes its tendency to see a minimal level of inherited material security and comfort as the usual prerequisite for this kind of virtue.

10

Professional ideologies: the making of a teaching corps

In the late eighteenth century the secular ethic of vocation became a vital idiom for new forms of collective consciousness as well as for new modes of individualism. The most striking case in point is the reform movement among teachers in the Latin schools and *Gymnasien*. Here again, though, a shift in vocabulary and rhetoric requires explanation. As early as the 1760s schoolmen had begun to fashion a professional ideology for their occupation. In the development of that ideology over the next two decades a larger trend is especially clear; the utilitarian ethic of Enlightenment rationalism was patterning into self-conscious – and self-serving – occupational identities. The rationalist ethic survived, albeit in muted form, into the nineteenth century; but it was overlaid by the idiom of *Bildung*, and the overlay signified important changes in defining the distinctive social status, intellectual foundation, and public function of an educated profession.[1]

[1] For an early example of the typical reform themes, see Martin Ehlers, *Gedanken von der zur Verbesserung der Schulen nothwendigen Erfordernissen* (Altona and Lübeck, 1766). Ehlers was a student of Gesner and an associate of Basedow and had become rector in Segeburg. Still useful as an introduction to school reform is Friedrich Paulsen, *Der gelehrte Unterricht im Zeichen des Neuhmanismus, 1740–1892, Geschichte des Gelehrten Unterrichts auf den deutschen Schulen und Universitäten vom Ausgang des Mittelalters bis zur Gegenwart*, vol. 2 (3rd ed.: Berlin and Leipzig, 1921); Conrad Rethwisch, *Der Staatsminister Freiherr von Zedlitz und Preussens höheres Schulwesen im Zeitalter Friedrichs des Grossen* (2nd ed.: Strasbourg, 1886); Paul Schwartz, *Die Gelehrtenschulen Preussens unter dem Oberschulkollegium (1787–1806) und das Abiturientenexamen*, 3 vols., Monumenta Germaniae Paedagogica, vols. 46, 48, 50 (Berlin, 1910–12). On reform in Prussia see also Karl-Ernst Jeismann, *Das preussische Gymnasium in Staat und Gesellschaft. Die Entstehung des Gymnasiums als Schule des Staates und der Gebildeten*, Industrielle Welt. Schriftenreihe des Arbeitskreises für moderne Sozialgeschichte, vol. 15 (Stuttgart, 1974); Detlef K. Müller, *Sozialstruktur und Schulsystem: Aspekte zum Strukturwandel des Schulwesens im 19 Jahrhundert*, Studien zum Wandel von Gesellschaft und Bildung im Neunzehnten Jahrhundert, vol. 7 (Göttingen, 1977). For regional studies see Franklin Kopitzsch, "Reformversuche und Reform der Gymnasien und Lateinschulen in Schleswig-Holstein im Zeitalter der Aufklärung," in idem, *Erziehungs- und Bildungsgeschichte Schleswig-Holsteins von der Aufklärung bis zum Kaiserreich* (Neumünster, 1981): 61–88; Hanno Schmitt, *Schulreform im aufgeklärten Absolutismus. Leistungen, Widersprüche, und Grenzen philanthropinischer Reformpraxis im Herzogtum Braunschweig – Wolfenbüttel 1785–1790*, Studien und Dokumentationen zur deutschen Bildungsgeschichte, vol. 12 (Weinheim and Basel, 1979); Volker Wehrmann, *Die Aufklärung in Lippe. Ihre Bedeutung für die Politik, Schule und Geistesleben* (Detmold, 1972).

The term "professional ideology" requires its own introduction. In recent decades, on both sides of the Atlantic, there has been a noticeable rise in public resentment of the wealth, status, and power attached to at least some species of professional expertise. The new mood has provoked sociologists and historians to probe the historical origins of modern professionalism. Why have some occupational groups succeeded in persuading both the surrounding society and the state that, by virtue of the knowledge they command, they have a legitimate claim to a distinctive status? On what grounds should they be trusted to serve as mediating agents of public authority in areas of vital importance to the society as a whole? Invariably professions have justified themselves by arguing that the knowledge in question includes an expertise indispensable to the public welfare; that the profession embodies (or will embody) both expert competence and disinterested dedication to a service ethic; that both attributes are guaranteed by competitive achievement in academic education, combined with specialized training under the control of the group itself.[2] Such claims are in some ways reminiscent of the corporate ideologies of old-regime Europe; but they also articulate distinctly modern forms of social consciousness, their conceptions of service, merit, and achievement originating in Enlightenment rationalism and anticipating (or reflecting) the class structures to which corporate hierarchies acceded. To characterize the rhetoric as ideology is to emphasize that it was (and is) self-serving, but not to imply, as is often implied in current attacks on the professions, a calculated effort to hoodwink the public. Quite the contrary: the underlying strength of the ideology lies in its enthusiasts' all too sincere equation of the role and status claimed for the profession with the only rational order of things, in their confidence that the self-interest of the group really does coincide with the public welfare.

At this generic level the ideologies of a wide variety of occupations in quite different historical environments can be seen as variations on a common logic. But the more recent sociological and historical literature on the professions has emphasized differences in national context that earlier models for "professionalization," generalizing as they did largely from the national experiences of England and the United States, tended to gloss over. The Anglo-American professional ideologies of the nineteenth century were concerned primarily with staking out well-protected monopolies within the rapidly expanding markets for various services and with asserting

[2] See esp. Thomas L. Haskell, ed., *The Authority of Experts. Studies in History and Theory* (Bloomington, Ind., 1984). This collection of essays is distinguished from most of the literature on professionalism and "professionalization" both by its historical depth and by its sensitivity to issues of epistemology and ethics. It should be of considerable help to historians (as well as sociologists) who want to extricate the analysis of the cultural significance of the modern professions from outworn models. For an example of the current rejection of professional claims see Randall Collins, *The Credential Society. An Historical Sociology of Education and Stratification* (New York, 1979).

new forms of cultural authority in response to the spread of market relations and the dissolution of traditional values that such relations seemed to portend. The obvious explanatory backdrop for both orientations was the breakneck expansion of industrial capitalism.[3] It is a reflection of a quite different national context and historical sequence for "professionalization" that in the last third of the eighteenth century German schoolmen already were sounding the themes that would become the stock-in-trade of nineteenth-century professional ideologies. The salient difference lies in the overarching (or underlying) agent of modernity; in the German states the development of public bureaucracies – of the administrative and judicial officialdom constituting the state – reached a relatively advanced stage before the expansion of industrial capitalism.

The precocity of teaching – its vanguard role in constructing the ideological profile of a modern professional world – was in direct response to the fact that it had been crippled by a dual legacy within old-regime society. In a context in which legitimate mobility was contingent on assuming a "public" office, teachers occupied quasi-offices, allowing only a marginal corporate status and relegating them to the fringe of an academic and official elite. This stigma was inseparable from another; for poor students without well-placed connections, the Latin schools were the dumping ground – and many never escaped it. If some ought never to have pursued academic studies (as the stereotype would have it), others were tragic victims of the blockage of talent and merit. In the course of securing teaching a new role and status, the reform movement aimed at making it a career open to talent by keeping out the unqualified and, as important, by guaranteeing upward mobility to deserving young men of plebeian origins. Accentuating utilitarian logic in some ways and dissolving its antinomies in others, the movement made the secular ethic of vocation an ideological rationale for both collective and individual mobility.

In modern professionalization, a specific kind of knowledge becomes a source of power, but the prestige of the group reflects the fact that power is exercised as a legitimate form of cultural authority. Here again the social situs of teaching accounts for its precocity. Precisely because the recruitment pool for the new profession would be unusually plebeian – because it would not derive its prestige from a corporate legacy – the aspiration to achieve a new status had to rest on a militant, far-reaching claim to exercise

[3] See, e.g., Burton J. Bledstein, *The Culture of Professionalism. The Middle Class and the Development of Higher Education in America* (New York, 1976); Thomas L. Haskell, "Professionalization as Cultural Reform," *Humanities in Society* 1:2 (1978): 103–14; Magali Sarfatti Larson, *The Rise of Professionalism. A Sociological Analysis* (Berkeley, Calif., ca. 1977). Larson's book is an important neo-Marxist contribution, relevant to the history of the professions in continental Europe despite its Anglo-American focus. For an enlightening assessment of Larson's argument, see the review article by Michael Schudson in *Theory and Society* 9 (1980): 215–29.

cultural authority. There is no better example of the effort to win recognition as a new "community of the competent," commanding a vital area of public service, that lay at the heart of professionalization.

But the social and institutional locus of the occupation meant that the quest for collective status, power, and authority had to operate on several levels and in several directions at once; in that regard teaching anticipates the complexity of the German variant on professionalization. At the local level, market dependence did not bring corrosive change; it operated within a web of local entanglements, keeping teachers in bondage to stubbornly traditional familes and communities within the institutional structure of the old regime. In the Anglo-American world, the ideological norm was the "free" profession; even when the state was expected to sanction professional monopolies with licensing procedures, freedom meant independence from public bureaucracies as well as relative invulnerability to market forces. The German variant – the one teachers' ideology adumbrated in the effort to escape local tangles – justified a direct symbiosis between professionalization and the expansion of the modern state.[4] The goal was that "half-bureaucratic, half-professional" status that would characterize the core of the German middle class in the nineteenth century.[5]

But the claim to exercise professional authority was not simply directed against old-regime constraints; it was also a response to distinctly modern threats, and by the turn of the century a meddling, potentially repressive state had become the chief among them. This is not to imply that in Ger-

[4] For an important analysis of a comparable professional ideology see Ute Frevert, *Krankheit als politisches Problem 1770–1880*, Kritische Studien zur Geschichtswissenschaft, vol. 62 (Göttingen, 1984). Frevert's book attests to the importance of Michel Foucault's work on "disciplines" in reorienting the history of the professions. See esp. *The Archaeology of Knowledge and The Discourse on Language*, trans. A. M. Sheridan Smith (New York, 1976). Foucault's efforts to define the relationship between social interests and ideas and to distinguish his own approach from that of intellectual history have not always been enlightening. For a helpful explication of the relevance of his thought to the history of the professions, see Jan Goldstein, "Foucault among the Sociologists: The 'Disciplines' and the History of the Professions," *History and Theory* 13 (1984): 170–92.

[5] Twenty years ago Lenore O'Boyle pointed to differences between the Anglo-American "free" professions and the continental "half-bureaucratic, half-professional" middle-class elite; but she may have oversimplified the ideological posture of the latter group by including it within a broadly liberal consensus. Lenore O'Boyle, "The Middle Class in Western Europe, 1815–1848," *American Historical Review* 71 (1966): 826–45. On the importance of the bureaucratic framework for "professionalization" in Germany see esp. Dietrich Rüschemeyer, *Lawyers and Their Society. A Comparative Study of the Legal Profession in Germany and in the United States* (Cambridge, Mass., 1973); idem, "Professionalisierung. Theoretische Probleme für die vergleichende Geschichtsforschung," *Geschichte und Gesellschaft* 6:3 (1980): 311–25. An important effort to sort out similarities and differences between Anglo-American and German "professionalization" and to distinguish kinds of professional "autonomy" is Charles E. McClelland, "Zur Professionalisierung der akademischen Berufe in Deutschland," in Werner Conze and Jürgen Kocka, eds., *Bildungsbürgertum im 19. Jahrhundert*, Teil 1 *Bildungssystem und Professionalisierung in internationalen Vergleichen* (Stuttgart, 1985): 233–47. For comparative perspectives see also Konrad H. Jarausch, ed., *The Transformation of Higher Learning, 1860–1930* (Stuttgart, 1982).

many the new professionalism and authoritarian government entered open confrontation. The conception of teaching itself as a career open to talent conveyed a characteristically German "bourgeois" aspiration, remarkably tame in comparison with the visceral hatred of an entire establishment that developed in the Parisian subintelligentsia on the eve of the Revolution. Radical opposition to the state was incompatible with the equation of profession and office; it would have pitted teachers against the very agent of progressive change in which they placed their hopes.

But political awareness and strategy can take a great variety of forms; we artificially narrow the eighteenth-century field of possibilities, and risk missing much of its nuance, by taking our defining criteria from nineteenth- and twentieth-century ideologies. If the claim to authority in professional ideology was "apolitical," it was so in the specific sense of aspiring to avoid the modern "liberal" arena of competing opinions and interests. The German professional alternative nonetheless projected a new public and, in a limited but important sense, a political space. *Beruf* as profession was seen as the essential vehicle of participation in modern public life; as in the traditional link between property and virtue in civic humanism, it would ground the political identity and the *vita activa* of the enlightened *Bürger*.[6] In the wake of Woellner's crackdown in Prussia, there was reason to wonder whether the reformers' vision of a public politics had been anything more than a momentary illusion. But illusion is the stuff of ideology. From this angle, as from others, the shift from utilitarian rationalism to neohumanism was as much an adjustment of strategy as it was a redefinition of objectives.

THE TEACHERS' CAUSE

By the 1780s it had become common for reform-minded schoolmen to use graduation exercises and other public events in their schools to carry their message to the public. On one such occasion at his gymnasium in Breslau, Lieberkühn contrasted the shameful recent past of schoolteaching with its hopeful present:

> How far behind the art and science of the doctor, the legal scholar, the pastor the noble and difficult art of the educator had to stand! How timidly even the better schoolmen drew back into the shadows!. . . Now more justice is being done to his

[6] On civic humanism see esp. Istvan Hont and Michael Ignatieff, eds., *Wealth and Virtue. The Shaping of Political Economy in the Scottish Enlightenment* (Cambridge, 1983); J. G. A. Pocock, *Virtue, Commerce, and History. Essays on Political Thought and History, Chiefly in the Eighteenth Century* (Cambridge, 1985). On the very different ideal of virtue that arose from the ranks of the Parisian subintelligentsia, see esp. Robert Darnton, "The High Enlightenment and the Low-Life of Literature," in idem, *The Literary Underground of the Old Regime* (Cambridge, Mass., 1982).

occupation everywhere; he can present himself with a modest awareness of his calling [*Berufs*]; the nobler and more comprehending portion of his fellow *Bürger* appreciate his merits. . . . The occupation of educators is now developing itself into a distinct profession [*Stand*], inspired by its particular spirit, performing its tasks as a distinct art, dedicated to it not merely out of necessity or coercion, but out of true inclination and, if I may say so, with a kind of artist's love![7]

There is no more succinct statement of the reformers' aspirations, and no better example of the distillation of eighteenth-century thought into a professional ideology. Traditionally relegated to the shadowy underlayer of the *Gelehrtenstand*, without the prestige and credibility accorded the university-educated doctors, jurists, and clergymen who formed its core, teachers now wanted their place in the sun. In their claim to that place, "profession," in its distinctly modern sense, joined the other meanings attached to *Beruf*, and the entire cluster of values about inner entelechy, work, merit, and service in the secular ethic of vocation became the idiom of a professional consciousness.

For all their confidence about winning over the "more comprehending portion" of the public, reformers like Lieberkühn were taking a great risk. If schoolmen were distinctly second-class citizens of the clerical estate, they also derived a certain minimal prestige and credibility from their association with its higher echelons. Now the reformers were bent on eradicating this clerical identity; the shabby entryway to the clerical edifice would become a separate but equal professional realm. What made this act of secession seem feasible in the early days of reform was the new "art" of pedagogy, and not simply because its fund of expertise could be said to require an entirely new training route, segregating future schoolmen from future cler-

[7] Philipp Julius Lieberkühn, "Rede von der ächten Verbesserung des Schulwesens in unsern Zeitalter," in idem, *Kleine Schriften, nebst dessen Lebensbeschreibung und einigen charakteristischen Briefen an Hrn. Professor Stuve*, ed. L. F. G. E. Gedike (Züllichau and Freystadt, 1791), pp. 227–28. This analysis of reform thought is culled from a great variety of sources; for representative contributions see Lieberkühn, *Kleine Schriften*; Friedrich Gedike, *Aristoteles und Basedow; oder, Fragmente über Erziehung und Schulwesen bei den Alten und Neuen* (Berlin and Leipzig, 1779); idem, *Gesammlete Schulschriften*, 2 vols. (Berlin, 1789–95); Friedrich Koch, *Einige Gedanken über die Bildung des Schulmannes* (Stettin, 1795); Georg David Koeler, *Ueber die Policey und äussere Einrichtung der Gymnasien* (Lemgo, 1789); Carl Ludwig Friedrich Lachmann, *Ueber die Umschaffung vieler unzweckmässigen Schulen in zweckmässig eingerichtete Bürgerschulen, und die Vereinigung der Militärschulen mit den Bürgerschulen* (Berlin, 1800); Friedrich Gabriel Resewitz, *Gedanken, Vorschläge und Wünsche zur Verbesserung der öffentlichen Erziehung als Materialen zur Pädagogik* (Berlin and Stettin, 1777–78); Johann Stuve, *Kleine Schriften gemeinnützigen Inhalts*, ed. Joachim Heinrich Campe (Berlin, 1794). There is also a substantial periodical literature; for especially relevant contributions see *Magazin für Schulen und die Erziehung Ueberhaupt*, ed. Johann Friedrich Scipperlin (Frankfurt and Leipzig, 1767–72); *Archiv für die ausübende Erziehungskunst*, ed. Karl Christian Heyler; *Pädagogisches Jahrbuch*, ed. Jeremias Nicolaus Eyring (Göttingen, 1783–88); *Allgemeine Revision des gesamten Schul- und Erziehungswesens*, ed. Joachim Heinrich Campe (Hamburg, 1785–92) (cited hereafter as AR); *Braunschweigisches Journal*, ed. Joachim Heinrich Campe et al. (Braunschweig, 1788–93) (cont'd. as *Schleswigsches Journal*).

gymen long before they left the universities. Teachers found in the pedagogical art what traditional learning had not offered; the school became, in its own right, a locus for the lifelong dedication to work that was supposed to give a sense of purpose to the enlightened *Bürger*. For the generation represented by Gesner and Ernesti, and more clearly for the next generation, the classroom ceased to be an appendage of the study; it became the central workplace for a new professional expertise requiring an early commitment, extensive training, and a lifelong effort to align practice more closely with theory and keep abreast of new developments in the field.

Rationalist theology helped woo young men away from mainstream clerical careers, in part by undercutting traditional motives and rationales for religious calling. If this shift of course was powered by a great deal of idealism, it also was taken with the awareness that, in income, status, and career prospects, teaching was still notoriously inferior to the clergy proper – hence the urgent note in reformers' insistence that young men dedicate themselves to teaching in response to the voice within, and not to the dictates of external circumstances. To men who had to justify a fateful turning point in their lives, the conversion to pedagogy became an act of self-affirmation, the commitment it required an ethical alternative to the self-denial of Pietist conversion. The celebration of work as the fulfillment of a "natural" inner entelechy had intensely personal meaning.

The reform-minded teacher had another reason to see his own career as a path freely chosen: his pressing need to distinguish himself from the great bulk of his colleagues. The enthusiasm for reform, gaining momentum over several generations from midcentury onward, produced a new breed, but they remained a small minority. The young militants of the 1780s were well aware that, as in earlier decades, teaching was usually a regrettable necessity, if not a last resort, for young men without alternatives. If reformers avoided (or at least overcame) the urge to escape to a pastorate, but at the same time resisted sinking into the bitter resignation to which so many of their colleagues succumbed, that was because they prided themselves on forming the vanguard of a profession in the making. It was essential to that self-image that their entry into teaching be explained as a commitment freely made, or at least that with the benefit of hindsight it turn out to have been the right road taken.

By 1788 Gedike had convinced himself that teaching was his true vocation, despite the fact that he had become a schoolman more by "accident" than by "choice" and had been determined to escape at the first opportunity.[8] If in his case the conviction of vocation was in response to gratifying career advancement, in others it was in defiance of bitter disappointments.

[8] Friedrich Gedike, "Jubilrede von den Freuden des Schulmanns" (Dec., 1788), in idem, *Schulschriften*, 1: 469–92.

Martin Ehlers, one of the pathbreakers, recalled that "strong natural inclinations" and a suitable "temperamental makeup" had combined with an appreciation of the "inner value" of the "school office" to propel him into teaching despite the "heroic sacrifice" it required.[9] In a letter to Campe in 1787, written in the hope of securing an appointment in Brunswick, Karl Traugott Thieme, a rector in Merseburg, complained that the benighted opposition to his reform efforts on the part of colleagues, superiors, and "a large segment of the public" deprived him of the personal satisfaction for which Gedike was so grateful. He would even accept a lower income, he assured Campe, "if only God would provide me in this life with the happiness of working with joy and consorting with people who recognize that I mean well." What made his predicament all the more tragic was the commitment he had brought to his work from the start; "I was not thrown into [teaching] by a theological shipwreck," he recalled, but despite "prospects" in the clergy "voluntarily devoted myself to school life in the conviction that I had an inner vocation for it."[10]

If the true teacher entered his calling out of choice rather than necessity, he was also born, not made. Professional training, as critical as it was, was not a substitute for suitable raw material. The rational alternative to a "theological shipweck" was the deliberate, guided self-examination needed to identify inborn talents and inclinations. Native intelligence, though indispensable for grasping the proper teaching method and mastering particular school subjects, would not compensate for a lack of innate traits of temperament. It was above all a natural affection for and ease with children that distinguished the true teacher from the ineffectual pedant. The sine qua non for an effective classroom lecturer, Gedike observed, was not erudition or even clarity, but a "liveliness" that "is more independent of theory and study than all other teaching skills, and is more than any other a gift of nature."[11]

It was one thing to contrast the born teacher with the pastor manqué, but quite another to extrude considerations of "birth" from the profile of a regenerated teaching corps. Some reformers looked forward to the day when the teaching profession, commanding "respectable" incomes and far more prestige, would have no trouble attracting suitable recruits from prosperous and "cultured" families, and outsiders without means would be the rare exceptions. But the more common tendency – one drawing strength from reformers' own conviction of vocation – was to turn an unfortunate

[9] See the "*Vorrede*" to Martin Ehlers, *Sammlung kleiner das Schul- und Erziehungswesen betreffender Schriften* (Flensburg and Leipzig, 1776).

[10] Thieme's letter to Campe (June 25, 1787) has been published in Schmitt, *Schulreform*, A-182 to A-184.

[11] Friedrich Gedike, "Einige Gedanken über den mündlichen Vortrag des Schulmanns," in idem, *Schulschriften*, 1: 416–17. See also, e.g., Ehlers, *Gedanken*, passim; Lieberkühn, *Kleine Schriften*, p. 242; Koch, *Einige Gedanken*, p. 15.

necessity into a peculiar virtue. The dumping ground of the learned estate would become a profession embodying the preference for "talent" over "birth" – and, in more inclusive terms, of individual choice over social ascription – in a rational society. It was to lure and hold this talent from below, but at the same time to compensate for its plebeian origins, that the occupation needed a dramatic upgrading.

If a rational society matched inner vocations to appropriate occupations, it also made the rewards for work contingent on the relative importance of its contribution to the general welfare. These were the twin axioms of professional ideology; the skeletal logic around which Martin Ehlers fleshed out a reform agenda in the mid-1760s, they became the formulaic mainstays of reformers' appeals for higher, more secure teaching incomes and a broad range of other improvements in the 1770s and 1780s.[12] The more effusive rhetoric was designed to demonstrate that the teaching corps, as neglected and impotent as it was in its present state, could be "one of the most useful professions in the state," if not "the most useful."[13] In a sense the claim itself was merely a variation on an old theme. It had long been more or less implicit in the corporate defense of legal privilege that the group in question in effect earned its status by virtue of its contribution to the social organism. Whereas in old-regime corporatism a historic status helped maintain a static order, however, reformers now claimed an entirely new status for teaching, appropriate to its awe-inspiring range of services in realizing a more rational future. Entrusted with new generations of the educated elite, teachers were in a unique position to disseminate the "useful" knowledge on which material progress depended, to uproot religious superstition, to inculcate the work discipline and incentive to achieve that distinguished the productive *Bürger* from the parasite, to instill loyalty to the state and respect for its laws, to implant the public spirit that would replace selfish familial and corporate mentalities.

The new status would be marked unequivocally by a new scale of teaching incomes. In the proverbial *misère* of German *Gelehrten*, the poverty-stricken schoolteacher was, and has remained, emblematic; but there were myriad degrees of misery, since the local variety of factors determining income level – the generosity of original endowments, their fate since the sixteenth century, demographic patterns, the state of the local economy, and so on – allowed nothing like a regularly graded scale. The rough distribution of incomes at the end of the century can be gauged from the inspection reports on Prussian schools, most of them in small towns, from 1788 to 1805. Our sample includes 219 teachers in 42 schools (out of a total of 224 regular teaching positions in these institutions) for whom both income and age were

[12] Ehlers, *Gedanken*, passim.

[13] See, e.g., Koeler, *Ueber die Policey*, esp. pp. 4–9; Lieberkühn, *Kleine Schriften*, passim; Gedike, *Schulschriften*, 1: 469–92.

Table 10.1. *Prussian schoolteachers: incomes*

Income[a]	Percentage
Less than 200 thaler	45.2 (99)[b]
200–99	29.2 (64)
300–99	16.9 (37)
400–99	3.7 (8)
500–99	3.2 (7)
600 and above	1.8 (4)
Total	100.0(219)

Note: Subtotals are in parentheses. The sample comprises 42 schools. Excluded were 5 vacant positions.

[a] Where the income as cantor, organist, sexton (*Küster*), university professor, or clerical official was indicated, it was excluded from the teaching income for the position. Most of the income estimates do *not* include the monetary value of the free lodgings provided for most teaching positions. Many also exclude the monetary value of free heating material and small contributions in kind.

[b] Two "assistant" positions (*Kollaborator*) at the *Stadtgymnasium* in Halle, each with 40 thaler and no other compensation, seemed too makeshift to be included in the sample. Other *Kollaborator* positions were included.

Source: Paul Schwartz, *Die Gelehrtenschulen Preussen unter dem Oberschulkollegium (1787–1806) und das Abiturientenexamen*, 3 vols., Monumenta Germaniae Paedagogica, vols. 46, 48, 50 (Berlin, 1910–12).

indicated. At its pinnacle stood two gymnasium directors in Berlin: Büsching with 996 thaler, and Gedike with 854 thaler. But they were practically in a class by themselves; the highest-paying positions in more than four-fifths of the schools were less than 500 thaler, and indeed in three-quarters of the schools they were less than 400 thaler. A hefty 74.4 percent of all the positions had less than 300 thaler, and nearly half – 45.2 percent – had less than 200 thaler (Table 10.1).

Where the poverty line lay was, of course, a relative judgment; in teachers' estimations, the right to fulfill basic human wants often shaded into a claim to "higher" but no less legitimate "needs," peculiar to educated men. What the figures demonstrate is that on the whole teachers' incomes stood well below those of any other group of university-educated men in public employment. Though not poverty-stricken, the rector making 400 thaler per year had reason to feel deprived when he thought about the considerably better endowed pastorates of local churches and the salaries of councilors in the administrative and judicial bureaucracies. Many of the teachers at the broad base of the pyramid, with incomes of less than 200 thaler, had free lodging; but most of them lacked the substantial contributions in kind that cushioned rural pastors against rising food prices. Those with families were probably closer in standard of living to unskilled laborers than to skilled artisans with small shops. The age distribution lends additional pathos to their situation. The declining percentages – from 30.1 in the 30–39 age group to 16.4 in the 50–59 group – are not due simply to natural attrition; clearly some teachers were moving into pastorates, though often after a long wait. But for many others the "waiting rooms" had become, or were well on their way to becoming, permanent abodes; 50.2 percent of the entire sample were over 40, and 29.6 percent were over 50. Many of those who stayed were relegated permanently to the bottom ranks. 68.9 percent of the 40–49 age group and 75.0 percent of the 50–59 age group had less than 300 thaler (42.2 percent of the former group, and 36.1 percent of the latter group, had less than 200 thaler!) (Table 10.2).

A low-paying position might suffice to support a single man en route to a pastorate, if only for a few years. It left older men with the unenviable choice of continuing in an involuntary bachelorhood or raising a family on the edge of poverty and plunging into debt when crises like inflationary food prices struck. Conscientious, qualified schoolmen ground down by the latter predicament were the most compelling argument for both a "respectable" income scale and career "prospects." One thinks of Rector Seeliger of the Grosse Schule in Potsdam, whose income of 244 thaler was neither unusually generous nor particularly abysmal. On his inspection tour in 1788, Gedike found Seeliger to be a devoted and skilled schoolman, but one suffering from real want. Having read "the best pedagogical writings" to compensate for the inadequacies of his early education, the forty-year-old rector found himself, in his own assessment, "an entirely propertyless man burdened with five children, with a pitiful income in an expensive town, sick in body, required to give instruction six to eight hours per day in order to be able to survive in need, with an extremely depressed temperament as a result of concern for his school and his own helplessness, and excluded from enjoyment of social recreation."[14]

In the more militant appeals for higher incomes, new expectations broke through the conventional pieties about the compensatory "inner" satisfactions of an ascetic devotion to duty and teachers' immunity to the *Luxus* spreading through the wealthier classes. The new tone admitted in all frankness that the teacher was only human; that he too had aspirations to a certain level of material comfort; that he too wanted his labor to be rewarded with a decent standard of living, well below the extravagance of the wealthy but attesting to a modest bourgeois affluence. In the logic of an emerging profes-

[14] Schwartz, *Gelehrtenschulen*, pp. 513–14. As a young man Winckelmann had endured one of these small-town positions, as conrector in Seehausen (Brandenburg); Carl Justi, *Winckelmann in Deutschland. Mit Skizzen zur Kunst- und Gelehrtengeschichte des achtzehnten Jahrhunderts* (Leipzig, 1866), pp. 117–22.

Table 10.2. *Prussian schoolteachers: distribution of incomes in age groups*

			Income (thaler)					
Age	Total	% of sample	Under 200	200–99	300–99	400–99	500–99	600 and over
20–29	43	19.6	69.8(30)	20.9 (9)	4.7 (2)	4.7(2)	—	—
30–39	66	30.1	37.9(25)	27.3(18)	28.8(19)	1.5(1)	3.0(2)	1.5(1)
40–49	45	20.6	42.2(19)	26.7(12)	13.3 (6)	4.4(2)	8.9(4)	4.4(2)
50–59	36	16.4	36.1(13)	38.9(14)	16.7 (6)	5.6(2)	2.8(1)	—
60–69	23	10.5	30.4 (7)	43.5(10)	17.4 (4)	4.4(1)	—	4.4(1)
70 and over	6	2.7	66.7 (4)	16.7 (1)	16.7 (1)	—	—	—

Note: Figures are percentages; subtotals in parentheses.

sional ideology, this was not to plead a case for blatant selfishness, but to make enlightened self-interest an instrument of service. Since teachers needed the rewards in question to function effectively, their self-interest coincided with the public welfare; in that limited but important sense, the familiar antinomy between duty and self-interest was bypassed in the vision of a professional mission.

Professional efficacy was a function of social authority; and the status underpinning that authority required a respectable scale of teaching incomes, commensurate with those of the clergy and other comparable groups. "The necessary respect for the teacher suffers in the less enlightened segment of the public and especially among the younger people subordinate to them," the staff of the Minden gymnasium explained in 1788, "when they cannot even show themselves publicly with the respectability suitable to the office and its dignity without being made ashamed by unmistakable marks of need."[15] The threadbare coat was an occupational handicap as well as a personal embarrassment. Even the needed reduction in daily hours of instruction was justified ultimately in these terms; the resulting leisure time would allow the teacher to "restore his powers," and hence would enhance his performance in the demanding task of instructing boys and young men day after day.[16]

The reformers were at once recasting traditional norms for corporate "station" and solidarity in utilitarian terms and arguing around the more inflexible prescriptions of the utilitarian ethic. Their logic harnessed the legitimate pursuit of self-interest to the functional imperatives of service. If it justified collective mobility for the occupation as a whole, it also sanctioned the kind of career mobility for individuals that old-style corporate bodies, relying heavily on legal and de facto inheritance to fill the ranks of their internal hierarchies, did not allow. Gedike was well aware that his own meteoric career was an exception to the rule. He had in mind the hundreds of men trapped in positions with paltry incomes, particularly in the stifling small-town environment of most Latin schools, when he lamented teachers' lack of "prospects in the future." What such men needed to sustain enthusiasm in office, he observed, was "the perspective accorded to every other *Stande* of lifting [oneself] in stages through outstanding *Verdienste* out of the narrow sphere into a wider, higher, more brilliant one."[17]

For all the inflated rhetoric about the preeminence of teaching in a hierarchy of more or less "public" functions, its rank-and-file practitioners

[15] Schwartz, *Gelehrtenschulen*, 3: 365. In a report to the Superior School Board on Aug. 24, 1802, Professor Fuchs of the gymnasium in Elbing was described as "a very good teacher"; but "in his entire exterior," the report added, "the oppression of his situation is visible." Fuchs had an income of 138 thaler, 45 groschen. Ibid., 1: 331.

[16] See esp. Friedrich Gedike, "Allgemeine Erfordernisse zur Verbesserung des Schulwesens," in idem, *Aristoteles*, pp. 237–64.

[17] Gedike, *Schulschriften*, 1: 471.

would have to accept a modest rung on the ladder of incomes and prestige in public employment; they could not expect to approach the heights of tenured administrative and judicial officialdom, even under a radically new dispensation. This obvious constraint on the occupation as a whole made it all the more vital to morale that teachers have "prospects" within it – that they be able to prove individual merit and reap the appropriate rewards. Appointment to a school directorship should be made in recognition of outstanding performance as a classroom teacher (and perhaps as a publisher in the field of education as well), even if that meant preferring a younger colleague to men with seniority. Movement from school to school (and from community to community) should be organized into an orderly promotion system, distributing appointments in schools with relatively high income scales and attractive teaching conditions to the most qualified applicants. The elite of the profession would be the schoolmen who, by dint of proven achievement in the field, ascended to supervisory positions in the new administrative hierarchies of public school systems.

In these calls for advancement, the passage from a secular ethic of vocation to a distinctly modern professionalism is especially well marked. Again, within the range of expectations appropriate to a new station, self-interest and service were reconciled; a profession that constituted itself as an outlet for legitimate ambition – so the underlying logic went – spurred its members to greater effectiveness and hence greater "usefulness."[18] If work was to be an appropriate vehicle for an inner calling, it had to provide ongoing possibilities for self-realization through disciplined achievement. A genuine profession structured a "career" (*Laufbahn*) in the modern sense; it embodied the principle of merit in its internal organization (if not in its recruitment) by carrying the deserving through an orderly progress, an ascending sequence of rewards. In the language of a longstanding Lutheran distinction, the predictable trajectory of the "external" *Beruf* would reflect – and confirm – the growth of the inner man. He grew in competition with others, but reformers – far from seeing a potential conflict between individual competition and corporate solidarity – saw the one as a cement for the other. To make a shared definition of merit the criterion for promotions was to provide a new and eminently defensible foundation for hierarchy within the profession.

With its alternative professional hierarchy, the new ideology modernized the meaning of corporate solidarity as well as vocational commitment. The problem was not simply that teachers were subject to degrading dependence on external patronage; their internecine warfare made it all the more difficult to command respect in the surrounding society. In the Latin schools

[18] See, e.g., Ehlers, *Gedanken*, pp. 309–11; Koch, *Einige Gedanken*, p. 13; Lachmann, *Umschaffung*, pp. 75–77; Koeler, *Ueber die Policey*, pp. 4–19.

and *Gymnasien* the more or less intricate hierarchies of official titles corresponded, at least roughly, to the hierarchies of grades, which were ranged in ascending order of prestige and desirability from the rudimentary lessons at the lower levels to the more scholarly instruction reserved for advanced pupils. But real power was another matter. The rector or director, usually in charge of the *Prima* and perhaps the *Sekunda*, might use his rank to override objections to promoting boys to his classes; but in the daily operation of the school each grade was the largely autonomous preserve of a single teacher, who received his own school fees. Nor were the titular hierarchies matched by regularly graded scales of incomes; fee rates in the entering grades were lower than at higher levels, but the total income for each position depended on the number of pupils at a particular grade level as well as the vagaries of local endowments over several centuries. Colleagues were apt to nurse grievances about income disparities, while the lack of an effective chain of command gave all the more significance to questions of precedence. The result – surely exaggerated in popular stereotype but confirmed in the reform literature – was that teachers were prone to engage in petty but bitter strife, caricaturing the concern with fine distinctions in rank in corporate bodies.[19]

Hence structuring careers within the profession went hand in hand with eliminating meaningless distinctions and establishing clear lines of authority. *Stand* as profession would embody a rationalized form of corporate solidarity, allowing experts to maintain a collective posture toward the public. In the 1780s – at the same time that they introduced multiple tracks for promoting pupils – Gedike and several other school directors set about welding their staffs into collegial bodies within a bureaucratic chain of command. In the formulation and execution of school policy the director became the presiding administrative officer, though he was expected to rely heavily on consultation with his colleagues. While his title commanded a higher income, the other members of the staff were not distinguished by title and might be equal in income as well. Their collegial equality was confirmed in the elaborate setups of larger schools. Each teacher would now be responsible for one subject in the entire hierarchy of grades, and the new emphasis was on the value and dignity of a shared art in all its applications. The teacher was first and foremost a practicing pedagogue, not a scholar in a particular field; if the traditional premium on scholarship had made the instruction of young boys in the entering grades a bothersome, low-status chore, the new dispensation made it the quintessence of the

[19] The ranks descended from director or rector (or both) to conrector, prorektor, subrector (or subconrector) and perhaps professor, to mere "colleagues" or "preceptors" or "collaborators." For examples of local hierarchies of teaching ranks and local income scales, see esp. Schwartz, *Gelehrtenschulen*, passim. On the internecine warfare among teachers see esp. the petition to the Superior School Board from the staff of the Rathslyceum in Stettin (Feb. 6, 1806), in ibid., 2: 94–96.

vocation – the task that, more than any other, was incompatible with old-style pedantry and demanded the gifts of the born teacher.[20]

In the last decades of the century reform-minded schoolmen found cause for anxiety as well as optimism in the dissolution of the traditional *Gelehrtenstand* and the assimilation of its constituent groups into a new service elite. This larger realignment promised to draw the teaching branch of the clergy out of its corporate ghetto and into a sphere of shared educational and professional credentials. Still epitomizing pedantic boorishness in the eyes of polite society, schoolmen of plebeian origins stood to benefit especially from standards of merit and refinement that transcended caste barriers. But Gedike's acceptance into a socially mixed, open elite of scholars and officials in Berlin was exceptional. It was a constant lament of the reform literature that even in "enlightened" circles teachers still faced contempt from other "educated men," bourgeois as well as noble.[21] Their insecurity on this score was in itself a measure of their lack of "worldly" (not to mention courtly) manners.

Achievement of an equal birthright in such circles obviously hinged on a new public awareness of the importance of teaching; on recognition of pedagogy as a genuine academic discipline; on the kind of education that, in addition to producing competent experts, would endow new teachers with a measure of polish despite their origins. In all these senses the qualified teacher would earn respect for his office. But the office would also have to make the man, and not simply by allowing him and his family to give visible expression to their "inner" refinement. Teachers sought a secure place in the ranks of public employment, and in that regard the traditional conditions and terms of their local employment constituted an enormous handicap. Mobility – both collective and individual – within an emerging class structure required a radical adjustment in the position of the academic school at the juncture of local society and state authority, and in the teacher's relationship to both.

The new profession could not constitute itself as a meritocratic career ladder so long as local communities retained their traditional right to make appointments. The reform literature is filled with complaints about the

20 See, e.g., Campe's preliminary draft of reform proposals in 1785–86, published in Schmitt, *Schulreform*, p. A-104; Koeler, *Ueber die Policey*, pp. 51–52; Lieberkühn, *Kleine Schriften*, p. 242; Gedike, "Allgemeine Erfordernisse"; Stuve, "Ueber ein wesentliches Hinderniss der zweckmässigen Einrichtung öffentlicher Stadtschulen," in idem, *Schriften*, pp. 236–63. Trapp, it should be noted, went so far as to argue against a "monarchical" organization of the school (i.e., with other teachers subordinate to a rector) and in favor of "a complete equality" among colleagues; AR 16 (1792): 74–144.

21 See esp. Gedike, *Schulschriften*, 1: 471; Stuve, "Ueber das Schulwesen," in idem, *Schriften*, 1: 202–3, 276. Koch observed that schoolmen would not require "the refined worldly tone of the courtier" but would need "intercourse with other groups [*Ständen*]" to avoid becoming "mere *Stubengelehrten*." Koch, *Einige Gedanken*, pp. 27–29.

incompetence of local officials to choose among applicants for vacant positions; about their apathy, if not their outright hostility, toward schoolmen; about the more or less blatant ways in which local connections made merit irrelevant. In the most commonly proposed alternative, local choice would be restricted to a few candidates who had been selected by provincial authorities strictly on the basis of merit and had been spared direct contact with the locals.[22] No less debilitating than teachers' "poverty" was their "dependence" within the webs of local society. Teachers struggling to make ends meet by giving private lessons, outside regular class hours, could not afford to antagonize the wealthier parents who used this service. As for the "official" income, rarely was more than a quarter of it in the form of a secure cash salary from the municipal treasury. Lack of tax resources and unwillingness to impose new burdens, reluctance to grant the school a higher priority in constricted local budgets, an implicit refusal to end teachers' traditional accountability to their neighbors – all combined to keep most towns committed to a congeries of more or less expedient support arrangements, most of them dating back to the Reformation. These involved unmediated dependencies on individual families, making the teacher's remuneration, by the standards of modern bureaucratic employment, more private than public.

Typically the most important source of cash was the weekly or monthly school fee, which was limited to families actually using the school. Rarely was its collection a responsibility of the local tax collector; each teacher received what was due him from his pupils, or made the rounds himself. In the smaller towns, where residents combined the practice of trades with farming, the teacher was also likely to receive seasonal contributions in kind from some families – particularly if he also served as parish organist or cantor. In other local customs, obligatory payment shaded into charity. Most common was the teacher's responsibility to lead the school choir at special occasions like weddings and funerals, and at the nocturnal performances before the homes of prominent *Bürger* during the Christmas and Easter seasons. The more or less voluntary donations at these events helped support needy pupils, but the accompanying teacher took a substantial share of the proceeds. The survival of these customs is in itself a measure of the paucity of municipal financial resources in eighteenth-century Germany, particularly in towns that had become (or had always been) provincial backwaters. At the same time it reflects a tenacious local definition of the schoolman as a kind of auxiliary clergyman, with an assigned role in sacramental ritual and seasonal liturgical events. But the contradiction between the teacher's assigned local "station" and his new self-image could not have

[22] See, e.g., Ehlers, *Gedanken*, pp. 185–90; Koeler, *Ueber die Policey*, pp. 54–57; Lachmann, *Umschaffung*, pp. 4–17; Stuve, "Ueber das Schulwesen," pp. 190–92.

been more stark. "At the end of the eighteenth century," the thirty-nine-year-old lyceum director in the town of Brandenburg observed in 1788, "no rational and fair-minded man will doubt that for men in public office it is extremely painful, and indeed it must be extremely detrimental to the usefulness of their function, to collect a part of their meager income on the streets and in front of doors."[23]

Multiple dependencies, entangling remuneration in the social and cultural fabric of local society, made the teacher vulnerable to personal retaliation. This situation had always made for a degree of friction with neighbors, but the spread of reform enthusiasm among new generations of teachers vastly increased the grounds for hostility on both sides. While the traditional terms of local employment had worked to conform teachers' conception of their task to locally defined needs, the mission of the new profession was to stand above local society, as the agent of a superior culture of rationality and public virtue. To the young militants entering the Latin schools in the 1770s and 1780s, the kinds of subordination and accountability inherent in existing arrangements seemed incompatible with this conception of a professional mission and status. Thieme's letter to Campe about his tribulations in Merseburg covers most of the reformers' *causi belli* with "the public" as well as with resistant colleagues:

Because I treat all pupils without distinction in a friendly and polite manner, and prefer creating good attitudes through an ethical approach to playing tricks on young people with dumb rules in a hunger to punish, I am charged with failing to maintain discipline and treating the pupils like gentlemen [*Herren*]. Because I appeal to the happy success of various good arrangements in foreign institutions, it is said that I wanted to transform the gymnasium into a Philanthropin. – Because I maintain that you should learn your mother tongue before you learn Latin and Greek, and that future tavernkeepers, shoemakers and farriers do not have to bother bungling through the drudgery of Latin grammatical exercises [*Donatplackerey*], people shriek that I hold the Latin and Greek languages in contempt, apparently because I do not understand them. Because I maintain that for the largest portion of pupils knowledge of nature, geography, history and mathematics (to date unknown things at this gymnasium!) are more necessary than critical knowledge of Greek and Latin, it is said that I want to do away with the old solid way of studying and introduce in its place a mania for facts [*Realiensucht*]. Because I maintain that in a school like ours religion rather than theology must be taught, and that forced church attendance, especially with our pitiful liturgy, produces contempt for the divine service and it would be better for the young people to hold devotional hours suitable to their specific needs, I am regarded as a man without religion, a seducer, a separatist, etc.[24]

One can easily imagine how arrogant and self-righteous these single-

[23] Schwartz, *Gelehrtenschulen*, 2: 426. For other complaints about these customs, see, e.g., ibid., pp. 255–56; Ehlers, *Gedanken*, pp. 218–20; Koeler, *Ueber die Policey*, pp. 30–32; Stuve, "Ueber das Schulwesen," p. 196.

[24] Schmitt, *Schulreform*, pp. A-182 to A-183.

minded professionals, fresh out of the universities and considerably younger than many of their pupils' fathers, must have seemed even to relatively enlightened parents and local officials. Moralistic intolerance of obstructive traditions, typical of the more rigid eighteenth-century species of rationalist idealism, had become the self-styled expert's contempt for uninitiated laymen (however well-educated they might be).[25] The reformer's dilemma was that his conviction of the righteousness of his cause made him no less vulnerable to reprisals. To insist on unpopular innovations in the curriculum or in discipline was to invite vexations in school fee (or wood fee) collection and arrears in payment, and perhaps to forfeit a part of the fee if parents could transfer their boys to a nearby school. In small towns contributions in kind gave parents ample leeway to express their displeasure; the bushel of rye might not be quite as full as it should be. The man who had to join his choirboys in "begging" charity in the streets was not in a position to defy opposition to his professional judgment in the school.

It was to liberate a new profession from these local entanglements that reformers looked to state intervention. The optimal solution was to make all teachers salaried state officials, but the required reordering of government spending priorities (or introduction of a new state tax) and willingness to ride roughshod over historic local rights could not be expected in the near future. If the state would not foot the bill, however, it could offer the direct protection of its overriding authority by requiring local communities to make teaching incomes truly "public." Short of creating a new local tax, municipal authorities could be made responsible for collecting the school fee and other payments into a central treasury, out of which teachers would receive secure salaries largely in cash. Thus face-to-face dependencies would accede to a mediate, impersonal relationship with the "public," allowing the professional to apply his expertise without undue lay interference.

The reformers were well aware that in the provisioning of salaries, as in the structuring of careers, the new professionals would have to accept the mediate role of local communities to a degree. Teaching nonetheless belonged in a statewide elite of educated professions because the mission of the academic schools, in contrast to that of "lower" or "popular" schools, was not primarily local in orientation. The public importance of *Gelehrtenschulen* lay in forming the entryway to the universities and the entire range of educated professions. Commanding that entryway was the expertise of the new profession; if its practitioners were to serve the interest of the society as a whole, they had to be a direct arm of state authority, operating free of local obstructions.[26] In the plans for an effective screening process

[25] The outstanding example is Lieberkühn, *Kleine Schriften.*

[26] It was in this sense that Lieberkühn called the schools "representatives" (*Stellvertreterinnen*) of the state. Lieberkühn, "Ueber den Werth und die Rechte der öffentlichen Erziehung," in idem, *Kleine Schriften*: 277–78. In Göttingen, Eyring reported, school reform had resulted

for university studies, this kind of professional autonomy went hand in hand with collegial solidarity. One of teachers' standard laments was that parents simply ignored their judgments when it came to deciding whether their sons were suitable for academic studies, how quickly they ought to advance through the grades, and whether they were "mature" enough to move on to the universities.[27] The conflicting interests of teachers at different grade levels made it difficult to form a united front against parental whims; whether a pupil was held back or pulled forward, one man's pecuniary gain was another's loss. Here above all the "independence" of a secure salary seemed indispensable; only then could the pedagogical experts enforce the regular promotion schedule and uniform standards for "maturity" that were so obviously in the public interest.

In the neocorporate approach, not uncommon among reform-minded teachers, the prestige of the new teaching corps would hinge ultimately on its ability to serve the educated and wealthier segments of the "public," though the imprimatur and protection of the state were still indispensable.[28] To the egalitarian reformers of the 1780s, intent on identifying and channeling a natural distribution of aptitudes, local disentanglement seemed all the more necessary; one critical measure of professional autonomy was whether the "objective" agents of a neutral state authority could promote talent from below despite entrenched social interests and "prejudice."[29] This was to carry the abstract symbiosis of professionalism and state-sponsored reform from above to a logical, though extreme, conclusion – and to ignore the degree to which the state, in the concrete, would remain committed to maintaining the de facto privileges attached to education and property.

from cooperation between state officials and the town *Patronat*; this contradicted the prevailing assumption "that all hindrance in the improvement and expansion of the school system of an entire land arises from the fact that the largest portion of the schools are under the *Patronat-Rechte* of the towns, whose obstructive privilege puts insurmountable difficulties in the way of any attempt at an improvement and any higher-striving power." "Allgemeine Nachricht, von der Veranlassung der Jubelfeierlichkeiten und ihrer Veranstaltung," *Pädagogisches Jahrbuch*, Stück 4–6 (1788): 5–9. On the centralizing impulse in reform and its roots in teachers' reactions against local dependence, see also Jeismann, *Das preussische Gymnasium*, pp. 37–74.

[27] For early examples see Johann Hinrich Fibing, *Kurze Entdeckung der vornehmsten Ursachen des frühzeitigen und höchstschädlichen Ziehens von Schulen nach Universitäten* (Oldenburg, 1753); Anton Brockhausen, *Betrachtung über die Hindernisse, die einen Schulmann abhalten* (Lemgo, 1775), pp. 5–10; Martin Ehlers, "Ob es ein sicheres Merkmal von der guten und rechtschaffenen Amtsführung eines Schulmannes sey, wenn er an seinem Ort allgemein geliebt und gelobt wird," in idem, *Sammlung*, pp. 23–70.

[28] Ehlers, like Basedow, seems to exemplify this approach; see esp. "Von der bey Zulassung und Beförderung der Jugend zum Studium nöthigen Behutsamkeit," in Ehlers, *Sammlung*, pp. 1–22. It also characterized the reform thought of most philanthropinists (including Campe and Trapp) in the 1780s and 1790s. See, e.g., Johann Stuve, *Nachricht von der Neu-Ruppinschen Schule vom Jahr 1783* (Züllichau, 1783), pp. 24–25; idem, "Ueber das Schulwesen," pp. 282–83. For other examples see Müller, *Sozialstruktur und Schulsystem*, esp. pp. 111–29.

[29] Gedike, Lieberkühn, and Böttiger (see Chapter 8) are the best examples, but see also Koeler, *Ueber die Policey*, pp. 21–24.

PEDAGOGY AND PHILOLOGY

The modern educated professions have constituted themselves as disciplinary communities, and typically the center of gravity – the institution generating a theoretical structure as well as a foundation in empirical research for the community and initiating new recruits into its mysteries – is the university. Germany led the way in these developments. Epitomized by the natural sciences by the mid-nineteenth century, the new professional ideal had already been anticipated in the formation of a new teaching corps for the reformed gymnasium.[30]

But the new disciplinary community that was taking shape in the academic schools in the early nineteenth century was very different from the one many reform-minded schoolmen of earlier generations had envisioned. As late as the 1790s, in the seminar for aspiring teachers Friedrich Gedike had established in Berlin, equal weight was being given to two fledgling "disciplines." One was the new pedagogy, taking its inspiration from Locke and Rousseau (as well as from classical sources); and the other was a revitalized classical scholarship, associated above all with Gesner and Heyne at Göttingen.[31] These had been the driving forces behind school reform for several decades, and to Gedike and many other schoolmen it seemed reasonable to assume that the new teaching corps would be the product of their marriage in a new training program. By the 1820s it was apparent that the marriage had been short-lived and that pedagogy had been the loser in the divorce settlement. The classical philologists who formed the core of a *Gymnasiallehrerstand* had received no formal training in the theory and method of pedagogy, which had not found a niche in the newly organized philosophy faculties at Berlin and other major universities. To this new breed, inspired by the scholarly idealism of Friedrich August Wolf and other mentors, the earlier enthusiasm for a pedagogical "discipline" epitomized the rigid, materialistic utilitarianism that their profession had escaped.[32]

[30] See esp. R. Steven Turner, "The Growth of Professorial Research in Prussia, 1818 to 1848 – Causes and Context," in *Historical Studies in the Physical Sciences*, ed. Russell McCormmach, 3 (1971): 137–82. Turner's work is particularly important for understanding the internal structure of the new "discipline-communities" (his term) and their relationship to the state. See also idem, "University Professors and Professorial Scholarship in Germany 1760–1806," in Lawrence Stone, ed., *The University in Society*, vol. 2: *Europe, Scotland, and the United States from the Sixteenth to the Twentieth Century* (Princeton, N.J., 1974): 495–531. Also informative on the rise and institutionalization of a new research imperative in the German universities is Charles E. McClelland, *State, Society, and University in Germany 1700–1914* (Cambridge, 1980), pp. 122–32, 151–89.

[31] Friedrich Gedike, "Ausführliche Nachricht von dem Seminarium für gelehrte Schulen (April 7, 1790)," in idem, *Schulschriften*, 2: 112–34. See also Koch, *Einige Gedanken*.

[32] On the shift to neohumanism within the teaching profession, see esp. Lenore O'Boyle, "Klassische Bildung und soziale Struktur in Deutschland zwischen 1800 und 1848," *Historische Zeitschrift* 207 (1968): 584–608. O'Boyle may be correct in attributing the hegemony of

New circumstances in the early nineteenth century certainly contributed to this turn of events, but the ascendancy of classical philology at the expense of pedagogy had begun several decades earlier. The initial stages can be traced through the careers of two remarkable personalities, Heyne at Göttingen and Wolf at Halle. Both rose from obscure origins and dependence on charity to eminence, and indeed to celebrity status, as teachers and scholars. But there the similarity ends; aside from the generational distance between them, their approaches to the philological seminar reflect the continuing relevance of an internal divide – a salient difference in origins and formative experience – between the outsiders and the insiders among poor students. Heyne, the older man, was an outsider who had barely managed to climb into academic life, while his younger rival had been groomed for an academic career from birth.

Heyne's autobiographical fragment is one of the more doleful narrations of childhood and youth in the eighteenth-century literature. A linen weaver at the mercy of merchant-suppliers, his father "was relegated entirely to poverty and its companions, timidity and faintheartedness" in his old age. In the son's childhood "the earliest game" was "deprivation."[33] He was able to pursue academic studies, despite his father's opposition, only by becoming the reluctant protégé of a local pastor who subjected him, as a kind of surrogate son, to imperious paternal authority, but at the same time – whether out of sheer carelessness or to keep him continually reminded of his dependence – was sporadic and stingy with the donations he needed to survive. As a student at Leipzig he was left to fend for himself for long periods:

> In this way I entered a life situation in which I was the prey of madness. Raised without being guided by principles, with an entirely undeveloped character, without friend, guide, advisor, I do not understand to this day how I endured in this helpless situation. What drove me on in the world was not ambition, not youthful imagination to be able one day to command a position among *Gelehrten*. I was accompanied relentlessly by the bitter feeling of lowliness, of the lack of a good upbringing and education in external things; and the awareness of awkwardness in social life. What had the most effect on me was stubbornness against fate. This gave me the courage

neohumanism in academic education in the first half of the nineteenth century to the classical philologists' ideological justification of their "new professional group" as a part of the ruling *Beamtenschaft*; but she ignores the origins of this shift in conceptions of *Wissenschaft* emerging in the late eighteenth century, and her concept of ideology does not do justice to the complexity of the new profession's claim to "public" authority. But see also the general comments on the relationship between humanistic education and professional status in idem, "A Possible Model for the Study of Nineteenth-Century Secondary Education in Europe," *Journal of Social History* 12 (Winter 1978): 236–47.

[33] Arnold Hermann Ludwig Heeren, *Christian Gottlob Heyne, biographisch dargestellt* (Göttingen, 1813), pp. 5–8. On Heyne see also Clemens Menze, *Wilhelm von Humboldt und Christian Gottlob Heyne* (Ratingen, 1966).

not to go under; everywhere to let things arise, although I might be entirely in the dust and might have to remain there.[34]

It was the solicitude of several professors, and especially of the great classicist Ernesti, that rescued Heyne from this precipice. But his prospects at the end of his studies were grim; he had chosen law over theology (probably less because he was attracted to the field than because he lacked a clerical vocation and wanted to spite his godfather), but lacked well-placed family connections and the independent means to finance an unpaid apprenticeship for a judicial office. In April 1752 he moved to Dresden in the hope of finding a savior in Count Bruhl, a state minister who had taken notice of him. When the great man finally deigned to bestow an appointment on him, it was as a copyist in his library, with the paltry yearly salary of 100 thaler. And that was only after leaving him to survive by his own devices for about a year. Heyne had gotten through the winter of 1753 as a tutor, but then had fallen into dire poverty and had had to sleep on the floor of a friend's room.[35]

To climb out of this predicament Heyne turned to scholarly publication. In 1761 his erudite and imaginative editions of classical texts won him the professorial appointment at Göttingen, where his household soon became one of the centers of polite society. He proved an appropriate successor to Gesner not only as a publishing scholar, but also as a seminar director. At Halle and elsewhere seminars for theology students had not enforced stringent admission standards, much less a competitive selection; their raison d'être was to dispense charity to the needy, and the requirements to attend lectures or to teach were minimal. To Heyne, as to Gesner, the mission of the philological seminar was to produce the nucleus of a new teaching corps, and from 1771 onward he used his position as inspector of the Latin school in nearby Ilfeld to provide a practical apprenticeship for seminar graduates. "Need" and "financial circumstances" were not the decisive criteria for awarding a relatively generous annual stipend of 50 reichsthaler to the nine regular seminar members. What mattered was the "inner" vocation, not "external" necessity. Applicants must have demonstrated that they had "good natural abilities" and "good morals" and must "show desire, eagerness, and an honest purpose to achieve a certain perfection in the humanities and especially in school disciplines."[36]

[34] Heeren, *Heyne*, pp. 24–25.

[35] Ibid., pp. 32–36.

[36] Heyne's description of the seminar has been published in Johann Stephan Pütter, *Versuch einer academischen Gelehrtengeschichte von der Georg-Augustus-Universität*, 2 vols. (Göttingen, 1765–88), 1: 248–49. The regular members of the seminar are listed in ibid., 2: 275–78. See also Paulsen, *Der gelehrte Unterricht*, p. 39. For background on seminars as university institutions, see Wilhelm Erben, "Die Entstehung der Universitäts-Seminare," *Internationale Monatsschrift für Wissenschaft, Kunst und Technik* (1913): 1247–64, 1335–47; Turner, "The Growth of Professorial Research"; McClelland, *State, Society, and University*, pp. 162–81.

Membership in the philological seminar became a much sought after honor, despite the unprecedented quantity and caliber of work required. That was due partly to the generous stipend, but above all to Heyne's celebrated ability to inspire students as a scholar-teacher.[37] One suspects that his very success gave him cause for concern; there was a marked tension between his long-term commitment to the creation of a new teaching profession and a deeply ingrained caution about his protégés' prospects. Social acceptance in Göttingen had not erased the earlier trauma of poverty and its insecurities. The lesson he drew from his own experience, evoked with unusual immediacy in the autobiographical fragment, was that young men without means and high-placed patrons could not afford to wander off the standard clerical career track, particularly when their alternative was a fledgling discipline offering limited and insecure prospects. Hence the delicate balance – while he expected his select few to prefer teaching, he also insisted that they regard it as a concentration within the larger field of theological studies.

And yet Heyne's cautionary advice aside, the seminar was offering theology students, and especially those without means, a clear professional alternative to the pastorate and the pulpit. By the 1780s that very impetus was producing men like Friedrich Jacobs, who defined themselves exclusively as schoolmen. And this was paralleled by another unintended effect: the shift in the disciplinary center of gravity. Heyne's genuine interest in the new pedagogy and in school reform was demonstrated in the plans he drew up for the Latin school in Ilfeld and the gymnasium in Göttingen.[38] But he was first and foremost a classical scholar, devoted to analyzing the linguistic and literary properties of Latin and Greek texts and interpreting them within the larger historical context of the ancient world. It was in this capacity that members of the philological seminar revered him as a model, and it was the initiation into the multifaceted classical scholarship he practiced – into the mysteries of new methods of textual analysis and interpretation – that exercised such appeal. One former disciple recalled Heyne's "quite unique talent in the explications of classical authors of antiquity to lead the listener right into the circle of ideas and feelings in which the

[37] Heyne's son-in-law recalled: "He soon reached the point where it was a distinction, an honor here in the eyes of the public to be a *Seminarist*; that when you left here you could take away no better recommendation than that you had been one. Now the better minds pressed for admission; it was no longer regarded as a form of charity. In this way and in this sense, one can say, he founded a school (he himself always protested against this expression); that is, in the sense that his methods of explicating the ancients were accepted, not in the sense that his opinions were accepted." Heeren, *Heyne*, p. 254.

[38] Christian Gottlob Heyne, "Nachricht von der gegenwärtigen Einrichtung des Königl. Pädagogii zu Ilfeld," *Archiv für die ausübende Erziehungskunst* 9 (1783): 40–119.

author wrote, so that he sees, feels and experiences the subjects with the author."[39]

These were young men who had been drilled in the sclerotic classicism of the Latin schools; Heyne wrought conversions to classical studies not only by offering them a disciplinary alternative to theology, but also by imparting a new intellectual vitality to a field of study that seemed to have been reduced to empty formalism. But if the recollections of former seminar members convey a sense of the new spirit Heyne breathed into ancient texts, they are conspicuously lacking in approving references to the pedagogical literature of the late eighteenth century. In his seminar Heyne was promoting the one-dimensional identification of academic teaching with classical scholarship that he opposed in principle.

What Heyne effected inadvertently Friedrich August Wolf promoted with awesome single-mindedness and more than a little cunning. Wolf's autobiographical fragment conveys not the bitterness of the outsider who had had to claw his way in, but the unshakable sense of identity derived from a familial and corporate tradition. In retrospect his parents – far from exemplifying the debilitating effects of poverty and insecurity – seemed to embody a bourgeois pride in maintaining standards of respectability on very little.[40] Thanks to the instruction provided by his father, a schoolteacher, he knew "much Latin and French" and "some Greek" by the end of his sixth year. Like other sons of obscure clergymen and schoolteachers, he had the enormous advantage of a corporate initiation within a local network of colleagues. Johann Conrad Hake, a new teacher in the Nordhausen gym-

[39] Recorded in the life history of Johann Friedrich Christoph Gräffe, in *Allgemeines Magazin für Prediger* 12:3 (1795): 11–12. Another former disciple, Johann Benjamin Koppe, recalled that to a "young theologian" like himself "the tasteful way in which Heyne taught this study [philology] and guided him to pursue it was totally new," and that "entirely new vistas were opened to him in Heyne's lectures on Greek antiquity, on art history, on Pindar and Homer." Ibid., 5:3 (1791): 325. The same form of seduction drew Arnold Hermann Ludwig Heeren, later to become Heyne's son-in-law, away from theology: and Heyne's encouraging words about his first "interpretation," he recalled, "decided [his] future life." Heeren, *Heyne*, p. 254.

[40] "Only the very observant outsider could have discovered signs of limited circumstances," he recalled, "and my mother wished to know nothing of poverty." "Entwurf einer Selbstbiographie," in *Friedrich August Wolf; ein Leben in Briefen*, ed. Siegfried Reiter, 3 vols. (Stuttgart, 1935), 2: 337–39. Wolf still lacks a major biography, but the basic narrative and a wealth of information are provided in J. F. J. Arnoldt, *Fr. Aug. Wolf in seinem Verhältnisse zum Schulwesen und zur Paedagogik* (Brunswick, 1861–62). Also useful, though tending more toward hagiography, is the early biography by Wolf's son-in-law; see Wilhelm Körte, *Leben und Studien Friedrich August Wolf's, des Philologen*, 2 vols. (Essen, 1833). For a balanced portrait, see Manfred Fuhrmann, "Friedrich August Wolf," *Deutsche Vierteljahrsschrift für Literaturwissenschaft und Geistesgeschichte* 33:2 (1959): 187–236. Wolf's contributions as a reformer are summarized in Paulsen, *Der gelehrte Unterricht*, pp. 210–29. On the degree of originality of Wolf's scholarship, see the recent judicious reassessments in Anthony Grafton, "Prolegomena to Friedrich August Wolf," *Journal of the Warburg and Courtauld Institutes* 44 (1981): 109–29; the Introduction to F. A. Wolf, *Prolegomena to Homer (1795)*, trans. and ed. Anthony Grafton, Glenn W. Most, and James E. G. Zetzel (Princeton, N.J., 1985).

nasium, took him under his wing and reinforced his father's tutelage in implanting a "love for thorough study of the ancient languages." Hake's encouragement and "intimate conversations" convinced him that as a *Primaner* he could ignore the regular classes in most subjects and "study by [himself] according to a fixed plan from morning to night, and indeed often through most of the night."[41]

Wolf liked to recall himself as an "autodidact," advancing to erudition entirely on his own. But it is more accurate to describe him as a precocious soloist within a corporate tradition, propelled by the constant approval of his father and colleagues and able to go it alone precisely because he had in effect inherited a collective scholarly ethos.[42] He also happened to be very bright, and the result was that he was far advanced beyond most of his peers by the time he arrived at Göttingen in 1777. One of the legends about his career is that, in an unprecedented gesture, he insisted on matriculating in philology rather than theology. To Heyne's objection that an exclusive devotion to philology would bring "no bread," he claimed to have responded that he "[had] known nothing of hunger to date" and "would consider devoting [himself] only to something to which [his] inclination drew him."[43] Admirers in awe of Wolf's temerity have missed the irony of this story; Wolf's commitment to a new professional identity was rooted in the corporate ethos of learning that it was in many ways fashioned to supersede.

This posture – part pride of caste, part modern professional consciousness – threatened to shipwreck Wolf's career at its very launching. The young virtuoso, proud of his scholarly accomplishments, faced in Heyne a patron who was eager to promote real talent but, in the words of his son-in-law, "expected . . . the obligations of reverence [*Pietät*] that in earlier times were taken for granted between the teacher and the pupil."[44] Refused admission to Heyne's collegium on Pindar, Wolf was too indignant to apply for a place in the philological seminar. Instead he continued his "autodidacticism"; attending courses only long enough to get reading lists, he preferred bouts of isolated work late into the night. This regimen endangered his health, but also produced results. Reputed to be something of a phenomenon, he began to attract an audience to his rooms for private lectures on Greek authors in the fall semester of 1778.[45]

Wolf's single-mindedness was not simply a matter of having a clear-cut

[41] "Entwurf einer Selbstbiographie," p. 338.

[42] Cf. the characterization of Wolf as a member of the "personal estate" (*persönlichen Standes*), detached from the corporate tradition of the old *Gelehrtenschule*, in Wilhelm Roessler, "Friedrich August Wolf. Ein Beitrag zum Verhältnis von 'Wissenschaft' und 'Pädagogik' um die Wende zum 19. Jahrhundert," *Bildung und Erziehung* 14 (1961): 143–67.

[43] "Entwurf einer Selbstbiographie," p. 339. See also Arnoldt, *Wolf*, pp. 28–31.

[44] Heeren, *Heyne*, p. 255.

[45] "Versuch einer Selbstbiographie," p. 340.

goal, and his talents were not limited to scholarship. He was also a pragmatist, adept at circumventing shoals and taking advantage of prevailing winds in plotting a course to a successful career in classical scholarship. In the early years Heyne – the most renowned classical scholar in Europe, with an influence over teaching and professorial appointments that extended far beyond Hanover – was an irremovable presence on his route. The open break between the two men did not occur until the mid-1790s, after Heyne had insinuated in a review that the original ideas in Wolf's pathbreaking *Prolegomena to Homer* were his own. Wolf's account of his student years in a letter to Heyne – a letter he published as their feud escalated – made it perfectly clear that he had never been a disciple and reproached the great man for his "unfriendly" and "crude" refusal to admit him to the Pindar collegium.[46] The palpable bitterness in this gesture is a measure of how difficult it must have been for Wolf to have waited so long to make it. But he *had* waited, and indeed for more than a decade and a half he had put a great deal of effort into winning and maintaining Heyne's patronage. In the summer of 1779 Wolf had accepted a position in Ilfeld, though it required that he swallow his pride and take the on-the-scene examination from which seminar members were exempt. "The man has abilities," Heyne wrote the Ilfeld rector, and the fact that "his character does not please me . . . cannot be the decisive consideration here."[47] Then and in later years, Wolf could not help making small gestures of defiance; but in his letters to Heyne he presented himself, ex post facto, as the student-disciple he had not in fact been, and was able to render the deference he had withheld face to face.[48]

Wolf understood that in academic careers no amount of virtuosity could compensate for the lack of a powerful sponsor. The other vital ingredient in the new discipline was scholarly publication, and here again Wolf proved a clever strategist. It was the relatively light teaching duties, allowing more time for scholarship, that had made the Ilfeld appointment preferable to a better-paying position Heyne had advised him to take. In his first publication, an edition of Plato's *Dialogues*, the introductory remarks and the use of German in the editorial notes were calculated to please Minister von Zedlitz and his two young protégés, Biester (his secretary) and Gedike, who wanted to make the classics more accessible to the educated public.[49] In 1783 this cultivation of the Prussian connection finally bore fruit; Wolf

[46] Friedrich August Wolf, *Briefe an Herrn Hofrath Heyne von Professor Wolf. Eine Beilage zum neuesten Untersuchungen über den Homer* (Berlin, 1797), esp. pp. 92–109.

[47] Arnoldt, *Wolf*, pp. 30–31.

[48] See, e.g., *Wolf; ein Leben in Briefen*, 1: 8–21, 82–83. A posture that may at first have expressed Wolf's grudging respect for Heyne's scholarly prowess eventually became sheer duplicity; as late as 1790, when he was already gloating over Voss's success at exposing Heyne's ineptitude in editing the *Georgics*, his occasional letters to the great man still rendered homage.

[49] "Versuch einer Selbstbiographie," p. 341. See also Wolf to Heyne, Oct. 16, 1782, in *Wolf; ein Leben in Briefen*, 1: 8–9.

was offered the appointment as inspector of the pedagogical seminar at Halle. Again practicing delayed gratification, he accepted an appointment that initially involved a considerable loss of income but offered the long-term prospect of a university career in classical scholarship. Wolf also knew very well that, if his ambitions for the Halle appointment were to be realized, he would have to change the mandate attached to it. The origins of the pedagogical institute lay in Semler's efforts in the late 1750s to supplement the theological seminar with a teacher training program. Schütz, the first inspector in charge of instruction, seems to have begun by emphasizing classical studies, but soon accommodated to Zedlitz's view of the institute as an experimental center for applying the basic precepts of Basedow's philanthropinism without the master's quirks. This orientation was dramatically confirmed when Schütz had to be replaced in 1779; the Ministry chose Ernst Christian Trapp, an outspoken disciple of Basedow, and in an unprecedented gesture of recognition of his new "discipline," installed him in a professorship of pedagogy.

Trapp lasted only a few years; he had made the mistake of leaping into a fierce theological dispute with the eminent Semler and had found it impossible to win acceptance among his colleagues and students without an established discipline.[50] Zedlitz and his Berlin advisors sought to replace him with a promising young scholar who would breathe new life into the pedagogical institute, but at the same time could counteract Halle's well-deserved reputation as a university that – in sharp contrast to its rival Göttingen – had neglected classical studies. They may originally have expected this combination from Wolf; but they clearly had doubts from the start, and when Heyne was consulted a second time – having sent a copy of Wolf's Plato edition to Zedlitz and having already recommended him for the position – he did not dispel them.[51] Wolf, aware that the seminar was already on the skids, was content to let it slide into oblivion. Aside from taking time and effort away from the research with which he planned to make his name, the seminar represented an intellectual threat to "his actual discipline." Wolf knew very well that the utilitarian preoccupations of Basedow,

[50] On the seminar and Trapp's appointment see Paulsen, *Der gelehrte Unterricht*, p. 82; Ernst Christian Trapp, *Versuch einer Pädagogik; mit Trapps hallischer Antrittsvorlesung Von der Nothwendigkeit, Erziehen und Unterrichten als eine eigne Kunst zu studiren*, ed. Ulrich Herrmann (1780: Paderborn, 1977), pp. 424–25. On Schütz's conception of the seminar, see Christian Gottfried Schütz, *Nachricht von der bey dem königl. theol. Seminarium zu Halle neuerrichteten Erziehungsanstalt und den dabey zur Bildung geschickter Schullehrer und Hofmeister getroffenen Einrichtungen* (Halle, 1778); idem, *Geschichte des Erziehungsinstituts bei dem theologischen Seminariums zu Halle* (Jena, 1781).

[51] Arnoldt, *Wolf*, p. 72. In response to Wolf's complaint that his pedagogical responsibilities were a nuisance, preventing him from "liv[ing] solely for [his] actual discipline," Heyne advised him to regard the institute as "the most useful part of your responsibilities, and the part that in the long run will bear fruits for your reputation and prestige in the public." Wolf to Heyne, Dec. 18, 1783, and Jan. 2, 1784, in *Wolf; ein Leben in Briefen*, 1: 13–18. Heyne's advice quoted in ibid., 3: 6.

Trapp, and others left classical studies at best a minor role in secondary education and that they had contempt for both the philological precision and the aesthetic sensitivity that the new classical scholarship required. To him the "how" of teaching was a function of its disciplinary substance, not a set of precepts applicable to all disciplines. The apprentice learned how to teach his subject by presenting it to peers in a rigorous seminar, under the guidance of a master scholar-teacher. Elevated to an autonomous discipline, pedagogy became mere disembodied theory.

Having let the pedagogical seminar go under, Wolf seized the opportunity to launch his alternative philological seminar when Zedlitz created the Superior School Board in 1787. Though initially intent on severing the connection with theology, he came to realize that it would be premature to require an exclusive commitment to teaching. But on the main point he prevailed. In its reaction to his initial proposal, the Ministry, probably at Gedike's instigation, expressed concern that the emphasis on classical scholarship would be at the expense of training in German and pedagogy. Wolf was more than willing to assure Berlin that German would not be neglected; but from behind protestations of modesty, he dug in his heels on the other issue. He had no competence in "theoretical pedagogy," he responded, and would have to abandon the project unless freed of the obligation to teach it. He was gambling that his proven ability to bring Halle badly needed prestige in classical studies would win the day – and it did. Wolf was given a free hand to draw up the charter the Ministry eventually approved, and it left no doubt that the raison d'être for the new seminar was the rigorous training of classical scholars.[52]

The key figures in the *Philologenstand* forming at the turn of the century came out of this seminar, and it was above all their conception of classical studies that shaped the new gymnasium. That Halle hosted the experiment is in itself remarkable; in June 1784, Wolf explained to Heyne why it was so difficult to follow his example at the Prussian university. His competitor for students' attention was August Hermann Niemeyer, who still supervised the seminar:

> He [Niemeyer] always reads something Greek or Latin there a few hours per week, instead of exercising the *Seminaristen*, as it actually should be. This collegium, since it is public, draws in everything that moves, and they hear – as he himself freely admits – nothing in the world but a nice-sounding German translation, filling the ears prettily. This is packed in the notebooks, and so the listeners depart intoxicated by the highly enthusiastic declamator, who has spoken such elegant German. Of rules of interpretation, or explanation of ancient customs, etc., and indeed of actual simple grammar they learn absolutely nothing. I have often not been able to com-

[52] See esp. Wolf's letters to Karl Abraham von Zedlitz (Jan. 27, 1787), Karl Christoph von Hoffmann (Sept. 6, 1787), and Friedrich Wilhelm II (Feb. 5, 1788), in *Wolf; ein Leben in Briefen*, 1: 52–57, 61–63.

prehend how many [students] regarded me indignantly when I said occasionally in a collegium: interpretation is a philosophical matter, in itself quite cold: one cannot become drunk on an author before one has gotten a firm grip on his meaning from the basics.[53]

That Wolf institutionalized his hard-nosed professionalism against such odds is a tribute to his teaching, which combined an awesome technical grasp of textual detail and historical erudition with an inspired ability to communicate the essential "spirit" of the work in question. Aside from his scholarly virtuosity, Wolf knew how to address the circumstances and aspirations of the highly qualified, well-motivated students his seminar attracted. Some kept open the possibility of a clerical career, but others – those who had never had a religious calling, or had come to doubt it – welcomed the opportunity to make an exclusive commitment to teaching. Wolf was careful to nourish that commitment and give it special prestige by forming the *Seminaristen* into an elite coterie, all welcomed in his home as well as his office, and some attaining the status of "friend" by the time they left Halle.

Wolf's conception of classical scholarship gave new generations of students an idealistic alternative not only to a tunnel-visioned *Brotstudium*, but also to the utilitarian ethic of "merit" their elders preached. In what would become the familiar vein of neohumanism, neophytes were reassured constantly that their effort was of a higher order of purity. While others struggled to attain "livings" as clergymen or to be "useful" in the standard sense, they were dedicated to the pursuit of scholarship for its own sake.[54] But again work itself remained sacrosanct; in Wolf and his disciples the new idiom blended quite naturally with a corporate legacy to make classical scholarship the locus par excellence of an academic work ethic. In a letter to Heyne in October 1787, Wolf described his "monotonous, work-filled life"; because of his "former disorderly and wild study" he often "need[ed] eight or more hours for one hour of lectures."[55] The young men Wolf praised in his seminar reports had what he called "iron and impassioned industry," without the youthful penchant for "autodidacticism" he had often had cause to regret. They were more disciplined versions of his earlier self, and some lent emphatic confirmation to the longstanding stereotype of the "regular persevering industry" to be found among poor students.[56] In the

[53] Wolf to Heyne, June 12, 1784, in ibid., pp. 27–28. See also Wolf's complaint about Niemeyer's efforts to denigrate his teaching methods among students; Wolf to Heyne, Oct. 30, 1784, in ibid., p. 32.

[54] See esp. Arnoldt, *Wolf*, pp. 88–89; "Zeugniss eines dankbaren Schülers," in ibid., pp. 265ff. (Beilage XIV).

[55] *Wolf; ein Leben in Briefen*, 1: 57.

[56] Wolf used the phrase "iron and impassioned industry" to describe a student to Heyne in October 1782; *Wolf; ein Leben in Briefen*, 1: 9. See also his reports on seminar members in ibid., pp. 70–73, 75–76. On the need for a "cold-blooded" publication strategy see esp. his advice to Ernst Gottlob Klose, a former *Seminarist*, in ibid., pp. 78–79, 85, 120–22.

course of molding such recruits into *Philologen*, Wolf gave a new scholarly substance to the ideal of teaching as a career rewarding merit and promoting talent from below.

This profile of Wolf is not meant to imply that the ascendancy of classical studies was due simply to one man's personal ambitions and accomplishments. Sometimes knowingly, sometimes with only a dim awareness of larger implications, Wolf served as the instrument of a process of disillusionment and reorientation in the emergence of a new profession. If teaching was to achieve professional status, as it was being defined at the turn of the century, schoolmen had to establish credibility for its claim to public authority. From the outset the reform movement looked to the state for an external source of credibility in the face of uncomprehending parents and local officials. But there was suddenly reason to question this strategy in the late 1780s, when Woellner's edicts in Prussia confronted teachers as well as pastors with the choice of bending the knee publicly to state-enforced Orthodoxy or risking removal from office. To reformers throughout North Germany the state, long idealized as a beacon of rationality, abruptly revealed its potential to serve as the repressive instrument of intolerance and obscurantism.

In an ironic about-face, Trapp and several other philanthropinists, having insisted that drastic state intervention was indispensable for the professionalization of teaching, now argued that secondary education should be left to flourish in a laissez-faire market. But their apostasy did not divert the mainstream of the reform movement; Wolf and his disciples were no less convinced than rationalist schoolmen that only the state could protect a new form of expertise from an uncomprehending laity.[57] This underlying continuity is in itself a measure of how tight the equation of modern profession and modern office had become – and of how important the bureaucratic legacy is to understanding the German alternative to an Anglo-American "liberal" profession.

But in the 1790s the need for an *internal* source of credibility became more urgent, as central premises of rationalist reform – about pedagogy as

[57] This underlying continuity is emphasized in the discussion of reactions to Woellner's crackdown in Jeismann, *Das preussische Gymnasium*, pp. 132–48. For background on the Woellner era, see esp. Paul Schwartz, *Der erste Kulturkampf in Preussen um Kirche und Schule (1788–1798)*, Monumenta Germaniae Paedagogica, vol. 58 (Berlin, 1925); Wolfgang Gericke, *Glaubenszeugnisse und Konfessionspolitik der Brandenburgischen Herrscher bis zur Preussischen Union 1540 bis 1815*, Union und Confession, vol. 6 (Bielefeld, 1977), pp. 91–95. On its long-term significance, cf. Fritz Valjavec, "Das Woellnersche Religionsedikt und seine geschichtliche Bedeutung," *Historisches Jahrbuch* 72 (1953): 386–400, which interprets the crackdown as "testimony for the shifting of the Enlightenment into politics, and for the birth pangs of Prussian liberalism." For the era's significance in inducing doubts about state intervention in education, see esp. AR 16 (1792): 1–43. On Wolf's attitude toward local authorities see his letter to Zedlitz, Jan. 12, 1788, in *Wolf; ein Leben in Briefen*, 1: 60.

a *Wissenschaft* and about its larger public context – lost credibility. To Gedike and others, the symbiosis of reform from above and professionalism implied that a progressive state would tolerate and be responsive to a new public politics. As it was celebrated in Gedike's "letters," in fact, the Berlin of the mid-1780s already had such a politics; that was why the reform from above emanating from its government ministries was legitimate, and why Prussia under Frederick the Great was an "enlightened" model for the rest of Germany. In 1773, in his widely read tract on "the usefulness of the pastorate," Spalding had called the clergy "the actual depositary of public morality." Ten years later Gedike was claiming the same role for an entire cluster of educated professions, including teaching. His conception of a public arena was shaped by the assumption that these professions were its moral conscience; their collective vision was the essential source of both "freedom in moral matters" and the "political improvements" such freedom produced.[58]

Old-regime absolutism, arrogating all public authority to itself, recognized opinion only as it emanated from isolated corporate enclaves and flowed through segregated channels. In the "enlightened" alternative, the state would provide itself with both moral guidance and expert opinion by allowing an entire educated "public" to constitute itself and respecting the autonomy of the professional disciplines that gave it an authoritative voice. It was not simply the importance of its service that distinguished an educated profession; its vision was more "public" than that of other occupations. As Lieberkühn explained, true "public spirit" was peculiar to certain professions in "public offices," including teaching; only a properly educated minority was capable of the "general point of view," encompassing "the whole of humanity, or at least our fellow *Bürger* and their welfare as our most important concern."[59] If this "point of view" was rooted in a liberal education, it was also – perhaps paradoxically from our perspective – inherent in the kind of expertise a profession commanded. Ultimately the public security of office was in recognition of the fact that professional knowledge was of a higher order; by its very nature a discipline – a *Wissenschaft* – conferred an ability to distinguish the welfare of the whole from narrow private interests and give it preference.

[58] See esp. the "Vierter Brief" and "Fünfter Brief," *Berlinische Monatsschrift* 2 (July-Dec., 1783): 542–52 (cited hereafter as BM); "Funfzehnter Brief," BM 3 (Jan.-June, 1784): 463–69. For Spalding's ideal of the pastoral office, see his *Ueber die Nutzbarkeit des Predigtamtes und deren Beförderung* (3rd ed.: Berlin, 1791), esp. pp. 31–32, 75–101.

[59] Lieberkühn, "Ueber den öffentlichen Geist des Schulmannes," in idem, *Kleine Schriften*, pp. 153–69. See also Gedike, *Schulschriften*, 1: 473–83. Particularly important on the development of a political "public" in the second half of the eighteenth century is Hans Erich Bödeker, "Prozesse und Strukturen politischer Bewusstseinsbildung der deutschen Aufklärung," in Hans Erich Bödeker and Ulrich Herrmann, eds., *Aufklärung als Politisierung – Politisierung als Aufklärung* (Hamburg, 1987), pp. 10–31.

By affording privileged insight into workings of nature that were not visible to the untrained eye, *Wissenschaft* perched the expert above private interests in an ethical as well as a cognitive sense. The fusion of theory and practice in its research promised a cumulative advance in objective understanding of the "laws," or at least of the "principles," of human "nature" in an area of vital social importance. Just as this kind of "scientific" objectivity was entirely compatible with, and indeed essential to, the practice of an "art," it was also the unimpeachable basis for a claim of *normative* authority. When "nature" was mapped into the jurisdictions of professional disciplines, it was not as the object of a merely functional rationality, in the service of ends sanctioned by tradition or some other, equally arbitrary authority. Nature was the ultimate arbiter in establishing the proper social organization and cultural order of priorities for a rational society. Ultimately a *Wissenschaft* should have an authoritative voice on public issues because it could guide society, despite its entrenched interests, into closer alignment with nature.

From one angle this conception of professional disciplines was not as far removed from the revolutionary ideology across the border as it might at first appear to be. Both can be said to have pitted an exalted vision of the political against the pettiness of mere politics, and in that sense both were profoundly hostile to the formation of a "liberal" political arena. Public politics was defined in terms of a unitary, transcendent principle, posed against the mere competition of interests and opinions. But French revolutionary ideology took shape in the vacuum caused by a cataclysm. Traditionally considered indivisible, the sovereign authority of the absolutist state seemed to have given way to a riot of selfish interests. In the very different context of Germany, the alternative professional ideal of Gedike's generation did not exhibit the same rhetorical stridency, categorical repudiation of the past, and obsessive claims about unity because it formed in a zone of accommodation between the state and its educated elite. What promised to forge unity – to transcend the mere clash of interests – in the French revolutionary definition of social objectives was the sacred Will of the People (or the Nation); legitimate authority lay in a form of leadership that gave direct, pure, and indeed "transparent" expression to popular sovereignty.[60] The German alternative claimed an unassailable cultural and

[60] On the French revolutionary ideal, see esp. François Furet, *Interpreting the French Revolution*, trans. Elborg Forster (1978: Cambridge, 1981), esp. pp. 25–61; Lynn Hunt, *Politics, Culture, and Class in the French Revolution* (Berkeley, Calif., 1984), pp. 39–47. By focusing on revolutionary ideology and the German concept of *Wissenschaft*, my analysis ignores a possible "third way" that would complicate the comparison in interesting ways. By the 1780s, the French Enlightenment had produced a concept of social science as "public knowledge" that differed from the German variant in requiring modern forms of political representation alongside the bureaucratic state, but also differed from the French revolutionary alternative in its claim of relative independence from a popular will. See the suggestive analysis in Keith

ultimately moral authority for disciplinary knowledge, which enabled its initiates to penetrate to nature through the transparent surface of society.

If the public openness of *Wissenschaft* marked a departure from corporate traditions, it also legitimated the authority of experts – of "communities of the competent" – over the lay public. Far from contradicting each other, this kind of elitism and the egalitarian approach to talent were corollaries within a single vision of a rational society. Gedike found a large grain of truth in the stereotype of the "learned cobbler" given to uninformed "speculation" about theological and political issues. Too many bright young men, forced into the trade, sought intellectual relief from its mindless drudgery. His conclusion was not that uneducated speculation should be deemed legitimate within a widened (i.e., democratized) public arena; the best way to avoid that prospect – to keep cobblers confined to their proper intellectual "sphere" – was to allow the talented to rise to intellectually challenging work.[61]

At least until the mid-1780s, the appeal of pedagogy lay precisely in its potential as a disciplinary authority in public life. The more egalitarian the reform objectives, the more the pedagogical image of nature was wielded as a normative foil – a reproach to privilege and a moral justification for the creation of a meritocratic order. And even in less far-reaching reform agendas the schoolroom became an empirical laboratory and the teacher its trained researcher. Here is Trapp's description of the dialectical process of induction and deduction in his *Versuch einer Pädagogik*:

> If we had a sufficient number of correctly made pedagogical observations and reliable experiences, we could write a correct and complete system of pedagogy of a kind that has not been available to date and cannot be; and if we had written the system we could put public education and school instruction on such a footing that there would be nothing more to change or improve. . . . As long as the world exists, there will always be something else for the physician and the pedagogue to observe and to notice, and the fund of experience in these two disciplines, which are quite analogous, and which I therefore name together without excluding many others, is a growth into infinity.
>
> But, if this is so, can one actually determine principles of education and develop a system of this art? Yes; but no principles that may not be in need of closer

Michael Baker, *Condorcet. From Natural Philosophy to Social Mathematics* (Chicago, 1975), esp. pp. 197–214. Also relevant is the discussion of the "consensual" and "usufructory" models of authority and the demonstration of the usufructory model in the career of Jean-Sylvan Bailly, in George Armstrong Kelly, *Victims, Authority, and the Terror. The Parallel Deaths of d'Orléans, Custine, Bailly and Malesherbes* (Chapel Hill, N.C., 1982), pp. 10–23, 149–210.

[61] Friedrich Gedike, "Ueber das Studium der Literarhistorie, nebst einem Beitrag zu dem Kapitel von gelehrten Schuster," BM 1 (Jan.-June 1783): 277–97. But cf. Müller, *Sozialstruktur und Schulsystem*, pp. 98–109. Müller's very different view of Gedike's political ideal is based on his reading of the anonymous "Neuer Weg zur Unsterblichkeit für Fürsten," BM 5 (1785): 239–47. But I do not find this piece as "democratic" as Müller does, and in any case I think it very unlikely that Gedike wrote it.

definition, limitation or expansion; no system that does not have its holes and lacks, even if they are not visible. . . . [But] one must work according to a definite plan, and this presumes principles and conclusions from principles, which are united in a whole. As soon as one educates people for civil society, one has a system, whether it be good or bad, poorly or well integrated. . . . What does the making of correct observations, reliable experiences entail? A great deal. A spirit free of prejudices and partisanship; a practiced eye; a penetrating look; a soft soul that accepts all impressions that the observed subjects make on it; a lively awareness of the possibility of erring, which leads to caution and repetition of the experiments.[62]

Trapp's notion of "system" anticipates the hubris as well as the humility of nineteenth-century scientific positivism. Within a decade neohumanism was contributing to and gaining strength from a growing awareness that, as an internal source of professional credibility, the would-be system might have inherent and fatal shortcomings. In neohumanism the claim of public authority became an effort to constitute a tradition in the face of flux – even as the profession sought emancipation from outworn familial and local traditions. In the programmatic writings of Wolf, Jacobs, and others, the very concept of a scholarly discipline formed in reaction against the modernity represented by crass commercialism, tunnel-visioned utilitarianism, and an emerging arena of myopic, ever fluctuating opinion. These were all of a piece in modern "civilization," which lacked the unitary spirit of a genuine *Cultur*. Within this multivalent cultural critique, the market – in the form of an increasingly commercialized literature – *was* a corrosive force. In the face of its rage for mere novelty and "popularity," the classical canon was a source of rigorous and fixed aesthetic standards.[63] But if the cult of the merely "useful" was particularly crass in commercial life, it also permeated a "political" universe in which the state – the rationalists' counterforce to entrenched familial and corporate interests – figured as a manipulative, potentially despotic force.

In this diagnosis rationalist pedagogy was a symptom, not an antidote. Part of the problem was that Trapp's laboratory was turning out to be more treacherous than he had expected. The more working schoolmen set about translating programmatic statements into praxis, the more they were impressed by the sheer difficulty of using the human material facing them as the raw data for generalizations about "nature." In the opposite direction,

[62] Trapp, *Versuch einer Pädagogik*, pp. 61–64. Cf. Herrmann's comments on Trapp's concept of a pedagogical discipline, in ibid., pp. 436–37.

[63] In many ways this neohumanistic version of professional knowledge anticipated nineteenth-century visions of a modern "clerisy," embodying a unitary spiritual power, although the latter drew more directly on Idealist epistemology and tended to regard academic professionalism as narrow specialization. A rich, broad-ranging analysis of this subject is Ben Knights, *The Idea of the Clerisy in the Nineteenth Century* (Cambridge, 1978). See esp. the differences between authoritative public knowledge and mere opinion in Knights's interpretation of John Stuart Mill (ibid., pp. 140–77) and his discussion of the rationales for "liberal education" (ibid., pp. 178–213).

deduction – the application of such generalizations to a heterogeneous collection of subjects – was proving no less problematic. In the 1780s, before the neohumanists began to attack their arbitrary schematism, rationalist pedagogues already were acknowledging a marked tension between their urge to classify pupils as early as possible in the interests of social utility and their increasing awareness that the unfolding of individual "natures" did not conform to the predictable scientific pattern of a "law." A "scientific" selection process ran the risk of giving undue importance to the short-term precocity of some and overlooking the long-term potential of others.[64]

In his "scholastic advice" to students at the turn of the century, Wolf added two more reasons for skepticism about the development of pedagogy into what he called a "philosophical system that reduces empirical rules and maxims to basic principles." One was that it was derivative; far from distilling laws from its own empirical research, pedagogy had to borrow theory from other disciplines.[65] Trapp's definition of individual "happiness" as a state of "pleasant experience" was typical of a widespread reliance on the crude tenets of materialist philosophy and psychology, and indeed he suggested that the new science of physiognomy might one day help to identify the innate "endowments" of young children.[66] Trapp saw no problem with this eclecticism, but over the next two decades its handicaps became glaring. One could undercut the scientific and moral authority of rationalist pedagogy – as the neohumanists did from the 1790s onward – simply by denying its borrowed premises.

Unable to generate an autonomous credibility, pedagogy was coming to seem too vulnerable to ideological appropriation from outside its ranks to constitute the disciplinary basis of a professional ideology. In Wolf's words, pedagogical theory was too implicated in "political questions" about "*desiderata*" that made life "sour" for "the practitioner."[67] To rationalists, Woellner's crackdown stood as a warning that the state could turn repressive; but neohumanists saw rationalist orthodoxy and Woellner's Orthodoxy as the two sides of one coin – as ideological variations on the threat of political manipulation. Utilitarian school reform already demonstrated how easily

[64] Seen in this light, Christian Garve's cautionary remarks reflected a trend; see his "Versuch über die Prüfung der Fähigkeiten," in idem, *Sämmtliche Werke*, 13 vols. (Breslau, 1801), 7: 9–88.

[65] Wilhelm Körte, ed., *Friedrich August Wolf über Erziehung, Schule, Universität ("Consilia Scholastica"). Aus Wolf's literarischem Nachlasse* (Quedlinburg and Leipzig, 1835), pp. 6–7. On Wolf's attitude toward rationalist pedagogy see also Fuhrmann, "Wolf," pp. 202–4. But cf. the assessment of Wolf's pedagogical contribution in Roessler, "Wolf." On the larger issue of the relationship between classical philology and pedagogy, see Clemens Menze, "Philologen und Pädagogen," in Hans Bokelmann and Hans Scheuerl, eds., *Der Aufbau erziehungswissenschaftlicher Studien und der Lehrberuf. Festschrift für Wilhelm Flitner zum 80. Geburtstag* (Heidelberg, 1970), pp. 252–73.

[66] Trapp, *Versuch einer Pädagogik*, esp. pp. 34–43.

[67] Körte, *Wolf über Erziehung*, p. 18.

the fledgling discipline of pedagogy could become the instrument of fundamentally inhumane state priorities. At the same time there was less and less prospect that pedagogy would yield the disciplinary consensus that might make it autonomous. To Trapp "the needs of society" had been as transparent as "human nature"; the new "system" would derive its "principles" from both.[68] But with the divergence between neocorporate and egalitarian versions of meritocracy, it was becoming increasingly obvious that the pedagogical definition of larger social "needs," like the state-enforced definition of the public welfare, was an ideological process.

Neohumanistic schoolmen at the turn of the century were as concerned as earlier reformers with establishing the moral authority of a public profession. The new classical studies seemed to offer precisely what pedagogy lacked. In his elaborate manifesto for an *Altertumswissenschaft*, Wolf was intent on demonstrating that the various forms of expertise required in the new discipline formed a "well-ordered" and "organic" whole. If the study of classical antiquity was interdisciplinary, it was also as self-contained as pedagogy was eclectic. While the pedagogue had to contend with a derivative, open-ended field, vulnerable to pressures from society and the state and hence to "political" appropriation by outsiders, the classicist commanded a clearly bounded intellectual jurisdiction. What gave the discipline clear borders was not simply its limited corpus of historical artifacts; its other advantage in that sense was that it could not be "popular." Since the essence of classical culture was distilled in its languages, Wolf and others insisted, the discipline was penetrable only by way of hard-won expertise in philology and textual criticism.[69]

The other source of disciplinary integrity was the subject itself. While the heterogeneity of the schoolroom-as-laboratory mitigated against systematic theory, the focus of classical studies – the culture of classical Greece – seemed to offer a scholarly community the prospect of ongoing penetration into an inherently unitary "spirit." Nature in the abstract – the rationalist standard – was replaced by the image of a specific historical culture. This was not to prefer empirical objectivity over moral authority; historical reconstruction promised a more credible – and more fruitful – union of the scientific and the normative. In the very process of achieving a unique refinement, classical Greece was seen to have exhibited human nature in its purest forms. Unlike the nature that pedagogy claimed to discern behind

[68] Trapp, *Versuch einer Pädagogik*, esp. pp. 44–45. For an approach similar to Trapp's in its naiveté see Johann Stuve, "Allgemeine Grundsätze der Erziehung, hergeleitet aus einer richtigen Kenntniss des Menschen . . .," AR 1 (1785): 232–382.

[69] Friedrich August Wolf, *Darstellung der Alterthumswissenschaft, nebst einer Auswahl seiner kleinen Schriften und literarischen Zugaben zu dessen Vorlesungen*, ed. S. F. W. Hoffmann (Leipzig, 1839), esp. pp. 6–8, 57–75; Friedrich Jacobs, "Zweck einer gelehrten Schule," in Rudolf Joerden, ed., *Dokumente des Neuhumanismus I*. Kleine Pädagogische Texte, vol. 17 (2nd ed.: Weinheim, 1962): 32–45.

a social surface, the natural model of Greece seemed detached from social bias by its very historical self-containment and distance.[70] In retrospect it is obvious enough that schoolmen like Jacobs projected their own social values onto classical Greece in the very process of extolling it as a model and using it as a standing reproach to their own commercialized, utilitarian, and – in the negative sense – politicized culture. But they thought they were taking the measure of modernity with an objective historical understanding of a superior culture. In that sense the new disciplinary community, using the more or less oblique method of invidious comparisons between past and present, claimed for itself the same public authority as moral arbiter that pedagogy had aspired to exercise.

This appeal of the new discipline as an internal source of credibility was inseparable from its advantages in structuring careers. There was more than a little of the old-style patron in Wolf's fatherly advice to his seminar protégés, and in his efforts to place them. But he also prepared and encouraged them to establish themselves by pursuing a "cold-blooded" publication strategy. What was needed was the kind of substantive scholarly contribution that was manageable for beginners but, unlike contributions to pedagogy, could be judged by criteria on which a community of scholars agreed. The apprentice established his credentials by applying his philological and historical skills to an ancient text or group of texts, and above all by sweeping away later accretions to reconstruct the original artifact. To Wolf it was outstanding proficiency in this kind of scholarship that ought to qualify schoolmen for the higher gymnasium grades, while the mediocre practitioners would be relegated to the lower ranks. That in itself is a measure of his distance from reformers like Lieberkühn and Gedike, whose efforts to eliminate invidious distinctions among grade levels reflected their conviction that mastery of the pedagogical art, and not scholarly prowess, was the critical professional qualification.[71]

In theory textual editing put the scholar "at the actual center of the entire field of classical studies."[72] Dissection and reconstruction of the particular text, however neglected the text had been and obscure it might seem, was a multifaceted entrée into the organic whole of the culture. As the epitome of scholarly expertise and the middle term between a well-cultivated personality and the historical *Cultur* that was its model, the dominant form of

[70] Wolf, *Darstellung*, pp. 52–53. This is not to deny that the new historical modes of thought within the German Enlightenment prepared the way for modern "historicism"; see the persuasive arguments in Peter Hans Reill, *The German Enlightenment and the Rise of Historicism* (Berkeley, Calif., 1975), and Hans Erich Bödeker, George G. Iggers, Jonathan B. Knudsen, and Peter H. Reill, eds., *Aufklärung und Geschichte. Studien zur deutschen Geschichtswissenschaft im 18. Jahrhundert* (Göttingen, 1986).

[71] See esp. *Wolf; ein Leben in Briefen*, 1: 209–10.

[72] Jacobs, "Zweck einer gelehrten Schule," p. 41. See also Wolf, *Darstellung*, esp. pp. 24–25.

publication would reflect the kind of professional personality Wolf aspired to produce. But in fact the gap between programmatic rhetoric and reality – a gap that would become glaring in the nineteenth-century *Philologenstand* – was already emerging among Wolf's students at the turn of the century. The theoretical claim to grasp the whole inevitably lost substance as careers in classical scholarship in the new *Gymnasien* and philosophy faculties came to be built increasingly on specialized, largely fragmented research. Wolf himself had an inkling of the danger; in his 1807 manifesto he warned that a new mania for detail, cut off from "general principles," threatened to produce confusion and as a result classical studies might forfeit its claim to be a unitary *Wissenschaft* in comparison with "the more rigorous disciplines" (*den strengern Disciplinen*).[73] But the momentum was there; the disciplinary credibility of the profession would soon be contradicted by the scholarship that launched and sustained its careers.

[73] Wolf, *Darstellung*, pp. 74–75. On Wolf's concept of research, see also Axel Horstmann, "Die 'Klassische Philologie' zwischen Humanismus und Historismus. Friedrich August Wolf und die Begründung der modernen Altertumswissenschaft," *Berichte zur Wissenschaftsgeschichte* 1 (1978): 51–70; idem, "Die Forschung in der Klassischen Philologie des 19. Jahrhunderts," in Alwin Diemer, ed., *Konzeption und Begriff der Forschung in den Wissenschaften des 19. Jahrhunderts*, Studien zur Wissenschaftstheorie, vol. 12 (Meisenheim am Glan, 1978), pp. 27–57. Anthony Grafton, "Polyhistor into *Philolog*: Notes on the Transformation of German Classical Scholarship, 1780–1850," *History of Universities* 3 (1983): 159–92, explores the ironies of the gap between theory and practice in the new *Altertumswissenschaft*.

11

The clerical identity

VOCATIONS, CAREERS, AND OFFICES

In the hagiography of every modern profession there is a heroic age of struggle. For German schoolmen, the struggle on one front pitted a fledgling profession against the clerical legacy that kept it fastened to an archaic identity. But when the schoolmen's act of secession is set in a larger process – when it is understood as a stage in the transformation of the learned estate into a *Bildungsbürgertum* – it can be seen to have occurred within the formation of a new consensus. In many respects teachers and clergymen fashioned similar ideological responses to analogous conditions, opportunities, and threats. There are underlying parallels in the initial impetus behind their formulations of professional ideologies and in their rhetorical shifts in gear from utilitarianism to neohumanism at the end of the century.[1]

While teachers reached for an entirely new status, reform-minded clergymen in the last decades of the eighteenth century felt compelled to react

[1] Generally the reform movements among teachers and clergymen have been considered separately, in part because the emphasis has been on the professional split between them from the late eighteenth century onward and in part because of the division of labor between the history of education and church history. A notable exception is Volker Wehrmann, *Die Aufklärung in Lippe. Ihre Bedeutung für Politik, Schule und Geistesleben* (Detmold, 1972). Christian Homrichhausen, "Evangelische Pfarrer in Deutschland," in Werner Conze and Jürgen Kocka, eds., *Bildungsbürgertum im 19. Jahrhundert*, Teil 1: *Bildungssystem und Professionalisierung in internationalen Vergleichen*, Industrielle Welt, vol. 38 (Stuttgart, 1985), pp. 248–78, includes background on the impact of Pietism and the Enlightenment. Still useful for the institutional and social conditions of clerical life is Georges Pariset, *L'Etat and les églises en Prusse sous Frédéric Guillaume Ier (1713–1740)* (Paris, 1897). For an interesting overview, stressing the social inferiority and the political subordination of the rural clergy, see Gerd Heinrich, "Amtsträgerschaft und Geistlichkeit. Zur Problematik der sekundären Führungsschichten in Brandenburg-Preussen 1450–1786," in Günther Franz, ed., *Beamtentum und Pfarrerstand 1400–1800. Büdener Vorträge 1967*, Deutsche Führungsschichte in der Neuzeit, vol. 5 (Limburg/Lahn, 1972): 179–238. An important recent addition to the literature on the clergy and its reform sentiments is John Stroup, *The Struggle for Identity in the Clerical Estate. Northwest German Protestant Opposition to Absolutist Policy in the Eighteenth Century*, Studies in the History of Church Thought, vol. 33 (Leiden, 1984). My analysis agrees with Stroup's in many respects and profited considerably from his detailed profile of the clergy on a regional scale as well as from his overarching interpretation of the shift from Enlightenment reform thought to neohumanism.

against a precipitous decline in the prestige of their order.[2] There was nothing new about this theme; one encounters the same lament in the early eighteenth century, especially among Pietist clergymen, and indeed in the immediate aftermath of the Thirty Years' War. But whereas the early Pietists traced the corruption of church life to the disruptions of war, clergymen a century later attributed the spread of irreligiosity to a superficial but nonetheless corrosive secular rationalism. Were popular attitudes toward the clergy actually changing? The very recurrence of alarm on this score gives pause for skepticism, and it is reinforced by clergymen's equally incessant complaints about popular attachment to obsolete confessional traditions.

What did confront clergymen was the dissolution of the learned estate. This was an accelerating process, opening new prospects for fashioning an up-to-date professional identity, but also raising the unsettling possibility that the ancient clerical order would not find a secure place in a new elite of educated professions. At first glance there might seem to have been little ground for anxiety on this score; the clergy still controlled one of the two main faculties at Protestant universities, and in the second half of the century theologians were still producing much of the published scholarship. Did not the order's hoary credentials as a learned body ensure that it would enjoy an analogous status in a new occupational hierarchy? But offsetting this advantage was the anomalous identity of the great majority of clergymen in a learned culture that was largely urban. While most educated men were concentrated in university towns and other centers, the uniqueness of the clergy as a learned profession lay in the fact that its pastorates, even in comparison with small-town Latin schools, were so dispersed. Village pastorates represented the farthest points to which academic learning and the doctrinal orthodoxy it was expected to uphold had penetrated the dense and often resistant culture of the rural masses.

It was above all in these rural outposts that clergymen faced the "poverty" most educated men were spared. Since pastorates were locally endowed and supported, they varied enormously in income level, even within a small region. Again deprivation was relative; in income even the occupant of a well-endowed village pastorate stood far below the pastor of a town cathedral, especially when the latter office was combined, as it often was, with a higher ecclesiastical post or a university appointment. Exaggeration was likely in figures cited to prove how poor the bulk of clergymen really were,

[2] For examples of the usual laments see, "Ueber die Verachtung des geistlichen Standes, so fern sie durch ihn selbst veranlasset wird," *Journal für Prediger* 16:1 (1785): 41–64 (cited hereafter as JP); Christian Benedikt Glörfeld, "Ueber die dem Landpredigerstande eigenen Uebel und deren Abhelfung," JP 18:4 (1787): 385–447; "Ueber die Bildung künftiger Landprediger," JP 19 (1787): 163–96. See also Alexandra Schlingensiepen-Pogge, *Das Sozialethos der lutherischen Aufklärungstheologie am Vorabend der Industriellen Revolution*, Göttinger Bausteine zur Geschichtswissenschaft, vol. 39 (Göttingen, 1967), pp. 183–91.

particularly in view of the tendency to underestimate the importance of land endowments and contributions in kind in insulating village pastors from the dramatic rises in food prices to which their colleagues in the towns were much more vulnerable. But estimates of income ranges by reliable observers leave no doubt that many positions had been poorly endowed from the start and that many more were made inadequate by inflation in the course of the eighteenth century. The lower strata of incomes tended to hover around the 300–thaler mark, and the very bottom was as low as 200 thaler; apparently some of the Latin school teachers who finally escaped to village pastorates experienced less improvement than they had expected.

In the eyes of clergymen, however, "poverty" was not the only reason village pastors were "disdained" by the educated urban elite. The other was their sheer isolation. One of the stock figures of clerical literature was the young theology graduate who sank into the obscurity of a village pastorate and could not climb out. If his *Brotstudium* had lasted only three or four semesters, as seemed increasingly the case, his link with the learned world was already tenuous. But even a stronger link was likely to snap over time. He might very well be the only university graduate in his community, and in the vast reaches of the countryside distance and poor traveling conditions meant that contacts with colleagues were necessarily infrequent. If he married the daughter of a local farmer he became "a peasant with his wife." In any case it was difficult to avoid being "peasantized" over the years. The need to farm the land endowments attached to their offices, or at least to manage them, dragged pastors down into the peasants' daily concerns; they became, in the words of a village pastor in lower Saxony, "entirely peasants, cattle and grain dealers."[3] Aside from the fact that the demands of farming left little time and energy for scholarship, the typical village pastor simply could not afford to maintain a decent library on his meager income, particularly if he had a large brood to feed.

There were village pastors who managed somehow to develop impressive scholarly libraries and who compensated for their physical isolation with far-flung correspondence. And as some clergymen pointed out, reality offered a broad spectrum of possibilities between the ideal of the pastor-scholar and the stereotype of his peasantized colleague; the pastor could limit his involvement in farming, particularly if he leased his land endowments, and he need not keep abreast of the latest scholarship to command respect and

[3] "Ueber die Bildung künftiger Landprediger," p. 175. On the intellectual isolation of the rural pastor and the problem of being "peasantized," see esp. "Wie wird ein Dorfprediger vor der Versuchung bewahret, sich und sein Amt immer mehr und mehr zu erniedrigen . . .?" JP 1 (1770): 283–92; "Von dem Ungange eines Predigers mit seinen Zuhörern, sonderlich auf dem Lande," JP 12 (1782): 144–70; "Ueber die Nothwendigkeit der moralischen Verbesserung des Predigerstandes," *Eusebia* 1 (1797): 122–26. It was "the contempt for the rural pastor" that induced Georg Heinrich Lang, a Special-superintendent in Trochtelfingen, to launch *Der Landprediger* in 1774; see the *Vorbericht* to the first volume.

eventually attain patriarchal status as the resident *Gelehrter*. But if the stereotype ignored a variety of accommodations, it recorded the precarious self-image many university graduates brought to village life. Likewise the peasantized pastor was a graphic reminder to colleagues that the broad base of the clerical pyramid threatened to drag down the entire order – to leave it hovering somewhere between the ignorant masses and the truly educated, largely urban elite. In 1790 Gottfried Less, a theology professor at Göttingen, voiced a widespread sentiment when he attributed the mounting contempt for religion and its ministers to the swarm of theology students "of the lowest station, lacking in culture, bad and raw in their attitudes and their manners."[4] Rural dispersion magnified the social handicap that the presence of poor students, and particularly of outsiders, already posed. The "peasantizing" of such recruits in rural outposts seemed less a shedding of learned culture than the confirmation of an inherited and perhaps ineradicable "baseness."

By the end of the century there was a wide spectrum of opinion on how to expunge this stigma. Johann August Nösselt, the presiding theologian at Halle, gave considerable weight to the minority view of the clergy as a career open to natural talent, even in the absence of "external" means. The stronger sentiment in the higher echelons of the clergy, and most noticeably in the professoriate, was to screen out the plebs in the process of reducing the supply of candidates.[5] But even within this social bias, reinforced by the corporate consciousness of clerical dynasties, it had become commonplace to define the clerical *Beruf* in the same secular language of nature that shaped teachers' self-image. This was in itself a striking measure of the extent to which the ascendancy of rationalist theology had eclipsed both Orthodoxy and Pietism. Despite the initial tendency in Lutheranism to regard the ministry as one of many outlets for Christian faith and charity in an "external" calling, some Orthodox theologians – responding to the threat of radical spiritualism – had made efficacy dependent on a sacral status derived from ordination and on the supernatural power inherent in Scripture. The Halle Pietists would have none of this; to them the sine qua

[4] Gottfried Less, *Ueber Christliches Lehr-Amt Dessen würdige Fürung, Und die schikliche Vorbereitung dazu* (Göttingen, 1790), pp. vi-vii, 72–75.

[5] Heyne and several other professors of lowly origins shared this view. For the spectrum of opinion, see, e.g., Johann August Nösselt, *Anweisung zur Bildung angehender Theologen*, 3 vols. (2nd enl. and rev. ed.: Halle, 1791), 2: 158–59; Less, *Ueber Christliches Lehr-Amt*; the memorandum by Heyne and other Göttingen professors, Feb. 4, 1788, in Göttingen Universitätsarchiv, 4 II a, file 31; I. C. Velthusen, "Einige Bemerkungen über die zu grosse Anzahl der Studirenden," *Neues Magazin für Schullehrer* 2:2 (1793): 347–52; Johann Samuel Fest, *Ueber die Vortheile und Gefahren der Armuth für Jünglinge auf der Academie* (Leipzig, 1784); Friedrich Erdmann August Heydenreich, *Ueber die zweckmässige Anwendung der Universitätsjahre. Ein Handbuch für Academisten, und die es werden wollen* (Leipzig, 1804), pp. 233–39. Stroup notes the predominance of "elitist" (or "exclusivist") tendencies in discussions of recruitment for the clergy, but ignores the minority sentiment for a more egalitarian selection; Stroup, *Struggle for Identity*, Appendix J.

non for an effective ministry was conversion, since only its wrenching transformation could make an "external" clerical calling the expression of an "inner fire."[6] Calling in this sense not only sanctified the occupancy of an "office," which would otherwise be mere sham; it also had the power to compensate for the absence of natural "gifts." Hence Francke, for all his concern with a *selectum ingeniorum*, was confident that the converted candidate would prove a "servant of the Lord" even if he had entered the clergy with the wrong motives and lacked the aptitude for scholarship.[7]

In rationalist theology, the ministry was thoroughly integrated into a social division of labor – one that would reflect the natural distribution of human resources in a rational society. Potential recruits were not urged to enter an "atonement struggle," but to make a rational decision after methodically identifying their God-given but natural capacities. Demonstrating the requisite character was not a matter of denying the natural self, but of harnessing its potential in disciplined academic achievement. The "external" calling might still refer to the office; but more often it was a shorthand for the ascriptive advantages of family wealth and "culture," and the issue was whether these should be considered essential to a clerical vocation. Even the neocorporate preference rejected as merely "accidental" much of the family-centered corporate tradition and charitable impulse that carried young men into the clergy. A certain minimal level of family wealth and "culture" might be indispensable, but the clergyman who insisted that his son follow in his footsteps, despite the boy's lack of abilities, was acting as irrationally as the artisan or peasant who, as a gesture of piety, dedicated his son to the church from birth. Patronage likewise was open to censure; the question was not whether patrons were instruments of providence or of "worldly" temptation, but whether they obstructed or facilitated a rational selection of qualified recruits.[8]

A reformed clergy, embodying this ideal of calling, would be a career open to talent, although it might not reach very far down the social scale for its recruits. Whether it should also form a structured career – whether clergymen should have the same opportunities for advancement to which teachers aspired – was a more delicate issue. In fact the clergy already had a loose hierarchy of incomes and prestige, with discernible career patterns. Among pastoral appointments the plums were senior positions in the cathedral churches of larger towns. These were usually the steppingstones

[6] Background in Stroup, *Struggle for Identity*, esp. pp. 29–42; Martin Schmidt, "Das pietistische Pfarrideal und seine altkirchliche Wurzeln," in Bernd Moeller and Gerhard Ruhbach, eds., *Bleibendes im Wandel der Kirchengeschichte. Kirchen-historische Studien* (Tübingen, 1973), pp. 211–50.

[7] See Chapter 5.

[8] See, e.g., Johann Lorenz Mosheim, *Sitten-Lehre der Heiligen Schrift* (4th rev. and enl. ed.: Helmstedt, 1753), pp. 517–34; Less, *Ueber Christliches Lehr-Amt*, pp. 62–63; Nösselt, *Anweisung*, 2: 158–59; Johann Georg Rosenmüller, *Anleitung für angehende Geistliche zur weisen und gemeinschaftlichen Verwaltung ihres Amtes* (Ulm, 1778), p. 10.

for the actual administrative elite – the regional inspectors and superintendents, and the consistorial councilors in provincial centers. The tenured professor still stood high in the pecking order, particularly when his professorial earnings were combined with the income attached to an office in ecclesiastical administration or a prestigious urban pastorate. To a degree the professoriate recruited in-house; chairs went to protégés of established scholars who had never left university life. But the pastor who made his mark in clerical publications – with a technical exercise in biblical scholarship, or with a collection of sermons, or simply with timely contributions on the issues of the day – could also ascend to a professorial appointment.

The biographical sketches published in the *Allgemeines Magazin für Prediger* at the end of the century represent a broad cross-section of this elite and include its senior members, on the edge of retirement or already retired, as well as its younger generation. They leave no doubt that career mobility was already a reality of life in the eighteenth-century clergy. In a sample of forty-two clergymen, nine had had four or more intercommunity promotions. Twenty-five of them had made three or more such moves, and only eleven of these were fifty years of age or older (out of nineteen in that age group).[9] And this is the tip of the iceberg; the most prestigious and lucrative urban pastorates formed the peak of a steep pyramid of pastoral appointments, most of them in villages and small towns, offering clergymen myriad opportunities to improve their incomes and other conditions of employment.

And yet in the second half of the century a widespread *Wanderlust* in the lower ranks was not being satisfied. The clerical literature is filled with laments about promising young men trapped in poorly endowed, remote, and stultifying village assignments, and with bitter complaints about the local procedures for filling vacancies. Even when the appointment was legally in the hands of the state government, local patrons – the estate lord, for example, or a clergyman on the scene – played an influential role. More often the new pastor was chosen by the estate lord exercising his ancient right of *Patronat*, or by the lay elders of the parish, or by the entire group of adult male parishioners. Disappointed office seekers tended to regard the latter, relatively democratic procedure as the most farcical, particularly when it included a "trial sermon" before the entire congregation. Ignorant laymen, concerned above all to find a preacher who met their standards for Sunday entertainment, were all too easily impressed by a demagogic performance in a booming voice. But in any case decisions were made behind the scenes. The most scandalous rumors were of candidates passing money under the table and of the bachelor agreeing to marry the deceased pastor's

[9] The sample from the *Allgemeines Magazin für Prediger* (cited hereafter as AMP) excludes twenty clergymen whose careers had been entirely within the universities, as well as six others whose careers seemed too eccentric.

widow (who might otherwise become a burden on the community) as a condition of his appointment. If outright nepotism did not come into play, "connections" within the community were indispensable – and obsequiousness toward the local powerbrokers was the order of the day.[10]

All this makes it understandable that poor students in clerical careers often seemed to confirm the prevailing stereotypes. There was the same degrading "dependence" on patrons, the same requirement of "servility," the same occasions for the ambitious young man to act without "honor." Clergymen had been inclined to agree that climbers in their own ranks were especially deserving of this moral censure. Mobility was suspect, and not simply because long tenure in a pastorate seemed necessary to win the confidence of a congregation and have an impact on it. In Halle Pietism, as in Lutheran Orthodoxy, patrons could be providential instruments in the "mediate" calling to a clerical office; but the opportunities and pressures of patronage were seen as tests of the passivity that only self-denial in conversion could effect. The true "servant of the Lord" did not actively seek an office; he waited for providence to point him to it and was careful not to mistake selfish motives for genuine responses to providential signs.

In the course of the eighteenth century this ideal of passivity retained considerable authority as a standard for condemning clerical careerism. But it came to coexist uneasily with mounting complaints about the lack of opportunities for advancement, and the result was a marked ambivalence about the considerable degree of career mobility that already existed. At midcentury Johann Lorenz Mosheim, the presiding theologian at Helmstedt, envisioned a three-tiered hierarchy of clerical careers, distinguished by levels of scholarly training and with crossovers only in rare cases. "So long as there are not reasons of great importance for doing otherwise," he wrote, "each should remain his entire life with the community to which he is assigned." Mosheim also called for new screening procedures to prevent "blind" decisions by parents and patrons from burdening the clergy with candidates lacking the requisite natural gifts. These two reforms seemed complementary; it would do little good to select qualified men if they were not required to develop strong bonds with their parishes and were not prevented from acquiring the habits of "servility" and hypocrisy that patronage demanded.[11]

[10] For complaints about appointment procedures see, e.g., "Ueber die Verachtung des geistlichen Standes," pp. 50–51; Glörfeld, "Ueber die dem Landpredigerstande eigenen Uebel," pp. 414–19; "Pastoralkorrespondenz," JP 6 (1799): 403–09; "Ueber die Nothwendigkeit der moralischen Verbesserung des Predigerstandes," pp. 39, 126; Johann Georg Gottfried Kiesling, *Briefe zur Bildung des Landpredigers*, vol. 2 (Hof and Plauen, 1787), pp. 283–90.

[11] Mosheim, *Sitten-Lehre*, pp. 517–34. Stroup, *Struggle for Identity*, pp. 50–81, rightly stresses Mosheim's defense of historic church rights against centralizing state interference; but Mosheim's reform thought also exemplifies a tension between this affinity with "political particularism" and a tendency to look to the state to reform clerical recruitment and rescue

That Mosheim wanted severe restrictions on career mobility is not surprising; his generation combined a degree of openness to rationalism with a solid attachment to the essentials of Orthodoxy and was strongly influenced by Pietism. But even in autobiographies written at the end of the century, Spalding and other prominent rationalists were still confirming the validity of traditional strictures by assuring their readers – and, one suspects, themselves – that their ascent from obscure origins to the heights of the clerical pyramid had not been motored by ambition. These were men who by upbringing, or as a result of a traumatic repudiation of Pietism in their youth, disdained the conversion experience as misguided enthusiasm, if not self-serving hypocrisy. They retraced the steps of their "inner" progress not in terms of receptivity to grace, but in the secular idiom of vocation. Where they nonetheless acknowledged the Pietist ideal was in repeated, almost formulaic claims that "calls" to new offices had materialized "accidentally" and "unexpectedly," often because patrons had interceded without their knowledge. While some had become convinced in retrospect that providence had guided their careers, others recalled in detail how providential signs at the time had persuaded them to accept particular appointments, despite their reluctance to do so.[12]

As heartfelt as they were, such assurances are a long way from the passive acceptance of God's Will that Francke had made a test of categorical self-denial. In the chemistry of its bonding with other values, recognition of providential intervention acted as a kind of solvent, dissolving guilt about the presence of ambition in decisions, or at least cleansing the conscience of its traces after the fact. That the solvent was still needed, even in a markedly rationalist mentality, is a measure of how deeply rooted clerical inhibitions about career advancement were. Yet in the second half of the century a new note of candor – a new willingness to confront the psychological reality of ambition and to allow it a degree of legitimacy in the fulfillment of a natural vocation – enters the discussion of clerical appointments. It is sounded, ever so tentatively, in Johann Georg Rosenmüller's introductory handbook for theology students, drawn from his lecture notes at Erlangen. As the son of a village towel maker and schoolmaster and as a former charity pupil, Rosenmüller was in a position to know about career opportunities. In the six years before his professorial appointment at Erlangen in 1773, he had occupied three pastorates. He went on to become a professor and superintendent at Giessen in 1783 and to combine the same

clergymen from dependencies on patrons and local communities. If state centralization seemed threatening in some respects, it seemed to promise emancipation in others.

[12] See, e.g., Johann Joachim Spalding, *Lebensbeschreibung von ihm selbst aufgesetzt*, ed. Georg Ludewig Spalding (Halle, 1804), esp. pp. 130–35; Anton Friedrich Büsching, *Eigene Lebensgeschichte* (Halle, 1789), passim. There are also numerous examples of this life perspective in the career sketches in AMP.

offices with the pastorate of the renowned Thomaskirche in Leipzig in 1787. By then Rosenmüller was fifty-one years old; since the completion of his university studies twenty-seven years earlier he had changed appointments (and communities) six times.

In the handbook Rosenmüller assured his readers that the "external call" (*vocationen externam*) to a particular office could be considered "providential," even though it came "indirectly, through men." But the candidate who expected God to use "quite extraordinary means" to lead patrons to choose him was guilty of "pride and vanity"; he must actually apply for a vacant position. If parishioners urged the pastor to stay but "providence" put "new obstacles" in the way of complying, he could "follow his new call with a good conscience." In choosing between two new appointments, he should ask which would provide the greater opportunity to "be useful"; but since this criterion could be very deceptive, it was also quite proper to consider "many external advantages for [his] health and for the better upbringing and support of [his] family."[13]

In the last decades of the century, many young clergymen may still have needed Rosenmüller's fine distinctions and tortuous logic to keep their moral bearings in the face of career opportunities and pitfalls. But his counsels came to seem dated as the view of appointments as rewards for individual merit, and hence as rungs on the ladder of a professional career, gained currency in the reform literature of the 1780s. It was a bit callous, a reviewer in the *Journal für Prediger* noted in 1788, to advise candidates surviving on "low incomes," and "well aware that they could fill more important positions with usefulness and God's approval," to trust in providence rather than apply for vacancies.[14] Sometimes drawing on firsthand experience in village outposts, spokesmen now openly voiced the frustrations and aspirations of young men at the broad base of the clerical pyramid. Christian Benedikt Glörfeld, the *Archdiakonus* in the town of Bernau in Brandenburg, claimed to speak for the majority of rural pastors, who lacked the "family connections" their colleagues in the towns enjoyed and could not practice "the art of sneaking in" through "devious means" and "tricks."

> . . . rural pastors, as soon as they have withdrawn from the great world into their rustic dwelling, are usually forgotten and can expect only to remain in their posts for the rest of their lives. How depressing is this prospect, and how sad it can make a man who does not want to bury his talents in a remote corner. . . . are not pastors as human as others? Should they spiritualize themselves completely and renounce everything earthly? Do you mean to find fault when, noticing that they would be more effective and could pursue their tasks with more enthusiasm if they did not

[13] Rosenmüller, *Anleitung*, esp. pp. 27–33. For the details of Rosenmüller's biography, see AMP 2 (1790): 85–90.

[14] See the review of Johann Casper Häseli, *Ueber das Anhalten und Bewerben um Predigerstellen*, in JP 20 (1788): 245–46.

have worries about subsistence, they have the blameless desire to see their circumstances improved?[15]

Glörfeld rejected patronage as an intolerable obstruction to enlightened ambition; instead the state should make rural pastorates an obligatory "seminary" to qualify for town appointments and should guarantee every clergyman the prospect of "advancing according to seniority and capacity."[16] This was typical of the tendency to regard village pastorates not as places in which to settle for a lifetime, but as launching points for structured career trajectories. In 1800 a village pastor in Grafschaft Hoya argued the advantages of beginning new candidates in "modest" rural posts, despite the tribulations he himself had experienced, but on the assumption that a staged advance to better positions would keep "merit and reward, worth and improvement of our external situation . . . in the proper balance and in the right relationship to one another."[17] In this view of the pastorate, as in the new conception of the teaching office, historic local rights were an imposing but surmountable obstacle. The most common proposal was to require communities to choose among a few candidates who had applied directly to the provincial consistory, without a trial sermon or any other local contacts, and who had already been deemed "meritorious" by its knowledgeable and "objective" councilors. Only with this circumvention of the "chicanery" and "cabales" of local notables, and of the ignorant preferences of the local population at large, would clergymen be able to pursue their legitimate ambitions with honor.[18]

Clergymen were no less insistent than teachers that their reform efforts were not to be confused with corporate selfishness. Once again sanctioned by the logic of a service ethic, group self-interest, far from threatening to collide with the welfare of the society as a whole, became the rational means to its promotion. It was to attract qualified men for a vital public mission, and to provide them with incentives for achievement in office, that the clergy needed a reform of appointment procedures and a host of other "improvements."

[15] Glörfeld, "Ueber die dem Landpredigerstande eigenen Uebel," pp. 415–17.

[16] Ibid., pp. 440–41.

[17] Müller, "Ueber die Nutzbarkeit der Verfahrungsart protestantischen Consistorien ihre Prediger von geringern auf bessere Pfarren zu versetzen," JP 38 (1800): 184. "What will stimulate us to continue with our *Bildung* and our studies," this pastor asked, "if we have to realize in distress that we are being overlooked despite all the integrity of our intentions, and that favoritism and recommendations always take precedence over merits?"

[18] See, e.g., Kiesling, *Briefe*, 2: 285–89; "Pastoralkorrespondenz," p. 406; Glörfeld, "Ueber die dem Landpredigerstande eigenen Uebel," pp. 414–19; "Ueber die Nothwendigkeit der moralischen Verbesserung," pp. 88–89; "Ueber die Prüfung der Candidaten zum Predigtamte. Was ist ihr Zweck? und was erfordert dieser?" *Eusebia* 3(1800): 197–248; Christian Dassel, "Worin soll die Tätigkeit der Prediger bestehen, und wie kann man dieselbe befördern?" *Eusebia* 3 (1800): 553–54.

To rationalist clergymen the mission itself seemed clear enough by the 1780s. In an extraordinarily popular book, Spalding had argued that the "usefulness" of the pastor consisted not only in teaching Christian doctrine, but also in disseminating the "public virtue" and the "community spirit" that was perfectly compatible with it. In the latter capacity the pastor was "the actual depository of public morality," inculcating in his congregation "industriousness, obedience, patient acceptance of burdens imposed, loyalty in service, honor in commerce and the trades, and the like."[19] In a sense, the utilitarian rationalism at the core of this vision reoriented a conception of the ministry fundamental to the Lutheran tradition. Spalding and like-minded colleagues could appeal to Luther's own view of the clergy not as a segregated caste with sacral, quasi-priestly functions, but as one more calling – albeit a critical one – integrated into Christian society. But this was integration in an entirely new key; what would now bind together minister and congregation was not the shared grace of a "priesthood of all believers," but the universal rationality of "virtue" (*Tugend*) and "usefulness."

Not surprisingly, the focus for this new mission was the rural pastorate. Since the late seventeenth century cameralist theorists had argued that an increase in the "usefulness " of the rural masses, and especially in their economic productivity, would both enhance their own "happiness" and bring enormous benefit to the state. In the eighteenth century economic objectives were incorporated into a larger assault on rural popular culture, aimed at ripping away the entire fabric of irrational norms and beliefs summoned up by the catchwords "prejudice" and "superstition." The enthusiasts of "enlightenment" in the educated elite had come to realize that the innate rationality of the peasant, though hidden beneath a crude exterior and often atrophied by the sheer drudgery of his life, could be tapped. But they also could not help but be aware that the notorious resistance to change in rural communities was greatly facilitated by their sheer inaccessibility. From this angle the dispersion of the clergy put it in a unique strategic position; the outreaches of Orthodoxy might become the conduits of enlightenment. As the only local bridge from the learned culture of rationality to the scattered masses of countrymen, the village pastor became the "popular educator" (*Volkserzieher*) or "popular enlightener" (*Volksaufklärer*) par excellence. It was in that capacity that he figured so prominently in a spate of rationalist idylls of the peasant-*Bürger*.[20]

19 Johann Joachim Spalding, *Ueber die Nutzbarkeit des Predigtamtes und deren Beförderung* (3rd, enl. ed.: Berlin, 1791), pp. 75–90, 100–1.

20 Perhaps the most famous examples of the new peasant literature were Christian Salzmann's *Sebastian Kluge* (1789) and Rudolf Zacharias Becker's *Das Not und Hülfs-Büchlein* (1788). The latter has received a highly informative commentary, placing it within the larger context of reform and its clerical leadership, in Reinhart Siegert, *Aufklärung und Volkslektüre Exemplarisch dargestellt an Rudolph Zacharias Becker und seinem 'Not-und Hülfsbüchlein'* (Frankfurt am Main, 1978). Still useful for the ideal of a rational peasant community and the key role assigned the

The initial impulse for this redefinition of the pastoral role came from outside the clerical ranks, and particularly from cameralism; but the clerical literature of the 1770s and 1780s made it central to an emergent professional ideology. If the clergy was to recover lost prestige, it would be by demonstrating its unique public "usefulness" in a functional hierarchy. With a reform of rural pastorates the rank and file – the men who from another standpoint seemed such a drag on its claim to learned status – would epitomize "merit" in and through "service."[21] While the ideal pastor remained a moral teacher in the 1770s and 1780s, he was also expected to compensate for the scarcity of other professional services in the countryside. The pastor familiar with new developments in scientific agronomy could use the example of his own farming, as well as his formal teaching, to encourage the peasants to introduce clover or potatoes, or to switch to a more efficient field rotation, or to cultivate silkworms. He could help alleviate local poverty by reorganizing poor relief and introducing "industry schools" for pauper children. With a little medical knowledge he could counteract the local ignorance and superstition about medical care that midwives and "quacks" perpetuated. As an informed mediator in local feuds, he could cure the peasants' notorious "mania for litigation," and with a basic knowledge of arithmetic and geometry he could serve as local surveyor.[22] There was a great deal of wishful thinking in all this; but in the 1770s and 1780s clergymen trained to fulfill this multifaceted mission proliferated throughout northern and central Germany, and at the turn of the century younger men

local pastor is Olga von Hippel, *Die pädagogische Dorfutopie der Aufklärung*, Göttingen Studien zur Pädagogik, Heft 31 (Langensalza, 1939). For background on the issue of popular (and esp. peasant) "enlightenment," see esp. Manfred Heinemann, *Schule im Vorfeld der Verwaltung. Die Entwicklung der preussischen Unterrichtsverwaltung von 1771–1800* (Göttingen, 1974); Walter Götze, *Die Begründung der Volksbildung in der Aufklärungsbewegung* (Langensalza, 1932); John G. Gagliardo, *From Pariah to Patriot; The Changing Image of the German Peasant, 1770–1840* (Lexington, Ky., 1969).

[21] The clerical periodical literature of the late eighteenth century is permeated with this reform sentiment and logic. For background on rationalist clergymen's conception of the new civic ethic and their efforts to disseminate it, see Schlingensiepen-Pogge, *Sozialethos*; Reinhard Krause, *Die Predigt der späten deutschen Aufklärung (1770–1805)*, Arbeiten zu Theologie, 2. Reihe, vol. 5 (Stuttgart, 1965). See also Dagobert de Levie, "Patriotism and Clerical Office: Germany 1767–1773," *Journal of the History of Ideas* 14 (1953): 622–27; Werner Schütz, "Die Kanzel als Katheder der Aufklärung," in *Wolfenbüttler Studien zur Aufklärung. Im Auftrag der Lessing-Akademie*, ed. Günter Schultz, vol. 1 (Wolfenbüttel, 1974), pp. 137–71; Joachim Whaley, "The Protestant Enlightenment in Germany," in Roy Porter and Mikuláás Teich, eds., *The Enlightenment in National Context* (London, 1981): 106–17. As this collection indicates, there is an increasing interest in the national variations on a distinctly moderate and heavily clerical "Protestant Enlightenment"; for an insightful study of a comparable reform sentiment and self-image among Scottish clergymen, see Richard B. Sher, *Church and University in the Scottish Enlightenment. The Moderate Literati of Edinburgh* (Princeton, N.J., 1985).

[22] On this utilitarian emphasis see esp. Stroup, *Struggle for Identity*, pp. 82–98; Krause, *Predigt*, pp. 118–45. For examples see Johann Heinrich Philipp Sextroh, *Ueber praktische Vorbereitungsanstalten zum Predigtamt. Nebst einer Nachricht vom Königlichen Pastoralinstitut in Göttingen* (Göttingen, 1783); Gotthilf Samuel Steinbart, *Vorschläge zu einer allgemeinen Schulverbesserung, insofern sie nicht Sache der Kirche sondern des Staates ist* (Züllichau, 1789).

were still taking them as models. These were the men who joined regional agronomy societies and tried to familiarize village schoolmasters with an "enlightened" pedagogy and curriculum. Though often concerned with doctrinal issues, they saw nothing wrong with using sermons as occasions for imparting "useful" information about farming and other subjects.[23]

The rural pastor who took up this "popular" mission had to strike a delicate balance in his posture toward the natives – one reflecting a new eagerness to bridge the enormous gap between learned and popular culture, but at the same time calculated to leave no doubt about his own social superiority as a "learned man" among the unlettered and unwashed. There was no room for a pedantic concern with doctrinal abstractions and technical points of exegesis in the new "popularity"; in sermons and other forums, the message had to be adapted both to the concrete circumstances of a particular local audience and to its narrowly bounded intellectual horizons. But if the pastor was to integrate his community into a larger culture, it was from an intellectual height to which they neither could nor should ascend. Clergymen shared the prevailing conviction that in the case of the peasantry it was especially important to keep enlightenment "relative" – that the prescription and the dosage must be calculated to make the toiling masses "happier" and more "useful" in their inherited stations. This cautious strategy coincided nicely with the utilitarian preoccupation with agronomy, medicine, and other concrete, practical subjects directly relevant to the countrymen's daily lives and not likely to infect them with intellectual and social pretensions that neither could nor should be satisfied.[24]

Again a service ethic justified the extrication of an educated profession from local entanglements. Intellectual superiority by itself would not suffice; the pastor would command sufficient authority as the emissary of a superior culture only if his office kept him at a safe social distance from the natives. Obviously he should not marry into one of the local peasant families; aside from the danger of being identified with one of the parties in local feuds, he would find it difficult to refuse a certain familiarity to inlaws. The "popular" approach required a certain friendliness and informality

[23] One of the most colorful and pugnacious examples of this type was Johann Moritz Schwager; see his autobiography in *Niederrheinisch-westfälische Blätter* 1:1 (1801): 33–93. See also Karl Aner, "Zwei märkische Landgeistliche aus der Aufklärungszeit," *Jahrbuch für Brandenburgische Kirchengeschichte* 17 (1919): 81–113; Franz Blanckmeister, "Ein sächischer Dorfprediger vor hundert Jahren. Zur Charakteristik der vulgär-rationalistischen Predigtweise," *"Halt was du hast." Zeitschrift für Pastoral Theologie*, ed. V. Fr. Oehler, 11 (Berlin, 1888): 337–54; Paul Luchtenberg, *Johannes Löh und die Aufklärung im Bergischen* (Köln and Opladen, 1965).

[24] Classic statements of this approach are Bernhard Siegfried Walther, *Ueber die Aufklärung des Landvolks* (Halle, 1782); Johann Wilhelm Reche, *Neuer Versuch über die Gränzen der Aufklärung* (Düsseldorf, 1789); J. M. S., "Soll man aufklären? und wie?", AMP 3 (1790): 284–304. On the strict limits usually imposed on popular enlightenment, see esp. Helmut König, *Zur Geschichte der Nationalerziehung in Deutschland im letzten Drittel des 18. Jahrhunderts*, Monumenta Paedagogica, vol. 1 (Berlin, 1960).

in dealings with parishioners, in contrast to the older style of stiff reserve; but under no circumstances was the pastor's relationship with his uneducated neighbors to assume the intimacy of social peers. He should not insult local families by refusing to attend their wedding feasts, but must be careful to leave before the liquor started flowing, the humor became crude, and the dancing strayed beyond the bounds of decorum. His sermons were to "descend" to the intellectual level of a village audience only to a point; they must never pander to popular ignorance. And so far as possible the pastor must avoid using dialect in his daily conversations as well as in sermons; it was above all his language, after all, that testified to the educational credentials he brought from outside, and perhaps to his superior breeding as well.[25]

Such counsels were permeated with clergymen's abiding sense of alienation from the traditional social norms and cultural values of village life. The grim reality of the countryside was "barbarism," a former village pastor reported in *Der Landprediger* in 1775, and that judgment was to be confirmed repeatedly in succeeding decades.[26] Clerical reform literature is perhaps our richest source for prevailing stereotypes of the peasant – for descriptions of his indifference to standards of "respectability" in dress and manner, his spitefulness toward neighbors and blind hostility to outsiders, his woeful ignorance about health and hygiene, his neglect of his children's education, his stubborn attachment to "superstition" in farming as well as in religious belief and observance, his alternating tightfistedness and absurd wastefulness. All this seemed to stand in ironic contrast to the purity of the natural setting, and indeed one of the tragic ironies was that the countrymen – the men closest to nature – often seemed too materialistic and blinkered to appreciate its beauties, much less to draw inspiration from them. It spoke volumes for the self-conscious isolation of the clergyman as an educated bourgeois – and for his inability to appreciate the priorities of another world – that this was often a source of bitter disappointment.

To a degree the clerical guardian of Orthodoxy in a village outpost, faced with popular religious beliefs still permeated with "paganism," also had reason to recoil from his neighbors. But now an "enlightened" intolerance for peasant culture, including its attachment to Orthodox doctrines and liturgical observances, intensified the alienation of educated men. Entering

25 See esp. Müller, "Wie verhält sich der Prediger in Absicht auf den Gebrauch der hochdeutschen Sprache . . . ?" *Neues Journal für Prediger* 17 (1799): 154–70. On the proper mix of "popularity" and distance see also B. i. N., "Von der Würde des Landgeistlichen und dessen Vortheilen vor dem Stadtgeistlichen in der Führung seines Amtes," *Der Landprediger* 1 (1774): 332–52; "Schmahlings Vorschläge, die Barbarey vom Lande zu treiben," *Der Landprediger* 2 (1775): 304–71, and 3 (1776): 1–94; J. W. Str., "Gedanken über den Beyfall der Prediger," JP 11:4 (1781): 385–412; "Von dem Umgange eines Predigers mit seinen Zuhörern, sonderlich auf dem Lande," JP 12 (1782): 144–70.

26 "Schmahlings Vorschläge."

office with this heightened consciousness of superiority, they were all the more anxious about their actual local status, as it was defined and enforced in the terms and conditions of rural pastorates. Their dilemma was not limited to an inability to maintain appearances on paltry incomes, though that often seemed exacerbated by the peasants' tendency to assess a man's personal "worth" merely by externals. To a degree teachers' envy of pastoral authority and prestige was misplaced; in fact in villages, and indeed in many small towns as well, the pastor stood in an analogous relationship with local families. Pastors who actually had to work the fields attached to their positions were probably rare; the more serious problem was that, as a small-scale farmer, the pastor was dependent on the largeholders to release hired hands, to lend him wagons to transport his harvest, to supply winter fodder for his animals. He could lease the land, but then he was beholden to local farmers to sell him foodstuffs they preferred to sell in town. And this was only one form of dependency on individual families, their obligations sometimes spelled out in contracts, but more often a matter of time-honored but informal custom. When the tithe was in kind, as it usually was, the local landholders obligated to supply it might skimp on quantity or quality, or deliver it late, or indeed insist that the pastor collect it himself. A more or less substantial portion of the pastor's cash income was in the form of "incidental" fees for services at weddings, baptisms, and funerals, often scaled according to the families' landholding status. If this arrangement seemed to make religion another market commodity, it also left the distinct impression that the pastor was the hireling of wealthier local families paying the higher rates. At the same time it put him in a painful conflict with families without means; for the pastor with a meager income it was a real sacrifice to exempt them from fee payment, but to insist on payment was to invite the charge of callous greed.[27]

By the very fact that the reform literature tended to dwell on these "vexations," it leaves an exaggerated impression of the extent of conflict between rural pastors and their congregations. What the proliferation of complaints in the last third of the century reflected was the injured self-estimations and frustrated idealism of a new breed, trained under rationalist

[27] For breakdowns of pastoral incomes, illustrating the usual variety of arrangements, see Luchtenberg, *Johannes Löh*, pp. 105–7, 255–57. For the usual complaints see, e.g., "Ueber die Verachtung," pp. 45–47; Glörfeld, "Ueber die dem Landpredigerstande eigenen Uebel," pp. 426–29; "Ueber die Nothwendigkeit der moralischen Verbesserung," pp. 63–64, 120–24; F. W. Wolfrath, "Ueber die Accidenzgefälle der Prediger," *Eusebia* 2 (1798): 107–214; "Versuch einer Vertheidigung des christlichen Lehramts, und der damit verbundenen Verrichtungen gegen Vorwürfe und Antipathie dieser Zeit," *Eusebia* 3 (1800): 34–37; "Welcher Beruf ist angenehmer und leichter, der eines Landpredigers oder eines Universitäts- und Hofpredigers?" *Eusebia* 3(1800): 296; Dassel, "Worin soll die Thätigkeit der Prediger bestehen," pp. 536–37; Friedrich Erdmann August Heydenreich, *Ueber den Charakter des Landmanns in religiöser Hinsicht. Ein Beytrag zur Psychologie für alle, welche auf das religiöse Bildungsgeschäft desselben Einfluss haben – vorzüglich für Landprediger* (Leipzig, 1800), pp. 82–83.

theologians at Halle and other universities. To such men the cost of frictionless integration into a small rural community was an intolerable degree of informal, highly personal accountability to an ignorant, tradition-bound laity. The aspiring "popular educator" shared a dilemma with his reform-minded colleague in a small-town Latin school; while his mission required that he stand above local society, as the agent of a profession operating largely free of lay control, he found his office densely ensnared in the local social fabric. Again the solution seemed to lay in the kind of outside intervention that only the state could supply. While some clergymen called for a secure salary, entirely or largely in cash, others reminded their colleagues that, for all its "vexations," income in kind had real advantages in inflationary times. But if traditional arrangements were to survive, it must be on new terms; by defining and enforcing local obligations, and above all by requiring local authorities to collect tithes and other contributions, the state would interpose the proper degree of impersonality between minister and flock. If the pastoral office was to be a conduit – if it was to be an effective agent of enlightened reform from above – it must also be an unassailably "public" pedestal.

THE CULTURE BEARERS

By the turn of the century the agenda for a reform of pastoral offices was fairly standard, but the overall conception of and rationale for professional autonomy was changing. The late 1780s had marked the beginning of a shift in the clerical ideal of public service and in the relationship to the state it implied.

Would the clergyman of the future be a "learned" man in any meaningful sense? As early as 1761 Johann Friedrich Jacobi, the highly respected general superintendent in Celle (Hanover), had confronted this question in an article on clerical education in the *Journal für Prediger*. Jacobi's theme was the blatant contradiction between, on the one hand, the extraordinary range of scholarly accomplishments expected of pastors and, on the other, their typically plebeian origins and their poverty in office. It simply made no sense, he argued, for most clergymen to study Greek, Hebrew, and the other "oriental" languages considered necessary for learned exegesis; they did not have the "cultured" background needed to master these scholarly tools during their brief studies, and in any case they would not be able to maintain scholarly libraries in office. Despite a utilitarian bent, evidenced especially by his efforts to encourage scientific farming, Jacobi was staunchly committed to Orthodoxy and continued to regard instruction in doctrine and spiritual counseling as the main responsibility of the pastor. The strength of his objections lay in a sober realism about the academic pretensions of his order, and the realism in turn was grounded in personal experience. He had in mind clergymen like his father, a village pastor who had struggled to educate three sons on a yearly income of 250 reichsthaler. It depressed him "to the point of tears" that "scholars with means" expected such men to purchase "costly" libraries. Jacobi was no less candid about his own accomplishments; even renowned scholars like Gesner had trouble keeping abreast of the latest philological scholarship in more than one language, he reminded his readers, and he for one had neither the time nor the intellectual capacity for such an effort.[28]

In the course of denying that the typical pastor could be a scholar, Jacobi posed the more provocative question whether his pastoral responsibilities actually required him to be one. This was the issue that provoked a parting of the ways in the 1780s. In 1785 Carl Friedrich Bahrdt, already a notorious radical among rationalist theologians, called for a thorough reorientation of pastoral training to produce "popular educators of public utility." Bahrdt's notable concession to tradition was to retain the study of Greek and Latin language and literature, though he managed to give a partisan twist to the usual view of its "liberal" effect by observing that he had never met a pastor "who was fond of and knowledgeable in the ancients and yet was blindly orthodox in his religion, obscure in his lectures, fanatical, or tasteless." But the usual range of courses in theology and ancillary disciplines produced pseudo-scholarly obscurantists, too stiff and ponderous to achieve the necessary "popularity." Explicitly omitted from Bahrdt's revised curriculum were Hebrew and other "oriental" languages, polemics, patristics, and church history. The emphasis was on "religion" (by which he meant a kind of moral anthropology) rather than theology, and on basic instruction in pedagogy, philosophy, natural history and physics, the arithmetic and geometry needed for surveying, agricultural economics, and the rudiments of medicine to improve health care.[29] A year later Campe, faced with clerical opposition to his plans for school reform in Brunswick-Wolfenbüttel, threw down the gauntlet with a roughly similar set of proposals. A bit less polemical in tone than Bahrdt, Campe actually went farther by suggesting that the future rural pastor prepare to practice rudimentary medicine and surgery by accompanying a doctor on hospital rounds during his last year of

[28] Johann Friedrich Jacobi, "Gedanken über die gewöhnliche Erziehung junger Geistlichen," JP 5 (1774): 51–81, 158–68, and his later defense of his views in idem, *Sämtliche Schriften*, 2 vols. (Hanover, 1781–83), 2: 368–87. Jacobi was one of the founders of the agricultural society at Celle. There is a balanced profile in Stroup, *Struggle for Identity*, Appendix B.

[29] Carl Friedrich Bahrdt, *Ueber das theologische Studium auf Universitäten* (Berlin, 1785), esp. pp. 62–98. See also the broader conception of a utilitarian civic ethic in idem, *Handbuch der Moral für den Bürgerstand* (Halle, 1789), and Ulrich Herrmann, "Die Kodifizierung bürgerlichen Bewusstseins in der deutschen Spätaufklärung – Carl Friedrich Bahrdts 'Handbuch der Moral für den Bürgerstand' aus dem Jahre 1789," in Rudolf Vierhaus, ed., *Bürger und Bürgerlichkeit im Zeitalter der Aufklärung*, Wolfenbütteler Studien zur Aufklärung, vol. 7 (Heidelberg, 1981): 321–33.

studies. Campe considered Greek as irrelevant as Hebrew, and it was only as a grudging concession, made unavoidable by the misguided reverence for a dead "*Symbolet*" of learning and wisdom, that he allowed for students to acquire a minimal ability to read a few Latin prose texts.[30]

Unlike Jacobi, Bahrdt and Campe espoused a radical Deism that had impelled their reform activism out of the clerical orbit entirely. If their extremism made them suspect, however, they could not be ignored; their criticisms and proposals drew on the same utilitarian reform sentiment that had been shaping a professional ideology among clergymen for several decades. Not surprisingly, the initial defensive reaction and the eventual shift in course were orchestrated by senior members of the professoriate. To declare theological and philological scholarship irrelevant to the professional mission of most clergymen was to question the very basis for a professorial elite, and indeed to undercut corporate privileges essential to their very livelihood at the universities. Bahrdt's attack was particularly unsettling, since he could claim to have an insider's view of the professoriate. Having grown up in Leipzig, where his father had been a theology professor, he had acquired a marked cynicism about the pretensions and empty rituals of university life. A personal scandal – he had gotten a local daughter pregnant – had suddenly ended his precocious academic career at Leipzig. In 1771 he had left a chair at Giessen, to the great relief of his Orthodox opponents there, to emulate Basedow in launching an experimental school for the new pedagogy. In the wake of this fiasco, Minister von Zedlitz had given him permission to teach at Halle, despite the protests of the theology faculty. Sheer notoriety may suffice to explain why hundreds of students flocked to the lectures of this new *Dozent* who had been excluded from a regular academic appointment.

In his pamphlet on pastoral training Bahrdt spoke from this position as former guild member-become-outsider. At present, he noted, students had no choice but to take the standard "bread courses," since testimonials of attendance at them were necessary to take the consistorial examination. Changing the examination content and eliminating the testimonials would at last break the hold of the "old gentlemen" – i.e., the tenured professors – who pocketed the fees that this monopoly guaranteed. Bahrdt relished the prospect that "many a *Privatdozent* (who now receives no requests at all for testimonials) would receive all the applause and many an old gentleman would remain a professor without an audience for his entire life."[31]

[30] Joachim Heinrich Campe, *Ueber einige verkannte, wenigstens ungenützte Mittel zur Beförderung der Industrie, der Bevölkerung und des öffentlichen Wohlstandes. In Zwei Fragmenten* (Wolfenbüttel, 1786), esp. pp. 59–61, 81–84. I have used the 1969 reprint by Sauer and Auvermann, Frankfurt am Main (Quellenschriften zur Industrieschulbewegung, vol. 2).

[31] Barhdt, *Ueber das theologische Studium*, pp. 118–29. For Bahrdt's own account of his tribulations see his *Geschichte seines Lebens, seiner Meinungen und Schicksale, von ihm selbst geschrieben* (Frankfurt am Main, 1790).

But there was a great deal more than fees at stake. Would the local pastor with the kind of training Bahrdt and Campe had in mind be in a position to "earn" a new "respect," or would he in fact be lacking in the credentials that commanded deference from the uneducated masses and ensured equality with other educated professionals? Campe had attempted to be reassuring on this score; unlike the pastor groomed in the old learning, who was an "alien," perhaps even "threatening" figure to the countrymen, his successor trained in "secular disciplines" would win "respect" as well as "trust" and indeed "love" as "the first man" in the community.[32] To the leading figures in the North German professoriate – Nösselt at Halle, Gottfried Less at Göttingen, Heinrich Philipp Conrad Henke and Johann Caspar Velthusen at Helmstedt – the prospects looked quite different. These were men who had apprenticed with the great scholars of the previous generation. Most of them were young enough to have developed a strong interest in the new classical scholarship as students, and indeed Nösselt and Henke had seriously considered scholarly careers as classicists. If they had become hostile to the Pietist equation of genuine religiosity with emotional turmoil and mystical "stirrings," that was in part because it seemed to offer an all too seductive escape from the disciplined study that understanding of doctrine and interpretation of scripture required. Hence a commitment to learning, far from being in conflict with their rationalist bent in theology, was an integral part of that preference. Their openness to a broader, more utilitarian definition of the pastoral role had gone hand in hand with the expectation that school reform would at last supply them with the "mature" students, well equipped in linguistic and literary studies, who could withstand the rigors of a truly scholarly program of theological studies.

Bahrdt and Campe provoked these professors to become more self-conscious and assertive about what they had always believed. There was room for differences of opinion about the proper role of revealed doctrine in pastoral teaching, but there could be no doubt that the social distance essential to the pastor's authority required scholarly credentials. As "popular educator" the rural pastor would simply dispense knowledge prepackaged for mass consumption. The enlightening mission threatened to make him a stand-in for all sorts of expertise and master of none, and hence to deprive his order of its own disciplinary jurisdiction within the larger intellectual preserve of the educated professions. At the same time "useful" knowledge, by drawing the pastor into the daily occupational concerns of the uneducated, and above all into their "material" preoccupations, threatened to bring him all too close to his parishioners. What he in fact needed – to borrow Campe's image – was the intellectual wherewithal to demonstrate that he was indeed an "alien man" from "another world."

[32] Campe, *Ueber einige verkannte, wenigstens ungenützte Mittel*, pp. 79–80.

With this concern about status made quite explicit and with this underlying implication of utilitarian reform clearly in mind, the theologians began to marshal arguments for keeping a modernized but unambiguously academic theology at the core of pastoral training. This was in part a matter of insisting that the pastor, even in a remote village, had to provide an authoritative interpretation of scripture and could not do so without the philological competence and historical knowledge needed for close textual analysis. Whereas the utilitarian emphasis had been on a versatile practical competence, the new theme was that the "field" to be mastered by every clergyman could not be reduced to the mere praxis of a craft. Like the new philosophy, theology had an imposing theoretical structure that had to be grasped systematically.[33] Initiates must acquire an understanding of the theoretical integrity of the "discipline" and of the research that moved it forward.

The task of the professoriate was to keep the educated public abreast of the research that continually expanded that structure and to familiarize students with both their results and their methods. It was with this conception of a university-based "discipline" that Nösselt, as spokesman for the academic senate at Halle, protested the direct subordination of Prussian universities to the new Superior School Board in 1788 and subsequent bureaucratic intrusions. Nösselt was in fact defending corporate privilege against state centralization, but the appeal to the historic legal rights of university faculties was hardly more than an afterthought in his argument. Corporate autonomy, in its professional mode, became the functional and meritocratic right of "the best men in the field," who had already proved themselves and required "freedom" from bureaucratic tutelage and paper work to conduct and publish original research.[34]

Inseparable from the concern that a reformed clergy might find itself without a scholarly jurisdiction was the alarm that it might lack a moral basis for autonomy. Again events in the late 1780s and early 1790s contributed to a new awareness of "political" implications. While Woellner's crackdown in Prussia posed the prospect of a state-imposed orthodoxy, the revolution in France raised the specter of a civic ideology entirely divested of Christian belief, and indeed opposed to the very existence of confessional churches. Even rationalist clergymen responded by becoming insistent on maintaining a distinction between the ultimate goal – the moral enlightenment with which clergymen were entrusted – and state-imposed reform.

[33] See, e.g., Less, *Ueber Christliches Lehr-Amt*, esp. pp. 17–22, 73–92; Nösselt, *Anweisung*; Johann Kaspar Velthusen, *Ueber die nächste Bestimmung des Landpredigerstandes. Ein durch Herrn Campes Fragmente veranlasster Beytrag zur Pastoraltheologie* (Helmstedt, 1787).

[34] The *Vorstellung* of 1788 and an excerpt from a report in 1801 were published in August Hermann Niemeyer, *Leben, Charakter, und Verdienste Johann August Nösselts. Nebst einer Sammlung einiger zum Theil ungedruckten Aufsätze, Briefe, und Fragmente*, 2 vols. (Halle, 1809), 2: 117–40.

In 1789 Johann Wilhelm Reche had published a typically utilitarian essay, emphasizing that the "needs" induced by popular enlightenment must not come into conflict with social duties. In his *Golden Mirror for Pastors*, published several years later, the unique mission of the pastorate is to disseminate and preserve the rational "moral culture" essential to the exercise of individual "moral freedom," and there is a new concern to prevent the state from imposing "external coercion" on both the pastor and his parishioners. The new language of Kantian philosophy has moderated utilitarianism to such an extent that the cultural jurisdiction of the clergy no longer is contained within a civic ideology and ultimately is superior to it. The clerical calling has become identical with the entire moral "person"; it is not to be judged by state-defined criteria for functional roles.[35]

As jolting as Woellner's crackdown and the revolution were to rationalists throughout North Germany, they only multiplied the political dimensions of a threat that clergymen had already begun to recognize. In the more radical reform agendas for pastoral training, utilitarianism à l'outrance raised an ironic possibility; the clergy, in the very process of fulfilling the "public" mission it had been claiming for several decades, might forfeit any credible right to a professional autonomy derived from an independent moral basis. Unable to generate and sustain a moral ideal within its own ranks, it might become merely the agent of a civic morality defined on high. Long assumed to reflect a universal standard of rationality, this civic morality now threatened to become a merely political instrument. Reche's implicit assumption was that the very purity of a rational morality would insure against that danger, but by then the more pronounced tendency was to adopt an alternative idiom for moral freedom. It was in the immediate clerical reactions to Campe's attacks that the distinctly neohumanistic distinction between the mere training of the *Bürger* and the cultivation of the "human being," particularly through a revitalized classical education, first revealed its potential for shaping professional ideologies.

The essential transition is mirrored in the career of Heinrich Philipp Conrad Henke, the director of the theological seminar at Helmstedt. Trained at Helmstedt in the early 1770s, Henke originally had aspired to a career as a schoolman, and in his enthusiasm for the new pedagogy had even made a pilgrimage to Basedow's Philanthropinum in 1776. When he switched to an academic career in theology, the rationalist clerical establishment welcomed him as one of its own. In the late 1790s his journal, *Eusebia*, provided a forum for complaints about inadequate and degrading pastoral incomes and the lack of career prospects in the clergy, accompanied by the usual appeals for state intervention. But as early as 1790, in key

35 Johann Wilhelm Reche, *Neuer Versuch über die Gränzen der Aufklärung* (Düsseldorf, 1789); idem, *Goldenen Spiegel für Prediger von einem Mitglied seines Standes* (ca. 1795), esp. pp. 20–26.

addresses on the "prospects for religion" and "complaints about the disdain for the clerical order," Henke had anticipated the rhetorical shift that *Eusebia* would exemplify. It was by enabling the *Mensch* to "become a better man by means of the guidance of religion," he emphasized in the first address, that the clergyman helped produce "a better *Bürger*."[36] In the second address he elaborated this distinction and its import:

> In the well-meaning intention of securing [the clergy] a proper and appropriate honor, some have described it in our day as a branch of the state service. Now however true it is that genuine religion at the same time is of the most considerable influence for order, peace and the welfare of the commonwealth, and that the more its spirit is spread among all classes of the people, the better off is the whole society; just as certain is it that religion is still not at all a concern of the person insofar as he is a *Bürger*, but rather is concerned with his entire purpose and destiny for the present and future world, with his immortal spirit. . . . the notion that teachers of religion are nothing but state-assigned and state-empowered spokesmen for good morals, civic loyalty and order is very one-sided and incomplete. Theirs is a higher calling, and the purpose of their labors extends further; they are speakers, interpreters, and heralds of the most important truths, guides, counselors, and companions of all their brethren in their striving after wisdom, virtue, and contentment, inner and eternal welfare. A calling that is all the more elevated and divine than any civil utilitarian service, since the destiny of man for these perfections is older and more important than all his social relationships, and since virtue is more than civic love for order, blessedness is more than civic welfare.[37]

In the 1790s Henke and other theologians integrated this language into clerical reform ideology, and in the early years of the next century younger colleagues confirmed its ascendancy. Utilitarian priorities were equated with a superficial materialism, despite the this-worldly asceticism that had marked the German cult of "useful" service and merit. In the alternative – an exalted "spiritual" cultivation – the capacity for religious experience and the innate potential for intellectual refinement were collapsed into a single purely "human" category. The result was often a murky blend; a renewed concern for salvation – i.e., for the afterlife – was conflated with a neohumanistic reverence for the "perfecting" of the purely human "personality" in this life. This adaptation lacked much of the radical thrust Humboldt and Schiller gave the ideal of *Bildung* in the 1790s. Clergymen intent on restoring the authority and prestige of the pastorate could hardly insist

[36] Heinrich Philipp Conrad Henke, *Frohe Aussichten für die Religion in die Zukunft* (2nd ed.: Helmstedt, 1801). On Henke's career see esp. Heinrich Wilhelm Justus Wolff and Georg Karl Bollmann, *Heinrich Philipp Conrad Henke. Denkwürdigkeiten aus seinem Leben und dankbare Erinnerungen an seine Verdienste* (Helmstedt and Leipzig, 1816). There is an excellent discussion of his thought in Stroup, *Struggle for Identity*, pp. 134–38.

[37] Heinrich Philipp Conrad Henke, *Beurtheilung der Klagen über Geringschätzung des Predigerstandes. Eine Rede, bey der Einführung eines neuen Priors des Kloster Michelstein am achten Sonntage nach Trinitatis 1790* (Helmstedt, 1790), pp. 32–33.

on the complete autonomy of an inner entelechy, not subject to any external standards, or make the ethical purely a product of the aesthetic. Such uncompromising individualism and aestheticism left room only for the guidance of a pedagogue; there was no place for a public arbiter of a collective morality presiding over an entire community. Likewise the new rhetoric could hardly assign the pastor to defend a realm of private conscience, assumed to be incompatible with the demands imposed on the *Bürger*; that might imply that reform – far from transforming the pastorate into a truly public pedestal under state sponsorship – would cut the symbiotic bond between church and state established in the early days of the Reformation.

The new rhetoric was designed to secure clergymen a public status commensurate with their service, but at the same time to prevent their reduction to political instruments of centralized authority. The pastor's contribution to public order and enlightened progress remained vital, but was now indirect; in the education of a congregation, as in the cultivation of an individual personality, public virtue developed only as the byproduct of a higher and purer "perfecting" of the essentially human. In a reworking of the ancient distinction between temporal and nontemporal spheres, "humanity" came to evoke an ethical and ultimately spiritual realm distinct from the merely "civic" duty to serve the state and the public welfare in a specific functional role. The rural pastor would still uplift from a distance; but now he would do so by radiating a cultivated sensibility, at once ethical and aesthetic. If his utilitarian role had been to inculcate a state-approved civic ethic from above, he would now preside over a "human" sphere at once morally superior and politically neutral.

This was to redefine the breadth of vision characteristic of an educated profession; the pastor's claim to superiority over merely private interests rested not on a utilitarian understanding of the "public welfare" and the proper role of local society in promoting it, but on the ability to lift his congregation above such immediate "material" concerns and make it aware of its part in the long-term spiritual "perfecting" of the society and indeed the entire species. The new clerical ideology in effect domesticated the utopian moment in neohumanism, and in so doing gave the pastoral office a unique status as the middle term between the "personality" of the cultivated Christian and the spiritual evolution of his local and national community. In the light of this ideal, contributors to *Eusebia* and other clerical journals at the turn of the century objected to lumping the pastor together with jurists and other public officials, despite his indisputable role and status as a public servant. While other officials were concerned with the particular functions of *Bürger* in civil society, the uniqueness of the pastor's cultural mission lay in his approach to people in their capacity as human beings. For that very reason the office – far from implying the narrowing that other forms of expertise entailed – required the well-rounded cultivation now evoked by the word *Bildung*. In the ideal image of the cultivated pastor, the *Mensch* and the *Bürger*, the personality and the office, became coterminous. The role of "popular educator" requires "constant cultivation" of both the intellect and the senses, a young clergyman reminded his colleagues in 1800, since "every pause in the striving after one's own perfection brings with it a standstill in the culture of the people."[38]

The rhetorical flights in such claims were not empty gestures. Their very stridency confirms that, for all the disillusionment with utilitarian objectives, an ethic of service remained indispensable to the professional claim to public authority. In the interaction between social experience and ideology that produced a modern *Bildungsbürgertum*, the language and logic of neohumanism did not nullify the rationalist service ethics that had emerged in specific occupational contexts; it reoriented them to more complex perceptions of threat. To characterize the rhetoric as an apolitical retreat into aesthetic and philosophical "inwardness" would be to miss its significance as a political form of collective self-defense. But the defense was not without its paradox; the "public" realm of culture and morality to which it laid claim was seen to transcend, not alter, social reality, and to hover above the merely political. If the clergy's vocational commitment to the "human" was pitted against the threat of a manipulative, dehumanizing *étatisme*, it was also defined more as an exercise of abstract moral suasion than as a possibility of open opposition to specific abuses of state power. The tendency was to assume that the roles of state servant, culture bearer, and moral conscience were, or at least would be, eminently compatible; the new rhetoric did not specify an ethical order of priorities in the event of an irreconcilable conflict between the pastor's official responsibility for maintaining public order and his guardianship over the realm of *Humanität*.

In the broad diffusion of a clerical ideology at the turn of the century, the new enthusiasm for *Bildung* did not simply sweep away the rationalist legacy. In a process of overlay and fusion the two idioms, stripped of their more vaulting claims, complemented each other in a fuzzy but serviceable professional self-image. The handbook for aspiring pastors published by Christian Victor Kindervater from 1802 to 1806 still registers the initial thrust of eighteenth-century reform thought, but is very distant from the utilitarian agenda popular in the 1780s. Kindervater himself was a blend

[38] Dassel, "Worin soll die Thätigkeit der Prediger bestehen," pp. 540–41. For other examples of the new rhetoric, see Stroup, *Struggle for Identity*, esp. pp. 139–41, 164–86. Stroup is correct, I think, to associate the clerical adoption of neohumanism with a "traditionalist particularism" in Hanover and Brunswick-Wolfenbüttel. But this is only one side of the story; the insistence on corporate independence vis-à-vis the state coexisted – in considerable tension – with an expectation that state-sponsored reform from above (i.e., a greater degree of centralization) would emancipate pastors from local tangles. I am suggesting that neohumanism offered an ideological (or at least rhetorical) resolution of this tension.

of old and new; born in 1758, he was a rationalist who contributed to the new classical scholarship, albeit only with editions and translations of Latin authors, and became a devotee of Kantian philosophy.

In Kindervater's handbook, the pastor in a "remote village" remained a missionary of enlightenment, confronting ignorance and narrow-mindedness. But now the missionary acted largely in his capacity as an exemplar of cultural refinement and as a moral guide; there was no point in acquiring a smattering of "useful" knowledge in medicine and other fields, and the sermon was no place for agricultural advice.[39] Kindervater was sounding a new note of realism, after decades of unfulfilled expectations. The young pastor was warned not to regard all peasants as "big, naive children," easily led around. If he entered his office expecting to sweep aside "prejudice" – to achieve the transformation of local life that the more extreme utilitarians had envisioned – he would founder on the social and institutional realities of the countryside and the sheer intractability of the peasant mentality.

But the point of this new modesty about professional efficacy was to ensure elite status, not to forgo it. While the utilitarian agenda had come to seem far-fetched, it still threatened to confirm a longstanding anxiety. "Peasantized" pastors still debased the collective prestige of the order, and their presence remained inseparable from the influx of plebeian recruits. Kindervater had in mind primarily the young man who had been raised in a crude – i.e., uneducated – home, who had borne the stigmas of charity and deprivation as a pupil and student, who had had to survive as a private tutor while waiting for an appointment, who entered office burdened with debts. To overcome these imposing handicaps – to maintain a precariously acquired sense of identity as an educated man and keep the proper social distance from the natives – required persistence in self-cultivation. The former poor student need not be intimidated by Kantian philosophy, though he should consider the "atheist" Fichte beyond the pale of respectable authors. Nor need he succumb to rural isolation; he could compensate for his lack of regular contact with other cultivated men by continuing his classical studies and making the Greek and Roman authors his "house guests."[40]

[39] Christian Victor Kindervater, *Ueber nützliche Verwaltung des Predigtamtes, Schulunterricht, Bildung der Gemeinden, und Lebensgenuss auf dem Lande*, 2 vols. (Leipzig, 1802–6), 1: 1–48. On Kindervater see Heinrich Doering, *Die deutschen Kanzleiredner des achtzehnten und neunzehnten Jahrhunderts* (Neustadt an der Orla, 1830), pp. 155–57. For a similarly modified approach to rural enlightenment, see Heydenreich, *Ueber den Charakter des Landmanns*.

[40] Kindervater, *Ueber nützliche Verwaltung*, 1: 1–19, 230–38, 271–308.

12

Radical visions: Johann Gottlieb Fichte

By the turn of the century Kantianism had become a respectable, if daring, persuasion in clerical circles; but its most promising acolyte seemed to have strayed beyond the pale. In the early 1790s the young Fichte had suddenly made his presence felt with applications of Kantian philosophy in the volatile areas of religion and politics. His *Attempt at a Critique of All Revelation*, published anonymously in 1792, was so Kantian that it was at first mistaken for the master's long-awaited statement on the subject. Welcomed by enthusiasts of the new philosophy, it confirmed others' fears of its anti-religious (or at least anticonfessional) animus. The *Critique* was immediately followed by an outspoken defense of the French Revolution. As the popular revolution in Paris was reaching its most radical and most violent stage, a young German philosopher argued for the right of the people to overthrow a tyrannical government and abolish the privileges of a corrupt aristocracy.[1] He was branded a Jacobin as well as an atheist, despite his stated conviction that Germany, unlike France, could avoid a violent revolution.

One need only compare these early writings with the famous *Addresses to the German Nation*, delivered in late 1807 and early 1808, to appreciate how difficult it has been for students of Fichte to sort out continuities and shifts in his construction of an Idealist philosophy. Over this decade and a half his thought moved in several "radical" directions at once; he can arguably be said to have anticipated socialism (or at least "state socialism") as well as totalitarian democracy and *völkisch* nationalism.[2] What follows is

[1] Johann Gottlieb Fichte, *Versuch einer Kritik aller Offenbarung* (Königsberg, 1792); idem, *Beiträge zur Berichtigung der Urteile des Publikums über die französische Revolution*, Teil 1: *Zur Beurteiling ihrer Rechtmässigkeit* (Danzig, 1793).

[2] For overviews of the imposing body of literature on Fichte, see Richard Saage, "Nachwort: Zur neueren Rezeption der politischen Philosophie Johann Gottlieb Fichtes," in Zwi Batscha and Richard Saage, eds., *Johann Gottlieb Fichte. Ausgewählte Politische Schriften* (Frankfurt am Main, 1977); Karl Hahn, *Staat, Erziehung und Wissenschaft bei J. G. Fichte*, Münchener Studien zur Politik, vol. 13 (Munich, 1969), pp. 1–22; Bernard Willms, *Die totale Freiheit. Fichtes politische Philosophie*, Staat und Politik, vol. 10 (Cologne and Opladen, 1967), pp. 1–14. Xavier Léon, *Fichte et son temps* 3 vols. (Paris, 1924–27), is a classic, often reflecting the nationalism of its era, but still useful for its analysis of Fichte's thought as well as for its rich biographical

not intended to resolve arguments about his place in political theory, but simply to illuminate recurrent tensions in his thought by tracing their origins and their several metamorphoses within the social and cultural milieu of academic mobility. This contextual approach confirms that Fichte's social consciousness is highly relevant to an understanding of his philosophy, even at its epistemological foundation; but it also points up how simplistic it can be to subsume the perceptions, resentments, and aspirations of men of his background and experience under an ideologically loaded definition of "bourgeois" (not to mention "proletarian") consciousness.[3] What was German about the young radical was not simply his Kantian inspiration; Fichte was confronting the choices that ideals of calling and vocation, with all they implied about the individual's relationship to nature, society, and the state, had posed throughout the eighteenth century. Obviously the imposing "system" he developed is too broadranging and too intricate to be reduced to a more or less oblique commentary on these themes. But in its occasionally eccentric but always revealing odyssey, the system encompassed the tension-ridden ideological field in which poor students and their academic mobility were perceived by the turn of the century.

In view of Fichte's origins, his professorial appointment as Reinhold's successor at Jena in 1794 is a particularly dramatic example of the new "mobility opportunities" Kantian philosophy was opening in university careers.[4] His family was uneducated, propertyless, and rural; the combination made him one of those especially rare exceptions among poor students. He

detail. George Armstrong Kelly, *Idealism, Politics, and History. Sources of Hegelian Thought* (Cambridge, 1969), pp. 181–285, is insightful on virtually all dimensions of Fichte's thought. Another important recent study is Zwi Batscha, *Gesellschaft und Staat in der politischen Philosophie Fichtes* (Frankfurt am Main, 1970). Batscha argues that society enjoyed a good deal of autonomy vis-à-vis the state in Fichte's conception of their proper relationship and that that autonomy in turn guaranteed a large measure of individual freedom. The argument is often persuasive, but may underestimate the authoritarian impulse that Willms, for example, emphasizes and identifies with "totalitarian democracy." See also Zwi Batscha, "Die Arbeit in der Sozialphilosophie Johann Gottlieb Fichtes," *Archiv für Sozialgeschichte* 12 (1972): 1–54, and Batscha's insightful introduction to *Ausgewählte Politische Schriften*.

[3] This is a notable shortcoming of Batscha's otherwise insightful study. Batscha is well aware that Fichte saw obstacles to his ideal of freedom in the de facto advantages derived from property ownership, as well as in the legal privileges attached to "birth" in the strict sense; nonetheless he finds Fichte articulating the consciousness of the property holders who, along with the "educated," constitute a modern *Mittelstand*. To say that Fichte "articulates in his philosophy the characteristics of the rising bourgeoisie [*aufsteigendes Bürgertums*]" is to substitute an ideological category for a social explanation. The underlying problem is that his interpretation is framed by a standard (in this case, Marxist) dichotomy between a progressive bourgeoisie (in the "objective" sense) and a reactionary aristocracy, and between capitalism and "feudalism," that does not do justice to its subtlety. See Batscha, *Gesellschaft und Staat*, esp. pp. 46–47, 221–28; idem, "Die Arbeit in der Sozialphilosophie Johann Gottlieb Fichtes," esp. p. 2. For a variation on the same problem, see Manfred Buhr, *Revolution und Philosophie. Die ursprüngliche Philosophie Johann Gottlieb Fichtes und die Französische Revolution* (Berlin, 1965).

[4] Hans H. Gerth, *Bürgerliche Intelligenz um 1800: Zur Soziologie des deutschen Frühliberalismus*, Kritische Studien zur Geschichtswissenschaft, vol. 19 (Göttingen, 1976), p. 44.

was the first of nine children born to Christian Fichte, a ribbon weaver in the village of Rammenau in the Oberlausitz (Saxony), and his wife Johanna Maria Dorothea. The special "tenderness" his father had always shown him, he later recalled, had been checked by an unsympathetic mother, opposed to favoring him at the expense of the other siblings.[5] The domestic tug-of-war was resolved by a particularly dramatic exercise of patronage. Already being groomed by the local pastor, the boy was called on to demonstrate his remarkable memory by repeating a sermon before Ernst Haubold von Miltitz, a visiting nobleman. Suitably impressed, Miltitz brought the prodigy back to his country estate, boarded him for several years with a nearby pastor, and arranged for his further education at the Saxon *Fürstenschule* at Pforta.[6]

As abrupt and decisive as this extrication had been, Fichte's ascent into another world was to be notably halting and precarious. Miltitz died in 1774, while his protégé was at Schulpforta, and at some point in Fichte's university studies Frau von Miltitz, having gotten the impression that he was wasting his time (and her money) at Leipzig, cut him off. He found himself deprived of both financial support and the well-placed patron indispensable to a young man of his background. Fichte spent most of the next decade in a seemingly endless succession of tutoring positions; always hoping to find the appointment that would at last secure connections and open "prospects," he invariably had to accept far less promising employment for want of an alternative means of survival.

In the fall of 1787 we find Fichte planning to leave a tutoring position in Saxony and still groping about for "prospects." "Shame and regret" about his "almost entirely wasted student years," he admitted in a letter to the vice-president of the High Consistory in Dresden, prevented him from turning to his other "patrons" for financial support to prepare for his qualifying examination in theology. By late November he was on another tack; since "nearly all the channels" for a clerical career were "closed," he had decided – though "not without the greatest inner struggle" – to prepare for a career in law, preferably by accompanying a young gentleman to a university as a private tutor.[7] Instead Fichte had to return to domestic employment in the fall of 1788 – this time as tutor to the children of

[5] Fichte to Marie Johanne Rahn, Mar. 15–16, 1790, in Johann Gottlieb Fichte. *Briefwechsel 1775–1793*, Gesamtausgabe der Bayerischen Akademie der Wissenschaften, III, vol. 1 (Stuttgart, 1968): 83. This well-annotated edition of the correspondence supersedes Johann Gottlieb Fichte, *Briefwechsel*, ed. Hans Schulz (2nd, enl. ed.: Leipzig, 1930). The *Gesamtausgabe*, which includes Fichte's unpublished fragments and early writings, will be referred to hereafter as GA.

[6] The story is well told in Léon, *Fichte et son temps*, 1: 29–38.

[7] GA, III, 1: 14–18. Fichte had felt that he needed a few months to make up for deficiencies, particularly in Hebrew. He announced his plan to study law to Christian Friedrich Pezold (Nov. 26, 1787), a university professor in Leipzig to whom he turned to secure a suitable tutoring position.

Antonius Ott, the wealthy owner of an inn in Zürich. His incessant battles with Frau Ott induced him to leave this employment in late March 1790. If he had been willing to remain in Zürich and immediately marry his devoted fiancée, Johanne Rahn, her income would have ended his recurrent penury. But he resisted this temptation – in part because he found the prospect of being a married man without an established career too embarrassing and in part because, as he later admitted to his brother, he felt in himself "too much power and drive" to accept the "yoke" of marriage and "spend [his] entire life as an everyday human being." It was a measure of his accumulated resentment about tutoring employments to date that he resolved not to accept another "obscure role" as "[the] *Informator* of the tender plants (indeed) of a petit bourgeois or a stingy little *Krautjunker*," only to be left to his own devices when the assignment ended. He had set his sights on a position that opened doors, preferably at a court, as tutor to a young prince.[8]

When Fichte returned to Leipzig in the spring of 1789 in pursuit of such employment, his only means of survival was hack literary work. Now too old to consort with students but lacking the contacts needed to gain entrée to prominent Leipzig families, he spent several months in "monotonous" isolation. On May 14, 1790, he penned an urgent appeal to his fiancée to send money, admitting that otherwise he saw "nothing before [him] but vexations, prostitutions, failure." To pay his debts promptly, he explained in an appeal to Dietrich von Miltitz (his patron's son) in early August, he had had to pawn all his clothes but the ones he was wearing. Meanwhile, returning to the hope of securing a pastorate in Saxony, he had traveled to Dresden to secure the patronage of the president of the High Consistory and, on his insistence, had written to Frau von Miltitz for a "pardon." But to no avail; "All my projects, up to the very last," he confided to his fiancée, "have evaporated."[9]

It was at this low ebb in his fortunes that Fichte found an "inner peace" and "freedom" in Kantian philosophy, but the discovery did nothing to improve his immediate prospects. The tutoring appointment that baled him out required a six-week trek across the eastern reaches of Germany to the von Plater household in Warsaw, and it proved a fiasco. Reacting indignantly to the countess's expectation that he be fluent in French and put off by her "condescending" welcome, Fichte resolved to leave and pressed to be compensated for his troubles with a half-year salary and the cost of the return

[8] Fichte to Samuel Gotthelf Fichte, Mar. 5, 1791, in ibid., p. 223; Fichte to Johann Friedrich Fritzsche, Dec. 27, 1789, in ibid., p. 45.

[9] Ibid., pp. 114–15, 140–51, 163–66. To make matters worse, he was acutely sensitive about his parents' – and particularly his mother's – disappointment. If they are "ashamed" of me, he wrote his brother in a particularly bitter letter, let them tell people I am "a village pastor somewhere." Fichte to Samuel Gotthelf Fichte, Jan. 3, 1791, in ibid., pp. 207–210.

trip.[10] He had to settle for considerably less and chose Königsberg – the nearest "emporium" (*Stapelstadt*) of learning, and the home of Kant – as his next resting place. There he wrote his *Critique of All Revelation*, and on August 18, 1791, he took the momentous step of submitting a draft of it for Kant's judgment. On September 1, having calculated that he faced destitution in two weeks, he drafted a tortuous request to Kant for a loan to finance his return trip to Saxony.[11] Kant demurred on the loan, but did find him still another tutoring position on an estate on the Baltic coast near Danzig.

Having resolved more than once to escape the tutoring syndrome, Fichte was now surprised to find himself settling dreamily into an idyllic retreat, complete with English and French gardens with "Chinese bridges," concerts and theater on the premises, and "fat sausages and good wine." It soon became apparent that the hardened veteran of the tutoring circuit found this household so appealing, despite his painfully acquired distaste for aristocratic manners, because he had fallen in love with the forty-two-year-old "angel in human form" who presided over it. The infatuation with Countess von Krockow lasted long enough to produce several most uncharacteristic displays of humility and contrition; but the countess and her husband soon found fault with his "moodiness" and his "passionate warmth in conversation," and by July he in turn had concluded that her "character" was "not what I at first thought it to be" and they would "never again be friends."[12] Disillusioned once more with "the world," he returned to the course he had avoided two years earlier. It was shortly after his marriage to Johanne Rahn in Zürich in October 1793 that he received the call to Jena.

These years as a student and tutor were the crucible of Fichte's intellectual development. Several years before his discovery of Kant, the need to fashion a personal identity – a need that was at once social and ethical – was already impelling him to construct a "system." The need became urgent as he experienced in acute form the marginality and extreme vulnerability of the poor student. Within the precarious etiquette of patronage, displays of humility and deference were de rigueur, but telltale signs of "baseness" were quickly spotted and acknowledgments of dependence easily became "servility." Fichte's recurrent dilemma was to win (or regain) sponsors without sacrificing that precious commodity called "honor." For the most part the

[10] Ibid., pp. 227–39. See also Fichte's description of his reception in Warsaw and his reaction to the countess as "a woman in the style of the great World," in "Tagebuch meiner Osterabreise aus Sachsen nach Polen, u. Preussland," in GA, II, 1: 410–11.

[11] Fichte to Immanuel Kant, Sept. 1–2, 1791, in GA, III, 1: 256–64. The available draft is worth comparing with the actual letter.

[12] Fichte to Johann Friedrich Pietzsch, Jan. 15, 1792, in ibid., pp. 280–82; Fichte to Johann Friedrich Schultz, late 1791–early 1792, in ibid., p. 275; Fichte to Luise von Krockow, June 29, 1792, in ibid., pp. 312–16; "Nöthige Aufklärung über gewisse Dinge. – um mögliche Misverständnisse zu heben" (written in June 1792), in GA, II, 2: 165–66.

letters to von Burgsdorff are abject pleas, complete with admissions of his earlier sins and present shortcomings, a healthy measure of flattery, and assurances of his devotion to the "fatherland" (which, we know from other letters, he considered pitifully backward); but "honor" impels him to assert the legitimacy of his pursuit of "truth" and to defend his aspiration to proclaim it from the pulpit rather than in the schoolroom.[13] In his laboriously formulated letter to Kant, the down-and-out student's cry for help becomes the scholar's assertion of personal integrity. One "pledge" for the requested loan is his reputation as a *Gelehrter*, which Kant would be in a position to destroy if he failed to pay the loan back. The other is his self-respect, which could not survive such a breach of "honor."[14]

But what social identity did Fichte's notion of honor entail? One answer can be gleaned from an unpublished fragment entitled "Incidental Thoughts on a Sleepless Night," written during a visit with his family on his way to Zürich in July 1788. These are the reflections of an embittered young man, associating the "extreme disdain and breadlessness" endured by scholars like himself with the "oppression" and exploitation suffered by the lower orders, and particularly by the peasantry, at the hands of an establishment of birth and wealth. *Luxus* has corrupted the entire society, but the most alarming decadence is to be found at the courts and among the landed nobility. The nobility's "laughable pride of pedigree" is matched only by the "money pride of the merchants," and "the claim that the nobleman is the support for the rights of the people" is an "absurdity." It was this social vision from the vantage point of the oppressed, combined with his newfound Kantian principles, that produced a defense of the French Revolution a few years later.[15]

But for all the moral conviction in his condemnation of the establishment and all the sense of personal victimization in his identification with the oppressed, the ribbon weaver's son had been thoroughly uprooted. Fichte did not need the professional self-image that gave schoolmen (and to an extent clergymen) a new sense of identity; he justified himself, in broader but no less modern terms, as a "scholar" (*Gelehrter*), and Kantianism reinforced a visceral confidence in his ability to win social acceptance in that capacity despite his origins. From one angle he faulted the corporate ghetto of traditional learning – the guild in which poor students were still expected to assume their modest places – for failing to imbue learned men with the proper interest in and respect for everyday occupational life. But if in that sense the "common learned *Handwerker*" was isolated from the lower or-

[13] GA, III, 1: 140–51.

[14] Ibid., pp. 256–64. In the final version of the letter, Fichte admitted that he had been "ashamed" to request the loan and offer these pledges face to face; but now, he added, he was "ashamed of the shame" that prevented him from doing so.

[15] "Zufällige Gedanken in einer schlaflosen Nacht," in GA, II, 1: 103–10.

ders, he also lacked the social credibility without which the scholar's claim of "power" was "laughable." In June 1794, shortly after moving to Jena, Fichte evoked for his brother Gotthelf the image of a "learned estate" climbing to "an ever higher rank" within a larger elite of wealth and education. In this modernized version of "the great world," learning enjoyed a new respect only if it was accompanied by the kind of "refinement" in speech and deportment that poor students seeking admission to the traditional *Gelehrtenstand* had not had to demonstrate. Proud to have finally secured a place in this elite in Jena, Fichte had no qualms about informing his twenty-two-year-old brother, who was still living at home but now aspired to follow in his footsteps, that it would take several years of schooling to compensate for his earlier "miseducation" (*Verbildung*) and improve his manners sufficiently. Gotthelf could begin with a brief visit to Jena, but without revealing their relationship; "If you appear as my brother, homes with which I am on close terms (and there are many) will insist that I introduce you to them: and that would not be pleasant for you, or for them, or for me."[16]

"Worthy of honor to you above everything," Fichte wrote in his "rules for self-examination" in 1791, "is the voice of duty."[17] His personality achieved an imposing solidity despite the countervailing pulls of his plebeian origins and his aspirations and despite a host of other centrifugal forces, because unflinching and unalloyed devotion to duty gave it a center of gravity. But on closer inspection this ethical core turns out to have combined alternatives that are not easily reconciled. From one angle, duty meant acceptance of a destiny imposed from without, and the issue was whether the imposition was to be interpreted in religious or secular terms. In his letters to his fiancée Fichte repeatedly professed his willingness to follow the "signs" of providential intervention in his life.[18] This posture may have been calculated to defend his departure and long absence in an idiom Johanne would accept; but it also attests to the personal meaning Fichte continued to derive from the Lutheran faith, strongly tinged with Pietism, with which he had been imbued as a child.

The theological explanation coexisted and occasionally fused with a fashionable philosophical alternative. The concept of "freedom," Fichte concluded from his initial plunge into philosophy, was an illusion, obscuring

16 Fichte to Samuel Gotthelf Fichte, June 24, 1794, in GA, III, 2: 150–53.

17 "Regeln der Selbstprüfung für das Jahr 1791," in GA, II, 1: 379. It was this ethical core of his "honor" that made him so anxious to pay his debts promptly, and so ashamed when he failed to do so. See, e.g., Fichte to Karl Gottlob Sonntag, July 7, 1791, in GA, III, 1: 248–51.

18 See, e.g., GA, III, 1: 71–73. Just before his departure from Zürich, Fichte assured Johanne that providence, which did not find it "too trivial" to "lower itself to our small whims and conventions," would not allow him to sink into destitution. Fichte to Marie Johanne Rahn, Mar. 15–16, 1790, in ibid., p. 83.

the fact that the activity of the mind and will, no less than that of the body, operated according to laws of material necessity. While there was "consolation" in discerning providential signs behind a seemingly endless series of trials and dilemmas, secular determinism also had its psychological compensations. He was not ashamed of his "blameless" destitution, Fichte assured Dietrich von Miltitz in early August 1791, but nonethless Frau von Miltitz (from whom he still hoped to secure a pardon) must not learn of it. She could never comprehend "how far need goes in a person like me, how guiltless he is, and what escapes he can be required to take."[19] This was to deny that the poor student was morally responsible for his behavior in the face of necessity; a philosophical preference for material necessity borders on becoming an appeal to social determinism. The suppliant finds a measure of honor in his "blameless" victimization by external forces, even as he becomes abject.

But there is a paradoxical duality in the young Fichte's view of the relationship between the "inner" and the "external," reminiscent of the tension between literal dogma and implicit tendency in the Pietist conversion experience. The Pietist exercise of self-discipline in an "atonement struggle" was meant, on one level, to produce a passive recipient of grace and instrument of providence; but long before Fichte's generation it sanctioned a kind of earned merit through personal achievement. In Fichte's conception of "duty" and "character development," this impulse is neither muted nor restrained. If iron self-discipline is meant to make him a willing instrument of providence (or at least to resign him to his fate), it is also the means to an emphatic voluntarism that impels "action" and produces an "effect" on the world. Hence in the same letter in which he appealed to "the plan of providence" to explain to Johanne why he could not pursue an academic career in Zürich, Fichte also confided to her, "I have only a passion, only a need, only a fullness of feeling of my self: to have an impact outside myself [*ausser mir zu würken*]."[20]

In Fichte's personality, self-denial in the Pietist sense has become willed self-mastery aimed at prevailing in a constant struggle against external obstacles and restraints. The struggle was on several fronts, but they were all of a piece in the perspective of this "disdained" and "breadless" young *Gelehrter*. Fichte's trust in providence did not prevent him from approaching his ascent from obscurity into "the great World" as a personal triumph. Having reached the heights of Jena, he impressed on his brother that the

[19] Fichte to Dietrich von Miltitz, early Aug., 1790, in ibid., pp. 164–65. On Fichte's early determinism, see esp. Reiner Preul, *Reflexion und Gefühl. Die Theologie Fichtes in seiner vorkanntischen Zeit* (Berlin, 1969). Determinism of this sort seems to have been implicit in the occasional note of fatalism in the face of "destiny" (*Schicksal*) (sometimes used interchangeably with "providence") or apparent "chance" (*Ohngefähr*) in letters to friends.

[20] Fichte to Marie Johanne Rahn, Mar. 2, 1790, in GA, III, 1: 73. See also his description of his "exercise in self-overcoming" (*Selbstüberwindung*) in ibid., pp. 172–73.

ascent was a kind of trial by ordeal. The willed self-mastery it required was not simply a matter of intellectual training; in erasing the traces of a harsh dialect and overcoming a "peasant" physical clumsiness, he had had to remake the social self by eradicating plebeian traits that were all too deeply rooted and making the credentials of the polite world an integral part of his personality. And yet if struggle required conformity in this sense, it was also a defiant assertion of the "honor" of the *Gelehrter* in the face of the prejudices of mere pedigree and wealth. In the Ott household, and again at Krockow, he had bristled at the slightest sign that his employees might be equating him with the domestic servants.[21] Like other tutors armed with an enlightened pedagogy, he had taken it upon himself to counteract the corrupting influence of the domestic environment, whether aristocratic or bourgeois, in "remolding" his pupils. From Leipzig he had looked back on the Zürich episode as "a ceaseless battle" in which he had "wanted to win and yet guarantee [himself] an honorable retreat."[22] He had brought the same militancy to his search for a pastorate in Saxony, despite the need to secure patrons. He was contemptuous of the enlightened young clergymen in Saxony who lacked the "power" to defy a "more than Spanish inquisition," and he would not "slink in the usual way" into a village pastorate. He expected "the dawn of better days" in the clerical order, he had written his fiancée; but "it is an enterprise that stimulates me," he had added, "to battle my way through [the] entrenchments and make a career despite them."[23]

Ultimately Fichte's defiant perseverance was nourished by the conviction that inner strength – sheer force of will – could override the force of external necessity. In his occasional meshing of free will and providence, the individual fulfilled his God-given assignment not by cultivating passivity, but by developing the inner self into the kind of iron-willed "character" that had an impact on the world.[24] In more concrete terms, the choice between necessity and will, passivity and "effect," was one between the impotence and obscurity of the typical scholar and the "action" in a public role, the "enterprise" that would effect change, to which he aspired. To the young Fichte the corruption of the existing order was so pervasive as to

21 Fichte to Anna Dorothea Ott, Aug. 20, 1789, in ibid., pp. 31–32; "Nöthige Aufklärung über gewisse Dinge," in GA, II, 2: 165–66.

22 "I succeeded," he added, "but you can see that it was a small exercise." Fichte to Friedrich August Weisshuhn, May 20, 1790, in GA, III, 1: 120. On his battles with Frau Ott, see also the notebook he kept for her enlightenment, as well as his private notes, originally published in Hans Schulz, *Johann Gottlieb Fichte als Hauslehrer*, Pädagogisches Magazin, Heft 709 (Langensalza, 1919). "I face insuperable obstacles in my efforts to remold [*umzuformen*] [my pupil]," he had reported from an earlier tutoring position. Fichte to Christian Friedrich Pezold, Nov. 26, 1787, in GA, III, 1: 17.

23 Fichte to Christian and Johanna Maria Dorothea Fichte, June 20, 1790, in GA, III, 1: 138; Fichte to Marie Johanne Rahn, Aug. 1, 1790, in ibid., pp. 155–56; Fichte to Marie Johanne Rahn, June 8, 1790, in ibid., p. 131.

24 For an interesting discussion of this interpenetration of themes, see Preul, *Reflexion und Gefühl*, esp. pp. 96–121.

suggest the impossibility of regeneration, at least in the immediate future. And yet his assertion of will took the form of a vaulting aspiration to regenerate his age. The "action" that he distinguished from mere "thinking" meant the power to transform people – to induce their moral rebirth – with his eloquence. The gifted scholar with whom he was taking private lessons in oratory, he reported to his fiancée from Leipzig, had spent his life "in darkness and unknown" because he lacked a "spirit of initiative"; but with the same oratorical skills his own "reputation" must be made, "or there is no justice in the world." Fichte's ambition to become a renowned preacher was rooted in the village boy's fascination with the pulpit as the only public platform he could hope to ascend; but now the platform had to be in a great center like Weimar, and the role he projected for himself had messianic undertones. It was in pursuit of this ambition that Fichte continued to hope for a clerical appointment, though he was contemptuous of the servility and hypocrisy it might require and though the village pastorates coveted by other young men of his background seemed intolerably obscure. At first his discovery of Kant seemed to confirm this plan; his mission as a preacher was now to popularize Kantian morality and "make [it] have an impact on the human heart through eloquence."[25] When he finally entered the academic career he had wanted to avoid, it was with this proselytizing fervor – and with the expectation that at Jena the lectern would be his pulpit.

Plebeian sympathies and elitist aspirations, freedom and necessity, hopeless corruption and imminent regeneration – these were the polarities in the young Fichte's orientation to his society and his age. In the subsequent construction of a philosophical system, they were not so much reconciled as reformulated. To explore the reformulations is to trace variations on some of the major themes of this study – and to follow some of the paths by which they found their way into nineteenth-century ideology.

FREEDOM, NECESSITY, AND DUTY

Faced with "the frustration of all [his] hopes," Fichte reported to his fiancée on September 5, 1790, he had suddenly found in Kantian philosophy "peace" and "an unbelievable exaltation above all earthly things." "I have accepted a nobler morality," he continued, "and instead of bothering with things outside myself I concern myself with myself."[26] In November he recounted the same experience to a friend:

[25] GA, III, 1: 130–31, 172. On his ambition to become a renowned preacher, see also Fichte to Friedrich August Weisshuhn, May 20, 1790, in ibid., p. 120; Fichte to Christoph Gottlob von Burgsdorff, July 1790, in ibid., p. 150.

[26] Fichte to Marie Johanne Rahn, Sept. 5, 1790, in ibid., pp. 170–71.

I came to Leipzig with a head that swarmed with great plans. Everything failed, and from so many soap bubbles all that was left over was the light foam from which they had formed. At first this disturbed my peace of mind a bit; and it was half in despair that I seized a *Partie* that I should have seized earlier. Since I could change nothing outside myself, I resolved to change what was inside me. I threw myself into philosophy, and indeed – and this is self-evident – into Kantianism. Here I found the antidote for the true source of my ill, and joy enough beyond that. The influence that this philosophy, and especially the moral part of it . . . has on the entire system of thought of a person, the revolution that has arisen through it especially in my way of thinking, is inconceivable. To you in particular I owe the admission that I now believe in the freedom of the person with my whole heart, and indeed realize that only on this assumption are duty, virtue, and morality in general possible.[27]

Fichte's exultation is a measure of the despair to which poverty, lack of prospects, and a sense of impotence as a superfluous *Gelehrter* had driven him. His evocations of a wrenching turn to introspection echo the language of conversion and convey a similar emotional intensity. The difference is that, in this conversion, inner peace was anything but the result of a retreat into passivity. The appeal of Kantianism lay in simultaneously investing the "voice of duty" with all the more authority and elevating an intuitive conviction of the freedom of the self-disciplined will into an unassailable philosophical truth.

Yet in a sense one of the polarities in the young Fichte's vision was simply reformulated. If Fichte's new ideal of moral freedom promised liberation from material necessity, it also allowed considerable scope to external coercive authority – in the form of a collective social will and the state that enforced it. It would be misleading to conclude from the later building blocks in Fichte's system – from his treatise on "the closed commercial state" (1800), for example, in contrast to the early Jena lectures on the "doctrine of knowledge" (*Wissenschaftslehre*) and "the mission of scholars" – that he eventually opted to tilt the scale to necessity in this new guise, at the expense of freedom. The system as a whole was designed to demonstrate the opposite; there would be less and less need for coercive authority, since freedom and duty would approach the point of perfect identity as society, though it could never fully realize the ideal of a rational order, advanced closer and closer to it. But within a theoretical edifice mounted on Idealist premises, the obligations as well as the rights involved in pursuing a vocation acquired increasingly concrete social dimensions. Here

[27] Fichte to Heinrich Nikolaus Achelis, Nov. 1790, in ibid., pp. 193–94. See also, e.g., Fichte to Friedrich August Weisshuhn, Aug.-Sept. 1790 (fragment), in ibid., p. 167; Fichte to Samuel Gotthelf Fichte, Mar. 5, 1791, in ibid., pp. 222–23. The Fichtean "picture of man as freedom" has aptly been described as "man discovering his proper calling in a perpetual contest with the inertia of his own alienations"; Leszek Kolakowski, *Main Currents of Marxism. Its Origins, Growth and Dissolution*, vol. 1: *The Founders* (New York, 1981), p. 54.

above all Fichte had to define both the broad scope for freedom in a rational polity and the necessary constraints on its exercise, and the internal tensions of his system approached the point of blatant contradiction.

In Fichte's version of Kantian transcendentalism, the attribution of a unique moral freedom to human beings was neither based on anything inherent in the natural order nor inferred from empirical observation of that order. More consequential than his mentor, Fichte refused to acknowledge any explanatory significance to an "objective" reality, existing outside and independent of consciousness. The standard division between subject and object not only encouraged an illusion of material necessity; it also obscured the all-embracing unity of consciousness, within which it was simply a logical impossibility for the I-as-object to be externalized, to become something extrasubjective. Considered as pure form, the indivisible "I" represented the irreducible, universal, and infinite source of the "moral law" that Fichte called Absolute Reason, and from that purely logical standpoint its freedom was likewise "absolute." As a moral being the "I" always strove to remain indivisible. It retained its freedom even as, with the "activity" (*Handeln*) of the will, it assumed a finite empirical identity. In this sense unconditional freedom, without which there could be no morality, characterized the uniquely human realm of rational *Intelligenz*.

The self-generating "I," incorporating sense objects into itself by free acts, always remained the starting point for causation. To the former determinist, faced with more than enough personal reasons for regarding himself as a helpless victim, the revolutionary insight was that neither he nor any other moral being was the object of coercion from without. Many young men of Fichte's generation derived intensely personal meaning from this a priori insight; but he may have been unique in finding in it a third way, a configuration of nature, reason and society – of natural freedom, rational self-discipline, and socially defined duty – that departed from rationalism and neohumanism while assimilating much of their spirit. In rationalist pedagogy, and indeed long before it assimilated Rousseau, the individual had been considered "free" to the measure that he could realize the innate entelechy of the natural self despite the exigencies of social existence. To Fichte the natural self – the cluster of innate capacities and inclinations he (following standard usage) called "forces" or "powers" (*Kräfte*) – belonged to the amoral realm of inert sense material and blind necessity that he evoked with the term *Natur*. Far from attributing a potentially liberating entelechy to these natural forces, he in effect made them the internal equivalent – the counterpart within the personality – to the potentially coercive, and indeed enslaving, external forces of physical nature. The moral autonomy of the rational will lay in prevailing over this threat; nature, both within and without, provided the resistant but malleable substance the will needed to substantiate the absolute I as an empirical – but still autonomous – personality.

If in Pietism freedom from doubt was effected by the infusion of grace, it now lay entirely within the individual consciousness, in an intuitive awareness of the transcendental ego. In Fichte's conversion to Kantianism, this shift not only justified a rejection of the Lutheran-Pietist ethic of passivity in the face of the Divine Will; it also opened a new angle for a radical critique of the status quo. The normative standard of reference was no longer an irreducible "nature" beneath the social surface and anterior to socialization; it had become an "absolute" self-identity, a self-referential insight into a spiritual unity anterior to natural being. The ethical impulse in this dynamic of ego formation often seems more akin to the rational self-discipline preached in the utilitarian ethic than to the blending of sensual and mental faculties in neohumanistic "cultivation." But in fact Fichte's conception of "freedom" was as opposed to the utilitarian *Bürger* as it was to the neohumanistic *Mensch*. At the same time that he denied to nature the emancipatory role it assumed in rationalist pedagogy, he rejected the countervailing rationalist tendency to equate reason with a socially imposed definition of duty and define the will as its socialized instrument. In Fichte's alternative vision, society realized an ideal of *Bildung* as multifaceted cultivation in the very process of subordinating nature to higher purposes. In a key passage in the lectures on "the mission of scholars," he explained that "absolute identity," the highest goal of human rationality, required that "all endowments be equally developed, all capacities be developed to the greatest possible perfection." Unavoidably the "influence of nature" initiated a process of unbalanced development; but reason eventually came to the rescue with a social "drive," inducing the individual consciousness to emulate others in its very effort to mold them in its image:

> [Reason] will see to it that each individual receives *directly from the hands of society* the entire complete *Bildung* he cannot acquire *directly from nature*. . . . reason is in a continual battle with nature; this war can never end, if we do not become gods; but it can and should make the influence of nature weaker and weaker, the rule of reason stronger and stronger; the latter should achieve over the former one victory after another. It may be that an individual can battle nature with success in his particular points of contact, but in all others is irresistibly dominated by nature. Now society is constituted, and stands for One Man; what the individual could not do is made possible by the united powers of all. Each battles individually, but the weakening of nature occurs through the collective struggle, and the victory that each individual achieves in his part comes to all.[28]

[28] Johann Gottlieb Fichte, *Von den Pflichten der Gelehrten. Jenaer Vorlesungen 1794–95*, ed. Reinhard Lauth, Hans Jacob, and Peter K. Schneider, Philosophische Bibliothek, vol. 274 (Hamburg, 1971), pp. 25–26.

Fichte's language of struggle remains rich in Pietist resonances, but now social solidarity has replaced the lonely struggle of conversion in the victory over natural corruption. As always, Fichte advanced from a priori insight; the "I" became conscious of its freedom only when confronted with another free consciousness. Freedom dictated that the I regard the other purely as an "end" or "purpose," as it regarded itself, and not as a mere "means" to its end; otherwise the individual consciousness contradicted itself by preferring a relationship of domination and subordination to one of "coordination," and invited others to reduce it to a means as well. It was because society constituted this "interaction [*Wechselwirkung*] of rational beings" that it was indispensable for the exercise of moral freedom and ultimately allowed reason to prevail. In intellectual life, the interaction took the form of mutual efforts to persuade, requiring mutual respect for autonomy.[29]

In one emphasis, this logic explained the establishment of a "state" as a collective effort to *maximize* individual freedom in an original "social contract." So long as the individual exercised his own freedom at others' expense – i.e., with others reduced to his means – and hence risked annihilation of his freedom by others in turn, human relationships inevitably were subjected to the "mechanical" laws of domination and subordination in a realm of blind necessity. The individual could be secure in the exercise of most of his freedom only if he transferred a small quotient of it to the collective authority of the state and its law. In this purely logical version of the progression from a state of nature to a social contract, the advance from pure consciousness to social relations remained an abstraction. But by the turn of the century freedom had acquired social substance in Fichte's definition of *Eigentum*, or property, as a "specific free activity," rather than as a "thing." If this definition had simply granted an entitlement to an object in recognition of the labor invested in it, it would have remained within the mainstream of eighteenth-century thought on property. But Fichte's point was that the labor itself constituted a "property"; the inalienable right was to the activity, and not to use of the objects modified by it. In a quintessentially Idealist preference, labor acquired social value for what it expressed in mutual communication of an inner, spiritual creativity, rather than for what it contributed and thus earned in the utilitarian sense. Seen in relation to the a priori case for "freedom," *Eigentum* in this sense conferred the autonomy needed to develop the consciousness in social "interaction"; it was the "sphere" of freedom guaranteed by the collectivity. If "activity" (*Handeln* or *Tätigkeit*) had originally referred only to acts (or, perhaps better, processes) of pure consciousness, it now evoked a social ethic of work.[30]

29 Fichte, *Von den Pflichten der Gelehrten*, pp. 12–21.

30 See esp. *Das System der Sittenlehre nach den Prinzipien der Wissenschaftslehre (1798)*, ed. Manfred Zahn, Philosophische Bibliothek, vol. 257 (Hamburg, 1963), pp. 288–97, and the more elaborate definition of an *Eigentumsrecht* in *Der geschlossene Handelsstaat*, in Batscha and

It was an ethic that found perverse resistance in the natural man, but nonetheless assimilated in spirit the eighteenth-century ideal of work discipline as the critical vehicle for self-realization, externalizing talents and other innate endowments in a socially useful modification of the environment. The radicalism of Fichte's reordering of priorities – of his methodical advance from a priori universals to concrete social activity – lay in inverting the more common eighteenth-century tendency to justify de facto privilege by appeal to a universal right. Property-as-thing, in the conventional view to which Fichte took exception, implied something that could in fact be enjoyed by some to the exclusion of others, even if the "natural" right to acquire it was extended in theory to all. In Fichte's conception of property as work and, in the more abstract but related sense, as the indispensable basis for "interaction," the possession of things could not prevent the universal exercise of a right to moral "freedom." So long as even one member of society was deprived of a "specific free activity" – i.e., of property-as-work – the freedom enjoyed by others was illegitimate.

Fichte's social radicalism did not stop at contradicting the neocorporate defense of de facto privilege. In his hands Idealist logic went well beyond conventional egalitarian reform, and indeed with an insistence on inalienable rights that had been notably absent from rationales for an egalitarian meritocracy of dutiful *Bürger*. It was the responsibility of the state to "install" every individual in an *Eigentum* by training him for a particular kind of work and to "protect" his use of it. In the ideal "commercial state" this guarantee of a right to work, and thereby to subsist at a decent level, allowed moral beings to treat each other as "ends" and reduce only things to the status of "means," and hence ensured the triumph of moral freedom over natural necessity. But work was an opportunity as well as a defense against exploitation; as the vital social expression of the rationally disciplined inner self, it promised maximum realization of potential. As early as the Jena lectures on "the mission of scholars," Fichte had derived another, closely related right from this Idealist version of vocation:

The choice of an occupation [*Standes*] is a choice through freedom; no person can be forced into any occupation, or be excluded from any occupation. Every individual activity, as well as every general arrangement [*Veranstaltung*] that proceeds from such coercion is illegitimate; aside from the fact that it is unwise to force a person into one occupation or keep him out of another, because no one can know com-

Saage, eds., *Schriften*, pp. 105–12. An "exclusive right" to *Eigentum*, Fichte insisted, applied not only when the "activity" involved use of a piece of physical property like land, but also – as in the case of skilled labor for a wage – when property in this narrower sense was absent. Indispensable for understanding Fichte's conception of labor and property is Batscha, "Die Arbeit in der Sozialphilosophie Johann Gottlieb Fichtes." See also Willms, *Die totale Freiheit*, pp. 104–8. Fichte was following Kant in rejecting the Lockean conception of property; for a lucid analysis of Kant's alternative approach, see Susan Meld Shell, *The Rights of Reason. A Study of Kant's Philosophy and Politics* (Toronto, 1980), esp. pp. 127–52.

pletely the particular talents of the other, and thereby often a member is completely lost for society, in that it is placed in the wrong position. Aside from that, it is in itself unjust; since it puts our action in contradiction with our practical conception of it. We wanted a *member* of society, and we produce a *tool* for it; we wanted a *co-worker* for our great plan, and we produce a *coerced, suffering instrument* for it.[31]

The bitterness of the marginal *Gelehrter* – of the young man who concluded on a "sleepless night" that "no nobility" and indeed "no *Stand*" should be "heritable" – has become an argument from philosophical principle. The argument is unmistakably Kantian in origin, but to appreciate its radical tenor one need only recall that, in his essay on "political right," Kant saw no need to reconcile his brief for opening careers to talent with his acceptance of the de facto advantage enjoyed by "fortuitous external property." To the former disciple, family wealth was not a "fortuitous" basis for freedom; its hereditary enjoyment by some threatened to deprive others of their right to freedom through work in an appropriate vocation. Like the neohumanists, Fichte refused to make the opening of careers to talent contingent on a social definition of "usefulness"; but he did not share their faith that a new breed of men, having cultivated themselves in insulation from society, would regenerate occupational life in the established order. It was to inspire "action" that he offered his normative ideal; though perhaps never to be fully realized, the vision of a rational society, guaranteeing *Eigentum* in Fichte's sense, was meant to demonstrate how much would have to change if actual social process was to promote freedom in and through work. If young men are to be free to choose their occupations after their reason has matured sufficiently, Fichte acknowledged in his ethics lectures, "much in human relationships would have to be very different from what it is now."[32]

But just two years later, in *The Closed Commercial State*, Fichte unraveled another logical thread, left implicit in this line of argument; and one of its inexorable conclusions was that the freedom to choose an occupation did not necessarily entail a right to enter it.[33] In a sense Fichte simply confirmed that his ideal of individual freedom, for all its daring in positing social rights, remained confined within familiar ethical inhibitions and prohibitions. In the *Beitrag*, where the argument was fashioned primarily to deny the legitimacy of the aristocracy's "feudal" privileges as a landowning class, Fichte had implicitly posed an open, competitive market against the traditional landlord-peasant relationship. But it soon became apparent that Fichte's rational alternative to the corporate hierarchy of the old regime did not find its ordering principle in a free market. His context for freedom in and through work (rather than in the use of objects modified by it) did not

[31] Fichte, *Von den Pflichten der Gelehrten*, pp. 29–30.
[32] Fichte, *System der Sittenlehre*, p. 269.
[33] The entire essay has been reprinted in Batscha and Saage, eds., *Schriften*, pp. 59–167.

assume, as an alternative theory of property assumed, that a natural harmony made state tutelage unnecessary. To leave the distribution of work to the "laws" of the market was to leave it to the same "blind" and "mechanical" necessity that governed physical nature.

Hence the countervailing thrust of his logic was to make the exercise of freedom contingent on – and indeed, in a more rational future, identical to – submission to the "voice of duty." In Fichte's application, the novelty of the Idealist reconciliation lay more in its point of departure than in its denouement; the social economy of the German utilitarian ethic now had an Idealist analogue, and the tenacious equation of unrestricted intergenerational mobility – the kind that the market, in principle, sanctioned – with the unleashing of blind, potentially destructive self-interest received a new philosophical imprimatur. The social contract was double-edged, in that a collectively enforced guarantee of freedom required collectively enforced limitations on its exercise. In the writings at the turn of the century, the initial preoccupation with keeping restrictions to a minimum was muted by a new concern with protecting individuals, and ultimately the society as a whole, from abuses of freedom. In this shift of emphasis, the social provision of individual freedom in "interaction" is conceived increasingly in terms of the "equilibrium" among *Stände* that had figured so large in rationalist social thought. These were not the old-regime corporate bodies, defined by legal rights (or privileges), but the constituent occupational groups in the functional hierarchy of a modern division of labor. But as in utilitarian visions of meritocracy, they nonetheless institutionalized a kind of corporate ethos, integrating individuals into work-focused solidarities and thereby providing the cement for the larger society. Just as individuals, as members of a *Stand*, entered a contract to respect each other's freedom in work, the *Stand* itself mediated their contract with the entire society. It was by ensuring coordination among the *Stände* – by preventing any occupational group from infringing on the "specific free activity" of any other – that the state guaranteed a right to work to individuals.[34]

Again the state derived its authority from an a priori definition of freedom and from the social embodiment of that definition in labor. But what gave momentum to state authority in this instance was Fichte's vision of progress. Here above all his Idealist conception of reason – for all its disdain for the "mechanical" reduction of human beings to "means" in rationalist reform thought – built on the set of assumptions and priorities in which mobility had been perceived throughout the eighteenth century. On one level the "perfecting" of society was a matter of Absolute Reason unfolding itself in the sense world or, more precisely, approaching in its temporal substan-

[34] On the evolution of Fichte's concept of *Stände*, see esp. *Von den Pflichten der Gelehrten*, pp. 21–32, and *System der Sittenlehre*, pp. 255–72, as well as the extensive discussion in *Der geschlossene Handelsstaat*.

tiality the unity it had never lost as form. But in its concrete historical evolution, the society that advanced toward – though it could never fully realize – Fichte's ideal *Vernunftstaat* was reminiscent of the dynamic social machine celebrated in cameralist and utilitarian visions of "perfectability." Despite a real empathy for Rousseau, based on a shared sense of alienation from a thoroughly corrupt age, Fichte did not subscribe to a Rousseauian explanation of the modern illness. There was no denying the extraordinary sensitivity of Rousseau's emotional response, he acknowledged to his student audience at Jena, but it was simply wrongheaded to attribute the complexity of the modern division of labor to the pursuit of artificial needs through false social roles. For the same reason that he rejected Rousseau's rural idyll of lost simplicity, in fact, Fichte also took exception to the neohumanists' nostalgia for the lost integration of *Mensch* and *Bürger* in classical Greece. The "golden age" lay not in a vanished past, but in a future in which the rule of reason would eliminate crude sensual needs and permit the disciplined cultivation of spirituality. It was to allow maximum time and freedom for such cultivation – and not for mere idleness, much less for the kind of spontaneous "play" Schiller had in mind – that physical labor would be reduced to a minimum. The road to an eventual age of "leisure" in this sense lay in rational devotion to work – through increased dominion over and exploitation of nature, in the form of an expansion of scientific knowledge and its technological applications.[35] In Fichte's scheme of things, in other words, moral as well as material progress required intensified specialization in a social division of labor. The functional *Stände* not only bound the individual to the whole; their intricate meshing moved the whole forward, and in that sense as well they were the social instruments of reason.

If coercive state authority ensured individual freedom within the limits of the original contract, the need to sustain collective progress made such authority all the more necessary. The distribution of *Bürger* among *Stände* could no more be left to the blind necessity of a "free" market than the availability of work affording subsistence. The advance of reason implied quite the contrary; to the measure that the division of labor became more complex, it was all the more incumbent on the state, as the temporal embodiment of rationality, to maintain an intricate "equilibrium" (*Gleichgewicht*) among the parts of the social mechanism. Once economic exchange was removed from the illusory freedom of the market and based on rational equivalents in work value, it would be possible to determine a proper proportion in the relative sizes of *Stände*. In practical terms the state, though it could not summarily assign a *Bürger* to any *Stand* when he came of age, must exclude him from the *Stand* of his choice if it was already "full," even,

[35] See esp. Fichte, *Von den Pflichten der Gelehrten*, pp. 44–54, where Fichte's version of progress is contrasted with Rousseau's pessimism.

one must infer, when his innate capacities and his education qualified him for it. This negative licensing procedure applied not only to agriculture, industrial production, and commerce, but also to the public officialdom supported by these sectors and indeed to each of its subgroups.[36]

Freedom of occupational choice cannot be restricted by any "individual activity" or "general arrangement," but the state is allowed and indeed required to exclude some aspirants from the occupations of their choice. One line of reasoning posed against the prevailing forms of social ascription an open, fluid society, with qualified young men of Fichte's background ascending with honor into a new elite within the universal sanction given to self-determination. The other imposed a rigid order on the new fluidity by subordinating individual aspirations to a collective definition of "need." In the name of "equilibrium" (and ultimately in the name of "freedom"), society could not rely on a self-adjusting market to distribute its human resources; instead the statist alternative – the alternative reformers had long considered essential to limiting access to academic education and public employment – received universal application.

Fichte saw no need to reconcile tensions at this level of specificity; he was convinced that the overall unity of his system, as a deduction from a priori truths, transcended its apparent contradictions. In fact his arguments for individual self-determination had never been intended to sanction the pursuit of self-interest. As always, freedom was inseparable from duty; the rational individual selected an occupation not to satisfy his personal "inclination" (*Neigung*), but to contribute as best he could to "the promotion of the purpose of reason" in society.[37] Parallel teleologies – one in history, the other in the individual consciousness – ensured that the exercise of freedom would become more and more rational in this sense. As society advanced in rational self-consciouness, it would in effect absorb the state into itself – or, to put it another way, it would have less need of the "external" coercive authority of an "emergency" state (*Notstaat*). With greater freedom in and through social interaction, the individual consciousness would be more and more able to reconstitute itself as a pure Absolute within the very sense world in which, by the nature of its activity, it had assumed a finite definition. Since the individual will and the collective will would approach the point of absolute unity, duty would no longer mean obligation imposed from without. Fichte's logic guaranteed what had been the ultimate promise of the rationalist ethic: that duty would be thoroughly internalized and hence would become completely voluntary – and completely reliable – submission to rational necessity. In such a society there would be less and less need to exclude a young man from a "full" occupation; the more

[36] Batscha and Saage, eds., *Schriften*, esp. pp. 77–95, 105–112.
[37] See esp. *System der Sittenlehre*, pp. 268–70.

commitment to duty became a purely rational – i.e., a purely moral – act of freedom, the more he could be expected to exclude himself.

ELITE AND MASS

Until his appointment at Jena the young Fichte faced in acute form the dilemma of the marginal poor student. Groomed to be a *Gelehrter* since his abrupt removal from family and native village, he continued to identify with the oppressed lower orders across an immense social distance. But he also prided himself on having achieved, or at least on having nearly achieved, a complete eradication of plebeian traits.

This ambiguity underlay another polarity that proved remarkably persistent. Fichte's system encompassed alternative visions of social hierarchy, overlapping to some degree, but nonetheless remaining in a state of uneasy coexistence. One was reminiscent of the utilitarian model for a progressive society; the learned estate would preside over and provide the intellectual energy for a dynamic occupational hierarchy as "enlightenment," in suitably popularized form, seeped down into the broad base of the social pyramid. The role of the educated professions was to produce and disseminate learning with direct social relevance – the kind of learning Fichte had posed against an outmoded corporate formalism in his early writings. Whereas this vision promised a more egalitarian integration of the "learned" into a larger community, the alternative made them a segregated and emphatically elitist vanguard. As the microcosm of a higher stage of human "perfecting," the learned estate would occupy a qualitatively superior cultural and ethical realm. The select few who ascended to its "public" space would hover above their society, transcend the historically conditioned cultural horizons of their age, and enjoy a unique freedom from the legal constraints to which ordinary *Bürger* were subject. This scenario reflected a distinctly Kantian – or, perhaps better, Idealist – preference for reason over merely instrumental rationality; but it also had much in common with the neohumanistic bifurcation into the cultivated few and the uninitiated mass and with the cognitive and normative claims for scholarly "disciplines" being made within professional ideologies, under the impact of neohumanism, at the turn of the century.[38]

With the spread of a spirit of free inquiry to "the unlearned *Publikum*," Fichte observed to his student audience in 1794, the scholar is ceasing to be "the pedant reeking with lamp oil, at home in the marketplaces of Athens and Rome but not in his hometown." Like many other young men of similar

[38] Cf. Batscha, *Gesellschaft und Staat*, esp. pp. 212–36. Especially relevant for the evolution of Fichte's conception of scholarship and its organization is Hahn, *Staat, Erziehung und Wissenschaft*.

background at the turn of the century, Fichte refused to assume the obsolete identity of a "common learned *Handwerker*" as the price for his admission to the educated elite. The urge to action could not be satisfied in the scholar's traditional corporate station.[39] This refusal found expression not only in his image of a new elite, merging education and property, but also in his conception of a new social hierarchy as a cultural continuum, posed against the corporate fragmentation of the old regime. Long after his conversion to Kantianism, the cameralist and utilitarian traditions are echoed in his censure of conventional scholarship for its snobbish ignorance of everyday occupational life; in his insistence that, in his efforts to advance his field, the professional scholar concern himself as much with empirical investigation of new "means" as with a priori insights about ends; in his equally emphatic concern with inculcating in a new generation of scholars the skills of communication needed to disseminate specialized knowledge. His repeated attributions of a new value and dignity to manual labor reflected in part the familiar utilitarian expectation that, in agriculture as well as in industry, advances in science and technology would reduce drudgery and allow more scope for the exercise of reason.

Again Fichte's Kantianism provided a new rationale for the egalitarian impulse in eighteenth-century rationalism. Now social definitions of merit and "usefulness" were assimilated to a higher ideal; performance of duty could have as much inner "value" in a lower *Stand* as in a higher one, because all *Stände* were equally indispensable to the advance of reason and hence, like Christians in the eyes of God, were equal before its "court." The import was still that moral equality sanctioned social inequality, albeit without justifying irrational privileges of birth. But it was to be a new kind of inequality – one in which the social relationships between higher and lower *Stände*, like relationships between individuals, would exemplify the "interaction" and "coordination" unique to moral beings, and not the reduction of objects to means that prevailed in nature. Reform still came from above, but it could not rely on the kind of authoritarian imposition that "enlightenment" in the rationalist sense had seemed to require. It would thrive on mutuality within an intricate division of labor; just as peasants and artisans had to become more receptive to the "advice" offered by their intellectual superiors, educated men had to abandon their corporate ghetto and develop the "social talents" of "receptivity" and "ability to communicate." The latter was not simply a matter of adapting the message to a popular mentality; it also required that in his use of moral suasion the scholar respect the moral "freedom" of the "lower popular classes."[40]

This ideal was posed against both old-regime corporatism and the authoritarian bureaucratic state threatening to replace it. Egalitarian def-

[39] *Von den Pflichten der Gelehrten*, pp. 102–05.
[40] Ibid., pp. 32–43; *System der Sittenlehre*, pp. 359–61.

erence toward scholars would be a voluntary form of respect, extended from one moral being to another; it would involve neither blind reverence for the honorific – i.e., merely external – credentials of corporate membership nor "slavish" subordination to the coercive authority of officialdom. But in another vision scholars hovered above the common lot of humanity as a self-sufficient breed apart. As late as 1805, in a series of lectures at Erlangen on "the nature of the scholar," Fichte acknowledged his personal need to reconcile these alternative profiles of an intellectual aristocracy:

> In the Divine Idea [the scholar] carries in himself the form of the future Age which one day must clothe itself with reality. . . . In every Age the Idea clothes itself in a new form, and seeks to shape the surrounding world in its image; and thus do continually arise new relations of the world to the Idea, and a new mode of opposition of the former to the latter. It is the business of the Scholar so to interpose in this strife as to reconcile the activity with the purity of his Idea, its influence with its dignity. His Idea must not lie concealed within him; it must go forth and lay hold upon the world, and he is urged to this activity by the deepest impulses of his nature. But the world is incapable of receiving this Idea in its purity; on the contrary, it strives to drag down the Idea to the level of its own vulgar thought. . . . What is more noble than the impulse to action, to sway the minds of men, and to compel their thoughts to the Holy and Divine? – and yet this impulse may become a temptation to represent the Holy in a common and familiar garb for the sake of popularity, and so to desecrate it. What is more noble than the deepest reverence for the Holy, and disdain and abnegation of everything vulgar and opposed to it? – and yet this very reverence might tempt some one to reject his age altogether, – to cast it from him and avoid intercourse with it.[41]

For Fichte the assumption of "learned" status had been a purifying rite of passage from the plebeian to the refined. Ultimately it was that experience, heightened in his initial enthusiasm for Kantian epistemology and receiving a quasi-religious confirmation within Idealist abstractions, that shaped his image of a new priesthood. Fichte often envisioned intellectual advance as the product of an intense competition of ideas, but his explicit rejection of a "liberal" market model for social relations had an implicit analogue in the intellectual sphere. Ideas were not opinions, claiming more or less empirical probability in a competition for social recognition. Their truth value lay in their degree of purity – i.e., in the degree to which they gave self-conscious expression to a priori principles, without being muddied by the merely empirical substance of sense experience. Likewise Fichte's priesthood was not a modern technocracy, its superior objectivity deriving from command of a morally neutral expertise. Ultimately advances in empirical understanding of "means" – i.e., in instrumental rationality – in a broad range of scholarly disciplines acquired authority in the service of a

41 *The Popular Works of Johann Gottlieb Fichte*, trans. William Smith, 2 vols. (4th ed.: London, 1889), 1: 271–72.

single normative vision derived from the philosophical source of truth common to all disciplines. The scholar was one of the select few initiated into this superior vision. It was as "the morally best human being of his age" in this sense that he "saw farther" than his contemporaries and pointed them toward a more rational future.[42]

Fichte's tendency to elevate the new learned estate to a higher order of purity was reinforced by his disillusionment with the public discourse of his age. By the absolute standard of his a priori procedure, normative authority could no more be derived from the neohumanist's intuitive historical understanding of the classical age than from the rationalist's more "mechanical" variety of empiricism. But like the new classical studies, his system claimed autonomy for a purified scholarship, generating its own ethical standards above the arena of social interests and mere politics. And as in neohumanism, that claim was prompted in part by the commercialization of the literary market, which seemed to signal the dissolution of all cultural – and ultimately moral – authority. Again Fichte's early experience on the margins of the *Gelehrtenstand* had left its mark; as an unemployed scholar in Leipzig, forced to try his hand at "trivial" novels and plays to survive, he had regarded the requirements of "the book traders" as one more intrusion on the "honor" and ultimately the freedom of the learned man.[43] His debut as a serious author in the early 1790s seemed to bring the reputation he sought; but over the next decade, as he was drawn into polemics and came to feel increasingly isolated even from Kantians, the kind of market for ideas created by commercial publishing became a symptom of the general corruption of the age. In its commercialized form, popularization created opinion at its worst – empirical knowledge in the form of a chaotic, ever changing, always superficial pluralism. His initial preference for the "eloquence" of the lecture now became a retreat into that oral format in the face of the deluge of print and the accompanying expansion of a pseudo-learned reading public.

It was in part to meet this threat that Fichte rested the normative authority of his ideal "republic of scholars" on a priori logic, rather than on the shaky foundation of tradition. But the ideal republic also addressed the underlying problem: the familiar conflict between the *Mensch* and the *Bürger*, the purely human and the socialized personality. Functionalism within the occupational ranks – the kind of collective rationality that Fichte considered indispensable to progress – had as its price a "certain half-ness and one-sidedness" in individual development. What distinguished membership in the republic

[42] See esp. *Von den Pflichten der Gelehrten*, pp. 40–42. The "totalitarian" potential of this vision of a new elite is suggested in Kolakowski, *Main Currents of Marxism*, 1: 54–56.

[43] GA, III, 1: 131–32. For his later view of the literary market, see esp. *Popular Works*, 1: 309–13. See also the insightful discussion of "public opinion" in Batscha, *Gesellschaft und Staat*, pp. 64–76.

of scholars from membership in a *Stand* was a serene detachment from narrow social interests and prejudices, analogous to the kind of privileged objectivity teachers and clergymen were claiming for their professional disciplines. The scholar embodied a more advanced stage in realization of the "general calling" as a human being, and hence his knowledge, however specialized it might be in some respects, was more objective in an ethical as well as a cognitive sense.

In the *System der Sittenlehre* (1798), Fichte distinguished the republic of letters from the historically bound community he called the "church" (*Kirche*). The "symbol" (*Symbol*) was the ethical consensus that bound a society as "church," and that was enforced in state law; unlike the pure ideal into which scholars had been initiated, it reflected the "imperfect" moral standards of society at a given stage of development. While most *Bürger* could legitimately be required to subscribe to this consensus, the republic was an "absolute democracy" in which no idea or line of research was forbidden and the "intellectually stronger" prevailed. It was also an open democracy, its members drawn from all *Stände*; but its higher arena for public discourse formed a privileged corporate jurisdiction, above the social division of labor as well as the flux of mere opinion.[44] Corporate privilege in this context meant a unique freedom; since the republic formed the microcosm of a more advanced stage of moral "perfectability," its members both required and merited exemption from the coercive restrictions necessarily imposed on those *Bürger* – i.e., the great majority of their contemporaries – confined within a less advanced stage of human evolution. For most *Bürger*, the coercive legal authority of the state closed the gap between freedom and duty; in the republic of letters there could be no legal coercion, because its members had to strive to achieve a rational exercise of complete freedom in and through complete devotion to duty.

Even at this rarefied level, Fichte's appreciation of the advance of knowledge as a *social* process is striking. But the advance occurred within a segregated "democracy," not in a larger process of social interaction. The new priesthood was a morally superior breed, its vision sharing in the absolute validity of the moral law, and its mission in authoritarian counterpoint to the new spirit of egalitarian deference. And yet precisely because its moral authority was exempted from the mere flux of empirical opinion and was in that sense detached from its own age, the priesthood was severely limited in its ability to influence the larger society directly. Fichte's lectures on Freemasonry in 1802–3 were one of several efforts to fuse the profiles of an enlightened intelligentsia, integrated into the larger society, and a serenely detached priesthood, and to reconcile authoritarian and egalitarian expectations. He imagined a properly organized lodge as a democratic "zone of reason" (*Vernunftgebiet*), with *Bürger* from a variety of *Stände* overcoming

[44] *System der Sittenlehre*, pp. 232–49.

the narrow-mindedness of occupational life in the course of developing each other into *Menschen*. While the lodge member involved in material production would lose "his mistrust, his shyness, his fear, his hatred and even his contempt" in the face of the better educated, he would also no longer be treated with "disdain." These "brothers" would in turn carry a new spirit of egalitarian sociability "out of the lodge and into the world." But if the order was an "open" corporation in these senses, it also had to be segregated and indeed secret. The very nature of the knowledge it generated – the normative vision of a "pure humanity" – required that this corporate melting pot be kept immune from contamination by the social division of labor from which it drew its members, as a kind of priesthood initiated into exclusive mysteries. Detachment in this sense was the other condition of its higher rationality.[45]

Fichte's alternative visions of hierarchy confronted the same questions that were being posed in professional ideologies at the turn of the century. Should all the university-educated professions participate equally in an intellectual democracy, or should the very nature of their public employment limit some to qualified membership in the republic of letters? Always proceeding from his new "science of knowledge," Fichte remained convinced that the prevailing fragmentation of academic learning would give way to a new unity. Students would specialize at the universities only after integrating into their personalities the Idealist "principles" that defined the normative "end" of each discipline, gave it internal coherence, and made it an integral part of a larger system of knowledge. Because their empirical expertise in various professions would remain inseparable from their understanding of and commitment to the moral law in its a priori purity, they would not cease to belong to the higher republic of scholars.

[45] The two lectures on Freemasonry are reprinted in Batscha and Saage, eds., *Schriften*, pp. 169–216. See esp. pp. 176–92. Though Fichte was projecting an ideal order, he had in mind the well-known social mixing in some existing lodges, including the one he had joined in Berlin. But the mixing would have its parameters; the lodge would combine "at least the two ends" of two "classes" – men concerned with "the education as well as the governance of spirit and heart" and those "provid[ing] for the needs of earthly life." Ibid., p. 191. In his lectures at Erlangen and in the memorandum he submitted to the Prussian government two years later, Fichte extended an analogous corporate status to reformed universities. Each university would constitute an autarchic community, with wealthier students and their *Kommilitonen* on scholarship enjoying equal support in a common household, distinguished by the same clothing as their professors, and thus forming the kind of egalitarian solidarity needed for intellectual freedom. While "academic freedom" of the old dispensation had allowed the professoriate to be oblivious to the excesses of a student subculture, professors now were to be moral guardians as well as intellectual mentors. But again freedom required corporate segregation and legal privilege; the university would remain beyond the reach of state law, since the rational freedom students had to learn to exercise was superior to the legal coercion facing ordinary *Bürger*. "Deduzierter Plan einer zu Berlin zu errichtenden höhern Lehranstalt, die in gehörigen Verbindung mit einer Akademie der Wissenschaften stehe," in Ernst Anrich, ed., *Die Idee der deutschen Universität. Die funf Grundschriften aus der Zeit ihrer Neubegründung durch klassischen Idealismus und romantischen Realismus* (Darmstadt, 1964), pp. 127–217.

If the republic and the "church" were linked as stages in the advance of a single Reason, however, the one lagged too far behind the other to be directly receptive to its higher rationality. The mediating role – the task of bridging stages – was assigned to the "teachers of the people" who would replace the existing clerical order and to "state officials." In their capacity as private authors, these were as free to express their dissent from the prevailing consensus as any other citizens of the republic; but as officials their efforts to persuade must always "proceed from" and operate within the *Symbol*, even though they saw beyond it and were aware of its inadequacies. Their responsibility as guardians of a historically conditioned consensus, in other words, attenuated their citizenship in the republic. The only exception – and for Fichte it was the key exception – was the university professor, whose state office and salary could in no way constrain his scholarly freedom. Responsible for initiating other scholars into the Ideal, the professor exercised his complete freedom from "the fetters of the church symbol" in office as well as in the higher altitudes of the republic.[46]

As "open" as it was in principle, the republic of scholars was not a free-floating intelligentsia. As in professional ideologies at the turn of the century, state office was assumed to be the only appropriate platform for an educated *Beruf*; the definition of a professional discipline operated within a received bureaucratic framework. In Fichte's system the ideal of *Wissenschaft* as a uniquely disinterested vocation, soaring above merely private interests – the ideal that underlay professional service ethics and claims to autonomy – received an imposing imprimatur; and so did the authority of the professoriate that guarded its mysteries. In this sense, Fichte simply shifted the intellectual center of gravity within the larger conception of a *Bildungsbürgertum* taking shape at the turn of the century, while confirming the fulcrum position of the university. But the implication of the shift was that, with the exception of university professors, the public exchange of ideas among "scholars" represented a higher order of freedom than the public profession of knowledge in office. This is not to imply that, in subordinating educated officials to the state-enforced consensus, Fichte obliged them to comply with a reactionary religious or political orthodoxy. But his conception of a two-tiered *Gelehrtenstand* contrasts with the more common – and the more naive – assumption that the *Bildung* of the individual, the autonomy of the professional, and the public responsibilities of the official were all of a piece. Again the difference lay ultimately in epistemology; to Fichte professional knowledge was inferior to pure scholarship for the simple reason that it could *not* generate a normative vision within itself. The source of that vision was a realm of philosophical insight, too far advanced

[46] *System der Sittenlehre*, pp. 232–49, 341–58; *Popular Works*, 1: 277–317.

beyond the empirical world of the professions to exercise direct social and cultural authority through it.

EDUCATING THE NATION

On December 13, 1807, before a small audience in the amphitheater of the Berlin Academy, Fichte began the series of fourteen lectures known as the *Addresses to the German Nation*. He had just returned to Berlin from Königsberg, where he had followed the Prussian government after Napoleon's victory at Jena and invasion of the kingdom.

The *Addresses* are often typical of the lofty philosophical posture Fichte preferred to assume; but more than anything else in his corpus, they reveal him formulating an immediate response to the events of his day. Almost without warning, the "system" becomes the framework for a militant nationalism. Though Fichte's nationalism rests on the eighteenth-century confidence that love of "the fatherland" was eminently compatible with a cosmopolitan devotion to "humanity," it often degenerates into a swaggering chauvinism and anticipates the *völkisch* ideology of the nineteenth century. But even in this new messianic key, Fichte continued to elaborate familiar themes and demonstrate ways of reconciling the polarities that had preoccupied him since youth.[47]

Fichte's very recourse to private lectures marked his growing isolation from and disillusionment with his age. In the early years at Jena, the students flocking to his Kantian sermons promised to form the nucleus of the new priesthood that would point society to a more rational order. But he ran afoul of student sentiment when he tried to arrange for the dissolution of the notorious *Orden* and, not without some reason, was blamed for complicity with the government. Apparently unable to protect him from student reprisals, the Weimar government also proved unwilling to allow him the unlimited intellectual freedom that he saw as essential to university life. In the spring of 1799 he was forced to resign under the accusation of atheism. Meanwhile his polemics had left him convinced of the futility of participating in a commercialized print culture, tolerating every brand of "opinion" only because it reduced ideas to mere fashions.

Contemptuous of the reading public, but lacking a university forum in Berlin, Fichte aired his thoughts on Freemasonry in private lectures in 1802–3. He used the same format for a sweeping historical diagnosis of "The Basic Characteristics of the Present Age" in 1806, and the 1807 *Addresses*

[47] On the place of nationalism in Fichte's larger system, see esp. Willms, *Die totale Freiheit*; Kelly, *Idealism, Politics and History*, pp. 248–85.

were intended as their sequel. In a sense the Napoleonic conquest had suddenly cleared – or, perhaps better, purified – the air for an oratorical appeal; thanks to French censorship, he observed with more than a hint of relief, "nothing else is left to us now but speech."[48] As in the early 1790s, universal corruption and potential regeneration entered immediate historical juxtaposition; and in the face of this new opportunity to have an "impact," Fichte's faith in the transforming power of the Word revived. To Fichte, as to so many others, it was the moral collapse of the entire Prussian population – and not the military failings of the army – that made the defeat so shameful. The collapse seemed to confirm his diagnosis of "the present age" as one of "complete sinfulness," marked above all by abandonment to materialistic selfishness. But it also marked a zero hour; having exhausted its capacity for decadence, the German nation as a whole found itself on the threshold of a new epoch of "free and deliberate development."

In the *Addresses* Fichte took it upon himself to bear witness to a "German love of fatherland" and to "the infinite value of its object."[49] The national rebirth he envisioned would extend over several generations, and he merely hoped to initiate the process through the small circle of educated men who formed his audience. If he was content to make a modest personal contribution, that was because his "nation" was now assigned an awesome role in the progress of the human species. The German nation, given little attention in earlier writings, became the vehicle for a new reconciliation of freedom and necessity. That so many Germans submitted passively to foreign conquest was a measure of the extent to which the German spirit had already been corrupted by "the deadly foreign spirit" of a materialistic rationalism, reducing human beings to mere instruments of external forces. Long before the French occupation, the rationalist state – the "mechanical" conception embodied in the Napoleonic regime – had become a model for German statesmen. But precisely because open resistance was impossible, the national assertion of will could take the form of a collective spiritual rebirth in the face of an illusory necessity. Inserted into the teleological schema Fichte had outlined in "The Characteristics of the Present Age," the German nation became for the human species what the *Gelehrtenstand* was for a given society; it was a vanguard collectivity, advancing the unfolding of reason in historical reality by pioneering the creation of a truly rational social order. In its very assertion of creative freedom – a creativity of which it alone among nations was capable – this community of Germans necessarily reflected and substantiated the universal moral law.[50]

If most Germans already were infected by "the deadly foreign spirit,"

[48] Johann Gottlieb Fichte, *Addresses to the German Nation*, ed. George A. Kelly (New York and Evanston, Ill., 1968), p. 133.
[49] Ibid., pp. 1–15.
[50] Ibid., pp. 114–29.

how was this creative leap forward to be initiated? The only way to prevent the present generation from contaminating its offspring was to separate *all* German children from their parents from an early age. A "universal German education" would initiate them into a "realm of pure thought" and would represent in microcosm the new "corporate body" of the German nation. This was a radical antidote indeed. Fichte's primary concern was not with building the kind of channel for a "cultivated" elite that neohumanists had in mind, but with institutionalizing a common initiation into the national community for all Germans, regardless of social origins. Hence there had to be a "total change" from the ground up, tearing down the barriers between a rudimentary "popular" instruction and an academic education reserved largely for "the richer classes."

Fichte's version of a "national" education may be said to have taken school reform to an extreme; but it did so by giving a radical – and appropriately philosophical – twist to the longstanding tendency, particularly in egalitarian reform, to regard the new school as an alternative jurisdiction, its standards of public virtue posed against the selfish social interests of families and classes. The difference was that the public mission of the school lay not in simulating nature, but in embodying an Idealist apotheosis of a national community. The nation soared above natural necessity, in that its collective will found its vital impulse, the life principle of its organic unity, in the a priori dictates of the moral law. Only by being completely incubated in the new schools would the next generation be able to absorb the "abstract, absolute and strictly universal" laws that "condition all possible mental activity," without "even hear[ing] that our vital impulses and actions can be directed toward our maintenance and our welfare . . . [and] that learning may be of some use for that purpose."[51]

Again Idealist logic had revolutionary implications. For the first generation, Fichte acknowledged, wealthier parents, accustomed to regarding higher education as their "private" concern, would be especially reluctant to entrust their children to the new schools; but in the interest of spiritual rebirth, the state would be acting entirely within its right in compelling them to do so. Compulsory participation in a truly "universal" public education, like compulsory military service, could not stop short of tearing down de facto class privileges. Fichte's radical dichotomy between a "realm of pure thought" and social reality, unlike the reconciliation of nature and society in neocorporate reform ideology, left no room for an underlying defense of "birth" in terms of familial upbringing and property. Instead it produced a denial of parental rights over children, and a transferral of parental authority to the state, that even the most radical eighteenth-century reformers had not dared.[52]

[51] Ibid., pp. 130–59.
[52] Ibid., pp. 160–74.

Fichte's compulsory school was meant not only to prevent property from making education a heritable privilege; it would also liberate the children of propertyless families from the disadvantages inherent in their inherited material circumstances. If the children of "the working classes" are not separated from their parents, he argued, "the hardship, the daily anxiety about making ends meet, the petty meanness and avarice, which occur here, [will] inevitably affect [them], drag them down, and prevent them from making a free flight into the world of thought."[53] In the *Addresses*, as in neohumanistic reform thought, material insecurity and deprivation seem all the more crippling in the light of an uncompromising ideal of personality development. But Fichte did not make this class experience sufficient grounds for excluding most sons of the lower orders from academic education; in his Idealist repudiation of social reality, ascriptive disadvantage became a form of the merely external coercion that could not be allowed to limit moral freedom in a truly rational society. For the propertyless above all, the new school's capacity to sustain "a free flight into the world of thought" was a function of its complete detachment from the social constraints of family and class.

The new school, then, was a completely egalitarian alternative to the prevailing social inequalities in education; but it might also be said of this national institution that it promised to realize the division between elite and mass that had extended like a geological fault through Fichte's earlier projections of a rational order. Fichte's alienation from the new print culture found expression in his claim that "reading and writing have been hitherto just the very instruments for enveloping men in mist and shadow and for making them conceited." For the great majority of pupils, a truly liberating education – one that penetrated to the a priori truth behind the mist and shadow – would rely on oral mastery of language until the very end, when they would be ready to "discover and use the letters." This form of mental learning would go hand in hand with an initiation to work in farming and artisanal trades. The purpose of manual labor was not simply to make the school community self-sufficient; Fichte hoped to realize within a national community the universal guarantee of moral autonomy in and through work. It was the introduction to a livelihood that would provide every future member of the "working classes" with a basis for "personal independence" – and thus empower him to contradict the current "principle" that "one must flatter, cringe, and be everyone's lackey if one wishes to live."[54]

The few pupils selected to be "scholars" were exceptions on both counts; they must be introduced to reading and writing at an early age, and the time others devoted to work they must spend in "solitary reflection." Their exceptional status within the school community reflected the fact that in

[53] Ibid., p. 139.
[54] Ibid., pp. 137–43, 155–56.

the regenerated nation, as in Fichte's earlier visions of a rational order, the learned estate was a kind of vanguard priesthood. While the members of other occupations merely maintained the species at "the stage of culture it has reached," the scholar "advanced" it by "see[ing] farther." To "understand the future," he must achieve the "unlimited skill in pure thought independent of phenomena" that his fellow citizens in ordinary occupations did not require. And yet even as Fichte once again elevated the learned few into a castelike elite, he also insisted that the elite "be able to implant [its conception of the future] in the present for its future development." The early mastery of reading and writing would segregate the future scholar from his fellows, but would equip him with the complete mastery of the native language needed to communicate his thoughts to his "people."[55]

A longstanding tension resurfaced here, but with a critical difference; under the pressure of events, Fichte had found a new reconciliation in his ideal of the German nation, and above all in his definition of that nation as an organic language community. What distinguished German-speaking people from the descendants of other originally Teutonic people – and the main target of this historical excursion was, of course, the French – was the linguistic continuity that made for a truly national cohesion. "The German speaks a language which has been alive ever since it first issued from the force of nature," he argued in the fourth address, "whereas the other Teutonic races speak a language which has movement on the surface only but is dead at the root." It was the difference between, on the one hand, a people whose cultural evolution reflected fundamental laws of linguistic development and, on the other, those "neo-Latin peoples" who had aborted their cultural growth by giving up their "mother tongue."

There is probably a good deal of unconscious borrowing from Herder and other eighteenth-century theorists, as well as from contemporaries like Humboldt, in this linguistic definition of "national character." But Fichte was also voicing a resentment of French cultural tutelage that had been mounting among educated Germans for several decades. The young tutor's defiant refusal to acknowledge social inferiority by apologizing for his rudimentary command of French, the German scholar's refusal to remain in the shadow of an apparently brilliant but superficial "foreign" culture, the patriot's outrage in the face of the conqueror – all were combined now in the *Addresses*. What had been a visceral reaction had become the philosopher's theoretical effort to demonstrate by way of language that the apparently inferior nation – the one that seemed to have willingly acknowledged its inferiority in the very enthusiasm with which it had aped French culture and that was now in danger of having it confirmed with the loss of

[55] Ibid., pp. 157–59.

its national independence – was in fact morally superior. The result was some of the most chauvinistic – and some of the silliest – passages in a rhetorical appeal not distinguished by either its tolerance or the modesty of its claims. If a Frenchman somehow had found his way into Fichte's audience, he would surely have been surprised to learn that he was "entirely without a mother tongue." In Fichte's linguistic pecking order, the prestige of a modern language no longer derived from its degree of consanguinity with Greek and Latin; what mattered was that it have an unbroken connection with a "natural" origin – that its development represent "the uninterrupted flow of a primitive language." Command of a "living" and superior language in this sense, the Frenchman would have discovered, not only gave the German a special affinity for Latin and Greek; it also enabled him to acquire a deeper understanding of French and other inferior neo-Latin languages than their native speakers.[56]

Fichte was not alone in blaming the Prussian collapse on the selfishness to which old-regime corporatism had degenerated under "mechanical" state tutelage or in concluding that national independence – culturally and ultimately in the political form of a nation-state – required a social coherence transcending class divisions as well as corporate distinctions. But he had special reason to conclude that the native integrity of their language had allowed the Germans to survive as a distinct national community, despite the ancient Roman imperium and the French imperium of the eighteenth century. The unique virtues he attributed to the native tongue reconciled his alternative visions of social hierarchy within a distinctly Idealist conception of an "organic" community. The uniqueness of the German language lay in fusing "mental culture" and "life" and hence in serving as the vehicle for rich interaction between the masses and an elite carrying "reason" forward. In the neo-Latin languages, "abstract concepts" were easily corrupted, since they were foreign imports divorced from the sensual reality of popular life. One result was that "the educated classes" came to regard "those classes who have no access to mental culture" as "a different species of humanity" and, far from trying to improve them with "loving sympathy," saw them as "nothing more than a blind instrument of their plans." If Germans avoided this class distance and exploitation, it was because in their "living language" the "supersensuous" was always "expressed by symbols of sense, comprehending at every step in complete unity the sum total of the sensuous and the mental life of the nation deposited in the language." Hence "the mass of the people" were "capable of education," while "the educators" could "test their discoveries on the people" and "wish to influence it." It was this symbiosis of educated and popular culture that had allowed the Germans to achieve a purification of Christianity in the Lu-

[56] Ibid., pp. 45–61.

theran Reformation. Now it was their historic destiny to carry humanity to a still higher stage of reason, under the leadership of Idealist philosophy.[57]

In this vision the *Volk* meant not the popular classes, but a national community transcending class divisions; and the abstractions of an apparently disembodied philosophy had become the quintessentially German expression of a national spirit. What Fichte had discovered in the "fundamental laws" of linguistic evolution was that the a priori abstractions of the Moral Law – like Luther's teachings and unlike the corrupted abstractions of "dead" languages – at once drew their nourishment from "life" at the broad base of the social pyramid and found a receptive soil in it. The elite vanguard of reason still "saw farther," but it had become a national priesthood – and in this organically rooted "republic of letters," the uprooted ribbon weaver's son at last had a "living" bond of communication with the world he had left.

The elite of "scholars" in the reborn nation would be a thorough meritocracy. Fichte knew from personal experience that the social distribution of "an excellent gift for learning and a conspicuous inclination for the world of ideas" had nothing to do with "so-called differences of birth." On the other hand, "every talent of that kind is a precious possession of the nation, and may not be taken from it," as it had been a property of the "public welfare" in utilitarian reform thought; and the development of talent was an exercise in individual freedom only in Fichte's paradoxical sense of that term.[58] In the national community, still more than in Fichte's earlier versions of a rational order, there is an authoritarian momentum to the a priori reconciliation of freedom and duty. Fichte now hales "Pestalozzian" pedagogy as the new medium of reconciliation, though the Pestalozzi of the *Addresses* is largely a symbol of a larger pedagogical sentiment with deep roots in the Enlightenment conception of "natural" self-realization as well as in neohumanism.

When Fichte pilloried utilitarian rationalism as a "clockwork pressure machine," he caught the duality of an ethic that sought to harness the motive force of self-interest to a degree, but at the same time was bent on suppressing it.[59] He also understood that in its pursuit of the ideal *Bürger* – in the reason-dominated hierarchy it sought to construct within the personality – rationalism had made the "art" of pedagogy in practice an exercise in manipulative intervention. The Pestalozzian alternative was to stimulate and guide the child's "self-activity." In Fichte's Idealist adaptation, the child engaged in self-activity by "creat[ing] spontaneously images which are not simply copies of reality, but can become its prototypes" – and by doing so out of sheer love for and pleasure in the images. But this was a spontaneity

[57] Ibid., esp. pp. 69, 107–08.
[58] Ibid., pp. 157–58.
[59] Ibid., esp. pp. 96–98.

in iron conformity with the higher laws of reason; it embodied the original Idealist paradox of the individual consciousness, exercising its freedom most fully by realizing the a priori necessity of a universal source. The difference was that the source – reason itself – no longer simply constituted a standard for "society"; it had become the vital spirit of a nation, sustained in its language and requiring the complete devotion of its members in all walks of life.[60]

This was to justify a drastic pedagogical intervention, and one may well wonder whether it would be distinguished from rationalist manipulation only within its own circular definition. If the new pedagogy was a "free" art, it was also "a reliable and deliberate art of fashioning in a man a stable and infallible good Will." The "freedom of the Will" on which the "old system" had relied was in effect destroyed by being swallowed up in necessity.[61] The underlying tensions in this new coupling of freedom and necessity were reflected in Fichte's mix of organic and mechanical metaphors. As an Idealist, opposed in principle to both the humanistic reverence for nature and the utilitarian conception of the state as an efficiently operating machine, he might have been expected to avoid both metaphors; instead each of them becomes a vehicle of mediation. The "art" of pedagogy lies not only in stimulating and guiding organic growth, but also in imposing on the individual consciousness the same rational artifice with which a self-conscious society orders itself. In the latter capacity, pedagogical artistry is also a mechanical application of coercive force, although organic spontaneity also has its analogue in a kind of mechanical self-propulsion. The object of the art is "pure morality," which "develops its own life spontaneously" within the pupil; but the pupil "goes forth at the proper time as a fixed and unchangeable machine produced by this art, which indeed could not go otherwise than as it has been regulated by the art, and needs no help at all, but continues of itself according to its own law."[62]

At this level of metaphor and a priori abstraction, the authoritarian momentum in Fichte's pedagogical strategy seems to lack substance. In the tenth address it acquires a motive force in social relationships. While knowledge itself sprang from sheer "love of and pleasure in learning," pedagogy must also exploit the "kind of love" that "fashions the life of action." This was the "instinct for honor," which in the child "appears first of all as the desire to be respected by those who inspire in him the highest respect":

Only insofar as the father is satisfied with him is he [the child] satisfied with himself. This is the natural love of the child for the father, not as the guardian of his sensuous well-being, but as the mirror, from which his own worth or worthlessness is reflected for him. Now, the father himself can easily connect with this love obedience and

[60] See esp. Kelly, *Idealism, Politics and History*, pp. 269–85.
[61] Fichte, *Addresses*, pp. 16–30.
[62] Ibid., p. 31.

every kind of self-denial . . . in the child [the instinct for mutual respect] begins as unconditional respect for adults and becomes the desire to be respected by them, and to measure by means of their actual respect how far he also should respect himself. . . . The adult has in himself his standard of self-esteem, and wishes to be respected by others only insofar as they have first of all made themselves worthy of his respect. . . . the aim of education is just to produce adult manhood in the sense that we have mentioned. Only when that aim is attained is education really completed and ended. Hitherto many men have remained children all their lives.[63]

It would be hard to find a more sanguine view of the compatibility between patriarchal authority and individual (male) autonomy – or a better example of the tendency to equate the specific cultural norms of the patriarchal family with moral absolutes. Fichte was absolved by his own logic from explaining exactly how this form of "self-control" and indeed "self-denial," developed in thrall to pedagogical extensions of the paternal will, would become adult "independence." In the light of eighteenth-century thinking about poor students and the dilemmas they faced, this return to a definition of duty in terms of "honor" – i.e., to the equation that had been Fichte's moral compass since youth – acquires special significance. Here the need for social approval is no longer the poor student's "ambition," its blind force threatening hierarchical stability. Suitably absolved of the "selfishness" with which it had been tainted, the "instinct for honor" has become a rational motive force for creating and perpetuating an organic community, transcending class divisions. Within the prescriptions of old-style paternalism, young men like Fichte had sought to preserve a core of inner integrity – of personal "honor" – despite their poverty and abject dependence. Now, in the rational order, integrity consisted in conforming to, and indeed in deriving self-respect from, the social authority of father-figures. Fichte had found another way to define individual freedom as completely voluntary dedication to the collectivity – one in which the pursuit of personal honor was completely subsumed under the imperatives of national honor.

[63] Ibid., pp. 147–49.

Epilogue

I

Fichte became a single-minded visionary, although his visions continued to exhibit a remarkable sensitivity to the aspirations and dilemmas of his generation. It was not his "republic of scholars," deriving its public authority from privileged insight into a priori philosophical truth, that came into being in the early nineteenth century. In neohumanistic rhetoric, something of the intellectual and moral autonomy in the face of state authority that Fichte reserved for university professors was extended to the rank-and-file professional jurisdictions of an emerging *Bildungsbürgertum*. But the new rhetoric had the effect of muffling, not reducing, the discordance between this rejection of state tutelage and the simultaneous reliance on state-sponsored reform. The prestige and security of state office also promised a mode of autonomy, indispensable if the new professionals were to be spared their predecessors' crippling accountability to local society.

Latent impulses in the Lutheran tradition, and particularly in Lutheran Pietism, contributed more or less inadvertently to the new ethic of profession and to the concept of office that was inseparable from it. But this ideological symbiosis of *Beruf* and *Amt* also marks a self-conscious departure from the sacred. It was a departure with its own iron inhibitions, easily ignored if we read back into it the individualism of the marketplace, or of contemporary liberal politics, or indeed of an "achievement society" in the contemporary sense. But its secularism was nonetheless distinctly modern. In the 1690s the original nucleus of "converted" students at Halle – the ones Francke had soon taken to recalling with nostalgia – had struggled to ward off the external temptations of the world by prevailing over "inner" corruption. The enemy within was the Old Adam – i.e., the natural man – and his powers were at their most insidious in the pretensions of reason. A century later, in the rationalist ethic of vocation, the lines of conflict between the inner and the exterior had been redrawn; the innate entelechy of the natural man was pitted against the external obstacles to his self-realization in an irrational social order. In the calling, self-discipline triumphed in denial of the natural self and in renunciation of the chimera of merely human achievement; the passive servant followed inner stirrings and external signs to an assigned "office" in the divine order. In the new dispensation, the yoke imposed on an abject "servant of the Lord" has acceded to the security and prestige awarded to the public servant, and the life course has formed into a structured career. The secular ethic of *Beruf* and *Amt* – i.e., of profession and office – defined a finely calibrated scale of legitimate expectations about income and status, and licensed the kind of self-disciplined achievement that propelled a sequential advance through school and professional life.

At the same time the old alloy of piety and eloquence – the ideal of Protestant humanism – was acceding to a neohumanistic amalgam of functional expertise and self-cultivation (*Bildung*). Honorific expertise – the kind old-style Latinity had epitomized – had been deflated beyond recovery; if it was to have value as a social currency, expertise had to take its place in a modern division of labor. But for all its importance in mapping that division and for all its power to deflate tradition, utilitarian rationalism had had a short-lived ascendancy. For the nineteenth-century *Gebildeten*, as for the traditional *Gelehrten*, the route to profession and office lay through the arduous rite of passage formed by the classical languages and their literature. In principle, induction into the new Hellenism was at the opposite pole from a corporate initiation; a quasi-religious reverence for the purely and uniquely human made the individual a free-floating personality, detached from social moorings and occupational demands. Ultimately the new idiom was so appealing because, in the conflict between the corporatism of the old regime and the rationalist version of modernity, it declared a plague on both houses. At the same time that its fusion of ethical idealism and aestheticism became the vital alternative to an atrophied corporate ideal of elegance, contemptuous of the merely utilitarian, it also attested to a mounting sense that the cult of utility, for all its concern with "welfare" and "happiness," portended a dehumanizing efficiency.

The prestige of the nineteenth-century *Bildungsbürgertum* rested on the duality of its self-image.[1] In the realm of ideology – reality is another matter – the educated professional was at once a "cultivated" (or "liberal") personality and a well-trained expert. The presence of poor students had contributed significantly to the formation of both images – as an imperfect anticipation of a future egalitarian meritocracy and as the constant reminder of a threat from below to be met by severely restricting the channel for academic mobility. One of the cruellest ironies was that the outsiders among poor students – those who had not enjoyed the advantage of a corporate

[1] Now indispensable on this subject is Werner Conze and Jürgen Kocka, eds., *Bildungsbürgertum im 19. Jahrhundert*, Teil 1: *Bildungssystem und Professionalisierung in internationalen Vergleichen*, Industrielle Welt, vol. 38 (Stuttgart, 1985).

patrimony – came to epitomize the obsolescence of a corporate tradition. Hothouse products of the schools, they embodied a kind of boorish "pedantry," at the opposite pole from worldly polish. And yet, unlike the sons of clergymen, outsiders also invited censure as the most obvious and alarming contradiction to the normative preference for inheritance that was central to old-regime corporatism.

On the other hand, there was no more emphatic example of the normative preference for "usefulness" in eighteenth-century rationalism – and indeed of its veritable cult of the utilitarian – than the attribution of true merit to the talented outsider. The peasant's or artisan's son who became a prominent *Gelehrter* represented at its purest the principle that natural talent, whatever its social source, became "merit" when it was harnessed to public needs and channeled into public service. Here Halle Pietism had provided a certain momentum, despite its very different order of priorities; there was an underlying affinity between the self-disciplined struggle toward conversion and the self-discipline of academic achievement, and between a *selectum ingeniorum* in the Pietist vision of a resanctified world and the opening of careers to talent in the utilitarian conception of a progressive society.

This debt to the enemy – to the religious "enthusiasm" derided by rationalists – did not prevent the egalitarian version of meritocracy from achieving a solid respectability within the German High Enlightenment. Opening careers to talent was not a matter of dismantling sponsorship from above, but of giving it a new structure; that approach – so different from the pariah mentality of the Grub Street egalitarianism across the border – reflects the fact that utilitarian rationalism had become the new orthodoxy of a reform-oriented academic and official establishment. Likewise egalitarian reform ideology, as radical as its social objectives were in context, typified the Enlightenment agenda for rationalizing society in its fusion of a strictly functional definition of merit with a bureaucratic impulse. If talent from below was not to go wasted for want of opportunity, old-style paternalism – the freewheeling particularism of traditional patronage – had to accede to the centralized, bureaucratic paternalism of the state and its professional educators.

The egalitarian version of the public school represented the German domestication of *Emile* at its most paradoxical. Only with the intrusion of public jurisdictions and bureaucratic procedures could society be recast in an abstract image of nature and could the social uses of talent be brought into closer alignment with its natural distribution. The paradox seems ominous in the light of our present disillusionment with the institutional impersonality and regimentation of public (and some private) schooling. If the schoolmen of Gedike's generation did not foresee this danger, that was in part because they were so confident that the teacher's fatherly interest in each pupil would soften – or, perhaps better, humanize – the bureaucratic impulse at the same time that it facilitated objective evaluation. Their naiveté on this score combined a certain nostalgia for the personal bonds of old-style patronage with an idealistic faith in the efficacy of the pedagogical art. In theory, the practitioner of the pedagogical art embodied the reconciliation of nature and society; pedagogical intervention fathomed and liberated the nature within, in all its uniqueness from child to child, as the objective instrument of social authority. More striking, though, is that to a degree impersonality was a desideratum, considered essential to the creation of a truly egalitarian order. The impersonality of the "objective" expert was a necessary antidote to social bias; it promised to release the public school from the grip of "privileged" families and to extricate poor students from the webs of dependence that had traditionally stigmatized them. This would become one of the operating assumptions in the liberal ideal of "equality of opportunity," in Germany and elsewhere. Its logic is less easily dismissed as naive, though it sits uncomfortably with our present mood of discontent with the dehumanizing effect of bureaucratic rationalization.

Much of what strikes us as naively optimistic about the various strains of reform ideology was concentrated in the increasing reliance on examinations. To Gedike, Humboldt, and others, the "art" of examining – like the art of pedagogy from which it derived – lay in applying impersonal objectivity in a way that probed an individual personality in a personal setting. The friendly examinations they described seem very far removed from the standardization and regimentation of bureaucratic credentialing in nineteenth-century schools and public employment. If personal bias was in principle rejected, social bias was in effect given free play; the very aura of objectivity – the same aura that made for so much confidence about the unimpeachable fairness of competitive classification and ranking in egalitarian reform – allowed the examination to become a finely tuned instrument of neocorporate ideology.[2]

In the formation of a neocorporate idiom, better adapted to the modern coupling of academic education and public employment than the traditional corporate defense of privilege, poor students and the issues they posed had also figured prominently. From one angle, to be sure, the outsider proved by default that personal "honor" was a kind of inheritance, an inbred corporate virtue. But from another the very absence of social veneer made him a more transparent subject; it was easier to identify and tap the uncorrupted potential of a "natural" human resource. The same need to prove himself – to earn admission through self-disciplined effort – that opened

[2] See esp. Friedrich Gedike, "Einige Gedanken über die Methode zu examiniren," in idem, *Gesammlete Schulschriften*, 2 vols. (Berlin, 1789–95), 2: 66–111; Clemens Menze, *Die Bildungsreform Wilhelm von Humboldts*, Das Bildungsproblem in der Geschichte des europäischen Erziehungsdenkens, vol. 13 (Hanover, 1975).

him to the charge of being a tunnel-visioned drudge could be welcomed as conducive to the very work ethic that utilitarian rationalism held sacred. It was in the face of these counterstereotypes – and in the need to prevent the opening of the floodgates that they might imply – that a neocorporate rationale for de facto (as opposed to de jure) privilege took shape. While the logic of corporatism was stretched well beyond a strict defense of pedigree and inherited legal right, utilitarian rationalism proved more receptive to an exclusive social coloration than the more abstract arguments for individual "merit" in the face of aristocratic privilege would suggest. This mutual adaptation repudiated, more or less, a "bourgeois" tradition of corporate learning as well as an aristocratic tradition of courtly politesse and liberality. If family upbringing was to remain a legitimate advantage, it must inculcate the kind of merit required in school and in public office. But neocorporatism also redefined, in an eminently modern idiom, the legitimate advantages of patrimony – and in a way that was especially beneficial to a bourgeoisie of education and property. In principle, merit and talent were individual attributes; but there was a lower class limit for the kinds of families in which, as a rule, the requisite cultural traits could be expected to take root, and a certain level of wealth was the normal precondition for their growth. This was to sanction de facto privilege in the very process of conceding the validity of universal standards.

Neohumanism, like the Sturm und Drang movement of the early 1770s, articulated a generational protest against rationalist orthodoxy and its implications for the work world of educated officialdom. The emancipatory thrust of its cultural individualism is nowhere more evident than in its application to poor students. To define freedom as self-cultivation was to offer a liberating alternative to both the harsh constrictions of the traditional *Brotstudium* and the kind of self-denial required in the utilitarian ethic. This kind of individualism not only refused to recognize the constraints of corporate membership; it also rejected flatly the rationalist quid pro quo, which made social ascent contingent on the restriction of individual growth to the state-defined requirements of service. But the neohumanists' emphatic preference for holistic growth over "mechanical" manipulation was in part a reaction against the bureaucratic impulse – the neat classification of school subjects, and ultimately of pupils' aptitudes – that was especially marked in egalitarian reform. And as a new source of standards imposed from above, *Bildung* yielded subtle grounds for excluding the disadvantaged. As the rationalists' specific intellectual and moral criteria for "talent" and "merit" acceded to a holistic ideal of the innately noble personality, the outsider's vulnerability to censure as an inveterately "base" interloper was in some respects magnified. Social bias was at once conveyed and obscured by the apparent universality and neutrality of an aesthetic ideal. Hence it is not surprising that, for all its insistence in principle on the need to detach the value of the individual from his social origins and affiliations, neohumanism was not committed to opening competition on an equal footing. It provided new rationales for admitting the few outsiders deemed truly exceptional – and for keeping the door wide open to unexceptional insiders.

II

Neither the neocorporate nor the egalitarian vision of meritocracy can be said to have triumphed in pure form in the reorganized *Gelehrtenschulen* and universities of the nineteenth century. Particularly in the law faculties, the universities retained their primary function of perpetuating a bourgeois elite of officials and professionals, its higher echelons merging to some degree with the service aristocracy, and its lower ranks peopled largely by clergymen and schoolteachers. There was room for a substantial minority of outsiders – far more than the eighteenth-century critics of poor students would have found tolerable. In times of expanding enrollments, in fact, the percentages of sons of artisans and petty officials may have been slightly higher in the nineteenth century. But what occurred in the course of the century was more a shift within these groups than a significant expansion in the presence of outsiders. The "new" lower middle class of petty officials moved toward parity with the "old" *Kleinbürgertum*, and for both groups the new philosophy faculties, leading to teaching careers in classical philology and other fields, gradually displaced the theology faculties as the chief conduits for academic mobility. At the end of the century, the broad mass of uneducated families – the great majority of the rural population and the rapidly expanding urban working classes – still had no more than a token presence. The minority of outsiders had not become the wedge for an egalitarian opening of careers in public employment.[3]

[3] See, e.g., Fritz K. Ringer, *Education and Society in Modern Europe* (Bloomington, Ind., 1978); Konrad H. Jarausch, *Students, Society, and Politics in Imperial Germany. The Rise of Academic Illiberalism* (Princeton, N.J., 1982); Rainer S. Elkar, *Junges Deutschland im polemischen Zeitalter: Das schleswig-holsteinische Bildungsbürgertum in der ersten Hälfte des 19. Jahrhunderts. Zur Bildungsrekrutierung und politischen Sozialisation* (Düsseldorf, 1979); Hartmut Titze, "Ueberfüllungskrisen in akademischen Karrieren. Eine Zyklustheorie," *Zeitschrift für Pädagogik* 27:2 (1981): 187–224; Margaret Kraul, *Gymnasium und Gesellschaft im Vormärz. Neuzeitliche Einheitsschule, städtische Gesellschaft und soziale Herkunft der Schüler*, Studien zum Wandel von Gesellschaft und Bildung im neunzehnten Jahrhundert, vol. 18 (Göttingen, 1980); Jürgen Apel, "Preussische Gymnasiallehrer 1820–1850. Soziale Herkunft, Studienverhalten, Studienerfolg nach Prüfungszeugnissen insbesondere der Bonner Schulamtskandidaten," *Vierteljahrschrift für Sozial- und Wirtschaftsgeschichte* 72:3 (1985): 353–68. At least in the first half of the nineteenth century, it now appears, the new gymnasium was more "socially open" than we had assumed. The key group in this regard were the "early leavers" – pupils who did not attain the *Abitur* but who represent the first step in a familial ascent into the academic and official elite over several generations. See esp. Detlef K. Müller, "The Process of Systematisation. The Case of German Secondary Education," in Detlef K. Müller, Fritz Ringer, and Brian Simon, eds., *The Rise of the Modern Educational System. Structural Change and Social Reproduction 1870–1920* (Cambridge, 1987).

The persistence of academic mobility was not due simply to the fact that stipends and other traditional forms of charity survived. In a sense the Protestant religious tradition that had engendered and sustained that charity since the early sixteenth century had become superfluous. In the Lutheran economy of salvation, "talent" was a loan, of value only when sanctified by the transformative power of grace; in the new economy of social progress, talent enjoyed a kind of autonomous value as an innate possession and – at least potentially, in its transformation into merit – as a legitimate form of property. But talented and otherwise meritorious outsiders were tolerable exceptions precisely because they were not seen as a social vanguard, pointing to an egalitarian future. Within the prevailing neocorporate logic, they were a qualified and safe extension of the commitment to individual achievement over "birth" – a commitment that served chiefly to justify the career rights of scions of upper bourgeois families in the face of aristocratic pedigrees and titles.

In access to academic education, social privilege attested to the cultural advantages still enjoyed by preindustrial status groups (the clergy remained the most striking case in point), even as it operated increasingly within the new economic inequalities of an industrial class structure. Thanks to the great proliferation of government statistics in the nineteenth century, this structural fit between education and society has been measured with admirable precision. The eighteenth century, with its pitifully sparse and scattered data, has been relatively neglected. But if we explore structure as process, with an eye to social relationships that are not given to statistical precision but nonetheless are revealing of the terms of inequality, the eighteenth-century lode of "impressionistic" evidence has a rich density. Likewise, if we approach the century with a sustained and respectful attention to ideas and their evolution in context, it tells us a great deal about why and how inequality was institutionalized in modern education. The point is not to isolate specific ideas as anticipations of the modern, but to explain how an entire cluster of ideas, with myriad affinities and binary oppositions, had formed into an ideological field by the turn of the century. The legacy of both religious and secular reform traditions, the persistence of corporate norms for hierarchy and attendant alarmism about social instability, the cultural terms of an emerging class consciousness – all conspired to keep the sponsorship of talent from below highly constricted.

Ambition, like talent, was often assumed to be an irreducible natural force; but it too was a normative construct. How could society reap the benefits of inborn talent and individual achievement without incurring the costs and risks of ambition? This was the recurrent dilemma posed by academic mobility in eighteenth-century society, and in response to it the ideological field took shape. The assumptions and norms brought to the dilemma may not have been uniquely German, but their configuration at least represents a distinctly German effort to avoid two extremes. One extreme was to leave the promotion of talent from below to old-style patronage. While some faulted patronage for not forming a secure ladder into the learned estate, others feared that it was opening the floodgates to the unqualified. Where these perceptions met was in a mounting awareness that the patron's highly individualized exercise of control could not be relied on to apply rigorous standards of merit and that the client's personal dependence was not conducive to developing the "honor" expected of an educated man.

As a form of control from above, the paternalism of the old dispensation lost credibility as it came to seem arbitrary in the light of rational standards. And yet the polar alternative – to make selection a product of unrestricted competition in an open market – remained virtually unthinkable despite the new appeal of market rationality at the turn of the century. In Adam Smith's model for equilibrium, as in much of eighteenth-century German social and ethical thought, ambition – the desire to improve one's lot in life – was both an instinctual urge and the calculated pursuit of self-interest. But from an ethical standpoint the radical new departure in Smithian political economy lay in transforming this calculating urge from a highly suspect motive (if not an actual vice) into a positive motive force. Ambition remained a form of selfishness, but it no longer threatened to spoil the social benefits of talent; under natural laws of self-adjustment in the market, it was the engine of their realization. Hence Smith could argue for the liberation of ambition at the base of the social pyramid as well as in its higher ranks. It was because workers could be expected to be ambitious – to strive to improve themselves – that higher wages could be seen as a spur to greater achievement rather than an invitation to sloth.[4]

In the positive stereotypes of poor students ambition was already credited to a degree with providing the incentive for self-disciplined achievement. But when Adam Bergk applied market logic in an argument for unrestricted access to the universities in 1800, he was defying a powerful historical momentum. Above all on the issue of academic mobility, more or less indigenous ethical traditions resisted a positive reevaluation of ambition. That issue – perhaps more than any other – came to register the tension between the natural rights of the *Mensch* and the obligations of the *Bürger*, between the promise of individual freedom and the dictates of collective order, in the German Enlightenment. A clear preference for the dutiful *Bürger* had already characterized cameralism, but this ethical priority had been reinforced, indirectly, but nonetheless powerfully, by the Pietist revival at the beginning of the century. Halle Pietism injected into the Lu-

[4] This aspect of Smith's thought is emphasized in Gertrude Himmelfarb, *The Idea of Poverty. England in the Early Industrial Age* (New York, 1985), pp. 42–63.

theran tradition the same uncompromising ideal of "this-worldly asceticism" that had sustained seventeenth-century Calvinism. Where Pietists saw natural depravity, rationalists found natural potential; but in its injunctions to disinterested service, the rationalist ethic of vocation nonetheless echoed the Pietist ethic of calling. If the rational *Bürger*'s self-discipline was not the converted Christian's self-effacement, it involved the same denial of instincts in the natural self and of the selfish calculations to which they gave rise. In both ethics, "selfishness" threatened the reconciliation of change and stability, movement and order. In a sense, the threat became more immediate as the Pietist aspiration to resanctify the world acceded to the rationalist vision of a *dynamic* equilibrium; now the hierarchical organization of society had to ensure stability in the very process of guaranteeing secular progress. What secularization changed was the source of the external imperative; whereas the converted Christian had found inner peace in submission to the Divine Will, the enlightened *Bürger* found "happiness" in subjection to the collective embodiment of reason – whether it took the form of state prohibitions or, preferably, was internalized as the dictates of conscience.

Neohumanism can be said to have taken the internalization of duty a step farther. In the very aspiration to revitalize conventional occupational roles, its enthusiasts implicitly accepted the established order. While their ideal of *Bildung* rejected the "mechanical" manipulation represented by state authority and its utilitarian priorities, it also made disinterested devotion to duty the product of spontaneous unfolding and integrative harmony in the organic growth of a personality. This new variant on this-worldly asceticism was the paradoxical counterpoint to an aesthetic celebration of the sensual. It makes understandable why the ascendancy of neohumanism proved so compatible with an upsurge of nationalism in the early nineteenth century. In neohumanism, the rationalist's self-discipline – the "mechanical" suppression of ambition and other illicit instincts within the self – was rendered unnecessary by the organic entelechy of the inner man; in nationalism (and here Fichte's *Addresses* were symptomatic of a larger shift), the analogous role that had been assigned the state vis-à-vis society in rationalist reform thought – its responsibility to subordinate individual self-interest to the collective need – promised to become superfluous as an organic ideal of national solidarity was realized.

All this is not to imply that German culture had no room for approval of the self-interested pursuit of ambition. By the turn of the century the new political economy commanded widespread enthusiasm in the German academic and official establishment. It played a vital role in the "revolution from above" in Prussia from 1806 onward and in similar reform efforts in other states. When it came to the practice of trades and to landownership, the replacement of corporate restrictions with an open market promised to unleash the vast reserves of human energy needed to create a national community and drive it forward. But in the new agenda for educational reform, the laissez-faire version of individual freedom – and the licensing of ambition it implied – was conspicuously absent; one of the received axioms was that the state must balance supply and demand – and must subordinate ambition to the requirements of social equilibrium – by keeping access to higher education more or less severely restricted. In a sense this is ironic; in the eighteenth century, the sphere of academic education and public employment had generated much of the secular reverence for talent as a vast natural resource. But it was precisely in that sphere, with its severely constricted boundaries and internal strains, that the social selection and promotion of talent seemed potentially too dangerous to be left to a self-adjusting market.

It was not simply in Germany that an oversupply of educated men seemed to threaten a particularly dangerous kind of failed mobility. The censorious stereotypes of poor students in eighteenth-century Germany had had their counterparts in France and other countries.[5] In the second half of the century, such stereotypes had distilled an incipient alarm about the growth of an intellectual proletariat, its members nursing deep resentments against a social order that failed to recognize and reward them. The alarm seemed to be dramatically confirmed by the "Grub Street Rousseauism" of the French Revolution. In the face of this specter, higher education may have been considered a critical exception to market logic throughout Europe. But the roots of this tenacious insistence on social equilibrium at the cost of individual freedom may be especially clear in Germany; the eighteenth-century legacy was a thick intertwining of religious and secular reform thought with traditional social norms and prescriptions.

Even the outer circle of consensus – the virtual unanimity on the need to avoid overcrowding – was as much a reflection of ideological assumptions about the social dangers of disequilibrium as it was a response to practical exigencies. In the inner core of alarmism about poor students, familiar social biases point to the tenacity of corporate norms. The functional hierarchy projected in utilitarian rationalism had no place for the legal demarcations of old-regime corporatism. But a simplification of hierarchy in that sense did not imply the brutal simplification of modern class dichotomies; with the dismantling of the legal scaffolding, other boundaries – in life-style, in cultural milieu, and ultimately in ethos – had to mark the fine gradations of a functional hierarchy, ascending from the mass of "common" occupations through the ranks of more or less "educated" and "public" professions. In this new order, the kind of mobility promised by "trade freedom"

[5] See, e.g., Harvey Chisick, *The Limits of Reform in the Enlightenment. Attitudes toward the Education of the Lower Classes in Eighteenth-Century France* (Princeton, N.J., 1981).

(*Gewerbefreiheit*) and unrestricted landownership was far less alarming than the kind embodied in the stereotypical poor student. Typically the ambitious artisan or peasant – like the typical worker in Smith's universe – was expected to improve himself within his station. If his entrepreneurial success lifted him into the ranks of substantial property, he at least had not exchanged a commercial world for an alien one – though this kind of mobility was nonetheless pilloried in the image of the *nouveaux riches*.

The concept of a professional career promised a kind of structure that the market did not allow, and for that very reason it admitted a controlled dosage of ambition into the public sphere of education and office. At the same time that the career sequence allowed and indeed encouraged ongoing expectations, it kept them confined to a clearly demarcated station. But when the focus shifts to entry into the professional elite, the outsiders among poor students represented an intergenerational leap across a great social and cultural divide – the bifurcation between the educated and the uneducated that had run through the corporate hierarchy of the old regime and that in some ways had widened with the qualitative distinction between cultivation and mere practical learning in neohumanism. The fate of the uprooted, malcontented poor student remained a potent cultural metaphor. In his very aspiration to win acceptance as a *Gelehrter*, despite his lack of both a cultural patrimony and material advantages, he attested to the alarming capacity of formal education to inflate expectations. Perhaps more than any other social type, the poor student in this guise remained a symbol of the tension between, on the one hand, the need to promote talent and stimulate achievement in a progressive society and, on the other, the need to limit expectations to the narrow boundaries of "station" in a well-ordered and stable society. If he was guilty of rampant materialism, his more characteristic transgression of limits lay in not bringing enough personal "honor" to his station, or, in the literal meaning of "ambition" (*Ehrgeiz*), in craving too much of it. In either case, he signaled the breakdown of a delicate balance between personal integrity and deference – the balance that bespoke a proper sense of station and bore witness to intricate quasi-corporate gradations in daily social intercourse.

From the late eighteenth century onward, these originally corporate norms and prescriptions for entry into (and exclusion from) the "learned estate" were assimilated into the elite consciousness of a modern *Bildungsbürgertum*, defining itself within an emerging class structure. Here again neohumanism articulated a continuity, even as it sought to liberate the individual personality from both the fetters of traditional corporate life and the tyranny of a utilitarian future. Its alternative to the utilitarian ethic of disinterested service was not to license ambition, but to apotheosize self-cultivation as a higher order of disinterestedness. Once again the outsider's effort to compensate for social disadvantage – whether that effort took the form of an instrumental approach to learning, or an openly ambitious competitiveness, or the calculating "servility" that was its mirror image – became the stigma of moral inferiority.

There are several cautionary tales in all this, though none of them yields a simple historical lesson for the changed circumstances of the late twentieth century. The credentialing process in higher education is no longer limited to a tiny elite of educated professions in public employment; in Germany, as in the United States, educational patents now extend to vast zones of semiprofessional "white collar" employment in both public and private bureaucracies. But at the same time the ideological spectrum on the relationship between education and mobility has widened to the left. In the late eighteenth century, when the new school was still a bold experiment yet to be realized, the appeal of "careers open to talent" lay in promising a kind of social justice that did not require tampering with the structure of inequality in the larger society. Now, after so many failed efforts to institutionalize equality of opportunity, the school seems more an instrument of inheritance than a potent agent of mobility. Critics on the left pose questions about social justice that the eighteenth-century vision of meritocracy, even at its most egalitarian, avoided. Does the reigning ideology of mobility through education, with its promise of equal opportunity for individuals, serve to legitimate gross disparities in wealth and power between groups? Can the promise be anything more than a chimera for much of the population so long as those disparities persist?

But within this new framework species of utilitarian rationalism and neohumanism continue to shape our thinking about mobility. Much of the current rhetoric on both sides obscures the moral choices that these ideological alternatives still pose and keeps us oblivious to the social biases that still accompany them. Arguably technocratic expertise, though a form of utilitarian knowledge par excellence, is also reminiscent of old-regime Latinity in its tendency to constitute a relatively neutral medium for competitive selection. At the same time the very fact that such expertise now occupies largely autonomous enclaves in higher education – i.e., that it is largely detached from the humanistic tradition – may serve to remove neocorporate prerequisites for entry into many desirable careers. But this kind of egalitarianism threatens its own abuses of power; the twentieth century has given us ample reason to fear, as the German neohumanists feared, that functional rationality reduces "duty" to blind conformity in a morally neutral universe. In the ideological celebration of an achievement society, the *Mensch* and the *Bürger* enter a new reconciliation; work becomes sacred both as the essential source of social validation and as the locus for individual self-fulfillment. But much of this is cant, obfuscating the fact that the individual must in effect renounce myriad potentialities in conforming to a collective definition of usefulness. Contemporary utilitarianism, like the eighteenth-century variety, proceeds from the familiar assumption that permission to climb the social ladder has its price. On that score, in fact, the difference between "sponsored" and "contest" mobility seems minimal; whether the regulating mechanism is the state or the market, the liberating entelechy of a unique inner "nature" is reduced to a standardized, programmed assignment in conformity with external demands.[6]

Does salvation lie in a recovery of nerve among contemporary neohumanists? I share the impulse, but wonder whether we are any more realistic, or any more conscious of our own biases, than our predecessors. Over the past two centuries neohumanists, for all their disgust with dehumanizing bureaucracy, have proved quite willing to purchase survival as the credentialing instruments of bureaucratic Leviathans – and have remained remarkably naive about the capacity of bureaucracy to absorb and neutralize their most powerful antidotes. The rhetoric has become more unreservedly egalitarian; but rhetoric cannot dispel the possibility that our literary humanism, like earlier varieties, requires cognitive and linguistic skills that only some children inherit. Like the German neohumanists, we deny absolute value to a utilitarian culture and reject our contemporaries' smug posture of superiority toward the past. But in the face of a thoroughly pluralistic and relativistic world, we too are convinced that full humanity can be achieved only on our terms. The issue is whether the terms have really become less exclusive and whether they now rest on more penetrating distinctions between the essential self and its social shell.

[6] See esp. John W. Meyer, "Myths of Socialization and Personality," in Thomas C. Heller, Morton Sosna, and David E. Wellbery, eds., *Reconstructing Individualism, Autonomy, Individuality, and the Self in Western Thought* (Stanford, Calif., 1986), pp. 208–21; John H. Schaar, "Equality of Opportunity, and Beyond," in J. Roland Pennock and John W. Chapman, eds., *Equality. Nomos IX* (New York, 1967), pp. 228–49.

Bibliographical note

The research for this book led me, by the nature of the subject, into a varied assortment of subfields in eighteenth-century studies, some crisscrossing regularly in the literature, some still rarely within hailing distance of each other. What follows is a highly selective bibliography, intended simply to acknowledge general debts that may have been neglected in the detail work of footnoting and to provide other scholars with useful points of departure onto new terrain.

Two broad-ranging and informative guides through German thought in the second half of the eighteenth century, with emphasis on social and political themes, are Klaus Epstein, *The Genesis of German Conservatism* (Princeton, N.J., 1966), and Jürgen Schlumbohm, *Freiheit. Die Anfänge der bürgerlichen Emanzipationsbewegung in Deutschland im Spiegel ihres Leitwortes (ca. 1760–1800)*, Geschichte und Gesellschaft, vol. 12 (Düsseldorf, 1975). Peter Hanns Reill, *The German Enlightenment and the Rise of Historicism* (Berkeley, Calif., 1975), offers a revealing perspective on many themes in eighteenth-century academic culture. My own understanding of continuities and changes in public discourse profited greatly from several of the contributions to *Geschichtliche Grundbegriffe. Historisches Lexikon zur politisch-sozialen Sprache in Deutschland*, 5 vols. (Stuttgart, 1972–84).

My route through the vast literature on German Protestantism in the early modern era marked my own preoccupations. Gerald Strauss, *Luther's House of Learning. Indoctrination of the Young in the German Reformation* (Baltimore and London, 1978), focuses on the reformers of Luther's generation and their immediate successors; but it identifies restraints, both in the nature of Lutheran reform objectives and in the obstacles to their realization, that persisted well beyond the sixteenth century. Gustaf Wingren, *Luther on Vocation*, trans. Carl C. Rasmussen (Philadelphia, 1957), is still the most lucid explication of Luther's theology of *Beruf*. Convenient introductions to the Pietist movement are F. Ernest Stoeffler, *German Pietism during the Eighteenth Century* (Leiden, 1973), and Martin Schmidt, *Pietismus* (Stuttgart, 1972). Francke's theology and reform thought are well represented in *August Hermann Francke. Werke in Auswahl*, ed. Erhard Peschke (Witten-Ruhr, 1969). The classic study of Francke's achievements at Halle is Carl Hinrichs, *Preussentum und Pietismus. Der Pietismus in Brandenburg-Preussen als religiös-soziale Reformbewegung* (Göttingen, 1971). It can be supplemented with Klaus Deppermann, *Der hallesche Pietismus und der preussische Staat unter Friedrich I (III)* (Göttingen, 1961), which is rich in institutional detail, and Wolf Oschlies, *Die Arbeits- und Berufspädagogik A. H. Franckes (1633–1727)*, Arbeiten zur Geschichte des Pietismus, vol. 6 (Witten, 1969), which brings out the social implications of Francke's theology.

It is becoming increasingly evident that the Enlightenment must be understood within its various national contexts. The militancy of the more celebrated French philosophes, intent on defying *l'infâme*, stands in contrast to the moderate reformism in countries where a Protestant establishment presided over the shift to rationalism. The distinctly Protestant contours of the German Enlightenment are surveyed in Joachim Whaley, "The Protestant Enlightenment in Germany," in Roy Porter and Mikuláás Teich, eds., *The Enlightenment in National Context* (London, 1981), pp. 106–17. Still indispensable on the distinctions among "rationalist" theologians, and for its profile of a rationalist clerical establishment, is Karl Aner, *Die Theologie der Lessingzeit* (Halle, 1929). The Protestant clerical contributions to Enlightenment reform thought are surveyed in Alexandra Schlingensiepen-Pogge, *Das Sozialethos der lutherischen Aufklärungstheologie am Vorabend der Industriellen Revolution*, Göttingen Bausteine zur Geschichtswissenschaft, vol. 39 (Göttingen, 1967).

There are many unanswered questions about the filiations and ruptures between Protestantism and other reform impulses. Marc Raeff, *The Well-Ordered Police State. Social and Institutional Change through Law in the Germanies and Russia, 1600–1800* (New Haven, Conn., and London, 1983), is insightful on the continuities between the Reformation and cameralist state policy and on the tensions inherent in successive reform agendas. Raeff's essay has the additional virtue of surveying policy across a variety of German states. The essential differences between "calling" and "vocation" are explained succinctly and with salient examples in Richard M. Douglas, "Talent and Vocation in Humanist and Protestant Thought," in Theodore K. Rabb and Jerrold E. Seigel, eds., *Action and Conviction in Early Modern Europe. Essays in Memory of E. H. Harbison* (Princeton, N.J., 1969), pp. 261–98. My understanding of the complex relationships between Pietism and rationalism was enhanced by Hinrich's *Preussentum und Pietismus* (cited above); by the analysis of rationalist diagnoses of Pietist "enthusiasm" in Hans-Jürgen Schings, *Melancholie und Aufklärung. Melancholiker und ihre Kritiker in Erfahrungsseelenkunde des 18. Jahrhunderts* (Stuttgart, 1977); and by the discussions of underlying continuities in Robert Minder, *Glaube, Skepsis und Rationalismus. Dargestellt aufgrund der autobiogra-*

phischen Schriften von Karl Philipp Moritz (1936: Frankfurt am Main, 1974). Both Minder and Schings, it should be noted, take Moritz's *Anton Reiser* as a key text. On the broader impact of Pietism, Gerhard Kaiser, *Pietismus und Patriotismus im literarischen Deutschland. Ein Beitrag zum Problem der Säkularisation* (Wiesbaden, 1961), and Koppel S. Pinson, *Pietism as a Factor in the Rise of German Nationalism* (New York, 1968), should also be consulted.

The formation of an educated *Bürgertum* in eighteenth-century Germany and the articulation of a distinctly "bourgeois" consciousness are subjects that have occupied several generations of historians and sociologists. Appropriately the focus has been on the officialdom of church and state, which supplied so many authors and so much of the readership in the emergence of an educated "public." Hans H. Gerth, *Bürgerliche Intelligenz um 1800. Zur Soziologie des deutschen Frühliberalismus*, ed. Ulrich Herrmann, Kritische Studien zur Geschichtswissenschaft, vol. 19 (Göttingen, 1976), is a reprint of a dissertation (originally published in 1935), with an informative introduction and updated bibliography. Gerth's essay has aged remarkably well; the density of its contextual detail remains impressive, and it still points us in fruitful directions. My own approach often diverges sharply from Wilhelm Roessler, *Die Entstehung des modernen Erziehungswesens in Deutschland* (Stuttgart, 1961); but Roessler's etiology of a modern bourgeois consciousness, like Gerth's, is imaginative and well documented. Two older monographs – Hans Rosenberg, *Bureaucracy, Aristocracy and Autocracy. The Prussian Experience 1660–1815* (Cambridge, Mass., 1958), and Joachim Lampe, *Aristokratie, Hofadel und Staatspatriziat in Kurhannover* (Göttingen, 1963) – are indispensable for understanding the tensions and accommodations between a service aristocracy and bourgeois officialdom in public employment. The same subject can be pursued in Bernd Wunder, *Priviligierung und Disziplinierung. Die Entstehung des Berufsbeamtentums in Bayern und Württemberg (1780–1825)* (Munich and Vienna, 1978), and Hans-Eberhard Mueller, *Bureaucracy, Education, and Monopoly. Civil Service Reforms in Prussia and England* (Berkeley, Calif., 1984). Martin Greiffenhagen, ed., *Das evangelische Pfarrhaus. Eine Kultur- und Sozialgeschichte* (Stuttgart, 1984), is a many-sided portrait of the pastorate, helpful for the eighteenth century despite its modern focus. There are useful profiles of the clerical branch of the *Bürgertum* in the early modern era in Günther Franz, ed., *Beamtentum und Pfarrerstand 1400–1800. Büdener Vorträge 1967*, Deutsche Führungsschichten in der Neuzeit, vol. 5 (Limburg/Lahn, 1972). Wolfgang Martens, *Die Botschaft der Tugend. Die Aufklärung im Spiegel der deutschen moralischen Wochenschriften* (Stuttgart, 1968), explores midcentury perceptions of aristocratic decadence and assertions of self-consciously bourgeois social norms.

The more recent efforts to construct a social profile of the *Bürgertum* and to practice a social history of ideas are demonstrated in Franklin Kopitzsch, ed., *Aufklärung, Absolutismus und Bürgertum in Deutschland. Zwolf Aufsätze,* Nymphenburger Texte zur Wissenschaft, vol. 24 (Munich, 1976) (Kopitzsch's essay includes an extensive bibliography), and Rudolf Vierhaus, ed., *Bürger und Bürgerlichkeit im Zeitalter der Aufklärung*, Wolfenbütteler Studien zur Aufklärung, vol. 7 (Heidelberg, 1981), which is particularly important for its nuanced and contextualized interpretations of the political (or in some cases, apolitical) orientation of the "bourgeois intelligentsia." The advantages of a biographical approach for exploring the social world and the social vision of the "enlightened" *Bürger*, and for understanding rationalism in relation to other currents of thought, are exemplified in Horst Möller, *Aufklärung in Preussen. Der Verleger, Publizist und Geschichtsschreiber Friedrich Nicolai*, Einzelveröffentlichungen der Historischen Kommission zu Berlin, vol. 15 (Berlin, 1974), and Mark Boulby, *Karl Philipp Moritz. At the Fringe of Genius* (Toronto, 1979). Ludwig Fertig, *Die Hofmeister. Ein Beitrag zur Geschichte des Lehrerstandes und der bürgerlichen Intelligenz* (Stuttgart, 1979), is invaluable not only for its extensive sample of primary sources on tutoring, but also for its subtly argued and richly documented introductory essay.

Herwig Blankertz, *Die Geschichte der Pädagogik. Von der Aufklärung bis zur Gegenwart* (Wetzlar, 1982), is a readable and concise introduction to a notoriously amorphous body of ideas. The outpouring of German literature on pedagogy and educational reform in the late eighteenth and early nineteenth centuries is staggering, but several collections allow forays into it. The utilitarian preoccupations of "philanthropinistic" reform are illustrated in *Johann Bernhard Basedow. Ausgewählte pädagogischen Schriften*, ed. A. Reble (Paderborn, 1965), and Herwig Blankertz, ed., *Bildung und Brauchbarkeit. Texte von Joachim Heinrich Campe und Peter Villaume zur Theorie utilitärer Erziehung* (Brunswick, 1965), while the shift to "general human education" is documented in Helmut König, *Schriften zur Nationalerziehung in Deutschland am Ende des 18. Jahrhunderts* (Berlin, 1954). Much of the literature marking the ascendancy of neohumanism, Idealism, and nationalism in the early nineteenth century can be found in *Friedrich Immanuel Niethammer. Philanthropinismus-Humanismus*, ed. Werner Hillebrecht, Kleine Pädagogische Texte, vol. 29 (1968); Helmut König, ed., *Deutsche Nationalerziehungspläne aus der Zeit des Befreiungskrieges* (Berlin, 1954); Rudolf Joerden, ed., *Dokumente des Neuhumanismus I*, Kleine Pädagogische Texte, vol. 17 (Weinheim, 1962); Ernst Anrich, ed., *Die Idee der deutschen Universität. Die funf Grundschriften aus der Zeit ihrer Neubegründung durch klassischen Idealismus und romantischen Realismus* (Darmstadt, 1964).

My own work on educational reform is indebted to several classics from an earlier era. Albert Pinloche, *La réforme de l'éducation en Allemagne au 18ème siècle. Basedow et le philanthropinisme* (Paris, 1889), includes lively narrative histories of Basedow's Philanthropinum and several other experimental schools, though Pinloche is sometimes intolerant of the quirks of their founders. The extensive analysis of archival records, including inspection reports, in Paul Schwartz, *Die Gelehrtenschulen Preussens unter dem Oberschulkollegium (1787–1806) und das Abiturientenexamen*, 3 vols., Monumenta Germaniae Paedagogica, vols. 46, 48, 50 (Berlin, 1910–12), makes it possible to study both the formulation of state reform policy in Prussia and the local conditions of the Latin schools and *Gymnasien*. Friedrich Paulsen, *Geschichte des gelehrten Unterrichts auf den deutschen Schulen und Universitäten vom Ausgang des Mittelalters bis zur Gegenwart. Mit besonderer Rücksicht auf den klassischen Unterricht*, 2 vols. (3rd, enl. ed.: Berlin, 1921), is now dated on the reform movements from the early eighteenth century onward; but there is no better description of the original vitality of the marriage of evangelical piety and humanistic scholarship in Reformation Germany and of its eventual ossification.

As the history of education has been drawn into the mainstream of historical research, the old-style *Ideengeschichte* of pedagogical theory, like narrowly administrative and institutional studies of the schools, has lost its raison d'être. For my purposes the most notable exception is Günther Dohmen, *Bildung und Schule. Die Entstehung des deutschen Bildungsbegriffs und die Entwicklung seines Verhältnisses zur Schule*, 2 vols. (Weinheim, 1965), which follows the themes of grace, natural entelechy, and pedagogical art through a long series of theorists and practitioners. An outstanding example of the more recent approach to educational ideas, at once theoretically informed and densely contextualized, is Clemens Menze, *Die Bildungsreform Wilhelm von Humboldts*, Das Bildungsproblem in der Geschichte des europäischen Erziehungsdenkens, vol. 13 (Hanover, 1975).

Helmut König helped point the study of both pedagogy and school reform in new directions with his *Zur Geschichte der Nationalerziehung in Deutschland im letzten Drittel des 18. Jahrhunderts*, Monumenta Paedagogica, vol. 1 (Berlin, 1960), and *Zur Geschichte der bürgerlichen Nationalerziehung in Deutschland zwischen 1807 und 1815*, 2 vols., Monumenta Paedagogica, vols. 12–13 (Berlin, 1973). König quotes extensively from sources that are not highly accessible, and despite his reliance on standard Marxist dichotomies (feudal vs. capitalist, bourgeoisie vs. aristocracy) he has a sharp eye for the social implications of reform thought. Two other innovative contributions are Karl-Ernst Jeismann, *Das preussische Gymnasium in Staat und Gesellschaft. Die Entstehung des Gymnasiums als Schule des Staates und der Gebildeten, 1787–1817*, Industrielle Welt. Schriftenreihe des Arbeitskreises für moderne Sozialgeschichte, vol. 15 (Stuttgart, 1974), and Hans Georg Herrlitz, *Studium als Standesprivileg. Die Entstehung des Maturitätsproblems im 18. Jahrhundert* (Frankfurt am Main, 1973), which helped shape my own thinking on the social issues posed by "poor students." Detlef K. Müller,

Sozialstruktur und Schulsystem: Aspekte zum Strukturwandel des Schulwesens im 19. Jahrhundert, Studien zum Wandel von Gesellschaft und Bildung im Neunzehnten Jahrhundert, vol. 7 (Göttingen, 1977), is primarily a quantitative study of the Berlin school system in the nineteenth century; but the introductory analysis of eighteenth-century reform currents explores the issue of social access to higher education by way of institutional blueprints and curriculum plans. The vast bibliography of primary and secondary literature in Wolfgang Neugebauer, *Absolutistischer Staat und Schulwirklichkeit in Brandenburg-Preussen*, Veröffentlichungen der Historischen Kommission zu Berlin, vol. 62 (Berlin and New York, 1985), pertains to eighteenth-century secondary schools as well as popular education and ranges well beyond the monograph's regional scope.

Since most of the recent research on German universities has focused on the modern institutions that took shape in the early nineteenth century, their eighteenth-century predecessors remain in relative obscurity. Roessler's *Die Entstehung des modernen Erziehungswesens* (cited above) provides background, as does Hellmuth Rössler and Günther Franz, eds., *Universität und Gelehrtenstand. 1400–1800. Büdinger Vorträge 1966*, Deutsche Führungsschichten in der Neuzeit, vol. 4 (Limburg/Lahn, 1970). Franz Eulenberg, *Die Frequenz der deutschen Universitäten von Ihrer Gründung bis zur Gegenwart* (Leipzig, 1904), is still the basic source on attendance patterns, and some of the extant data on the social composition of the eighteenth-century student population are interpreted from a comparative perspective in Fritz K. Ringer, *Education and Society in Modern Europe* (Bloomington, Ind., 1978). There is much to be learned about the professoriate and the intellectual climate of the universities in Reill, *The German Enlightenment and the Rise of Historicism* (cited above). R. Steven Turner has made two seminal contributions on the reforms of the eighteenth and early nineteenth centuries: "University Reformers and Professorial Scholarship in Germany 1760–1806," in Lawrence Stone, ed., *The University in Society*, vol. 2: *Europe, Scotland and the United States from the Sixteenth to the Twentieth Century* (Princeton, N.J., 1974), pp. 495–531, and "The Growth of Professorial Research in Prussia, 1818 to 1848 – Causes and Context," in Russell McCormmach, ed., *Historical Studies in the Physical Sciences* 3 (1971), pp. 137–82.

For want of recent research on which to build, Charles E. McClelland, *State, Society, and University in Germany 1700–1814* (Cambridge, 1980), moves quickly through the eighteenth century. Nonetheless McClelland is able to use his own research for a particularly original assessment of the significance of the new university at Göttingen. The fact that the eighteenth-century records in university archives are sparse and fragmentary, at least in comparison with those for the modern era, is of course discouraging; but to judge by my archival soundings in Göttingen and Halle, they contain much unused material on the kinds of charity distributed to students, on the student subculture, and on the careers and daily preoccupations of the professoriate. Likewise there is still much to be gleaned from earlier secondary literature, despite its very different purposes; a useful guide is Wilhelm Erman and Ewald Horn, eds., *Bibliographie der deutschen Universitäten*, vols. 1–3 (Berlin and Leipzig, 1904–5).

Some of the concerns of the new, interdisciplinary history of education are exemplified in Peter Lundgreen, *Sozialgeschichte der deutschen Schule im Ueberblick*, Teil 1: *1770–1918* (Göttingen, 1980). To repeat a complaint aired in the Introduction, much remains to be done in complementing quantitative analyses of social and institutional structures, and of mobility rates within them, with qualitative research on social norms and cultural meanings. The anthropological orientation that is enlivening the history of popular culture would also be appropriate for subjects – e.g., the reciprocal bonds and obligations of patron-client relationships, the corporate dimensions of school life, the significance of Latinity within old-regime society – on which contemporary sociological models do not shed light. The neglect on this score is confirmed by the bibliography surveyed in Konrad H. Jarausch, "The Old 'New History of Education': A German Reconsideration," *History of Education Quarterly* 26:2 (1986): 225–41.

The new history of education must also be brought into closer alignment with the history of the family, which has had a relatively slow start in German historiography. Eighteenth-century background on family types is provided in Heidi Rosenbaum, *Formen der Familie. Untersuchungen zum Zusammenhang von Familienverhältnissen, Sozialstruktur und sozialem Wandel in der deutschen Gesellschaft des 19. Jahrhunderts* (Frankfurt am Main, 1982), and Helmut Möller, *Die kleinbürgerliche Familie im 18. Jahrhundert: Verhalten und Gruppenkultur*, Schriften zur Volksforschung, vol. 3 (Berlin, 1969), explores the social and cultural values of urban artisans. An innovative interdisciplinary contribution on the relationship between home and school is Jürgen Schlumbohm, "'Traditional' Collectivity and 'Modern' Individuality: Some Questions and Suggestions for the Historical Study of Socialization. The Examples of the German Lower and Upper Bourgeoisies around 1800," *Social History* 5:1 (Jan. 1980): 71–103. Fertig, *Die Hofmeister* (cited above), reminds us of the continuing importance of domestic education in the eighteenth century and sets tutoring within changing domestic contexts, particularly in aristocratic milieus.

A promising partnership has formed between the new history of education and the nascent history of the professions. Our growing awareness of the distinctiveness of the German context for "professionalization," at least in comparison with that of England and the United States, can be gauged from Dietrich Rüschemeyer, "Professionalisierung. Theoretische Probleme für die vergleichende Geschichtsforschung," *Geschichte und Ge-*

sellschaft 6:3 (1980): 311–25; R. Steven Turner, "The '*Bildungsbürgertum*' and the Learned Professions in Prussia, 1770–1830: The Origins of a Class," *Histoire sociale – Social History* 13:25 (May 1980): 105–35; Werner Conze and Jürgen Kocka, eds., *Bildungsbürgertum im 19. Jahrhundert*, Teil 1: *Bildungssystem und Professionalisierung in internationalen Vergleichen* (Stuttgart, 1985). Particularly helpful on the social, moral, and epistemological issues raised by the modern professions since their origins are Magali Sarfatti Larson, *The Rise of Professionalism. A Sociological Analysis* (Berkeley, Calif., 1977); Thomas L. Haskell, ed., *The Authority of Experts. Studies in History and Theory* (Bloomington, Ind., 1984).

This book has made several intrusions into literary studies, and along the way I have tried to acknowledge my debts to both the classics of *Germanistik* and more recent critical literature. I would only emphasize what the text is designed to demonstrate: that the autobiographical literature of eighteenth- and early-nineteenth-century Germany offers myriad possibilities for meshing historical and literary analysis. Historians interested in the wide variety of autobiographical texts, and in the generic categories and interpretive methods now being applied to them, should consult Klaus-Detlef Müller, *Autobiographie und Roman. Studien zur literarischen Autobiographie der Goethezeit* (Tübingen, 1976), and Günter Niggl, *Geschichte der deutschen Autobiographie im 18. Jahrhundert* (Stuttgart, 1977).

Index

Index

SWANSEA UNIVERSITY COLLEGE
LIBRARY
Classmark: LC 191.8.G2 Lav
Location: Miners' Library
Accession No:
Univ Wales Swansea
WITHDRAWN FROM STOCK
Library
1007809186

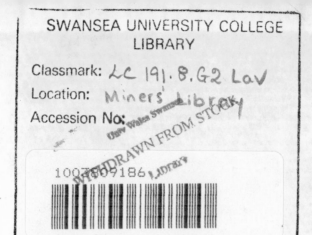